NAVWEPS 01-60ABA-1

A-5 Vigilante
Pilot's Flight Operating Instructions

by U.S. Navy

NATOPS Flight Manual
NAVY MODEL
A-5A AIRCRAFT

THIS PUBLICATION SUPERSEDES NAVWEPS 01-60ABA-1
DATED 1 FEBRUARY 1964

THIS PUBLICATION TO BE USED IN CONJUNCTION WITH
SUPPLEMENTAL NATOPS FLIGHT MANUAL NAVWEPS 01-60ABA-1A
FOR NAVY MODEL A-5A AIRCRAFT

PUBLISHED BY DIRECTION OF
THE CHIEF OF NAVAL OPERATIONS

©2012 Periscope Film LLC
All Rights Reserved
ISBN #978-1-937684-72-3

- SERVICE CHANGES / ENGINES / FUEL SYSTEM
- ELECTRICAL SYSTEM / HYDRAULIC SYSTEMS
- FLIGHT CONTROLS / UTILITY SYSTEMS
- CANOPIES / ESCAPE SYSTEM
- AIR CONDITIONING / OXYGEN / ICS/CNI
- LIGHTING/INSTRUMENTS / RADAR ALTIMETER / SERVICING
- NORMAL PROCEDURES
- FLIGHT PROCEDURES
- EMERGENCY PROCEDURES / ALL-WEATHER / COMMUNICATIONS
- WEAPON SYSTEMS / STANDARDIZATION / EVALUATION

NAVWEPS 01-60ABA-1

NATOPS Flight Manual

NAVY MODEL

A-5A AIRCRAFT

THIS PUBLICATION SUPERSEDES NAVWEPS 01-60ABA-1
DATED 1 FEBRUARY 1964

THIS PUBLICATION TO BE USED IN CONJUNCTION WITH
SUPPLEMENTAL NATOPS FLIGHT MANUAL NAVWEPS 01-60ABA-1A
FOR NAVY MODEL A-5A AIRCRAFT

PUBLISHED BY DIRECTION OF
THE CHIEF OF NAVAL OPERATIONS

- SERVICE CHANGES / ENGINES / FUEL SYSTEM
- ELECTRICAL SYSTEM / HYDRAULIC SYSTEMS
- FLIGHT CONTROLS / UTILITY SYSTEMS
- CANOPIES / ESCAPE SYSTEM
- AIR CONDITIONING / OXYGEN / ICS/CNI
- LIGHTING/INSTRUMENTS / RADAR ALTIMETER / SERVICING
- NORMAL PROCEDURES
- FLIGHT PROCEDURES
- EMERGENCY PROCEDURES / ALL-WEATHER / COMMUNICATIONS
- WEAPON SYSTEMS / STANDARDIZATION / EVALUATION

NAVWEPS 01-60ABA-1

NATOPS Flight Manual

NAVY MODEL

A-5A AIRCRAFT

THIS PUBLICATION SUPERSEDES NAVWEPS 01-60ABA-1
DATED 1 FEBRUARY 1964

THIS PUBLICATION TO BE USED IN CONJUNCTION WITH
SUPPLEMENTAL NATOPS FLIGHT MANUAL NAVWEPS 01-60ABA-1A
FOR NAVY MODEL A-5A AIRCRAFT

PUBLISHED BY DIRECTION OF
THE CHIEF OF NAVAL OPERATIONS

SERVICE CHANGES / ENGINES / FUEL SYSTEM
ELECTRICAL SYSTEM / HYDRAULIC SYSTEMS
FLIGHT CONTROLS / UTILITY SYSTEMS
CANOPIES / ESCAPE SYSTEM
AIR CONDITIONING / OXYGEN / ICS/CNI
LIGHTING/INSTRUMENTS / RADAR ALTIMETER / SERVICING
NORMAL PROCEDURES
FLIGHT PROCEDURES
EMERGENCY PROCEDURES / ALL-WEATHER / COMMUNICATIONS
WEAPON SYSTEMS / STANDARDIZATION / EVALUATION

1 May 1965

NAVWEPS 01-60ABA-1

Reproduction for non-military use of the information or illustrations contained in this publication is not permitted without specific approval of the issuing service. The policy for use of Classified Publications is established for the Air Force in AFR 205-1 and for the Navy in Navy Regulations, Article 1509.

LIST OF CHANGED PAGES ISSUED
INSERT LATEST CHANGED PAGES. DESTROY SUPERSEDED PAGES.

NOTE: The portion of the text affected by the current change is indicated by a vertical line in the outer margins of the page.

ADDITIONAL COPIES OF THIS PUBLICATION MAY BE OBTAINED AS FOLLOWS: BuWeps

USAF ACTIVITIES. — In accordance with Technical Order No. 00-5-2.

NAVY ACTIVITIES. — Use Publications and Forms Order Blank (NavWeps 140) and submit in accordance with instructions listed thereon.

For listing of available material and details of distribution see NavSandA P-2002, Section 8, and NavWeps 00-500A.

A

NAVWEPS 01-60ABA-1

INTERIM CHANGE SUMMARY

The following Interim Changes have been either canceled or incorporated in this NATOPS Flight Manual:

Canceled or Previously Incorporated
No. 1 through No. 6

Incorporated in This Change on Pages Indicated
No. 7   Page 173
No. 8   Pages 64, 181, 182

INTERIM CHANGES OUTSTANDING: (to be maintained by custodian of NATOPS Flight Manual)

Number   *Date*   *Purpose*

DEPARTMENT OF THE NAVY
OFFICE OF THE CHIEF OF NAVAL OPERATIONS
WASHINGTON 25, D.C.

1 May 1965

LETTER OF PROMULGATION

1. The Naval Aviation Training and Operating Procedures Standardization Program (NATOPS) is a positive approach towards improving combat readiness and achieving a substantial reduction in the aircraft accident rate. Standardization, based on professional knowledge and experience, provides the basis for development of an efficient and sound operational procedure. The standardization program is not planned to stifle individual initiative but rather, it will aid the Commanding Officer in increasing his unit's combat potential without reducing his command prestige or responsibility.

2. This Manual is published for the purpose of standardizing ground and flight procedures and does not include combat tactics. Compliance with the stipulated manual procedure is mandatory. However, to remain effective this manual must be dynamic. It must stimulate rather than stifle individual thinking. Since aviation is a continuing progressive profession, it is both desirable and necessary that new ideas and new techniques be expeditiously formulated and incorporated. It is a user's publication, prepared by and for users, and kept current by the users in order to achieve maximum readiness and safety in the most efficient and economical manner. Should conflict exist between this manual and other publications, this manual will govern.

3. Check lists and other pertinent extracts from this publication necessary to normal operations and training should be made and may be carried in Naval aircraft for use therein. It is forbidden to make copies of this entire publication or major portions thereof without specific authority of the Chief of Naval Operations.

4. This manual supersedes the A-5A NATOPS Flight Manual, dated 1 February 1964, and is effective on receipt.

J. S. THACH
Vice Admiral, USN
Deputy Chief of Naval Operations (Air)

TABLE OF CONTENTS

Section I	THE AIRCRAFT*	1
Part 1	General Description	1
Part 2	Systems*	11
Part 3	Aircraft Servicing	111
Part 4	Aircraft Operating Limitations Refer to the Supplemental NATOPS Flight Manual (NAVWEPS 01-60ABA-1A)	
Section II	INDOCTRINATION	119
Section III	NORMAL PROCEDURES	121
Part 1	Briefing and Debriefing	121
Part 2	Mission Planning	123
Part 3	Shore-based Procedures (Pilot)	127
Part 4	Carrier-based Procedures (Pilot)	139
Part 5	Normal Procedures (Systems Operator)	148A
Section IV	FLIGHT PROCEDURES*	149
Section V	EMERGENCY PROCEDURES	163
Section VI	ALL-WEATHER OPERATION	183
Section VII	COMMUNICATIONS PROCEDURES	191
Section VIII	WEAPONS SYSTEMS	193
Section IX	FLIGHT CREW COORDINATION Refer to the Supplemental NATOPS Flight Manual (NAVWEPS 01-60ABA-1A)	
Section X	STANDARDIZATION EVALUATION	197
Part 1	Standardization Evaluation Program	197
Part 2	A-5A Pilot/Systems Operator Standardization Evaluation Form	211
Part 3	Pilot Standardization Evaluation Worksheets	215
Part 4	Systems Operator Standardization Evaluation Worksheets	233
Section XI	PERFORMANCE DATA Refer to the Supplemental NATOPS Flight Manual (NAVWEPS 01-60ABA-1A)	
Alphabetical Index		251

*Also refer to the Supplemental NATOPS Flight Manual (NAVWEPS 01-60ABA-1A)

Foreword

THE NATOPS FLIGHT PUBLICATIONS ARE ABOARD!

A-5A-1-0-14

SCOPE

This NATOPS Flight Manual (NAVWEPS 01-60ABA-1) and the classified Confidential Supplemental NATOPS Flight Manual (NAVWEPS 01-60ABA-1A) contain information and procedures (based on the latest available data) necessary for safe and efficient operation of A-5A aircraft.

Each issue of the NATOPS Flight Manual will be reviewed by the Model Manager concerned. Suggested changes should be sent to him or to your Evaluators for coordination.

The NATOPS Pocket Check List (NAVWEPS 01-60ABA-1B) reflects official NATOPS procedures and is arranged as a ready reference to operating procedures, servicing requirements, and assential performance data. Check List arrangement is as follows:

EMERGENCY PROCEDURES
REFERENCE DATA
SPECIAL PROCEDURES
NORMAL PROCEDURES

CHANGES

Changes to these publications are published as directed by the Chief of Naval Operations. Change stripes (heavy vertical lines in margins) indicate specific changes to text material. Flight crews must be cognizant of all pertinent technical directives, since these may cover critical flight restrictions or new procedures not yet incorporated by change.

NATOPS Changes or BuWeps Interim Changes, which point out safety-of-flight items, should be placed at the front of this manual until the Interim Change Summary (flyleaf preceding the Table of Contents) indicates that the information has been incorporated by change. This means that the flyleaf must always be consulted before using the manual.

To determine whether your copy of the manual is the latest issue or contains the latest changes, consult NavSandA Publication 2002, Section VIII, Part C.

CHANGE RECOMMENDATIONS

An example of the NATOPS Manual/NATOPS Flight Manual/Flight Manual Change Recommendation Form (OPNAV Form 3500-22) is included in the front of this manual. Recommendations for changes to this manual are classified as Urgent or Routine and may be submitted by anyone.

Urgent change recommendations are those which involve safety of flight and require immediate promulgation. They are submitted by PRIORITY message directly to the NATOPS Advisory Group member in the chain of command. Advisory Group members process Urgent change recommendations in accordance with OPNAV Instructions 3510.9B.

Routine change recommendations are submitted to the Model Manager (Commanding Officer, RECONATI-CRON 3, NAS Sanford, Florida) on OPNAV Form 3500-22.

MANUAL ARRANGEMENT

In addition to the Table of Contents preceding this Foreword, an Alphabetical Index is provided at the end of both the NATOPS Flight Manual and the Supplemental NATOPS Flight Manual for referencing specific subjects and illustrations. An understanding of the general contents of each section will simplify locating the information you desire.

NAVWEPS 01-60ABA-1
Foreword

SECTION I — THE AIRCRAFT

Part 1, General Description—An introduction to the aircraft.

Part 2, Systems—Description and operation of all major systems, including normal and emergency operation.

Part 3, Aircraft Servicing—Description and operating procedures for complete servicing, including starting units, danger areas, and turning radius.

Part 4, Aircraft Operating Limitations—Restrictions for operation of the aircraft, engines, and systems which must be observed for safe flight.

SECTION II — INDOCTRINATION

A resumé of required training and equipment for compliance with the NATOPS program.

SECTION III — NORMAL PROCEDURES

Part 1, Briefing and Debriefing—A general outline of requirements.

Part 2, Mission Planning—A guide to effective planning, including responsibilities, forms, and cruise planning.

Part 3, Shore-based Procedures (Pilot)—Standard normal procedures used to conduct VFR nontactical flight from an on-shore station.

Part 4, Carrier-based Procedures (Pilot)—Standard normal procedures used to conduct VFR nontactical flight from a carrier.

Part 5, Normal Procedures (Systems Operator)—Standard normal, unclassified procedures for conduct of normal missions.

SECTION IV — FLIGHT PROCEDURES

A summary of standard in-flight procedures, and the latest available data concerning aircraft characteristics throughout all phases of flight.

SECTION V — EMERGENCY PROCEDURES

Standard procedures to be followed during any emergency which could reasonably be expected.

SECTION VI — ALL-WEATHER OPERATION

Additional information and procedures required for flight under all weather conditions.

SECTION VII — COMMUNICATIONS PROCEDURES

Procedures utilized to standardize all forms of communications, including the use of electronic navigation equipment.

SECTION VIII — WEAPONS SYSTEMS

Operational procedures for effective utilization of the aircraft armament system in all modes, plus information on store loading and practice bombing.

SECTION IX — FLIGHT CREW COORDINATION

Attack mode check lists for both the pilot and the systems operator.

SECTION X — STANDARDIZATION EVALUATION

Part 1, Standardization Evaluation Program—The concept, applicability, definitions, and outlines of grading criteria for the A-5A Standardization Evaluation Program.

Part 2, A-5A Pilot/Systems Operator Standardization Evaluation Form

Part 3, Pilot Standardization Evaluation Worksheets

Part 4, Systems Operator Standardization Evaluation Worksheets

SECTION XI — PERFORMANCE DATA

Graphic and tabular data of aircraft performance to be used for effective mission planning.

AIRCRAFT BUREAU NUMBERS

Each aircraft has its Bureau Number painted on the side of the aft fuselage, followed by a Block Number for series identification. These numbers are designated in groups as follows:

BLOCK	NAA NUMBERS	BUREAU NUMBERS
NH-10	11 — 21	146702, 147850 through 147859
NH-15	22 — 25	147860 through 147863
NH-20	26 — 32	148924 through 148930
NH-25	33	148931
NH-30	34, 35	148932, 148933
NH-35	36, 37	149276, 149277
NH-40	38 — 45	149278 through 149285
NH-45	46 — 59	149286 through 149299

Note

- Aircraft NH-01 and NH-05, Bureau Numbers 145157 through 146701, are not covered by this manual.
- Aircraft modified through updating by the contractor may be recognized by an appropriate change in Block Number. NH-10 aircraft become NH-11, NH-15 aircraft become NH-16, etc.
- *This manual describes all A-5A aircraft (NH-10 and subsequent) not converted to the RA-5C configuration.*

WARNINGS, CAUTIONS, AND NOTES

Three types of attention-gaining devices are employed in the NATOPS Flight Manual. The type of device used depends upon the degree of hazard involved should crew members disregard or fail to perform the procedure. A functional interpretation of each type is as follows:

WARNING

Operating information which, if ignored, can result in personal injury or loss of life.

CAUTION

Additional operating information which is important in preventing damage to or destruction of the aircraft or its equipment.

Note

An operating procedure or information which is included for a more complete understanding.

iii

Section 1
Part 1

NAVWEPS 01-60ABA-1

MODEL A-5A AIRCRAFT

VIGILANTE

Figure 1-1

the aircraft
Section I

TABLE OF CONTENTS

PART 1—GENERAL DESCRIPTION 1	Wheel Brakes 70
The Aircraft 1	Fold Systems 72
Aircraft Service/Airframe Changes Listing 5	Canopies 74
Aircraft Loading 9	Escape System 75
PART 2—SYSTEMS 11	Escape System Operation 80
Engines 11	Air Conditioning and Pressurization System ... 82
Engine Characteristics 17	Oxygen Systems 88
Air Induction System 18	Intercommunications System (ICS) 90
Engine Operating Procedures 24	Communications-Navigation-Identification
Aircraft Fuel Supply System 25	System (CNI) 92
Fuel System Operation 31	Lighting Systems 98
Buddy Tanker Refueling System 32	Warning, Caution, and Advisory Indicators ... 101
Air Refueling Procedures (Receiver) 36	Instruments 101
Electrical Power Supply System 37	Angle-of-attack System 103
Hydraulic Power Supply Systems 41	Gyrocompass System 105
Pneumatic Power Supply System 49	Radar Altimeter 106A
Flight Control Systems 49	PART 3—AIRCRAFT SERVICING 111
Automatic Flight Control System (AFCS) ... 59	External Power and Air Requirements 111
Flight Control Systems Operation 62	Military Specifications 114
Speed Brakes 65	External Power Units 114
Wing Flaps and Droop Leading Edge 65	Refueling 114
Landing Gear 68	Systems Servicing 118
Arresting Gear 69	Danger Areas 118
Nose Wheel Steering 70	Ground Handling 118A

PART 1 — GENERAL DESCRIPTION

THE AIRCRAFT

The A-5A is a two-place, two-engine attack aircraft, designed for carrier- and land-based operation. It is capable of supersonic high- and low-altitude special and conventional weapon delivery. The aircraft is characterized by a relatively long nose section, a sharply swept, shoulder-mounted wing, a tall vertical stabilizer, and large, rectangular air intakes. The vertical stabilizer, the wings, and the radome may be folded to facilitate hangar deck storage. Lateral control is provided by a system of spoiler-deflectors which are also used as speed brakes. Provisions are incorporated for both internal and external store carriage and release. The aircraft can be refueled in flight. All-weather attack is directed by the bomb directing set and utilizes automatic flight control. The flight control systems provide improved supersonic and low-speed handling qualities through a pitch augmentation system and a yaw damper. Landing speeds and angle of attack are reduced by full-span, powered droop leading edges and a wing flap surface boundary layer control system. For gross weight and cg data, refer to AIRCRAFT LOADING, in this section.

Section I
Part 1

NAVWEPS 01-60ABA-1

GENERAL ARRANGEMENT

1. PITOT-STATIC BOOM
2. AIR REFUELING PROBE (RETRACTABLE)
3. RADAR ANTENNA (AN/ASB-12)
4. REFUELING PROBE LIGHT
5. FORWARD ELECTRONIC COMPARTMENT (AUTONAVIGATOR-RADAR-TV)
6. WINDSCREEN RADIATION SHIELD
7. PILOT'S PROJECTED DISPLAY INDICATOR (AN/ASB-12)
8. NAVIGATIONAL-BOMBING COMPUTER (AN/ASB-12)
9. LIQUID OXYGEN CONVERTER
10. RADAR PASSIVE WARNING ANTENNA
11. MAIN ELECTRONICS BAY
12. IFF-SIF ANTENNA
13. FUSELAGE SUMP FUEL TANK
14. INTEGRAL WING FUEL TANK
15. ANTI-COLLISION LIGHT
16. AFT FUEL (SADDLE) TANK
17. FORMATION LIGHT
18. VERTICAL STABILIZER FOLD LINE
19. TACAN-COMM DUPLEX ANTENNA
20. POSITION AND BUDDY TANKER LIGHTS
21. FUEL SYSTEM OVERBOARD VENT OUTLET
22. TAIL BOOM ECM ANTENNA
23. TAILCONE (EXPENDABLE)
24. FUEL DUMP TUBE
25. ARRESTING HOOK BUMPER
26. ARRESTING HOOK
27. ENGINE STARTING AIR RECEPTACLE
28. CATAPULT HOLDBACK
29. ECM ANTENNA
30. CATAPULT HOOKS
31. EMERGENCY RAM-AIR TURBINE
32. EXTERNAL ELECTRICAL AND COOLING AIR ACCESS
33. APPROACH LIGHTS
34. TAXI LIGHT
35. AUX BRAKE ACCUMULATOR REPEATER GAGE
36. DELETED
37. CANOPY JETTISON AIR BOTTLES
38. ADF ANTENNA
39. ELECTRONIC ALTIMETER ANTENNA
40. UHF COMM ANTENNA
41. AIR REFUELING REFERENCE LIGHT

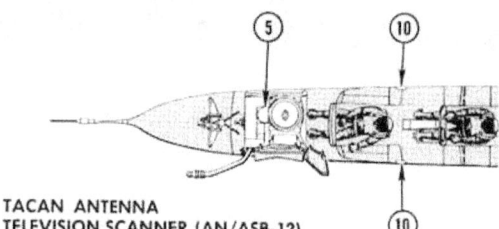

42. TACAN ANTENNA
43. TELEVISION SCANNER (AN/ASB-12)
44. INTERNAL STORE AND EJECTION GUN
45. ECM RADAR RECEIVER ANTENNAS
46. WING FOLD LINE
47. WING TIP POSITION LIGHT
48. 400-GALLON DROP TANK
49. FLAP EMERGENCY/CANOPY NORMAL AIR BOTTLE
50. BOMB BAY FUEL CANS (EXPENDABLE)
51. HYDRAULIC RESERVOIRS

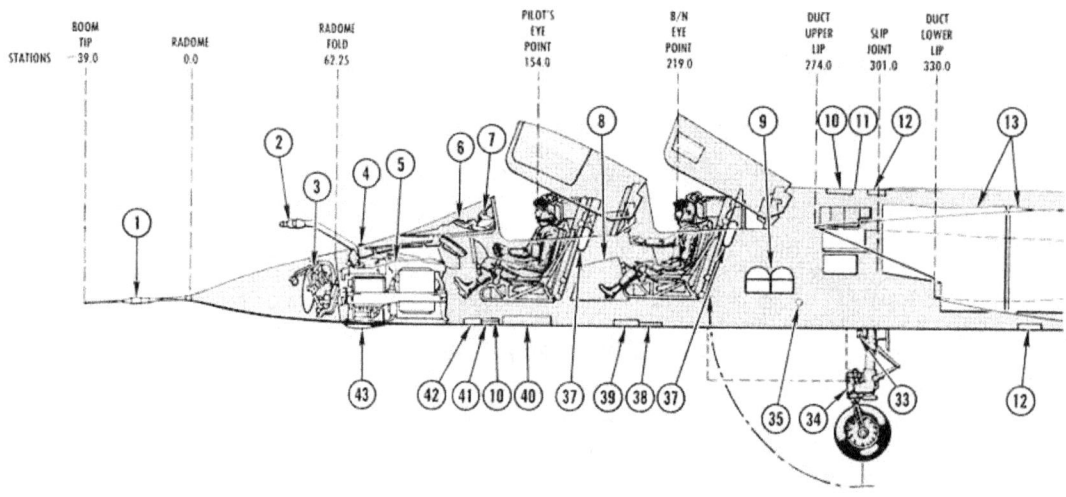

Figure 1-2 (Sheet 1)

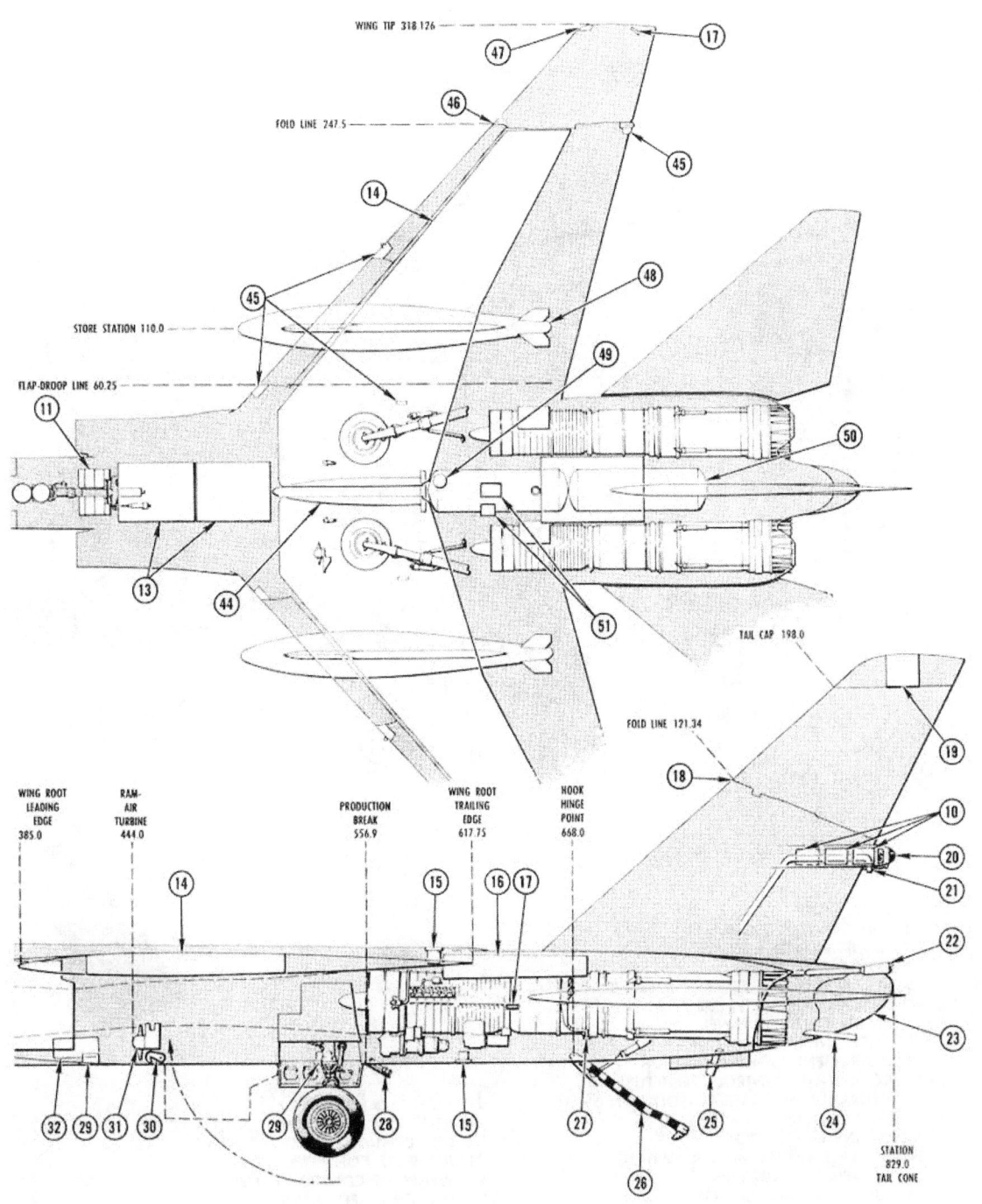

Figure 1-2 (Sheet 2)

Section I
Part 1

NAVWEPS 01-60ABA-1

PILOT'S LEFT CONSOLE

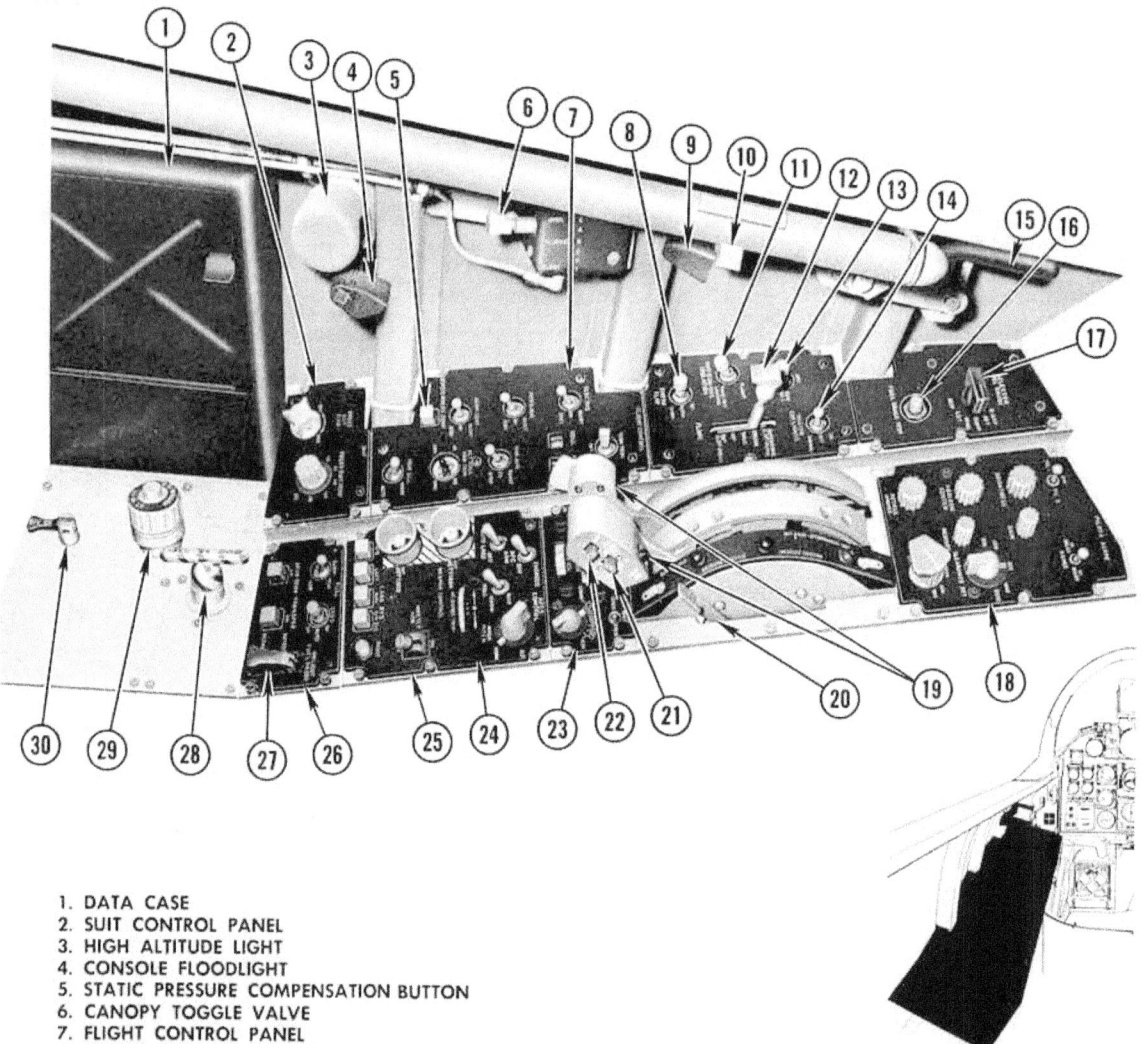

1. DATA CASE
2. SUIT CONTROL PANEL
3. HIGH ALTITUDE LIGHT
4. CONSOLE FLOODLIGHT
5. STATIC PRESSURE COMPENSATION BUTTON
6. CANOPY TOGGLE VALVE
7. FLIGHT CONTROL PANEL
8. EMERGENCY FLAP SWITCH
9. INSTRUMENT PANEL FLOODLIGHT
10. COCKPIT AIR CONTROL (VENT TUBE)
11. HYDRAULIC SUBSYSTEMS ISOLATION SWITCH
12. FLAP SWITCH
13. ENGINE FIRE SWITCH
14. EXTERIOR LIGHTS MASTER SWITCH
15. CATAPULT HAND GRIP
16. FUEL GAGE TEST BUTTON
17. FUEL GAGE SELECTOR
18. PILOT'S SCOPE CONTROL PANEL
19. EMERGENCY IGNITION BUTTONS
20. THROTTLE FRICTION LEVER
21. SPEED BRAKE SWITCH
22. INTERCOM — TRANSMIT SWITCH
23. UHF COMM CONTROL PANEL
24. AIRCRAFT CONTROL PANEL
25. WEAPONS CONTROL PANEL
26. FUEL TRANSFER PANEL
27. IN-FLIGHT FUEL PROBE CONTROL SWITCH
28. SPEED BRAKE DUMP HANDLE
29. ANTI "G" VALVE
30. OXYGEN SUPPLY VALVE

A3J-1-1-00-38H

Figure 1-3

4

AIRCRAFT DIMENSIONS

Overall static dimensions of the aircraft are as follows:
Wing span .... 53.02 feet
   wings folded .... 42.00 feet
Length .... 76.55 feet
   vertical stabilizer and radome folded .... 65.37 feet
Height .... 19.37 feet
   vertical stabilizer folded .... 15.50 feet

THE COCKPITS

The pilot and systems operator are provided separate, connected cockpits. Control of cockpit temperature and pressurization is maintained primarily by the pilot. All primary flight controls and indicators are installed in the pilot's cockpit. All primary controls and indicators for navigation and bombing are installed in the systems operator's cockpit.

WARNING INDICATORS

Warning indicators for FIRE and OXYGEN are installed in both cockpits. Refer to WARNING, CAUTION, AND ADVISORY INDICATORS, in Part 2 of this section.

AIRCRAFT SERVICE/AIRFRAME CHANGES LISTING

Past changes to aircraft, after delivery to the Navy, have been known as Aircraft Service Changes (ASC's). Future changes to the aircraft will be known as Airframe Changes (AFC's), beginning with A-5 Airframe Change 86, as directed by BuWeps Instruction 5215.8, dated 30 January 1963. The Aircraft Service Changes and Airframe Changes listing contains ASC's and AFC's applicable to A-5A aircraft, and includes only those changes affecting procedures or systems description which are considered necessary information for pilot and systems operator operation of the aircraft. Each change is listed along with the affected aircraft (by Bureau Number), its purpose, and the degree of urgency (category). A complete listing and summary of Aircraft Service Changes and Airframe Changes applicable to the aircraft can be found in the NavSandA Publications 2002, Section VIII, Parts C and D.

Note
AVC's, EMC's, Avionics Bulletins, etc, are not listed, but may be referenced in this manual.

SERVICE/AIRFRAME CHANGE NO.	AIRCRAFT AFFECTED (BUREAU NO.)	SUBJECT AND PURPOSE	CATEGORY
7	All	AVIONICS (a) Installs ECM provisions.	Record
10	All	ENGINE (a) Provides anti-icing protection for engine nose domes.	Urgent
27	All	ENGINE CONTROLS (a) Provides a catapult handgrip usable for both the Military and Maximum Thrust throttle positions.	Routine
29	146702 — 149285	CONDITIONING SYSTEM (a) Changes airflow distribution and temperature control point (80°F). (b) Adds automatic parallel cooling controlled by throttle position for ground operations.	Routine
38	All	CONDITIONING SYSTEM (a) Permits pilot and systems operator to receive pressure suit cooling air from electronic equipment cooling air receptacle.	Routine
42	All	PITCH AUGMENTATION AND AFCS (a) Provides "g" command system. (b) Reinstates MACH hold mode. (c) Installs DROOPS caution "Q" box. (d) Installs longitudinal stick damper.	Urgent
43	All	AVIONICS (a) Replaces interval timer and modifies COMBAT/TRAINING audio bombing tone.	Routine

Section I
Part 1

PILOT'S INSTRUMENT PANEL

(TYPICAL)

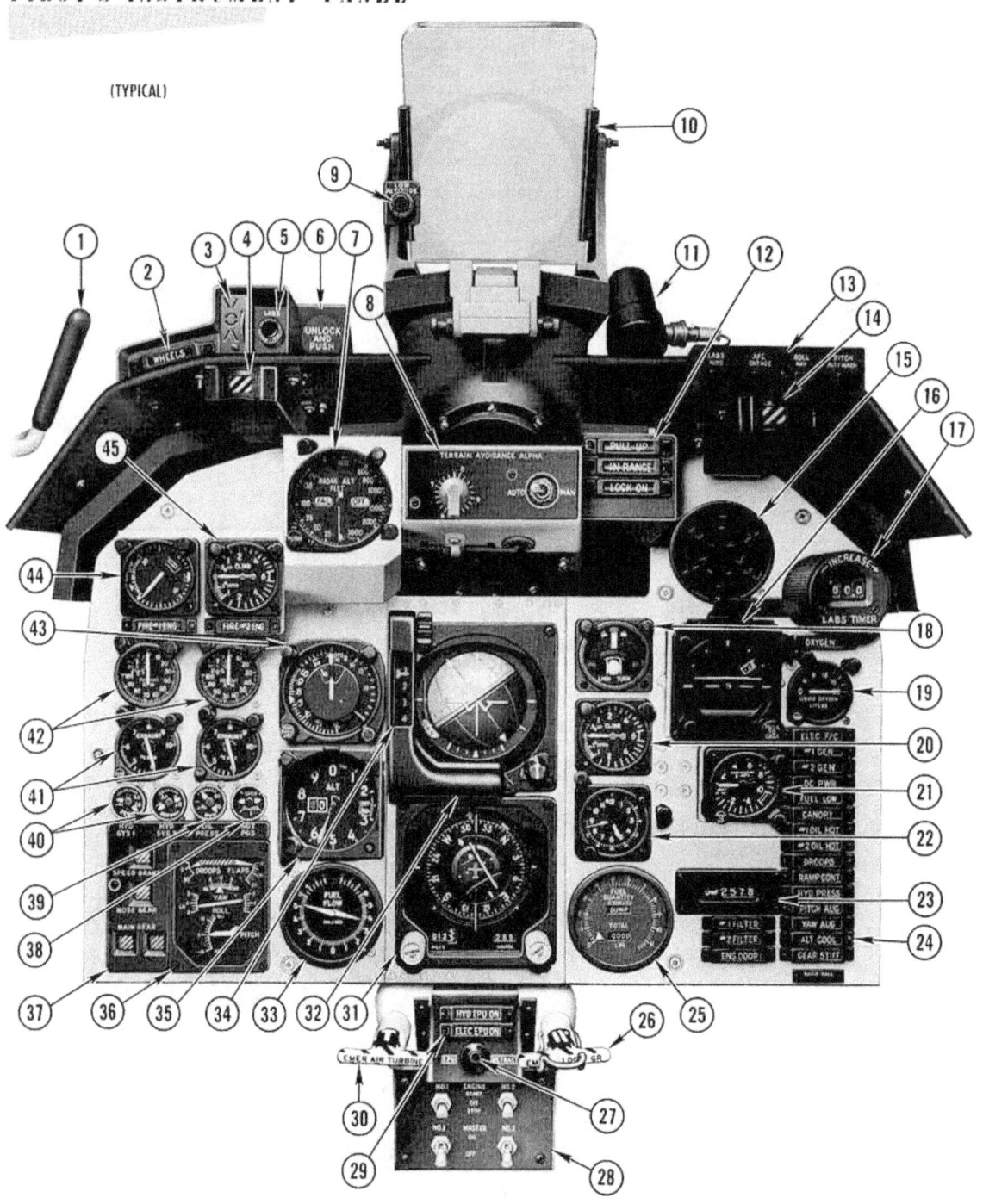

Figure 1-4 (Sheet 1)

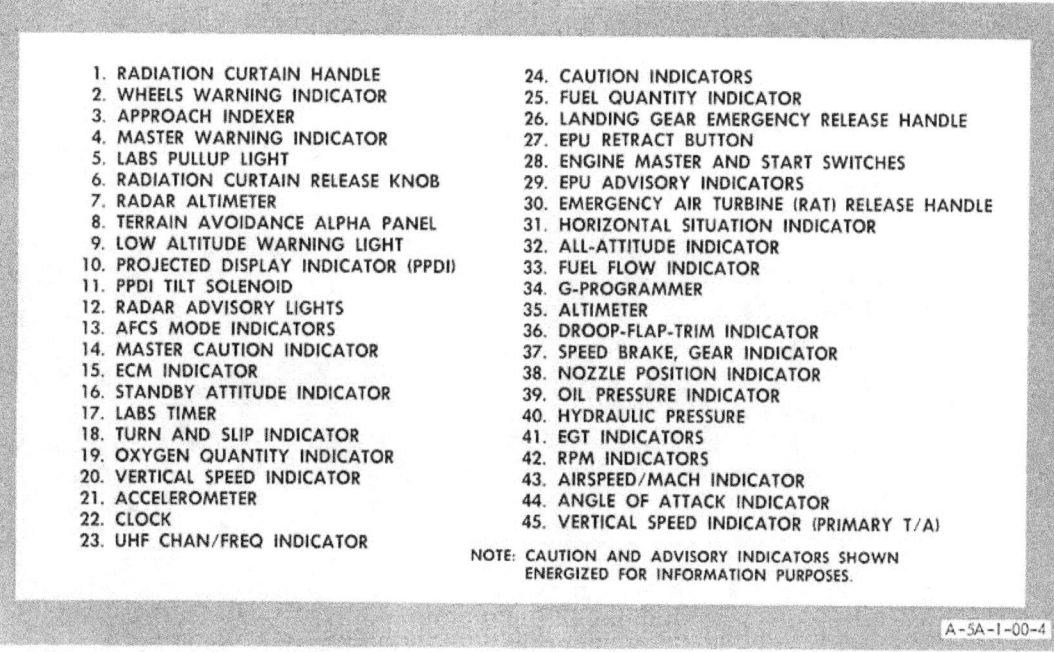

Figure 1-4 (Sheet 2)

SERVICE/AIRFRAME CHANGE NO.	AIRCRAFT AFFECTED (BUREAU NO.)	SUBJECT AND PURPOSE	CATEGORY
58	All	AFCS/AUTO-LABS (a) Installs AFCS advisory indicators. (b) Indicates inadvertent disengagement of AFCS. (c) Provides positive indication of LABS mode selection.	Routine
81	All	MASTER WARNING AND CAUTION SYSTEM (a) Provides pilot with method of dimming master warning and caution indicators during night operations.	Urgent
101	All	CANOPY (a) Modifies manual release system. (b) Provides automatic uplock for manual opening.	Urgent
103	All	ARRESTING GEAR (a) Installs redesigned bumper assembly.	Urgent
112	All	BOMB DIRECTING SET (a) Adds inertial autonavigator preheat capability.	Urgent
129	All	NOSE WHEEL STEERING (a) Installs provisions for improved control.	Urgent

Section I
Part 1

NAVWEPS 01-60ABA-1

PILOT'S RIGHT CONSOLE

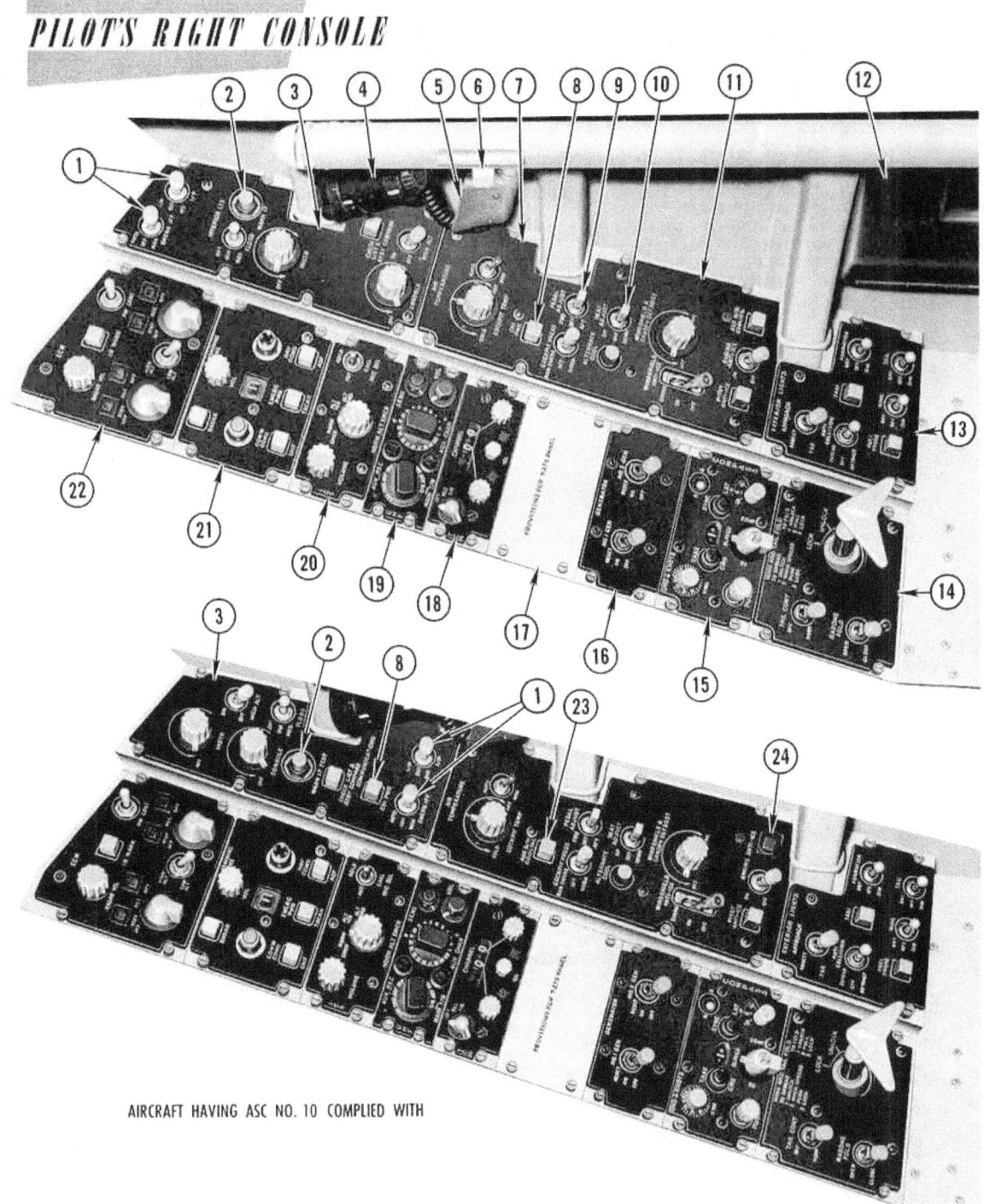

AIRCRAFT HAVING ASC NO. 10 COMPLIED WITH

A3J-1-1-00-39F

Figure 1-4A (Sheet 1)

1. IFF CONTROL SWITCHES
2. WARNING LIGHTS TEST BUTTON
3. INTERIOR LIGHTS CONTROL PANEL
4. EMERGENCY LIGHT
5. INSTRUMENT FLOODLIGHT
6. COCKPIT AIR VENT CONTROL (VENT TUBE)
7. AIR TEMPERATURE CONTROL PANEL
8. CNI POWER BUTTON
9. PEDAL ADJUST SWITCH
10. SEAT ADJUST SWITCH
11. ANTI-ICE CONTROL PANEL
12. RELIEF BAG AND SIGHT FILTER STOWAGE CASE
13. EXTERIOR LIGHTS CONTROL PANEL
14. FOLD SYSTEMS CONTROL PANEL
15. COMPASS CONTROL PANEL
16. GENERATOR CONTROL PANEL
17. PROVISIONS FOR T-375 OR AN/AWW-1 CONTROL PANEL
18. TACAN CONTROL PANEL
19. AUXILIARY RECEIVER CONTROL PANEL
20. ICS CONTROL PANEL
21. AUDIO SELECTOR PANEL
22. ECM CONTROL PANEL
23. AUX B/N COOLING BUTTON
24. ENGINE ANTI-ICE INDICATOR

A-5A-1-00-5

Figure 1-4A (Sheet 2)

AIRCRAFT LOADING

The following table and figure 1-4E provide a simplified method of calculating aircraft gross weight and center-of-gravity location. Procedures consist of adding the weights of all items carried to the average basic weight and algebraically adding load item incremental index values to the basic weight index. Final index is then used with take-off gross weight to determine cg location in percent MAC.

- Average Basic Weight—33,800 pounds.
- Arm—518.50.
- Weight Index—80.6.

Note

Basic weight is typical average from Chart C of the Handbook of Weight and Balance Data (NAVWEPS 01-1B-40) for delivered aircraft and includes:

- Trapped fuel.
- Trapped and operating engine oil.
- Full oxygen service and emergency controllers.
- Seat kits, including parakits, pans, and parachutes.

ITEM	WEIGHT (POUNDS)	INCREMENTAL CG INDEX
Pilot	200	−3.6
Systems Operator	200	−2.9
Forward Can (empty)	163	−0.3
Mid Can (empty)	163	+0.5
Aft Can (empty)	163	+1.3
Carriage (2 cans)	67	+0.4
Carriage (3 cans)	104	+0.3
Tail Cone (universal)	80	+1.2
Tail Cone (refueling)	73	+1.1
Buddy Tanker Can	251	−0.3
Buddy Tanker Carriage	133	+0.4
Tanker Reel/Drogue	382	+4.6
Drogue Carriage	31	+0.4
MK 28 Internal Store	1885	−1.4
Carriage (MK 28 store)	100	+0.1
MK 27 Internal Store	3020	−5.8
Carriage (MK 27 store)	86	Negligible
Stabilizing Fins (store train)	92	+1.0
Gun (store ejection)	146	−0.2
Pylon (Mod B)	328	−0.3
Pylon (cast)	475	−0.5
Drop Tank (empty)	260	−0.4
Power Pod (RCPP-105-1)	2000	−5.3
MK 28 External Store (free-fall)	2037	−4.4
MK 57 External Store	485	−0.9
MK 82 General Purpose	532	−1.4
MK 83 General Purpose	1000	−2.5
MK 84 General Purpose	2000	−4.6
Aero 8A PBC (empty)	380	−0.7
MK 76 (4)	100	−0.2
MK 89 (4)	224	−0.5
MK 106 (4)	18	Negligible
A/A37B-3 PMBR	163	−0.4
Landing Gear Operation:		
DOWN to UP	—	−3.1
UP to DOWN	—	+3.1

Section I
Part 1

NAVWEPS 01-60ABA-1

NAVIGATOR'S LEFT CONSOLE

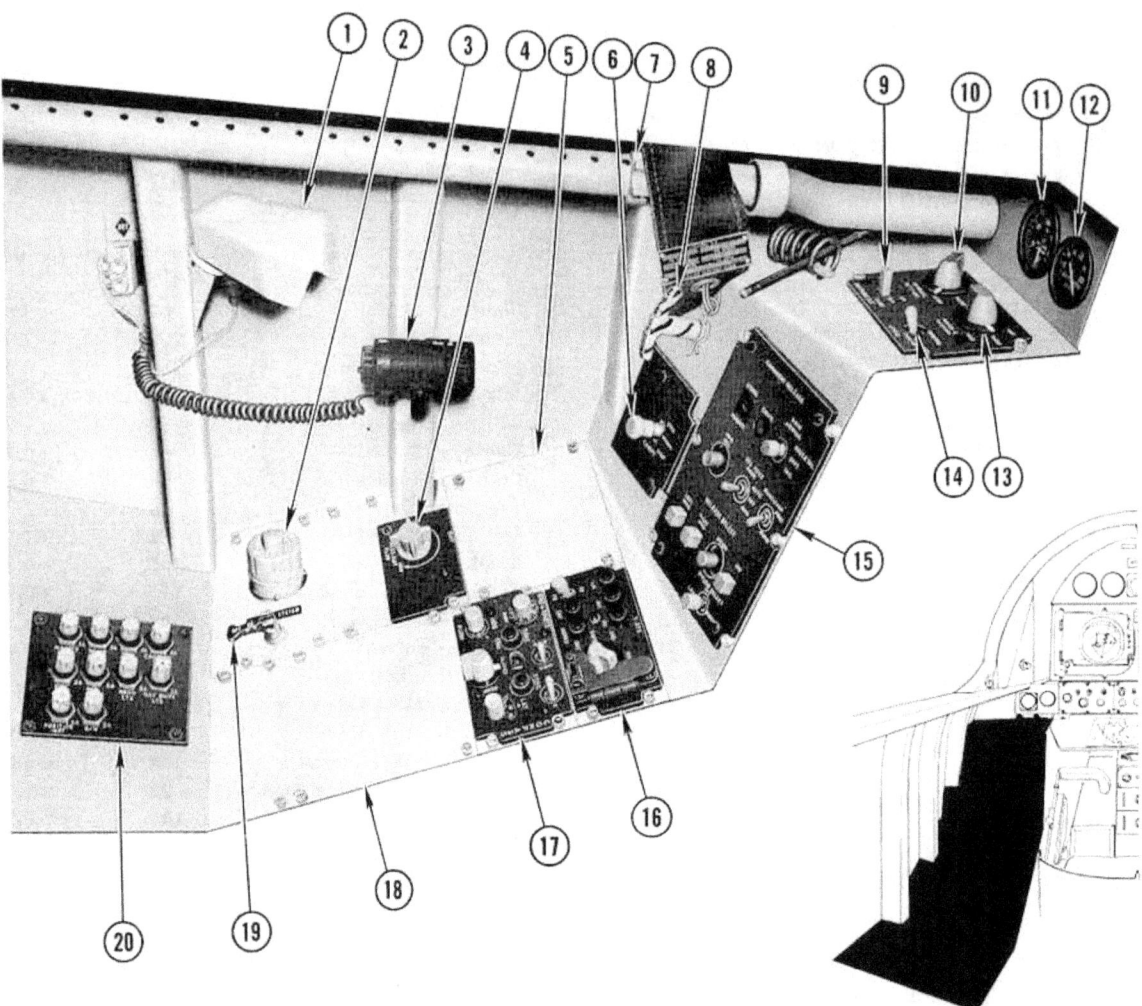

1. CONSOLE FLOODLIGHT
2. ANTI "G" SUIT VALVE
3. EMERGENCY LIGHT
4. PRESSURE SUIT FLOW KNOB
5. PROVISIONS FOR ECM EQUIPMENT
6. CANOPY TOGGLE VALVE
7. COCKPIT AIR CONTROL
8. CANOPY EMERGENCY JETTISON HANDLE
9. ALTITUDE SET SWITCH
10. ALTITUDE MODE KNOB
11. COCKPIT PRESSURE ALTIMETER
12. LIQUID OXYGEN QUANTITY INDICATOR
13. RANGE AND BEARING KNOB
14. SPEED SELECT SWITCH (TRUE AIR/GROUND)
15. ARMAMENT RELEASE PANEL
16. T-375 OR AN/AWW-1 ARMAMENT CONTROL PANEL
17. COMPASS CONTROL PANEL
18. PROVISIONS FOR BUDDY TANKER PANEL
19. OXYGEN SYSTEM SUPPLY VALVE
20. FUSE PANEL

A3J-1-1-00-52C

Figure 1-4B

NAVIGATOR'S DISPLAY PANEL

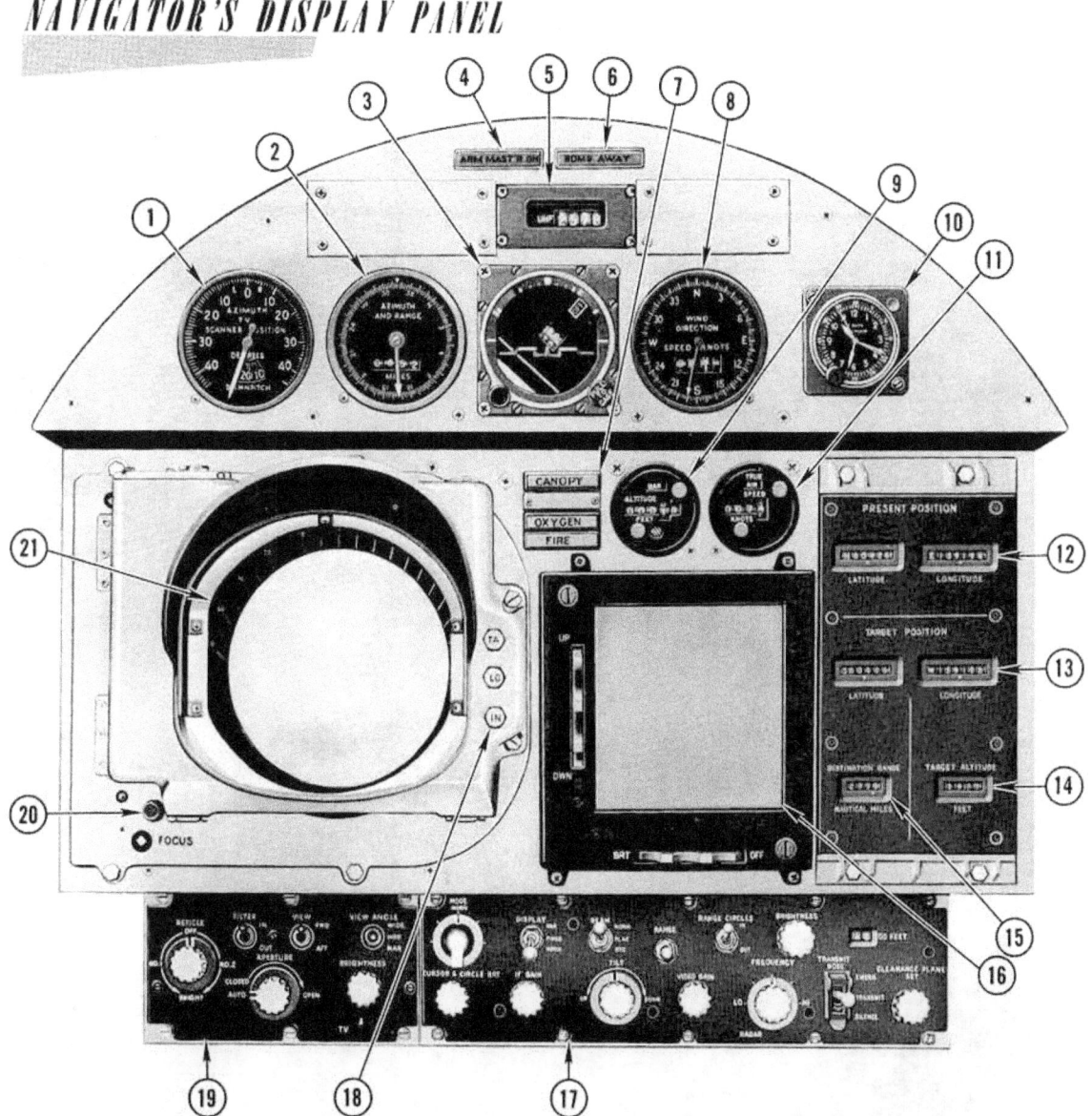

1. TV SCANNER POSITION INDICATOR
2. AZIMUTH AND RANGE INDICATOR
3. ATTITUDE INDICATOR
4. ARMAMENT MASTER ON ADVISORY LIGHT
5. UHF CHANNEL/FREQUENCY INDICATOR
6. BOMB AWAY ADVISORY LIGHT
7. WARNING AND ADVISORY LIGHTS
8. WIND, SPEED AND DIRECTION INDICATOR
9. RADAR-BARO ALTIMETER
10. CLOCK
11. TRUE AIRSPEED/GROUND SPEED INDICATOR
12. PRESENT POSITION INDICATOR
13. TARGET POSITION INDICATOR
14. TARGET ALTITUDE INDICATOR
15. DESTINATION RANGE INDICATOR
16. DATA VIEWER
17. RADAR CONTROL PANEL
18. RADAR ADVISORY LIGHTS
19. TELEVISION CONTROL PANEL
20. FOCUS CONTROL
21. RADAR-TV INDICATOR

Figure 1-4C

NAVIGATOR'S RIGHT CONSOLE

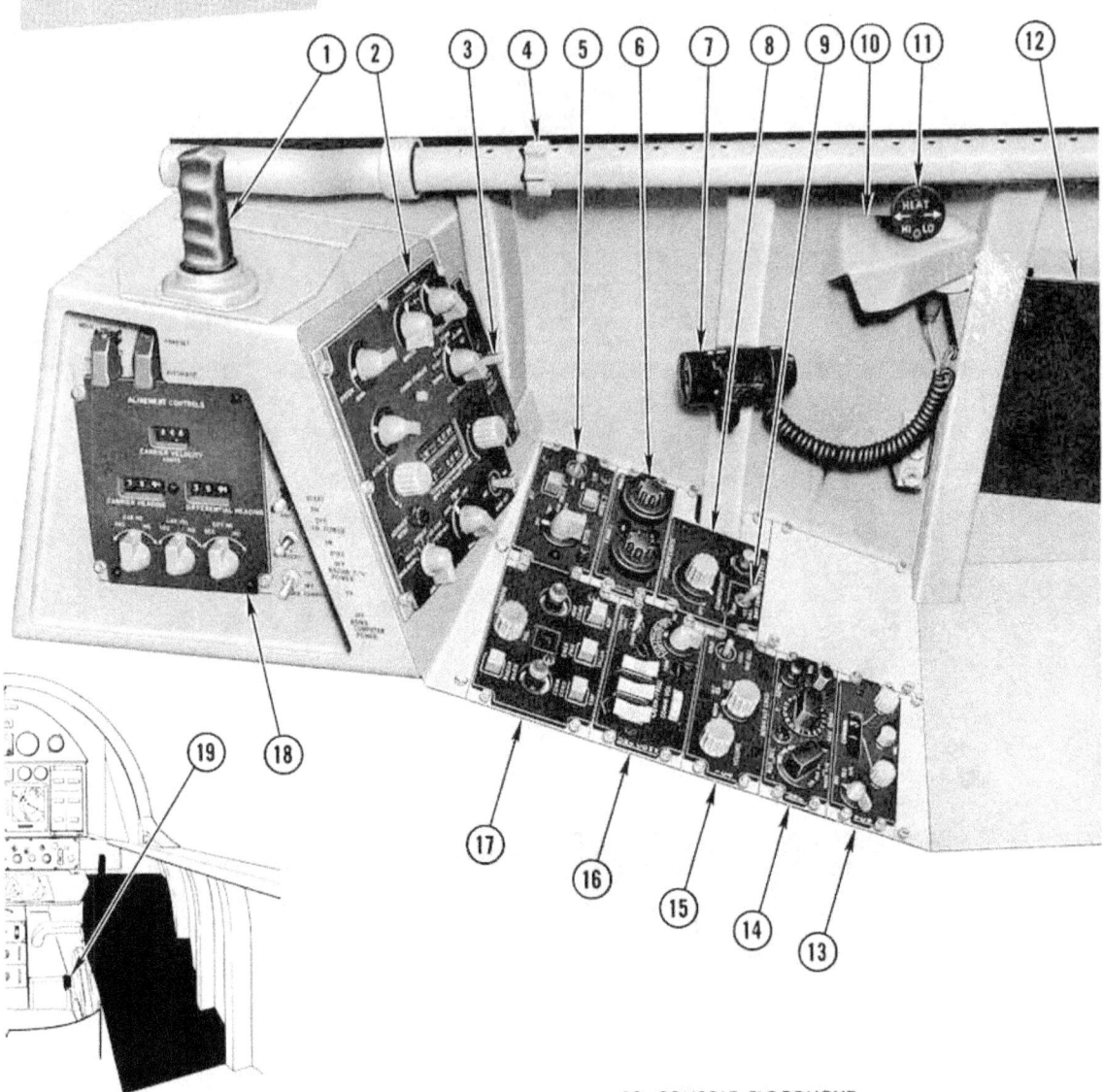

1. CURSOR CONTROL HANDLE
2. BOMBING-NAVIGATION CONTROL PANEL
3. SEAT ADJUST SWITCH
4. COCKPIT AIR CONTROL
5. IFF CONTROL PANEL
6. SIF CONTROL PANEL
7. EMERGENCY LIGHT
8. INTERIOR LIGHTS CONTROL PANEL
9. TRANSMIT CONTROL SWITCH
10. CONSOLE FLOODLIGHT
11. COCKPIT HEAT LEVER
12. STOWAGE CASE
13. TACAN CONTROL PANEL
14. AUXILIARY RECEIVER CONTROL PANEL
15. ICS CONTROL PANEL
16. UHF COMM CONTROL PANEL
17. ICS AUDIO SELECT PANEL
18. ALIGNMENT CONTROL PANEL
19. FOOT-OPERATED MICROPHONE SWITCH

Figure 1-4D

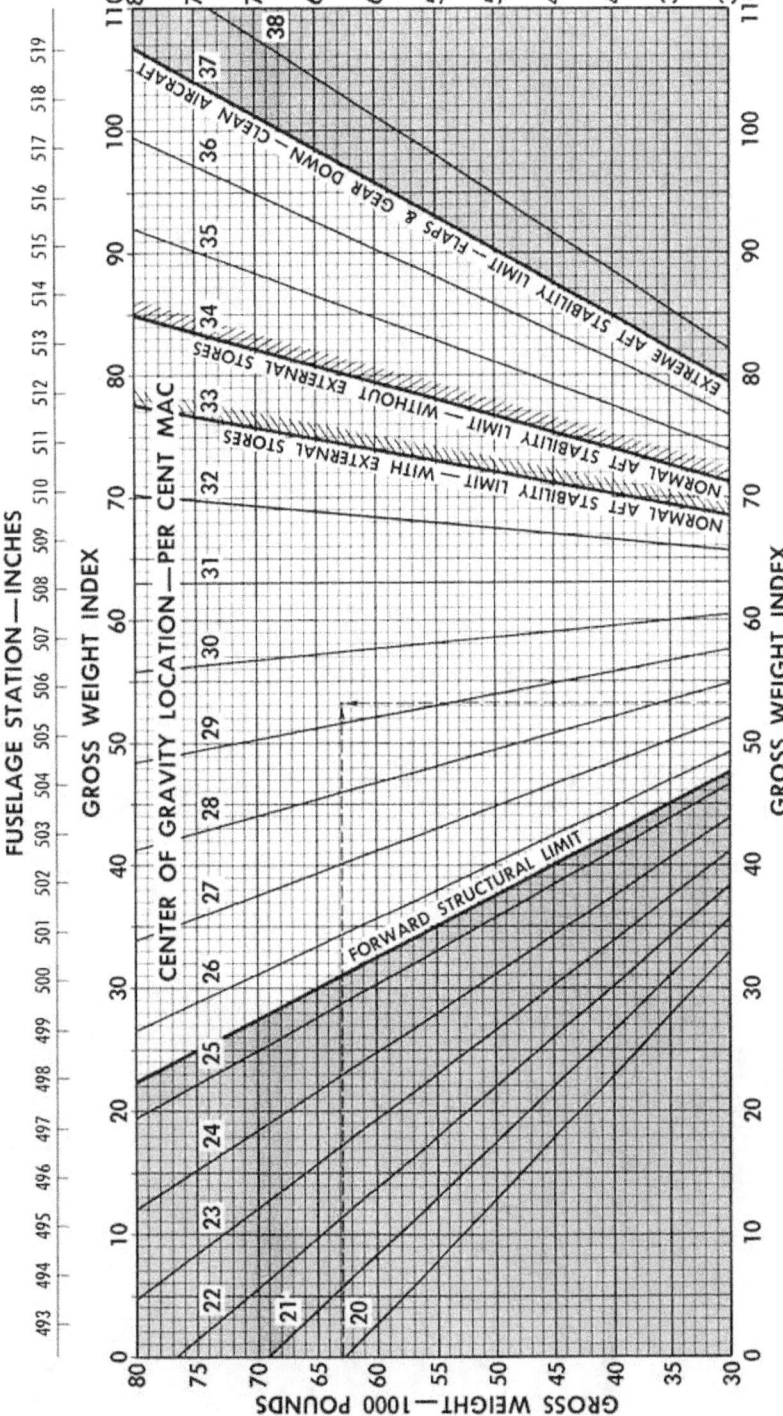

Figure 1-4E

ITEM	WEIGHT (POUNDS)	INCREMENTAL CG INDEX
Fuel:		
Sump Tank	4726	−34.3
Wing Tank	9452	−2.4
Aft Tank	884	+5.8
Forward Can (bomb bay)	2006	−3.4
Mid Can (bomb bay)	2006	+6.9
Aft Can (bomb bay)	2006	+16.7
Buddy Tanker Can	1972	−3.4
Drop Tank	2720	−5.7
Partial Fuel Load Data: (JP-5, Standard Day)		
Sump Tank	4000	−29.0
	3000	−21.8
	2000	−14.5
	1000	−7.3
Wing Tank	9000	−2.3
	8000	−2.0
	7000	−1.8
	6000	−1.5
	5000	−1.3
	4000	−1.0
	2000	−0.5
	1000	−0.3
Aft Tank	800	+5.2
	600	+3.9
	400	+2.6
	200	+1.3
Buddy Tanker or Forward Can	1500	−2.6
	1000	−1.7
	500	−0.9
Mid Can	1500	+5.2
	1000	+3.4
	500	+1.7
Aft Can	1500	+12.5
	1000	+8.3
	500	+4.2

ITEM	WEIGHT (POUNDS)	INCREMENTAL CG INDEX
Drop Tank (each)	2000	−4.2
	1500	−3.2
	1000	−2.1
	500	−1.1

Note

Weights and incremental cg index values are given for *single units*. If two are carried (e.g., pylons and drop tanks), *double* given weight and index values.

CAUTION

The center-of-gravity location method presented should be used only as a check for small changes in configuration. For each *new* configuration (not previously calculated), the Handbook of Weight and Balance Data (NAVWEPS 01-1B-40) *must* be used.

COMPUTING GROSS WEIGHT AND CG

1. Add weights of all load items for the desired configuration to the average basic weight provided. Total is take-off gross weight.

2. Note basic weight cg index number (80.6). Add (algebraically, using the given sign convention) the incremental index numbers of all load items for desired configuration to this value. Final sum is take-off gross weight cg index.

3. Enter the cg locator (figure 1-4E) with take-off gross weight and final cg index. Project gross weight horizontally and index number vertically.

The meeting point may be read in cg, percent MAC. Be certain this point falls in a useful area on the chart.

Note

- A detailed discussion on the gross weight/index method is presented in Section VII of Basic Technical Order, Weight and Balance (T.O. 1-1B-50).

- If a specific aircraft weight from Chart C of the Handbook of Weight and Balance Data (NAVWEPS 01-1B-40) is used in lieu of the average shown, the following formula should be used to arrive at basic cg index:

$$\text{Index} = 63 \frac{\text{Basic Weight } (508.11 - \text{Basic Arm})}{20,000}$$

- For items not listed, the following formula should be used to arrive at incremental cg index number:

$$\text{Increment} = (-) \left(\frac{\text{Item Weight } [508.11 - \text{Item Arm}]}{20,000} \right)$$

- Arms are locations in terms of fuselage station reference, and are shown in Charts A and E of the Handbook of Weight and Balance Data (NAVWEPS 01-1B-40).

EXAMPLE:

Find take-off gross weight and cg location for the long-range (three cans, two drop tanks) configuration.

ITEM	WEIGHT (POUNDS)	INCREMENTAL CG INDEX
Average Basic Weight	33,800	80.6
Pilot	200	−3.6
Systems Operator	200	−2.9
Forward Can	163	−0.3
Mid Can	163	+0.5
Aft Can	163	+1.3
Carriage (3 cans)	104	+0.3
Tail Cone (universal)	80	+1.2
Sump Tank Fuel	4,726	−34.3
Wing Tank Fuel	9,452	−2.4
Aft Tank Fuel	884	+5.8
Forward Can Fuel	2,006	−3.4
Mid Can Fuel	2,006	+6.9
Aft Can Fuel	2,006	+16.7
Pylons (2)	950	−1.0
Drop Tanks (2)	520	−0.8
Drop Tank Fuel (2)	5,440	−11.4
Take-off Gross Weight Take-off CG Index	62,863	53.2

Enter figure 1-4E to determine cg in percent MAC.

Take-off cg location = 29.3 percent MAC.

PART 2 — SYSTEMS

ENGINES

The aircraft is powered by two J79-GE-8 (8A) axial-flow, turbojet engines, each developing a maximum thrust of approximately 17,000 pounds in full afterburner at 100% rpm (7685 rpm) under sea level conditions. The Military Thrust rating is 10,900 pounds. Engine components include variable inlet guide vanes (heated for anti-icing), variable stator vanes in the first six stages of the 17-stage compressor, a three-stage turbine, and 10 annular-flow combustion chambers. Variable-thrust afterburning and a hydromechanically controlled, converging-diverging aerodynamic exhaust nozzle are also incorporated.

ENGINE FUEL SYSTEMS

Fuel flow to the combustion chambers is controlled to establish and maintain desired rpm under various engine operating conditions. The main fuel controls combine inputs of throttle position, compressor inlet temperature, engine speed, and compressor discharge pressure in metering fuel for combustion. They also position the variable stator vanes for optimum compressor performance. Throttle linkage simultaneously provides coordinated signals to the main fuel control, nozzle area control, and afterburner control. Fuel flows from the main fuel control through a flowmeter and an oil cooler into the pressurizing and drain valve, then to the 10 fuel nozzles for spray injection. See figure 1-5. As engine operating power is selected by the throttles, fuel is regulated for changes in compressor inlet temperature and discharge pressure. A fuel cutoff valve within the fuel control unit stops fuel flow to the combustion chambers when the throttles are retarded to OFF.

ENGINE-DRIVEN FUEL PUMPS

Before entering the main fuel control, the low-pressure fuel supply is boosted to high pressure by an engine-driven pump located on the bottom of each engine accessory section. This pump is composed of an impeller-type booster element and single positive displacement, gear-type pumping elements.

MAIN FUEL CONTROLS

Independent hydromechanical fuel control units meter fuel flow to establish and maintain engine rpm. They also initiate afterburner operation, and regulate servo pressure to control the inlet guide vanes and variable stator blades for optimum engine compressor performance. During steady-state operation, fuel metering is controlled by a governor in response to throttle position. The fuel control units limit engine maximum rpm at low compressor inlet temperatures and raise engine minimum rpm at high compressor inlet temperatures.

OIL COOLERS

Each engine is equipped with a main oil cooler and an afterburner oil cooler to reduce and control the temperature of scavenged oil. This is accomplished by using the fuel supply as a coolant. During cold engine operation, the coolers bypass scavenged oil until oil temperature reaches normal operating limits. The coolers also bypass scavenged oil when oil inlet/outlet differential pressure exceeds maximum limits. The afterburner cooler bypasses fuel when the fuel inlet/outlet differential pressure exceeds a maximum limit; however, the main cooler does not bypass fuel under any conditions.

FUEL FILTERS

Two main filters are mounted on the engine, upstream of the fuel control unit. Should the low-pressure filter become clogged, a pressure drop of approximately 25 psi will cause the fuel filter pressure switch to actuate. A filter caution light is provided as an indication that the filter has clogged and that bypass will occur if the pressure continues to drop. The high-pressure fuel filter is provided with a bypass but no warning light. Two fuel filter caution indicators (figure 1-7) are installed on the instrument panel in the pilot's cockpit. An indication of impending fuel filter bypass is provided by differential pressure sensing switches which are set to energize their respective caution indicators before sufficient pressure drop occurs to cause opening of the bypass valve. Should illumination of a FILTER caution indicator be accompanied by fuel flow fluctuations exceeding ±300 pounds per hour, the flight should be discontinued, the fuel filter inspected, and corrective action taken prior to the next flight.

OIL SUPPLY SYSTEMS

Each engine is provided with a pressure-type oil supply system. In addition to providing necessary lubrication, the system also supplies oil to the constant-speed drive units and to the variable exhaust nozzle system. An oil tank is mounted on the compressor housing of each engine. Each engine oil tank has a usable capacity of 5.2 gallons. This supply is sufficient for an 8-hour air refueling mission. The tanks are designed so that failure or leakage of a constant-speed drive unit will not cause engine oil starvation. The oil scavenge systems filter and cool oil from the lubrication, engine hydraulic, and constant-speed drive systems and return the oil to the tanks for re-use. After scavenged oil passes through the engine filter, it flows through the afterburner oil cooler and then through the main oil cooler. If the temperature in the oil tank reaches 295°F, an overheat thermoswitch turns on the applicable OIL HOT caution indicator (figure 1-7) on the pilot's instrument panel. The main and

Section I
Part 2

NAVWEPS 01-60ABA-1

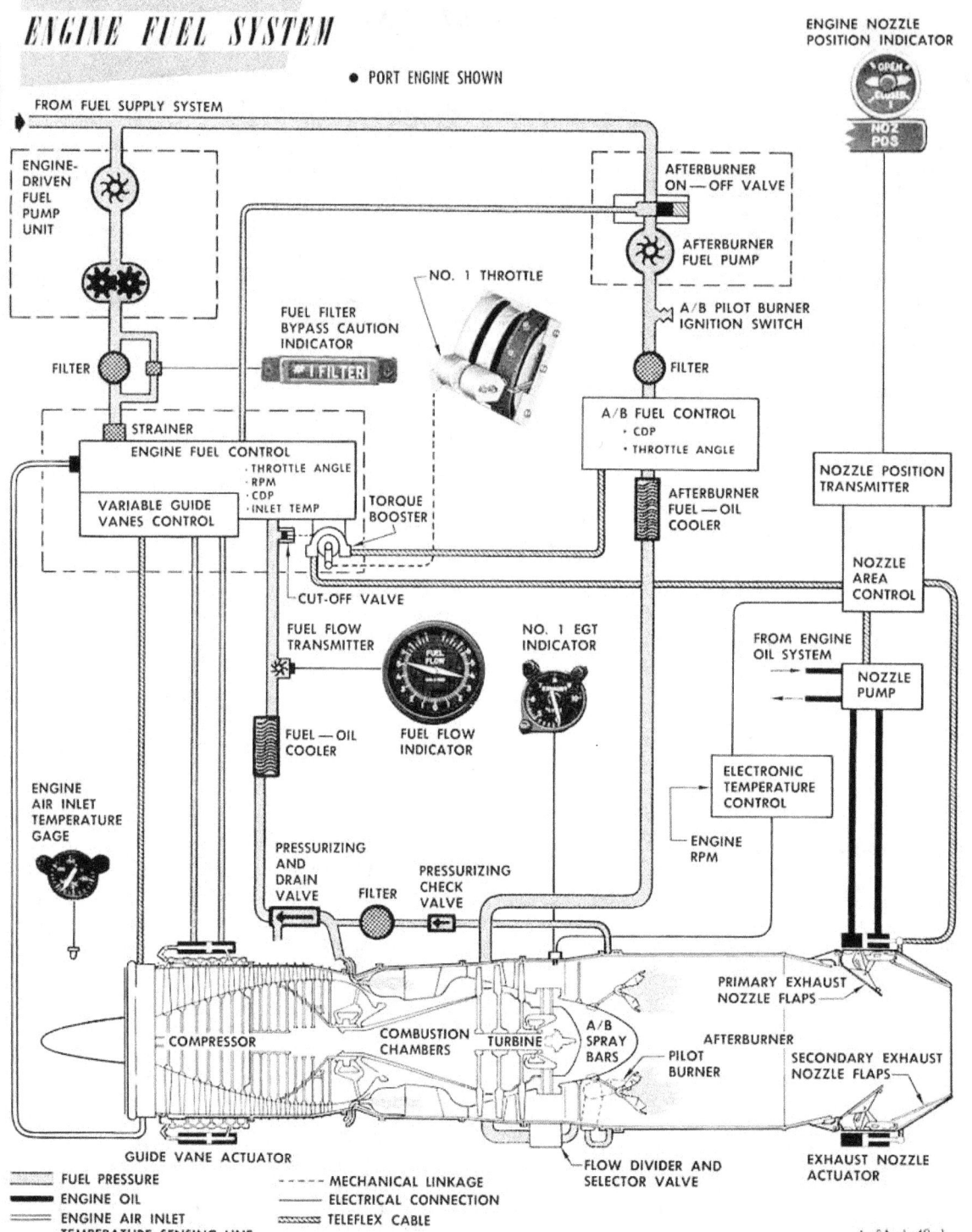

Figure 1-5

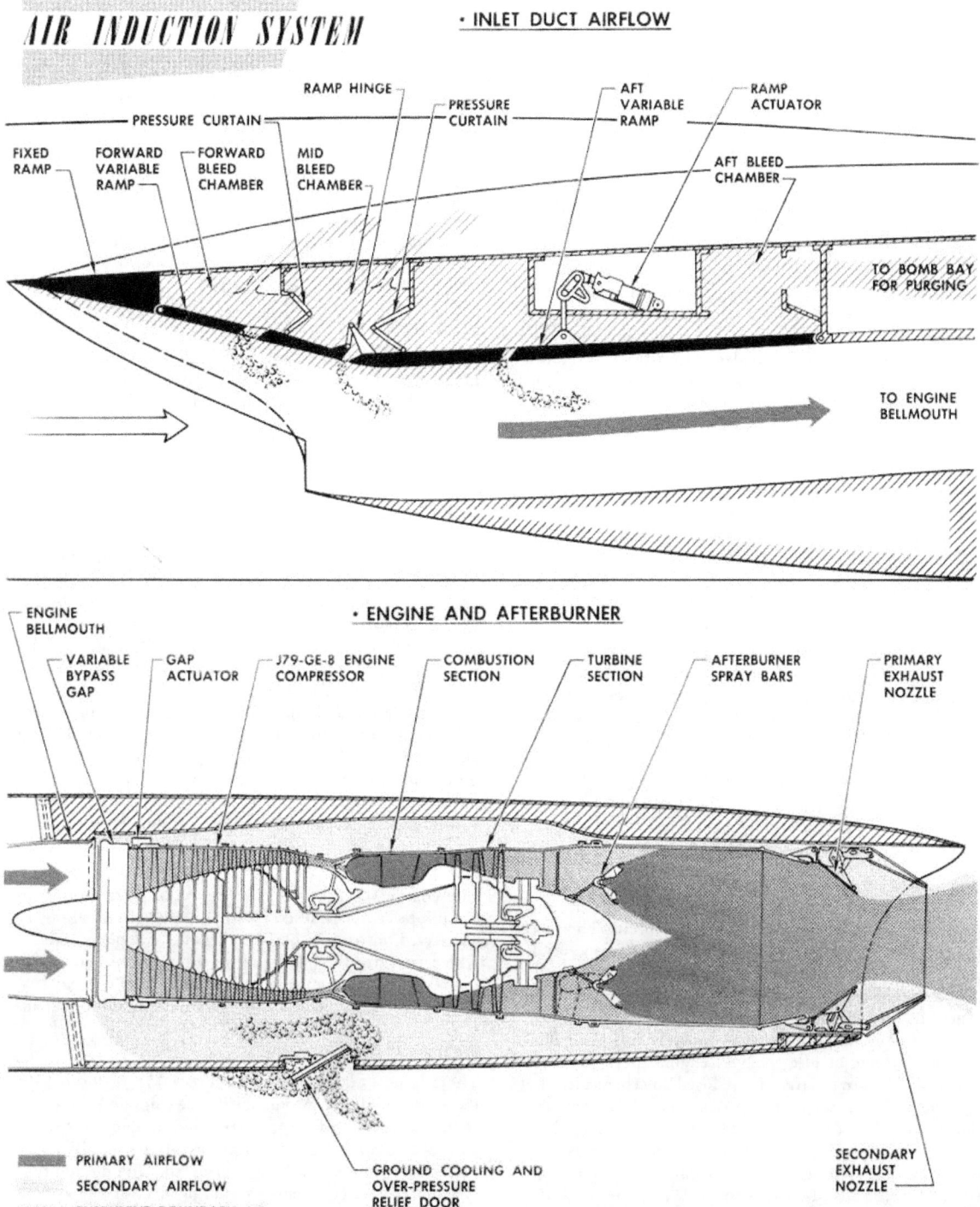

Figure 1-6

afterburner oil coolers transfer oil heat to the fuel passing through the coolers. The oil tanks, gear cases, and sumps are interconnected and vented to a common overboard vent through a pressurizing valve which maintains approximately 4 to 5 psi above ambient pressure at any altitude.

AFTERBURNERS

A variable-thrust afterburner is installed on each engine. The afterburners are self-igniting and self-controlled by separate torch igniters, afterburner fuel pumps, and fuel control units. When afterburner power is selected by moving the throttles to the MIN AFTERBURNER position or beyond, fuel is pumped under high pressure to the afterburner fuel control units, which schedule fuel to the afterburner manifolds and sectors through flow dividers. Afterburning fuel flow is divided into core and annulus flows. Core flow is injected in a small area near the center of the exhaust gas stream. As fuel flow increases, the afterburner fuel control schedules the additional fuel to the annular area around this central core. As afterburning is selected, the afterburner ignition units supply ignition to the pilot burners, which, in turn, ignite the fuel spray. Afterburner thrust may be varied between MIN and MAX for both engines or for either engine independently.

Note

On engines having Power Plant Change No. 8 complied with, the afterburner torch igniters are extinguished when afterburning is terminated. In addition, the torch igniters do not operate when the emerging electrical power unit (RAT) is the only source of electrical power, AB light-offs under this condition may be late and hard, since AB fuel is ignited by the main engine exhaust gas stream.

VARIABLE AREA EXHAUST NOZZLES

The variable area exhaust nozzles control engine exhaust area in order to maintain exhaust gas temperature and engine thrust at optimum within design limits. This feature is primarily important for efficient engine operation at military power and in the afterburner power range. The variable exhaust nozzle control systems utilize engine oil for hydraulic power to position the nozzle actuators. The nozzles are approximately full open during starting and at idle rpm. As engine speed increases above idle, nozzle area is reduced mechanically by throttle position until, at approximately 79% rpm, the nozzle stops closing. The nozzle is modulated according to EGT and rpm requirements while rpm is increased in the cruise power range. After reaching 100% rpm, continued throttle advance closes the nozzle farther until the maximum operating EGT [625 ($\pm$10) °C] is reached. The nozzle area is then modulated to maintain approximately 625°C by amplified signals from the EGT thermocouple harness. As AB light-off rpm drop (rollback) starts, the nozzles are monitored open by increasing EGT (temperature limiting) and modulated to maintain maximum operating EGT. Exhaust temperature and rpm signals electronically control the nozzle for maximum performance during rapid throttle movements.

VARIABLE STATORS AND INLET GUIDE VANES

The engine inlet guide vanes and the first six stages of stator vanes are variable. The system is linked mechanically and is controlled by the main fuel control unit. It is powered by actuators using fuel as the hydraulic medium. The system acts to position the stator and guide vanes as a function of rpm and compressor inlet temperature. This provides maximum compressor efficiency and stall-free acceleration and deceleration.

STARTING SYSTEM

Turbine impingement starting provisions are incorporated. The starting air receptacles are located on the outboard sides of the aft fuselage. See figure 1-40. A manifold supplies external air through seven ports to impinge directly upon the second-stage turbine wheel, providing starting torque to the engine rotor assembly. The starting system provides a connection for automatic shutoff of external air and engine ignition; however, the normal procedure includes the pilot signaling for starting air shutoff as the engine speed reaches approximately 45% rpm. With external electrical power connected and the desired engine master switch positioned to ON, momentarily moving the corresponding engine starter switch to START completes a circuit to the external starting air cart, providing air for engine rotation. Movement of the throttle from OFF to IDLE completes the ignition circuit and opens the fuel control unit cutoff valve. Light-off occurs at 10% to 15% rpm, but starting air aids in developing higher engine speed. When engine rpm reaches approximately 3300 (45%) rpm, the centrifugal switch mounted on the rear gearbox opens, shutting off external starting air and engine ignition.

ENGINE MASTER SWITCHES

The engine MASTER switches (figure 1-7) are located on the pilot's center pedestal. With external electrical power connected, moving either switch to ON completes circuits which energize the boost pumps in the sump and saddle tanks. Subsequent movement of the throttle from OFF to IDLE initiates operation of the engine ignition system.

ENGINE START SWITCHES

The engine START switches (figure 1-7) are located on the center pedestal. Momentarily moving either a START switch to START, with the corresponding engine MASTER switch ON, completes electrical circuits to supply air to the starting system and energizes the engine ignition system. This circuit remains energized until the engine attains approximately 45% rpm, at which time a speed-sensing switch cuts off the external starting air supply. An engine start may be aborted at any time by moving the throttle to OFF and momentarily moving the engine START switch to STOP.

ENGINE FIRE SWITCH

The ENGINE FIRE switch (figure 1-7), operates engine bay fuel and hydraulic shutoff valves. The firewall shutoff valves are actuated to the open position by the engine master switch circuits.

Note

Use of the ENGINE FIRE switch may cause cavitation damage to engine-driven fuel and hydraulic pumps. If the ENGINE FIRE switch is used, it should be left in the selected position (ENG NO. 1 or ENG NO. 2) and the corresponding engine MASTER switch moved to OFF. Ground inspection of all engine systems will be required.

THROTTLES

The engines are controlled by separate throttles (figure 1-7), located in a quadrant on the left console. The No. 1 throttle grip incorporates a plate-type handguard. Throttle stops are provided for positive control of engine power setting and to prevent inadvertent engine shutdown. Throttle stops provided are OFF, IDLE, MIL (military), MIN AFTERBURNER (minimum afterburner), and MAX AFTERBURNER (maximum power). The throttle linkages incorporate restriction cams or "gates." This restriction to throttle aft movement occurs at a quadrant position corresponding to approximately 78% rpm and serves as a caution that further rpm decrease will result in loss of BLC effectiveness. A throttle friction lever (figure 1-7) is mounted on the inboard side of the throttle quadrant for use as a throttle lock and force control. The No. 2 throttle grip contains a radio and ICS microphone switch and a speed brake switch.

EMERGENCY IGNITION BUTTONS

An emergency ignition button (figure 1-7) is installed in the forward face of each throttle grip. These buttons provide engine ignition system operation for air starts. Providing essential a-c bus power is available and the respective engine MASTER switches are on, the system is energized when the emergency ignition buttons are depressed. The ram-air turbine-powered emergency power unit can provide the essential a-c bus electrical power for ignition if both generators are inoperative.

CATAPULT HANDGRIP

An adjustable catapult handgrip (figure 1-7) is mounted on the cockpit bulkhead above and forward of the throttle quadrant. It is spring-loaded to the stowed position and is pulled down and aft to aid in holding the throttles at the Military Thrust power setting during catapulting. On some aircraft,* the handgrip may be set for MIL or MAX AFTERBURNER position.

EGT INDICATORS

An exhaust gas temperature indicator for each engine (figure 1-7) is located on the instrument panel. A press TEST button is provided on each indicator. Depressing the button causes temperature indication to increase to a stop above 1000°C. Upon releasing the button, the needle should return to its original indication. Electrical power for operation of the EGT indicators is supplied by the essential a-c bus. No power-off warning is provided; however, the indicators "freeze" upon power failure. For maximum exhaust gas temperatures, refer to Section I, Part 4, of the Supplemental NATOPS Flight Manual (NAVWEPS 01-60ABA-1A).

TACHOMETERS

A tachometer for each engine (figure 1-7) is located on the instrument panel. They are calibrated in percent of engine speed in rpm and are powered by their respective engine tachometer generators. Engine top speed (100%) corresponds to 7685 rpm. Failure of a tachometer generator results in failure of the indicator, the rpm reading falling to zero.

NOZZLE POSITION INDICATOR

A single miniature indicator located on the pilot's instrument panel (figure 1-7) reflects the position of both afterburner nozzles. The indicators are powered by the essential d-c bus and receive electrical position signals from the nozzle area controllers, indicating nozzle position from fully closed to fully open.

FUEL FLOW INDICATOR

A fuel flow indicator (figure 1-7) is located on the instrument panel. This dual-needle instrument indicates engine fuel consumption in thousands of pounds per hour flow and is scaled in varying increments from 0 to 12. The indicator is powered by the essential instrument a-c bus. Interruption of electrical power freezes the indication.

Note

Fuel flow to the afterburners is not indicated.

OIL PRESSURE INDICATOR

The oil pressure indicator (figure 1-7) is an electrically operated, dual-needle instrument, receiving electrical inputs from two direct, engine-mounted oil pressure transmitters. The indicator is powered by the essential instrument a-c bus. Loss of electrical power causes the indicator needles to remain at their last position. For engine oil pressure limits, refer to Section I, Part 4, of the Supplemental NATOPS Flight Manual (NAVWEPS 01-60ABA-1A).

RAMP CONTROL SWITCH

The ramp control switch (figure 1-7) is located on the left console and is used to start or restore normal variable ramp operation. After engine start, this switch should be held in RESET until the RAMP CONT caution indicator goes out. If the ramp control system cannot be reset, the ramp control switch should be left in STBY.

*Aircraft having ASC 27 complied with

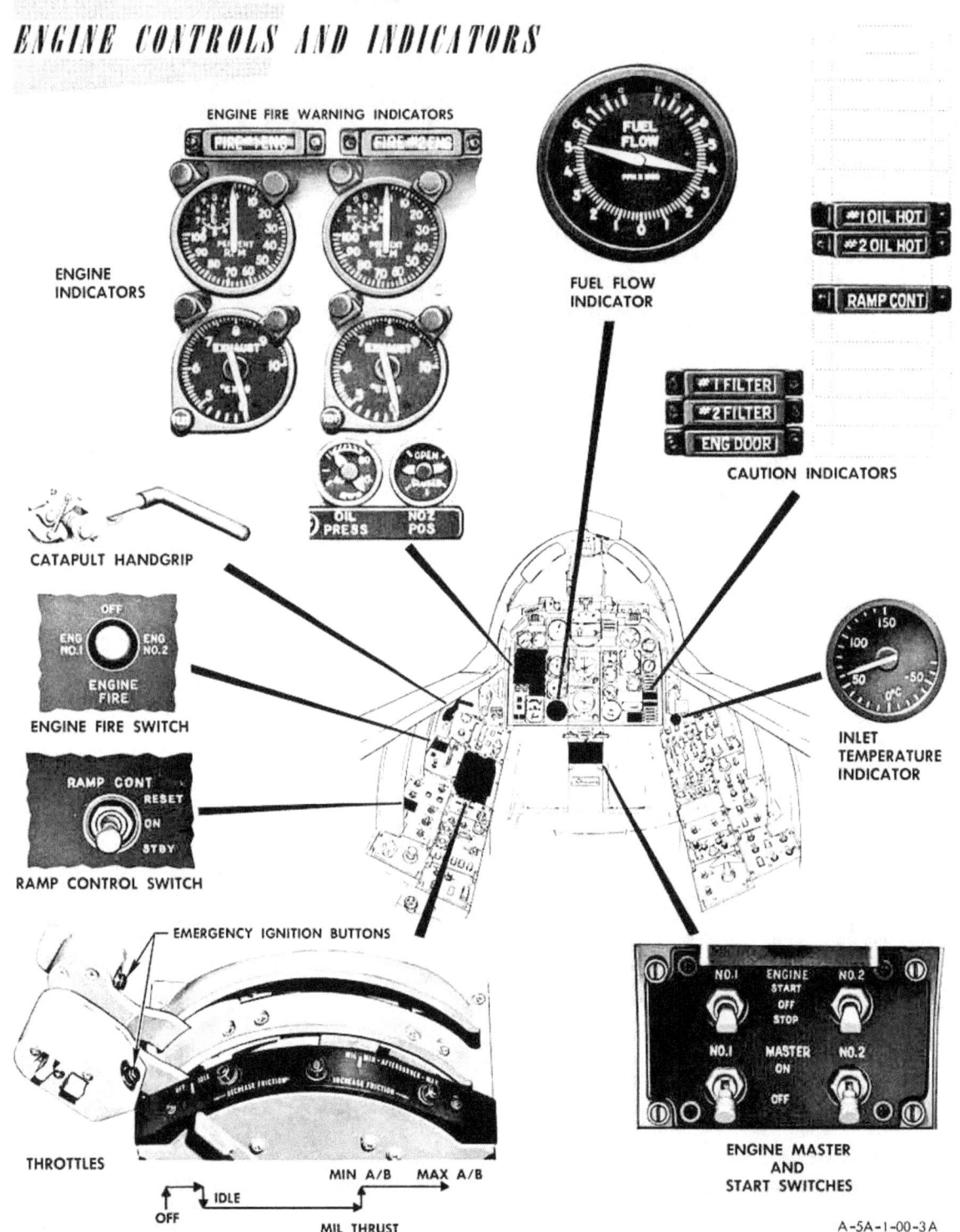

Figure 1-7

Flight with inoperative inlet control must be conducted at reduced Mach number. Refer to Section I, Part 4, of the Supplemental NATOPS Flight Manual (NAVWEPS 01-60ABA-1A).

RAMP CONTROL CAUTION INDICATOR

The ramp control caution indicator (RAMP CONT, figure 1-7) is located on the pilot's instrument panel. Illumination indicates a failure of the hydraulic or the electrical control system, or both. If the malfunction is transient, the ramp control switch may be used to restore normal system operation.

ENGINE CHARACTERISTICS

The J79-GE-8 (8A) engine displays positive control characteristics over its entire range of thrust. At all power settings above approximately 79% rpm, variable exhaust nozzle area is automatically controlled as a function of EGT and throttle position, except during accelerations. At lower power settings, nozzle area is a direct function of throttle position. Normal Thrust is reached at 96% rpm. This is the highest continuous (nonlimited) setting. Military Thrust is reached at maximum sustained EGT and fuel flow at 100% rpm (above approximately 40°F compressor inlet temperature), and is marked at MIL on the quadrant.

ACCELERATION

During normal operation, engine accelerations can be made from any power setting without encountering compressor stall or exceeding EGT limits. For slow accelerations, the exhaust nozzle closes directly with throttle advance until maximum operating EGT is reached. For "burst" accelerations, closure of the nozzle is limited by combined signals of engine rpm and EGT in the nozzle controller ("speed derivative control"), effecting an extremely fast acceleration rate. Time to accelerate from IDLE to MIL averages 4 to 7 seconds (BLC off), and may increase to approximately 10 seconds with BLC operating, depending upon initial airspeed. For accelerations, the exhaust nozzle control system overrides the throttle mechanical schedule at engine speeds as low as 79% rpm, modulating the area larger or smaller to control EGT. Maximum engine speed and ground idle speed are ground adjusted at the engine main fuel control unit.

GOVERNOR OVERRIDE

The main fuel control unit senses compressor inlet temperature to override governor maximum speed and flight idle schedules under varying inlet temperature conditions.

RPM/EGT CUTBACK

At ambient temperatures less than approximately 40°F, the maximum engine mass airflow rating may be exceeded at 100% rpm. Mass airflow is limited, therefore, by lowering engine maximum rpm below this temperature. As compressor inlet temperature (CIT) decreases from approximately 4° to −54°C, engine top speed decreases from 100% to 92%. EGT decreases as rpm drops below approximately 98%. As a typical example, −27°C CIT (approximately 21,000 feet under standard conditions) results in a cutback from 100% rpm and 625°C EGT to about 96% rpm and 616°C EGT.

FLIGHT IDLE RESET

To reduce the effects of insufficient engine airflow on reduction of throttle setting at supersonic speeds, the minimum idle rpm schedule of the main fuel control unit is reset by the governor override. As CIT increases from 57° to 110°C, minimum idle rpm increases from 65% to 100%. Once reset has occurred, rpm cannot be throttle-reduced until CIT is reduced.

AFTERBURNERS

The afterburners should light off within a maximum of 3 seconds after the throttles are moved outboard of the MIL detent and forward into afterburner range. Lights should be obtained at any engine rpm above approximately 90%, and any "hard" or late light should not be accepted as normal. As the throttles are advanced in afterburner range, thrust increase should be smooth and positive, displaying direct control with the throttles. Fuel flow to the afterburners is not indicated. However, combined engine and afterburner fuel flow at MAX AFTERBURNER is approximately four times that of the engine at Military Thrust.

VARIABLE NOZZLES

The variable area exhaust nozzle system schedules engine nozzle area to obtain optimum thrust while maintaining EGT within design limits. During throttle bursts, speed derivative signals (engine speed and EGT) cause the nozzle amplifier to compare rates of rpm and EGT change, scheduling nozzle opening accordingly. As the engine accelerates to near the Military Thrust limit, the nozzle area controller modulates nozzle area, maintaining EGT within steady-state limits. A malfunction in the nozzle hydraulic (engine oil) system causes the nozzle to freeze or drift open, resulting in excessive EGT or loss of EGT and thrust.

Section 1
Part 2

AIR INDUCTION SYSTEM

The air induction system (figure 1-6) provides a stable air supply at sufficient total pressure and controlled velocity to ensure maximum engine efficiency under varying flight conditions. Inlet air pressure recovery is accomplished through controlled velocity reduction by variable ramps. Each inlet duct contains three ramps. The first ramp is a fixed, 6-degree wedge. The second ramp has a slot-perforated surface for bleeding turbulent boundary layer air and is hydraulically variable from 1½ to 23 degrees down. The third ramp is separated from the second ramp by a 1¾-inch slot and moves with the second ramp to form a variable geometric inlet. The ramp system reduces duct air velocity and increases pressure recovery through creation of a series of shock waves in the air stream ahead of the duct lip. To match engine demand with duct supply, an electrically driven, modulating bypass gap is mounted around the front frame of each engine. The gaps pass excess duct airflow around the engines, through the engine compartments, and out the afterburner ejector nozzles. The excess air provides the secondary airflow for engine compartment and engine cooling. The ramps and gaps are automatically scheduled and controlled by an electrical inlet control system. An rpm sensing override circuit provides ramp and duct overload protection in the event of rpm reduction at high supersonic speeds.

SECONDARY AIRFLOW

The air induction system provides air for cooling the engines and engine compartments and supplies air to the variable area exhaust nozzles. During flight, inlet duct air in excess of that required for efficient engine operation is guided around the compressor inlets and into the engine compartments. This airflow cools the engine compartments and flows overboard between the primary and secondary exhaust nozzle flaps. The air creates an aerodynamic convergent-divergent nozzle for the engine primary exhaust flow. During ground operation and with the flaps or landing gear extended, engine compartment cooling air is provided by the engine cooling and overpressure doors, which also provide engine primary air through reverse airflow.

ENGINE PRESSURE RELIEF DOORS

A motor-operated, bungee-loaded door is installed on the bottom center section of each engine compartment. During ground operation or in-flight operation with the flaps extended 25 degrees or more or with the landing gear extended, the doors open to provide outside air for engine compartment cooling and additional primary air for engine operation. Should engine compartment pressure exceed 8 psi, the pressure opens the door, because of the off-center mounting of its hinge, far enough to allow bungee action to complete full opening. The doors are then automatically closed electrically when engine compartment pressure is reduced to less than 7 psi. If the doors remain open (caution light on) after reducing power or airspeed, the remainder of the flight should be conducted at subsonic speeds and below 35,000 feet. On the ground, the doors can be opened by turning on an engine master switch if a source of electrical power is provided.

ENGINE DOOR CAUTION INDICATOR

The engine door caution indicator (ENG DOOR, figure 1-7) is illuminated whenever either engine compartment cooling and overpressure door is open. Illumination on the ground is normal. Illumination during flight with the landing gear and flaps retracted indicates engine compartment overpressure due to incorrect scheduling of the secondary air gaps. Should this occur, excessive airspeed, altitude, and power settings must be avoided to prevent possible internal structural damage.

AIR INDUCTION SYSTEM OPERATION

The air induction system is designed to provide an air supply to the engine at high-pressure recovery with low inlet drag. The system includes variable geometry inlets, variable secondary air bypass gaps, and an automatic control system. The inlet control system is composed of amplifiers which combine electronic signal inputs of duct static pressure, ambient pressure, and aircraft Mach number to control the variable inlet ramps and bypass gaps. Portions of both the forward and aft variable ramps are slotted and separated by an additional 1½-inch slot for removing ramp turbulent boundary layer airflow. This air is directed into plenum chambers above the ramps. The aft plenum air is routed into the bomb bay for cooling and purging; forward and mid plenum air passes overboard through vents at the top of each duct. A cooling and overpressure relief door, located on the underside of each engine compartment, provides engine compartment overpressure relief as necessary under high "Q" conditions, and cooling air

Pages 19 through 22, figures 1-8 through 1-10 deleted.

and engine supplementary air during low-speed and ground operation. Refer to ENGINE PRESSURE RELIEF DOORS, in this section.

INLET CONTROL

Protection against duct airflow instability is required for the air induction system at high Mach numbers during power reductions and in the event of engine or fuel control failure. To prevent severe inlet buzz, the affected ramp will fully extend to the 23-degree (down) position whenever the airspeed is above 1.3 Mach and the engine rpm drops below approximately 94.5%, either by pilot action or a failure. This will not illuminate the RAMP CONT caution indicator, since the monitor circuit, which normally indicates failure if the ramps are more than 3 degrees apart, is bypassed in this case. When speed drops below 1.3 indicated Mach number or rpm is increased above approximately 94.5%, the monitor circuit will be reactivated and will indicate failure. Holding the ramp control switch in RESET until the failure light goes out will then reset the ramp to the normal schedule. Should this light not extinguish, the ramps must be observed externally to determine their relative positions.

VARIABLE RAMPS

Below 0.95 Mach, the variable ramps are maintained in the fully retracted position with the inlet control system reset in normal operation. Above 0.95 Mach, the variable ramps are automatically positioned by hydraulic actuators in accordance with a programmed schedule, increasing to about 14 degrees down at maximum speed. At high supersonic speeds, inlet airflow is decelerated through two oblique waves and a normal shock wave. The ramp schedule provides duct airflow with high-pressure recovery for good engine performance throughout the airspeed envelope.

Ramp Monitor

Should a failure occur which results in the inlet control system driving the ramps to positions differing by more than 3 degrees, the control system will monitor off, providing a "fail-safe" mode of operation. Should this occur, the ramp control caution indicator will illuminate and the ramps will be driven by air load slowly toward the fully retracted position. Under these conditions, if the system cannot be reset, flight speed should be limited to 1.3 indicated Mach number. To provide improved single-engine efficiency, turning off the windmilling engine MASTER switch will bypass the monitor circuit and drive the respective ramp to the 23-degree extended (down) position, reducing windmilling drag.

CAUTION

- Moving an engine MASTER switch to OFF at any Mach number above 0.3 will cause the corresponding ramp to extend (down) regardless of engine operation or rpm.

- Subsequent to ramp control system failure, DO NOT repeatedly or continuously hold the RAMP CONT switch in RESET if reset is not successful. The RESET position overrides the ramp monitor circuit and hydraulic shutoff to the ramp actuators. This condition may cause the ramps to be driven full down, resulting in a large loss of thrust.

To protect the aircraft from a failure of one of the above override circuits at low speed, neither ramp will extend to the full down position when the aircraft speed is below 0.3 Mach number regardless of other conditions. If speed is reduced below 0.3 Mach number when one ramp is extended, the RAMP CONT indicator will illuminate. The ramps should then be reset, returning the extended ramp to schedule. If the RAMP CONT caution indicator cannot be extinguished by resetting the ramps, the ramp will move slowly to the fully retracted position.

BYPASS GAPS

A variable area secondary air gap, located around each engine immediately ahead of the compressor inlet, acts to properly match engine airflow demand and inlet duct supply. These gaps, which are actuated by electrically powered jackscrews, can modulate from a maximum of 80 square inches opening to a minimum of 30 square inches. Below 1.3 Mach, there is no requirement to decrease the bypass area, and the gaps are maintained at 80 square inches. Above 1.3 Mach, the gaps are operated in a modulating schedule of decreasing area as a function of duct static pressure, ambient pressure, and aircraft Mach number. Should a failure occur in the inlet control system, the gaps are immediately driven to full open (80 square inches) compensating for the increased airflow during ramp retraction under air load. Air which is directed into the engine compartments by the gaps is used for engine and structural cooling and is ejected through the secondary nozzle of the variable area afterburner. Utilizing the bypass air in this manner forms an aerodynamic convergent-divergent exhaust nozzle, increasing engine thrust up to 5 percent. The gaps also serve to minimize inlet drag and match engine and inlet airflow.

Duct Airflow Instability

In the event of improper variable ramp angle scheduling at speeds above 1.3 Mach, the position of the duct normal shock wave becomes unstable and may alternately enter and leave the duct, causing rapid fluctuations in pressure. If caused by faulty ramp scheduling, this instability is characterized by a low amplitude, moderate frequency buffet which increases in intensity with increasing Mach number. If caused by structural failure of an inlet ramp or failure of an engine rpm sensing switch during a power reduction, fully developed inlet buzz may occur. Refer to Section IV. Should airflow instability or buzz onset occur, Mach number should be reduced as quickly as possible by extending speed brakes and retarding the throttles to not less than Military Thrust. If this buffet coincides with illumination of the RAMP CONT caution indicator, reset should also be attempted. Normally, if engine rpm is reduced to less than 94.5% rpm above 1.3 Mach, the engine rpm switch extends the ramp of the affected inlet to the full down position (23 degrees) to preclude inlet buzz. When rpm is re-established above the rpm switch limit, the RAMP CONT caution indicator will illuminate and the ramp control system should be reset.

ENGINE OPERATING PROCEDURES

ENGINE STARTING

Engine ground starting requires both external a-c electrical power and engine starting air. Normal starts may be made with or without automatic shutoff of the air source, using the RCPP-105-1 pod or RCPT-105-3 unit. When using the automatic feature (electrical connection from aircraft to air unit), flow of start air begins when the engine START switch is moved to START, ignition operation is automatic, and start air is shut off automatically when an engine rpm of about 45% is reached. During pilot-controlled starts (electrical connection not used), the pilot must signal for airflow, depress the EMER IGN button to obtain ignition, and signal for airflow shutoff at about 45% rpm. During pilot-controlled starts, the engine START switches need not be used, since airflow is direct to the impingement starting ducts. For complete engine operating procedures, refer to Sections III and IV.

ALTERNATE STARTS

Alternate starts may be made using GTC-85 or USAF MA-1 or MA-1A GTC units. These units are designed to operate with air turbine starting systems, and are not capable of providing the volume of air required for normal turbine impingement starts. The procedure for alternate starts is nearly identical to that for normal starts, except that maximum obtainable engine rpm (approximately 8%) should be attained before moving the throttle from OFF, and the throttle should be modulated between OFF and IDLE to maintain EGT between 675° and 700°C during acceleration to IDLE. When EGT stabilizes or approximately 30% rpm is reached, the throttle may be moved to the IDLE stop.

CAUTION

Engine start should not be attempted with flaps extended. Engine compressor loss due to BLC flow may cause false or hanging starts. If flaps are extended, move the flap control switch to CRUISE or SUPERSONIC, move the engine START switch to START or signal for airflow, and delay moving the throttle to IDLE until the flaps have retracted.

AIRCRAFT FUEL SUPPLY SYSTEM

The aircraft fuel supply system (figure 1-11), includes the sump tank, aft (saddle) fuselage tank, integral wing tanks, provisions for three bomb bay fuel cans, and two 400-gallon drop tanks. The fuselage sump tank, located immediately forward of the bomb bay, contains two dual-speed boost pumps (high-duty at afterburner selection), each incorporating standpipes for inverted flight. All fuel from the other tanks is transferred into the sump tank and directed to the engine-driven fuel pumps. The integral wing tanks contain two dual-speed transfer pumps and two scavenge pumps. The wing transfer pumps switch to high-duty during afterburner operation, when wing fuel is being dumped, and during buddy tanker transfer operation. The scavenge pumps ensure movement of fuel from the outer portion of the wing tanks to the transfer pumps. The aft fuselage saddle tank is located above the bomb bay, forward of the vertical stabilizer. It contains a level control valve and two transfer pumps. During flight, the wing, sump, and saddle tanks are pressurized to approximately 5.5 psi by air from the air conditioning and pressurization system. The tanks are depressurized when the landing gear or air refueling probe is extended. Fuel system pressurization prevents excessive fuel boil-off and improves boost pump performance and engine suction feed in either normal or inverted flight at all altitudes. A fuel-air separator is incorporated in the forward boost pump feed line in the sump tank between the pump and the engine fuel feed manifold. Should the pump become temporarily uncovered, such as during flight with a nose-high attitude and low fuel state, the fuel-air separator allows any air in the fuel to escape back into the tank instead of feeding to the engine.

INTERNAL FUEL TANKS

The internal fuel tanks consist of a fuselage sump tank, two integral wing tanks, and an aft fuselage (saddle) tank.

BOMB BAY FUEL CANS

For normal mission, two expendable fuel cans are installed in the linear bomb bay. For long-range ferry missions, three cans may be installed. Bomb bay can fuel is transferred directly to the sump tank by air pressure at 25 psi from the air conditioning and pressurization system. The solenoid-operated pressurization valve is normally open to assure fuel transfer in the event of electrical failure. Provisions are also made for installation of a buddy tanker refueling package in the linear bomb bay. Refer to BUDDY TANKER REFUELING SYSTEM, in this section.

DROP TANKS

Two 400-gallon drop tanks can be installed at the external store stations. When drop tank fuel is selected, the tanks are pressurized by 14 psi air pressure, forcing fuel directly into the sump and wing tanks. The tanks can be released in flight by using the armament release system. If the emergency jettison button is used, the tanks are released without forced ejection. Refer to ARMAMENT SYSTEM, in Section I, Part 2, of the Supplemental NATOPS Flight Manual (NAVWEPS 01-60ABA-1A).

Section I
Part 2

NAVWEPS 01-60ABA-1

AIRCRAFT FUEL SUPPLY SYSTEM

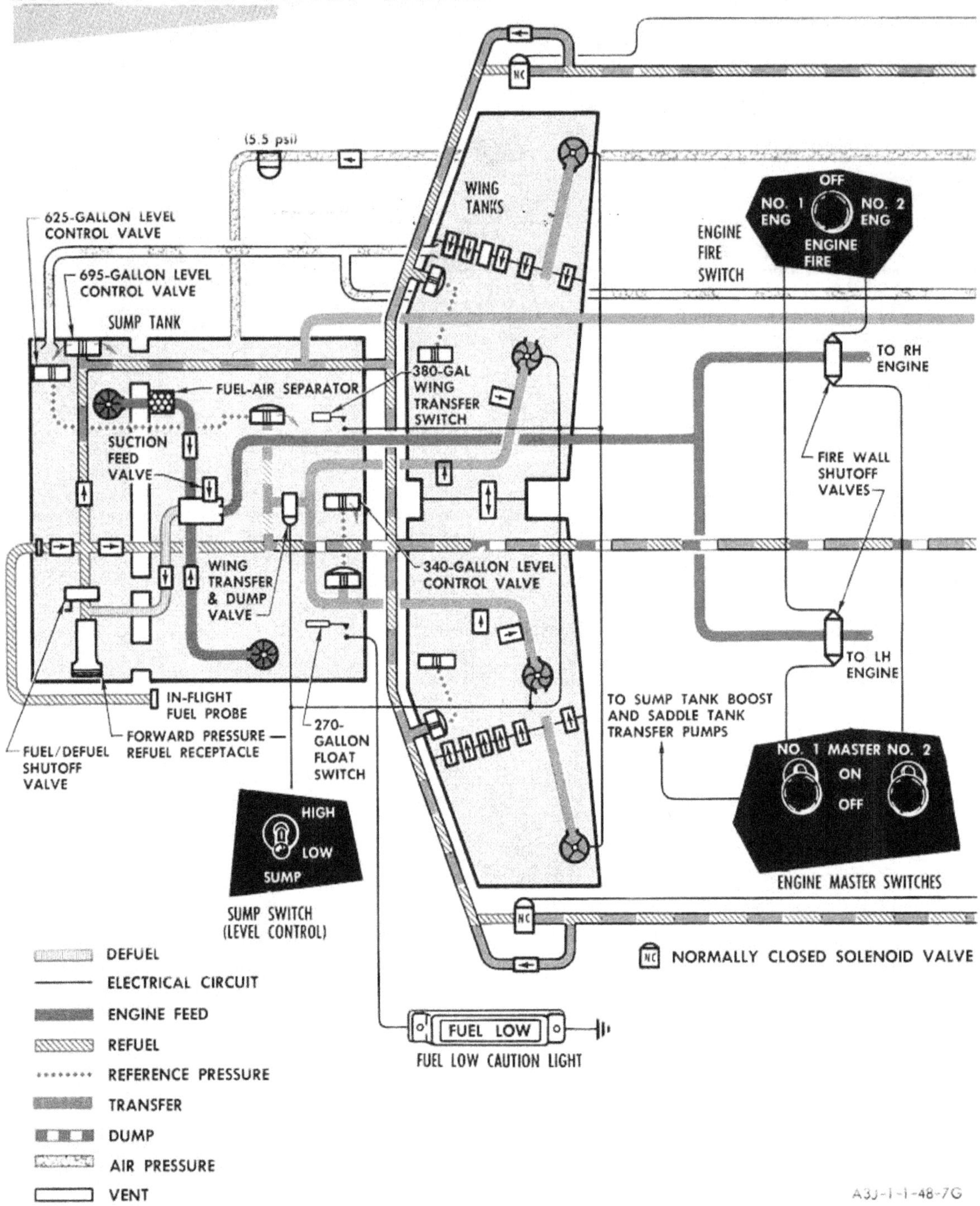

- 625-GALLON LEVEL CONTROL VALVE
- 695-GALLON LEVEL CONTROL VALVE
- SUMP TANK
- (5.5 psi)
- WING TANKS
- ENGINE FIRE SWITCH
- OFF / NO. 1 ENG / NO. 2 ENG / ENGINE FIRE
- FUEL-AIR SEPARATOR
- 380-GAL WING TRANSFER SWITCH
- TO RH ENGINE
- SUCTION FEED VALVE
- FIRE WALL SHUTOFF VALVES
- WING TRANSFER & DUMP VALVE
- 340-GALLON LEVEL CONTROL VALVE
- IN-FLIGHT FUEL PROBE
- FORWARD PRESSURE REFUEL RECEPTACLE
- 270-GALLON FLOAT SWITCH
- TO LH ENGINE
- TO SUMP TANK BOOST AND SADDLE TANK TRANSFER PUMPS
- FUEL/DEFUEL SHUTOFF VALVE
- NO. 1 MASTER / NO. 2 / ON / OFF
- ENGINE MASTER SWITCHES
- HIGH / LOW / SUMP
- SUMP SWITCH (LEVEL CONTROL)
- NC — NORMALLY CLOSED SOLENOID VALVE
- FUEL LOW
- FUEL LOW CAUTION LIGHT

Legend:
- DEFUEL
- ELECTRICAL CIRCUIT
- ENGINE FEED
- REFUEL
- REFERENCE PRESSURE
- TRANSFER
- DUMP
- AIR PRESSURE
- VENT

Figure 1-11 (Sheet 1)

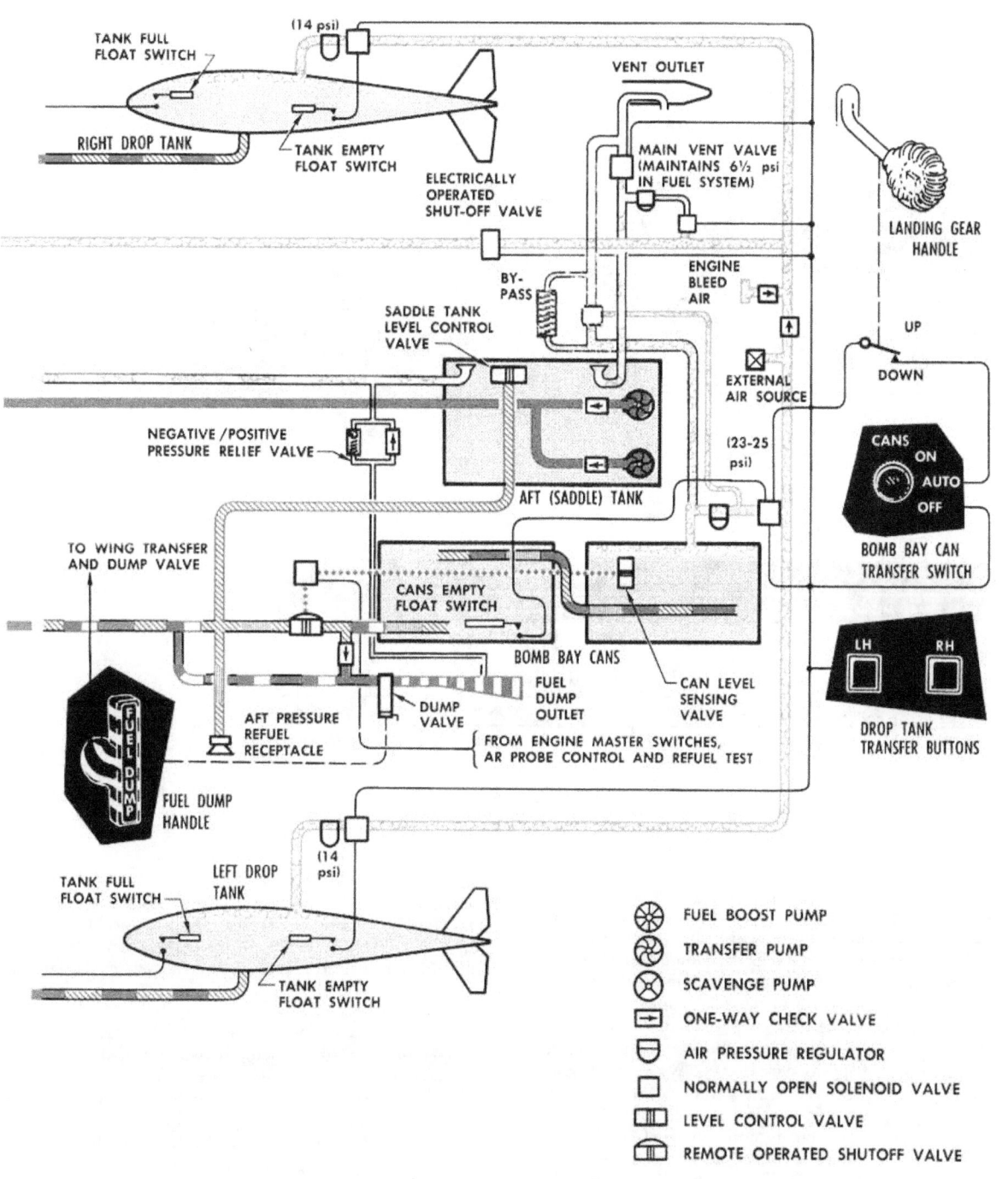

Figure 1-11 (Sheet 2)

- JP-5 FUEL (6.8 POUNDS/GAL STANDARD DAY ONLY)
- FOR JP-4 FUEL USE 6.5 POUNDS/GAL FOR STANDARD DAY

TANK CAPACITIES

TANK	GALLONS	POUNDS
SUMP TANK	695	4726
WING TANKS	1390	9452
AFT (SADDLE) TANK	130	884
BOMB BAY CAN (EACH)	295	2006
BUDDY TANK	290	1972
DROP TANK (EACH)	400	2720

APPROXIMATE USABLE FUEL TOTALS

NORMAL MISSION		LONG RANGE MISSION		FERRY MISSION		BUDDY TANKER MISSION	
SUMP TANKS WING TANKS SADDLE TANK BOMB BAY CANS (2)		NORMAL MISSION PLUS DROP TANKS (2)		LONG RANGE MISSION PLUS ADDITIONAL BOMB BAY CAN		LONG RANGE MISSION PLUS BUDDY PACKAGE	
GALLONS	POUNDS	GALLONS	POUNDS	GALLONS	POUNDS	GALLONS	POUNDS
2805	19,074	3605	24,514	3900	26,520	3895	26,486

Figure 1-11A

FUEL TRANSFER

Normal transfer of fuel from the individual tanks is controlled by level control valves in the sump tank. As total fuel remaining decreases, the valves maintain a definite sump tank level, depending upon which tank is transferring. This provides automatic control of aircraft center of gravity. The sump tank boost pumps and the saddle tank transfer pumps will operate when electrical power is available and either engine master switch is positioned to ON. With the engine MASTER switch ON, saddle tank fuel is sequenced to transfer when sump fuel is less than the full level of approximately 4700 pounds until depleted. Bomb bay can transfer is sequenced when sump level is less than 4250 pounds if the bomb bay CANS transfer switch is in the AUTO or ON position. In AUTO, bomb bay can fuel is prevented from transferring while the landing gear handle is in the DOWN position. Wing tank fuel transfers automatically when sump quantity falls below the 2300-pound level. If the SUMP switch is placed in HIGH (as for buddy tanker operations), wing fuel is sequenced to transfer to the sump tank when sump level falls below the 4250-pound level. Drop tank fuel transfer, when selected by the pilot, will maintain a 4700-pound sump level at Military Thrust above approximately 7500 feet MSL with one tank selected (at any altitude with both tanks selected) until drop tank is exhausted.

Note

At medium and low altitudes with the engines operating at afterburner power settings, drop tank fuel transfer may not be sufficient to maintain a full sump tank. Should this occur, the sump fuel level may drop until the 4700-pound level control valve is uncovered to allow transfer of bomb bay can fuel when selected.

Normal procedures require the CANS transfer switch be placed in AUTO and the SUMP switch at LOW at all times unless the buddy tanker package is installed. Drop tank and bomb bay can fuel transfer pressurization is vented and shuts off automatically upon fuel depletion. Refer to FUEL SYSTEM OPERATION, in this section.

Note

When the bomb bay fuel cans are nearly empty, cycling of the can pressurization system may occur, due to the alternate actuation of the float switch by changing fuel levels. This cycling may be accompanied by a mild "rumbling" which will continue until the forward can is empty or the CANS transfer switch is turned off, depressurizing the bomb bay cans.

FUEL VENTING

All fuel tanks are pressurized and provisions are made for venting as follows:

1. The wing and sump tanks vent into the saddle tank and from there vent through the normally open main vent valve into the vent outlet pipe. The main vent valve is electrically energized (closed) when the landing gear is retracted. It will relieve the vent pressure at approximately 6.5 psig.
2. A negative/positive relief valve is provided in the wing and sump tank vent line (negative relief during defueling and positive relief for a clogged overboard vent). This valve is connected to the fuel dump outlet.
3. The bomb bay cans vent directly through a separate line, containing a pneumatically operated vent shutoff valve, to the vent outlet pipe. The shutoff valve is open for can venting and closed when the cans are pressurized. A bomb bay can relief valve bypasses any overpressurization to the vent outlet.
4. Drop tank pressure relief valves vent excessive air pressure overboard.

FUEL DUMPING

The pilot may dump wing and bomb bay can fuel through a line at the aft end of the linear bomb bay if the necessity arises. Refer to FUEL DUMP HANDLE, in this section. Bomb bay can fuel is dumped by engine compressor bleed pressure in approximately 3 minutes if two cans are installed and in 5 minutes if three cans are installed. At normal (nose high) flight attitudes, wing tank fuel is dumped at 1600 to 1800 pounds per minute. In the event of bomb bay can pressurization failure, the aft can may be dumped by gravity in about 10 to 15 minutes. Under these conditions, the forward can will not dump, due to lack of sufficient air pressure. For dumping the aft can (2000 pounds), optimum aircraft attitude is a zero pitch angle.

CAUTION

Dumping bomb bay can fuel with the sump switch in HIGH can result in loss of total fuel to a level as low as 1700 pounds. It is recommended that LOW sump be selected prior to dumping bomb bay can fuel and the sump tank quantity be closely monitored during fuel dumping as a method of preventing inadvertent loss of total fuel.

CAUTION

If the dump handle is left in the wing dumping position after the wing tanks are dry, total fuel may be lost to 1700 pounds, regardless of sump switch position. It is recommended that wing and total quantity be monitored and that the dump handle be returned to the off position when the desired amount of fuel remains to prevent inadvertent loss of sump tank fuel.

REFUELING

GROUND PRESSURE REFUELING

All internal tanks may be refueled in approximately 5 minutes through two pressure refueling receptacles. The forward receptacle is located aft of the nose gear well and the aft receptacle is located inboard and aft of the left main landing gear well. Aircraft with drop tanks can be refueled in approximately 7½ minutes. External electrical power is required for refueling the drop tanks and level control valve testing. The aft refueling receptacle can be used to fill only the saddle tank and the bomb bay cans and to fill the sump tank to the 4250-pound level. The drop tanks may be filled at gravity fueling points, if desired. Refer to Part 3, in this section.

Note

After refueling, the push-pull refuel-defuel selector valve, located in the forward receptacle access, must be pushed to the FLIGHT AND DEFUELING position and the position securing pin must also be installed.

AIR REFUELING

An air refueling system is installed to extend mission range and endurance. The system consists of a hydraulically actuated, retractable probe and line connections to the pressure refueling system.

Hookup is accomplished by flying the probe into the cone-shaped drogue being trailed by the tanker. After making contact, the pilot of the receiving aircraft decreases the distance between his aircraft and the tanker until at least 6 feet of hose has rewound onto the reel. This action automatically starts fuel flow through the hose. At the system design receiving rate of about 2000 pounds per minute, a normal air refueling may be accomplished in 3½ to 4 minutes. Normal extension of the air refueling probe depressurizes the internal fuel system for refueling operations. Refer to AIR REFUELING in Section IV.

Note

To air refuel drop tanks, the DROP TANK TRANSFER buttons must be released (pressure off) to depressurize the tanks.

SUMP SWITCH

The sump switch, located on the fuel transfer panel (26, figure 1-3), provides control of the sump fuel level. Normal sequencing requires selecting the LOW position. Buddy tanker operations require that the SUMP switch be positioned to HIGH. Moving the SUMP switch to HIGH opens the wing dump and transfer gate valve, transferring wing tank fuel to the sump tank at any time sump level is less than approximately 4250 pounds. The HIGH sump level capability is provided for center-of-gravity control during buddy tanker operations. Although internal transfer of wing fuel to the buddy can is independent of sump switch position, the HIGH position allows simultaneous transfer of wing fuel to both the sump tank and the buddy fuel can when sequenced by the respective level control valves. The HIGH sump position also serves as an alternate method of initiating wing fuel transfer to the sump tank in the event of transfer failure in the LOW position.

Note

Prior to shutting down the engines or pulling electrical power after flight, it is recommended that the sump switch be checked in the LOW position. If this check is not made, fuel from the wing and sump tanks may gravitate through the wing transfer valve, causing the bomb bay cans to overfill. This results in fuel overboarding and, under some conditions, an aft center of gravity.

CANS TRANSFER SWITCH

The CANS transfer switch on the fuel transfer panel (26, figure 1-3) is located on the pilot's left console. Normal bomb bay can transfer is initiated by placing the switch to AUTO prior to take-off. After the aircraft is airborne, moving the landing gear handle to the UP position will allow the cans to pressurize. Use of the ON position allows bomb bay can pressurization regardless of landing gear handle position. In the buddy configuration, the switch must be OFF to prevent transfer of the buddy fuel to the sump tank and the subsequent need to transfer additional wing fuel back to the bomb bay cans for buddy tanker operations.

CAUTION

All catapult take-offs are made with the CANS transfer switch in AUTO. Catapult launches with the cans pressurized may cause overstress failure of the cans with attendant fuel loss and explosion hazard. For gear down operations, such as FMLP and GCA, the CANS transfer switch should be moved to ON.

Note

Should a sequencing malfunction allow the wing tanks to empty with the bomb bay cans full, an excessively aft center-of-gravity condition can result. Bomb bay can fuel should be transferred or dumped prior to landing. Refer to FUEL SYSTEM OPERATION WITH BUDDY TANKER, in this section.

DROP TANK TRANSFER BUTTONS

Drop tank fuel is selected by mechanical push buttons located on the fuel transfer panel (26, figure 1-3). Fuel transfer from either or both tanks is selected by depressing the buttons, marked LH or RH. Drop tank fuel transfer may be stopped by depressing and releasing the buttons again. This action stops the flow of pressurization air and vents the tank to atmosphere.

IN-FLIGHT FUEL PROBE SWITCH

The INFLIGHT FUEL PROBE switch (27, figure 1-3) is located on the pilot's left console. When the switch is moved to EXTEND, the probe is actuated forward to the extended position. This automatically dumps fuel system pressurization (5.5 psi) and bomb bay can transfer pressure (25 psi); however, drop tank pressurization is not affected. When the switch is moved to RETRACT, the probe is actuated aft to the retracted position and fuel remaining in the probe is automatically purged into the sump tank by air from the windshield anti-ice and rain removal system. Probe extension or retraction requires 5 to 10 seconds.

FUEL DUMP HANDLE

The fuel dump handle (2, figure 1-23) is located on the pilot's left forward console. The fuel dump handle has two positions. When the handle is pulled straight back, the bomb bay cans are pressurized, the dump tube is extended, and bomb bay fuel is dumped overboard. If the handle is further rotated 45 degrees to the right, the wing transfer and dump valve opens, the wing transfer pumps switch to high-duty, and wing fuel is dumped overboard via the dump tube. Primary bus a-c electrical power is required for operation of the wing transfer pumps. In case of transfer pump failure, however, some dumping will occur because of the 5.5 psi differential pressure in the tank. Dump rate is improved by maintaining a normal flight (nose-high) attitude.

CAUTION

Before dumping bomb bay fuel, ensure that the SUMP switch is placed in the LOW position. This allows the wing transfer dump valve to remain closed, preventing inadvertent loss of wing fuel during bomb bay can dumping.

> **CAUTION**
>
> Do not attempt to dump fuel from the bomb bay cans with the SUMP switch at HIGH and the air refueling probe extended, unless required in an emergency to reduce total weight. In this condition, the cans are vented and wing fuel only will be dumped.

FUEL QUANTITY INDICATOR

A fuel quantity indicator (25, figure 1-4) is installed on the pilot's instrument panel. By using the fuel gage selector (17, figure 1-3), total fuel or fuel quantity in an individual tank may be checked. Total fuel quantity is indicated by a digital counter, calibrated in pounds remaining. In the B BAY, WING, LDT, RDT, or AFT position of the fuel gage selector, individual tank quantity is indicated by the pointer, while the total fuel counter remains fixed at the indication before selection. In the normal SUMP position, sump tank level is indicated by the pointer, while total fuel remaining is read continuously on the counter. A press-to-test button is provided to check the indicator for normal operation. When the test button is pressed, the needle and totalizer should run down scale. Upon releasing the button, the needle should return to its original position.

FUEL LOW CAUTION INDICATOR

The fuel low caution indicator (FUEL LOW, figure 1-4) automatically illuminates when the fuel level in the sump tank reaches approximately 1700 to 1900 pounds.

FUEL SYSTEM OPERATION

The normal transfer of wing, saddle tank, and bomb bay can fuel to the sump tank is automatic. Drop tank fuel must be manually selected. With external electrical power connected, placing either engine MASTER switch to ON activates the sump tank boost and aft tank transfer pumps. Prior to take-off, the CANS transfer switch should be in AUTO or OFF, the sump switch LOW, and drop tank transfer buttons selected off. Fuel from the aft fuselage tank will maintain the sump tank level at approximately 4700 pounds if engine flow rate does not exceed a total of 7500 pounds per hour. If take-off is delayed and saddle tank fuel is exhausted, sump tank level may be maintained at approximately 4700 pounds (625 gallons) by moving the CANS transfer switch ON. This procedure allows can fuel to transfer to the sump, maintaining a favorable center-of-gravity condition. After the desired sump tank level is attained and prior to take-off, return CANS transfer switch to AUTO or OFF.

> **Note**
>
> Approximately 1200 pounds of fuel are required for a normal start, average field-taxi, take-off, and acceleration to best climb speed.

> **CAUTION**
>
> If one full and one empty drop tank are installed, selection of on-deck transfer of the full tank alone results in transfer of fuel into the empty tank.

NORMAL FUEL SEQUENCE

Normal sequencing results in the following sump indications:

TANK BEING TRANSFERRED	SUMP TANK FUEL LEVEL CONTROL VALVE SETTING (GALLONS)	SUMP TANK LEVEL INDICATION (POUNDS)
Drop tanks	695	4700
Saddle tank	695	4700
Bomb bay	625	4250
Wing	340	1900 to 2300
Sump (low level)	270	1600 to 1950

(Sump indications are based on JP-5 fuel, at 6.8 pounds per gallon on a Standard Day.)

> **Note**
>
> Sump level varies with pitch attitude during bomb bay fuel transfer. In a Maximum Thrust climb at low altitude, sump fuel as low as 2200 to 2400 pounds may be anticipated.

Drop tank fuel transfer is selected after take-off. Under normal conditions, the drop tanks will keep the sump tank full (4700 pounds) and will keep the wing tanks filled until drop tank fuel is exhausted. When the drop tanks are empty, approximately 17,900 pounds (two bomb bay cans) or 20,000 pounds (three bomb bay cans) of fuel will remain. DROP TANK TRANSFER buttons should be released to off (up) prior to air refueling to depressurize tanks and allow proper venting. Drop tank transfer will normally be left on for all other flight operations.

When the landing gear handle is raised to the UP position, the internal fuel tanks pressurize. While the cans are feeding, a 4250-pound (625-gallon) level is maintained in the sump tank.

> **Note**
>
> "Rumbling" may occur when cans are nearly empty, caused by alternate actuation of the float switch with changing fuel level. This rumbling stops when the forward can is empty or when bomb bay cans are depressurized.

When bomb bay can fuel is exhausted, approximately 13,000 pounds of fuel will remain.

> **CAUTION**
>
> The CANS transfer switch should be moved to ON prior to take-off to check for positive transfer. Prior to catapult launch, return the switch to AUTO or OFF. Allow approximately 2 minutes to pressurize cans. Failure to transfer bomb bay can fuel results in an aft center-of-gravity condition, seriously affecting pitch control during a landing approach. During landing gear down operations (such as FCLP, bounce, and GCA approach), bomb bay fuel transfer is not available unless the CANS transfer switch is in the ON position.

Normal consumption will drop the sump tank level to approximately 2300 pounds (340 gallons) and the wing tank pumps will maintain this level until wing tank fuel is exhausted. The FUEL LOW caution indicator will be illuminated when the remaining fuel reaches approximately 1840 pounds (270 gallons).

Note

- Before dumping bomb bay fuel, check that the SUMP switch is in LOW. Otherwise, fuel from the opened wing transfer valve, along with sump tank fuel, will be forced through the wing-to-sump level control valve by pressure differential between the sump tank (5.6 psi) and the fuel dump tube (ambient).

- If bomb bay can dumping is attempted with the air refueling probe extended, fuel will dump by gravity only. If the SUMP switch is also at HIGH, wing fuel will be dumped with the handle in the bomb bay dump position.

TOUCH-AND-GO OPERATIONS

For carrier touch-and-go operations, or FMLP operations with empty wing tanks and landing gear down, the CANS transfer switch must be in the ON position to obtain fuel transfer. The switch should be returned to the AUTO or OFF position, prior to each arrested landing or catapult launch.

Note

To minimize the amount of fuel transferred from the saddle tank to the empty wing tanks for catapult launches:

(a) Leave the CANS transfer switch at AUTO or OFF until external power is disconnected.

(b) Leave the engine MASTER switches OFF until just prior to starting engines.

(c) Place the SUMP fuel switch in the HIGH position until engine start to ensure transfer of any wing fuel into the sump tank as soon as possible.

(d) The SUMP switch should always be placed in the LOW position prior to dumping fuel or securing engines.

INVERTED FLIGHT

The sump tank boost pumps incorporate inverted flight standpipes controlled by gravity-sensitive valves. During negative-g flight, essentially all sump tank fuel is available for continuous flow to the engines. Negative-g flight restrictions are a result of engine lubrication system capabilities. Refer to Section I, Part 4, of the Supplemental NATOPS Flight Manual (NAVWEPS 01-60ABA-1A).

BUDDY TANKER REFUELING SYSTEM

The buddy tanker package is designed to provide refueling tanker capabilities. The total capacity of the bomb bay installation can be transferred, used to extend range, or dumped, as operationally required. The package installation consists of a 290-gallon buddy tank, two bomb bay fuel cans, a reel with 78 feet of hose, a pump unit, and a flow scheduler. The nonjettisonable package is installed in the linear bomb bay. Operation of the buddy tanker system is controlled by the navigator through the buddy tanker control panel (figure 1-13). The aircraft fuel system provides fuel for additional tanker capacity. Prior to take-off on a buddy tanker mission, the pilot must check bomb bay can transfer OFF and move the SUMP switch to HIGH. This allows wing tank fuel to transfer, maintaining a 4250-pound level in the sump tank during tanker transfer operations.

> **CAUTION**
>
> - Prior to extending the hose for refueling, move the CANS transfer switch to ON until several hundred pounds of bomb bay can fuel is transferred. This procedure prevents possible venting of fuel from the tanker overboard vent on receiver disengagement.
>
> - The buddy tanker refueling system should not be operated above 39,000 feet.

When installed, the buddy tanker control panel (figure 1-13) is located on the navigator's left console.

HOSE CONTROL SWITCH

The HOSE CONTROL switch (4, figure 1-13) controls the trail and rewind operation of the hose and drogue. Placing the switch to TRAIL extends the hose full length and turns on the hose floodlight in the vertical stabilizer fuel vent fairing. While the hose is extending, the IN

BUDDY TANKER FUEL SYSTEM

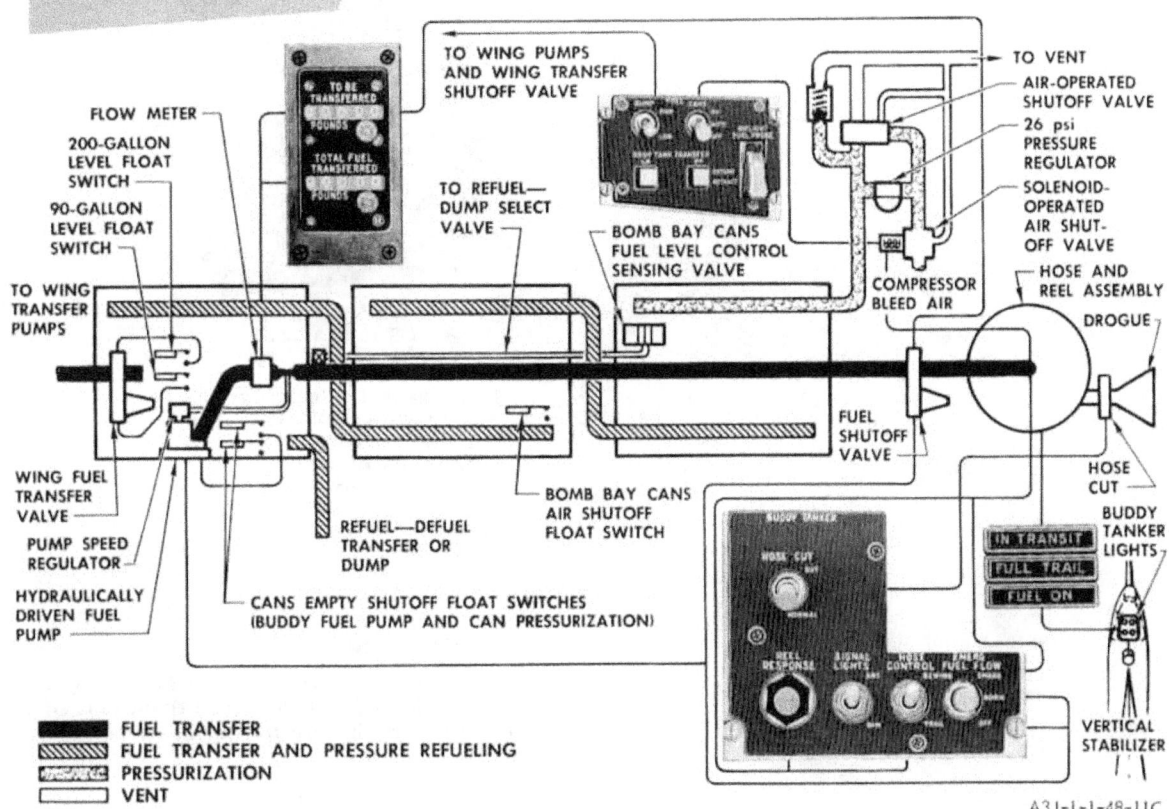

Figure 1-12

TRANSIT light will come on. When the hose is fully extended, the FULL TRAIL light will come on and the IN TRANSIT light will extinguish.

WARNING

Ensure that the HOSE CONTROL switch is in the REWIND position prior to starting engines. With this switch in TRAIL, the presence of electrical and hydraulic power will cause the hose to unwind, resulting in damage to the hose and reel.

Note

Do not attempt to dump bomb bay fuel with the HOSE CONTROL switch in TRAIL as wing fuel will be inadvertently dumped. Should it become necessary to dump bomb bay can and buddy tank fuel, it is recommended that the HOSE CONTROL switch first be placed in REWIND.

EMERGENCY FUEL FLOW SWITCH

The emergency fuel flow switch (3, figure 1-13) permits the operator to allow automatic fuel transfer or, in emergency or training conditions, to extend the hose and select transfer of fuel to the receiver aircraft. The OFF position may be used to turn off fuel flow at any time governing the fuel quantity transferred to any receiver. Emergency fuel flow operation is indicated to the receiving aircraft by the illumination of a red light on the vertical stabilizer. In true emergencies, the light indicates the hose is dead and lacks reel response. The OFF position can be used to make practice hookups without fuel transfer.

REEL RESPONSE BUTTON

The REEL RESPONSE button (6, figure 1-13) is used to compensate for changes in aerodynamic load on the drogue caused by altitude and/or airspeed variation. If the tanker aircraft changes airspeed by 10 knots and/or altitude by 1000 feet, reel response should be reset. When altitude and/or airspeed is stabilized, momen-

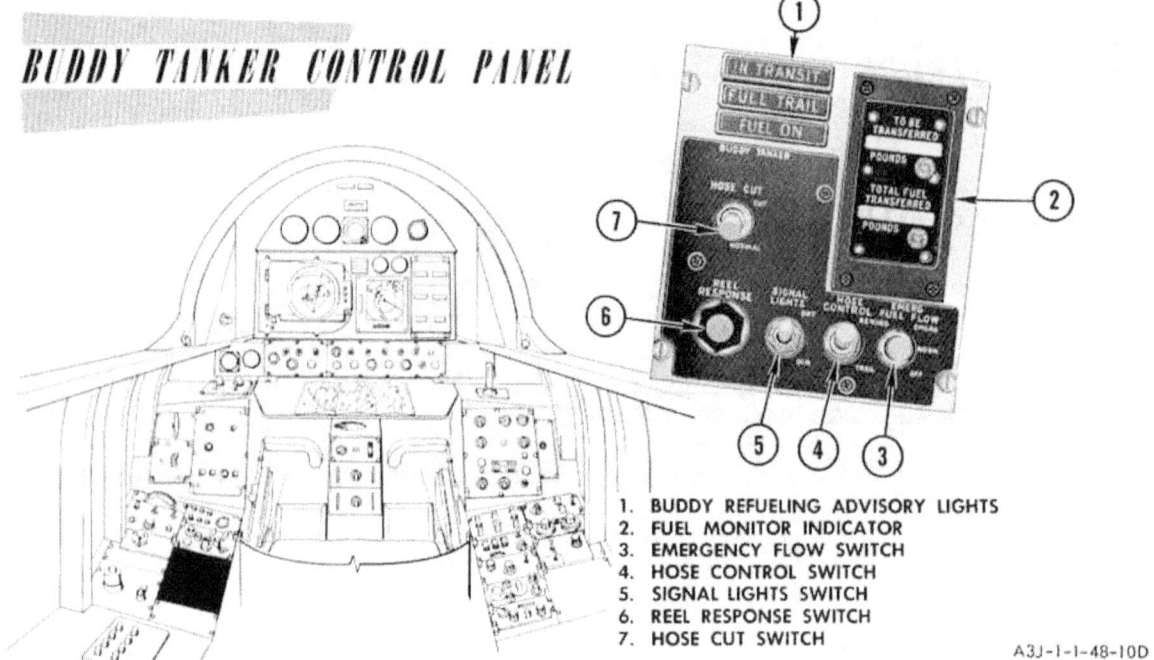

Figure 1-13

tarily depress the button. Without resetting reel response, a decrease in aerodynamic load on the drogue can cause the hose to reel in. An increase will render reel response inadequate to take up the slack in the hose when contact is made with the receiver aircraft.

HOSE CUT SWITCH

The HOSE CUT switch (7, figure 1-13) is provided for emergency guillotining of the hose. If hose will not retract or rewind when the REWIND position of the hose control switch is selected, the operator may move the HOSE CUT switch to CUT. This will actuate an explosive guillotine at the hose reel which cuts the hose, allowing the aircraft to land without the trailing hose. The CUT position also operates relays and valves which shut off the fuel supply and electrical and hydraulic power to the package.

WARNING

To minimize the possibility of fuel collecting in the bomb bay, the HOSE CUT switch should be left in CUT once it is operated.

SIGNAL LIGHTS SWITCH

The intensity of the signal lights on the vertical stabilizer is controlled by the SIGNAL LIGHTS switch (5, figure 1-13).

IN TRANSIT LIGHT

When the hose and drogue are unwinding or rewinding, the IN TRANSIT light (1, figure 1-13) illuminates. The light will extinguish when the drogue reaches the FULL TRAIL position.

Note

With the buddy panel installed, the IN TRANSIT, FULL TRAIL, and FUEL ON lights are tested by depressing the navigator's indicating lights test button.

FULL TRAIL LIGHTS

The yellow FULL TRAIL lights (1, figure 1-13) on buddy tanker control panel and vertical stabilizer will illuminate when the hose and drogue are at full extension. When these lights illuminate, the system is ready to allow contact to be made by the receiver aircraft.

FUEL ON LIGHTS

The green FUEL ON lights (1, figure 1-13) on the buddy tanker control panel and vertical stabilizer indicate that the buddy tanker transfer pump is operating and fuel should be transferring. The light will remain on as long as the pump is operating.

Note

The FUEL ON light can be illuminated without fuel being transferred if the fuel to be transferred indicator is set to zero or the EMERG FUEL FLOW switch is in the OFF position.

FUEL TO BE TRANSFERRED INDICATOR

The fuel TO BE TRANSFERRED indicator (2, figure 1-13) is a digital-type meter located on the buddy tanker control panel. The meter indicates pounds of fuel to be transferred to the receiver aircraft. Through the use of a reset knob on the meter, the tanker operator manually sets the meter for the amount of fuel to be transferred before each hookup of a receiver aircraft. As fuel is transferred, the meter indications will decrease toward zero. When zero is reached, fuel transfer is automatically shut off.

Note

- If the fuel TO BE TRANSFERRED indicator is at zero, the buddy fuel shutoff valve will remain closed, precluding any possibility of fuel transfer except during emergency fuel flow.
- With the EMERG FUEL FLOW switch to EMERG, automatic shutoff is inoperative.

TOTAL FUEL TRANSFERRED INDICATOR

The TOTAL FUEL TRANSFERRED indicator (2, figure 1-13) indicates the total pounds of fuel delivered from the tanker aircraft. Through the use of the associated reset knob, the indicator should be set to zero before each refueling mission.

FUEL SYSTEM OPERATION WITH BUDDY TANKER

With the buddy tanker package installed, the pilot must check the CANS transfer switch OFF and place the SUMP switch in the HIGH position after starting engines. This turns on the wing transfer pumps immediately and causes them to maintain a sump level of approximately 4250 pounds. When the navigator moves the HOSE CONTROL switch to TRAIL, the buddy fuel shutoff valve opens. When the hose goes to full trail, the wing pumps are switched to high duty and hydraulic power is made available for operating the refueling pump. The bomb bay cans and buddy tank are pressurized and the refueling pump is turned on after the hose has been pushed in at least six feet from full trail to the refueling range. The cans and buddy tank are depressurized after the cans are emptied. Fuel can be transferred to a receiver at a rate of approximately 2050 pounds per minute at 55 psig nozzle pressure.

Note

If an excessive fuel transfer rate is noted on the TO BE TRANSFERRED indicator, loss of the air refueling hose or drogue may be indicated. In this event, place the emergency flow switch to OFF.

When the 90-gallon fuel level is reached in the buddy tank, the wing transfer valve opens and wing fuel is transferred to the buddy tank until the 200-gallon level is reached. Fuel transfer to the buddy tank then ceases until the 90-gallon level is again reached. When the drogue is out of the refueling range limits as the receiver aircraft breaks contact, the refueling pump is turned off and the cans are depressurized (if they have not been emptied and depressurized previously). The systems operator moves the HOSE CONTROL switch to REWIND, which returns the wing transfer pump to normal duty and closes the wing transfer valve. The remaining buddy tank and bomb bay can fuel can be transferred to the sump by selecting CANS transfer switch to ON or AUTO. Fuel available for transfer includes all fuel other than sump fuel.

Note

If the buddy tank and bomb bay cans contain fuel after the refueling mission, the SUMP switch should be moved to LOW and the CANS transfer switch moved to AUTO or ON, in order to transfer the fuel to the sump tank for engine feed.

Should it become necessary to reduce gross weight, such as during an engine failure after take-off, fuel in the buddy tank, bomb bay cans or ferry can installations may be dumped by pulling the fuel dump handle to the first detent. Fuel is dumped at approximately 2050 pounds per minute for all bomb bay loading configurations. If dumping is attempted while the air refueling hose is at full trail, the buddy tank receives fuel transfer from the wing tanks each time the 90-gallon level is reached. All wing fuel can be depleted in this manner.

CAUTION

- To prevent dumping more fuel than is intended, monitor the total fuel quantity indicator during dumping operations.
- Unless safe flight cannot otherwise be maintained, fuel dumping is not recommended during afterburner operation, because of fire hazard.

BUDDY TANKER PROCEDURE

For complete procedures, refer to Section III, Part 5. The fuel TO BE TRANSFERRED and TOTAL FUEL TRANSFERRED indicators should be preset before clearing receiver aircraft into position. In addition, a check should be made to ensure that the pilot has moved the CANS transfer switch to AUTO or ON for a sufficient length of time to transfer several hundred pounds of bomb bay can fuel into the aircraft system. The TV sight may be used to monitor receiver aircraft and to check the condition of the hose and drogue. Following hose trail, reel response should be checked as outlined in Section III, Part 5. After hookup is achieved, illumination of the FUEL ON light indicates normal transfer of fuel is occurring. On disengagement, the FUEL ON light goes out and the FULL TRAIL light comes on. Between receiver aircraft hookups, the REEL RESPONSE button should be depressed momentarily if speed has changed more than 10 knots or altitude more than 1000 feet. After fuel transfer is complete, the HOSE CONTROL switch is moved to REWIND and the pilot moves the CANS transfer switch to AUTO or ON, transferring any remaining fuel to the aircraft internal system.

BUDDY TANKER EMERGENCY OPERATION

Should failure of the No. 2 hydraulic system or a malfunction in the buddy tanker system occur, the hose may be trailed by moving the EMERG FUEL FLOW switch to EMERG, then to OFF after the hose is trailed. In emergency trail, the hose is unlocked and is unwound from the reel by the aerodynamic drag of the drogue canopy. Excessive trail rate is prevented by a brake which is integral with the reel. With the EMERG FUEL FLOW switch at EMERG, gravity flow fuel pressure is present in the drogue. The EMERG FUEL FLOW switch must be returned to OFF to allow receiver hookup, then moved to EMERG to transfer fuel.

AIR REFUELING PROCEDURES (RECEIVER)

For complete procedures, refer to Section IV. Any planned air refueling will be thoroughly prebriefed. Prior to refueling, tanker/receiver equipment compatibility must be definitely determined. Refueling probe extension is limited to 280 KIAS, and the normal range of airspeed for refueling operation is 250 to 270 KIAS. Drop tank transfer and pitch augmentation will be secured, and the electric flight control system may be secured, prior to hookup attempts. Caution must be exercised to avoid high-rate closure or departure on the trailed drogue to prevent possible FOD from damaged drogue canopies. For night refueling, complete familiarity with tanker signal lights is required. These lights are color-coded as follows: amber—drogue at full trail; green—fuel on (transferring).

CAUTION

If the tanker hose loops on initial contact, or will not retract, a tanker malfunction exists. DO NOT ATTEMPT FURTHER ENGAGEMENTS unless an emergency dictates refueling is mandatory.

ELECTRICAL POWER SUPPLY SYSTEM

A-C POWER

The basic aircraft electrical power source is a 400-cycle, constant-frequency, alternating-current system supplying three-phase power (A, B, C rotation) at 115 volts per phase. Across any two phases, power measures 200 volts. Normal a-c power is provided by two engine-driven generators. Essential a-c and d-c bus power can be provided by an emergency power unit which is driven by a ram-air turbine.

GENERATORS

A 30-kva, a-c generator is driven by a constant-speed drive on each engine, providing a total system capacity of 60 kva. The generators are cooled by passing oil from the engine oil tank through the frame and shaft of each generator.

Constant-speed Drives

The constant-speed drives are hydromechanical transmissions which, by differential action, convert variable engine speed to a constant speed to drive the generators. A governor system is provided to serve two functions: to control the drive output speed and to provide overspeed and underspeed protection. A pressure-sensitive switch is included in the circuit to disconnect generator output from the system in the event of an underspeed or overspeed condition. In the event of an overspeed condition, the generator will trip and cannot be reset until the engine has been shut down. If a generator drops out because of a temporary underspeed condition, operation is usually regained automatically without needing resetting. Constant-speed drive operation should be checked at engine shutdown after each flight by noting generator cutout rpm with external electrical power applied. Refer to GENERATOR-OUT CAUTION INDICATORS, in this section.

A-C POWER DISTRIBUTION

The a-c power distribution system is composed of two independent systems. The No. 1 system is normally energized by the left-hand generator and consists of the No. 1 primary bus and the monitored buses. The No. 2 system is normally fed from the right-hand generator and consists of the No. 2 primary and essential buses. If the output of either generator falls below approximately 95 volts, the generator is automatically disconnected and both bus systems are connected by means of line contactors to receive power from the operating generator. Normally, power is supplied by the a-c generators to the primary buses which energize the monitored and essential buses. The monitored buses supply nonessential distribution which is cut off when one generator has failed and the aircraft is in afterburner operation. This ensures sufficient a-c power to the remaining electrical system when fuel boost and wing transfer pumps are on high duty for afterburning during single-generator operation. The essential a-c bus supplies power to equipment essential to navigation and communications. The essential bus is normally connected to the No. 2 primary bus, but in the event of failure of the No. 2 generator, power will be supplied by the No. 1 generator to the No. 2 primary and essential buses. The essential bus can also be powered by the ram-air turbine-driven emergency power unit. During ground operations with external electrical power applied to the aircraft, some electronic components (see cooled components in figure 1-14) require cooling air to prevent overheating under certain conditions. Electrical power to this equipment is controlled by relays, an external cooling air temperature sensor, and an external cooling air hose receptacle switch. For normal ground operation of cooled equipment, cooling air must not exceed 115 (± 5)°F for 15 consecutive seconds. In the event of insufficient cooling airflow, faulty hose connection, or abnormal air temperature, electrical power to the equipment is interrupted by the relays.

EXTERNAL POWER

For ground operation of all buses, external a-c electrical power must be supplied. For ground operation of all equipment, cooling air (optimum 80°F) must also be supplied. The external power access is located on the left side of the fuselage, forward of the main gear. Two indicator lights are mounted beside the external power receptacles and will come on when the generators are operating and ready to connect into the system. Although external power can be removed when either of these lights comes on, the disconnect should be delayed until both lights on. Removal of the external power plug automatically transfers the electrical load to the aircraft electrical power system. If external cooling air supply is utilized for ground operation of cooled equipment, the nozzle must be properly connected and air temperature must not be excessive. A contact switch in the receptacle deenergizes cooled equipment until a temperature sensor completes the circuit, or until the hose is disconnected. If autonavigator alinement procedure has been initiated, care should be taken to disconnect external electrical power prior to removing cooling air. This precludes bomb directing set power interruption and loss of alinement.

Note

The electrical power source for starting must be a 25-kva (minimum), 115-volt, three-phase (A, B, C rotation), 400-cycle unit.

D-C POWER

D-C power is obtained by utilizing two d-c converters (transformer-rectifiers), a primary and an alternate, to provide 28 volts dc to various systems.

D-C POWER DISTRIBUTION

The d-c power distribution system is composed of the primary bus and the essential bus. The two buses are connected and receive power from the No. 1 primary a-c bus through the primary d-c converter. Should d-c

Section I
Part 2

NAVWEPS 01-60ABA-1

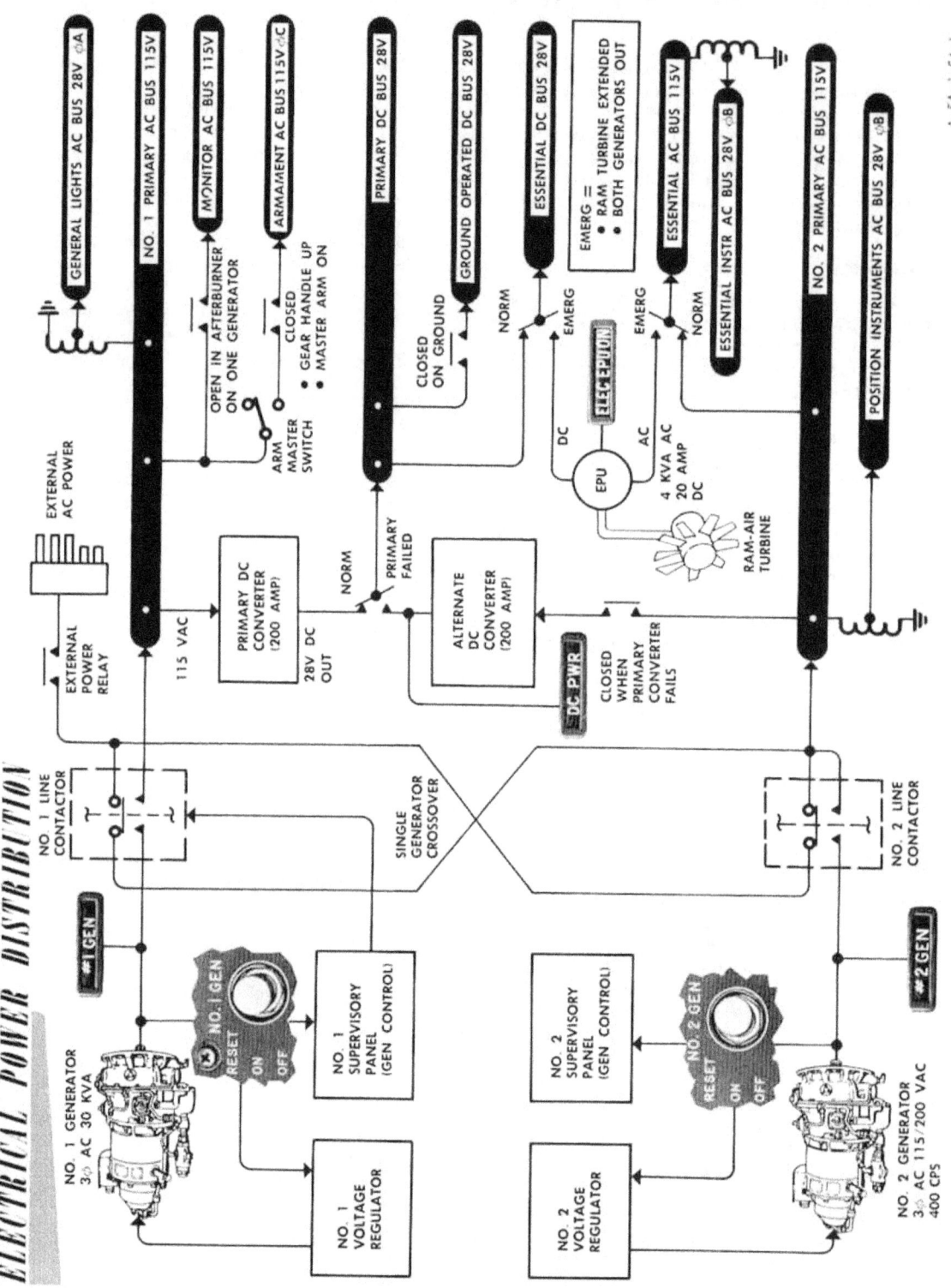

Figure 1-14 (Sheet 1)

NAVWEPS 01-60ABA-1

Section I
Part 2

POWER DISTRIBUTION

NO. 1 PRIMARY AC BUS

AIR DATA SYSTEM
AWW-1
ARM INITIATION
ARM MASTER
BOMB/NAV SYSTEM
BUDDY TRANSFER
FORWARD BOOST (SUMP)
GROUND SAFETY
LH WING TRANSFER PUMP
(F) NAV STANDBY GYRO HORIZON
(F) NAV COCKPIT WHITE LIGHTS
NO. 1 A/B IGNITION
(F) PILOT CONSOLE LIGHTS
(F) PILOT INSTR LIGHTS
PRI DC CONVERTER
RADAR
(F) RELEASE CONTROL
STORE & PYLON RELEASE
TAXI LIGHT

GENERAL LIGHTS AC BUS‡

AR PROBE LIGHT
EXTERIOR LIGHTS
EXTERIOR LIGHTS DIM
NAV RED FLOOD LIGHTS
PILOT HIGH ALT LIGHTS
WING LIGHTS

MONITOR AC BUS
LOST ON ONE GEN A/B OPERATION

AFT SEAT ADJUST
AN/ALQ-41†
AN/ALQ-51†
ENGINE ANTI-ICE
ENGINE COOLING DOORS
FORWARD SEAT ADJUST
IR ECM (PROVISIONS)
NO. 1 AFT TANK PUMP
NO. 2 AFT TANK PUMP
PEDAL ADJUST
RADAR ALTIMETER
RADOME FOLD
SCAVENGE PUMPS
SUMP/WING TFR PUMP HIGH DUTY
TACAN

ARMAMENT AC BUS

(F) NO. 1 STORE EJECTION
(F) NO. 2 STORE EJECTION

ESSENTIAL AC BUS

AFT BOOST PUMP (SUMP)
ALTERNATE COOLING
ALTERNATE TRIM
✓ CENTER PEDESTAL Cφ
CABIN COOL
CNI (IFF)
EQUIP COOL
✓ FIRE EXT & SHUTOFF
FLAP & DROOP CONTROL
(F) FLAP-DROOP-TRIM INDICATOR
FLIGHT REF SET (AN/ASN-26)
FUEL LOW
(F) FUEL QTY (SUMP) INDICATOR
(F) FUEL QTY (TOTAL) INDICATOR
INDICATING LIGHTS TEST
(F) INSTRUMENT TRANSFORMER
INFLIGHT REFUEL
(F) J-8 GYRO (Cφ)
✓ NAV ESSENTIAL TRANSFORMER
NO. 1 ESSENTIAL JETTISON
NO. 2 ESSENTIAL JETTISON
(F) NO. 1 EGT
(F) NO. 2 EGT
NO. 1 FIRE DETECTOR
NO. 2 FIRE DETECTOR
✓ NO. 1 FUEL SHUTOFF
✓ NO. 2 FUEL SHUTOFF
✓ NO. 1 START & IGNITION
✓ NO. 2 START & IGNITION
(F) OXYGEN QUANTITY INDICATOR
(F) PILOT ESSENTIAL TRANSFORMER
(F) INSTRUMENT VIBRATOR
PITOT HEATER
SUIT TEMPERATURE
RAM AIR

ESSENTIAL INSTRUMENT AC BUS

ALT INSTRUMENT POWER
CNI
FLIGHT REF SET
(F) FUEL FLOW INDICATOR
(F) HYD PRESS INDICATORS
(F) OIL PRESS INDICATOR

POSITION INSTRUMENT AC BUS

AZIMUTH & RANGE INDICATOR
HORIZONTAL SITUATION INDICATOR

NO. 2 PRIMARY AC BUS

AIR DATA SYSTEM
ALT DC CONVERTER
AUTO FLIGHT
BOMB/NAV SYSTEM
CNI
DC CONVERTER CONTROL
ELEC FLIGHT CONTROL
MONITOR BUS CONTROL
NO. 2 A/B IGNITION
POSITION INSTRUMENTS
HSI
INLET RAMPS
LAT & DIR TRIM (NOR)
NO. 1 GAP ACTUATOR
NO. 2 GAP ACTUATOR
NO. 1 NOZZLE CONTROL*
NO. 2 NOZZLE CONTROL*
PITCH AUG AIR DATA
RH WING TRANSFER PUMP
YAW AUG

ESSENTIAL DC BUS

✓ CABIN PRESSURE
✓ CNI ESSENTIAL
✓ EMERGENCY FLAP
✓ EMER JETTISON CONTROL
✓ FLIGHT REF SET
✓ FUEL GAGE DC
✓ FUEL SEQUENCING
✓ ICS RELAY POWER
✓ INDICATORS & TEST NO. 1
✓ INDICATORS & TEST NO. 2
✓ INLET RAMPS
✓ LANDING GEAR INDICATOR
✓ NAV ICS
✓ NOZZLE POSITION††
✓ PILOT ICS
✓ TURN & BANK INDICATOR
✓ WINDSHIELD DEFROST & ANTI-ICE
✓ YAW DAMPER

PRIMARY DC BUS

ACTIVE ECM
AIR TEMP DETECTOR
AIR TURBINE RETRACT
ALQ-41
ALQ-51
ANGLE OF ATTACK
ANTI-COLLISION LIGHTS
AR PROBE LIGHT
BUDDY TANKER
B/N AUX HEATING
CANOPY SEAL
CNI PRI NO. 1
CNI PRI NO. 2
ELEC FLIGHT CONTROL
EMERGENCY BUDDY TANKER
ENGINE OIL COOL
EPU ELEC INDICATOR
FLAP SHUTOFF
FUEL TRANSFER
FWD BOOST PUMP CONTROL
HYDRAULIC ISOLATION
LABS DC
LANDING GEAR CONTROL
NOSE WHEEL STEERING
HOOK & APPROACH LIGHTS
NO. 1 ALT SUPV POWER
NO. 2 ALT SUPV POWER
NO. 1 STORE RELEASE
NO. 2 STORE RELEASE
PNEUMATIC PRESSURE
PASSIVE WARNING SHUTTERS
PITCH AUG
PEDAL SHAKER & ACCEL
WING-TAIL FOLD & AUX COOL

GROUND OPERATED DC BUS

FUEL PUMP TEST
MAINTENANCE LIGHTS
REFUEL TEST & DEFUEL

✓ COCKPIT CIRCUIT BREAKER
(F) FUSE
* AIRCRAFT 146702 THROUGH 147863
† AIRCRAFT HAVING ASC NO. 7 COMPLIED WITH
†† AIRCRAFT 148924 AND SUBSEQUENT

Figure 1-14 (Sheet 2)

39

Section I
Part 2

NAVWEPS 01-60ABA-1

bus voltage fall from 28 volts to 24 volts for 30 seconds, or should bus voltage drop to zero for 6 seconds, the system will automatically switch the d-c buses over to receive power from the alternate d-c converter. If the alternate converter should fail, the essential d-c bus can receive power from the emergency power unit if the ram-air turbine is extended.

EMERGENCY ELECTRICAL POWER UNIT

In the event of a complete primary electrical power failure, emergency a-c and d-c power is obtained from a hydraulically driven motor-generator unit. This unit is supplied with hydraulic power by a ram-air turbine pump unit which can be extended and retracted as desired. The emergency generator provides 4-kva, 400-cycle, three-phase, 115-volt a-c power and 28-volt, 20-ampere d-c power for the essential buses automatically upon extension of the ram-air turbine. It is a self-cooled, constant-frequency unit which is capable of providing sufficient electrical power to effect an air start and make an emergency landing. Refer to RAM-AIR TURBINE OPERATION, in this section. If the emergency ram-air turbine is supplying emergency hydraulic pressure as well as electrical power, excessive flight control movements may cause momentary shutoff of the electrical emergency power unit, thus extinguishing the ELEC EPU ON advisory indicator and deenergizing the essential buses.

ELECTRONICS POWER SUPPLY

Electrical power for the electronic equipment is provided by the No. 2 primary, the monitored, and the essential a-c buses, as well as the primary and essential d-c buses. Ground operation of the electronic equipment is available when external electrical power and cooling air are applied. External cooling air as well as external electrical power is required for electronic equipment operation on the ground when the engines are not operating. Electrical power to the cooled equipment is controlled by an overheat thermoswitch when the ground cooling unit nozzle engages a switch in the ground cooling air receptacle. This thermoswitch interrupts power to the cooled equipment of excessive temperature is sensed for a period of 15 seconds or more.

ELECTRICAL CIRCUIT PROTECTION DEVICES

The aircraft electrical power distribution circuits are protected by circuit breakers, voltage limiters, and fuses. The pilot's circuit-breaker and limiter panel (figure 1-15)

CIRCUIT BREAKERS AND LIMITERS

AFT OF RIGHT CONSOLE

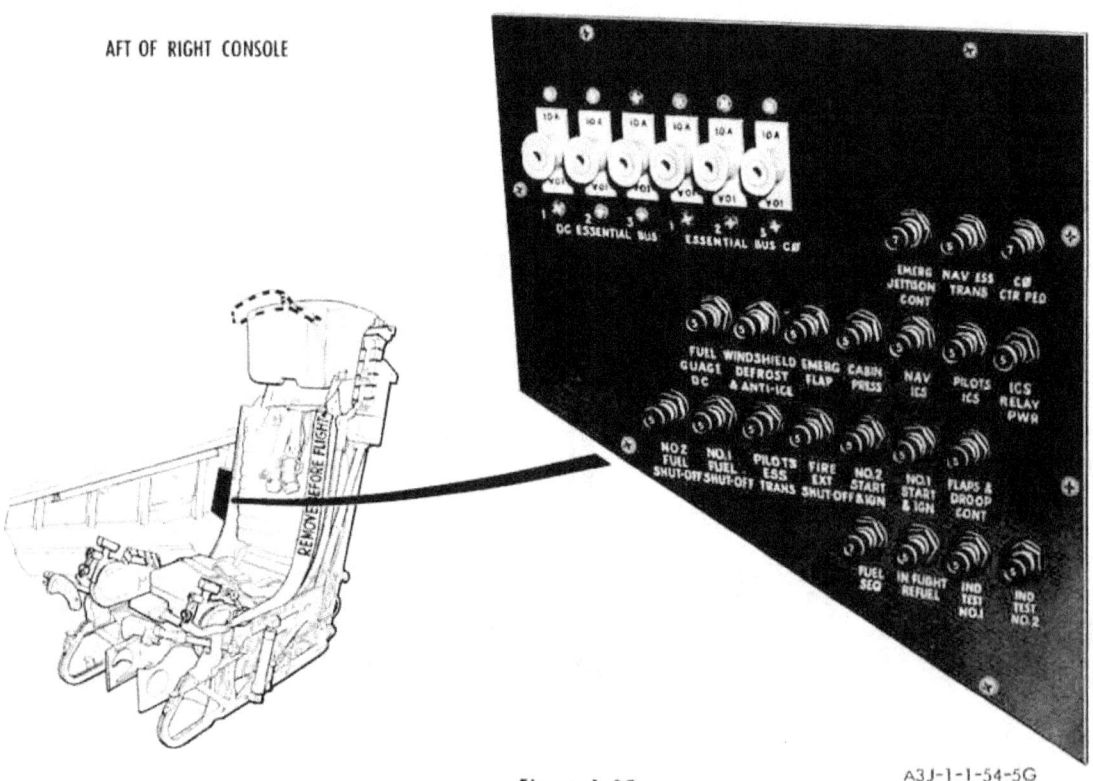

Figure 1-15

A3J-1-1-54-5G

40

is located aft of the right console. The voltage limiters located on this panel protect essential a-c and d-c bus components. Protection for the instrument and lighting circuits is provided by fuses in the pilot's center pedestal and on the navigator's left console. The main bus distribution circuit-breaker panels are located in the electrical distribution bay above the nose wheel well and are not normally accessible to the pilot for inspection.

CONTROLS AND INDICATORS

GENERATOR SWITCHES

A control switch for each generator is located on the pilot's right console (16, figure 1-4A). The generator switches have three positions (OFF, ON, and RESET) and are maintained in either the ON or the OFF position. The a-c generators will assume the electrical load when external power is removed if the engines are up to idle speed and generator output voltage and frequency are within limits. Should the generator-on indicator lights at the external power receptacle remain extinguished after engine start is complete, the pilot will be advised and the generator switches should be held momentarily in RESET and released. If an attempt is made to reset the generator circuit while a fault still exists in the system, the circuit will reset and trip again. Additional reset attempts will result in no response.

Note

Properly operating generators will reset automatically as engine rpm builds. However, if the generator switches were placed in OFF prior to engine shutdown on the previous flight, the generators must be reset by the pilot during start. External power should not be disconnected until both generators are "on the line" or reset. This prevents interruptions in electrical power which will cause loss of auto-navigator alinement.

GENERATOR-OUT CAUTION INDICATORS

Generator-out caution indicators (#1 GEN and #2 GEN, figure 1-4) are located on the pilot's instrument panel. Each indicator is automatically illuminated when its respective generator line contactor is not connected to the bus system. In the event of loss of both generators, all cockpit lights will extinguish, including the generator-out caution indicators, unless external power is applied or the emergency ram-air turbine is extended.

Note

On engine shutdown with external power applied, check that the generator-out caution indicators illuminate at not less than 28% to 30% engine rpm. Illumination at lower rpm should be noted on the "yellow sheet" for maintenance corrective action.

Generator-on Lights

A generator-on indicator light for each generator is located near the external power receptacles. The lights will be illuminated when generator output is at proper frequency and voltage, at which time it is permissible to disconnect external power.

D-C POWER CAUTION INDICATOR

A d-c power caution indicator (DC PWR, figure 1-4) is provided in the pilot's cockpit. This indicator signifies that the primary d-c converter is inoperative. Subsequent failure of the alternate d-c converter is indicated by the appearance of "power-off" warning flags, including barber poles in the landing gear and speed brake position indicators.

EMERGENCY ELECTRICAL INDICATOR

An emergency electrical indicator (ELEC EPU ON, figure 1-4) is installed on the pilot's center pedestal. This green light is illuminated when the RAT is extended and the emergency power unit is supplying the required a-c and d-c voltages. Proper operation of the emergency electrical system is indicated by restoration of power to essential indicators such as the landing gear and speed brake position indicators and AAI.

RAM-AIR TURBINE OPERATION

For flight test procedures used to check RAT operational integrity, refer to FLIGHT TEST PROCEDURES in Section IV.

HYDRAULIC POWER SUPPLY SYSTEMS

Hydraulic power is supplied by two separate systems. Both systems have two independent pumps, a reservoir, and separate lines, delivering a basic no-flow pressure of 2800 to 3250 psi. The reservoirs are pressurized to provide adequate fluid supply to the engine-driven pumps under all conditions. Both the No. 1 and No. 2 systems are used to power the vertical stabilizer, horizontal stabilizer, and spoiler-deflector systems. Operation of the flight control systems on one system produces no noticeable difference from two-system operation for normal low-rate control movements. Sudden, high-rate longitudinal or lateral stick movements can, however, drop single-system pressure sufficiently to cause momentary stiffness. Should operating pressure in either system fall below approximately 650 psi, a pressure-operated switch energizes the master and HYD PRESS caution indicators. With the engines at equal rpm, operating pressure of a pump in either system should be within 300 psi of the opposing pump at all times.

NO. 1 SYSTEM

The No. 1 system provides hydraulic power to the basic flight control systems. In the event of complete failure of both No. 1 system pumps, pressure may be restored in this system by the emergency ram-air turbine (RAT).

NO. 2 SYSTEM

The No. 2 system provides power to all basic flight control surface actuators, the droop leading edge, and all

Section I
Part 2

NAVWEPS 01-60ABA-1

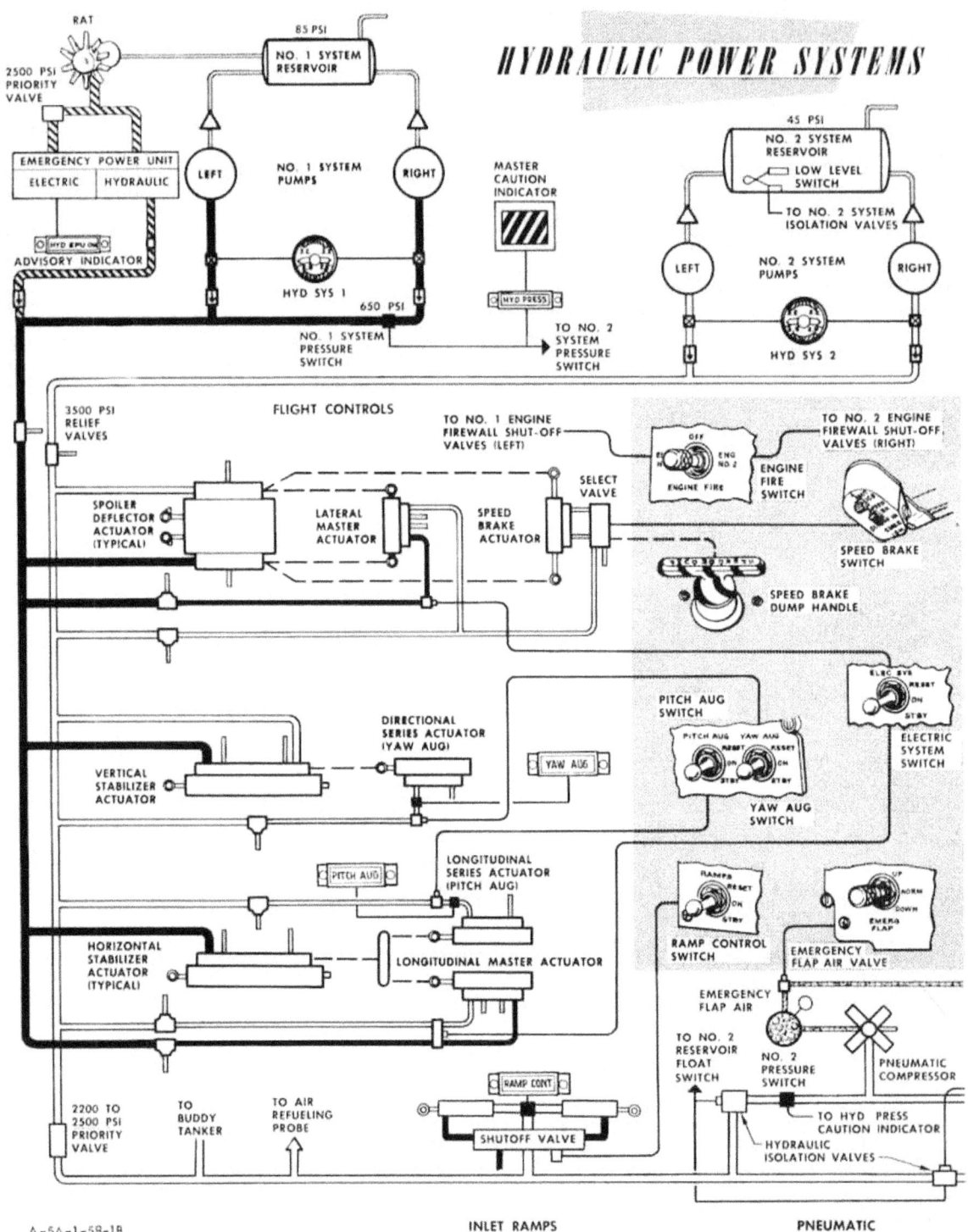

Figure 1-16 (Sheet 1)

NAVWEPS 01-60ABA-1

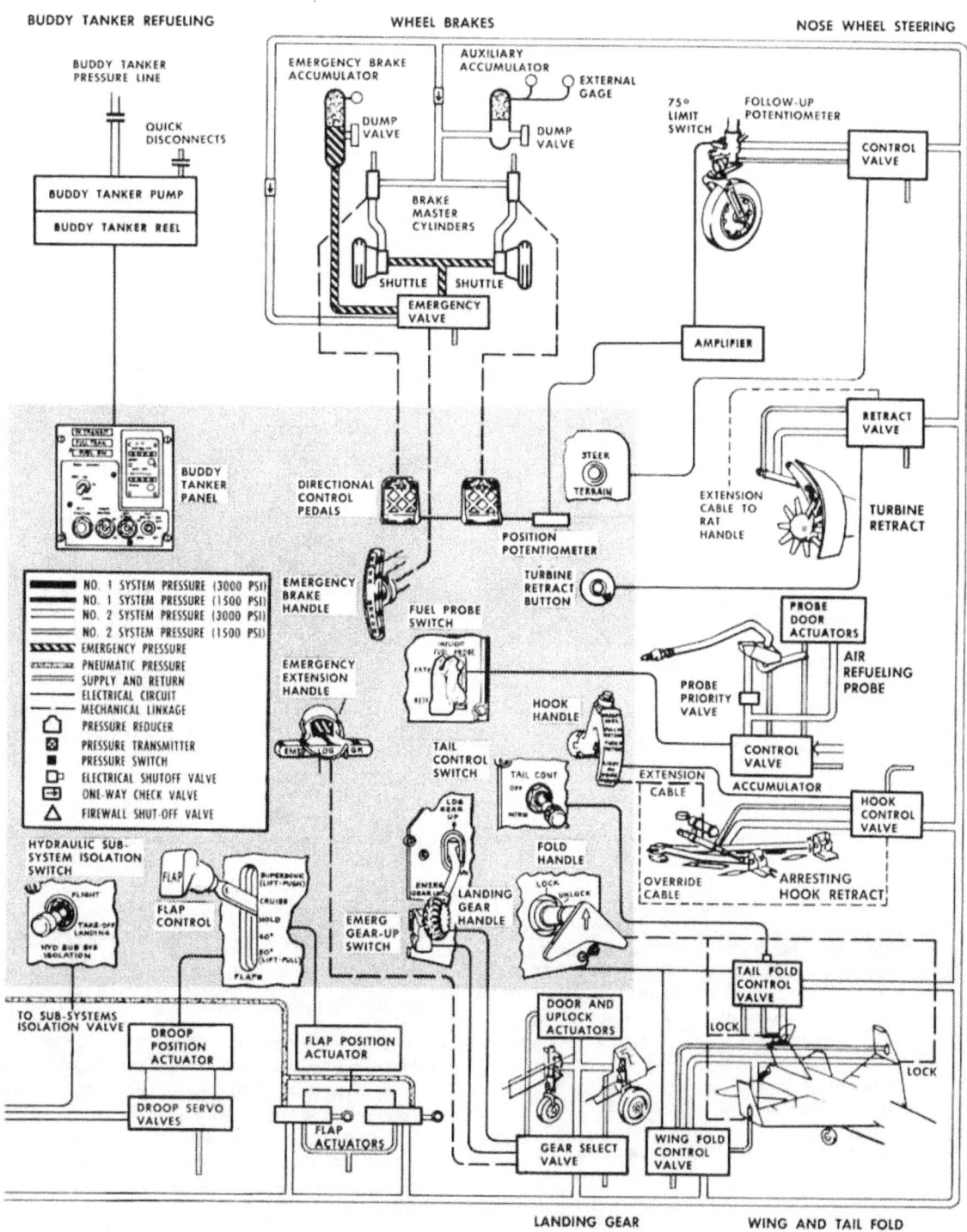

Figure 1-16 (Sheet 2)

other hydraulically operated systems and components. No. 2 system pressure is reduced to approximately 1500 psi for use in the pitch and yaw augmentation systems and the lateral and longitudinal flight control master actuators. No. 2 system pressure is used at 3000 psi to operate the landing gear, flaps, droops, arresting hook retraction, nose wheel steering, wheel brakes, fuel probe, pneumatic compressor, wing/tail fold, inlet variable ramps, ram-air turbine retract, and speed brake systems. In addition, No. 2 pressure operates the buddy tanker fuel transfer pump if installed. The No. 2 system incorporates two isolation valves downstream of components essential to the mission such as the flight control system, speed brakes, ramp control system, air refueling probe actuator, and buddy tanker package. In addition, a 2200 psi priority valve assures pressure for the flight controls at all times. Both isolation valves are controlled electrically by a float level control switch in the hydraulic reservoir. In the event of loss of hydraulic fluid, both isolation valves close in order to maintain hydraulic pressure to essential hydraulic services. One isolation valve can be controlled by the pilot through the hydraulic subsystems isolation switch. Refer to HYDRAULIC SUBSYSTEMS ISOLATION SWITCH, in this section.

HYDRAULIC PRESSURE INDICATORS

Two miniature indicators are installed on the instrument panel (40, figure 1-4). The No. 1 and No. 2 system indicators each have two needles to provide indications for both left and right engine pumps. No indication of emergency power unit hydraulic pressure is provided except for the HYD EPU ON advisory indicator on the center pedestal. The hydraulic pressure indicators receive power from the a-c essential instrument bus.

HYDRAULIC PRESSURE CAUTION INDICATOR

A HYD PRESS caution indicator on the instrument panel (figure 1-4) is provided to warn the pilot when hydraulic system output falls below a safe minimum. Loss of pressure from one pump does not illuminate the indicator, but the affected pressure indicator needle will show the loss. The caution indicator illuminates if the pressure in either system falls below approximately 650 psi. The HYD PRESS caution indicator will go out if the RAT is the only source of No. 1 system pressure.

Note

Illumination of the caution indicator with no immediate pressure drop indicated for either system is an indication that a hydraulic isolation valve has closed and loss of fluid in the No. 2 system reservoir has occurred, and that subsystems powered by the No. 2 system will be inoperative.

HYDRAULIC SUBSYSTEMS ISOLATION SWITCH

The subsystems isolation switch (11, figure 1-3) is located on the left console. This two-position switch is labeled TAKE-OFF/LANDING and FLIGHT. The FLIGHT position enables the pilot to close one of the subsystems isolation valves in the No. 2 hydraulic system. This valve shuts off hydraulic pressure to subsystems not required during normal cruising flight and prevents fluid loss in the event of a suspected leak. Isolated systems include the landing gear, flaps, normal wheel brake power, emergency wheel brakes, nose wheel steering, tail fold, wing fold, arresting gear retract, and ram-air turbine retract. The switch must be placed in the TAKE-OFF/LANDING position for ram-air turbine retraction and all flight operations requiring the use of isolated subsystems. After returning to the TAKE-OFF/LANDING position, emergency operation of the isolated hydraulic subsystems may still be required. In the event a No. 2 hydraulic system leak depletes reservoir level to the automatic isolation point, selecting FLIGHT has no effect as the reservoir float switch overrides the cockpit switch.

EMERGENCY HYDRAULIC POWER

Should both No. 1 system pumps fail without loss of fluid, system pressure may be restored by extending the emergency ram-air turbine. At speeds at and above 150 KIAS, this turbine will supply sufficient pressure for operation of the flight controls at normal movement rates. Lateral control movements should be restricted to minimum rate. Under normal operation, the EPU hydraulic pump is isolated from system pressure by check valves. The emergency electrical power unit is hydraulically driven by the ram-air turbine. Retraction of the ram-air turbine is accomplished through use of No. 2 hydraulic system pressure.

AIR TURBINE HANDLE

The air turbine handle (30, figure 1-4), is located on the left-hand side of the center pedestal. This handle is labeled EMER AIR TURBINE. Pulling the handle releases the turbine door-locking mechanism, allowing an actuator bungee to push the turbine into the air stream. The air stream then pulls the turbine to the fully extended position.

TURBINE RETRACT BUTTON

Pushing the turbine retract button (27, figure 1-4) on the center pedestal operates the turbine retract solenoid valve, causing No. 2 hydraulic system pressure to actuate the air turbine retract cylinder. The button must be held depressed for approximately 4 seconds or until turbine is fully retracted. Upon release of the button, the ELEC EPU ON and HYD EPU ON indicators should be extinguished.

Note

The hydraulic subsystems isolation switch must be in the TAKE-OFF/LANDING position before the air turbine can be retracted.

Pages 45 through 48 deleted.

Emergency Hydraulic Indicator

An emergency hydraulic indicator (HYD EPU ON, 29, figure 1-4) is installed on the center pedestal. When electrical power is available from either or both engine-driven generators, this green light is illuminated when hydraulic pressure generated by the ram-air turbine-driven emergency power unit exceeds approximately 1750 psi. This light will extinguish if emergency pressure drops below approximately 1450 psi. When no electric power is available from the engine-driven generators, the HYD EPU ON advisory light can illuminate only if the emergency electrical power unit is operating (above 2500 psi). Refer to EMERGENCY ELECTRICAL POWER UNIT, in this section.

PNEUMATIC POWER SUPPLY SYSTEM

The pneumatic power supply system provides high-pressure air for canopy normal operation, canopy emergency jettison, and emergency flap extension. Separate pressure storage bottles are provided for the canopy jettison and emergency flap extension system. The emergency flap bottle provides pressure for normal canopy operation. The pneumatic system bottles are precharged to 3200 psi, prior to flight, through the pneumatic service panel under the aircraft, inboard of the right main landing gear. The panel also contains test switches for emergency flap system isolation and the pneumatic compressor. During flight, a hydraulic motor-driven air compressor maintains the bottles at 3000 psi. The compressor is powered by the No. 2 hydraulic system. An oil servicing point for the compressor is located in the right main gear well. A canopy pneumatic control toggle valve and a canopy emergency jettison "T" handle are provided in each cockpit, and an external toggle valve is provided for each canopy. Refer to CANOPIES, in this section.

FLIGHT CONTROL SYSTEMS

For schematic diagrams of the flight control systems, see figures 1-17, 1-18, and 1-19. Longitudinal and directional control is provided by one-piece slabs and a spoiler-deflector system is provided for lateral control. The flight control systems are hydraulically powered and irreversible. Control forces are simulated by artificial feel bungees installed in the mechanical linkage. Control of the longitudinal and lateral systems is through master actuators and mechanical linkage, which, in turn, operates full-powered hydraulic surface actuators. The directional control system is a direct, mechanically controlled, hydraulically powered system. The longitudinal and directional systems are augmented for optimum control characteristics at various altitudes and airspeeds. A priority valve in the No. 2 hydraulic system prevents pressure from being directed to other than the flight control actuators if the system drops below 2200 psi. The hydromechanical system consists of the control stick and directional control pedals, connecting mechanical linkage, the control surfaces, the tandem master and control surface actuators, and associated flight control hydraulic systems. Normal pilot control inputs are electrically transmitted to the master actuators (when the electric flight control system is engaged) but the basic mechanical system operates in parallel with the electric system and will automatically take over to transmit stick inputs to the master actuator if the electric flight control system should fail or is not used. When pitch augmentation is engaged, horizontal stabilizer displacement is varied by a series actuator at a mechanical summing point for near-constant aircraft response to control stick inputs at all altitudes and at airspeeds above 0.55 Mach.

CONTROL STICK

The pilot's control stick (figure 1-20) incorporates a normal pitch trim wheel, a five-position normal roll trim/stand-by pitch trim button, a STEER/TERRAIN (nose wheel steering/radar action) button, a flight control systems disable ("kill") button, and an armament initiation trigger. For a description of the trim controls on the stick grip and flight control panel, refer to TRIM SYSTEMS, in this section.

DIRECTIONAL CONTROL PEDALS

The directional control pedals are of the conventional hanging type, with an electrical adjustment fore and aft of the centered position. A stall warning pedal shaker is provided, which vibrates the pedals if local angle of attack exceeds 15 units.

HORIZONTAL STABILIZERS

The horizontal stabilizers, constructed in two one-piece slabs, are attached to spindle fittings on the fuselage below the vertical stabilizer. These control surfaces have a travel range of 15 degrees leading edge up and 18 degrees leading edge down. Changes in pitch trim are made by small movements of the entire surface. Changes in lateral (roll) trim are accomplished by differential deflection of the horizontal stabilizers.

VERTICAL STABILIZER

The vertical stabilizer is a one-piece, all-movable surface. Total surface travel is 16 degrees; 8 degrees either side of center. Vertical stabilizer travel is regulated by a ratio-changing mechanism controlled by the position of the wing flaps. Stabilizer travel varies linearly from 2 degrees left or right (with flaps up) to 8 degrees left or right (with flaps down 25 degrees or more). A position light, buddy tanker signal lights, and a fuel overboard vent are installed in a fairing on the trailing edge of this surface.

Section 1
Part 2

NAVWEPS 01-60ABA-1

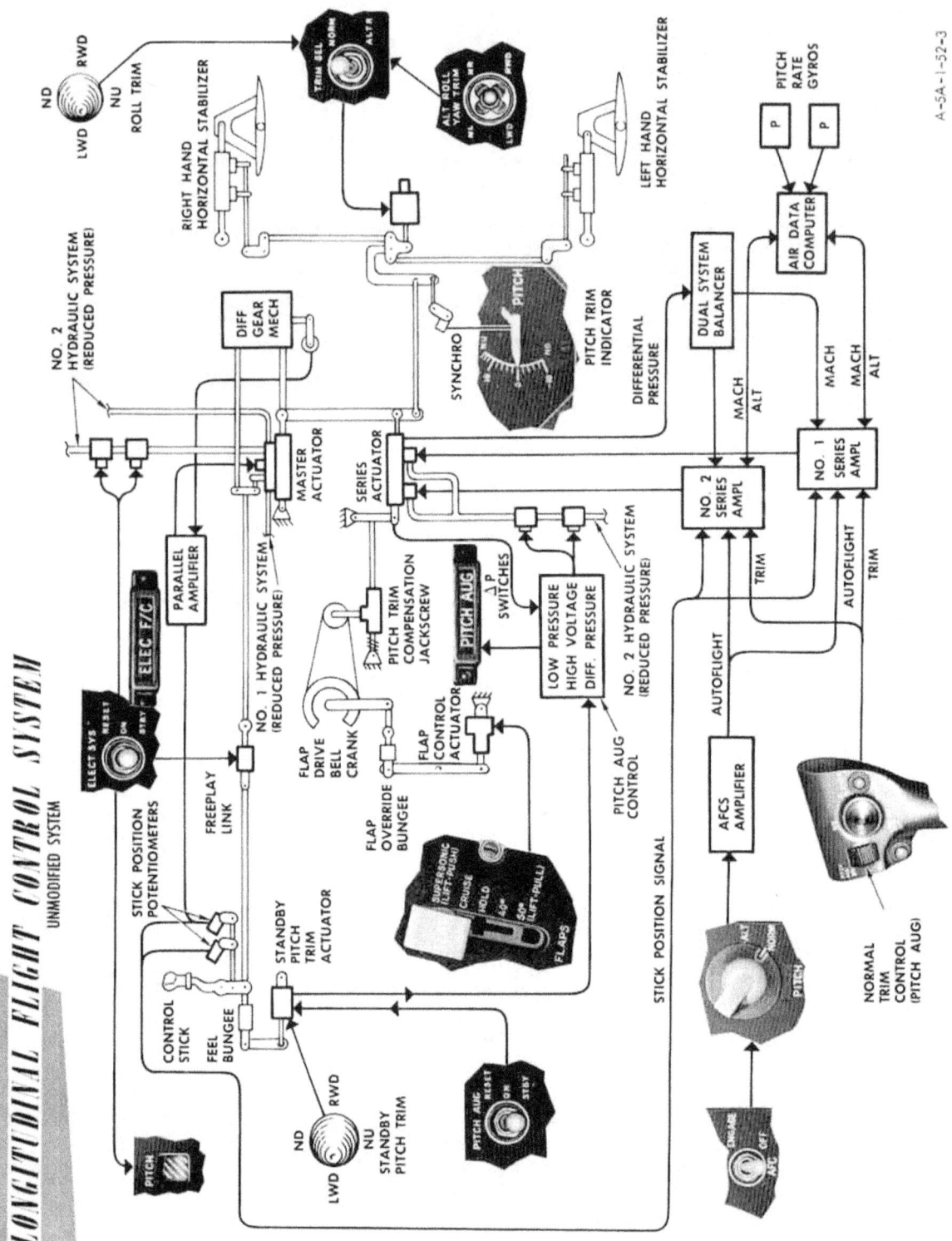

Figure 1-17 (Sheet 1)

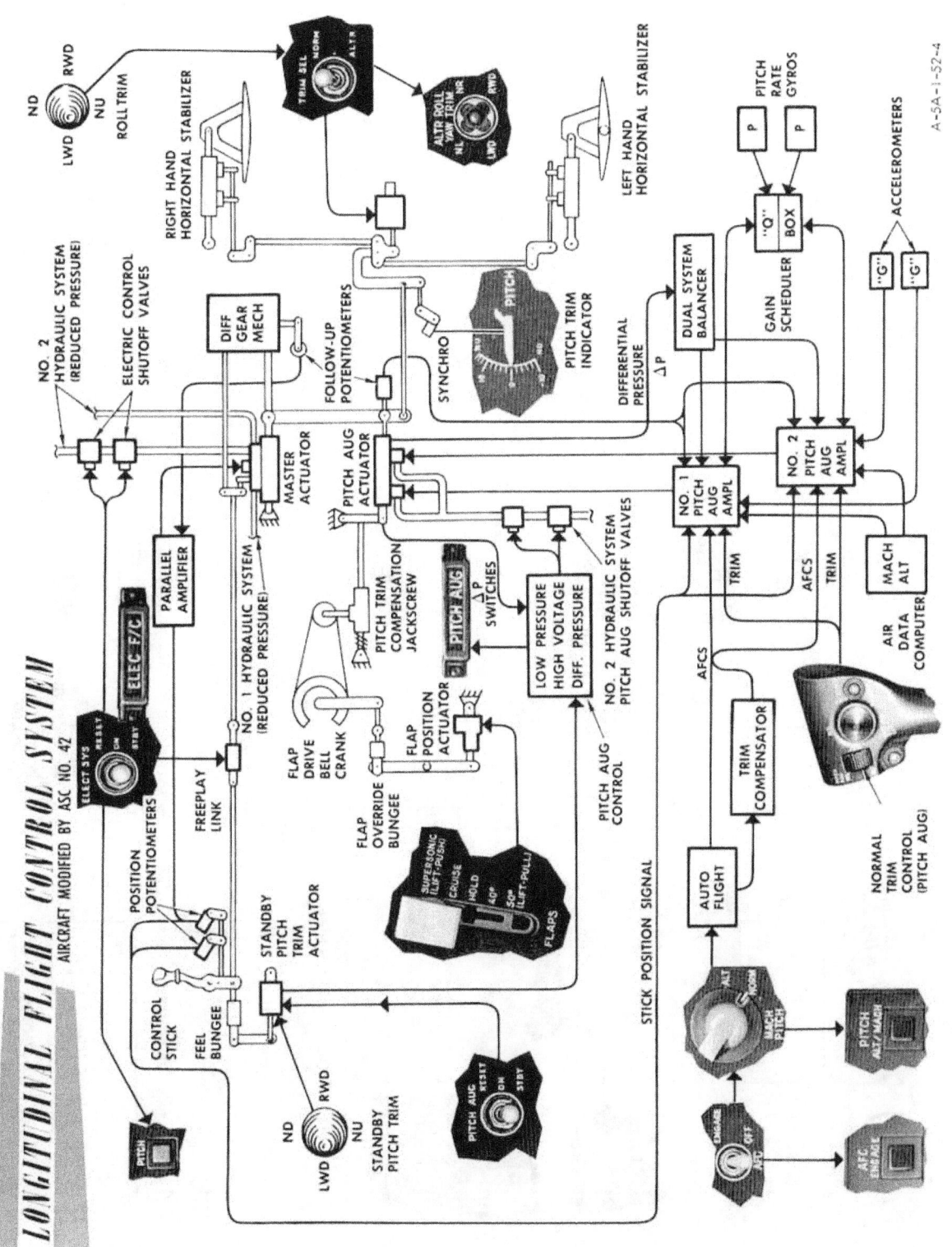

Figure 1-17 (Sheet 2)

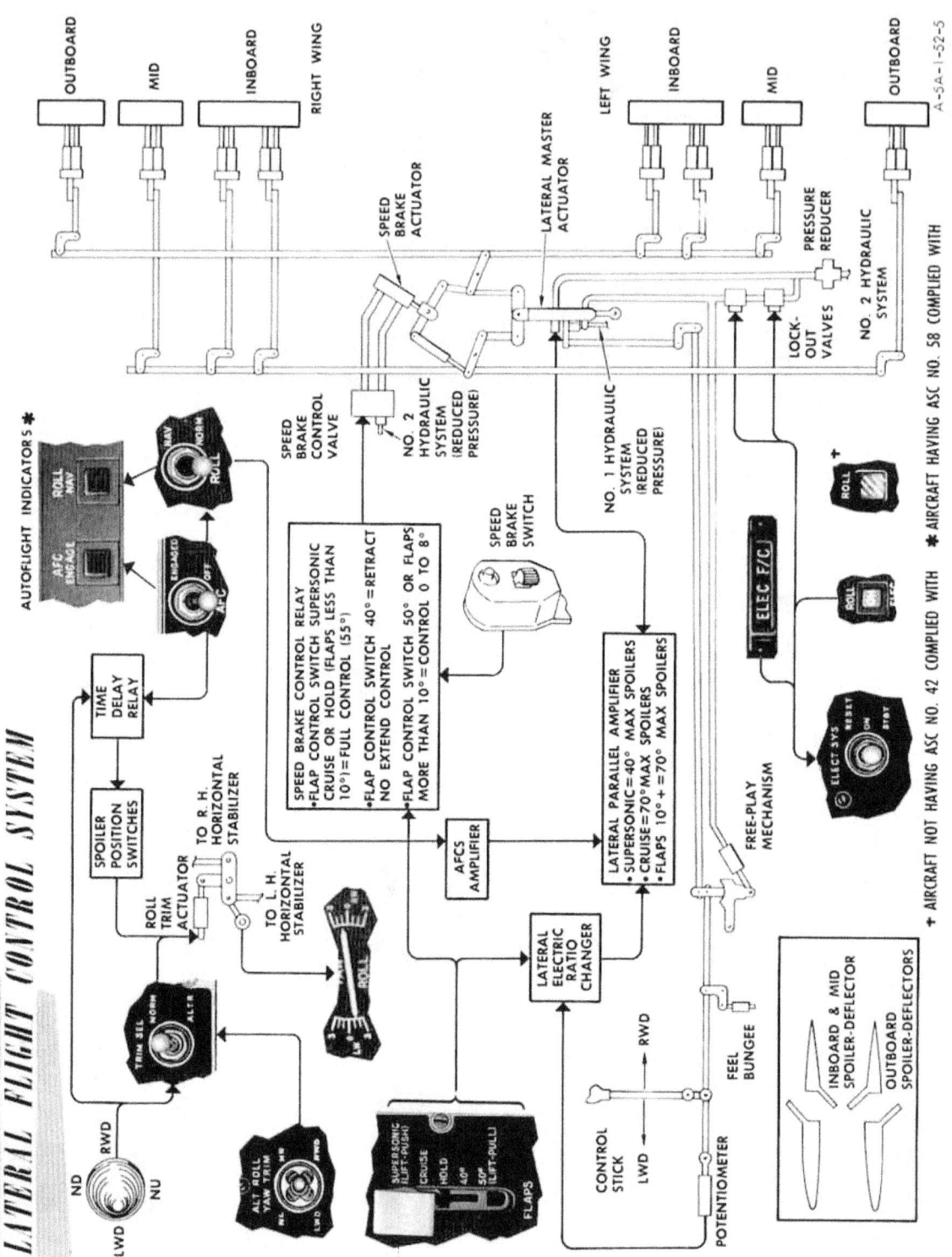

Figure 1-18

NAVWEPS 01-60ABA-1

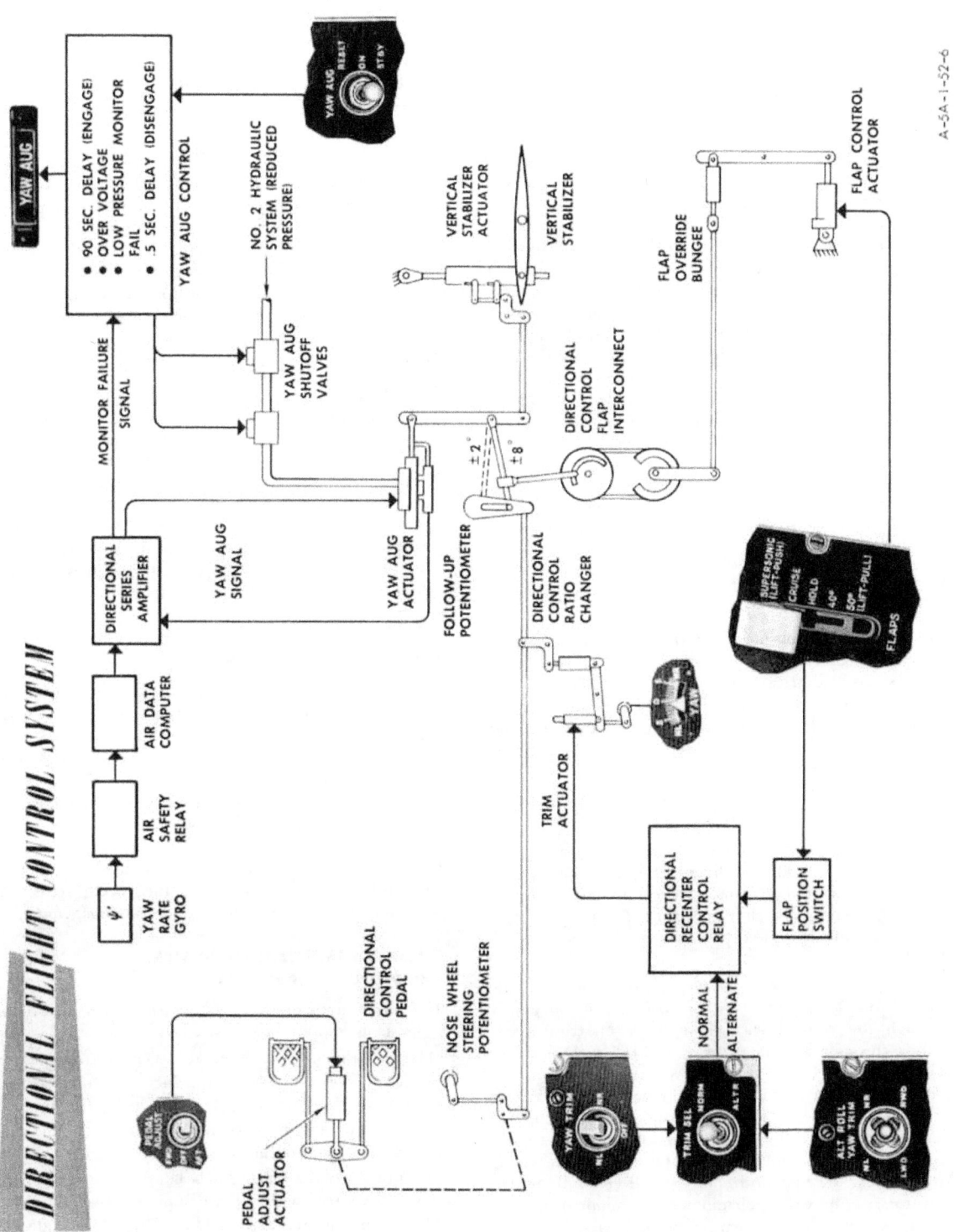

Figure 1-19

SPOILER-DEFLECTORS

Lateral control is provided by an arrangement of conventional and inverted spoilers and deflectors located on the inboard wing panels. The conventional spoilers, located at the mid and inboard positions, open a maximum of 70 degrees. The deflectors, located on the lower surfaces under the conventional spoilers, open a maximum of 35 degrees. The outboard spoilers and deflectors are inverted, the spoilers being on the lower surfaces and the deflectors on the upper surfaces. The inverted spoilers open a maximum of 70 degrees and the outboard deflectors open a maximum of 39 degrees. The spoilers and deflectors are mechanically interconnected so that hydraulically powered movement of the spoilers results in movement of the deflectors. During rolling maneuvers, the inverted spoiler and deflector on the outside wing induce drag, offsetting the yaw effect of the mid and inboard spoilers on the inside wing. A series of override bungees is installed in the mechanical linkage to the spoiler actuators, consisting of one bungee for each inverted spoiler and one for each set of inboard and mid spoilers. These bungees allow continuous operation of the lateral system in the event one set of actuators should fail. The spoiler-deflectors are also used for speed brakes. Refer to SPEED BRAKES, in this section.

LONGITUDINAL AND LATERAL ELECTRIC SYSTEMS

The longitudinal and lateral electric systems are designed to provide control for the corresponding hydromechanical systems. Electrical operation eliminates mechanical system friction and provides reduced breakout force for longitudinal and lateral control. The various series and parallel actuator servo valves require No. 2 hydraulic system pressure for operation.

Note

If both the No. 2 hydraulic pressure indicators are below 1000 psi, disengaging the electric flight control system will prevent longitudinal and lateral trim shifts resulting from abnormally low hydraulic pressures.

The master actuator servo valves for both systems are capable of accepting either mechanical commands through the control stick linkage, or electrical commands through amplifiers from control stick position potentiometers. During electrical operation, stick movement produces a signal from the potentiometers which is amplified and fed into the lateral and longitudinal master actuators. The master actuators respond to the command signals, mechanically positioning the control valves of the horizontal stabilizer and spoiler actuators. Follow-up potentiometers, mounted in the master actuator linkage, send a position signal back to the amplifier, nullifying the command signal when the proper control surface position is reached. Longitudinal electric system operation independent of the mechanical system is maintained by a free-play mechanism which acts as a clutch in the mechanical linkage. This free-play mechanism is disengaged during electrical operation and the mechanical linkage aft of the free-play mechanism is forced to follow movements of the control stick through master actuator movements.

Note

Should a malfunction cause a hard-over control movement, the pilot can return the system to mechanical control by (1) depressing the "kill" button on the stick grip, (2) selecting the stand-by position of the electric system switch, or (3) restraining the control stick by applying a stick force to oppose the control movement.

Lateral Ratio Changer

To reduce lateral control sensitivity and prevent excessive roll rates at high speed, the electric flight control system (figure 1-18) provides for an electrical change in control stick-to-spoiler ratio through the flap control system. With the electrical system operating, lateral control is restricted to 40 degrees inboard and mid and 48 degrees outboard spoiler deflection with SUPERSONIC droops selected. With the electric flight control systems disengaged and/or with CRUISE (5 degrees) or more droop deflection, the lateral control system operates at the full ratio.

Lateral Free-play Mechanism

The lateral free-play mechanism is a hydromechanical device consisting of a hydraulically extended, spring-retracted actuator and associated linkages. No. 2 hydraulic system pressure to operate the actuator is provided from the lateral master actuator shutoff valves. When the electric system is operative, hydraulic pressure extends the actuator and unlocks the mechanical movement from the cable system. If the electric system is switched off or fails, the solenoid-operated shutoff valves close off hydraulic power and the spring returns the free-play mechanism into mechanical engagement.

PITCH AUGMENTATION SYSTEM (MODIFIED BY ASC 42)

The pitch augmentation system provides relatively constant pitch control characteristics over the entire range of speed and altitude attainable. The system provides constant "feel" (stick movement and force requirements), and accepts control signals from the pitch axis of the automatic flight control system (AFCS). The system provides nonlinear horizontal stabilizer position control below 0.25 Mach, pitch damping above 0.3 Mach, and "g" control with pitch damping above 0.55 Mach. All components are dual for fail safety, and include pitch rate measuring gyro pitch accelerometers, electronic (series) amplifiers, and a hydraulic (series) servo actuator in series with the mechanical (pilot-controlled) system. The series actuator, acting through independent linkage, operates the horizontal stabilizer actuators, adding to or subtracting from the control authority of the pilot's electrical or mechanical input. A differential pressure transducer in the series actuator constantly compares the operating pressures of the dual pistons of the series actuator, providing a signal proportional to the unbalance. The balancer corrects the signal to the servo valves, resulting in equal piston pressures. Differential pressure switches in the actuator will shut off the system in the event of an unbalance beyond balancer capability. A failure of the No. 2 hydraulic system will also shut off the system through operation of hydraulic pressure switches.

Note
Electrical components of the pitch augmentation system must be allowed to warm up for 1½ minutes and flight control hydraulic pressure must be within normal limits before the system can be reset for operation.

CONSTANT CONTROL FEEL

The pitch augmentation system provides desirable longitudinal control system feel at all airspeeds and altitudes. At low speeds (below 0.25 Mach), the pilot has a direct, stick-to-stabilizer ratio for positive control of pitch attitude. As airspeed increases above 0.25 Mach, air data computer inputs increase, providing a combination of direct stick-to-stabilizer control and direct command of normal acceleration ("g") through the augmentation system. Above 0.55 Mach, the system has transitioned to a "g" command system with pitch damping, producing a requirement for constant stick force and stick displacement per change in "g."

Note
Automatic horizontal stabilizer modulation and pitch trim changes through the pitch augmentation system are not followed by the control stick.

PITCH DAMPING

Above 0.3 Mach, the pitch augmentation system provides pitch damping, stabilizing the aircraft during short-term pitch oscillations. Should longitudinal oscillations occur because of pilot input or turbulence, the pitch rate gyros and accelerometers detect the motion and convert it to an electrical signal. The signal is then fed to the series amplifiers, which control the longitudinal series actuator, acting to damp out the oscillations.

PITCH AUGMENTATION SYSTEM (UNMODIFIED)

Systems not modified by ASC No. 42 consist of paired pitch rate gyros, series amplifiers, and a dual hydraulic servo actuator. The air data computer processes pitch rate signals with true Mach number gain scheduling to produce a "Mach × pitch rate" signal for comparison with the "g" commanded by pilot input. Pitch trim with pitch augmentation engaged differs in that the system does not compensate for speed increase or reduction from trimmed speed, requiring pilot to return to the desired stick-free condition.

YAW DAMPER

The directional control system is equipped with a yaw damper. The system consists of a yaw rate measuring gyro, Mach number and altitude potentiometer gain scheduling in the air data computer, a yaw amplifier (directional series), and a hydraulic servo actuator, installed in series with the mechanical system. The directional series actuator controls the vertical stabilizer actuator without affecting control pedal position. A yaw rate results in a signal from the gyro, which is shaped by potentiometers for Mach number and pressure altitude in the air data computer. The signal is then fed to the amplifier, which boosts the signal and relays it to the directional series actuator. The series actuator then causes the vertical stabilizer actuator to move, stabilizing the aircraft about the yaw axis. The air data computer outputs (true Mach number and true pressure altitude), when integrated with the yaw rate signal, result in proper yaw damping corrections at all airspeeds and altitudes. The output signal of the yaw rate gyro is fed to the yaw damper amplifier through a contact of the ground safety relay. When the weight of the aircraft is on the extended landing gear, the damper is rendered insensitive to yaw gyro output, eliminating spurious vertical stabilizer movements during ground operation.

CAUTION
If a rapid, undamped oscillation of the vertical stabilizer is encountered during taxi or other ground operation, indicating a ground safety relay failure, disengage yaw augmentation system immediately. Abrupt rudder pedal inputs or rough terrain may result in rapid, self-sustaining oscillations through ±1 degree at a maximum rate of 10 degrees per second. A ground relay failure will have no effect on airborne performance; however, if a known failure exists, yaw damper (augmentation) system should be disengaged before landing rollout.

The authority of the yaw damper system is limited to ±1 degree of vertical stabilizer travel and is independent of the flap mechanical ratio changes. This limited travel feature prevents yaw damper malfunctions from damaging the aircraft.

CONTROLS AND INDICATORS

ELECTRIC SYSTEM SWITCH

The electric system switch (figure 1-20) is located on the flight control panel. This three-position (STBY, RESET, and ON) spring-loaded switch controls the longitudinal and lateral electric systems. To place the systems in operation, hold this switch in RESET until both the pitch and roll indicating windows show a blank and the ELEC F/C caution indicator goes out; then release the electric system switch to the ON position. This action disengages the free-play links in the mechanical systems,

Section 1
Part 2

NAVWEPS 01-60ABA-1

FLIGHT CONTROLS AND INDICATORS

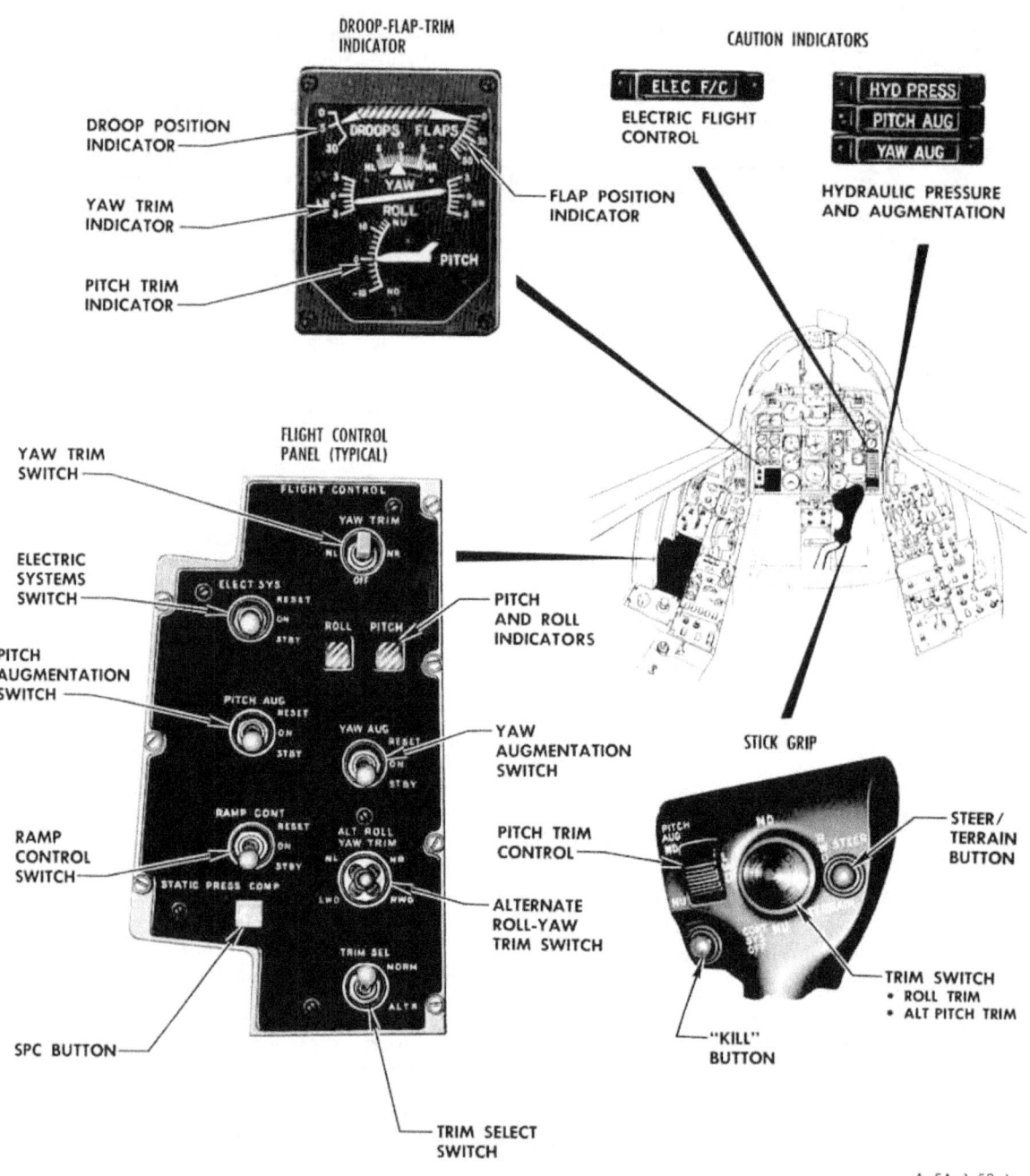

Figure 1-20

energizes the lateral and longitudinal master actuators in the electrical mode of operation, and completes the circuit to the pitch and roll electric system indicators.

Note

The electric system switch may be used to reset one system even though the other system will not remain engaged.

Roll and Pitch Indicators

The electric system roll and pitch indicators (figure 1-20) are located on the flight control panel, adjacent to the electric system switch. These windows show a barber pole if the mechanical control system is in operation. During electrical operation, these windows display a blank which blends with the control panel.

Electric Flight Control Caution Indicator

The ELEC F/C caution indicator (figure 1-20) is illuminated when either the longitudinal or lateral electric system is disengaged.

CONTROL SYSTEMS DISABLE ("KILL") BUTTON

Depressing the "kill" button (figure 1-20) disengages the electric flight control, pitch augmentation, and automatic flight control systems. Aircraft control is then accomplished through the mechanical flight control system. The flight control electric, pitch augmentation, or autoflight systems may be re-engaged at any time after "kill" button use by resetting individual control switches.

CAUTION

When depressing the "kill" button, the pilot should be prepared to compensate for any pitch trim changes associated with pitch augmentation disengagement.

Note

The yaw augmentation system cannot be disengaged by depressing the "kill" button.

PITCH AUGMENTATION SWITCH

The pitch augmentation switch (PITCH AUG, figure 1-20) is located on the flight control panel. This switch has three positions: STBY, RESET, and ON. When the system is inoperative, the PITCH AUG caution indicator is illuminated. To place the system in operation, hold the switch in RESET until the PITCH AUG caution indicator goes out, then release the switch to the ON position. This action moves the stick to a neutral position by centering and deactivating the stand-by pitch trim actuator, energizes the pitch augmentation hydraulic shutoff valves, and energizes a holding circuit for system operation, extinguishing the PITCH AUG caution indicator. In the event pitch augmentation dropout is caused by a transient condition, the system may be reset after the trouble clears.

Pitch Augmentation Caution Indicator

The pitch augmentation caution indicator (PITCH AUG, figure 1-20) is located on the pilot's instrument panel. This light will be illuminated whenever pitch augmentation is not engaged.

CAUTION

Failure of the pitch augmentation system may be accompanied by a change in pitch trim and stick position under power approach conditions. A moderate to rapid change in stick force may be required to maintain attitude. Subsequent to pitch augmentation failure, all pitch trim changes must be made through the stand-by pitch trim switch.

YAW AUGMENTATION SWITCH

The yaw augmentation switch (YAW AUG, figure 1-20) is located on the flight control panel. This switch has three positions: STBY, ON, and RESET. When the system is inoperative, the YAW AUG caution indicator will be on. To place the system in operation, hold the switch in RESET until the YAW AUG caution indicator goes out, then release the switch to ON. This action opens hydraulic shutoff valves and energizes a holding circuit for system operation, extinguishing the YAW AUG caution indicator.

Yaw Augmentation Caution Indicator

The yaw augmentation caution indicator (YAW AUG, figure 1-20) is installed on the pilot's instrument panel. This light will be illuminated whenever yaw augmentation is not engaged.

CAUTION

Under some circumstances, such as an internal failure of the yaw rate gyro, the yaw augmentation system may not operate properly while the YAW AUG caution indicator remains off and the system remains engaged. Should undamped yaw oscillations be noted with the YAW AUG caution light off, move the yaw augmentation switch to STBY, and exercise caution in maneuvers involving high roll rates or roll reversals.

TRIM SYSTEMS

PITCH TRIM

Normal pitch trim is provided through the pitch augmentation system. The system trims the aircraft without changing the neutral position of the control stick. Below 0.25 Mach, the pitch trim control functions as a position trim control, removing longitudinal control stick forces for a desired horizontal stabilizer position. Above 0.55 Mach, the pitch trim control functions as a "g" trim control. The desired "g" is automatically maintained by a change in aircraft pitch attitude. The pitch augmentation system changes the position of the horizontal stabilizers to coincide with the setting of the trim wheel.

STAND-BY PITCH TRIM

A stand-by pitch trim system is provided for pitch trim control in the event pitch augmentation shuts off. This system trims longitudinal stick forces by changing the "no load" position of the control stick artificial feel bungee, moving the stick with trim. Stand-by pitch trim is limited to 2 degrees nose-up and 6.75 degrees nose-down. Should the pitch augmentation system fail, the stand-by pitch trim switch may be used to trim out the control force change which occurs as a result of the centering of the longitudinal series actuator. The system operates on either primary or essential bus a-c power and is available, in the event both generators fail, by using the emergency ram-air turbine. The trim select switch need not be placed in ALTR to utilize the stand-by pitch trim switch unless both generators fail and the emergency ram-air turbine is used as the source of electrical power.

Note

Severity of the trim change on dropout of pitch augmentation depends upon the amount of displacement trimmed into the system through the longitudinal series actuator. At approach speeds, considerable displacement is present with all forces trimmed out. A failure which causes pitch augmentation to monitor off under these conditions usually results in a substantial nose-down pitch with an increase in back stick force and position required to hold pitch attitude.

LATERAL TRIM

Normal lateral (roll) trim is provided through differential displacement of the horizontal stabilizers. An electrical actuator is connected through reversing linkage to the control valves of the horizontal stabilizer actuators. When the lateral trim switch is moved, the electrical trim actuator causes differential displacement of the horizontal stabilizers, trimming the aircraft about the roll axis.

Note

An override bungee is provided in the lateral trim linkage to allow any lateral trim to be removed if full nose-up or nose-down longitudinal control displacement is required. The lateral trim will automatically return when the control stick is returned toward neutral.

DIRECTIONAL TRIM

The aircraft is trimmed about the yaw axis by changing the "no load" position of the directional artificial feel bungee. As the yaw trim switch is moved, the directional control pedals assume a new "no load" position, and the vertical stabilizer is displaced, trimming the aircraft about the yaw axis. The authority of the directional trim system and the total travel of the vertical stabilizer are controlled through the flap mechanical ratio changer. With the flaps extended more than 30 degrees, 6 degrees of left or right trim can be obtained. With the flaps extended less than 25 degrees or retracted (SUPERSONIC or CRUISE), trim is restricted to 1½ degrees of left or right travel. To prevent a radical trim change during flap extension, the yaw trim actuator incorporates a centering feature which returns stabilizer trim toward neutral during the ratio change.

Note

A full yaw trim indication (7 units) results from either the 1½- or 6-degree stabilizer position.

ALTERNATE ROLL/YAW TRIM

When selected, the alternate roll/yaw trim system will assume operation of lateral and directional trim in the event of normal trim switch or electric system failure. This system is powered by the essential a-c bus and, if necessary, may be operated on power supplied by the emergency ram-air turbine.

AUTOMATIC FLAP TRIM

An automatic pitch trim correction during extension or retraction of the flaps is provided by a mechanical interconnect between the flaps and the longitudinal series actuator. This mechanism moves the longitudinal series actuator assembly a distance proportional to flap deflection, compensating for the pitch trim changes resulting from variation of boundary layer airflow effect. For a 50-degree flap selection, 8 degrees aircraft nose-down (stabilizer leading edge up) trim change is provided without changing the trimmed neutral position of the control stick. Since the interconnect is mechanical, it operates during all modes of longitudinal system operation: pitch augmentation engaged or stand-by, and electric flight control system engaged or stand-by.

Note

Should flap extension be selected with the control stick full forward, flap deflection may be restricted. Normal flap actuation resumes when the stick is allowed to return toward neutral.

CONTROLS AND INDICATORS

Trim Select Switch

The trim select switch (TRIM SEL, figure 1-20) is located at the rear of the pilot's flight control panel. This switch has two positions: NORM and ALTR. In the NORM position, primary a-c bus power is supplied to the normal yaw trim and roll trim circuits. The ALTR position is used in the event of electric system or trim switch failure to transfer control of roll and yaw trim to the alternate roll/yaw trim switch, and to shift the electrical power supply for all trim circuits to the essential a-c bus.

Pitch Trim Control

Normal pitch trim is adjusted through a rotary synchro-type control (figure 1-20) installed on the face of the control stick grip. This control [NU (nose up), ND (nose down)] enables the pilot to trim horizontal stabilizer position and normal acceleration ("g") through the pitch augmentation system. Below 0.25 Mach, the pitch trim control is used to trim horizontal stabilizer position, relieving control stick loads during take-off and landing. Above 0.55 Mach, the pitch trim control is a means of trimming "g" or stick force. Trim control rotation establishes a reference signal for the trim synchronizer in the longitudinal series amplifier. Summing circuits in the amplifier compare the reference signal with actual "g" signals measured by a pair of pitch accelerometers. The result is an error signal which is sent to the series actuator, causing the aircraft to nose up or down, seeking a nulled condition.

Note

- On aircraft not modified by ASC 42, constant normal acceleration factor ("g") is not maintained during accelerations and decelerations. Pitch trim input is required for speed changes.
- Rotating the pitch trim control too fast can cause an erroneous or null signal condition, resulting in either no trim response or a momentary reverse response.

Normal Roll/Stand-by Pitch Trim Switch

The normal roll/stand-by pitch trim switch (figure 1-20) is located on the control stick grip, to the right of the pitch trim control. This switch is spring-loaded to neutral (off) from four trimming positions. The lateral positions are LWD (left wing down) and RWD (right wing down). These positions control normal lateral trim through differential displacement of the horizontal stabilizers. The vertical positions are NU (nose up) and ND (nose down). These positions may be used to trim out longitudinal stick forces with the pitch augmentation system inoperative.

Yaw Trim Switch

The yaw trim switch (figure 1-20) is located on the flight control panel. Yaw trim is controlled by holding this switch to NL (nose left) or NR (nose right) until the undesirable load is removed from the control pedals.

Alternate Roll/Yaw Trim Switch

The ALT ROLL/YAW TRIM switch (figure 1-20) provides control of roll and yaw trim with the TRIM SEL switch at ALTR. In the event of failure of the normal roll or yaw trim circuits, undesirable stick loads or yawed flight can be corrected by using this switch as desired.

Droop, Flap, and Trim Indicator

All trim positions and droop and flap positions are indicated by a single unit (figure 1-20) installed on the instrument panel. Droop position is indicated at the 0-, 5-, and 30-degree positions, the pointer resting at the 5-degree position without electrical power. Flap position is indicated from 0 to 50 degrees. Vertical stabilizer trim is indicated from 0 to 7 units nose left and nose right. Actual stabilizer yaw trim position depends upon whether the flaps are up or down. Horizontal stabilizer differential displacement (roll trim) is indicated from 0 to 3 units wing up or down for either wing. Horizontal stabilizer position is indicated from 0 to 12 units nose up and from 0 to 12 units nose down. The pitch needle is a miniature aircraft, indicating the resulting aircraft attitude reaction to a given trim setting.

Note

- All trim indications are in UNITS of trim displacement and are NOT directly proportional to surface movement in degrees.
- The pitch trim indicator provides an indication of horizontal stabilizer movement and position during either trim operated or direct (control stick) flight control movements.
- During flap retraction, the yaw trim indicator will not move. When the stabilizer shift occurs, the indicator will remain at the position indicated since the indicator reflects the percentage of total trim rather than actual surface position.
- With flaps up, full yaw trim is indicated as 7 units although only 1½ degrees of actuator travel has occurred.

AUTOMATIC FLIGHT CONTROL SYSTEM (AFCS)

The AFCS is designed to provide automatic control of the longitudinal and lateral flight control systems above 0.5 Mach and 500 feet above the ground. During normal AFCS operation, the pilot can make control stick attitude corrections (stick-steering) within limits without disengaging the system. The AFCS acts through components of the longitudinal and the lateral flight control systems. Command signals to the system are heading, pitch, and roll synchro inputs generated by the flight reference set, Mach number or altitude signals from the air data computer, or steering error signals from the bomb directing set. These systems direct commands to the flight control system through the pitch augmentation (longitudinal series) and lateral electric system amplifiers. The AFCS provides NORM (hold bank, hold pitch, or hold heading), ALT (hold altitude), MACH (hold Mach*), and NAV (autonavigation) modes of operation. In addition, the AFCS provides automatic LABS maneuvers as an alternate method of weapon delivery.

NORMAL MODE

Normal mode AFCS operation provides "hold pitch" control within 1 degree of the desired pitch attitude and "hold heading" control within ½ degree of flight reference set heading output. Aircraft attitude limits in this mode are plus or minus 55 degrees of pitch and plus or minus 60 degrees of bank. Pilot stick-steering

*Aircraft having ASC 42 complied with

AUTOFLIGHT CONTROLS AND INDICATORS

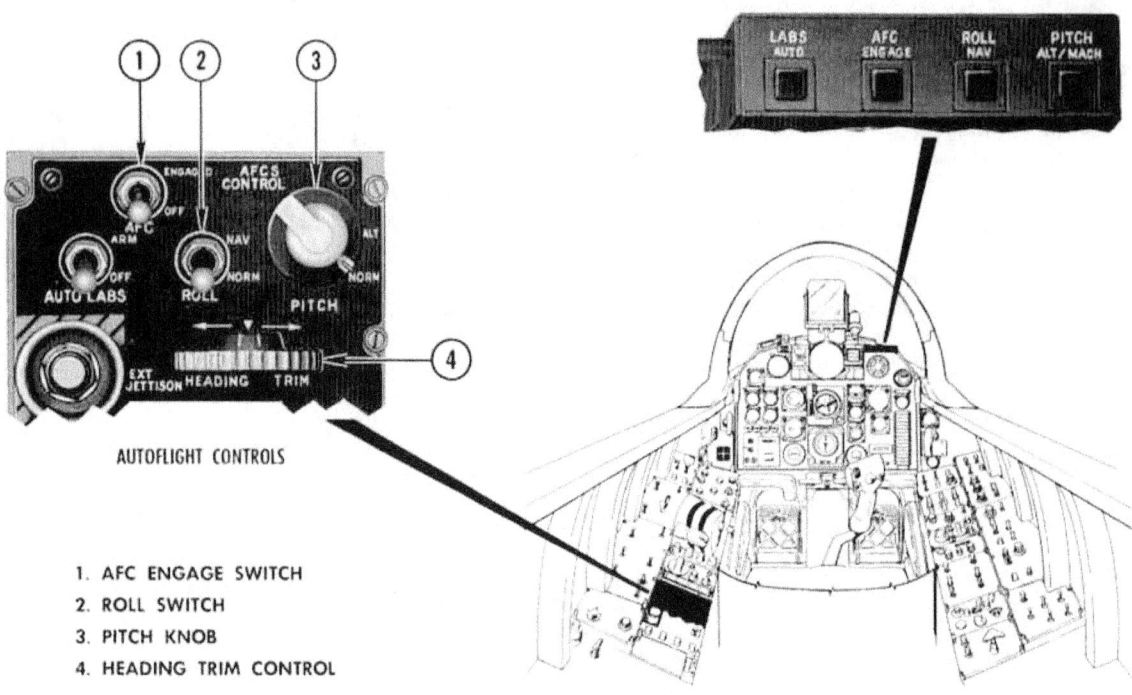

1. AFC ENGAGE SWITCH
2. ROLL SWITCH
3. PITCH KNOB
4. HEADING TRIM CONTROL

*AIRCRAFT HAVING ASC NO. 58 COMPLIED WITH

Figure 1-21

corrections to these limits may be initiated at any time in this mode without disengaging the system. For stick-steering corrections, a 1-pound breakout force is required. Release of stick-steering breakout force at a bank angle of less than 5 degrees results in AFCS resumption of "hold heading" control. A stick-steering correction with stick centering at between 5 and 60 degrees of bank will switch the lateral system to "hold bank," resulting in a sustained, coordinated turn at the existing bank angle. This turn will be maintained until the aircraft is stick-steered to within 5 degrees of the wings level attitude and the control stick is centered, or until the NAV mode is selected. Should the pilot make a stick-steering correction in pitch, the longitudinal system will revert to "hold pitch" and will maintain the pitch angle at stick release, up to the 55-degree limit. A pilot-initiated correction of more than 55-degree pitch or 60-degree bank will disengage the autoflight system.

ALTITUDE MODE

The altitude mode of operation is a function of the longitudinal control system, utilizing true pressure altitude signals from the air data computer. Altitude is maintained within plus or minus 50 feet (or 2 percent, whichever is less) above 10,000 feet, and plus or minus 30 feet below 10,000 feet. A longitudinal stick-steering correction reverts the system to "hold pitch." After the aircraft has been leveled at the new altitude, the ALT mode may be reselected. A load factor limiting device prevents AFCS pitch corrections from exceeding plus or minus 1 "g" from the load factor existing prior to correction.

> **CAUTION**
>
> Changing SPC mode while in hold altitude (ALT), at subsonic speeds, will cause aircraft pitch response, with severity depending on altitude and Mach number at time of change.

MACH MODE*

The MACH (hold Mach number) mode is a function of the pitch augmentation and autoflight systems, utilizing Mach number signal output of the air data computer. This mode modulates aircraft pitch attitude to maintain true Mach number within 0.01 Mach of that present

*Aircraft having ASC 42 complied with

at time of mode selection. On aircraft not having ASC 42 complied with, the MACH position of the AFCS PITCH knob is inoperative and obscured.

CAUTION

- Do not change SPC mode while in MACH mode.
- Do not engage MACH hold while at low altitude or in rough air.

NAV MODE

The roll switch may be placed to NAV as soon as desired after the AFCS is engaged. The aircraft will turn on course for the selected destination. The longitudinal system will continue to operate in the selected mode. Refer to BOMB DIRECTING SET, AN/ASB-12, in Section I, Part 2, of the Supplemental NATOPS Flight Manual (NAVWEPS 01-60ABA-1A).

AUTO-LABS

Refer to LABS OPERATION, in Section I, Part 2, of the Supplemental NATOPS Flight Manual (NAVWEPS 01-60ABA-1A).

CONTROLS AND INDICATORS

AUTOFLIGHT INDICATORS*

The autoflight indicators (figure 1-21) are mounted directly above the master caution indicator on the instrument panel shroud. During flight with the AFC switch at OFF, these indicators are blank. With the AFC switch at ENGAGED, the AFC ENGAGE indicator shows "ON." The ROLL NAV indicator displays "ON" only with the AFCS engaged, the ROLL switch positioned to NAV, and an operating bomb directing set installed. The PITCH ALT/MACH indicator displays "ON" with the PITCH knob at ALT for the hold altitude mode. For a description of the LABS AUTO indicator, refer to LABS OPERATION, in Section I, Part 2, of the Supplemental NATOPS Flight Manual (NAVWEPS 01-60ABA-1A).

AFC SWITCH

The AFC switch (1, figure 1-21) has two positions: OFF and ENGAGED. The electronic components of the AFCS are energized and warmed up when external or aircraft electrical power and cooling air are applied. After the electric flight control and pitch augmentation systems are engaged, placing this switch to ENGAGED, during flight within AFCS attitude limits, places the AFCS in operation. Should these limits be exceeded while stick-steering, the system will automatically disengage and the AFC switch will return to the OFF position.

PITCH KNOB

The PITCH knob (3, figure 1-21) is a three-position rotary selector, with ALT (hold altitude), NORM (hold pitch), and MACH (hold Mach number) positions.

Note

On aircraft not having ASC 42 complied with, the MACH mode is inoperative and the knob position obscured.

After the AFCS has been engaged in the NORM mode and the aircraft is flying at the desired altitude, the PITCH knob may be moved to the ALT position. A stick-steering pitch correction moves the knob from ALT to NORM. Once the correction is concluded and breakout force is relieved from the control stick, the knob may be repositioned as desired.

ROLL SWITCH

The ROLL switch (2, figure 1-21) has two positions: NORM and NAV. The NORM position provides "hold heading" or "hold bank" control and provides heading trim. Refer to HEADING TRIM CONTROL, in this section. With the ROLL switch in NORM, stick-steering is available. Steering corrections will revert the system to "hold bank" if the control breakout force is relieved at more than a 5-degree bank angle. The AFCS will then maintain a coordinated turn at the bank angle existing at stick release. To return to "hold heading," the aircraft must be stick-steered to a bank angle of less than 5 degrees and the control stick centered. The NAV position locks out the heading input of the flight reference set and supplies a steering signal from the bomb directing set. The use of stick-steering for heading corrections causes the lateral system to revert from NAV to NORM mode operation.

AUTO LABS SWITCH

Refer to LABS OPERATION, in Section I, Part 2, of the Supplemental NATOPS Flight Manual (NAVWEPS 01-60ABA-1A).

HEADING TRIM CONTROL

The HEADING TRIM control (4, figure 1-21) provides vernier-type trim control of aircraft heading in the roll NORM (hold heading) mode. Should a heading change be desired, the pilot may roll this control toward the desired direction of heading correction. The aircraft will roll into a coordinated turn and roll out when a commensurate number of degrees of heading has been passed.

CONTROL SYSTEMS DISABLE ("KILL") BUTTON

A "kill" button (figure 1-20) is provided on the lower left portion of the control stick grip face. Should a malfunction occur in the AFCS, the pitch augmentation system, or the pitch or roll electric systems, all systems may be disabled by depressing this button. This action will position the AFC switch to OFF, disengage the electric flight control systems, and disable pitch augmentation.

AFCS OPERATION

NORMAL MODE

1. Above 500 feet, check the PITCH knob and ROLL switch at NORM and move the AFC switch to ENGAGED.

   Note the AFC ENGAGE indicator "ON." If the system is engaged in a turn, the aircraft will

*Aircraft having ASC 58 complied with

hold existing bank angle until changed by control stick steering.
2. Control climb Mach number by stick-steering pitch attitude as desired.
3. Make all fine heading changes by rotating the HEADING TRIM control.
4. Turns are accomplished by stick-steering the roll-in and rollout.

Note
- The PITCH AUG trim control is inoperative in the pitch NORM and ALT modes.
- Should turbulence cause the aircraft to exceed AFCS stick-steering limits, the AFCS will remain engaged and will return the aircraft to the previous attitude.
- Failure of the pitch augmentation or electric flight control systems results in loss of AFCS operation.

ALTITUDE MODE
1. When the desired altitude is reached, stick-steer the aircraft to a level attitude and move the PITCH knob to ALT.
2. Check PITCH ALT/MACH indicator "ON."
3. When accelerating or decelerating through the transonic speed range, a transient pitch effect may occur due to compressibility effects of the transonic speed range on the air data computer pressure sensing and compensation system. If this transient effect is considered objectionable, the NORM (hold pitch) mode of the AFCS can be selected. When above or below this speed range, the ALT mode of operation can then be reselected.

NAV MODE
1. When desired after take-off, engage AFCS in the pitch and roll NORM mode.
2. Stick-steer the aircraft to approximate heading desired and move the ROLL switch to NAV.
3. Check ROLL NAV indicator "ON."

Note
The NAV mode is operable only when the bomb directing set is in operation.

4. If a stick-steering heading change is made, the ROLL switch will move to NORM and the ROLL NAV indicator will go blank. When the aircraft is returned to the desired course, return the ROLL switch to NAV to resume operation.

MACH MODE*
1. With the AFCS engaged, establish Mach number as desired.
2. PITCH knob—MACH.
3. Check PITCH ALT/MACH indicator "ON."
4. Adjust power as required for altitude control.

AUTO-LABS
The AFCS may be used in performing automatic LABS maneuvers on bomb directing set targets or on any target through the LABS system. Refer to Section I, Part 2, of the Supplemental NATOPS Flight Manual (NAVWEPS 01-60ABA-1A).

FLIGHT CONTROL SYSTEMS OPERATION
LONGITUDINAL CONTROL

The longitudinal system is augmented to provide ease of control throughout the entire speed and altitude range of operation. Below 0.25 Mach, the system provides positive horizontal stabilizer position response to control stick movements for take-off and landing. As airspeed is increased above 0.25 Mach, a transition begins which changes the system from a "position" system to a "rate" system at 0.55 Mach. Pitch damping is operative at all speeds above 0.3 Mach. Above 0.5 Mach, control stick deflection commands a "g" force rather than a set stabilizer position. During normal operation with pitch augmentation, a stick force of 5.6 pounds and a stick movement of 3/4 inch commands 1 "g" of additional acceleration. These control force and deflection characteristics are constant above 0.55 Mach over the entire operating range of speed and altitude. By moving the control stick and then holding it fixed, the pilot generates a "g" command signal proportional to stick movement. The pitch augmentation system holds aircraft acceleration at the "g" commanded by comparing the command signal with detected acceleration signal.

PITCH AUGMENTATION OFF

With pitch augmentation disengaged or inoperative, variations in airspeed and altitude result in changing requirements for control stick movement and force, and the aircraft handles in a manner similar to that of slower, transonic aircraft not having augmented flight controls. In addition, loss of pitch damping requires cautious handling and trimming in the transonic speed range to prevent pilot-induced oscillations. Available aircraft nose-up (stick aft) horizontal stabilizer displacement is reduced by approximately 6 degrees, and pitch corrections at low speeds require larger stick movements than when operating with pitch augmentation engaged. Refer to LOW-SPEED FLIGHT, in Section IV.

PITCH AUGMENTATION ON

With pitch augmentation operating, stick displacement required remains constant above 0.55 Mach, and stick position is not changed when the pitch trim control is rotated. The pitch augmentation system tends to maintain zero pitch rate whenever the stick is in the neutral longitudinal position. As a result of this characteristic, aircraft normal load factor varies with bank angle. During a "normal rate" 360-degree roll, the pitch augmentation system will tend to stabilize the aircraft to 0 "g" at 90 degrees, −1 "g" at 180 degrees, 0 "g" at 270 degrees, and back to 1 "g" at wings level. Therefore, to maintain positive 1 "g" during a 360-degree roll, pilot longitudinal control is necessary.

*Aircraft having ASC 42 complied with

NAVWEPS 01-60ABA-1

Section I
Part 2

CAUTION

Pitch augmentation dropout during high-g maneuvers may cause the aircraft to pitch up or "dig-in," requiring a change in stick force at a moderate rate. If dropout occurs during transonic turns or pull-ups, the resultant change in "g" (±1.5 "g" without pilot correction) could exceed structural limits. Upon illumination of the PITCH AUG and master caution indicators, relax stick pressure until the trim transient is complete (15 to 18 seconds). Use stand-by pitch trim for all subsequent pitch trim changes.

LATERAL CONTROL

With the spoiler-deflector system, adequate roll-rate capability is provided for low-speed flight. More than adequate roll rate is available to transonic speeds, where a slight decrease is noted. Maximum roll rate again increases at medium and high supersonic speeds.

LATERAL CONTROL EFFECTIVENESS

At low airspeeds, the aerodynamic effectiveness of the spoilers is considerably greater with flaps extended than with flaps retracted. In order to ensure adequate lateral control for asymmetrical store loadings or possible engine failure, flaps should not be retracted below 200 knots.

DIRECTIONAL CONTROL

The all-movable, hydraulically powered vertical stabilizer provides excellent directional control throughout the aircraft operational envelope. Full control pedal displacement produces 2 degrees of stabilizer deflection with the flaps retracted and 8 degrees of stabilizer deflection with the flaps extended.

DIRECTIONAL RATIO CHANGER

The change in vertical stabilizer deflection ratio flaps-up to flaps-down is accomplished through a ratio changing mechanism, operated by mechanical linkage attached to the flap actuating linkage. The directional shift begins at 0 degrees, and the shift is complete when the flaps reach 50 degrees. The vertical stabilizer ratio mechanism has no effect on directional control pedal travel.

WARNING

To avoid any danger of overloading the vertical stabilizer, abrupt control pedal movements should be avoided at airspeeds above 600 knots IAS.

TRIM OPERATION

LATERAL TRIM

Because of a trim interaction characteristic of this system, a large lateral trim change may require some longitudinal trim change.

DIRECTIONAL TRIM

Because of trim interaction, a change in directional trim usually requires a slight change in lateral trim.

Directional Trim Centering

To prevent a large magnification of any trim setting upon flap extension, the vertical stabilizer trim actuator is returned toward neutral as the flaps extend to 25 degrees. During flap extension, the trim indicator follows the trim actuator toward zero. Directional retrimming may be required following flap extension.

PITCH AUGMENTATION OPERATION

The pitch augmentation system consists of an electrically controlled, tandem piston hydraulic actuator, effectively in series with the master actuator (parallel system). See figure 1-17. Augmented system operation provides relatively constant stick force and displacement per "g," position trim at low speeds, "g" command at high speeds, and pitch damping. The augmentation system controls the movements of the series actuator, which is attached to a mixer bell crank in the longitudinal control linkage. The final mixer bell crank output to the surface actuators is the algebraic sum of movements of both the master actuator (parallel system) and the series actuator (augmentation system). Each half of the tandem series actuator is controlled by a separate servo valve which accepts inputs from one-half of the dual electronic systems. The output of these valves is constantly measured and a dual system balancer acts to equalize the output of the series amplifiers. Should an unbalance in signal beyond the capability of the balancer exist for more than 2 seconds, differential pressure switches in the servo valve disable the system, allowing the series actuator to center and illuminating the PITCH AUG caution indicator. If the condition which caused the unbalance is transient, the system may be reset through the pitch augmentation switch.

LOW-SPEED OPERATION

In the low-speed mode, pilot stick movement produces direct stabilizer response for precise control of pitch attitude during take-off or landing. Normally, position trim is provided at low speeds through the trim control synchro on the stick grip. The trim control synchro output is directed to the series amplifiers, commanding a stabilizer position change equivalent to trim control rotation. All position trim corrections are made through the series actuator; therefore, stick neutral position is not affected.

PITCH DAMPING

Above 0.3 Mach, the system provides damping of short-period pitch oscillations. This feature is provided by modifying pitch rate signals from a pitch rate sensing gyro. The pitch rate signal is washed out to eliminate the steady-state signal such as that produced during a pull-up and/or a stabilized turn, and to allow only changes in the pitch rate signals to pass through. The pitch rate signals are summed with other inputs in the series amplifiers, and stabilizer position is modulated to maintain an effective zero pitch rate change.

HIGH-SPEED OPERATION

At high speeds (above 0.55 Mach), the stick position potentiometer output functions as a "g" command. This is accomplished by transition from series actuator follow-up (position system) to a "g" command system. During this mode of operation, the pitch trim control acts as a "g" trim control, allowing the pilot to trim normal acceleration number as desired. Trim synchronizers in the series amplifiers maintain "g" error at zero when the system is disengaged and maintain the aircraft at the trimmed "g" state once the trimmed setting is established. Stick position potentiometer output is transmitted to the series actuators as a "g" command at the rate of one additional "g" for each $3/4$ inch of stick travel. As the "g" change begins, pitch accelerometers send a signal into the series amplifiers, where the signal is compared with stick position input. Stabilizer position is varied by the resultant series amplifier signal, and "g" force is maintained at the value commanded by control stick input. Constant stick force per "g" is automatically provided above 0.55 Mach, as the artificial feel bungee in the control linkage exerts a 5.6-pound force for every $3/4$ inch of stick travel. When no acceleration change signal is present (no stick movement or trim control input), the series amplifier signal maintains the aircraft at the steady-state acceleration, providing constant normal acceleration.

Note

On systems not modified by ASC 42, the "Mach × pitch rate" (MΘ) environment produces aircraft pitch changes due to speed changes, introducing positive static stability.

SPEED BRAKES

Positive deceleration with small longitudinal trim change is provided through the lateral flight control surfaces by a system which opens all spoilers and deflectors simultaneously. The spoiler speed brake system is electrically controlled and operated by the No. 2 hydraulic system. When the speed brake switch is moved to OUT, hydraulic pressure is ported to a spring-loaded speed brake actuator, which positions the lateral system mechanical linkage to obtain any desired position to a maximum deflection of 55 degrees.

Normal lateral control is provided with the speed brake in any position through differential movement of the spoiler-deflectors from speed brake position. An interconnect is provided, which retracts the spoiler speed brake to 8 degrees open when the flap control switch is placed in the 50-degree position. The speed brakes can then be controlled only between closed and 8 degrees with the speed brake switch. The speed brakes close automatically when the flap control switch is moved to the 40-degree position. An override switch, mounted on the flap linkage, also retracts the speed brakes to 8 degrees when the flaps are lowered more than 10 degrees, regardless of flap control switch position.

SPEED BRAKE SWITCH

A speed brake switch (21, figure 1-3) is located on the No. 2 throttle grip. This thumb-actuated switch has three positions: OUT (aft), IN (forward), and OFF (center). The switch is spring-loaded to OFF (neutral) from the OUT position.

SPEED BRAKE DUMP HANDLE

A speed brake dump handle (28, figure 1-3) is located at the rear of the pilot's left console. This handle permits manual dumping of hydraulic pressure in the speed brake selector valve to return in the event of electrical or No. 2 hydraulic system failure. This allows the spring-loaded speed brake actuator to move the spoiler-deflector control linkage to the closed position. This handle is held in the dump position by a ratchet incorporated in the handle shaft. To return the handle to the down position, the handle must be twisted clockwise. Spring action will return the handle to the console.

SPEED BRAKE INDICATOR

A speed brake indicator (37, figure 1-4) is located on the pilot's instrument panel. The indicator shows the open ("OUT") and closed ("IN") positions of the speed brake and displays a barber pole during speed brake movement, during the absence of electrical power, and whenever the speed brake is stopped in an intermediate position.

SPEED BRAKE OPERATION

CHARACTERISTICS

Speed brake extension at subsonic speeds is accompanied by an easily controlled nose-down pitch and moderate airframe buffet. Extension at supersonic speeds is characterized by high deceleration forces and speed brakes should be extended in increments with extension limited to approximately one-half until less than Mach 1.0. When decelerating through 1.0 Mach, pitch trim may reverse and pilot-induced oscillation may be encountered, particularly with pitch augmentation inoperative.

Note

- The inverted spoilers will not extend fully at speeds corresponding to 500 KEAS or higher.
- A slight increase in roll sensitivity may be noted as the speed brakes open and close.

WING FLAPS AND DROOP LEADING EDGE

WING FLAPS

The trailing edge wing flaps are electrically controlled and hydraulically operated by No. 2 hydraulic system pressure. Flap synchronization is provided through a mechanical interconnect. No-load hydraulic flap extension and retraction require approximately 8 seconds.

CAUTION

Extension of the flaps with either forward engine access door open will result in damage to the flaps, the access door, or both.

Section I
Part 2
NAVWEPS 01-60ABA-1

FLAP AND DROOP CONTROLS

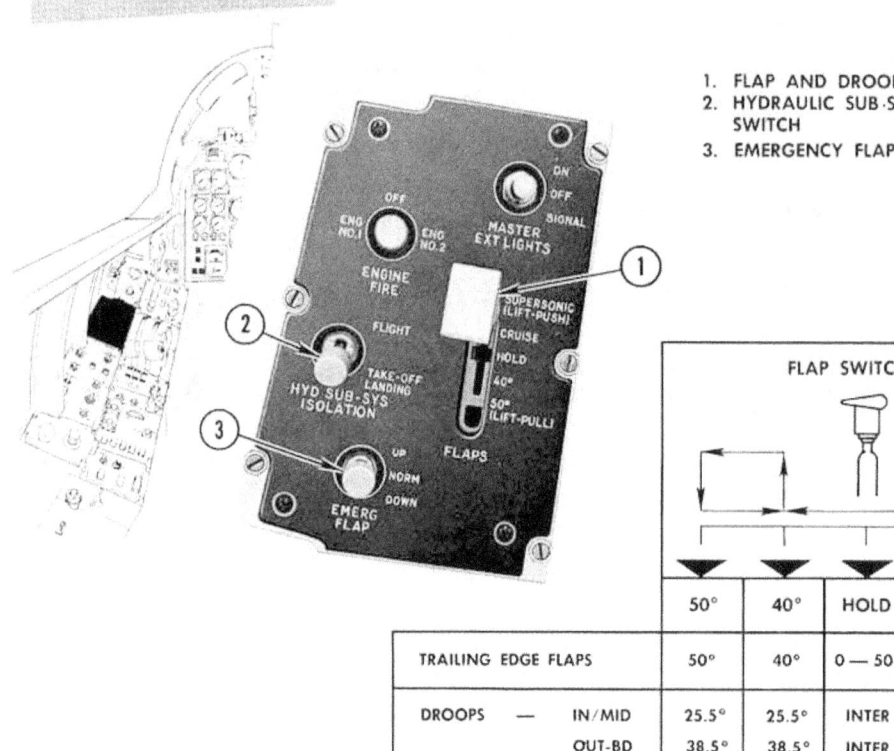

1. FLAP AND DROOP CONTROL SWITCH
2. HYDRAULIC SUB-SYSTEMS ISOLATION SWITCH
3. EMERGENCY FLAP SWITCH

FLAP SWITCH OPERATION					
	50°	40°	HOLD	CRUISE	SUPERSONIC
TRAILING EDGE FLAPS	50°	40°	0 — 50°	0°	0°
DROOPS — IN/MID	25.5°	25.5°	INTER	3°	0°
OUT-BD	38.5°	38.5°	INTER	5°	0°
AVAILABLE SPEED BRAKE	0 — 8°	NONE	①	55°	55°

① Flaps less than 9° = Full speed brake available.
  Flaps more than 10° = Speed brakes not available.

FLAP CONTROL FUNCTIONS		
FLAP POSITION	FLAP SWITCH POSITION	FUNCTION
0°	SUPERSONIC	Spoiler-deflector travel limited to 40/48 degrees.
	CRUISE	Spoiler-deflector travel unlimited (70 degrees). Droops caution indicator (A/B range).
25° — 30°	HOLD, 40° OR 50°	Engine door indicator (flaps 25° or more). Directional ratio change and trim centering. Lateral control transfer — 10° to 30° flaps.
40°	40°	Speed brakes retracted and disabled.
0 — 50°	HOLD, 40° OR 50°	Wheels warning light — flaps down 35° or more with either throttle retarded below approximately 85 to 90% engine rpm. Pitch trim compensation of horizontal stabilizers throughout flap range. BLC full flow — 50° flaps.
	50°	Speed brakes restricted: 0 to 8°.

A-5A-1-52-2

Figure 1-22

FLAP INTERCONNECT

Compensation for pitch trim change due to flap extension or retraction is accomplished by a flap interconnection which mechanically repositions the pitch augmentation actuator, thus moving the horizontal stabilizers to a new trimmed position. Mechanical interconnection also produces a ratio change in available vertical stabilizer travel with control pedal deflection and directional trim dependent upon actual position of the flap. Full lateral electric flight control spoiler deflection and automatic speed brake retraction to 8 degrees are controlled by an interconnect system through flap control switch position. An override switch (mounted on the flap actuator) is incorporated in parallel with the flap switch control circuit to allow full spoiler throw and automatic speed brake retraction whenever the flaps are extended 10 degrees or more.

DROOP LEADING EDGE

Full wing span droop leading edges are installed on each wing. Each droop leading edge consists of three mechanically controlled sections. The outboard section operates on linkage separate from the inboard sections, and has an actual maximum extension of 38.5 degrees, while the mid and inboard sections extend to a maximum of 25.5 degrees.

Note
Though actual individual droop position exceeds that of the indicator, 0, 5, and 30 degrees are used for easier reference.

Activation of the wing flaps automatically positions these surfaces through a series of jackscrews driven by No. 2 hydraulic system powered motors. The combined change in airfoil resulting from lowered wing flaps and drooped leading edge sections increases lift and lowers stall speeds. For flight at less than transonic speeds, the CRUISE position provides best performance. In this position, all droop leading edge sections are lowered to 5 degrees. Since the droop actuators are not capable of withstanding supersonic speeds, the leading edges are fully retracted by placing the flap control switch in SUPERSONIC. On the *extend* cycle (flap control switch in 40° or 50°), the droops begin extending toward 30 degrees when the flaps pass 25 degrees. On the *retract* cycle (flap control switch in CRUISE), the droops begin retracting toward 5 degrees when the flaps pass through 30 degrees. Droop operation lags flap movement. Selection of HOLD with flaps between 0 and 50 degrees results in the droops stopping at an intermediate position between 0 and 30 degrees.

BOUNDARY LAYER CONTROL

Boundary layer control operation is automatically coordinated with wing flap operation. Boundary layer control decreases the airspeed and angle of attack required for approach and landing, and also minimizes the amount of aircraft rotation required for lift-off. A boundary layer control valve, installed in the compressor bleed line from each engine, directs high-velocity air over the landing flaps, beginning when the flaps leave the fully retracted position. Flow reaches maximum when the flaps are extended approximately 40 degrees and the valves are full open at 50 degrees. This high-velocity flow effectively increases lift and reduces angle of attack required in the landing configuration.

FLAP CONTROL SWITCH

The flap control switch (1, figure 1-22) is located outboard of the engine throttle quadrant on the pilot's left console. Operation of the flaps, droop leading edge and automatic speed brake retraction, lateral control ratio, and directional trim centering are coordinated through the use of this switch. The flap control switch has 50°, 40°, HOLD, CRUISE, and SUPERSONIC positions. The positions of the flap control switch function as shown in figure 1-22. The flap control switch may be moved directly between the 40°, HOLD, and CRUISE positions, but must be lifted and moved into and out of SUPERSONIC and lifted and moved into the 50° position. The flap control switch may be pushed directly from the 50° position to the 40° position. If the switch is lifted while in the 50° position, a mechanical stop prevents movement to the HOLD or CRUISE position.

Note
To prevent inadvertent movement directly from SUPERSONIC to HOLD, the flap control switch must be dropped into CRUISE position before HOLD can be selected.

FLAP/DROOP POSITION INDICATORS

Refer to DROOP, FLAP, AND TRIM INDICATOR, in this section.

Droops Caution Indicator

The droops caution indicator (DROOPS, figure 1-4) is installed to caution the pilot not to continue accelerating with droops in CRUISE. With the flap control switch in CRUISE and either or both throttles at minimum afterburner or higher, this indicator is illuminated. When the flap control switch is moved to SUPERSONIC, or the throttles are retarded past minimum afterburner, the indicator goes out. On aircraft modified by ASC No. 42, illumination of the DROOPS caution indicator is an automatic function of airspeed with the flap control switch in the CRUISE position. With the droops in CRUISE, the light will illuminate at speeds exceeding approximately 360 KIAS or 0.95 Mach, whichever is less.

EMERGENCY FLAP SWITCH

A three-position emergency flap switch (3, figure 1-22) is provided on the left console, aft of the flap control switch. In the event of failure of the No. 2 hydraulic system, moving the flap control switch to 50° and the emergency flap switch to DOWN will extend the flaps to 50 degrees by emergency air pressure from the pneumatic system. Air-oil separation during use of the emergency pneumatic system is provided by a floating piston, which is inactive during normal operation. If the switch is returned to NORM after emergency extension, the flaps are locked down.

Loss of essential power does not affect flaps after emergency extension.

WARNING

An UP position is provided for use in the event air load retraction is required after emergency extension. Use of this position is NOT recommended because of the danger of asymmetrical air loads causing mechanism failure with subsequent split-flap conditions.

FLAP EMERGENCY EXTENSION

The flaps may be extended by the emergency pneumatic method for any failure. The lateral ratio changer (40- versus 70-degree spoilers) operates on emergency flap extension through a switch which is actuated as the flaps extend through 10 degrees. To extend the flaps by the emergency method, reduce speed to less than 190 KIAS, move the EMERG FLAP switch to DOWN, and place the flap control switch to 50°.

Note

Full (50°) flaps may not be obtained until airspeed is reduced to less than 170 KIAS.

LANDING GEAR

The retractable tricycle landing gear is electrically controlled and hydraulically operated. The landing gear swings forward on retraction, the main gear rotating 90 degrees and locking into the fuselage. Normal retraction requires 7 to 9 seconds. In the event of hydraulic failure, the forward retraction feature allows the gear to be extended by gravity and air load by pulling the emergency gear handle. The wheel well doors are electrically sequenced to open whenever the gear is in any unlocked position. The strut and trunnion fairing doors are mechanically linked to, and retracted by, the landing gear struts.

Note

The gear fairing and wheel well doors do not close after landing gear emergency extension.

LANDING GEAR HANDLE

The landing gear handle (3, figure 1-23) is located on the left forward console in the pilot's cockpit.

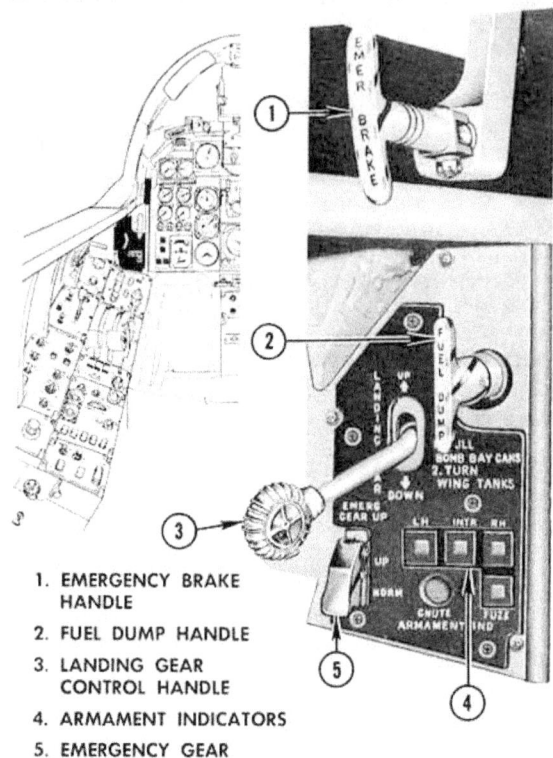

PILOT'S LEFT FORWARD CONSOLE

1. EMERGENCY BRAKE HANDLE
2. FUEL DUMP HANDLE
3. LANDING GEAR CONTROL HANDLE
4. ARMAMENT INDICATORS
5. EMERGENCY GEAR UP SWITCH

Figure 1-23

EMERGENCY GEAR UP SWITCH

A guarded emergency gear up switch (5, figure 1-23) is installed on the left forward console in the pilot's cockpit. This switch is provided for retracting the landing gear in the event of control switch or circuit breaker malfunction. Should emergency retraction in flight be necessary, the switch may be moved to the UP position to retract the gear.

WARNING

With electrical and hydraulic power available, moving the emergency gear up switch to UP bypasses the normal gear retraction circuit, unlocks the gear door uplocks and landing gear downlocks, and sequences the landing gear system to retract. Should a failure in the ground or air safety contacts of the landing gear control relay occur, the gear may retract with the weight of the aircraft on the gear.

LANDING GEAR WARNING LIGHT

The landing gear handle (3, figure 1-23) contains a red warning light. This light will illuminate during normal operation whenever the landing gear is not locked in the position called for by the landing gear handle. After gear retraction, the light remains on if any gear or door does not lock in the retracted position. After extending, the light stays on if the gear fails to lock down. The warning light will not be illuminated should the gear doors and fairing doors fail to close with the gear locked down. Turning the instrument lights knob out of OFF connects this light to a reduced power source for dim lighting.

LANDING GEAR POSITION INDICATOR

A landing gear position indicator (37, figure 1-4) is installed on the pilot's instrument panel. This indicator contains a window for each landing gear, indicating "UP," "DN," or a barber pole for an unsafe condition or the absence of electrical power.

WHEELS WARNING INDICATOR

The WHEELS warning indicator (2, figure 1-4) is installed on the pilot's instrument panel shroud. This indicator is illuminated and the master warning indicator will flash whenever either throttle is retarded to a position corresponding to approximately 85% to 90% engine rpm and the landing flaps are extended 35 degrees or more, if the landing gear handle is *not down*. There is no dimming feature for this indicator. The WHEELS warning indicator is powered by the essential d-c bus and can operate on emergency electrical power from the ram-air turbine-powered emergency power unit.

Note

Extinguishing of the WHEELS warning indicator is not an indication that the gear is locked down.

LANDING GEAR EMERGENCY EXTENSION HANDLE

A landing gear emergency extension handle (26, figure 1-4) is installed on the right side of the center pedestal. When the retaining safety clip is pushed down and the handle is pulled outward and held at full travel (approximately 15 inches), all gear and fairing door uplocks are released, allowing gravity and air loads to extend the gear to the down and locked position.

GEAR STIFF Caution Indicator

The GEAR STIFF caution indicator (figure 1-4) is provided to indicate the hydraulically extended and stiffened, catapulting position of the nose gear strut.

Note

The nose gear stiff system is deactivated.

LANDING GEAR OPERATION

Landing gear normal retraction occurs in three phases: (1) doors open, (2) gear retracts, and (3) doors close. Failure of either the gear to retract or the doors to close causes the landing gear warning light to remain illuminated and the position indicator to remain barber-poled. Landing gear normal extension occurs in reverse order to retraction.

Note

The landing gear doors are normally closed when the aircraft is on deck. They may be opened by moving the GEAR DOOR switch (electrical power access panel) to OPEN with hydraulic and electrical power available. During preflight inspection, ensure that the switch is positioned to NORMAL.

CAUTION

If the doors are open on engine start, they will close abruptly as No. 2 hydraulic system pressure builds. Ensure that all ground personnel are clear prior to starting engines.

ARRESTING GEAR

The arresting hook is located on the aft lower fuselage and is hinged adjacent to the root of the horizontal stabilizer leading edges. The V-shaped arresting gear is faired into the fuselage by mechanically operated trunnion, hook point doors, and beam fairing doors. The hook is retracted by No. 2 hydraulic pressure and extended by a piston-type air hydraulic accumulator.

Hook point doors are installed to cover the hook point when the arresting gear is retracted. These doors are opened and closed mechanically by the hook during the cycle. An air-oil hook bumper unit prevents the hook from bouncing into the access well during arrested landings and retracts before the hook is retracted.

ARRESTING HOOK HANDLE

An arresting hook handle (5, figure 1-24) is located on the pilot's right forward console. The hook is extended by pulling the handle aft approximately 5 inches. This unlocks the doors, releases the hook uplock, and allows the hook to drop by gravity, assisted by air pressure in a snubber actuator. The hook may not reach the fully extended position until airspeed is reduced to the point at which gravity and accumulator load can overcome the force of the air stream. The arresting gear may be retracted by turning the handle counter-clockwise and pushing it into the console. This allows No. 2 hydraulic system pressure to act upon the bottom of the actuator, retracting the hook. Hook extension is not dependent upon hydraulic system pressure or electrical power; therefore, no separate emergency system is provided. Should the control valve stick in the "hook up" position, a mechanical override linkage forces the valve to the "hook down" position.

HOOK WARNING LIGHT

The hook warning light is located on top of the arresting hook handle. This red light will come on any time the arresting hook is not in the position selected by the arresting hook handle. Should the control cable break between the handle and the control sector, the hook warning light will illuminate and the hook will extend, regardless of handle position. A control cable break between the sector and the emergency bungee causes the hook and doors to unlock, but the hook warning light will remain off and the hook will remain retracted until the handle is pulled.

CAUTION

- On some aircraft,* a hook malfunction can be caused by out-of-phase sequencing of the hook and hook bumper. Do not reselect extend (after positioning hook to retract) until hook has completely retracted. When hook has completely retracted, warning light will be off.

- Should the hook warning light flicker (on and off) in flight, check that the HYD SUBSYS ISOLATION switch is in FLIGHT, to prevent damage to the hook cylinder. (This will usually result in a steadily illuminated hook warning light.)

NOSE WHEEL STEERING

Nose wheel steering to 75 (±5) degrees either side of center is available through the directional control pedals when the STEER/TERRAIN button is depressed. When the button is not depressed, the nose wheel is in the damping, swiveling configuration which allows 360-degree swiveling of the nose wheel for ground handling purposes and unlimited steering deflection through differential braking. As a safety feature, the nose wheel steering system will operate only when the weight of the aircraft is on the main landing gear. On some aircraft,† nose wheel steering will engage with aircraft weight on either or both main landing gear.

Note
A yaw trim change during nose wheel steering operation repositions the control pedals, turning the nose wheel.

STEER/TERRAIN BUTTON

A momentary contact button, labeled STEER/TERRAIN, is located on the control stick grip (figure 1-20). Nose wheel steering is activated by holding the button depressed, and control is maintained through movement of the directional control pedals. The STEER/TERRAIN button is also used as a radar mode control when the aircraft is in flight. The button functions as a terrain avoidance clearance plane control or as a ranging radar initiating control, depending upon bomb directing set control settings. Refer to BOMB DIRECTING SET, AN/ASB-12, in Section I, Part 2, of the Supplemental NATOPS Flight Manual (NAVWEPS 01-60ABA-1A).

WHEEL BRAKES

The brake system consists of two independent hydraulic systems: the normal brake system and the emergency brake system. They are completely separate down to the shuttle valve at each main gear wheel. The normal system consists of a power brake valve with an integral manual master cylinder, and auxiliary accumulator, and necessary lines and hoses. The power brake valves, one for each wheel, provide differential pressure at the wheel in proportion to the degree the pedals are depressed. Hydraulic pressure from the No. 2 hydraulic system is metered from the system to each brake unit. When no system or accumulator pressure is available, the valve automatically transfers to its master cylinder portion and acts as a manual pressure generating unit. The hydraulic accumulator in the normal system is capable of a minimum of three maximum brake applications and up to as many as 12 lesser applications of a magnitude necessary to stop a fully loaded aircraft during ground handling operations. An externally

---

*Aircraft not having AFC 103 complied with
†Aircraft having AFC 129 complied with

mounted brake accumulator pressure indicator is located on the left side of the forward fuselage, just ahead of the intake duct. This repeater gage should show a precharge of 800 psi (or 3000 psi if the hydraulic system has been operating and pressure is not bled), and is used to check that adequate accumulator pressure is available for power-off braking.

EMERGENCY BRAKES

The emergency brake system receives pressure from the No. 2 hydraulic system and consists of a power metering valve, an accumulator, and necessary lines and hoses. The system is operated by an emergency brake handle located in the pilot's left forward console (1, figure 1-23), and provides pressure to both main gear wheels simultaneously in proportion to the extent the handle is pulled. Optimum emergency braking is obtained by slowly pulling outward on the handle, increasing braking force as speed decreases. The accumulator provides a minimum of three maximum brake applications and up to as many as 12 lesser applications. This is similar to the normal braking system.

Note

For field landings utilizing emergency brakes, it is recommended that the emergency brakes be used first to conserve auxiliary brake accumulator action for directional control in the last stages of landing rollout.

WHEEL BRAKE SYSTEMS OPERATION

The wheel brake systems are capable of stopping the aircraft under nearly all mission conditions. In addition to normal full power braking, limited duration braking is supplied by the auxiliary brake accumulator. An emergency brake system is provided, and marginally effective power-off manual braking can be obtained.

NORMAL BRAKE SYSTEM

Normal braking requires relatively light pedal forces and pedal deflection. Up to 85 pounds force is normally sufficient for rollout braking at typical gross weights. Directional control is easily maintained in the event of nose wheel steering failure, and differential braking can be used to execute turns exceeding the 75-degree swivel of the nose wheel steering system.

Note

- A pedal force of about 100 pounds is required to hold the aircraft with both engines at Military Thrust.
- Provided gross weight is sufficient to prevent tire skidding, properly operating brakes will hold the aircraft at MIN AFTERBURNER.

For a discussion of optimum braking technique, refer to STOPPING THE AIRCRAFT, in Section III, Part 3.

WHEEL BRAKE EMERGENCY OPERATION

Note

Upon first indication of any brake malfunction, the aircraft should be maneuvered off the duty runway and towed in. Should brake failure occur on the catapult, pull the emergency brake handle, signal the catapult office, and down the aircraft.

BRAKING WITH HYDRAULIC FAILURE

In the event of failure of the No. 2 hydraulic system or during towing operations, the charge in the auxiliary brake accumulator may be used to obtain braking. If a single increasing pressure application is used, sufficient power is available to stop. Approximately three "on and off" type applications are available with a fully charged auxiliary accumulator, and up to 12 lesser applications of the "towing and spotting" type. Auxiliary brake accumulator charge for ground operation is indicated by a repeater gage on the left fuselage below the aft cockpit.

CAUTION

On depletion of the auxiliary accumulator, brake pedal forces increase rapidly and emergency or manual braking is required.

EMERGENCY BRAKES

The fully charged emergency brake accumulator provides a maximum of four full "on and off" applications of pressure at equal force to both brakes. Operation with the emergency brake handle is similar to that obtained through the pedals with the auxiliary accumulator, except that both brakes are operated simultaneously. A single application of emergency braking is normally sufficient to stop the aircraft if the handle is pulled gently until deceleration is felt, then pulled slowly outward, increasing force as speed decreases.

Note

For emergency landings with failure of the No. 2 hydraulic system, it is recommended that emergency braking be used to decelerate after using aerodynamic braking, controlling direction with rudder, and conserving auxiliary brake accumulator (pedal braking) for directional control just before stopping.

WARNING

A sudden pull on the emergency brake handle may lock the main wheels, causing tire failure and possible loss of directional control. Optimum technique is to slowly pull the emergency handle until deceleration is detected. Handle displacement can be increased as speed decreases.

MANUAL BRAKES

If both the normal and emergency brake accumulators are exhausted, marginally effective manual braking may be obtained through the master cylinder action of the brake valves. The pedals must be pumped to build up pressure, then a HARD braking force applied (up to 300 pounds).

Note

When new brake assemblies are installed, it is recommended that the pilot be notified and that several applications of moderate braking be applied while taxiing out for flight. This procedure will wear off the metal protective primer, reducing smoking on landing rollout.

FOLD SYSTEMS
WING AND TAIL FOLD

Power folding of the wings and vertical stabilizer is accomplished by No. 2 hydraulic system pressure. A hydraulic lock valve is provided in the wing fold line to prevent inadvertent wing spreading in the event of hydraulic pressure loss during wing folding, and to maintain the folded position when hydraulic pressure is removed. A manual override lever is installed on the wing fold lock valve to permit manual spreading of the wings. A similar lever on the tail fold control valve (located on the bottom of the aft fuselage) also allows manual folding and unfolding of the vertical stabilizer. Positive hydraulic sequencing actuates the lockpins upon completion of the wing spread cycle. Manually operated locks, actuated from the cockpit, secure the lockpins in position. Folding and unfolding of the wings and vertical stabilizer can be accomplished simultaneously by using the fold control handle. The wings can be cycled independently, if desired, by selecting the OFF position of the tail control switch.

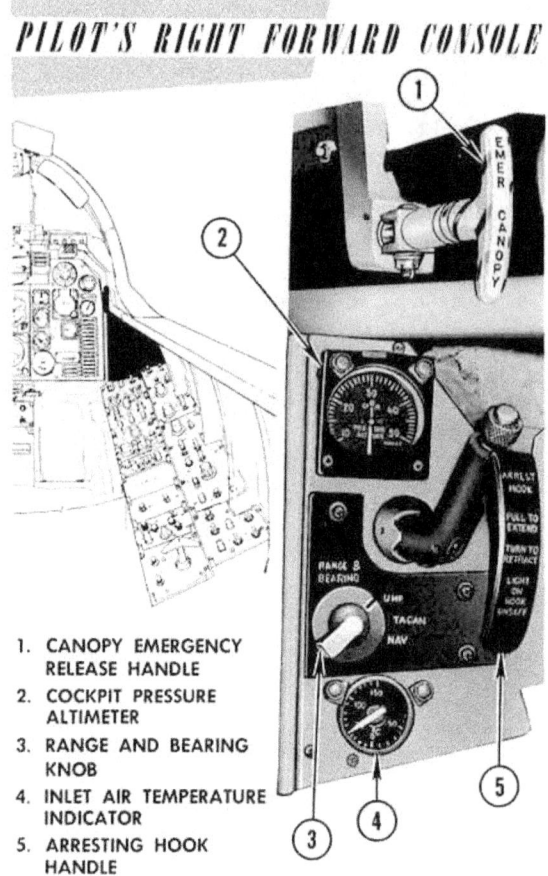

PILOT'S RIGHT FORWARD CONSOLE

1. CANOPY EMERGENCY RELEASE HANDLE
2. COCKPIT PRESSURE ALTIMETER
3. RANGE AND BEARING KNOB
4. INLET AIR TEMPERATURE INDICATOR
5. ARRESTING HOOK HANDLE

A3J-1-1-00-21B

Figure 1-24

FOLD CONTROL HANDLE

Operation of the wing and tail fold system is controlled by the use of the fold control handle (figure 1-24A), installed at the rear of the pilot's right-hand console. With the wings folded, clockwise rotation of the handle to the UNLOCK position spreads the wings and extends the vertical stabilizer. The pilot should then pause for 10 seconds to ensure that the wing and tail lockpins have been sequenced into position. The handle should then be pushed down and twisted counterclockwise to the LOCK position. This action provides mechanical security for the wing and tail hydraulic lockpins.

Note

The handle must be lifted slightly before it can be moved to either the locked or unlocked position.

For wing and tail folding, this procedure is reversed.

CAUTION

If the wings are folded, check that the control handle is in the LOCK position prior to engine start.

Tail Control Switch

A tail control switch (figure 1-24A) is used to select simultaneous folding of the outboard wing panels and the vertical stabilizer (NORM position), or folding of the outboard wing panels only (OFF position).

Wing and Tail Fold Warning Flags

Red warning flags are installed at the fold lines of the wings and vertical stabilizer. These flags extend when the fold control handle is pulled (unlocked) and retract when the handle is pushed in (locked).

RADOME FOLD

To permit access to the radar compartment and to facilitate handling, the radome can be opened and rotated upward and aft through operation of an electrical actuator. A warning flag protrudes on each side of the radome as an indication that the latches are not locked. An interlock relay prevents operation of the fold circuit from the pilot's cockpit, unless the aircraft is on the ground and the radar antenna is in its stowed position.

RADOME FOLD SWITCH

Moving the two-position radome fold switch (figure 1-24A) to OPEN supplies monitored bus a-c electrical power to a latch drive motor. When the latches are fully unlocked, the fold actuator extends, opening the radome. Moving the switch to CLOSE causes the actuator to retract the radome toward the closed position until a limit switch energizes the locking latches. This mechanically positions the warning flags flush with the radome exterior.

External Control Switch

An external radome fold control switch (interlock bypass) is installed inside the right jowl door aft of the radome. This switch is used to open or close the radome with the aircraft electrical system energized and the cockpit radome fold switch at OPEN.

Note

Should radome fold fail to operate when selected, check that the external control switch is positioned to CLOSE.

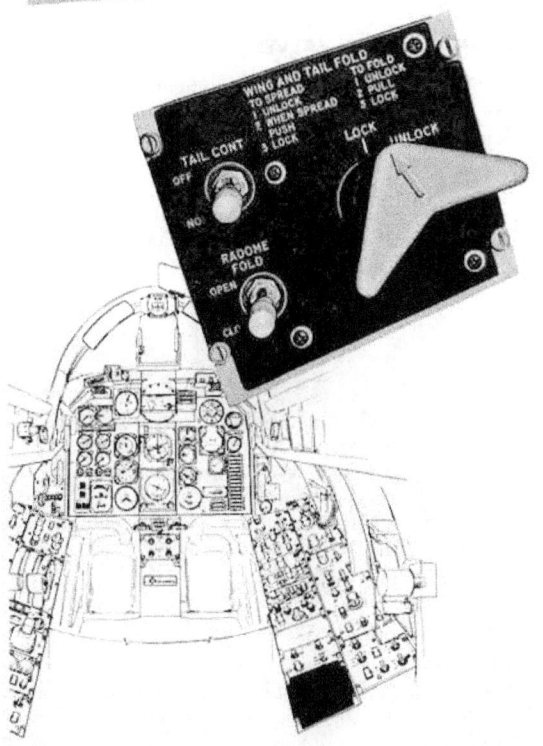

Figure 1-24A

CANOPIES

The pilot's and systems operator's cockpits are provided with separate jettisonable, clamshell canopies. The pilot's canopy is of conventional design. The systems operator's canopy is primarily of metal construction with a small window on each side, restricting the amount of light in the cockpit for monitoring radar and television equipment. A sliding shade arrangement is installed for both windows in the systems operator's canopy for darkening the cockpit. Both canopies are opened and closed by pneumatic cylinders, which are controlled by pneumatic toggle valves installed in each cockpit. Power for canopy operation is supplied by the aircraft pneumatic compressor system and an air storage bottle with 3000 psi pressure reduced to 450 psi. The emergency flap system air pressure supply is utilized, providing approximately 25 canopy cycles. An emergency air bottle is also provided for each canopy, supplying 3000 psi air for emergency jettison. When normal opening is initiated, the canopies move rearward approximately 1 inch to unlock, then swing upward 33 degrees to the fully open position. Normal opening or closing time is approximately 5 seconds.

Note

During the closing or opening cycle, the canopy may "bounce" slightly. This is not an abnormal condition.

CANOPY TOGGLE VALVES

The pilot's canopy toggle valve (6, figure 1-3) is located above the left console. The systems operator's canopy toggle valve is located on the left forward console. These three-position pneumatic toggle valves are marked CLOSE, NORMAL, and OPEN and are spring-loaded to the NORMAL position. Prior to actuating the canopy, hold the toggle valve momentarily in the same position as the canopy to prevent possible rough operation.

CAUTION

Should the canopy toggle valve be held momentarily to OPEN at any time after the canopy is closed (before take-off), ensure that the canopy is locked by holding the toggle valve in CLOSED. This will prevent possible in-flight loss of the canopy due to movement of the locking overcenter linkage.

EXTERNAL TOGGLE VALVES

A toggle valve for each canopy is installed in a canopy control access below the pilot's left-hand canopy skirt. These toggles are used for normal external opening or closing of either canopy and utilize the canopy pneumatic system.

CANOPY JETTISON HANDLES

A canopy jettison handle (1, figure 1-24, and 8, figure 1-4B) is installed in each cockpit. By pulling these handles aft approximately 1 inch, independent emergency release of the canopies is achieved.

CAUTION

Canopies should not be jettisoned when the aircraft is stationary, since canopy trajectory is greatly affected by wind. Under no-wind conditions, the forward canopy will fall directly on the aft cockpit. Manual canopy release should be used when aircraft is stationary, except in extreme emergencies.

CANOPY MANUAL RELEASE HANDLES

EXTERNAL RELEASE HANDLES

Two external manual release handles are installed on each canopy, one on each side. A square push button, located just aft of each handle, must be depressed to release the handle. Once the handle springs out, it should be pulled full forward to a latched position. By using both external handles, two men can remove either canopy. This is accomplished by pushing the latched handles aft with moderate force until the canopy moves upward slightly and aft about 1 inch. The canopy may then be lifted about its pivot point. If the canopy is opened manually, the mechanical uplock must be set to allow the canopy to remain in position. On modified aircraft,* manual opening of the canopy allows an automatic, ratchet-type uplock to hold the canopy in one of three positions (10 degrees, 20 degrees, or full open), as desired.

Note

- The canopy is physically disconnected from the actuator when the manual release handles are used. Raise the canopy just enough to allow rotation of the uplock handle. Should the canopy rollers come out of the tracks, the canopy may jam.
- No canopy external jettison provisions are installed.

INTERNAL RELEASE HANDLES

Both canopies are equipped with an internal release handle on the left side of the skirt. These handles operate the same linkage as the external release handles.

*Aircraft having AFC 101 complied with

To operate, the handle lock is pushed forward, allowing the handle to spring out and downward. On some aircraft,* an aft force of up to 250 pounds may be required to unlock the overcenter linkage and move the canopy aft 1 inch to free the hooks. On modified aircraft,† approximately 50 pounds force is required to unlock the linkage, and only a small force is then required to move the canopy aft. After manually opening the canopy on the ground, the actuator must be reconnected and pressurized to the up position for normal operation. On modified aircraft,† the automatic uplock pawl must be stowed for normal operation.

Note

During in-flight manual release, the canopy should depart after moving about 1 inch.

WARNING

When attempting in-flight manual release, grasp the handle PALM UP, with the thumb TUCKED IN, as serious injury can occur as the canopy departs. The handle should be operated in as close to the vertical position as possible.

Disconnect Override Handles

Both canopies are equipped with an actuator disconnect override handle under an access door on the left rear portion of the frame. When rotated counterclockwise, these handles prevent disconnection of the canopy manual release mechanism from the canopy actuators. If manual access to the cockpits is required under high wind conditions, using these override handles will prevent inadvertent canopy loss. To assure disconnection of the canopy actuator rod end, the handle must be in the down position immediately prior to raising the canopy after the canopy has moved aft. The canopy should then be raised to a minimum height sufficient to allow engaging the canopy uplocks. If the canopy is raised too high, the canopy guide rollers will separate from the guide rails.

MANUAL UPLOCK HANDLES

Each canopy is provided with a manual uplock and handle. These handles are located directly aft of the ejection seat headrests and are a part of the canopy operating mechanism. If the canopies are opened and it is desired that they remain open for a prolonged period, the manual uplocks should be engaged by rotating the manual uplock handles aft until the indicator flag reads "UPLOCK ENGAGED." To unlock the canopies, rotate the handles forward until the forward lock indicator reads "UPLOCK DISENGAGED," and the aft indicator retracts from sight.

Note

To relieve binding of the canopy manual uplocks, pressurize the up side of the canopy actuators by holding the canopy toggle valves to OPEN for at least 5 seconds before disengaging.

CANOPY CAUTION LIGHTS

Each cockpit is provided with a canopy caution light. These lights are located in the caution light bank on the main instrument panel in the front cockpit and on the top center portion of the main instrument panel in the rear cockpit. The pilot's caution light is a flip-flop type which is energized when one or both canopies are unlocked and electrical power is applied to the circuit from the generators or external power units. The systems operator's caution light will come on only when his canopy is unlocked. An electrical interconnect between the two canopies requires that both canopies be closed and locked before the pilot's light will go out.

ESCAPE SYSTEM

The escape system provides safe emergency egress from the aircraft under nearly all flight conditions. If aircraft attitude and rate of sink are within seat recovery capability, escape is possible at ground level at speeds as low as approximately 100 knots. For minimum safe ejection altitudes, see figure 1-26.

Note

Ejection of the aft seat can be initiated by the pilot or the systems operator. Refer to EJECTION INTERCONNECT, in this section.

EJECTION SEATS

The ejection seats (figure 1-25) are designed to provide integrated crew environmental services (personal disconnect), as well as safe escape under nearly all flight conditions. The seat bucket is electrically adjustable through a vertical range of 5 inches, while the headrest remains stationary. The seat is equipped with an NB-7E personnel parachute, requiring use of the standard integrated harness garment.

Note

Crew members will personally connect parachute riser and lap strap "Rocket-Jet" fittings when entering, and disconnect when leaving, the aircraft to maintain skill and check for proper operation.

Seat ejection is initiated by pulling the face curtain handle forward and down sharply to full travel, or by turning (unlocking) and pulling either alternate ejection knob. After ejection is initiated, the crewman is automatically positioned in the proper ejection posture by ballistic prepositioning devices. Postejection sequencing provides automatic seat trajectory stabilization and descent to below 13,000 feet, crew member/seat separation, and automatic parachute deployment. Escape from the seat in the event of ditching or crash landing is provided by a single handle, which severs or releases all

*Aircraft not having AFC 101 complied with
†Aircraft having AFC 101 complied with

connections to the seat. A hinged lift plate, attached to the bottom of the seat, is opened as the seat rises on ejection. This plate provides additional aerodynamic lift and stability as the seat enters the air stream.

CATAPULT ROCKETS

Seat ejection thrust is provided by a single unit catapult rocket. When actuated, the catapult portion fires, thrusting the seat up the rails and clear of the cockpit. As the seat leaves the rails, the rocket portion ignites, providing a directionally and longitudinally stable thrust. This force is sufficient to propel the seat to a height of approximately 125 feet above the aircraft flight path at average cruise speeds, providing ample height for separation and deployment.

DROGUE PARACHUTES

A 52-inch diameter, stabilizing drogue parachute is installed in each headrest. On ejection, the drogue chute is deployed by a thruster actuated by a lanyard which is pulled as the seat ascends the rails. For ejections at high altitudes (above 13,000 feet), the drogue chute remains attached to the seat, providing stabilized crewman/seat free-fall to 13,000 feet, where automatic crewman separation and personnel parachute deployment sequencing takes place. On crewman/seat separation, the drogue lower riser attachments are released, allowing the seat to rotate forward about the upper riser attach points simultaneously with separation bladder inflation. As the crewman leaves the seat, the parachute "pulloff" lanyard extends to its full 14-foot length. The drogue upper attachments are then released from the seat, allowing the drogue to deploy the main chute canopy. After 0.5 second of "pulloff" lanyard tension, a small ballistic cutter separates the drogue from the main parachute.

INERTIA REEL

A ballistically operated inertia reel provides crew member retention in an upright position during maneuvering, deceleration, and ejection. The reel may be manually locked and unlocked during normal use by the shoulder harness lock handle. The reel mechanism is attached to the upper portion of the personnel parachute by a strap which, when in the unlocked condition of the reel, allows the crew member to lean forward as desired. When locked by the handle or a 2- to 3-g deceleration, the reel prevents any further play-out. On ejection, the inertia reel ballistic device is actuated, winding in the strap and restraining the crew member in the retracted position in the seat.

KNEE BAR AND FOOT RETRACTORS

During the initial phase of seat ejection, leg positioning and restraint and positioning of the lower torso are accomplished by lowering the seat bucket to bottom, lifting the knees, and locking the feet in foot wells. The knee-raising bar contacts the legs behind the knees. As the knees are lifted, the feet fall into foot wells, and the wells are closed by hooks. If acceleration is being experienced, such that the feet will not fall into the wells, the hooks contact the lower legs and push the feet into the wells. On automatic crewman/seat separation, the foot retractors are ballistically ejected from their housing rods, and the knee bar is mechanically freed. The foot retractors can be manually spring-ejected by placing the thumb and forefinger behind a release on each retractor rod and pushing down and forward, parallel to the rod.

SEPARATION SYSTEM

The automatic seat/man separation system consists of a preset aneroid, a ballistic thruster, and ballistically operated mechanical release devices or cutters. The seat remains in the stabilized attitude until it has decelerated to separation velocity and descended below 13,000 feet. Then, simultaneously, the lower drogue chute risers, leg hooks, and harness release attachments are released, and separation bladders, located under the survival kit and behind the personnel parachute, are inflated. Refer to ESCAPE SYSTEM OPERATION, in this section.

Separation Aneroid Indicator

A separation aneroid indicator is installed behind an inspection hole in the back of the seat. The indicator is viewed by unlocking the shoulder harness, leaning the parachute forward, and moving the seat back separation bladder to one side. A satisfactory aneroid is indicated if only white can be seen in the inspection window.

Note

At field elevations of 5000 feet and higher, it is acceptable for a small portion of red to be visible in the inspection window.

SURVIVAL KIT

A land and water survival kit is installed in the seat bucket. This kit contains the emergency high-pressure oxygen supply and a standard PK-2 life raft and survival package. The pressure gage for the emergency oxygen system, along with its emergency pull-ring, is located on the left forward portion of the kit as viewed by the seated crew member.

WARNING

Do not use supplemental seat cushions on top of the survival kit. Serious injury can result on ejection due to cushion compression and seat center-of-gravity movement.

Note

During the ejection sequence, the emergency oxygen system is automatically operated. If the crew member is wearing a full pressure suit, emergency pressurization of the suit is provided above 35,000 feet during seat/man free-fall.

EJECTION SEAT

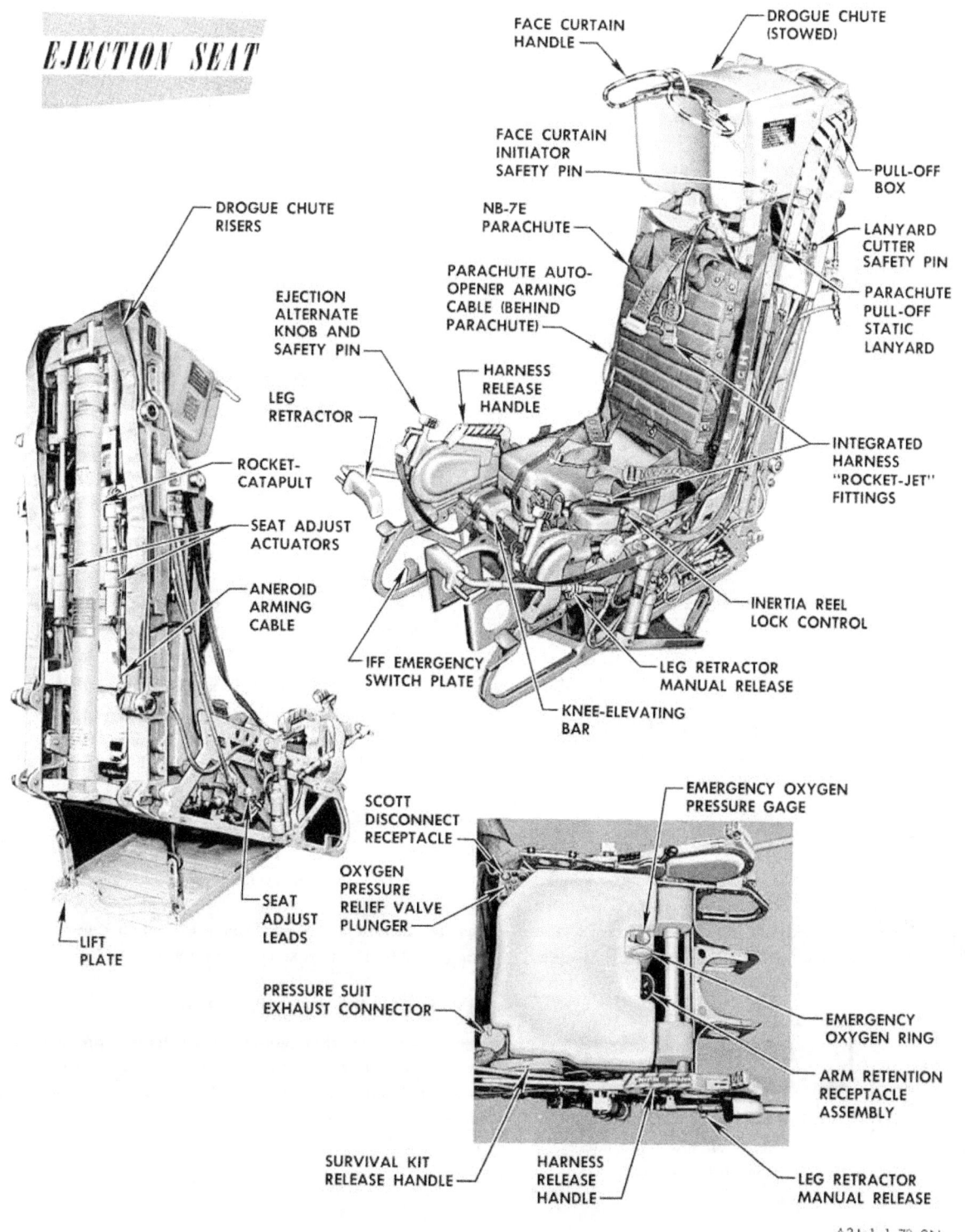

Figure 1-25

After crewman/seat separation and parachute deployment, the survival kit and raft are manually deployed for water landing by pulling a yellow handle on the right side of the kit. As the raft and equipment package falls to the full length of its retaining lanyard (about 15 feet), the life raft is automatically inflated by its integral CO_2 bottle. A retractable knife for emergency cutting of parachute shroud lines is located in the kit release handle.

SEAT ADJUST SWITCH

The seat adjust switch (10, figure 1-4A, and 3, figure 1-4D) is located on the right console. This switch provides electrically operated seat height adjustment. The seat adjust circuit is inoperative with one generator inoperative.

HARNESS LOCK HANDLE

The harness lock handle (figure 1-25) is located on the left side of the seat. Moving the handle to the LOCK (forward) position prevents the crew member from leaning forward by locking the inertia reel. The reel may be unlocked by leaning back to remove tension from the reel and moving the handle back to UNLOCK. If the reel is locked automatically, the reel may be unlocked by cycling the handle.

EJECTION INTERCONNECT

The ejection seats are connected by a system of ballistic lines and a delay device to allow the pilot to operate the escape sequence in both cockpits. This interconnect does not allow the systems operator to eject the pilot, nor does it in any way affect the systems operator's ability to initiate his own ejection. In the event of an emergency, initiation of ejection by the pilot jettisons both canopies. The aft seat is then automatically ejected, followed approximately 0.75 second later by the forward seat. This sequence provides safe separation from the canopies and ensures crew member separation.

WARNING

On being warned of emergency ejection by the pilot, the systems operator should immediately assume the erect position for ejection.

HARNESS RELEASE HANDLE

The harness release (ditching) handle (figure 1-25) allows complete crew member separation from the seat through the action of this single handle. When pulled up through full travel, this handle releases the following:

1. Survival kit hold-down attachments.
2. Parachute static "pulloff" lanyard.
3. Shoulder harness and lap belt attach points.
4. Parachute automatic opener (if seat is NOT ejected).

WARNING

- After ejection, the harness release handle may be used, if desired, to override the automatic separation and chute deployment sequence. The parachute automatic opener is armed on separation from the seat. If, however, the harness release handle is used to obtain freedom from the seat for *unejected bail-out*, the automatic opener cable is *released* and the *manual "D" ring* must be pulled to obtain parachute deployment.

- Manual separation at high altitudes can result in severe tumbling or spinning, causing possible injury or death.

FACE CURTAIN

The face curtain is stowed in the seat headrest. The curtain "B" handle, in the event ejection is to be initiated, should be gripped firmly with both hands and pulled sharply outward and down over the head in one continuous motion (approximately 18 inches).

ALTERNATE EJECTION PULL-KNOBS

The alternate ejection pull-knobs are located on each side of the seat frame at the knee position. To operate, either knob must be turned inward 90 degrees to unlock (about 40 inch-pounds torque force), then pulled upward 3/4 inch with a force of about 30 pounds to initiate ejection.

MINIMUM SAFE EJECTION ALTITUDES

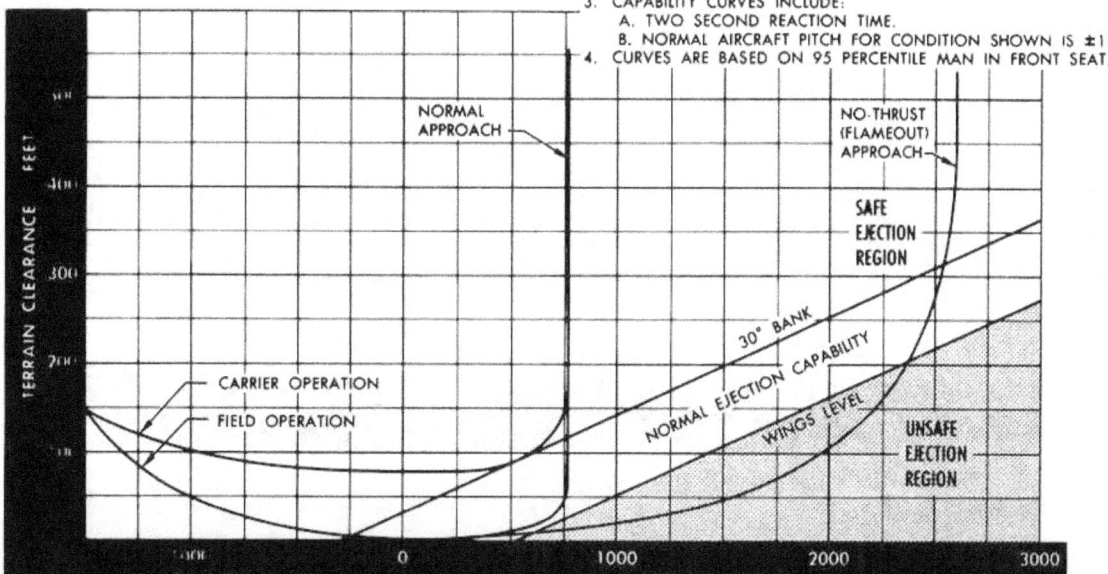

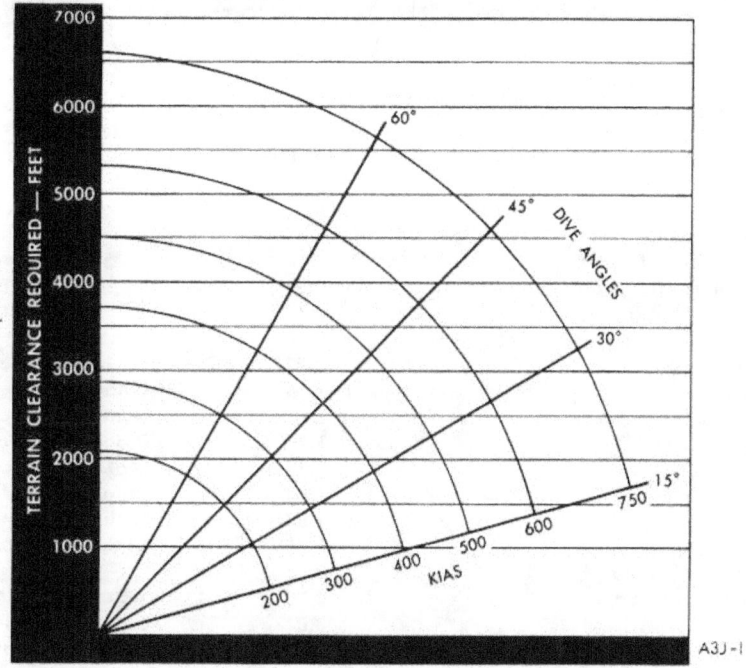

Figure 1-26

Section I
Part 2

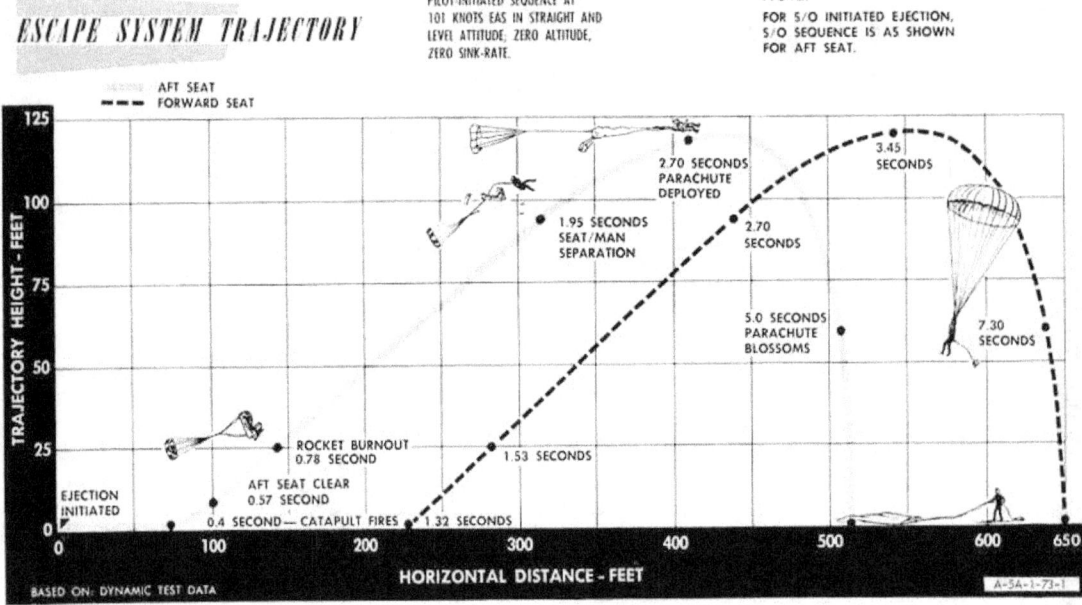

Figure 1-27

ESCAPE SYSTEM OPERATION

Once initiated, operation of the ejection and escape sequence is entirely automatic. For minimum safe ejection altitudes, see figure 1-26. Figure 1-27 illustrates the escape system trajectory. The following table is a chronology of a pilot-initiated, ground-level ejection (100 KEAS), with escape and recovery of both crew members.

AFT SEAT	TIME IN SECONDS (CUMULATIVE)	FRONT SEAT
—	Zero	Initiation
Canopy jettisoned	0.10	Canopy jettisoned
Seat bottomed, S/O restrained	0.20	Seat bottomed, pilot restrained
Front canopy clear	0.30	↑
Catapult fired	0.40	
Separation aneroid armed	0.50	(0.75-second delay)
Drogue chute deployed	0.52	
Seat clear of cockpit	0.57	
Drogue chute inflated	0.58	
Rocket burnout	0.78	↓
	1.15	Catapult fired
	1.25	Separation aneroid armed
↑	1.27	Drogue chute deployed
(Stabilized ascent)	1.32	Seat clear of cockpit
	1.33	Drogue chute inflated
↓	1.53	Rocket burnout
Seat/man separation	1.95	(Stabilized ascent)
Separation complete	2.26	—
Parachute deployed	2.70	Seat/man separation
—	3.01	Separation complete
—	3.45	Parachute deployed
Parachute inflated	5.00	
—	7.30	Parachute inflated

AIR CONDITIONING SYSTEM

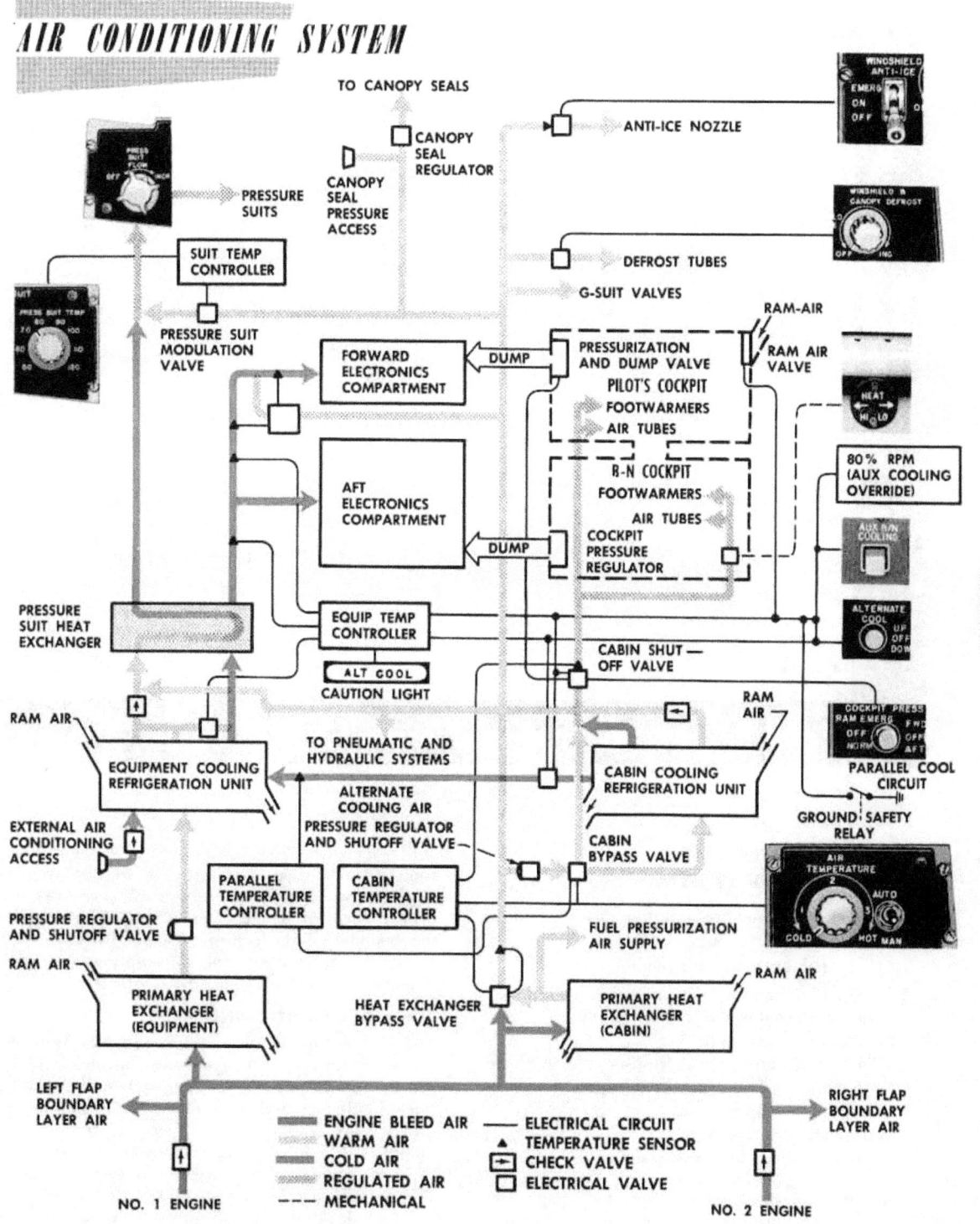

Figure 1-28

COCKPIT PRESSURIZATION SCHEDULE

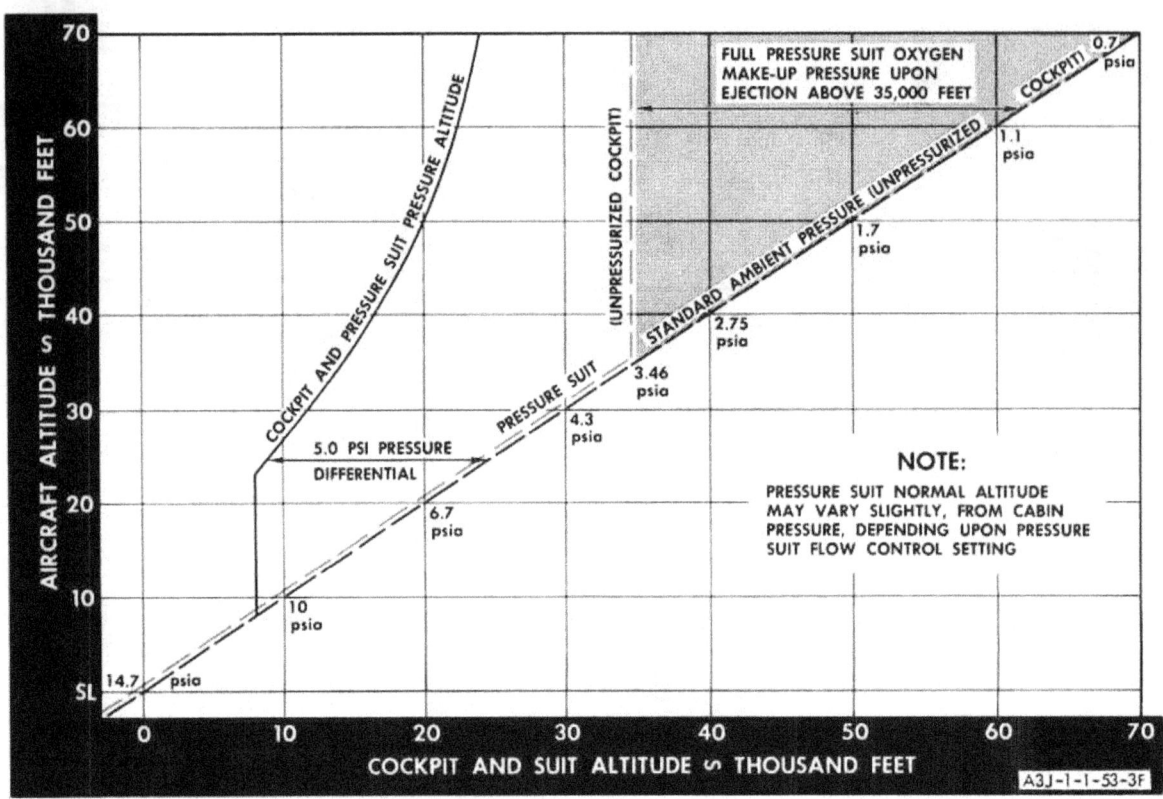

Figure 1-29

AIR CONDITIONING AND PRESSURIZATION SYSTEM

The air conditioning and pressurization system performs the following functions:

1. Cockpit and pressure suit conditioning.
2. Cockpit and pressure suit pressurization.
3. Equipment cooling and pressurization.
4. Anti-G suit operation.
5. Windshield and canopy defrosting and windshield anti-icing.
6. Engine anti-icing.
7. Pneumatic system supply.
8. Hydraulic reservoir pressurization.

The final stage of each engine compressor is tapped at three points to supply hot, high-pressure air. The compressor air is routed to primary heat exchangers on each side of the aircraft, where it is cooled to approximately 300°F by ram air from the engine intake ducts. The compressor bleed air lines to the heat exchangers are cross-connected for single-engine operation and are equipped with check valves to prevent backflow in the event of engine failure. Between the check valves and primary heat exchangers, air is tapped off to supply the boundary layer control system. Turbine refrigeration units further cool the air supply as required for system operation. See figure 1-28.

COCKPIT CONDITIONING

The cockpit conditioning system provides a regulated air supply for cockpit temperature control, cockpit pressurization, windshield and canopy defrosting, and windshield anti-icing and rain removal. In addition, this system provides a source of pressurized air for the canopy seals, air data computer, liquid oxygen bay, ECM waveguide, radar, inertial autonavigator platform, aircraft fuel supply system, and hydraulic reservoirs, and provides supercharging air to the pneumatic system air compressor. Cockpit air conditioning is accomplished by manual or automatic mixing of warm air from the primary heat exchanger with cold air from the cockpit refrigeration unit.

COCKPIT TEMPERATURE KNOB

The cockpit temperature knob (COCKPIT TEMP, 3, figure 1-30) is operated in conjunction with the AUTO/MAN switch in controlling cockpit conditioning supply air temperature. With the AUTO/MAN switch in MAN, the knob directly controls cockpit supply line air temperature through mixing of engine compressor and refrigerated air in the supply line. With the switch in AUTO, cockpit conditioning supply air temperature is maintained constant at the knob setting by an automatic temperature sensor and the primary cabin heat exchanger bypass valve.

CAUTION

Before taking off in humid weather, place the cockpit pressure switch to RAM EMERG.

When operating in AUTO, a change in flight conditions (altitude or Mach number) may require a change in knob setting to maintain the desired temperature. When operating in MAN, changes in power setting or flight conditions will require more frequent changes in selected setting to maintain cockpit temperature as desired. The cockpit temperature knob can be used to modify uncomfortable cockpit temperatures caused by defrost system operation.

AUTO/MAN SWITCH

The AUTO/MAN switch (4, figure 1-30) provides automatic or manual control of cockpit supply air temperature. The AUTO position allows the temperature control system to maintain cockpit supply air temperature automatically at the preset position of the cockpit temperature knob. Should the cockpit supply air temperature become uncontrollable because of system malfunction, the switch should be placed in the MAN position and the cockpit supply air temperature should be controlled manually with the cockpit temperature knob. Should an extreme temperature malfunction occur when the pressure suit is being worn, the extreme temperature may be offset by manually changing suit temperature. It may be desirable to move the cockpit pressure switch to RAM EMERG or to turn the defrosters on for additional heat as applicable.

Ventilation Outlets

Cockpit ventilation is provided by footwarmers and air distribution tubes, located below the canopy rails on both sides of each cockpit. Airflow direction is controlled through manual rotation of the ventilation tubes.

Navigator's Heat Lever

The navigator's heat lever (12, figure 1-30) controls the flow of additional hot air to the rear cockpit. This air is ducted through a variable control valve from the defrosting system to supplement normal cockpit air conditioning and compensate for the temperature difference between cockpits.

COCKPIT CONDITIONING OPERATION

To operate the cockpit conditioning system, proceed as follows:

1. AUTO/MAN switch—AUTO.
2. Cockpit temperature knob—mid-position (2).
3. Cockpit pressure switch—NORM.

WARNING

If fuel fumes are noted in the cockpit after starting the right-hand engine, shut down immediately and "down" the aircraft, as a definite fire hazard may exist.

4. Navigator's heat lever—mid-position.
5. Windshield and canopy defrost knob—on as desired. Some defrost flow should be maintained during all pressure suit operations to ensure adequate warmth for the pressure suit conditioning lines.
6. The pilot controls cockpit temperature by rotating the cockpit temperature knob toward HOT or COLD as desired. If additional heat is required, move the windshield and canopy defrost knob toward INC as necessary.
7. If formation of cockpit fog is anticipated during take-off or approach, it is recommended that the cockpit pressure switch be positioned to OFF and that canopy defrost be operated at maximum.

Note

Excessive cockpit heat resulting from defrost airflow can be modified by use of the cockpit temperature knob.

8. Aft cockpit temperature is controlled by moving the heat control lever toward LO (aft) or HI (forward).
9. If automatic temperature control fails, move the AUTO/MAN switch to MAN and control temperature directly with the cockpit temperature knob.

Note

Should temperature controller failure during flight cause fog formation in the cockpit, the best corrective action is to utilize windshield and canopy defrost airflow as required. Turning the cockpit pressure switch OFF also aids fog dissipation, if pressurization is not required.

CONDITIONING AND PRESSURIZATION CONTROLS

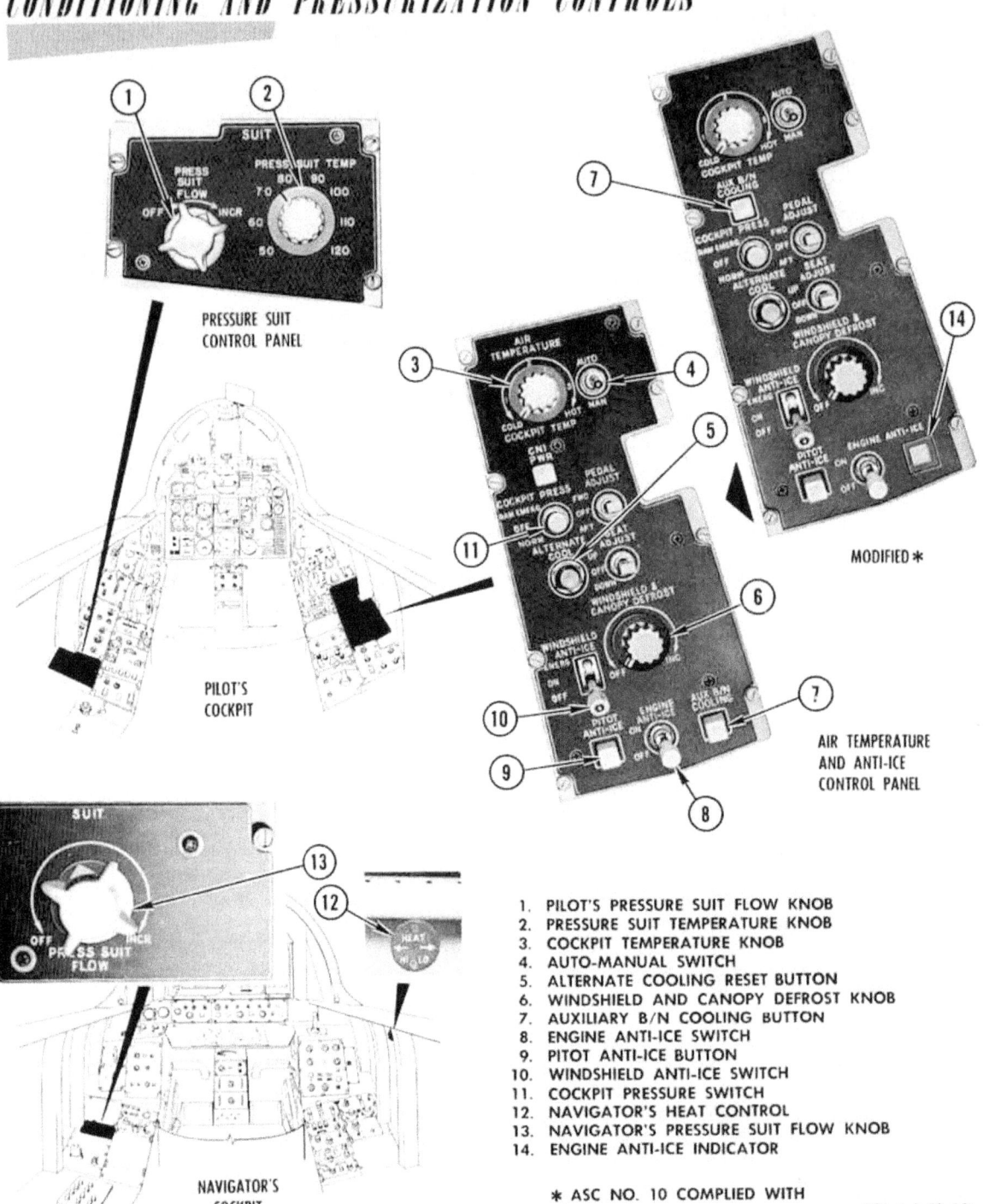

1. PILOT'S PRESSURE SUIT FLOW KNOB
2. PRESSURE SUIT TEMPERATURE KNOB
3. COCKPIT TEMPERATURE KNOB
4. AUTO-MANUAL SWITCH
5. ALTERNATE COOLING RESET BUTTON
6. WINDSHIELD AND CANOPY DEFROST KNOB
7. AUXILIARY B/N COOLING BUTTON
8. ENGINE ANTI-ICE SWITCH
9. PITOT ANTI-ICE BUTTON
10. WINDSHIELD ANTI-ICE SWITCH
11. COCKPIT PRESSURE SWITCH
12. NAVIGATOR'S HEAT CONTROL
13. NAVIGATOR'S PRESSURE SUIT FLOW KNOB
14. ENGINE ANTI-ICE INDICATOR

* ASC NO. 10 COMPLIED WITH

Figure 1-30

10. If emergency cockpit cooling is mandatory, check the windshield and canopy defrost knob OFF and move the cockpit pressure switch to RAM EMERG. A reduction in airspeed may also be required.

COCKPIT PRESSURIZATION

The cockpit pressurization system pressurizes and ventilates the cockpits. A cockpit pressure regulator, mounted aft of the navigator's left console, maintains the following pressure schedule. See figure 1-29.

1. An unpressurized cockpit to 8000 feet MSL.
2. A constant 8000-foot level pressure from 8000 to approximately 23,400 feet MSL.
3. A constant 5.0-psi differential pressure at all altitudes above approximately 23,400 feet MSL.

In the event of pressure regulator failure, a combination dump, vacuum pressure relief valve prevents cockpit pressure differential from exceeding approximately 5.5 psi. The vacuum relief function of this valve prevents cockpit pressure from falling below a pressure level 0.25 psi less than atmospheric pressure, thus avoiding possible canopy or cockpit structural collapse. Cockpit ventilation is achieved by exhausting cockpit air through the cockpit pressure regulator into the main electronics bay and through the combination dump, vacuum pressure relief valve into the forward electronics bay.

COCKPIT PRESSURE SWITCH

The cockpit pressure switch (11, figure 1-30), located on the pilot's air temperature control panel, has three positions: NORM, OFF, and RAM EMERG. In the OFF position, there is no cockpit pressurization or ventilation. In the NORM position, automatic cockpit pressurization and ventilation are provided according to the schedule shown in figure 1-29. If cockpit air is contaminated by smoke or fumes, placing the cockpit pressure switch to RAM EMERG will ventilate the cockpits.

Note

In the OFF and RAM EMERG positions of the cockpit pressure switch, crew member environment may be modified with the pressure suit controls or by turning on the windshield and canopy defrost system.

COCKPIT PRESSURE ALTIMETER

The cockpit pressure altimeter (2, figure 1-24) indicates cockpit pressure altitude in feet. When the full pressure suit is worn, altitude is indicated by a suit-mounted altimeter.

COCKPIT PRESSURIZATION OPERATION

The cockpit pressurization system operates automatically when the engines are operating and the canopies are closed to maintain the schedule shown in figure 1-29.

To initiate and monitor system operation, proceed as follows:

1. Cockpit pressure switch—NORM.
2. Canopy—closed (CANOPY caution indicator out).
3. Check cockpit pressure altimeter for normal schedule.

Note

In the event of equipment conditioning system failure, cockpit pressurization flow is lost upon initiation of alternate cooling, and cockpit altitude rapidly approaches the ambient pressure level.

4. If normal operation cannot be obtained through use of the alternate cooling reset button, reduce altitude as necessary for safe flight.
5. If ram-air ventilation is desired, move the cockpit pressure switch to RAM EMERG.

CAUTION

If a crack should develop in the windshield, move the cockpit pressure switch to OFF, descend, reduce airspeed to minimum, and land as soon as possible.

EQUIPMENT CONDITIONING

Electronic equipment conditioning is accomplished by air from the electronic cooling refrigeration unit. This air is used to control the environment of components such as the a-c power supervisory panels, voltage regulators, autoflight control system, bomb directing set, and other equipment. These components must be supplied with cooling air during ground operation prior to and during engine starting. The cooling air must be supplied to the equipment whenever external electrical power is supplied to the components. See figure 1-40 (sheet 2) for usable equipment and system requirements.

Note

The equipment conditioning system has priority over the cockpit conditioning and pressurization systems in the event of a malfunction of the equipment conditioning refrigeration unit.

ALTERNATE COOLING

The equipment and cockpit conditioning systems are interconnected to increase total system reliability. If the equipment refrigeration unit air temperature exceeds limits, an overheat thermoswitch, located in the equipment refrigeration unit discharge line, energizes two relays which accomplish the switching required for alternate cooling to supply equipment cooling air from the cabin refrigeration unit. If the overheat condition is eliminated, normal cooling system operation may be restored by depressing the alternate cooling reset button.

Section I
Part 2

AUXILIARY B/N COOLING AND HEATING*

During ground operation (aircraft weight on the landing gear), the air supply for cockpit conditioning and pressurization is automatically diverted to supplement electronic equipment cooling in a manner identical to alternate cooling. This is required during low engine rpm operation to supply adequate cooling air to electronic components. Automatic operation of the auxiliary cooling function is selected through the pilot's AUX B/N COOLING button. Auxiliary cooling is automatically terminated during ground operation through a sector switch which actuates at a throttle angle corresponding to approximately 80% rpm. In addition to auxiliary cooling, automatic auxiliary heating prevents overcooling of the bomb directing set during extended high-altitude operation. Warm air from the pressure suit supply line is diverted to the bomb directing set to provide temperatures above minimum limits.

Note

Operation of pressure suit conditioning and pressurization is not affected during auxiliary cooling operation; however, if the pressure suit is worn, utilization of the defrost system airflow for crew member warmth may be required during extended high-altitude operation.

Alternate Cooling Reset Button

The alternate cooling reset button (ALTERNATE COOL, 5, figure 1-30) is located on the air temperature control panel. This button is used to regain normal equipment conditioning flow.

Alternate Cooling Caution Indicator

The alternate cooling caution indicator (figure 1-4) is located on the pilot's instrument panel. This indicator illuminates if cockpit conditioning and pressurization air supply has been diverted to the equipment conditioning system.

Auxiliary B/N Cooling Button*

The AUX B/N COOLING button (7, figure 1-30) is depressed to select automatic ground operation of the auxiliary cooling function, which overrides normal cockpit conditioning and pressurization under overheat conditions. Depressing and releasing the button to its off (up) position deenergizes the auxiliary cooling bypass.

Note

The AUX B/N COOLING button is to remain depressed at all times with an operational bomb directing set installed.

EQUIPMENT CONDITIONING OPERATION

Normal operation of the equipment conditioning system is entirely automatic. If the ALT COOL caution indicator is illuminated prior to take-off, proceed as follows:

1. Increase engine speed to 85% rpm or higher.
2. Depress the alternate cooling reset button until the ALT COOL caution indicator extinguishes.
3. If the ALT COOL indicator illuminates after button release, it can be assumed that the equipment conditioning system has failed and cockpit conditioning and pressurization will not be available.

If the ALT COOL caution indicator illuminates in flight, proceed as follows:

1. Depress the alternate cooling reset button.
2. If the indicator illuminates after 15 seconds, increase engine rpm and airspeed and again attempt reset.
3. If the indicator still illuminates after button release, it can be assumed that the equipment conditioning system has failed.

PRESSURE SUIT CONDITIONING

Hot air from the equipment cooling secondary heat exchanger is cooled by cold air from the equipment cooling refrigeration unit in the pressure suit heat exchanger. This moderate temperature air, and warm air from the defrost and anti-ice ducts, is directed to the pressure suit controller, where it is mixed for use in pressure suit ventilation and temperature control. Suit conditioning airflow is directed through the composite disconnects approximately 3.0 psi above cockpit pressure. Pressurization air is supplied from points downstream of the two secondary heat exchangers. The pressure schedule is shown in figure 1-29.

SUIT TEMPERATURE KNOB

The PRESS SUIT TEMP knob (2, figure 1-30) is located on the suit control panel in the pilot's cockpit and controls the temperature of both crew member's suits. Pressure suit temperature may be controlled from 50° to 120°F.

SUIT FLOW KNOBS

The suit flow knobs (1 and 13, figure 1-30) are located on the left console in both cockpits. The pilot's flow knob must be turned more than 5 degrees from the OFF position so that the pressure suit temperature knob can be used to control the temperature of the air flowing into the suits.

PRESSURE SUIT OPERATION

Prior to starting engines, the crew members' pressure suits are ventilated from an external cooling air source

*Aircraft having ASC 29 complied with

(figure 1-40). The crew members may regulate external pressure suit airflow by using the PRESS SUIT FLOW knobs on the suit panels in each cockpit. The temperature of the external cooling air is controlled at the source; however, effective temperature control is achieved through flow adjustment.

Note

On modified aircraft,* suit ground conditioning air is provided from the main cooling air receptacle.

It is recommended that defrost system airflow be utilized to ensure adequate heat for pressure suit airflow. Above 35,000 feet cockpit altitude, a suit pressure corresponding to approximately 34,500 feet is maintained in the event of loss of cockpit pressurization. The liquid oxygen system provides suit pressurization automatically in the event both the normal and alternate systems fail due to a system malfunction or a dual flame-out. Refer to OXYGEN SYSTEMS, in this section. If extreme suit temperature cannot be controlled normally, the PRESS SUIT FLOW knob should be turned off, initiating automatic emergency operation through the oxygen system. Cockpit temperature should be maintained high enough to reduce faceplate fogging.

Note

- If pressure suit flight is made following an overnight cold soak of the aircraft below 32°F, move the suit flow knobs to the full INCR position with the pilot's PRESS SUIT TEMP knob at 70° for about 5 minutes prior to take-off. This procedure will preclude possible ice-up of the pressure suit flow controller in the personnel disconnect.
- To preclude possible suit inflation and crew member incapacitation due to a malfunction during take-off, the suit flow knobs should be left OFF and one glove left open until the aircraft is airborne.

ANTI-G SUIT OPERATION

The anti-ice and rain removal line of the cockpit conditioning system is tapped as a source of pressurized air for anti-G suit operation. G-suit air is routed to an anti-G valve on the left console in both cockpits. On demand, the air flows into the suits through the composite disconnects.

ANTI-G SUIT VALVES

The anti-G valves each consist of a spring-balanced valve which is opened when positive "g" force is sufficient to overcome valve spring tension. The top of each valve may be turned to select a HI (1.5 psi per "g") or LO (1.0 psi per "g") suit pressure during accelerations. A manual operation button is incorporated for checking valve operation. Anti-G suit operation is entirely automatic. To ease discomfort caused by long-duration flight, the anti-G valve manual button can be depressed to provide changes in suit pressure.

DEFROST AND ANTI-ICE SYSTEMS

The hot air supply of the cockpit conditioning primary heat exchanger provides windshield and canopy defrosting and windshield external anti-ice and rain removal. When the pilot's canopy is closed, 300°F air is available to the defrost and anti-ice valves for system operation.

WINDSHIELD AND CANOPY DEFROST KNOB

A windshield and canopy defrost knob is provided on the anti-ice control panel (6, figure 1-30). With this knob, a flow of windshield and canopy defrost air is routed through perforated tubing around the lower inside surfaces of the windshield and canopy. This knob should be turned on well in advance of descent from high altitudes so that the large area of the canopy may be warmed thoroughly before being exposed to warm moist air at lower altitudes. During adverse flying weather, it may be necessary to maintain continuous defrost flow to keep the windshield and canopy clear. Defrost flow is turned on and increased as desired by turning the knob clockwise from the OFF position.

Note

Should defrost airflow become unadjustable (no knob response), defrost valve action may be regained through ON/OFF switching of the windshield anti-ice system. Do not, however, leave the WINDSHIELD ANTI-ICE switch in the ON position.

WINDSHIELD ANTI-ICE SWITCH

The windshield anti-ice switch (10, figure 1-30) is located on the anti-ice control panel. This switch has three positions: OFF, ON, and EMERG. During flight in adverse weather, especially during precision instrument approaches in icing conditions or precipitation, this switch should be in the ON position. High-velocity, hot air is directed onto the outer surface of the windshield to remove rain droplets or ice crystals for improvement of pilot visibility. A safety provision for overpressure and/or overtemperature is built into the anti-icing and rain removal system. Should anti-icing air temperature exceed 360°F or nozzle pressure exceed 50 psi, a sensing circuit returns the switch to the OFF position. Should

*Aircraft having ASC 38 complied with

airflow be needed for flight safety under these conditions, the switch can be lifted and moved from ON into the EMERG position, where a detent holds it in place and overrides the safety features.

> **CAUTION**
>
> The windshield anti-icing and rain removal system should be operated in the EMERG position only when absolutely essential, as the airflow temperature and pressure safety devices are overridden. The EMERG position should never be used on the ground except for take-off, and then only if absolutely necessary. If used on the ground, select EMERG for a *maximum of 5 seconds,* then select OFF for at least 60 seconds before reselecting EMERG.

Note

Any time the EMERG position has been used, a notation should be made on the yellow sheet, and the windshield should be inspected for overtemperature damage.

PITOT ANTI-ICE BUTTON

When depressed, the pitot anti-ice button (9, figure 1-30) provides a-c essential bus power to heater elements in the airstream direction detector probe and in the pitot-static boom.

ENGINE ANTI-ICE SWITCH

Engine anti-ice airflow is controlled by the engine anti-ice switch (8, figure 1-30), a two-position switch (ON/OFF) located on the pilot's right console. Moving this switch to ON opens a solenoid-operated valve which regulates the flow of hot air internally through the struts and guide vanes. On some aircraft,* this switch also controls flow of anti-icing air to the engine accessory bullet nose. The air is discharged out the trailing edge of the guide vanes and from the engine bullet nose into the engine.

Engine Anti-ice Indicator

On some aircraft,* the engine anti-ice indicator displays "ON" when the engine anti-ice switch is ON, both engine anti-ice air valves have opened, and air is flowing as required. Lack of an "ON" indication means either a valve malfunction or loss of power to the indicator.

DEFROST AND ANTI-ICE OPERATION

For flight under adverse weather conditions, set the defrost and anti-ice controls as follows:

1. WINDSHIELD & CANOPY DEFROST knob—as desired.
   For warm, humid conditions, a defrost setting of about one-half is recommended. The cockpit temperature knob can be used to modify the temperature, if necessary.
2. WINDSHIELD ANTI-ICE switch—as desired.
   If precipitation limits visibility, move this switch to ON.
3. PITOT ANTI-ICE button—Depress.
4. ENGINE ANTI-ICE switch—ON as desired.
   The ENGINE ANTI-ICE switch should be moved to ON whenever visible moisture is encountered and ambient temperature is at or near the freezing point.

> **CAUTION**
>
> The only cockpit indications of failure of the pilot anti-icing system are abnormal pitot-static instrument readings when icing occurs. Should failure occur under icing conditions, boom icing can also cause undesired changes in inlet ramp operation. If such icing should occur at low or cruising airspeeds, placing the RAMP CONT switch to STBY will prevent the ramps from being extended toward full down which could cause loss of engine airflow and possible flameout.

OXYGEN SYSTEMS

Two independent oxygen systems are installed. The normal breathing oxygen supply is provided by a liquid oxygen conversion system. An emergency oxygen supply is incorporated into the survival kit in each seat, providing emergency breathing supply and emergency pressure suit inflation when actuated. The seat composite disconnect provides connection to both normal and emergency oxygen systems.

Note

The Scott disconnect upper block should be checked immediately for proper connection in the event of oxygen flow interruption.

NORMAL OXYGEN SYSTEM

A 20-liter liquid oxygen system is installed, which is supplied by separate 10-liter converters. Liquid oxygen is evaporated under controlled pressure and routed at 70 psi to the cockpit supply valves. The oxygen conversion system is located in the aft portion of the nose wheel well, above the well cover. See figure 1-31 for oxygen system duration.

*Aircraft having ASC 10 complied with

Note

The forward converter must be installed to obtain an operational system. If the aft converter is removed, a dummy capacitor must be installed to obtain oxygen quantity indication. The dummy disconnects must be connected to prevent liquid oxygen spillage into the electronics bay.

OXYGEN SUPPLY VALVES

An oxygen system supply ON/OFF valve (30, figure 1-3) is provided on the left console. To obtain oxygen pressure at the composite disconnect, the valve control lever is moved to the ON (forward) position.

Oxygen Quantity Indicators

An oxygen quantity indicator (19, figure 1-4) is installed in both cockpits. The forward cockpit indicator contains an amplifier which receives power from the essential a-c electrical bus. The aft cockpit indicator is a repeater instrument, connected to the forward indicator. Up to 20 liters is indicated in increments of 1 liter. An indicator test button is located on the pilot's indicator.

OXYGEN WARNING INDICATORS

An oxygen warning indicator is mounted on the instrument panel in both cockpits. These red warning indicators come on if the liquid quantity in the conversion system drops below 0.8 liter or if build-up pressure falls below 45 psi in the systems operator's system and below 45 psi for more than 4 seconds in the pilot's system. The warning light circuit may be checked by use of the warning lights test button (5, figure 1-35).

EMERGENCY OXYGEN SYSTEM

A high-pressure (1800 psi), gaseous, emergency oxygen supply bottle is installed in each of the seat-mounted survival kits. Utilization of this supply is automatic upon initiation of ejection. A manual ring is provided on each survival kit for obtaining emergency oxygen flow. If used as an emergency breathing supply with the standard mask, up to 20 minutes normal breathing is available without cockpit pressurization. If used to supply both emergency breathing and pressure suit, the supply is sufficient to permit emergency seat/man free-fall descent to a safe altitude.

Note

With a good pressure suit, there is no decrease in time available on emergency oxygen pressurization, since minor leakage is made up by air which is exhaled into the suit.

EMERGENCY OXYGEN PRESSURE GAGES

An emergency oxygen supply pressure gage is installed in each survival kit. For all flights, this gage should read a minimum of 1800 psi and a maximum of 2200 psi.

EMERGENCY OXYGEN RINGS

An emergency oxygen manual actuator ring is installed on the survival kits near the pressure gage. If emergency oxygen flow is required, this ring should be pulled sharply upward, separating it from the survival kit.

PERSONAL COMPOSITE DISCONNECT

A Scott composite disconnect is installed at the left rear corner of the ejection seat. The composite disconnect consists of three separate blocks. These three blocks (upper, intermediate, and lower) are joined together to form the junction for the personal leads from the crewman to the aircraft. The lower disconnect block is attached to the cockpit floor with a cable, which remains in the aircraft at all times. The intermediate block is fastened to the survival kit as a permanent part and has an oxygen port connected to the emergency oxygen bottle in the survival kit. Lanyards are routed to the intermediate block for actuation of the pressure suit exhaust disconnect and the emergency oxygen supply valve. On ejection, the lower block (attached to the cockpit floor by a lanyard) separates from the intermediate block, leaving the intermediate and upper blocks connected. This connection provides emergency oxygen flow to the crewman upon descent. The upper block is attached to the intermediate block after entering the cockpit. The upper block is available in four configurations. They are the standard garment personal lead and the short, medium, and long full pressure suit personal leads. All four configurations have a manual release handle cable assembly (yellow pear). This manual release assembly is used to cock the upper block mechanism for connection with the intermediate block to release the upper block prior to leaving the cockpit. The standard garment personal lead assembly (upper block) is used with conventional nonpressurized flying garments. The upper block is composed of an anti-G suit hose, oxygen hose, and a communications cable assembly.

OXYGEN SYSTEMS OPERATION

NORMAL

Normal operation of the oxygen system is fully automatic, requiring only that the crew members be properly connected and that the supply valves be positioned to ON. In either the standard mask or full pressure suit

OXYGEN DURATION

AIRCRAFT ALTITUDE		COCKPIT ALTITUDE		HOURS vs TWO CREW MEMBERS	OXYGEN QUANTITY in LITERS						LESS THAN 0.8
FEET X1000	PSIA	FEET X1000	PSIA		20	16	12	8	4	2	
70	0.65	24.2	5.65		20.5	16.4	12.3	8.2	4.1	2.0	EMERGENCY DESCEND TO ALTITUDE NOT REQUIRING OXYGEN
60	1.05	22.6	6.05		19.1	15.3	11.5	7.6	3.8	1.9	
50	1.69	20.3	6.69		17.2	13.7	10.3	6.9	3.4	1.7	
45	2.14	18.6	7.14		15.9	12.7	9.5	6.4	3.2	1.6	
40	2.72	16.8	7.72		14.6	11.7	8.8	5.8	2.9	1.5	
35	3.46	14.6	8.46		13.1	10.5	7.9	5.2	2.6	1.3	
30	4.36	12.0	9.36		11.6	9.3	7.0	4.7	2.3	1.2	
25	5.45	9.2	10.45		10.4	8.3	6.2	4.1	2.1	1.0	
20	6.75	8.0	10.91		9.9	7.9	5.9	4.0	2.0	.9	
8	10.91	8.0	10.91		9.9	7.9	5.9	4.0	2.0	.9	
5	12.23	5.0	12.23		8.9	7.1	5.3	3.6	1.8	.8	
SEA LEVEL	14.70	SEA LEVEL	14.70		7.5	6.0	4.5	3.0	1.5	.7	

Figure 1-31

configuration, 100 percent oxygen is supplied to the crew when the oxygen supply ON/OFF valves are in the ON position. Ensure the position of the emergency oxygen bottle manual actuation ring on the survival kit. Check the operation of the warning system with the warning lights test button.

Preflight

Before each flight, inspect the oxygen system components as follows:

1. Check survival kit emergency oxygen pressure—1800 to 2200 psi.
2. Check liquid oxygen quantity indicator—20 liters.
3. Press the oxygen test button on gage. Check needle rundown. During the test, when the indication is 0.8 liter and below, the OXYGEN warning indicator should illuminate. Upon releasing the test button, the needle should continue to its original setting and the OXYGEN warning indicator should extinguish.

WARNING

If preflight inspection reveals that the system has been empty for several hours or if the system has been left open because of replacement of parts, without all lines and components having been capped or plugged, complete system purge and refilling is mandatory before flight.

EMERGENCY

The first indication of oxygen supply exhaustion will be illumination of the OXYGEN warning indicator. If the warning light circuit is defective and the liquid oxygen quantity indicator is not periodically checked, system supply exhaustion will be indicated by a sudden onset of difficult inhalation. If this occurs, immediately pull the emergency oxygen supply ring and descend to an altitude where oxygen is not required.

WARNING

- Should the OXYGEN warning indicator illuminate in flight and more than 0.8 liter of oxygen is aboard, a system malfunction has occurred. Check the Scott disconnect upper block for proper connection. Descend to a safe cockpit altitude and be prepared to pull emergency oxygen supply ring upon noting a restriction to inhalation.
- Emergency oxygen flow is not available if the Scott upper block becomes disconnected.

SUIT EMERGENCY PRESSURIZATION

The oxygen system supplies suit pressurization in the event of complete failure of the aircraft air conditioning and pressurization system above 35,000 feet. The sequence of events which results in the aircraft oxygen system being used for suit pressurization is completely automatic and requires no attention from the crew members. With the pressure suit, oxygen system pressure will adequately protect the crew members for descent and landing from any altitude.

INTERCOMMUNICATIONS SYSTEM (ICS)

The ICS provides communication between cockpits, serves as a selector station and audio amplifier for ECM and CNI subsystems, and provides communication between the cockpits and ground crew. The system incorporates a basic control unit installed in each cockpit, consisting of two transistorized amplifiers, their controls, and a panel of selector switches. Two remote ICS stations, one located in the external canopy control access and another near the external electrical power receptacle, may be utilized by the ground crew members for aircraft preflight and starting checks or during bomb directing set preflight operations. The ICS is powered by the essential d-c bus and is thus operative through the emergency ram-air turbine power unit in the event of dual generator failure. For a listing of electronic equipment, see figure 1-32.

MICROPHONE SWITCHES

The pilot's microphone switch is located on the No. 2 throttle grip. The microphone switch has two positions: ICS and XMIT. The ICS position (down) is used for intercommunication with the aft cockpit or the external ground stations. The XMIT position (up) actuates the main communications transmitter. For aft cockpit communications, a foot-operated microphone switch is provided on the right footrest. The ICS position of the microphone switch and the aft cockpit foot-operated ICS switch duplicate the function of the ICS CALL position of the microphone select switch.

ICS FUNCTION SELECTOR

The function selector (C2, figure 1-33) has four positions: EMER, NORM, ALT ICS, and ALT RAD. These functions are as follows:

POSITION	FUNCTION
NORM	NORMAL ICS OPERATION. The ICS and radio amplifiers are operative.
ALT RAD	USED IF RADIO AMPLIFIER FAILS. ICS amplifier handles ICS output as well as all incoming signals.
ALT ICS	USED IF ICS AMPLIFIER FAILS. Radio amplifier handles ICS output as well as all incoming signals.
EMER	EMERGENCY COMMUNICATIONS. Used if both amplifiers in either control unit fail. Provides UHF communications, TACAN, and ADF signals direct to the headphones, plus intercom through UHF communications sidetone. (AN/APR-18 audio is not provided.)

ICS VOLUME KNOB

The volume knob (C1, figure 1-33) controls ICS audio level without affecting the level of selected receivers.

MICROPHONE SELECT SWITCH

The microphone select switch (MIC SEL, C3, figure 1-33) is independent of the ICS function selector and has three positions: COLD, HOT, and CALL. If the MIC SEL switches in both cockpits are not in the same position, the momentary CALL position may be used, or the microphone switch on the throttle held in ICS.

AUDIO SELECT BUTTONS

Audio select buttons (B1, 4, 5, 6, figure 1-33) are positioned forward of the ICS control panel. These buttons may be depressed to monitor the audio output from the communications, navigation, and ECM systems receivers. All receivers, or as many as desired for monitoring, can be selected. Audio monitoring of the following components is controlled by these buttons.

BUTTON	COMPONENT
UHF	UHF communications radio
TACAN	UHF navigation
ADF	Auxiliary receiver
RADAR WARN	Radar passive warning receiver

TABLE OF ELECTRONIC EQUIPMENT

EQUIPMENT	FUNCTION	CHARACTERISTICS	CONTROL PILOT	NAVIGATOR
COMMUNICATIONS — NAVIGATION — IDENTIFICATION AN/ASQ-56				
UHF Comm Unit	Voice Communications	1750 Frequencies	Left Console	Right Console
TACAN Unit	Station Range, Bearing	126 Channels	Right Console	Right Console
IFF/SIF Unit	IFF (Radar Identification) SIF (Selective Identification)	Mode 1-73 Codes Mode 3-77 Codes	Right Console Emerg Only	Right Console
AUX UHF Unit	Auxiliary UHF Receiver and ADF Unit	20 Present Channels	Right Console	Right Console
ASSOCIATED ELECTRONIC EQUIPMENT				
ICS	Intercommunication Cockpit and External	Cockpit/External	Right Console	Right Console
AN/APN-120	Radar Altimeter Height Above Terrain	Pilot — 0 to 3000 feet B/N — 500 to 75,000 feet	Instrument Panel	Instrument Control Panel
AN/ASN-26	Flight Reference Set	Attitude Reference Compass and Labs	Right Console	Right Console
ECM	Electronic Countermeasures	[Refer to the Supplemental Flight Manual (NAVWEPS 01-60ABA-1A)]		
AN/ASB-12	Bomb Directing Set	[Refer to the Supplemental Flight Manual (NAVWEPS 01-60ABA-1A)]		

Figure 1-32

ICS OPERATION

The ICS is operative when the aircraft electrical system is energized by external or generator power. With the ICS function selector in the NORM position, reception of main UHF signals and any other selected receiver signals is available, provided the selected receivers are energized. Simultaneous monitoring of navigation and ECM equipment is accomplished through the associated audio select buttons by controlling the volume through the individual UHF, TACAN, and ECM system volume controls. To operate the ICS, proceed as follows:

NORMAL

1. ICS function selector—NORM.
2. Adjust ICS volume as desired.
3. MIC SEL switch—COLD.
   Check ICS operation, using microphone switch ICS position.
4. Recheck the ICS.
   MIC SEL switch—as desired.

EXTERNAL STATIONS

For communication with the Plane Captain or crewman during starting or postflight procedure, use the ICS as follows:

1. ICS function selectors—NORM (both cockpits).
2. MIC SEL switches—HOT (both cockpits).
3. Increase ICS volume as required.
4. Establish communication with external stations.

LOSS OF NORMAL MODE

If a crew member loses ICS contact, proceed as follows:

1. ICS function selector—ALT ICS.
2. Check intercommunication as in normal operation.

If selected receiver signals fail:

1. ICS function selector—ALT RAD.
2. If signals are regained, the ICS intercom amplifier has assumed the function of the failed intercom radio amplifier.

LOSS OF ALTERNATE MODE

Should NORM and ALT ICS fail, intercommunications may be regained as follows:

1. ICS function selector—EMER.
2. Systems operator's transmit control switch—RADIO.
3. UHF audio select button—Depress.
4. COMM VOL control—maximum.
5. Proceed as for normal radio communications.

COMMUNICATIONS-NAVIGATION-IDENTIFICATION SYSTEM (CNI)

CNI POWER BUTTON

The CNI power button (8, figure 1-4A) is located on the pilot's right console, forward of the cockpit pressure switch. With external electrical power and cooling air applied, depressing the CNI power button provides amplifier warm-up voltage to CNI system components.

Note

Operation of CNI system components should be delayed at least 90 seconds to allow warm-up.

EMERGENCY POWER INDICATOR

The emergency power indicator (B7, figure 1-33), normally blank, will flip to "ON" if a CNI power supply malfunction occurs. An "ON" indication denotes that the main communications transmitter is operating on reduced power. In this event, the TACAN unit is inoperative and IFF and SIF may also be inoperative, depending on the extent and type of malfunction. This indicator does not reveal the operating status of the auxiliary receiver unit.

UHF COMMUNICATIONS UNIT

The UHF communications unit (UHF COMM) transmits and receives AM signals in the frequency range from 225.0 to 399.9 megacycles. Through this unit, either crew member may select any of 20 preset channels, standard military emergency frequency, or manually tune to any of 1750 transmitter-receiver frequencies.

COMMUNICATIONS COMMAND BUTTON

The COMM COMD button (B8, figure 1-33) is used to assume command of the main and auxiliary UHF communications units. The button contains a dimmable green indicating light. The button in the cockpit having command is illuminated.

MODE SELECTOR

The communications mode selector (COMM/AUX, H2, figure 1-33) is used to control the operation of both the main and auxiliary UHF communications units. With this selector, the main unit can be operated as a transmitter-receiver, with or without monitoring of the military emergency (guard) frequency, or as an ADF receiver for navigation purposes. The auxiliary receiver can be used as an ADF receiver or to monitor the military emergency frequency.

VOLUME CONTROL

The COMM VOL control (H4, figure 1-33) is used to turn on the UHF communications unit and control main UHF receiver volume. With CNI power on, UHF unit power is reduced to warm-up condition by rotating the control counterclockwise to the OFF detent.

CNI CONTROLS

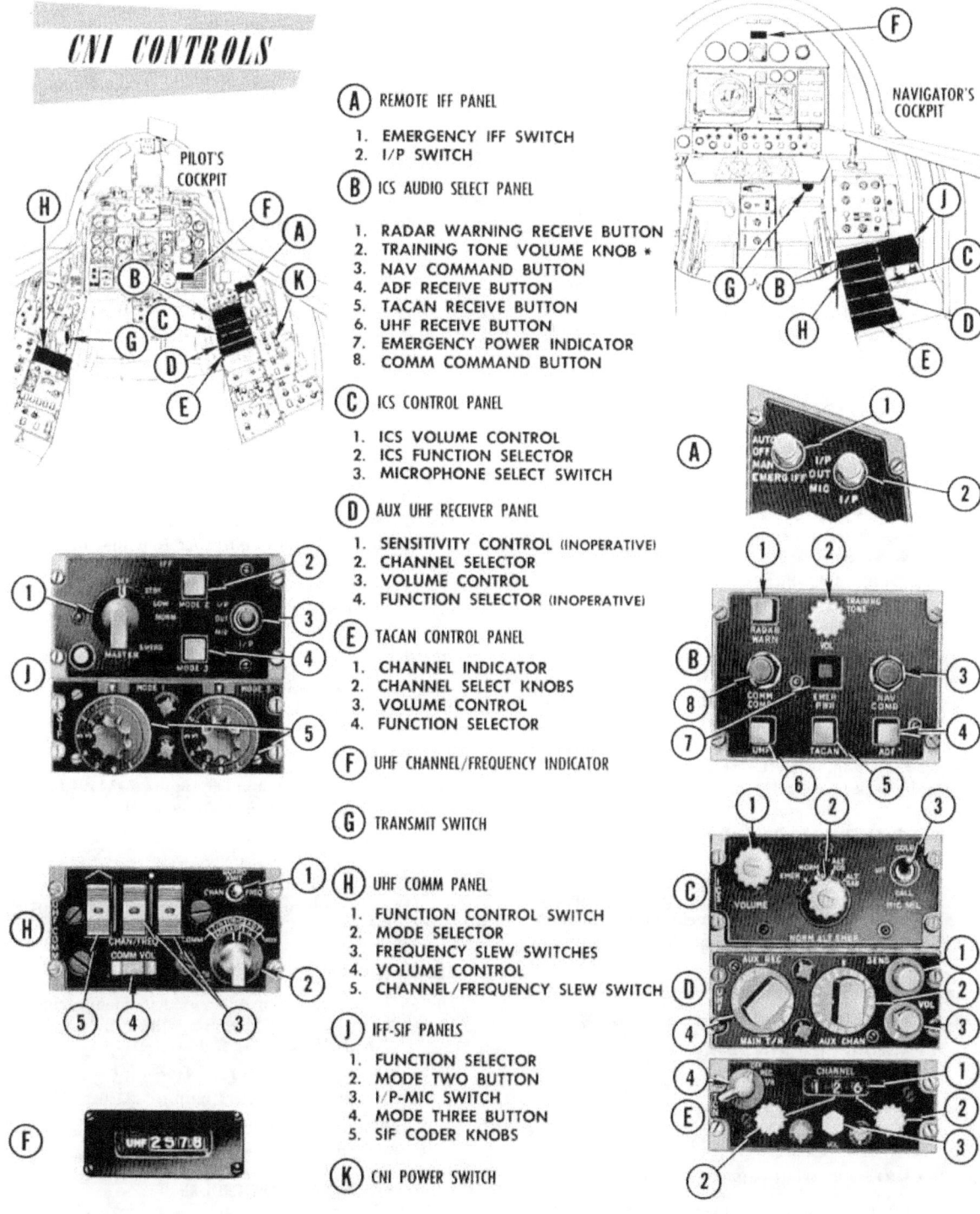

A. REMOTE IFF PANEL
  1. EMERGENCY IFF SWITCH
  2. I/P SWITCH

B. ICS AUDIO SELECT PANEL
  1. RADAR WARNING RECEIVE BUTTON
  2. TRAINING TONE VOLUME KNOB *
  3. NAV COMMAND BUTTON
  4. ADF RECEIVE BUTTON
  5. TACAN RECEIVE BUTTON
  6. UHF RECEIVE BUTTON
  7. EMERGENCY POWER INDICATOR
  8. COMM COMMAND BUTTON

C. ICS CONTROL PANEL
  1. ICS VOLUME CONTROL
  2. ICS FUNCTION SELECTOR
  3. MICROPHONE SELECT SWITCH

D. AUX UHF RECEIVER PANEL
  1. SENSITIVITY CONTROL (INOPERATIVE)
  2. CHANNEL SELECTOR
  3. VOLUME CONTROL
  4. FUNCTION SELECTOR (INOPERATIVE)

E. TACAN CONTROL PANEL
  1. CHANNEL INDICATOR
  2. CHANNEL SELECT KNOBS
  3. VOLUME CONTROL
  4. FUNCTION SELECTOR

F. UHF CHANNEL/FREQUENCY INDICATOR

G. TRANSMIT SWITCH

H. UHF COMM PANEL
  1. FUNCTION CONTROL SWITCH
  2. MODE SELECTOR
  3. FREQUENCY SLEW SWITCHES
  4. VOLUME CONTROL
  5. CHANNEL/FREQUENCY SLEW SWITCH

J. IFF-SIF PANELS
  1. FUNCTION SELECTOR
  2. MODE TWO BUTTON
  3. I/P-MIC SWITCH
  4. MODE THREE BUTTON
  5. SIF CODER KNOBS

K. CNI POWER SWITCH

*AIRCRAFT HAVING ASC 43 COMPLIED WITH

Figure 1-33

FUNCTION CONTROL SWITCH

The function control switch (H1, figure 1-33) is used to select the transmitter frequency option of the main UHF unit. The function control switch operates as follows:

POSITION	FUNCTION
CHAN	Operation in mode preset channel (using the left-hand UHF slewing switch).
GUARD XMIT	Main unit is automatically tuned to military emergency frequency (243.0 mc).
FREQ	Operation in manual tuning mode (any of 1750 frequencies using all three UHF slewing switches).

CHANNEL/FREQUENCY SLEW SWITCHES

The channel/frequency slew switches (H3, 5, figure 1-33) are used to select operating frequency or channel of the main UHF unit through touch-tuning. With the function control switch in CHAN, the left switch is used to select the desired channel, 1 through 20. With the function control switch in FREQ, all three switches are used to select frequency between 225.0 and 399.9 megacycles. When the function control switch is in the GUARD XMIT position, the touch-tuning circuits are inoperative.

CHANNEL/FREQUENCY INDICATORS

A channel/frequency remote indicator (F, figure 1-33) is installed in both cockpits. This indicator reads the operating channel (1 through 20 or GUARD) or the selected frequency between 225.0 and 399.9 megacycles. When the slewing switches are operated, the indicator changes reading in pulses at a rate of approximately three digits per second.

UHF COMMUNICATIONS OPERATION

Note
If the UHF equipment is to be operated prior to engine start, external equipment cooling air and electrical power must be connected.

1. CNI power button—Depress.
2. COMM VOL—Rotate to right as desired.
3. Mode (COMM/AUX) selector—T/R—ADF or T/R+G—ADF.
4. Function control switch—CHAN.
5. COMM COMD button—Depress; check illuminated.
6. UHF audio select button—Depress.
7. Operate channel (left) slewing switch, setting desired channel into channel/frequency indicator.
8. After allowing 90 seconds for warm-up, check communications as desired.
9. To select a manual frequency, move the function control switch to FREQ and, using the slewing switches, set desired frequency in channel/frequency indicator.
10. To secure the main UHF unit, rotate the COMM VOL control left to OFF.

MAIN UHF/ADF PROCEDURE

For main receiver ADF operation, proceed as follows:

1. Function control switch—CHAN or FREQ.
2. Set desired channel or frequency into channel/frequency indicator.
3. Mode (COMM/AUX) selector—ADF—G.
4. Range and bearing knob—UHF.
5. Observe bearing to selected facility indicated on the horizontal situation indicator.

AUXILIARY UHF RECEIVER

The auxiliary UHF receiver provides ADF operation and emergency reception on 20 preset channels between 265.0 and 284.9 megacycles. The auxiliary receiver is controlled through the lower row of functions of the communications mode selector on the main UHF control panel. Auxiliary receiver channels are selected with the AUX CHAN knob on the auxiliary receiver control panel.

CHANNEL KNOB

The AUX CHAN knob (D2, figure 1-33) selects any of the 20 preset auxiliary receiver channels.

VOLUME KNOB

The auxiliary VOL knob (D3, figure 1-33) is used to control auxiliary receiver volume level.

Note
The AUX REC function selector and sensitivity (SENS) knob are not operational in this installation.

AUXILIARY RECEIVER OPERATION

The auxiliary receiver may be used to monitor military emergency frequency while using the main receiver in the ADF mode. Proceed as follows:

1. Mode (COMM/AUX) selector—ADF—G.
2. UHF, ADF audio select buttons—Depress.
3. Range and bearing selector—UHF.
4. Auxiliary volume—as desired.

AUXILIARY UHF/ADF PROCEDURE

For navigation purposes, the auxiliary receiver is used in the ADF mode as follows:

1. Mode (COMM/AUX) selector—T/R—ADF or T/R+G—ADF.

2. ADF audio select button—Depress if desired and adjust auxiliary volume.
3. AUX CHAN knob—desired channel.
4. Range and bearing selector—UHF.
5. Observe bearing to facility on the horizontal situation indicator.

TACAN

The TACAN (Tactical Air Navigation) unit operates in conjunction with land-, ship-, or aircraft-based beacons in the UHF band from 1025 to 1150 megacycles. This band is divided into channels separated by 1 megacycle, providing 126 channels. This TACAN unit presents magnetic bearing, course deviation, and slant-range distance to a maximum of 196 nautical miles from surface-based beacons. Distance, bearing, and course information are presented to the pilot by the horizontal situation indicator and to the systems operator by the azimuth and range indicator.

FUNCTION SELECTOR

The TACAN function selector (E4, figure 1-33) is used to turn on the unit and select mode of operation. Function selector positions operate the TACAN as follows:

POSITION	FUNCTION
OFF	System secured.
REC (Receive)	Unit receives and indicates magnetic bearing and course deviation to selected station.
T/R (Transmit/Receive)	Unit receives and indicates magnetic bearing, course deviation, and slant-range distance in nautical miles to selected station.

CHANNEL KNOBS

The TACAN channel knobs (E2, figure 1-33) are used to select operating channels 001 to 126.

Note

- Channels 127, 128, and 129 may be selected but are not operative.
- Approximately 12 seconds are normally required for channel change and lock-on.

VOLUME KNOB

The volume knob (E3, figure 1-33) allows control of TACAN beacon audio identification signals when selected through the TACAN audio select button. No identification signal is present while the unit is searching for a newly selected channel.

TACAN OPERATION

To operate the TACAN, proceed as follows:

1. CNI power button—Depress.
2. TACAN audio select button—Depress.
3. TACAN function selector—REC or T/R.
4. NAV COMD button—Depress.
5. Range and bearing selector—TACAN.
6. Select desired beacon channel.
7. Adjust volume and identify beacon.

Note

When TACAN is initially turned on, up to approximately 20 seconds may be required to obtain lock-on.

8. Observe bearing on horizontal situation indicator.
9. Set desired course into HSI and observe deviation.
10. To secure the TACAN, move the function selector to OFF.

Note

- Garbled or unreadable station identification signals are a reliable indication of a malfunction of the aircraft unit or the surface station. Unless confirmed by known landmarks or ship sighting, range and bearing displays accompanied by an unreadable identifier should not be trusted.
- TACAN may occasionally lock on to a false bearing which is 40 degrees, or any multiple of 40 degrees, in error on either side of the correct bearing. Switching to another channel and then returning to the desired channel should recycle the search mode. This deficiency does not affect the distance indication provided by the TACAN unit.

RANGE AND BEARING KNOBS

A range and bearing knob (3, figure 1-24) is installed in each cockpit to provide selection of signal source from the UHF communications system (UHF), TACAN (TACAN), or the bomb directing set (NAV) for navigation display. The knobs are independent so that each crew member can select a separate source. In the UHF position, the bearing pointer of the horizontal situation indicator or the system operator's azimuth and range indicator displays magnetic bearing to the selected radio facility. In TACAN, these indicators display magnetic bearing and distance (as selected) to the TACAN beacon. In NAV, the horizontal situation indicator or the system operator's azimuth and range indicator displays bearing and distance to selected bomb directing set navigation checkpoint or target. Refer to Section I, Part 2, of the Supplemental NATOPS Flight Manual (NAVWEPS 01-60ABA-1A).

HORIZONTAL SITUATION INDICATOR (HSI)

The horizontal situation indicator (figure 1-34) provides selected radio and bomb directing set navigation displays. Within 46.5 nautical miles of target with the bomb directing set operating in the BOMB mode, the indicator shows magnetic bearing and distance to the weapon release point. The compass ring (4, figure 1-34) is controlled by the flight reference set, duplicating the heading indication of the all-attitude indicator. The bearing pointer (2) indicates magnetic bearing to station or destination. The heading marker (5) indicates desired heading as adjusted with the heading set knob (14). During TACAN operation, the course pointer, the course deviation bar, and the reciprocal course pointer (8, 1, and 15) form a single arrow when flight path is on the selected course. The deviation bar (1) is deflected when the flight is off the selected course. Selection of the desired inbound or outbound course is made by setting the desired course into the course setting indicator (12) with the course set knob (11). Mode of operation indicator lights are provided on the face of the instrument.

ADF MODE

When homing on a selected UHF communications unit or auxiliary UHF receiver channel (range and bearing selector at UHF), the UHF light (10, figure 1-34) appears. The course deviation bar (1) is locked at center and the distance indicating window (13) is covered by a shutter. Magnetic bearing to the selected station is indicated by the bearing pointer (2).

TACAN MODE

With TACAN operating and the range and bearing selector at TACAN, magnetic bearing to selected station is indicated by the bearing pointer (2, figure 1-34), and the TAC light (6) is visible in the upper right corner of the instrument. "TO/FROM" indication is provided by an arrow (9) which appears near the center of the instrument. Depending on position of the aircraft relative to selected course, the head of this arrow will appear near either end of the course deviation bar. The deviation bar (1) slides to either side to indicate displacement from selected course (12). Each deviation dot under the bar indicates 2½ degrees displacement. The distance indicating window (13) displays TACAN range up to 196 nautical miles (T/R) and the 1000 digit is hidden by a shutter. If the TACAN is switched from T/R to REC, the entire window is covered.

Note

When changing TACAN channel (range and bearing selector at TACAN), the course deviation bar centers, the bearing pointer searches, and the distance window flag appears until lock-on is achieved.

NAV AND BOMB MODES

Refer to Section I, Part 2, of the Supplemental NATOPS Flight Manual (NAVWEPS 01-60ABA-1A).

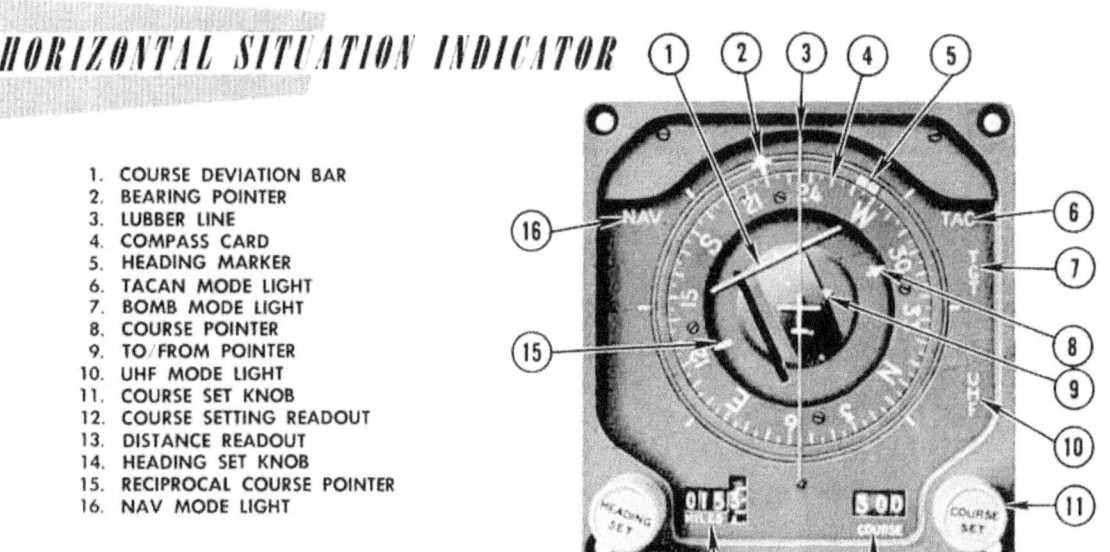

HORIZONTAL SITUATION INDICATOR

1. COURSE DEVIATION BAR
2. BEARING POINTER
3. LUBBER LINE
4. COMPASS CARD
5. HEADING MARKER
6. TACAN MODE LIGHT
7. BOMB MODE LIGHT
8. COURSE POINTER
9. TO/FROM POINTER
10. UHF MODE LIGHT
11. COURSE SET KNOB
12. COURSE SETTING READOUT
13. DISTANCE READOUT
14. HEADING SET KNOB
15. RECIPROCAL COURSE POINTER
16. NAV MODE LIGHT

Figure 1-34

IDENTIFICATION UNITS (IFF AND SIF)

The IFF/SIF transponder units provide coded display responses, along with the basic video return of the aircraft, on the scope of any properly equipped and interrogating air or surface radar. The IFF unit (Identification, Friend or Foe) supplies a basic reply pulse in any of three modes. The SIF unit (Selective Identification Feature) provides coded response for the three basic modes. In-flight selection of 70 codes is available for MODE 1, and 77 codes are available for MODE 3. MODE 2, the classified military identification mode, is preset by maintenance personnel, and is not available for in-flight SIF code selection. In addition to the military identification applications, navigation assistance, traffic separation, and distress identification are available through the IFF/SIF system. If preselected by the pilot, the IFF automatically responds in the emergency mode upon ejection of either crew member.

Note

- Operation of SIF requires that the NORM/MOD switch on the SIF unit in the electronics bay be set to MOD. NORM position results in a basic IFF response (no SIF). Ground stations equipped with SIF are not capable of receiving unmodified IFF signals.

- Master controls for the IFF and SIF units are installed in the aft cockpit only. Flight in positive control areas is not normally permitted without operational SIF.

- An emergency IFF mode switch is located on the pilot's right-hand console and an emergency IFF switch is under each crew member's seat. Refer to EMERG IFF SWITCH, in this section.

IFF/SIF CONTROLS

MASTER Function Selector

The MASTER function selector (aft cockpit, J1, figure 1-33) controls operation of the IFF/SIF system in any or all selected modes. With the SIF unit NORM/MOD switch at MOD, the MASTER function selector supplies power for SIF operation. The MASTER function selector operates the system as follows:

OPERATION	POSITION
OFF	Partial filament power (90 seconds after CNI power is turned on).
STBY	Warmed up and ready.
LOW	Mode 1, low power, plus Mode 2 and Mode 3 as selected.
NORM	Mode 1, normal power, plus Mode 2 and Mode 3 as selected.
EMERG	Four Mode 1 replies, normal power (plus three Mode 3, Code 77 replies in modified aircraft).

Note

- Pilot selection of MAN (EMERG IFF switch) overrides all positions of the systems operator's MASTER function selector, including OFF. Direct selection of MAN with the MASTER function selector at OFF requires no delay before response is available if CNI power has been on for at least 90 seconds.

- Aircraft modified by Avionics Change 170 respond automatically in Mode 3, Code 77, during emergency operation. The MODE 3 button need *not* be depressed to obtain this feature.

MODE 2 and MODE 3 Buttons

The MODE 2 and MODE 3 buttons (aft cockpit, J2, J4, figure 1-33) provide selection of transponder operation in two additional modes. MODE 2 is the classified military mode of identification. MODE 3 is used in conjunction with civilian and some military agencies, such as FAA Air Traffic Control Centers and GCA or CCA. MODE 2 and MODE 3 can be selected separately or simultaneously, and are initiated in the LOW or NORM positions of the MASTER function selector.

Identify Position (I/P) Switch

The I/P switch (both cockpits, A2, figure 1-33) allows a radar agency to single out, by radio request, an individual aircraft in a high-density traffic area. The I/P position is momentary, requiring the switch to be held in position. The MIC position, which may be selected permanently, provides IFF I/P response on holding the microphone switch in XMIT (pilot) or depressing the foot-operated microphone switch (systems operator). The I/P position provides a 30-second response, after which IFF response returns to normal. The I/P function operates in the various modes as follows (modes assumed selected):

NORM/MOD SWITCH POSITION	MODE 1	MODE 2	MODE 3	RESPONSE
NORM	Double reply	Normal reply	Normal reply	IFF only
MOD	Double reply	Normal reply	Normal reply*	IFF/SIF

*On aircraft having Avionics Bulletin 46 complied with, the IFF is capable of transmitting an I/P response in Mode 3. Without this modification, positive identification with some FAA Centers may require momentary selection of STBY or making identifying terms.

SIF MODE 1 and MODE 3 Code Dials

The MODE 1 and MODE 3 code dials are two concentric-type switches. The outer dial sets the first digit of the MODE 1 or MODE 3 codes, while the inner dial sets the second digit.

EMERG IFF Switch

The EMERG IFF switch (A1, figure 1-33) is used to select IFF emergency response. The EMERG IFF switch has three positions: MAN, OFF, and AUTO. In OFF, the IFF emergency mode is deenergized and control maintained at the systems operator's IFF control panel. The MAN (manual) position is used to select emergency IFF response, overriding the systems operator's MASTER function selector. The AUTO position is selected to prepare the system to respond in the emergency mode in the event of ejection. Automatic IFF emergency response will not occur with the switch in the OFF position, which may be used over territory where the emergency transmission would be considered undesirable.

IFF/SIF OPERATION (SYSTEMS OPERATOR)

1. MASTER function selector—STBY.
2. Position MODE 1 and MODE 3 SIF code dials to desired codes.
    The outer dial selects "tens," the inner dial selects units.
3. I/P switch—OUT.
4. MASTER function selector—NORM, as directed.
5. Rotate MASTER function selector to LOW (partial sensitivity) when requested to do so by properly identified assisting agency.

Note

Low position is utilized for surface tracking when close to the radar facility.

6. Set MODE 2 and MODE 3 buttons as requested.
7. For emergency operation, press dial stop and rotate MASTER function selector to EMERG.
    The IFF will automatically transmit an emergency response when interrogated.

Note

On aircraft not having AVC 170 complied with, the SIF MODE 3 dial must be set to Code 77 to ensure that all FFA SIF-equipped radar sites are aware of the EMERG squawk.

8. To secure the IFF/SIF, rotate MASTER function selector to OFF.

PILOT'S IFF PROCEDURES

1. EMERG IFF switch—AUTO for normal operations (or OFF only if no automatic emergency IFF response is desired for tactical reasons).
2. For "Squawk Flash" or "Ident" requests, hold I/P switch momentarily in I/P as directed, or place I/P switch in MIC and hold the microphone switch in XMIT, as desired.

Note

- On aircraft not having Avionics Bulletin 46 complied with, the I/P function in MODE 3 is not available.
- The MAN position of the EMERG IFF switch overrides any position of the systems operator's MASTER function selector, including OFF.
- Prior to flight with the aft cockpit unoccupied, ensure that the IFF MASTER function selector is positioned to NORM, the MODE 3 button is depressed, the I/P switch (aft cockpit) is at OUT, and the desired IFR or VFR MODE 3 SIF code is selected.

LIGHTING SYSTEMS

EXTERIOR LIGHTS

Exterior lighting equipment consists of wing and tail position lights, low-intensity formation lights, retractable, rotating anticollision lights, a taxi light, and approach lights. Lights and their controls are as follows:

POSITION LIGHTS

Position lights are located on the wing tips and the vertical stabilizer. Controls for the position lights are located on the exterior lighting panel on the pilot's right console.

ANTICOLLISION LIGHTS

Retractable, rotating anticollision lights are installed on the top of the fuselage and on the bottom aft of the systems operator's cockpit. The anticollision lights can be utilized as steady, white fuselage position lights by placing the exterior lights master switch to ON with the anti-collision switch at RETRACT.

TAXI LIGHT

A single taxi light is located on the nose wheel landing gear.

FORMATION LIGHTS

The aircraft is equipped with wing tip and fuselage low-intensity formation lights. The fuselage formation lights are installed aft of each wing trailing edge. The wing tip formation lights are single units with lenses on both the upper and lower surfaces, permitting the lights to be viewed from positions above and below the lead aircraft.

AIR REFUELING REFERENCE LIGHT

An amber air refueling reference light is installed on the underside of the forward fuselage below the pilot's cockpit. This light is controlled by the formation lights switch and is slightly dimmer than the other formation lights except when the air refueling hose is trailed, at which time the light is energized to full brilliance.

FUEL PROBE LIGHT

A retractable light is installed in the upper left nose section forward of the windshield for illumination of the fuel probe. This red-lensed light is controlled by the fuel probe light button and extends and retracts with the probe.

APPROACH LIGHTS

Refer to ANGLE-OF-ATTACK SYSTEM, in this section.

EXTERIOR LIGHTS MASTER SWITCH

The exterior lights master switch (1, figure 1-35) is located on the left console immediately forward of the flap control switch. This toggle switch has ON, OFF, and SIGNAL positions. The exterior lights master switch must be moved from the OFF position before the anticollision or position lights can be illuminated. The purpose of the switch is to enable the pilot to signal for night catapult and to extinguish the exterior lights after a night carrier landing. When the switch is positioned to ON, all position lights will be illuminated if their individual switches are at BRT or DIM and the anticollision light is at RETRACT. When the switch is *held* in the SIGNAL position, it will perform the same function as it does when in the ON position. If one or both of the wing or taillight switches is positioned to BRT or DIM, the corresponding position lights will be illuminated as long as the exterior lights master switch is held in SIGNAL. The taxi light and the approach lights system are not part of the exterior lights master circuit.

Note

At least one of the position light switches must be in the BRT or DIM position for a signal application.

WING AND TAILLIGHT SWITCHES

The function and brightness of the wing and tail position lights are controlled by two selector switches (11, 12, figure 1-35) on the exterior lights control panel.

ANTICOLLISION LIGHTS SWITCH

The anticollision lights switch (14, figure 1-35) controls the retractable anticollision lights through the exterior lights master switch as follows:

MASTER LIGHTS SWITCH POSITION	EXTEND	ANTICOLLISION LIGHTS SWITCH POSITION		
		OFF	RETRACT	
OFF	*	Off	*	
ON	Extend—Rotate	Off	Position Light	
SIGNAL	Extend—Rotate	Off	Position Light	

*Extension, retraction, and illumination power is supplied by the exterior lights master switch. If the anticollision lights are extended and the master switch moved to OFF, the anticollision lights extinguish and remain extended. To ensure retraction in flight, move the anticollision lights switch to RETRACT and hesitate approximately 5 seconds before placing the exterior lights master switch to OFF.

FORMATION LIGHTS SWITCH

A formation lights switch (10, figure 1-35) is installed on the exterior lights control panel. This switch has BRT, DIM, and OFF positions.

FUEL PROBE LIGHT BUTTON

The fuel probe light button (13, figure 1-35) is provided for control of night illumination of the extended air refueling probe. Depressing the button extends and illuminates the light if the probe is extended. Redepressing and releasing the button turns out the light and retracts the assembly.

APPROACH LIGHTS SWITCH

The flashing function of the approach lights and approach indexer may be bypassed for field carrier landing practice or carrier touch-and-go by selecting the T & G position of the approach lights switch (8, figure 1-35), located on the exterior lights control panel.

TAXI LIGHT BUTTON

The taxi light button (9, figure 1-35) is located on the exterior lights panel. During night operations, the taxi light is illuminated by depressing the button and is extinguished by redepressing and releasing the button. If the light is on when the landing gear is retracted, the light will extinguish, and will illuminate on extension if the button is left depressed.

PILOT'S INTERIOR LIGHTS

The following interior cockpit lighting is installed:

1. Right and left console red floodlights.
2. Right and left console white high-altitude lights.
3. Console refractor panels red lights (indirect).
4. Individual red instrument lighting (instrument panel).
5. Indirect red lighting for checkoff lists and stand-by compass.
6. Warning, caution, and advisory lights.
7. Left and right emergency lights.

PILOT'S INTERIOR LIGHTS CONTROLS

FLOODLIGHTS SWITCH

The intensity of console red floodlighting is controlled by the FLOOD switch (4, figure 1-35). On/off selection is made through the CONSOLE lights knob. The FLOOD switch allows BRT, DIM, or MED selection.

INSTRUMENT LIGHTS KNOB

The brightness of individual instrument lights and checkoff lists lights is controlled by the INSTR knob (3, figure 1-35). When the knob is turned clockwise from the OFF position for night operation, the following lights are automatically dimmed: landing gear warning light, hook warning light, compass SYNC and TAKE CMD lights, HSI function lights, LABS light, radar advisory lights, and the master warning and caution indicators.

CONSOLE LIGHTS KNOB

The console lights intensity is controlled by the CONSOLE knob (2, figure 1-35).

HIGH-ALTITUDE LIGHTS SWITCH

The high-altitude lights are selected through the HIGH ALT switch (7, figure 1-35).

CHECK LISTS AND STAND-BY COMPASS BUTTON

Lighting of the take-off and landing check lists and stand-by compass is controlled through the CHECK LIST & STBY COMPASS button (6, figure 1-35). The check lists lights intensity is dependent upon CONSOLE knob position.

WARNING LIGHTS TEST BUTTON

The WARN LT TEST button (5, figure 1-35) provides an operational check of all cockpit caution, warning, and advisory indicators.

EMERGENCY LIGHT

The cockpit emergency light (4, figure 1-4A) provides mobile utility or emergency white or red light. Illumination and brightness is controlled by a rheostat on the back of the light. A small button, located on the rheostat, provides momentary full bright intensity. The lens at the front of the light may be rotated to provide four light patterns: white spot, white flood, red spot, and red flood. This light is provided by the essential a-c bus and may be operated with power supplied by the RAT-driven emergency unit.

SYSTEMS OPERATOR'S INTERIOR LIGHTS

The system's operator's cockpit is equipped with the following interior lights:

1. White incandescent compartment lighting.
2. Warning, caution, and advisory lights.
3. Red floodlights.

SYSTEMS OPERATOR'S INTERIOR LIGHTS CONTROLS

COMPARTMENT LIGHTS KNOB

Brightness of the white incandescent compartment lights is controlled through the COMPARTMENT lights knob (16, figure 1-35).

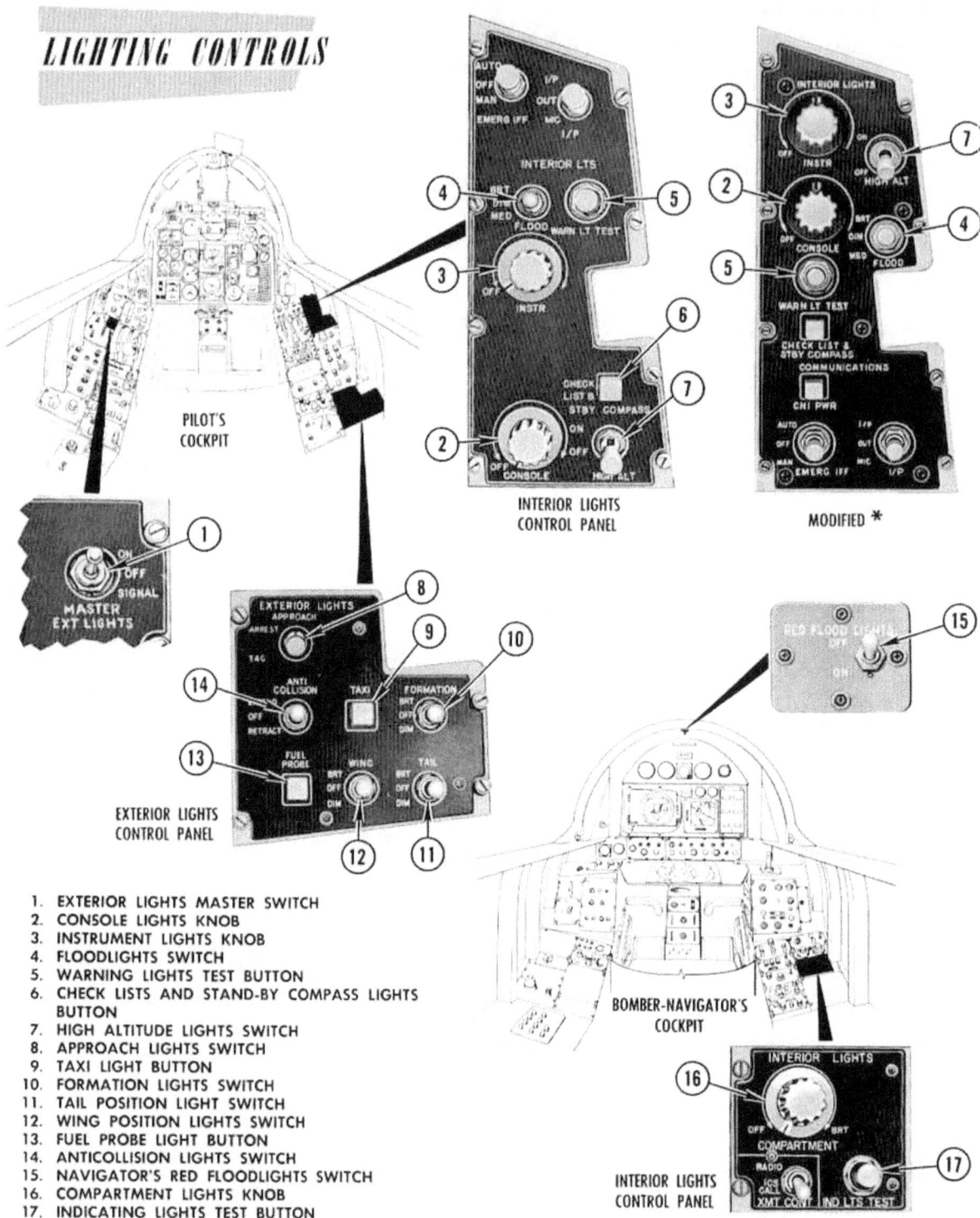

Figure 1-35

RED FLOODLIGHTS SWITCH

The red floodlights are controlled by a switch (15, figure 1-35) on the fairing above the systems operator's instrument panel.

INDICATING LIGHTS TEST BUTTON

The indicating lights test button (17, figure 1-35) operationally tests all aft cockpit warning, caution, and advisory lights.

MISCELLANEOUS LIGHTING

Interior lighting of the bomb bay is provided by four dome lights. The electronics compartment is lighted by a single floodlight. These lights are controlled by the BOMB BAY LTS switch, located on the external power access panel. See figure 1-40.

WARNING, CAUTION, AND ADVISORY INDICATORS

The warning, caution, and advisory indicator system consists of yellow caution indicators, red warning indicators, and green and yellow advisory lights. All indicators are automatically dimmed when the instrument lights are turned on for night operations. The warning and caution indicators are of a flip-shutter design, appearing black until energized.

WARNING INDICATORS

The red FIRE #1 ENG and FIRE #2 ENG warning indicators are installed on the upper left portion of the pilot's instrument panel (figure 1-4). The red OXYGEN warning indicator is located on the upper right of the instrument panel. Single FIRE and OXYGEN warning lights are installed on the system's operator's instrument panel. Three additional warning indicators are installed on the pilot's instrument panel: the WHEELS warning indicator, the illuminated landing gear handle, and the hook handle-mounted warning light.

CAUTION INDICATORS

A bank of yellow caution indicators is installed on the lower right portion of the pilot's instrument panel (figure 1-4). A single caution light (CANOPY) is installed on the systems operator's instrument panel.

MASTER WARNING AND MASTER CAUTION INDICATORS

A master warning and a master caution indicator are installed under the instrument panel shroud in the pilot's cockpit. These barber-poled, rotating lights are designed to draw the pilot's attention to a warning or caution indicator which might otherwise be missed. The master warning and caution indicators are turned off by depressing and releasing the face of the light assemblies.

Note

- On aircraft having ASC 81 complied with, the potential brightness of the master warning and caution indicators is reduced by moving the INSTR lights knob from OFF.
- The master warning indicator is *not* energized by the landing gear handle or hook handle warning light circuits. The master warning indicator is energized by the FIRE #1 ENG, FIRE #2 ENG, OXYGEN, and WHEELS warning indicators only.

ADVISORY LIGHTS

Yellow and green advisory lights are installed on the consoles in both cockpits and on the pilot's center pedestal. The console-mounted advisory lights indicate the operational status and cockpit in command of the various communications and navigation equipment.

WARNING LIGHTS TEST BUTTONS

A warning lights test button is installed on the right console in each cockpit. The crew members can depress their respective buttons to test operation of the indicating lights. In addition to testing the lights, depressing these buttons also provides functional checks of the fire warning system, armament indicating circuits, and the CNI emergency power indicator.

INSTRUMENTS

A standard group of pitot-static instruments is provided: airspeed/Mach indicator, counter-pointer altimeter, and vertical speed indicators. The pitot-static system receives ram and static pressure through the radome-mounted pitot boom. The pitot-static instruments, the inlet control, pitch augmentation, and autoflight systems, the yaw damper, and the bomb directing set receive corrected static pressure input from a pressure compensator in the air data computer. This corrected static pressure feature may be disabled by the pilot in the event of a suspected malfunction in the air data computer. In addition to the pitot-static group, other flight instruments include an all-attitude indicator, an angle-of-attack indicator, an accelerometer, a turn-and-bank indicator, and a stand-by attitude indicator for use in the event of failure of the all-attitude indicator. The pilot's navigation instruments include a horizontal situation indicator (HSI), a stand-by magnetic compass, and a clock. The systems operator's cockpit is provided with an azimuth and range indicator, a clock, wind speed and direction and true airspeed/ground speed indicators. Engine instruments and other system indicators are described with their applicable systems in this section.

AIR DATA COMPUTER

The air data computer is an analog device which receives static and pitot pressures from the pitot-static boom, indicated angle of attack from the airstream direction detector (right forward fuselage), and total temperature from a probe mounted in the right inlet duct. An electrical output of altitude is provided to the inlet duct control system and flight control augmentation systems. A pneumatic output of altitude is provided for the pilot's altimeter, airspeed, Mach, and vertical speed indicators. Mach number is computed from the ratio of static and pitot pressures, and electrical outputs are provided for pitch augmentation, inlet duct and autoflight control systems. Electrical outputs of altitude which can be corrected for local atmospheric pressure variation from standard conditions are supplied to the bomb directing set and displayed in the systems operator's cockpit. The correction is made by the systems operator's setting in known terrain elevation and selecting the BARO CAL mode, which uses the radar altimeter. True airspeed is computed from Mach number and total temperature, and electircal outputs are provided to the bomb directing set and flight reference set and displayed in the systems operator's cockpit. True angle of attack is computed from indicated angle of attack and Mach number, and electrical outputs are provided to the AN/ASB-12 radar antenna (in the alpha AUTO mode of terrain avoidance) and to the bombing computer. Normal velocity is computed from TAS and true angle of attack for the bombing computer.

STATIC PRESSURE COMPENSATOR (SPC)

Indicated static pressure is corrected for position error by a static pressure compensator (pneumatic generator) in the air data computer. The output pressure, controlled by Mach number, is supplied to the pilot's flight instruments (airspeed, altitude, and vertical speed) and is converted to electrical outputs which are provided for the pitch augmentation inlet duct and autoflight control systems.

SPC BUTTON

Depressing the SPC button (5, figure 1-3) routes the output of the SPC to the instruments. Subsequently depressing (releasing) the button (away from the panel) routes indicated static pressure from the pitot-static boom directly to the instruments and to the altitude computing portions of the ADC. The resulting display will be lower than actual altitude and airspeed. See figure 11-5 of the Supplemental NATOPS Flight Manual (NAVWEPS 01-60ABA-1A). The SPC button will have no effect on the true airspeed display in the systems operator's cockpit. Some malfunctions of the SPC mechanism which cause erroneous output will initiate a fail-safe condition. In order to attain the next most accurate static pressure, the SPC is automatically bypassed and indicated static pressure is routed to the pilot's pressure-operated instruments and to the altitude computing portions of the air data computer. A barber pole is displayed in the systems operator's radar/barometric altimeter when operating in the BARO mode. Because some inert failures cannot be detected by this fail-safe feature, cockpit control is provided.

Note

The error which can be introduced by the SPC is nearly equal to the amount of error present at landing touchdown speeds. Because of this, and due to the possibility of a failure at a critical time, it is recommended that the SPC be turned off for landings.

CAUTION

With the SPC turned off during a catapult launch, rate of descent and loss of altitude may be indicated on the cockpit instruments as a transient condition, due to increased position error in the airspeed system as airspeed increases, and due to longitudinal acceleration affecting the air pressure in the pitot-static line.

ALL-ATTITUDE INDICATOR

The all-attitude indicator (figure 1-36) is an electrically operated servodriven instrument which displays aircraft attitude and heading 360 degrees about all axes. Basically, the indicator consists of a $3\frac{3}{4}$-inch sphere suspended in a sealed case. The sphere is capable of unrestricted movement around three axes, representing the relative movement of the earth and sky as viewed from the cockpit. A trim knob in the lower right-hand corner of the instrument rotates the sphere for change in zero pitch reference. Aircraft roll while in a vertical pitch attitude results in a heading change indication. Pitch angle reference marks are placed at 30 and 60 degrees above the horizon line, on each vertical heading reference line. The heading numerals are inverted during inverted flight. A vertical pointer is provided which indicates errors in lateral steering for the NAV or BOMB modes of the bomb directing set. The pointer indicates linear steering error left or right of the true run-in course. The pointer also provides roll/yaw deviation error during alternate LABS pull-ups. The vertical indices are equivalent to 5 degrees from the true run-in course. The indicator receives power through its own amplifier from the essential a-c bus. A red "OFF" flag becomes visible at the lower left of the sphere when the indicator is not receiving normal power or has sustained internal power supply failure. In addition, the horizon sphere may roll to an extreme angle.

CAUTION

Should the "OFF" flag of the all-attitude indicator appear in flight, the instrument is *immediately* unreliable. If necessary, refer to the stand-by attitude indicator on the instrument panel.

During flight under instrument conditions, a periodic cross-check between the all-attitude indicator and the

ALL-ATTITUDE INDICATOR

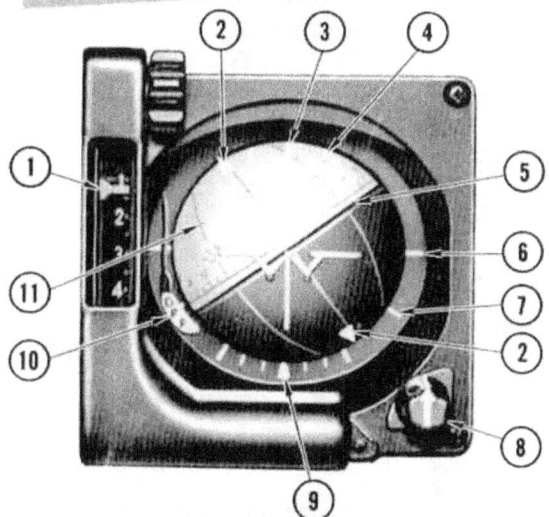

1. LABS "G"-PROGRAMMER (REFER TO NATOPS SUPPLEMENTAL FLIGHT MANUAL)
2. ROLL POINTER
3. LATERAL STEERING AND ROLL-YAW POINTER
4. 5-DEGREE STEERING MARKS
5. HORIZON LINE AND HEADING SCALE
6. 90-DEGREE BANK MARKER
7. 60-DEGREE BANK MARKER
8. PITCH TRIM KNOB
9. BANK SCALE (0, 10, 20, 30 DEGREES)
10. OFF FLAG
11. PITCH REFERENCE MARKS (30 DEGREES)

Figure 1-36

stand-by attitude indicator is recommended. Maneuvering flight with airspeed changes of 35 knots or more can cause the flight reference gyro platform to erect to a false vertical component. This causes the all-attitude indicator to display erroneous wing-down indications of up to 10 degrees. Under normal flight conditions, the gyro platform corrects transient wing-down indications at a rate of approximately 5 degrees per minute.

G-PROGRAMMER

A G-programmer is mounted on the left side of the instrument bezel of the all-attitude indicator. This indicator is used during loft or toss bombing maneuvers. The desired "g" index may be alined with the horizon bar of the all-attitude indicator by means of a knob at the top of the instrument. Upon activation by the pull-up signal from the bomb directing set, weapon initiation trigger, or LABS timer, a motor-driven pointer moves down scale at a predetermined rate. During manual pull-ups, keeping the pointer alined with the moving reference pointer by steadily increasing control stick back pressure assures proper entry into the weapon delivery maneuver. The programmer is inoperative when the autoflight control system is engaged.

STAND-BY ATTITUDE INDICATOR

A stand-by attitude indicator (16, figure 1-4) is provided for the pilot's emergency use in case of malfunction of the flight reference set or the all-attitude indicator. The indicator is electrically operated and will permit rolls and loops without tumbling the gyro. If a malfunction occurs as a result of a power failure, a warning flag becomes visible, indicating "OFF." When not in use, the indicator face is obscured from view by a spring-loaded cover.

AIRSPEED/MACH INDICATOR

The airspeed/Mach indicator (43, figure 1-4) is a pressure-operated instrument which presents calibrated Mach number and airspeed in knots to the pilot. The instrument receives total pressure from the pitot-static boom and true static pressure from the air data computer. Should the static pressure compensator fail, or if the SPC button is released to the off position because of unreliable airspeed or altitude instrument readings, the indications will read IAS, indicated Mach, and indicated altitude (with no correction for static pressure system error). The instrument provides indicated airspeed readings from 80 to 850 knots on a fixed dial and from 0.4 to 2.5 Mach on a moving scale.

INLET AIR TEMPERATURE INDICATOR

An inlet air temperature indicator (4, figure 1-24) is installed on the pilot's right forward console. This indicator (−70° to 150°C) presents the free air stream total temperature, measured at the engine inlet duct. This temperature can be used to determine ambient air temperature effects on flight performance by considering aircraft Mach number. Refer to Section XI, of the Supplemental NATOPS Flight Manual (NAVWEPS 01-60ABA-1A).

ANGLE-OF-ATTACK SYSTEM

The angle-of-attack system consists of an airstream direction detector and an angle-of-attack indicator which controls the approach lights on the nose landing gear and the pilot's approach indexer. Refer to APPROACH LIGHTS, in this section. The airstream direction detector is located on the right side of the fuselage, forward of the right intake duct. The detector alines with the direction of the local air stream and sends a resultant signal voltage to the angle-of-attack indicator. The detector probe is electrically heated through the pitot anti-ice circuit.

ANGLE-OF-ATTACK INDICATOR

The angle-of-attack indicator (44, figure 1-4) displays aircraft local angle of attack as sensed by the airstream direction detector. This indicator operates whenever d-c electrical power is available (d-c converter operating), and requires no control initiation by the pilot. The face of the indicator is adjusted to place the nominal approach angle of attack (13½ units) under an index at the 3-o'clock position. An "OFF" flag, located near the center

Section I
Part 2

NAVWEPS 01-60ABA-1

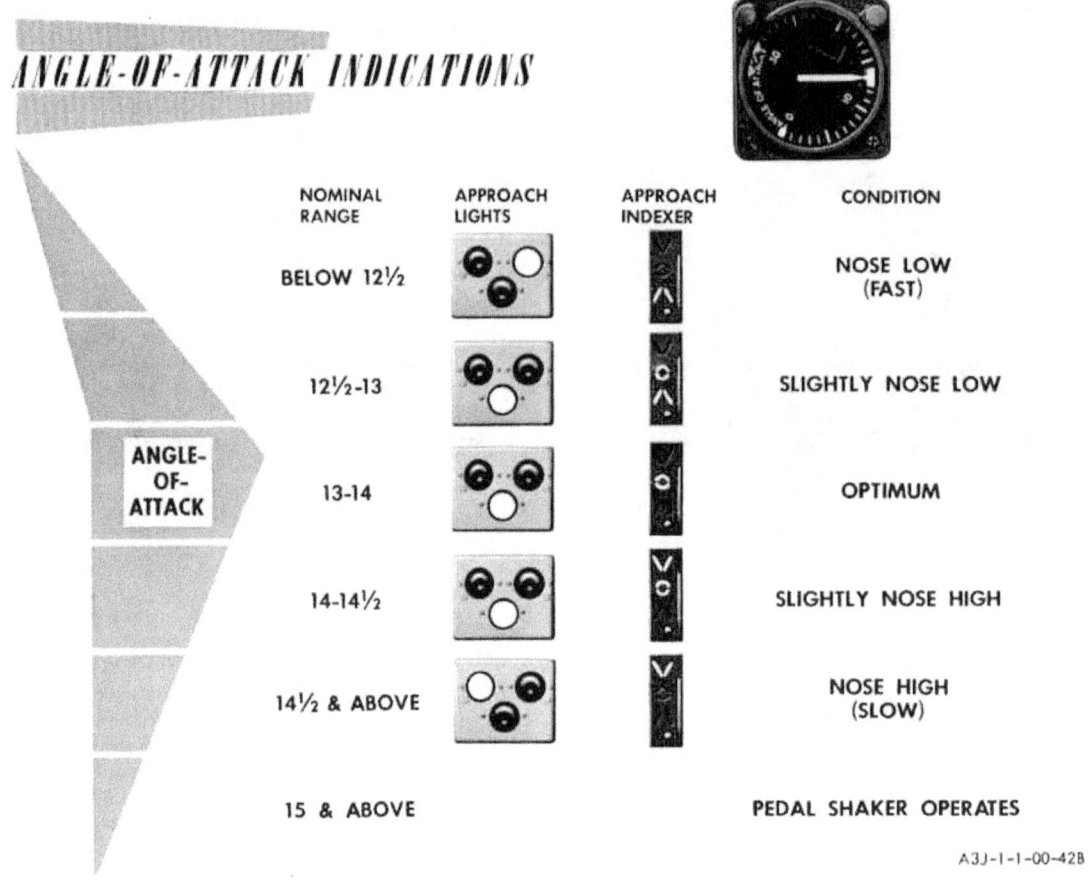

Figure 1-37

of the indicator, appears in the event of failure. In the event of failure or when not powered, the indicator pointer may rest at any point on the dial. A system of cam-operated switches within the indicator operates the approach lights and approach indexer.

APPROACH INDEXER

The approach light system is supplemented in the pilot's cockpit by the approach indexer (figure 1-37). The indexer is illuminated under the same conditions as the approach lights, since operation is also controlled by the position of the landing gear and arresting hook. The indexer is also controlled by the hook bypass relay and will flash if the landing gear is locked down and the hook is up or unlocked (with the approach lights switch in ARREST). The red-lighted approach indexer is located on the instrument panel shroud and is a visual aid to the pilot in determining the optimum landing approach attitude. A press-to-test button and a mechanical dimmer controlled by a knurled wheel are incorporated. The wheel may be rotated upward to provide dimming, as desired, through rotation of polaroid lenses on each indexer lamp. No control action is required from the pilot to utilize the approach light and approach indexer systems. For indications of the angle-of-attack system, see figure 1-37.

APPROACH LIGHTS

The approach lights, installed on the nose gear strut, aid the Landing Signal Officer in determining aircraft landing approach attitude. These lights signify fast (red), "Roger" (amber), and slow (green) approach attitudes, respectively, as viewed by the landing signal officer. The approach light system is automatic. It is activated when the landing gear is down and locked and is controlled by the angle-of-attack indicator. Refer to ANGLE-OF-ATTACK INDICATOR, in this section. When the landing gear and arresting hook are down, the applicable approach light is on "steady." If the landing gear is down and the hook is retracted, the applicable approach light is on "steady" or flashing, as controlled by the approach lights switch. The approach light system is dimmed for night operations by placing the exterior lights master switch to ON. The approach lights are extinguished when the weight of the aircraft compresses the landing gear struts.

GYROCOMPASS SYSTEM

The flight reference set, AN/ASN-26, provides precision heading information regardless of aircraft geographic latitude and flight attitude. Three modes of compass operation are available to the crew members in each cockpit. The normal mode of compass operation is designated the SLAVED mode and provides a gyro-stabilized magnetic heading indication. An alternate mode of operation is the directional gyro (DG) mode which is used during operation in high latitudes, bomb directing set stand-by navigation mode, and failure of the SLAVED mode. For emergency compass operation, a magnetic induction compass reference is used and is designated the compass (COMP) mode.

COMMAND BUTTONS

The compass control panels are equipped with a TAKE CMD (take command) button (2, figure 1-38). Either crew member can take command of the compass system by momentarily depressing the TAKE CMD button. Command of the system is indicated by steady illumination of a dimmable green light within the button.

HEMISPHERE SWITCH

The hemisphere switch (5, figure 1-38) provides controlled reversal of the correction voltages from the ground speed and latitude dials for the hemisphere (north or south) in which flight is being conducted.

MODE SELECTOR

The compass mode selector (7, figure 1-38) is used to select compass modes of operation. Three modes of operation are available: DG (directional gyro), SLAVED, and COMP (compass).

SYNCHRONIZING BUTTON

The SYNC button (4, figure 1-38) activates a fast servo loop which overrides the normal compass slaving rate of 2 degrees per minute, thus providing synchronization of heading presentation with magnetic heading in 10 seconds maximum during SLAVED mode operation. Synchronization is accomplished automatically on initial turn-on or reselection of the SLAVED mode, but may be initiated as desired by depressing the button momentarily. An amber light, which may be dimmed for night operation, is incorporated within the button. During synchronization, the light should come on, indicating continuity of electrical power to the fast slave servo. The annunciator needle should center and the SYNC button indicator light should extinguish when synchronization is achieved.

Note

The SYNC light illuminates momentarily when compass mode is changed.

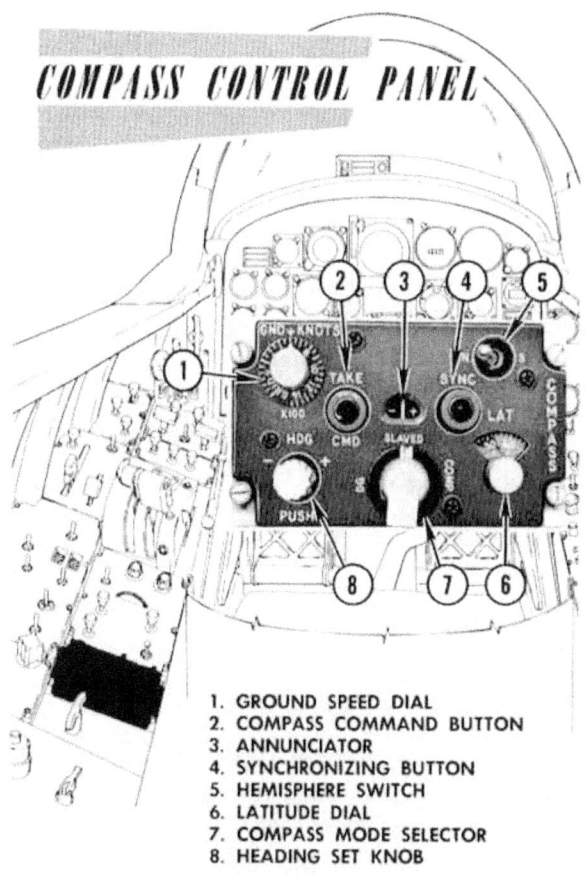

COMPASS CONTROL PANEL

1. GROUND SPEED DIAL
2. COMPASS COMMAND BUTTON
3. ANNUNCIATOR
4. SYNCHRONIZING BUTTON
5. HEMISPHERE SWITCH
6. LATITUDE DIAL
7. COMPASS MODE SELECTOR
8. HEADING SET KNOB

A3J-1-1-71-4B

Figure 1-38

GROUND SPEED DIAL

The ground speed dial (1, figure 1-38) introduces the proper correction for system drift caused by the east-west component of aircraft velocity, and accurate settings are required only in the DG mode. When operating the AN/ASB-12 bomb directing set in STBY-NAV mode, DG should be selected and the ground speed dial used to set in proper compass drift rate correction.

LATITUDE DIAL

The LAT dial (6, figure 1-38) is used to manually set known flight latitude to the heading compensator, in conjunction with ground speed, when operating in the DG mode, such as during AN/ASB-12 STBY-NAV operation. The LAT dial should be manually adjusted upon each 5-degree change of latitude in DG mode.

ANNUNCIATOR

The annunciator (3, figure 1-38) provides visual indication of the error in synchronization existing between the signals from the magnetic induction compass transmitter and the gyro-stabilized platform (directional gyro) heading indication. With the annunciator indicating minus or plus, the heading indications of all instruments are in corresponding error in the SLAVED mode.

HEADING SET KNOB

The heading set knob (8, figure 1-38) is used, in conjunction with the DG and SLAVED modes of compass operation, to manually synchronize heading signals from the induction compass transmitter and the gyro-stabilized platform. The heading set knob is provided for manually changing, left or right, the heading indications of the all-attitude indicator, the azimuth and range indicator, and the magnetic heading pointer of the course deviation indicator. Synchronization is achieved by turning the knob left or right (— and + directions) until the annunciator needle is centered.

ALL-ATTITUDE INDICATOR

Aircraft heading is displayed by the sphere of the AAI in all modes of compass system operation. Refer to INSTRUMENTS and see figure 1-36, in this section.

HORIZONTAL SITUATION INDICATOR

The compass ring of the HSI (figure 1-34) is driven by the compass system in all modes of operation.

Note

Heading indications of the AAI, HSI, and the aft cockpit azimuth and range indicator should agree at all times.

COMPASS SYSTEM OPERATION

Compass components of the flight reference set receive electrical power when external power is applied or when the engine-driven generators are producing proper voltage. In the event that one or both engine-driven generators fail, the compass system is fully operational with electrical power from one generator or from the ram-air turbine. On initial application of electrical power, the compass control in the forward cockpit is in command of the compass system. It is recommended that before command is transferred, the crew member taking command select compass mode to coincide with the control presently in command.

SLAVED (NORMAL)

The SLAVED mode is normally used during all flights at latitudes where magnetic induction compass sensing is reliable. In this mode, signals from the flight reference set gyro-stabilized platform and the induction compass transmitter are integrated in the heading compensator. Heading compensator output is then fed to the AAI, HSI, and the aft cockpit azimuth and range indicator. Should gyro heading differ from magnetic, as will normally be the case when selecting the SLAVED mode, the control will synchronize the AAI sphere and the azimuth and range indicator to aircraft magnetic heading at the rate of approximately 18 degrees per second. Should this "fast slaving" be desired, the crew member in command of the compass system may depress his SYNC button momentarily and observe the annunciator and the amber light within the button. When synchronization is accomplished, the annunciator needle will be centered between the minus and plus signs and the amber light will be extinguished.

1. After the AAI erects, check that the compass mode selector is in the SLAVED position.
2. Check the annunciator needle and depress the synchronizing button if the needle is not centered.

Note

- Do not depress the SYNC button until the wings are spread and locked.
- Synchronization should NOT be attempted during turns or radical maneuvers, or in conditions of extreme turbulence. Erratic indications may result from the turn and acceleration errors may be imposed upon the magnetic induction compass transmitter.
- The synchronizing button should not be *held* down, as the fast slave circuit is operated by a thermal time-delay relay. Slaving synchronization should be achieved within 10 seconds after the button is momentarily depressed.

DG (ALTERNATE)

If the compass SLAVED mode fails to operate properly during STBY-NAV mode operation of the AN/ASB-12 bomb directing set, the DG mode should be selected. In addition, at high latitudes (usually above 60 degrees) where magnetic heading is unreliable, the output of the magnetic induction compass transmitter should be cut out by selecting the DG mode. In this mode, the flight reference gyro alone transmits electrical signals through the heading compensator to the heading indicating instruments. Automatic correction for apparent drift and east-west ground speed is accomplished by adjusting the ground speed dial for each major speed change and adjusting the LAT dial upon each 5 degrees of change in latitude.

1. Compass mode selector—DG.
2. Hemisphere switch—as applicable.
3. LAT dial—local.
4. When established at stabilized climb, cruise, or descent ground speeds, set computed ground speed into the ground speed dial.
   Average ground speed settings may be desired during climbs and descents.
5. Correct heading indication with the heading set knob as desired.

Note

- The SYNC button should not be used in the DG or COMP modes at it will have no effect. The heading set knob should be used in DG mode.
- A manual/doppler (MAN/DOP) toggle switch is installed on some compass control panels. Set the MAN/DOP switch to MAN for all operating modes.

COMP (EMERGENCY)

The COMP mode of operation is used in the event of malfunction of both the SLAVED and DG modes. Selection of the COMP mode utilizes the unstabilized signal of the magnetic induction compass transmitter. The heading presentation is that of a basic earth inductor compass and is provided for use as a stand-by system.

1. Ensure adequate electrical power is available.
2. Compass mode selector—COMP.
3. Observe unstabilized magnetic heading.
4. Periodically cross-reference the stand-by magnetic compass.

CAUTION

The COMP mode of operation should only be used in the event of component damage or malfunction. The COMP mode is subject to turning and acceleration errors associated with all induction compass transmitters and magnetic compasses, and is also affected by local magnetic variations. During operation in the COMP mode, it is recommended that 20 degrees of bank angle not be exceeded if minimum turn error is desired.

STAND-BY MAGNETIC COMPASS

A common Air Path stand-by magnetic compass is installed with the sunvisor on the canopy bow.

RADAR ALTIMETER

The radar altimeter, which is part of the electronic altimeter set, AN/APN-120, furnishes accurate altitude calibration data to the air data computer for correction of barometric altitude factor used by the bomb directing set. In addition, the set furnishes precision height-above-terrain data from terrain level to 75,000 feet to the crew members. The set consists of two independent sections: a low system and a high system, operating from a common power supply.

Note

Accurate radar altimeter indication is dependent upon level aircraft attitude.

HIGH-ALTITUDE SYSTEM (SYSTEMS OPERATOR)

The high-altitude system measures aircraft altitude from 500 to approximately 75,000 feet, within pitch and bank attitude limits of approximately 30 degrees. A signal from the high-altitude system is transmitted to the system operator's radar/barometric altimeter when the radar mode of operation is selected. The high system operates on the pulse propagation principle at a frequency of 4225 megacycles. Time relay between pulse transmission and reception is converted into aircraft altitude above the terrain. Below 500 feet, the high system switches to input from the low-altitude system. The high system continues to transmit, but all signals are generated by the FM-CW (low) system. Operational tolerance of the high-altitude system (above 500 feet) is ±22 feet.

LOW-ALTITUDE SYSTEM (PILOT)

The low-altitude system measures aircraft height above terrain from ground level to 3000 feet. An automatic turn-on signal from the high system (in RADAR mode) energizes the pilot's low-altitude system below approximately 4000 (+500/−700) feet above the terrain. If the high system is in BARO mode, the barometric altitude shaft of the air data computer causes automatic low system turn-on at approximately 4000 feet ABOVE MEAN SEA LEVEL. The low system utilizes a frequency-modulated, continuous-wave (FM-CW) radio transmission at a frequency of 4300 megacycles, by which the measure of altitude is accomplished through monitoring of frequency differential between transmitted and received signal. In the event automatic turn-on does not occur, as indicated by appearance of the "FAIL" flag when the aircraft is below 3000 feet, the pilot can obtain low system operation through an override button located on the indicator. The LOW ALTITUDE warning light and the systems operator's radar/barometric altimeter are operated by the low system below 500 feet above the ground.

MODE AND CALIBRATION CONTROLS (SYSTEMS OPERATOR)

ALTITUDE MODE KNOB

The systems operator's ALTITUDE mode knob (8, figure 1-39) has four positions: RADAR CAL, RADAR, BARO, and BARO CAL. These positions function as follows:

POSITION	FUNCTION
RADAR CAL (Radar Calibrate)	Used during ground test by maintenance personnel, with an rf energy-absorbing hat under the system antenna, or in flight to determine high system operation and calibration accuracy. Proper operation and calibration is indicated by a 00000 (±22)-foot indication on the systems operator's radar/barometric altimeter.

Note
- Radar calibration at high altitudes is impractical because of the time required to complete the slewing operation.
- Do not select RADAR CAL or leave the altitude mode knob in RADAR while the aircraft is on deck.

RADAR	The electronic altimeter energizes the systems operator's radar/barometric altimeter and the "RDR" mode flag is displayed.

Note
Failure of the high system above 500 feet results in BARO mode operation.

BARO (Barometric)	Corrected barometric altitude is displayed in the systems operator's radar/barometric altimeter and the "BAR" mode flag is displayed. A barber pole is displayed in the systems operator's radar/barometric altimeter if the SPC is OFF or failed.
BARO CAL (Barometric Calibrate)	Selected to correct indicated barometric altitude by correcting the air data computer with radar height plus a pre-flight set-in of calibration point terrain elevation.

Note
In aircraft not having bomb directing set, AN/ASB-12, installed, BARO CAL mode is inoperative.

RADAR ALTIMETER CONTROLS AND INDICATORS

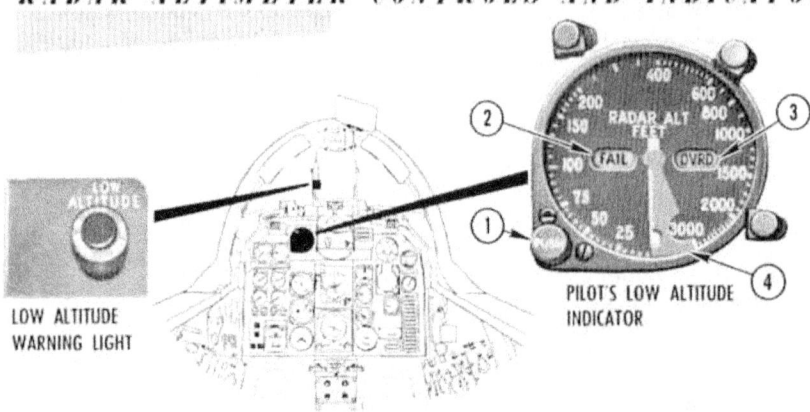

1. LOW ALTITUDE OVERRIDE BUTTON
2. FAIL FLAG
3. OFF/OVRD FLAG
4. POINTER MASK
5. RADAR BAROMETRIC MODE FLAG
6. FAIL FLAG
7. ALTITUDE SET SWITCH
8. ALTITUDE MODE KNOB
9. RANGE AND BEARING KNOB
10. SPEED SELECT SWITCH

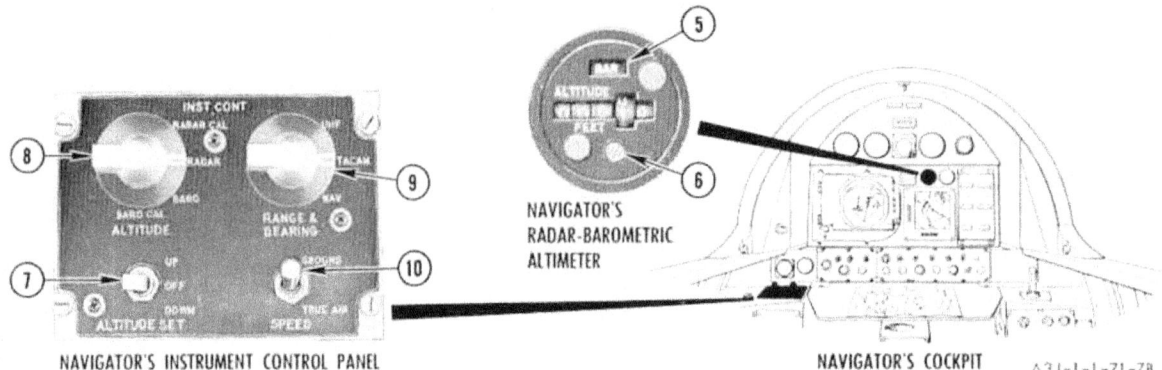

Figure 1-39

ALTITUDE SET SWITCH

The altitude set switch (7, figure 1-39) is used by the navigator to correct the radar/barometric altimeter in the barometric mode. Prior to take-off, desired elevation may be set into the altimeter by moving the switch to UP or DOWN and releasing the switch at the corrected indication.

LOW-ALTITUDE INDICATOR (PILOT)

The low-altitude indicator (figure 1-39) provides an indication of height above terrain from approximately 3000 feet to ground level (ground level, or zero, corresponds to a point 10 feet above the terrain). The indicator face contains a "FAIL" indicating window (2, figure 1-39) and an "OFF/OVRD" (override) indicating window (3, figure 1-39). During normal operation below 3000 feet above the terrain, both windows display a blank (black) space. In the event of low system failure, the "FAIL" flag is displayed and the indicating pointer retreats behind a mask (4, figure 1-39).

OVERRIDE BUTTON

An override push button on the face of indicator (1, figure 1-39) is used to activate the low system transmitter on descent in the event the "OFF" flag fails to disappear automatically at approximately 3300 feet above the ground. When low system transmitter operation is initiated through depressing the button, the "OVRD" flag is displayed. When altitude is regained, the button should again be depressed in order to shut off the low-altitude system and return to automatic operation; otherwise, sensitivity of the navigator's high-altitude system is reduced.

Note

In override mode above 5000 feet, the low-altitude indicator may display a momentary erroneous reading (with a "FAIL" flag showing) of 1500 feet if the navigator shifts from RADAR to the BARO mode. The indicator then returns to the proper reading.

LOW-ALTITUDE WARNING LIGHT

The LOW ALTITUDE warning light is installed on the left side of the PPDI. This red light, used during terrain avoidance, low-altitude flight, illuminates whenever aircraft clearance above the terrain is less than 400 feet. Operation of this light depends on proper function of the low-altitude portion of the electronic altimeter. Refer to TERRAIN AVOIDANCE, in Section I, Part 2, of the Supplemental NATOPS Flight Manual (NAVWEPS 01-60ABA-1A).

HIGH SYSTEM OPERATION (SYSTEMS OPERATOR)

The systems operator's radar/barometric altimeter provides a direct, digital read-out of aircraft height above terrain in feet. Control of the altimeter is the responsibility of the systems operator. Successful bombing missions depend, in part, on accurate altitude information. BARO mode altitude should be monitored during bomb runs, as barometric altitude is a direct input to the bombing computers. It is important to BARO CAL the radar altimeter periodically, so that, should the high system fail, BARO mode altitude information will be accurate. When the high system is disabled (overridden) or failed below 3000 feet, high system information is unreliable in any radar mode.

1. Prior to application of electrical power, move ALTITUDE mode knob to BARO.
   Check indication with known field elevation and correct indication through use of the ALTITUDE SET switch.
2. After take-off, move ALTITUDE mode knob to RADAR CAL.
   Indicator should run to 00000 (± 22) feet.
3. Select RADAR or BARO as desired.

BAROMETRIC CALIBRATION

To calibrate the radar/barometric altimeter and air data computer over a preset checkpoint, proceed as follows:

1. ALTITUDE mode knob—Hold in BARO CAL until the radar/barometric altimeter stabilizes.
   Target elevation displayed on the target altitude indicator will be added to radar altitude.
2. Release ALTITUDE mode knob to BARO, or select RADAR, as desired.

Note

Barometric calibration should always be performed prior to updating the autonavigator TV or cursor correction).

ALTIMETER CALIBRATION (ADDITIONAL CHECKPOINT)

To perform a barometric calibration over a checkpoint other than one previously stored, proceed as follows:

1. SYSTEM MODE knob—TARGET SET.
2. COORD SELECT knob—ALT.

3. Using the cursor control handle, slew known elevation into the target altitude indicator.
4. When over checkpoint, move the ALTITUDE mode knob to BARO CAL and hold until the radar/barometric altimeter stabilizes.
5. COORD SELECT knob—NORMAL.
6. SYSTEM MODE knob—NAV (if desired).
7. ALTITUDE mode knob—BARO or RADAR, as desired.

BAROMETRIC CALIBRATION WITHOUT BOMB DIRECTING SET

To correct barometric altitude indication in aircraft not having a bomb directing set installed, proceed as follows:

1. ALTITUDE mode knob—RADAR.
   Note radar altitude indication.
2. Add indicated value to known checkpoint elevation.
3. ALTITUDE mode knob—BARO.
4. Correct indicator to sum of radar altitude and checkpoint elevation through use of the ALTITUDE SET switch.

LOW SYSTEM OPERATION (PILOT)

Prior to take-off, the indicator should read 0 feet. During climb-out above 3300 feet, the "OFF" and "FAIL" flags appear and the pointer is driven behind the mask. As altitude is decreased to 4000 (+500/−700) feet, the "OFF" flag should disappear. Below 3000 feet, radar altitude is indicated. If the pointer should remain masked and the "OFF" flag is displayed below an estimated 3000 feet above the terrain, depress the override button. Radar altitude is then displayed and the "OVRD" flag is visible.

CAUTION

When penetrating near mountainous terrain, the override button should be depressed departing cruising or holding altitude. This procedure allows the low-altitude system to energize as radar altitude decreases to approximately 4000 feet, regardless of high system mode selection.

Note

The low-altitude system should not be operated continuously in override (with "OVRD" flag displayed) above 4000 (+500/−700) feet above the terrain. Failure of the low system can cause erroneous altitude indications on the systems operator's radar/barometric altimeter.

Section I
Part 2

NAVWEPS 01-60ABA-1

PILOT'S COCKPIT

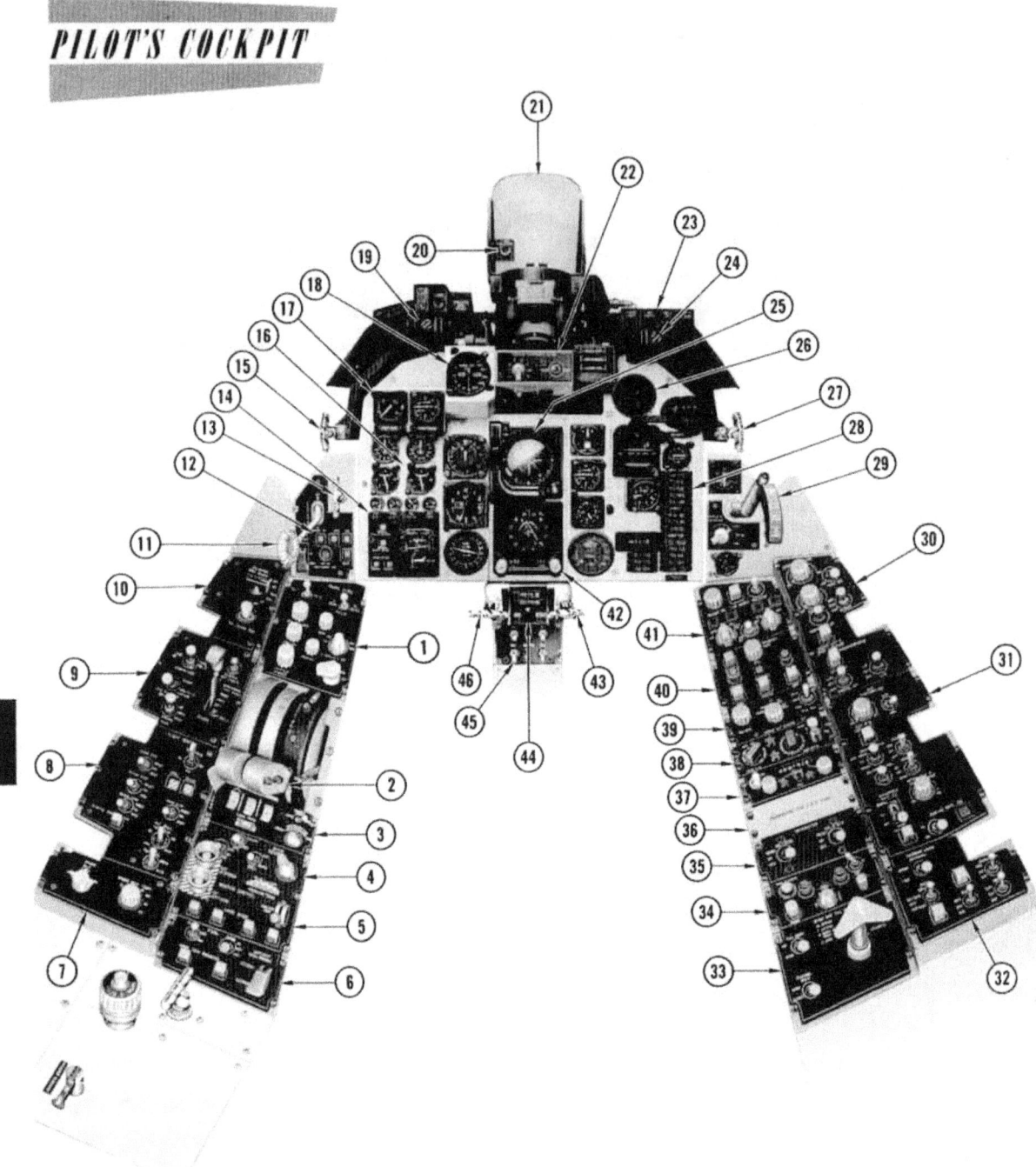

Figure 1-39A (Sheet 1)

1. PILOT'S SCOPE PANEL
2. THROTTLES
3. UHF COMM CONTROL PANEL
4. AUTO-FLIGHT CONTROL PANEL
5. WEAPONS CONTROL PANEL
6. FUEL CONTROLS
7. SUIT CONTROL PANEL
8. FLIGHT CONTROL PANEL
9. FLAP/DROOP CONTROL PANEL
10. FUEL QUANTITY CONTROLS
11. LANDING GEAR HANDLE
12. ARMAMENT INDICATORS
13. FUEL DUMP HANDLE
14. GEAR, SPEEDBRAKE, DROOP, FLAP, AND TRIM INDICATORS
15. EMERGENCY BRAKE HANDLE
16. ENGINE INDICATORS
17. ANGLE OF ATTACK INDICATOR
18. RADAR ALTIMETER (LOW)
19. MASTER WARNING LIGHT
20. RADAR LOW-ALTITUDE WARNING LIGHT
21. PILOT'S PROJECTED DISPLAY INDICATOR
22. T/A ALPHA CONTROL PANEL
23. AFCS INDICATORS
24. MASTER CAUTION LIGHT
25. ALL-ATTITUDE INDICATOR (AAI)
26. ECM INDICATOR
27. CANOPY JETTISON HANDLE
28. CAUTION INDICATORS
29. ARRESTING HOOK HANDLE
30. INTERIOR LIGHTS CONTROL PANEL
31. AIR TEMPERATURE AND ANTI-ICE CONTROL PANEL
32. EXTERIOR LIGHTS CONTROL PANEL
33. WING AND TAIL FOLD CONTROL PANEL
34. COMPASS CONTROL PANEL
35. GENERATOR CONTROL PANEL
36. PROVISIONS FOR T-375 AMAC PANEL
37. TACAN CONTROL PANEL
38. UHF AUXILIARY RECEIVER CONTROL PANEL
39. INTERCOM CONTROL PANEL
40. AUDIO SELECT CONTROLS
41. ECM CONTROL PANEL
42. HORIZONTAL SITUATION INDICATOR (HSI)
43. EMERGENCY LANDING GEAR RELEASE HANDLE
44. RAT RETRACT BUTTON
45. ENGINE START CONTROLS
46. RAT RELEASE HANDLE

A-5A-1-00-2A

Figure 1-39A (Sheet 2)

Section I
Part 2

NAVWEPS 01-60ABA-1

NAVIGATOR'S COCKPIT

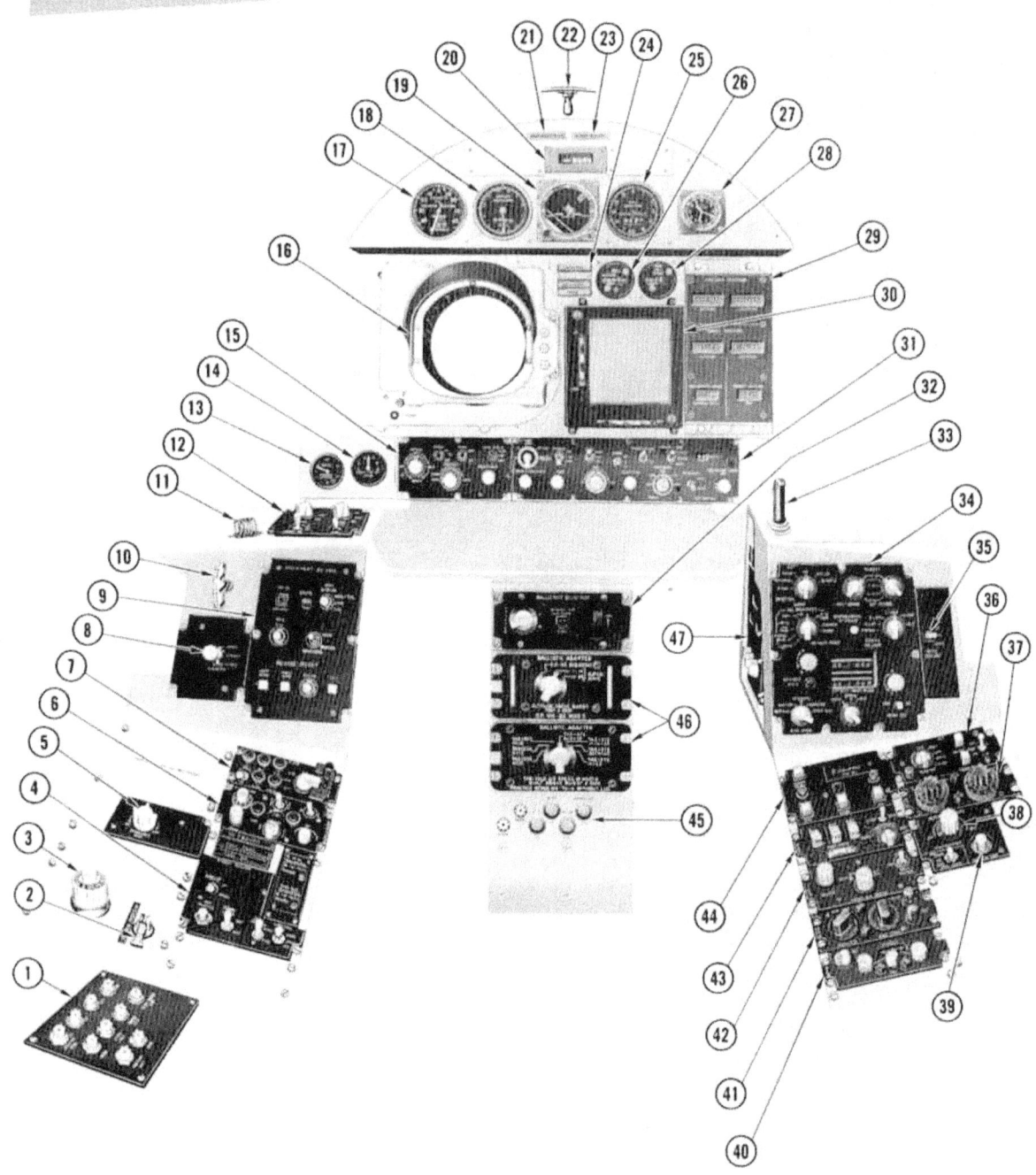

Figure 1-39B (Sheet 1)

1. FUSE PANEL
2. OXYGEN VALVE
3. G-SUIT VALVE
4. BUDDY TANKER PANEL
5. PRESSURE SUIT FLOW KNOB
6. COMPASS CONTROL PANEL
7. T-375 OR AN/AWW-1 PANEL
8. CANOPY TOGGLE
9. ARMAMENT RELEASE PANEL
10. CANOPY JETTISON HANDLE
11. PENCIL HOLDER
12. INSTRUMENT CONTROL PANEL
13. COCKPIT PRESSURE ALTIMETER
14. OXYGEN QUANTITY INDICATOR
15. TV CONTROL PANEL
16. RADAR-TV INDICATOR
17. TV SCAN INDICATOR
18. AZIMUTH AND RANGE INDICATOR
19. ATTITUDE INDICATOR
20. CHANNEL/FREQUENCY INDICATOR
21. ARM MASTER "ON" LIGHT
22. NAVIGATOR'S RED LIGHTS SWITCH
23. BOMB AWAY LIGHT
24. WARNING AND CAUTION LIGHTS
25. WIND SPEED AND DIRECTION INDICATOR
26. RADAR-BAROMETRIC ALTIMETER
27. CLOCK
28. TRUE AIRSPEED/GROUNDSPEED INDICATOR
29. POSITION AND DESTINATION INDICATOR
30. DATA VIEWER
31. RADAR CONTROL PANEL
32. BALLISTICS SELECTOR PANEL
33. CURSOR CONTROL HANDLE
34. BOMBING-NAVIGATION CONTROL PANEL
35. SEAT ADJUST SWITCH
36. IFF CONTROL PANEL
37. SIF CONTROL PANEL
38. INTERIOR LIGHTS CONTROL PANEL
39. INDICATING LIGHTS TEST BUTTON
40. TACAN CONTROL PANEL
41. AUXILIARY RECEIVER PANEL
42. ICS CONTROL PANEL
43. UHF COMMUNICATIONS PANEL
44. AUDIO SELECT PANEL
45. B/N FUSES
46. BALLISTIC ADAPTER MODULES (TYPICAL)
47. ALINEMENT CONTROL PANEL

Figure 1-39B (Sheet 2)

PART 3 — AIRCRAFT SERVICING

Normally, the aircraft will be serviced by qualified maintenance personnel and servicing will not require flight crew supervision. However, navigation flights, diversions, weather alternates, and NATO operations may require the use of various bases. Therefore, the flight crew must have a knowledge of aircraft servicing procedures sufficient to accomplish normal aircraft turn-around-type servicing. Reference to the following procedures and figure 1-40, or the NATOPS Pocket Check List (NAVWEPS 01-60ABA-1B), should be sufficient to ensure proper aircraft servicing by transient maintenance personnel under the supervision of the flight crew.

EXTERNAL POWER AND AIR REQUIREMENTS

The aircraft requires external electrical power, cooling air, and engine starting air.

ELECTRICAL

For ground operation of all buses, external a-c electrical power must be applied. The external power receptacle is located on the left side of the fuselage, forward of the main gear, at access number 74. Electrical power required is 115 volts, 400 cycles, three-phase (A, B, C rotation), ac, 30 kva. Two indicator lights (green) are mounted beside the external power receptacles and will come on when the generators are operating and ready to connect into the system. Although external power can be removed when either of these lights comes on, the disconnect should be delayed until both lights are on. Removal of the external power plug automatically transfers the electrical load to the aircraft electrical power system and extinguishes the generator-out caution indicators on the pilot's instrument panel. Refer to EXTERNAL POWER UNITS, in this section, for a listing of units which provide acceptable a-c power output.

Note

For instructions on the use of USAF electrical power units, refer to General Airframe Bulletin No. 2 dated 22 July 1963.

COOLING AIR

An external cooling air supply is required for ground operation of cooled equipment. The nozzle must be properly connected in the external power receptacle at access number 74 and air temperature must not be excessive. A contact switch in the receptacle deenergizes cooled equipment until a temperature sensor completes the circuit, or until the hose is disconnected. When available, the E7304 conditioned air dump valve should be used when applying external cooling air to ensure properly controlled air at the correct temperature and pressure for operation of electrically powered equipment. If autonavigator alinement procedure has been initiated, care should be taken to disconnect external electrical power prior to removing cooling air. This precludes bomb directing set power interruption and loss of alinement. Desired cooling air requirements are 4.0 psig clear air at 80°F temperature. Refer to EXTERNAL POWER UNITS, in this section, for a listing of usable cooling air units.

ENGINE STARTING AIR

The aircraft engines have an impingement starting system requiring 180 pounds per minute, 75 psia (5:1) airflow. Engine starting air connections are located on the lower left side of each engine at access numbers 109:1 and 155:1. Refer to EXTERNAL POWER UNITS, in this section, for a listing of usable engine starting air units.

POWER UNITS (RCPP-105-1 AND RCPT-105-3)

The RCPP-105-1 power unit is a streamlined, self-contained, air-transportable ground support pod. The RCPT-105-3 power unit is a trailerized, non-air-transportable version of the RCPP-105-1 unit. Internal components include a gas turbine compressor, a 60-kva a-c generator, a turbine refrigeration unit, the required fuel and oil supply, and controls. The pod provides air at 70°F for conditioning use, and engine starting air at 186 pounds per minute, 156.6 in Hg. For ground aircraft systems operation, 60-kva, 400-cycle a-c electrical power is provided. During the engine start cycle, pod-provided cooling airflow is automatically interrupted. The power pod can be carried on either inboard wing station, although it is normally transported on the left since the pod refueling receptacle is located on the left fuselage above the main gear wheel door. The pod can be refueled on the ground from the aircraft supply, either by gravity flow or under pressure from the wing transfer pumps. In emergencies, the pod may be jettisoned by the pilot through use of the external jettison button.

B/N AUXILIARY POWER UNIT

The E7488 B/N auxiliary power unit ("chin package") is a self-contained power unit, designed to be attached to the lower forward fuselage. Internal components include an internal combustion engine, an a-c generator, refrigeration unit, required fuel supply, and necessary equipment for mounting. Its purpose is to provide uninterrupted electrical power and temperature-conditioned air to the bomb directing set for alinement operations prior to take-off and for turnaround missions.

Section I
Part 3

NAVWEPS 01-60ABA-1

SERVICING

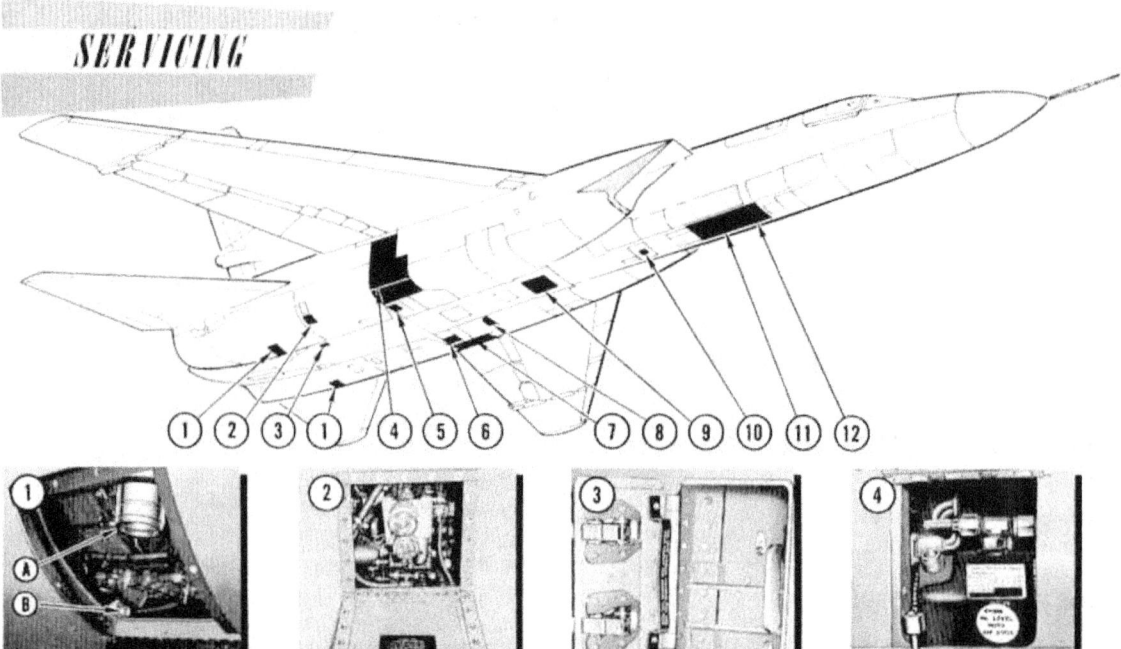

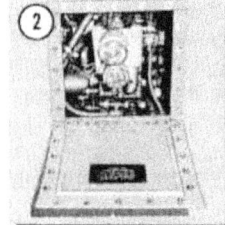

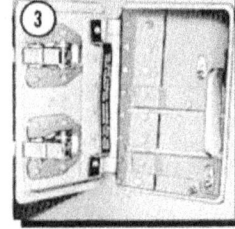

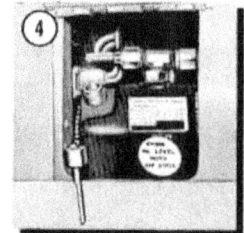

1. GROUND STARTING AIR CONNECTION (RIGHT SIDE SHOWN)
   A. AIR CONNECTION
   B. REMOTE START CUT-OUT ELECTRIC CONNECTOR

2. OIL TANK FILLER ACCESS (ON EACH SIDE)
   TANK CAPACITY
   5.2 GAL EACH

3. MANUAL TAIL FOLD ACCESS DOOR

4. PNEUMATIC COMPRESSOR OIL RESERVOIR

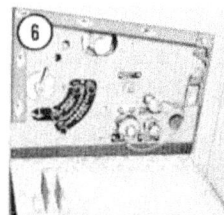

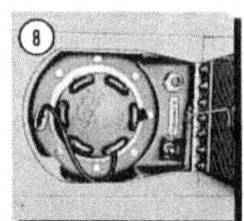

5. PNEUMATIC SYSTEM SERVICE PANEL
   PRECHARGE —
   2800 TO 3200 PSI

6. HYDRAULIC SYSTEMS SERVICE PANEL
   NO. 1 RES — 2.31 GAL
   NO. 2 RES — 5.67 GAL

7. EMERGENCY BRAKE ACCUMULATOR SERVICE PANEL (LEFT GEAR WELL)
   PRECHARGE — 1000 PSI

8. AFT GROUND REFUELING RECEPTACLE
   (SUMP, AFT AND BOMB BAY TANKS ONLY)

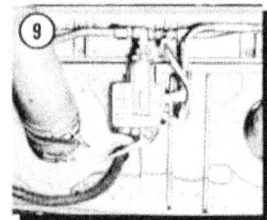

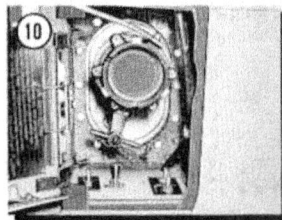

9. MANUAL WING FOLD VALVE

10. FORWARD (SINGLE-POINT) REFUELING RECEPTACLE

11. LIQUID OXYGEN SERVICE
    10 LITERS EACH CONVERTER

A3J-1-1-00-9L

Figure 1-40 (Sheet 1)

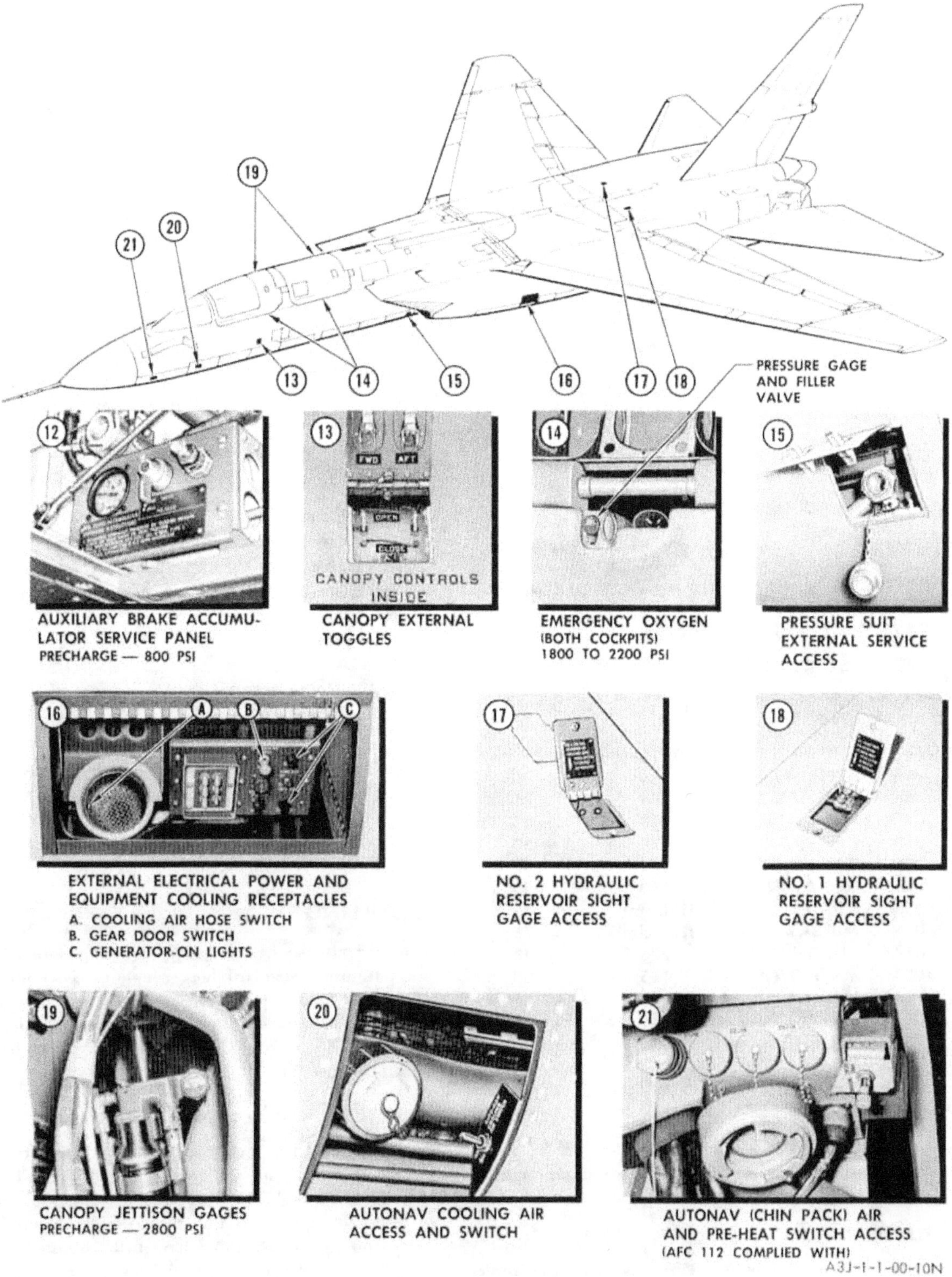

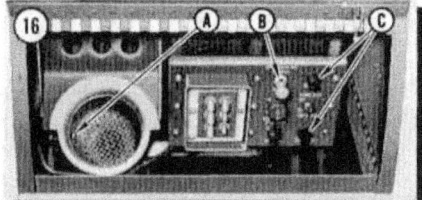

19
20
21
13
14
15
16
17
18
PRESSURE GAGE AND FILLER VALVE
12
AUXILIARY BRAKE ACCUMULATOR SERVICE PANEL
PRECHARGE — 800 PSI
13
FWD
AFT
OPEN
CLOSE
CANOPY CONTROLS INSIDE
CANOPY EXTERNAL TOGGLES
14
EMERGENCY OXYGEN
(BOTH COCKPITS)
1800 TO 2200 PSI
15
PRESSURE SUIT EXTERNAL SERVICE ACCESS
16
A
B
C
EXTERNAL ELECTRICAL POWER AND EQUIPMENT COOLING RECEPTACLES
A. COOLING AIR HOSE SWITCH
B. GEAR DOOR SWITCH
C. GENERATOR-ON LIGHTS
17
NO. 2 HYDRAULIC RESERVOIR SIGHT GAGE ACCESS
18
NO. 1 HYDRAULIC RESERVOIR SIGHT GAGE ACCESS
19
CANOPY JETTISON GAGES
PRECHARGE — 2800 PSI
20
AUTONAV COOLING AIR ACCESS AND SWITCH
21
AUTONAV (CHIN PACK) AIR AND PRE-HEAT SWITCH ACCESS
(AFC 112 COMPLIED WITH)
A3J-1-1-00-10N

Figure 1-40 (Sheet 2)

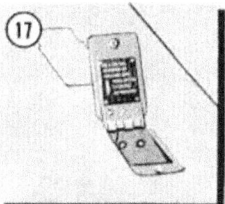

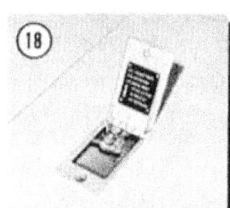

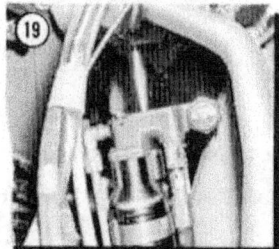

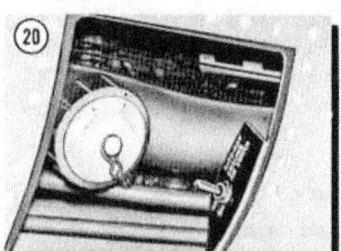

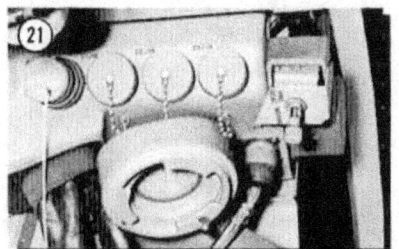

MILITARY SPECIFICATIONS

The following materials are required to service the aircraft:

MATERIALS	MILITARY SPECIFICATION
Fuel	
Primary—JP-5	MIL-J-5624 (NATO F-44)
Alternate—JP-4	MIL-J-5624 (NATO F-40)
Emergency—AVGAS	MIL-G-5572 (NATO F-22)
—Jet A	AVTUR 40 (NATO F-30)
—Jet A-1	AVTUR 50 (NATO F-34)
Hydraulic Fluid (red)	MIL-H-5606 (NATO H-515)
Engine Oil	
Primary	MIL-L-23699 (Wep)
Cold Alternate	MIL-L-7808 (NATO O-148)
Lubricating Oil	MIL-L-6085 (NATO O-147)
Dry Nitrogen	MIL-N-6011 (BBN-411A) Type I
Oxygen	
Gaseous (high pressure)	MIL-O-21749 (Wep), Type I
Liquid	MIL-O-21749 (Wep), Type II
	MIL-O-27210 (USAF)

EXTERNAL POWER UNITS

ENGINE STARTING AIR

Airflow required for normal start is 180 pounds per minute, 75 psia.

SERVICE	UNIT	POUNDS PER MINUTE	OUTPUT (PSIA)
USN	RCPP-105-1	186	75
USN	RCPT-105-3	186	75
USN	GTC-85-15*	110	50
USN	GTC-85-24*	120	50
USN	GTC-85-28*	122	52
USN	GTC-85-72†	150	50
USN	MA-1E*	(120 cfm)	45
USN	MD-3A†	(180 cfm)	75
USAF	CTC-0-105-2	236	78
USAF	MA-1 GTC*	115	50
USAF	MA-1A*	82	45
USAF	MA-2†	150	65
USAF	502-7D (Boeing)†	182	53
USAF	MA-1MP*	117	40
USAF	MA-2MP*	110	45
USAF	MA-3MP†	150	60

*Acceptable with two units Y-connected

†For alternate start, modulate throttle to maintain EGT less than 700°C

ELECTRICAL

Electrical power required is 115 volts, 400 cycles, three-phase (A, B, C rotation), ac, 30 kva, four-wire.

USN UNITS	USAF UNITS
RCPP-105-1	AF/M32A-10
RCPT-105-3	B-10, B-10A, B-10B
NC-5, NC-6	MD-3, MD-3A
NC-7, NC-8	MD-3M
NC-10, NC-12	MA-1MP, MA-2MP
	MA-3MP

Note

USAF electrical units must have AN3430-2A cables, with jumper installed between pins "E" and "F." Refer to General Airframe Bulletin No. 2 dated 22 July 1963.

COOLING AIR

Cooling air requirements are as follows:

	INPUT AIR TEMPERATURE	
RECEPTACLE	70°F	50°F
Main	31.2 pm, 6.2 psig	19.2 pm, 3.0 psig
Forward (A/N)	—	6.0 pm, 0.58 psig

USN UNITS	USAF UNITS
RCPP-105-1	MA-3, MA-7
RCPT-105-3	MA-8, A/M32C-6
NR-2, NR-3	555R
NR-4, NR-5	
NR-7, NR-8	
MD-3A	
E7488 (chin package)	

Note

Electrical power should always be removed before removing cooling air. Use conditioned air dump valve assembly (E7304) if available to regulate the cooling airflow and temperature at the main receptacle.

REFUELING

The aircraft may be refueled by deck edge hoses, trucks, or pits, using standard hose couplings. Fuel flow rate desired is 40 to 50 psig and is not to exceed 60 psig. JP-5 fuel should be used (JP-4 can be used as an alternate, and AVGAS or NATO Jet A or Jet A-1 can be used in an emergency).

Note

If AVGAS is used, the main and afterburner fuel control specific gravity should be set for 0.72. If flight time exceeds 5 hours, a fuel nozzle and hot section inspection is required. Top engine speed may have to be adjusted, as lower fuel specific gravity may cause a slight drop in maximum rpm.

DANGER AREAS

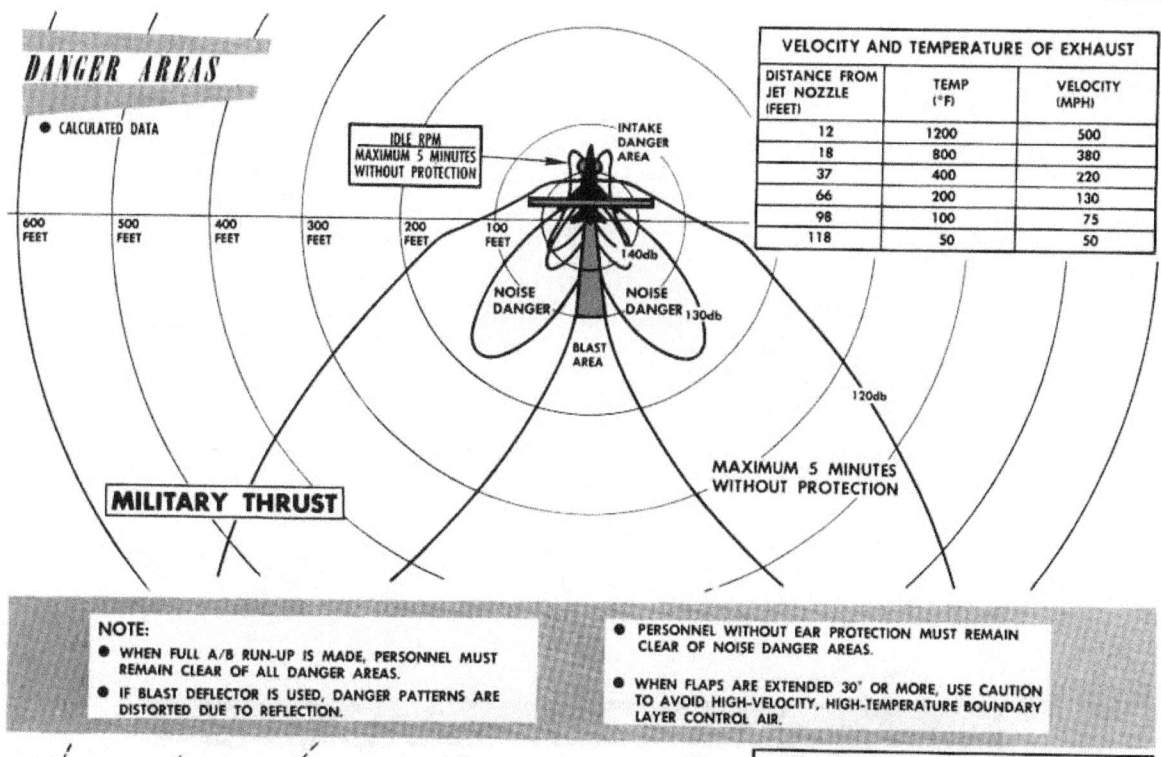

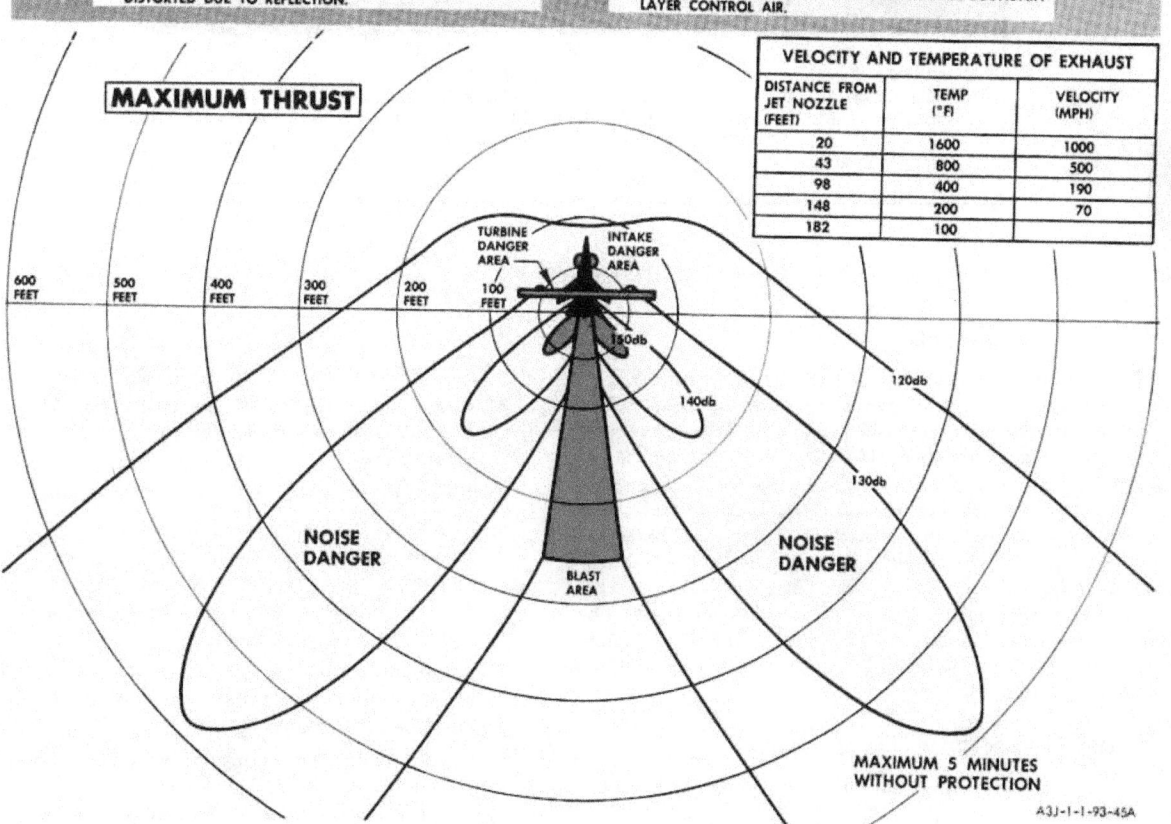

Figure 1-41

TURNING RADIUS

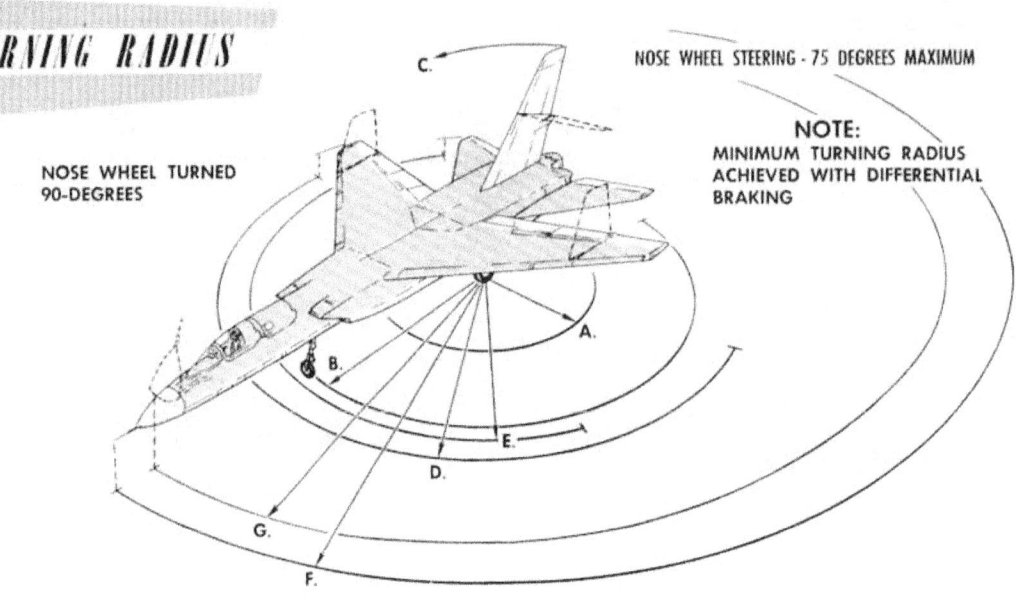

Figure 1-42

TURNING RADIUS

A. MAIN GEAR .... 11.62 FT.	WING (FOLDED) .... 28.00 FT.
B. NOSE GEAR .... 21.82 FT.	E. HORIZONTAL STABILIZER .. 32.14 FT.
C. VERTICAL STABILIZER (SPREAD) 19.40 FT.	F. RADOME (UNFOLDED) .... 49.83 FT.
(FOLDED) .15.5 FT.	G. RADOME (FOLDED) ...... 43.12 FT.
D. WING (SPREAD) .... 34.86 FT.	

GROUND PRESSURE REFUELING

All internal fuel tanks may be refueled in approximately 5 minutes through two pressure refueling receptacles. The forward receptacle is located aft of the nose gear well at access number 215 and the aft receptacle is located inboard and aft of the left main landing gear well at access number 84. Aircraft with drop tanks can be refueled in approximately 7½ minutes. External electrical power is required for refueling the drop tanks and level control valve testing. The aft refueling receptacle can be used to fill only the aft tank and the bomb bay cans, and to fill the sump tank to the 4250-pound level. The drop tanks may be filled at gravity fueling points, if desired.

NORMAL PROCEDURE

For normal refueling, the following procedure is to be followed:

1. Inspect main fuel vent on vertical stabilizer for freedom from obstructions.

2. Inspect vent valve sensing line outlet (under right afterburner) for freedom from obstructions.

3. Inspect ambient sensing line outlets (lower fuselage inboard of right main gear) for freedom from obstructions.

4. Ensure that the aircraft is properly grounded.

5. Check the following cockpit switches:
   (a) Engine MASTER switches—OFF.
   (b) INFLIGHT FUEL PROBE switch—RETRACT.
   (c) Bomb bay CANS transfer switch—AUTO.
   (d) SUMP switch—LOW.

6. External electrical power unit must be connected and operating for level control valve shutoff test and drop tank refueling.

7. Check forward refueling receptacle handle pin pulled and handle pulled down.
   See instructions inside receptacle access door.

8. Check hose coupling attached to forward receptacle and properly grounded.

9. For decreased refueling time, a second hose may be attached to the aft refueling receptacle.

Note

If difficulty is encountered in attaching the hose to the receptacle or if leakage occurs, a spanner wrench adjustment to the nozzle may correct the problem.

10. Early in the refueling process, check operation of level control valve shutoff function by holding the TEST switch in the forward receptacle access in PRIMARY, then SECONDARY, noting hose jerk and that fuel flow nearly stops within 15 seconds in each position.

If external tanks are installed, hold the EXTERNAL TANK REFUEL TEST switch momentarily in TEST simultaneously with the primary and secondary valve check.

CAUTION

If fuel flow does not drop during this check, immediately stop refueling and investigate. Failure of the valves to check fuel flow can result in overfilling, fuel overboarding, and possible damage to the aft or sump tanks.

11. Shut down refueling equipment immediately after step 10.
12. Pull forward receptacle handle to FLIGHT AND DEFUELING position.
13. Reapply refueling pressure to the forward receptacle.

    The refueling equipment should show no fuel flow, indicating that the refuel/defuel selector valve is properly closed.

14. Shut off refueling pressure and return the fuel valve handle to the down position.
15. Continue refueling until fuel flow stops automatically.
16. When refueling is complete (fuel flow ceases), check the fuel quantity indicator with the fuel tank selector to ensure all tanks are filled as desired.
    Refer to Section I, Part 2, for fuel quantities.
17. Check refueling hoses removed, check the forward receptacle handle pushed in to the FLIGHT AND DEFUELING position, and check the securing pin in place.
18. Check receptacle doors closed and check for excessive drainage or overboarding.

REFUELING AIRCRAFT WITH ENGINES RUNNING

The operational need for refueling the aircraft with the engines running is of primary concern when aboard ship and participating in Carrier Qualifications. Also, occasions may arise when the necessary ground support equipment is not available for starting the engines (as in a divert situation), and refueling with engines running becomes necessary. The following procedures are primarily for shipboard operations and are slanted toward Carrier Qualifications, but they may be modified as the situation requires.

1. Use HOT mike or hand signals with ground crew.
2. Report fuel state, fuel required, and whether "carqual" or full load is required.
3. On signal, INFLIGHT FUEL PROBE—EXTEND.
4. When ready, signal crew to start refueling. *Monitor fuel quantity indicator closely.* Warn ground crew when 1000 pounds short of desired total. Order "Stop fuel" when 200 pounds short of desired total.
5. Check all tanks for desired load. If satisfactory, report total fuel (and gross weight for "carqual") to the ground crew.
6. On signal, INFLIGHT FUEL PROBE—RETRACT.
7. If overfueling or wrong tank fill occurs, and transfer is not feasible, report aircraft "down" to ground crew. Request instructions from tower.
8. Observe safety precautions:
   (a) Engine power—IDLE.
   (b) Ground crew—Watch for loose clothing, caps, etc, around air intake ducts.
   (c) Be familiar with aircraft gross weight limits (CAT, ARREST).
   (d) Check proper trim settings for fuel loads.

PARTIAL FUEL LOAD PROCEDURE

When a partial fuel load is desired, the aft refueling receptacle should be used to prevent fuel entering the wing tanks and drop tanks. The following procedure can then be used by the pilot to preclude any asymmetrical load caused by fuel entering the wing tanks:

1. Prior to turning either engine MASTER switch ON, place the bomb bay CANS transfer switch to AUTO or OFF until external electrical power is disconnected from the aircraft.
2. Leave engine MASTER switches OFF until ready to start engines.
3. If any fuel remains in the wing tanks, selecting the HIGH position of the SUMP switch will further reduce the possibility of asymmetric loading.
4. The SUMP switch should be placed in LOW after the wing tanks are empty or prior to engine shutdown.

Note

A leaking refuel/defuel valve allows recirculation of fuel within the sump tank (from the boost pumps and back through the sump level control valve). Although some sump fuel may transfer to the wing tanks, the amount will be small due to the relatively high cracking pressure of the wing refueling level control valves.

SYSTEMS SERVICING

HYDRAULIC

The hydraulic systems are serviced with red hydraulic fluid at access number 90. The temperature of the fluid must be near ambient when checking the systems. The systems must be serviced if the red light is on or if the level in the reservoir sight gage is at REFILL. The sight gages may be checked through access numbers 103 and 170 on top of the aft fuselage. The spoiler speed brakes must be closed during servicing. Servicing pressure should be 80 to 110 psig at 1.5 gpm flow rate. Do not exceed 120 psig or 1.5 gpm. After servicing, the reservoirs are to be pressurized at 60 to 110 psig with dry nitrogen.

CAPACITIES	U.S. GAL	LITERS
No. 1 Reservoir	2.30	8.71
No. 1 System	6.70	25.36
No. 2 Reservoir	5.67	21.46
No. 2 System	16.80	63.60

The hydraulic system accumulators are serviced with dry nitrogen. The auxiliary brake accumulator is serviced in the nose wheel well and should be precharged to 800 ($\pm$50) psig. The emergency brake accumulator is serviced in the left-hand main gear well and is precharged to 1000 ($\pm$50) psig.

ENGINE OIL

The engines are serviced through access numbers 97.1 and 162. Servicing should be accomplished within 30 minutes after engine shutdown. If this time limit is exceeded, the engine transfer gearbox must be drained of excess oil. Fill the system until about one pint of oil overflows out the overboard drain. Fill capacity for each engine is 5.2 gallons (19.7 liters).

Note

MIL-L-23699 (Wep) oil is normally used. For starting ambient temperatures below $-40°F$, MIL-L-7808 oil should be used.

ARRESTING GEAR SNUBBER AND BUMPER

Service the arresting gear snubber and bumper with hydraulic fluid and dry nitrogen. Service instructions are shown on the snubber and bumper plates. The snubber is serviced at access number 154 and the gear must be lowered to service the bumper.

LANDING GEAR STRUTS

The landing gear struts are serviced with hydraulic fluid and dry nitrogen. The main strut extension should measure 8 9/16 ($\pm$1/4) inches between the torque arm pins for all gross weights and temperatures. For nose gear strut extension, refer to the instruction plate on the top aft side of the landing gear strut.

OXYGEN SYSTEMS

The liquid oxygen system is serviced in the nose wheel well. Two 10-liter bottles are installed, and may be removed from the aircraft for servicing if desired. The emergency seat kit bottles are serviced with high-pressure oxygen. Fill to 1800 psi minimum (black area on gage).

PNEUMATIC SYSTEMS

The pneumatic system storage bottles are serviced to 2800 to 3200 psig with clean, dry air or with dry nitrogen at access number 177. The pneumatic compressor reservoir is serviced in the right-hand main gear well. Lubricating oil, MIL-L-6085, is used. The oil level is checked with a dip stick attached to the filler cap. The filler cap is to be safety-wired after servicing.

TIRES

All tires are serviced with dry air or dry nitrogen.

TIRES	GROSS WEIGHT (POUNDS)	ASHORE (PSI)	AFLOAT (PSI)
Main Gear, 36 x 11, Type VII, 24-ply	35,000	120	250
	40,000	140	250
	45,000	160	250
	50,000	175	250
	55,000	195	250
	60,000	215	250
	63,000	225	250
Nose Gear, 26 x 6.6 Type VII, 16-ply	All	150	325

PITOT-STATIC DRAINS

Pitot-static drains are located inside the radome fold and under access numbers 68 and 222. Remove the caps, drain any moisture, and replace the caps.

HIGH-PRESSURE AIR VALVES

The landing gear struts, arresting gear snubber, arresting hook bumper, hydraulic accumulators and pneumatic system have high-pressure air valves. After servicing, these valves must be tightened and torqued. Torque values are:

Valve body	100—110 inch-pounds
Valve swivel nut	50—70 inch-pounds
Emergency canopy bottle drain plug	15—20 inch-pounds

DANGER AREAS

NOISE AREAS

This aircraft, like all jet aircraft, has engines installed which produce noise and heat blast when operating. See figure 1-41. Danger areas are to be avoided and protective ear covering *must* be worn in noise danger areas.

MOVABLE SURFACES

When electrical and hydraulic power are applied to the aircraft, there are numerous movable surfaces which can cause injury to personnel and damage to the aircraft and equipment if these surfaces are inadvertently operated. Only *qualified* personnel should be permitted to be in the cockpits or to operate these movable surfaces.

GROUND HANDLING

TURNING RADIUS

While being taxied, the nose wheel is steerable up to 75 degrees either side of center. The shortest turning radius is made with full nose wheel steering and differential braking. For congested area movement, it is recommended that the aircraft be towed rather than taxied. See figure 1-42.

TOWING

For towing operations, the nose wheel is full swiveling. The aircraft can be towed by the nose gear, using a Navy universal tow bar (NT-2 Model 3 or similar) of suitable length. For towing operations, proceed as follows:

1. Ensure landing gear pins are installed.

2. Check normal and emergency brake accumulators for proper charge.

3. A qualified person mans the pilot's cockpit and is familiar with the aircraft brake system.

TABLE OF CONTENTS

Introduction 119
Training 119
Flight Crew Requirements 120
Personal Equipment Requirements 120

INTRODUCTION

The standardized procedures in this manual are directed primarily to operational squadrons, but are also used as a basis for establishing procedures within the training squadrons. The assumption is made that flight crew members reporting to operational squadrons will have qualified in basic readiness training in a Heavy Attack Training Squadron. The training for basic readiness received in the training squadrons consists of approximately 112 flight hours, which include 87 hours basic training and 25 hours FCLP, plus day and night carrier qualification. Training to attain final readiness is accomplished in the operational squadrons. It is important that all flight crews realize a maximum of training during each operational flight. The following requirements apply for pilot qualifications:

First flight—6 WST periods.

Night flight—10 hours.

FCLP—50 hours (15 night).

Carrier landings—8 day, 12 night.

Unit commanding officers are authorized to waive any of the minimum flight qualification or ground training requirements in writing if recent experience in similar aircraft models so warrants.

In the interest of brevity, reference is made within this manual to Naval Warfare Publications and other appropriate directives.

TRAINING

Each squadron will establish and maintain a ground and flight training syllabus in order to keep flight crew members current in all phases of training necessary to the maintenance of a high degree of combat readiness. In addition to the basic squadron training program, other specialized training required by various directives is specified in the following paragraphs.

Note
Training requirements, checkout procedures, and weather minimums for Ferry Squadrons are governed by the provisions contained in the OPNAVINST 3710.6 series.

WEAPONS SYSTEM TRAINER (WST)

The weapons system trainer is available through the Carrier Readiness Air Wing (CRAW). Refresher periods on emergency procedures will be scheduled at least quarterly for each pilot. The WST will also be used for instrument training. Pilots will be scheduled periodically in order to maintain a high level of instrument proficiency. Systems operator refresher periods will be scheduled after protracted time away from the system, and for assistance in overcoming personal technique errors.

LOW-PRESSURE CHAMBER

All personnel flying in jet aircraft are required to maintain current qualification in a low-pressure chamber. All personnel will receive pressure suit indoctrination and checkout prior to conducting any flight over 50,000 feet.

EJECTION SEAT

An ejection seat trainer will be used to initially qualify/refresh flight crew members every 2 years. In addition, each crew member will receive basic instruction in the A-5A ejection seat while undergoing CRAW training. A review lecture and checkout will be given quarterly in the A-5A ejection system, utilizing the CRAW ejection seat trainer.

SURVIVAL TRAINING

Each crew member will qualify in the following phases of training:

1. Night vision—when reporting from nonoperational duty.
2. Dilbert Dunker—every 2 years.
3. Swimming tests—every 2 years.
4. Underwater breathing—every 2 years.
5. Helicopter rescue—every 2 years.
6. Parachute harness release and drag—every 2 years.

MOBILE SURVIVAL TRAINING

A mobile survival trainer makes periodic visits to the local NAS. All crew members will be scheduled to attend every 2 years.

FLIGHT CREW REQUIREMENTS

The crew will normally consist of a pilot and a systems operator both of whom will meet the requirement for basic readiness. A minimum crew consisting of a pilot may be used during FMLP and carrier qualification. Duties of the flight crew members are as follows:

PILOT

1. Has complete responsibility for the aircraft and its assigned mission and the performance of the S/O in his specified flight duties.
2. Ensures safe and proper operation of the aircraft in accordance with standard procedures.
3. Supervises adequate and continued training of the systems operator.
4. Delegates duties to the S/O and ensures that all duties are properly understood.

SYSTEMS OPERATOR

1. Completely prepares for solution of the weapons system bombing problem.
2. Prepares for and properly conducts aircraft navigation.
3. Ensures that the navigation bag, with appropriate contents, is carried in the aircraft.
4. Inspects for security and condition of bomb load.
5. Assists in the preflight preparation of the aircraft.
6. Gives a postflight debriefing of the weapons system operation.
7. Assists in other duties as directed by the pilot.

PERSONAL EQUIPMENT REQUIREMENTS

Appropriate flying equipment will be worn by all personnel flying in the aircraft. They will be familiar with the operation and use of all required survival equipment. All survival equipment will be secured in such a manner that it is easily accessible and will not be lost during an emergency. Equipment to be worn is listed in the following paragraph.

TEMPERATE CLIMATE (LOW AND MEDIUM ALTITUDE)

	WINTER	SUMMER
1. MA-2 integrated torso harness with MK-3C life preserver (the MA-2P harness assembly with MK-IV life preserver will be worn only with the full pressure suit or the MK 5/5A exposure suit)	x	x
2. Antibuffet helmet painted and rigged in accordance with latest survival bulletin	x	x
3. A-13A oxygen mask with appropriate retention fittings	x	x
4. Flight suit	x	x
5. Anti-G suit	x	x
6. Approved survival knife and sheath	x	x
7. Lace-up, ankle-length boots	x	x
8. Wool or thermal socks	x	x
9. Flight gloves	x	x
10. Identification tags	x	x
11. Winter trousers or thermal underwear	x	
12. .38-caliber pistol with tracer ammunition	x	x

Note

An approved signaling device is authorized as a substitute for the pistol when operational and/or security conditions warrant.

13. Flashlight with red lens (night only)	x	x
14. Personal survival kit	x	x

OVER-WATER FLIGHTS

The full pressure suit or anti-exposure suit will be worn on all over-water flights when the water temperature is 59°F or below, or outside air temperature is 32°F or below, or the combined air/water temperature is 120°F or below. During daylight, within gliding distance of land, the exposure suit need not be worn if water temperature is above 50°F. Operational Commanders may waive the requirement for wearing all types of anti-exposure suits if a possibility exists that high ambient cockpit temperature could cause extreme fatigue and dehydration.

HIGH-ALTITUDE/HIGH-SPEED FLIGHTS

For flights above 50,000 feet, both crew members will wear the full pressure suit with all approved accessories, in lieu of all other personal equipment.

normal procedures

PART 1 — BRIEFING AND DEBRIEFING

TABLE OF CONTENTS

PART 1—BRIEFING AND DEBRIEFING 121	Launch Procedure 141
General Briefing 121	Rendezvous and Departure 141
Operational Briefings 122	Recovery Procedures 141
Debriefing 122	Carrier Instrument Procedures 144
PART 2—MISSION PLANNING 123	Night Carrier Operations 146
Subsonic/Supersonic Missions 123	Lost Communications 146
Specific Responsibilities—Mission Planning 123	PART 5—NORMAL PROCEDURES
Operational Mission Planning 123	(SYSTEMS OPERATOR) 148A
Navigation Planning 123	Crew Duties 148A
Crew Planning Requirements 123	Before Entering Aircraft 148A
Fuel Planning 124	Entering Aircraft 148A
Navigation Bag Check List (Flight Crew) 125	Cockpit Check (A/N Prealined) 148A
Mission Check List 125	Autonavigator Alinement 148B
PART 3—SHORE-BASED PROCEDURES	Stand-by Nav Turn-on 148D
(PILOT) 127	After Starting 148E
Scheduling 127	Before Taxi 148E
Line Operations 127	Before Take-off 148E
Taxi, Take-off, and Landing 132A	After Take-off 148E
Stopping the Aircraft 138	In-flight Procedures 148E
PART 4—CARRIER-BASED PROCEDURES 139	Malfunction Check Lists 148G
Command Responsibility 139	Emergency Tanker 148M
Scheduling 139	Before Landing 148M
Briefing 139	After Landing 148N
Flight Operations 139	Systems Shutdown 148N

Successful execution of an assigned mission demands complete familiarity with its requirements. The nature of the assigned mission will determine briefing format and persons responsible for delivering the briefing. If possible, both crew members will attend all mission briefings. It is the responsibility of the Operations Officer to see that correct and complete briefings are conducted. Briefing duties will be assigned to specific individuals of the various squadron departments by the Operations Officer.

GENERAL BRIEFING

The general briefing applies to mission training flights, competitive exercises, operational readiness tests, and flight operations conducted in accordance with Operations Orders. The general briefing will be conducted as soon as possible after receiving the Operations Order, generally not later than 48 hours prior to launch time.

OPERATIONAL BRIEFINGS

TARGET BRIEFING

The target briefing encompasses all phases of flight planning and includes a thorough crew evaluation of all available intelligence information.

INTELLIGENCE PLANNING/BRIEFING

1. Friendly/enemy forces.
2. Current intelligence.
3. Targeting (visual/radar).

WEATHER BRIEFING

1. Local.
2. Destination, alternate.
3. Enroute.

MISSION PLANNING BRIEFINGS

Mission briefings will normally include the information noted in the following paragraphs.

OPERATIONAL MISSION PLANNING

1. Primary mission.
2. Secondary mission.
3. Operations area.
4. Control agency.
5. Communications.
6. TOT.

GENERAL OPERATIONS BRIEFING

1. Aircraft assignment.
2. Call signs.
3. Deck spot and launch order.

WEAPONS BRIEFING

1. Loading.
2. Safety.
3. Arming, dearming.
4. Duds/jettison procedure.
5. Special route assignments.

NAVIGATION BRIEFING

1. Climb-out.
2. Cruise control, fuel oxygen.
3. Marshal, penetration, GCA/CCA.
4. Recovery.

FORMATION (FLIGHT LEADER'S BRIEFING)

When formation flying is scheduled, the designated leader or senior pilot, if no leader is assigned, will conduct the required briefing. This briefing will cover the following points:

1. Radio frequencies to be used.
2. Location and type rendezvous to be used.
3. Position of each aircraft in the formation.
4. Airspeed and altitude to be used for the rendezvous.
5. Alternate leaders, in case the designated leader fails to become airborne.
6. Type mission to be flown.
7. Lost communications procedure.

FINAL BRIEFING

The final briefing will take place just prior to manning aircraft. At this time, all other information needed by the crew in order to accomplish the flight will be available. This briefing will usually start 1½ hours before launch time. When attending this briefing, the crew will be in flight clothing (including pressure suit) appropriate to the mission.

DEBRIEFING

A thorough debriefing is necessary to obtain maximum value from tactical or training flights. The postflight debriefing will be conducted by the Air Intelligence Officer and/or his assistant, under the supervision of the Operations Officer. The debriefing will be conducted as soon as practicable following recovery of the flight. A standard debriefing form, tailored to meet the tactical mission, will be utilized in order to ensure that no items are overlooked.

PART 2 — MISSION PLANNING

The ease and success with which a mission is accomplished is directly affected by the preplanning process. Thorough, detailed planning is mandatory and is a crew function. Training will emphasize the necessity for coordination and delineation of responsibilities. Both crew members must be thoroughly acquainted with all aspects of the mission and must understand the manner in which each is to assist the other in performance of assigned tasks. All delivery missions should be planned to include an alternate mode of delivery to cover the possibility of failure of the AN/ASB-12 bomb directing set.

SUBSONIC/SUPERSONIC MISSIONS

Subsonic missions will be planned, using the performance data in Section XI of the Supplemental NATOPS Flight Manual (NAVWEPS 01-60ABA-1A), aerologic information, and weapons criteria. Missions requiring a supersonic dash will be planned in a similar manner, except that for the cruise control portion of the planning, a "canned" problem approach will be used. Refer to FUEL PLANNING, in this section.

SPECIFIC RESPONSIBILITIES — MISSION PLANNING

PILOT AND SYSTEMS OPERATOR

1. Briefings.
2. Mission delivery methods and tactics.
3. Mission profile/master time schedule.

PILOT

1. Aircraft performance factors.
2. Route card, including fuel control log.
3. Communications.
4. DD-175 or other appropriate flight clearance form.
5. Target study/planning.

SYSTEMS OPERATOR

1. Target study/planning.
2. Target and checkpoint data check list.
3. Weapons check list.
4. Navigation route log.
5. Navigation portion of DD-175.
6. NAVWEPS Special Weapons Check Lists.

Note
Use Chapters 2 and 3 of the Supplement to NWIP 41-3 for other mission planning tactical considerations.

OPERATIONAL MISSION PLANNING

PLANNING FORMS

When proper planning precedes the mission, the crew conducts the mission primarily by means of check lists and logs. The following check lists are used in mission planning:

1. NAVWEPS Special Weapons Check Lists, or applicable conventional weapons check lists.
2. Mission check lists, used to ensure complete planning and conduct of the flight.
   Refer to MISSION CHECK LIST, in this section. The mission check list provides a basis for construction of the mission profile/master time schedule, which is used to ensure complete, accurate, and timely accomplishment of each specific item thereon. The profile/master time schedule includes:
   (a) Navigation information.
   (b) Fuel control and management.
   (c) Mission data, such as bomb-safe line, weapons arming, etc.
   (d) Monitor control points.
   (e) Altitude, speed, and time control.
3. Navigation log.
4. Fuel control log.
5. Target and checkpoint data check list.
6. Weapons tactic check list.

NAVIGATION PLANNING

FACTORS

Factors to be considered in navigation planning include:

1. Mission operational requirements.
1A. Radar/visual checkpoints.
2. Range-to-target or total radius.
3. Weather, including wind, contrails, and cloud cover.
4. Weapons criteria.
5. TOT.
6. Enemy defense criteria.

CREW PLANNING REQUIREMENTS

1. Completeness of navigation bag [refer to NAVIGATION BAG CHECK LIST (FLIGHT CREW), in this section].
2. Operational and weather briefings.
3. Preparation of two sets of suitable scale charts, depicting the intended flight path, diversionary fields, and other data as may be pertinent.
4. Preparation of pilot's route card.
5. Preparation of DD-175 or other required flight plan.

Section III
Part 2

6. When ship-based, knowledge of PIM and condition of ship's navigational aids.
7. Ensuring that required code books and tables are aboard aircraft.
8. For supersonic missions, ensuring that the appropriate "canned" profiles are drawn and studied.
9. Preparation of navigation log and completion of navigation portion of the profile/master time schedule.

MINIMUM NAVIGATION REQUIREMENTS

1. Over land—a minimum of two fixes hourly.
2. Over water—a minimum of two dead reckoning positions hourly.
3. A running plot of autonavigator positions and winds shall be maintained as dictated by the mission.

FUEL PLANNING

The A-5A fuel planning problem is a complex one, stemming from the great variety of attack modes, plus the wide latitude in altitudes and airspeeds. A preflight fuel plan will be incorporated on the route cards for all flights. The latest REST computer will be used for the cruise control computations. If these computers are not available, or if aircraft configuration makes their use impractical, the performance data in Section XI of the Supplemental NATOPS Flight Manual (NAVWEPS 01-60ABA-1A) will be used.

All jet aircraft respond to certain performance parameters. The three most important of these, and the ones upon which specific range depend are (1) gross weight, (2) ambient air pressure, and (3) Mach number. The performance data in Section XI of the Supplemental NATOPS Flight Manual (NAVWEPS 01-60ABA-1A) indicate range or specific range for various altitudes (i.e., ambient air pressure), weights, and Mach numbers. Also indicated are engine rpm, fuel flow, and TAS. These last, however, are dependent upon Standard Day conditions. For other than standard conditions, the first three factors (weight, altitude, and Mach number) are the controlling parameters. On a warmer-than-standard day, engine rpm, fuel flow, and TAS will all be higher than indicated in the curves; however, if proper Mach number is flown, specific range will be accurate.

Note
To obtain the specific range indicated, FLY MACH NUMBER. Do not fly power settings, fuel flow, or TAS. To do so will result in inaccuracies if the day is nonstandard.

SPEED
Missions fall into two categories: (1) entirely subsonic, and (2) partially supersonic. The planning for these two missions differs, and is covered separately as follows.

SUBSONIC MISSIONS
The subsonic mission will be planned, using either the performance data in Section XI of the Supplemental NATOPS Flight Manual (NAVWEPS 01-60ABA-1A), or the A-5A REST computer. Both sources are accurate, easy to use, and contain all required instructions for proper use. Each mission will be planned separately, based upon requirements.

SUPERSONIC MISSIONS
Fuel consumption at high speeds is very high, and small errors in planning can result in gross errors in available fuel. In addition, temperature plays an important role in the overall range. Because of the difficulty in accurate planning, and the possibility of serious error, all supersonic missions will be based on "canned" profiles. Each squadron will develop as many representative profiles as required for the targets assigned, with alternate profiles for hot and cold days. For actual missions, the crew will select a profile which contains as much or more range than the mission, and this profile will be flown. The crews will provide themselves with alternate profiles to be used if the temperature at altitude proves to be hotter or colder than standard. Specifically, profiles for 10 degrees cold, 10 degrees hot, and 20 degrees hot will be carried on each supersonic mission. Enroute to the target, and within 10 minutes of selecting afterburning, the pilot will determine outside temperature from the inlet temperature gage. (At 0.9 Mach above 36,000 feet, the inlet temperature should read −21°C for a Standard Day.) At this time, the pilot will decide which profile will be used and delay or anticipate afterburning selection as indicated.

SINGLE-ENGINE FLIGHT
Single-engine specific fuel consumption for the A-5A indicates that "singling-up" will not result in an increase in range. Pilots will refrain from shutting down an engine in flight for this purpose.

FUEL CONTROL LOG
The pilot's route card will include a fuel control log, indicating planned fuel remaining at each navigational checkpoint, the IP, and over the target. In addition, supersonic flights will include fuel remaining at the start of the supersonic run, at the end of each minute of afterburner operation, and at the end of the supersonic run. The crew will monitor fuel closely to determine whether the flight is proceeding as planned. *This is most important on supersonic missions, where an extra minute of afterburning can cost 60 nautical miles overall range.* Fuel computations will be based on forecast winds. However, in applying winds, *all* predicted head-wind factor, but only *half* of any tail-wind factor will be applied.

FUEL REQUIREMENTS
It is evident that the fuel requirements for a mission will be dependent upon the type of mission, the flight profile selected, the ordnance load assigned, and aircraft gross

weight. A realistic determination of the fuel requirements can be established only after consideration of all the following elements:

1. Maximum fuel available based on configuration, ordnance/weapons load, basic operating weight of the aircraft, and maximum take-off gross weight.
2. Fuel required for ground operation, i.e., turn-up and taxi to take-off position.
3. Fuel required for take-off and climb to cruise altitude.
4. Fuel required for cruise in accordance with the mission profile.
5. Fuel required for descent at destination.
6. Fuel required for the alternate, holding, and reserve.

Fuel requirements will be calculated to allow for the following amounts of fuel upon return:

1. VFR conditions—2000 pounds at the break.
2. IFR conditions—2200 pounds at filed alternate approach fix.

Note

For carrier-based operation, plan for landing at maximum allowable gross weight.

Pilots are responsible for adhering to the minimum fuel requirements as stated in current OPNAV Instructions. A reserve of 1500 pounds constitutes a low state.

BINGO FUEL

Bingo fuel may be defined as the fuel state required to enable the aircraft to proceed to a designated airfield and land with minimum safe fuel remaining. It is particularly applicable to shipboard operations within a reasonable range of a land mass, but may be applied to exercises conducted with an airfield as the operating base where the mission requires a maximum endurance on station. The Operations Officer is responsible for publishing a fuel planning card which will facilitate an accurate and rapid determination of Bingo fuel requirements. Bingo cards are predicted on the following:

1. VFR.
    (a) Starting at sea level.
    (b) Arriving at the break with 1500 pounds remaining.
2. IFR.
    (a) Starting at sea level.
    (b) Arriving overhead destination at 20,000 feet with 2200 pounds remaining.

NAVIGATION BAG CHECK LIST (FLIGHT CREW)

ITEM	PILOT	SYSTEMS OPERATOR
1. NATOPS Pocket Check List (NAVWEPS 01-60ABA-1B)	x	x
2. Flashlight with red lens (night or cross-country only)	x	x
3. FLIP Enroute Supplement	x	x
4. Enroute High Altitude Charts	x	x
5. Area Arrival Charts (as required)		x
6. Enroute Low Altitude Charts		x
7. Terminal (High Altitude) Charts	x	x
8. Navigation Charts (area of flight)	x	x
9. REST Computer, A-5A	x	
10. Dividers and plotter		x

MISSION CHECK LIST

The following items listed will be used as a guide in the preparation of mission check lists. Only those items applicable to the type mission flown need be considered.

NAVIGATION

1. PIM.
2. TAS/GS checks.
3. (Deleted.)
4. Pressure pattern D readings.
5. Checkpoint coordinates and elevations.
6. Bearings and distances enroute.
7. Variation.
8. Control lines and times.
9. TOT and TT.

WEAPONS

1. Pre-take-off check.
2. Post-take-off check.
3. Arming check.
4. Pre-drop check.
5. Abort check.

FUEL MANAGEMENT

1. Climb, descent, and cruise data.
2. Bomb bay and wing transfer data.
3. Fuel control log.

DETECTION

1. EW.
2. GCI.
3. Aircraft or missile intercept point.

Section III
Part 2

BOMB SYSTEM
1. Computer ballistics.
2. Offsets.
3. Target coordinates and elevations.
   (a) Aimpoint/checkpoint coordinates and elevations.
4. Target intelligence (radar).
   (a) Target intelligence (TA/visual).
5. Altitude options.

AIRCRAFT ARMAMENT
1. Bomb release selectors and options.
   (a) Mode select.
   (b) Release select.
   (c) Arming.
   (d) Weapons monitor and control.
   (e) Jettison.
   (f) Primary/secondary options.

TACTICAL
1. EMCON.
   (a) Radar.
   (b) Communications and Navaids.
2. Radio signals.
3. Thermal shields.
4. Bomb-safe line.
5. Target defenses.
6. DECM operation.
7. Abort procedures.

REPORTS
1. ADIZ.
2. Tactical control.

PART 3 — SHORE-BASED PROCEDURES (PILOT)

When based ashore, the squadron is responsible through the local wing and/or fleet air commander to the appropriate type commander.

SCHEDULING

LONG-RANGE PLANNING SCHEDULES

Weekly and monthly flight planning schedules will be published to assist the orderly progress of training and the planning of maintenance.

DAILY FLIGHT SCHEDULE

The daily flight schedule will be prepared by the Flight Officer or Schedule Officer. When approved by the Commanding Officer, the daily flight schedule has the authority of a direct order of the Commanding Officer. The daily flight schedule will include the following information:

1. Name of the Operations Duty Officer.
2. Time of sunrise and sunset.
3. Schedule of flights, to include:
    (a) Briefing times.
    (b) Take-off times.
    (c) Flight duration.
    (d) Flight crews.
    (e) Aircraft, fuel load, and ordnance.
    (f) Mission.
    (g) Flight leaders (when appropriate).

LINE OPERATIONS

MANNING AIRCRAFT

Following the final briefing (and filing of flight plans, if required) the pilot will review previous aircraft discrepancies and sign the yellow sheet. The systems operator will review previous weapons system discrepancies. Crews will man aircraft at least 30 minutes prior to scheduled launch time. A thorough preflight inspection and an orderly, methodical, prestart check will be made. If pressure suits are worn, the preflight check may be made by a qualified crew other than the flight crew.

BEFORE ENTERING AIRCRAFT

1. Conduct aircraft exterior inspection. See figure 3-1.
2. External units—connected and operating.
    An RCPP-105-1/RCPT-105-3 or equivalent unit, or a 400-cycle, three-phase (A, B, C rotation), 120-volt, 30-kva electrical unit and a suitable engine start air unit are required. If the bomb directing set is to be alined, cooling air is also required.

AFT COCKPIT CHECK (SOLO FLIGHT)

1. Oxygen—OFF.
2. IFF/SIF—NORM/as desired.
3. HOSE CONTROL switch—REWIND.
4. Seat and parachute—secured.
5. Loose gear—stowed.
6. AN POWER, BOMB COMPUTER POWER, and RADAR/TV POWER switches—OFF.
7. Canopy (listen for "pop")—closed.

ENTERING AIRCRAFT

1. Inspect seat and canopy (figures 3-2 and 3-3).
2. Canopy uplock—ENGAGED.
3. Canopy emergency air bottle—2800 psi (minimum).
4. Emergency oxygen—1800 psi.
5. Seat quick-disconnects—fastened/safetied.
6. Disconnect block—Fasten/check.
7. Oxygen—OFF.
8. Relief plunger—Depress.
9. Yellow knob—Pull.
10. Disconnect block—Mate.
11. Oxygen—ON.
12. Lines—Pull to check.
13. Harness—Fasten/Adjust.

Note
Crew members will personally fasten and become proficient at fastening the "Rocket-Jet" fittings and adjusting the integrated harness.

PRESTART CHECK

1. Seat/canopy safety pins (four)—removed (after entry).
2. Canopy uplock—disengaged (Plane Captain).
3. SPEED BR DUMP handle—down.
4. Bomb bay CANS transfer switch—AUTO.
5. SUMP switch—LOW (HIGH for FMLP, carqual, or tanker).
6. DROP TANK TRANSFER buttons—up (OFF).
7. INFLIGHT FUEL PROBE switch—RETRACT. Lift cover to check.
8. MASTER ARM switch—OFF.
9. SPC button—up (OFF).
10. AFC switch—OFF.
11. UHF selector—as desired. Rotate COMM VOL control right to approximate volume desired.
12. FLAPS—CRUISE or SUPERSONIC.

Section III
Part 3
NAVWEPS 01-60ABA-1

EXTERIOR INSPECTION

A) LEFT NOSE
1. Air refueling probe — RETRACTED. Check all doors flush.
2. Radome — SECURE. Check lock flag flush if closed.
3. TV scanner condition — CHECK.
4. Pitot boom cover — REMOVED. Check pitot boom condition.

B) RIGHT NOSE
1. Radome lock flag flush, if closed.
2. Angle-of-attack probe cover — REMOVED. Check probe condition.

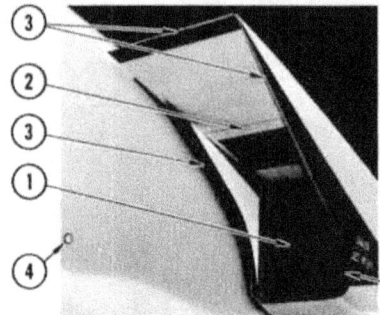

Q) LEFT INTAKE
1. Duct cover — REMOVED, Duct-CLEAR.
2. Ramp — RETRACTED, check condition.
3. Condition of leading edges — CHECK.
4. Auxiliary brake accumulator repeater gage — 800 psi.

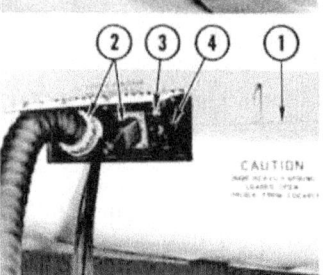

P) LEFT-FORWARD FUSELAGE
1. Ram-air turbine — RETRACTED. check lock-pin flush with fuselage.
2. External electrical power and air conditioning units connected and operating.
3. Ground door switch — NORMAL.
4. Bomb bay lights switch — OFF.

N) LEFT MAIN GEAR (SEE F)
1. Tire condition — CHECK.
2. Brake back-up plate — FREE. Check for ⅜ inch rotational freedom.
3. Strut extension — 8-9/16 inches.
4. Door condition — CHECK.
5. Emergency brake accumulator — 1000 psi. (Under pull-out door on inner bulkhead)
6. Safety lock — REMOVED.

M) LEFT WING
1. Position and formation lights condition — CHECK.
2. Wing fold area for leaks — CHECK.
3. ECM antenna condition — CHECK.
4. If installed, drop tank and pylon safety pins — REMOVED.
5. Droops, spoilers for hydraulic leaks — CHECK.

OPERATIONAL CHECK
1. All covers, jury struts — REMOVED.
2. Chocks — IN PLACE.
3. Doors, fasteners, exposed lines — SECURED.
4. Tires, brake stacks — CHECKED/FREE.
5. IFF/TACAN lobing switches — ON.
6. Radome lock flags — FLUSH.
7. Ramps — FULLY RETRACTED.
8. Engine Intakes — CLEAR.
9. RAT — RETRACTED.

L) LEFT STABILIZER AND AFT FUSELAGE (SEE H)
1. Trailing edge guard — REMOVED.
2. Stabilizer condition — CHECK.
3. Engine access doors — SECURE. Check fasteners flush with surface.
4. Fuselage formation light condition — CHECK.

A3J-1-1-00-45D

Figure 3-1 (Sheet 1)

NAVWEPS 01-60ABA-1
Section III
Part 3

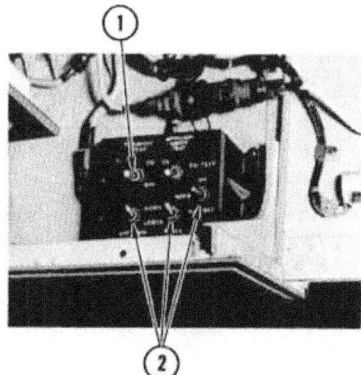

C NOSE GEAR
1. Tire condition — CHECK.
2. Steer-damp unit condition — CHECK.
3. Strut extension — See MIM chart. (Between upper and lower torque arm pins.)
4. Approach lights condition — CHECK.
5. Manual lock handle — UNLOCKED AND REMOVED.
6. Taxi light condition — CHECK.

D NOSE GEAR WELL
1. Training tone switch — AS DESIRED.
2. UHF COMM, TACAN, AUX REC switches — NORMAL.
3. Auxiliary brake accumulator — 800 psi. (right bulkhead)

E RIGHT INTAKE (SEE Q)
1. Duct cover — REMOVED Duct — CLEAR.
2. Ramp — RETRACTED Check condition.
3. Condition of leading edges — CHECK.

K VERTICAL STABILIZER
1. Position light condition — CHECK.
2. Buddy tanker lights condition — CHECK.
3. Fuel overboard vent — UNDAMAGED. Check for fuel drainage.
4. ECM antennas condition — CHECK.
5. Tail cap antenna cover condition — CHECK.
6. Leading edge condition — CHECK.

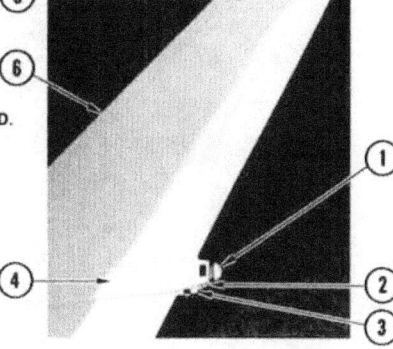

F RIGHT MAIN GEAR
1. Fuel vents — Clear (inboard).
2. Tire condition — CHECK.
3. Brake back-up plate — FREE. Check for 3/8 inch rotational freedom.
4. Strut extensions — 8-9/16 inches. (Between torque arm connector pins).
5. Door condition — CHECK.
6. Pneumatic system accumulator pressure — 2700 psi. (Inboard of right main gear door).
7. Safety lock — REMOVED.

G RIGHT WING (SEE M)
1. Droops and spoilers for hydraulic leaks — CHECK.
2. If installed, drop tank and pylon safety pins — REMOVED
3. ECM antenna condition — CHECK
4. Wing fold area for leaks — CHECK.
5. Position and formation light condition — CHECK.

J ENGINE OUTLETS
1. Exhaust nozzle covers — REMOVED.
2. Afterburner nozzle flaps — UNDAMAGED. Check for freedom of movement.
3. Spray bars — CHECK. Check for signs of warpage or breaks.
4. Tail cone — SECURE.
5. Fuel dump tube — RETRACTED.

H RIGHT STABILIZER AND AFT FUSELAGE
1. Fuselage formation light condition — CHECK.
2. Arresting hook fairing doors — CLOSED.
3. Engine access doors — SECURE. (Check fasteners flush with surface)
4. Stabilizer condition — CHECK.
5. Trailing edge guard — REMOVED.

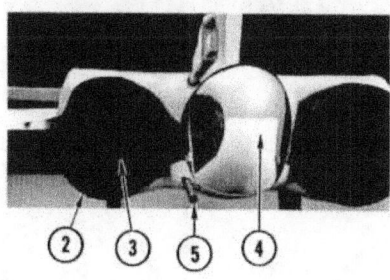
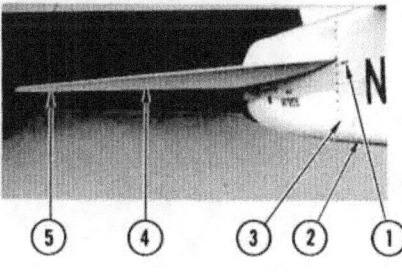

A3J-1-1-00-46D

Figure 3-1 (Sheet 2)

Section III
Part 3

NAVWEPS 01-60ABA-1

CANOPY AND SEAT INSPECTION

APPLICABLE TO BOTH COCKPITS

1. Canopy uplock — ENGAGED
2. Thermal radiation shield — CHECK CONDITION
3. Sun visor and standby compass — CHECK CONDITION
4. Face curtain handle — STOWED
5. Canopy emergency air bottle — 2800 psi (minimum)
   (Pilot — right side) (B/N — left side)
6. Right ejection seat quick disconnect — MATED AND SAFETY-WIRED
7. Ditching handle — DOWN AND SECURE
8. Ejection knob safety pins — INSTALLED
9. Right leg retractor — SECURE
10. Canopy jettison handle safety pin — INSTALLED
11. Arm retention cable and latch — STOWED
12. Left leg retractor — SECURE
13. Emergency oxygen gage — 1800 psi
14. Lap straps — CHECK CONDITION AND SECURITY
    (Pull straps to check seat kit securely retained)
15. Shoulder harness lock handle — UNLOCK
16. Pull parachute pack forward and check:

> **CAUTION**
>
> BE SURE PULL-OFF LANYARD IS NOT PULLED WHEN CHUTE IS TILTED FORWARD

(a) Shoulder harness lock operation
(b) Shoulder harness disconnect — SECURE
(c) Pull-off static lanyard pocket — SECURE
(d) Parachute opener arming cable — SECURE
(e) Aneroid power device indicator — CHECK
   (Pull right side of separation back bladder aside and check indicator through inspection hole
   White — SAFE   Red — UNACCEPTABLE

NOTE:
At elevations of 5000 feet or above, a small portion of the red flag being visible is acceptable.

17. Personnel disconnect (Scott) — CHECK CONDITION
18. Shoulder straps and arm retention rollers — CHECK CONDITION AND SECURITY
19. Face curtain safety pin — INSTALLED
20. Left ejection seat quick disconnect — MATED AND SAFETY-WIRED
21. Pull-off lanyard box — CHECK

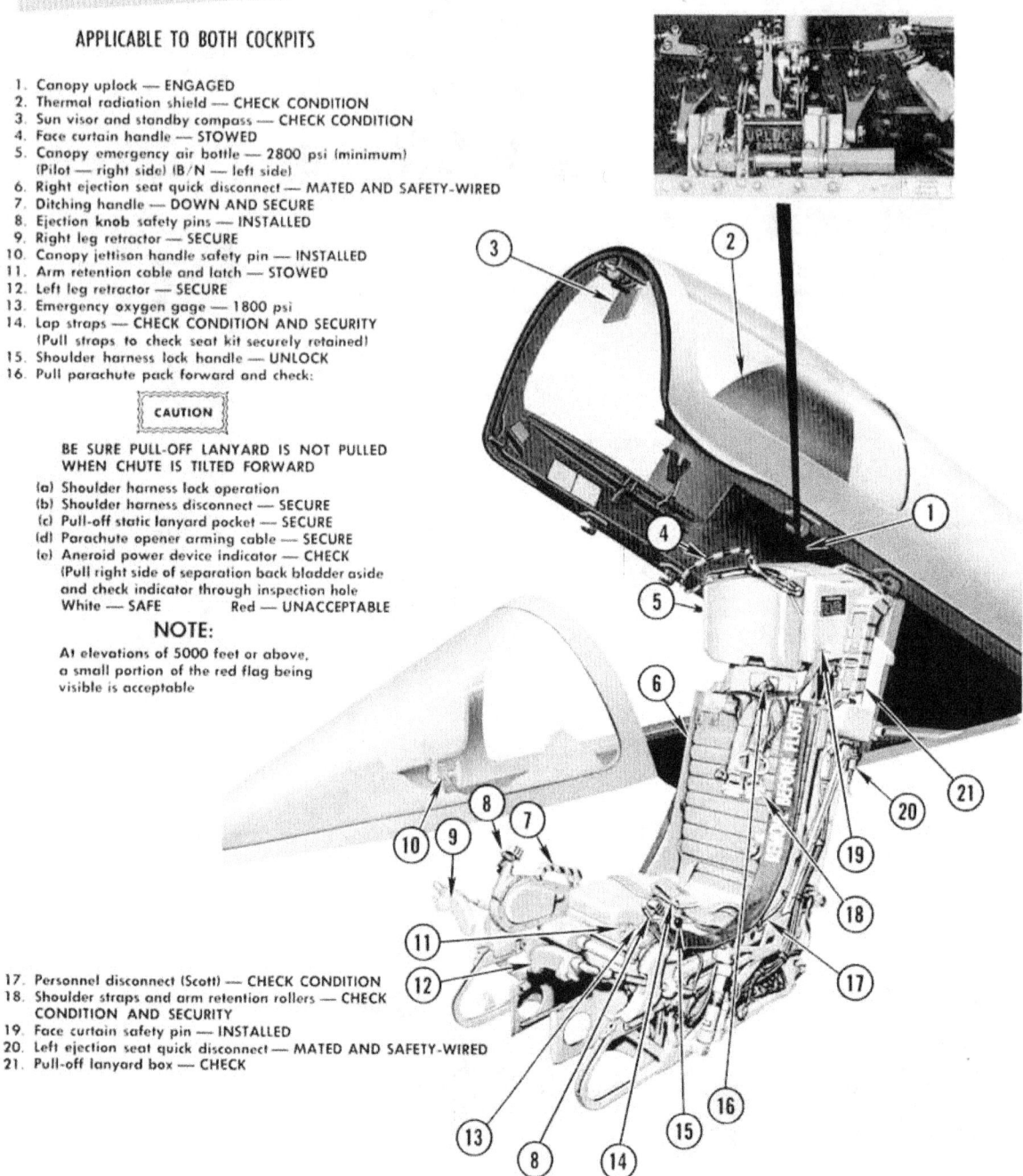

Figure 3-2

ENTERING THE COCKPITS

Figure 3-3

13. EMERG FLAP switch—NORM.
14. HYD SUB-SYS ISOLATION switch—TAKE-OFF/LANDING.
15. ENGINE FIRE switch—OFF.
16. Fuel quantity—check total and individual tank quantities.
    (a) FUEL GAUGE TEST button—TEST (Press).
    (b) Check gage for rundown and return.
17. LANDING GEAR control handle—DOWN.
18. EMERG GR UP switch—NORM.
    Lift guard to check.
19. FUEL DUMP handle—in.
20. EGT indicators—TEST.
21. EMER AIR TURBINE handle (RAT)—in.
22. EMER LDG GR handle—in and guarded.
23. EMER CANOPY jettison handle—in.
24. ARREST HOOK handle—in.
25. Oxygen quantity gage—check, Test.
    Check gage for rundown and return.
26. CNI PWR button—ON (Depress).
27. AUX B/N COOLING button—ON (Depress).
28. TAIL CONT switch—same position as tail.
29. WING AND TAIL FOLD handle—same position as wings.
30. EMERG IFF switch—AUTO.
31. WARN LT TEST button—Press, Test.
32. COCKPIT TEMP knob—2.0.
33. COCKPIT PRESS switch—NORM.
34. WINDSHIELD & CANOPY DEFROST knob—OFF.
35. WINDSHIELD ANTI-ICE switch—OFF.
36. PITOT and ENGINE ANTI-ICE switches—OFF.
37. NAV COMD button—as desired.
38. Compass TAKE CMD button—as desired.
39. Circuit breakers—in.
40. Interior lights—as desired.
41. Exterior lights—as desired.

STARTING ENGINES (WITH RCPP-105 ELECTRICAL CONNECTION)

1. Throttles—OFF.
2. Engine MASTER switches—ON.

Note

Either engine may be started first.

3. NO. 2 START switch—START.
   Check starting air ready and signal before starting.
4. 10% rpm—throttle to IDLE.
   Check engine instruments for normal start.
5. At 45% rpm, NO. 2 START switch—STOP.
6. NO. 2 GEN switch—RESET.
7. Repeat steps 3 through 6 for No. 1 engine.
8. External power and air—check with S/O (Disconnect when ready).
   Disconnect electrical power before disconnecting cooling air.
9. HYD SYS 1, HYD SYS 2 pressure indicators—3000 (±250) psi.
10. Check generator caution indicators out.

STARTING ENGINES (WITHOUT RCPP-105 ELECTRICAL CONNECTION)

1. Throttles—OFF.
2. Engine MASTER switches—ON.
3. Signal crewman to start air (connected engine should start monitoring).
4. 10% rpm—Depress/Hold EMER IGN, Move No. 2 throttle to IDLE.
   While holding EMER IGN, move throttle to IDLE, and hold button down until engine light-off definitely occurs.
5. At 45% rpm—Signal crewman to secure air.
6. NO. 2 GEN switch—RESET.
7. Repeat steps 3 through 6 for No. 1 engine.
8. External power and air—check with S/O (Disconnect when ready).
   Disconnect electrical power before disconnecting cooling air.
9. HYD SYS 1, HYD SYS 2 pressure indicators—3000 (±250) psi.
10. Check generator caution indicators out.

ALTERNATE START (GTC-85 OR MA-1A UNIT)

When performing a start with alternate units, proceed as follows:

1. Throttles—OFF.
2. Engine MASTER switches—ON.
3. Signal crewman to start air (connected engine should start motoring).

Note

Engine acceleration is slow, requiring as much as 1 minute to reach maximum obtainable rpm (6% to 9%).

4. At maximum obtainable rpm, depress and hold No. 2 engine EMER IGN button and move throttle outboard and forward approximately halfway to IDLE.
5. Modulate throttle position below IDLE to maintain EGT below 700°C during acceleration.
6. At 30% rpm, or when EGT stabilizes, move throttle to IDLE.
7. At 45% rpm, signal crewman to secure air and hold START switch to STOP.
8. NO. 2 GEN switch—RESET.
9. Repeat steps 3 through 8 for other engine.
10. External power and air—check with S/O (Disconnect when ready).
11. HYD SYS 1, HYD SYS 2 pressure indicators—3000 (±250) psi.
12. Check generator caution indicators out.

FLIGHT CONTROL AND PRETAXI CHECK (ABBREVIATED)

Note

- For complete flight control check procedures, refer to FLIGHT TEST PROCEDURES, in Section IV.
- Use the rearview mirror to check spoiler and vertical stabilizer action. The Plane Captain should check ALL surfaces for proper action and full deflection.

CAUTION

Flight control checks will be conducted under positive control of the Plane Captain. They will not be initiated until the Plane Captain can see that all personnel and equipment are clear of the control surfaces.

1. Canopies—CLOSED.
   (a) Listen for "pop."
   (b) Check CANOPY caution indicator out after "pop."
2. Wings and tail—spread and locked.
3. RAMP CONT switch—RESET.
   Check RAMP CONT caution indicator out.
4. TRIM SEL switch—ALTR.
   Check ALT ROLL/YAW TRIM and alternate pitch trim in each direction.
5. TRIM SEL switch—NORM.
   Check normal roll, yaw, and pitch trim in each direction.

6. YAW AUG switch—RESET.
   Check YAW AUG caution indicator out.
7. ELEC SYS (flight control) switch—RESET.
   (a) Check ELEC F/C caution indicator out.
   (b) Check PITCH and ROLL indicators—blank or "ON."
8. PITCH AUG switch—RESET (ON SIGNAL ONLY).
   Check, set pitch trim 8 units nose-up.
9. PITCH AUG switch—STBY.
10. Speed brake switch—OUT.
    Check spoiler action.
11. Flap control switch—50°.
    (a) Check speed brakes retract to 8 degrees.
    (b) Check spoiler action.
12. Flap control switch—40°.
    (a) Check speed brakes fully retracted.
    (b) Check spoiler action.
13. Flap control switch—CRUISE.
    (a) Check flaps retracted, droops 5 degrees.
    (b) Check spoiler action.
14. Pitch trim—check 1.3 units nose-up.
    PITCH AUG switch—RESET.
15. Vertical, horizontal stabilizers—check full travel. ON SIGNAL ONLY, check 18 degrees nose-up, 15 degrees nose-down.
16. Move stick rapidly forward, then full left and rapidly right.
    (a) Check ELEC F/C caution indicator on and PITCH, ROLL indicators blank or barber-poled.
    (b) ELEC SYS switch—RESET.
17. Move stick rapidly aft, then full right and rapidly left.
    (a) Check ELEC F/C caution indicator on and PITCH, ROLL indicators blank or barber-poled.
    (b) ELEC SYS switch—RESET.
18. Disable ("kill") button—Depress.
    Check ELEC F/C and PITCH AUG caution indicators on, ELEC SYS and PITCH AUG switches at STBY.
19. Operate flight controls—check normal and full travel.
    Check pitch trim indicators—18 degrees nose-up, 8 degrees nose-down.
20. PITCH AUG and ELEC SYS switches—RESET, if desired.
21. CNI command lights—as desired.
22. Compass—set and slaved.
23. External power and cooling air—removed.
24. Bomb bay CANS transfer switch—ON.
25. Air refueling probe—check operation.
26. Canopy defrost and windshield anti-ice systems—check operation.

TAXI, TAKE-OFF, AND LANDING

TAXI PROCEDURES

1. When taxiing in close quarters (within 10 feet of obstructions), there shall be a director in front and a wing tip walker at each wing to ensure safe clearance of obstructions. The crew shall be alert to spot any obstructions which the aircraft might strike.
2. Check the brakes before getting into close quarters. Once clear of close quarters, check emergency brake operation.
3. The aircraft can be taxied using minimum power and nose wheel steering. To start, it is usually necessary to increase rpm to about 80%. Once moving, retard throttles as appropriate. If excess power is required to taxi, check for dragging brakes.

Note

If brakes are dragging, down the aircraft.

4. Do not brake against nose wheel steering. Center the nose wheel before stopping.

AIR CONDITIONING/DEFROST PROCEDURE

1. Pressurization should not be used during take-off when high humidity exists.
2. Prior to take-off, operate canopy defrost, cockpit ventilation, and windshield anti-ice systems to blow any possible water out of the air vents.

Note

For operational AN/ASB-12 flights, do not operate the engines at less than 80% rpm with flaps extended for more than 2 minutes when ambient temperature exceeds 100°F. With flaps extended, advancing power above 80% rpm will ensure adequate system cooling.

FUEL CONSERVATION

While taxiing to take-off position, the take-off check list shall be completed. On long-range flights or where

NAVWEPS 01-60ABA-1

Section III
Part 3

TYPICAL TAKE-OFF

ALL CONFIGURATIONS

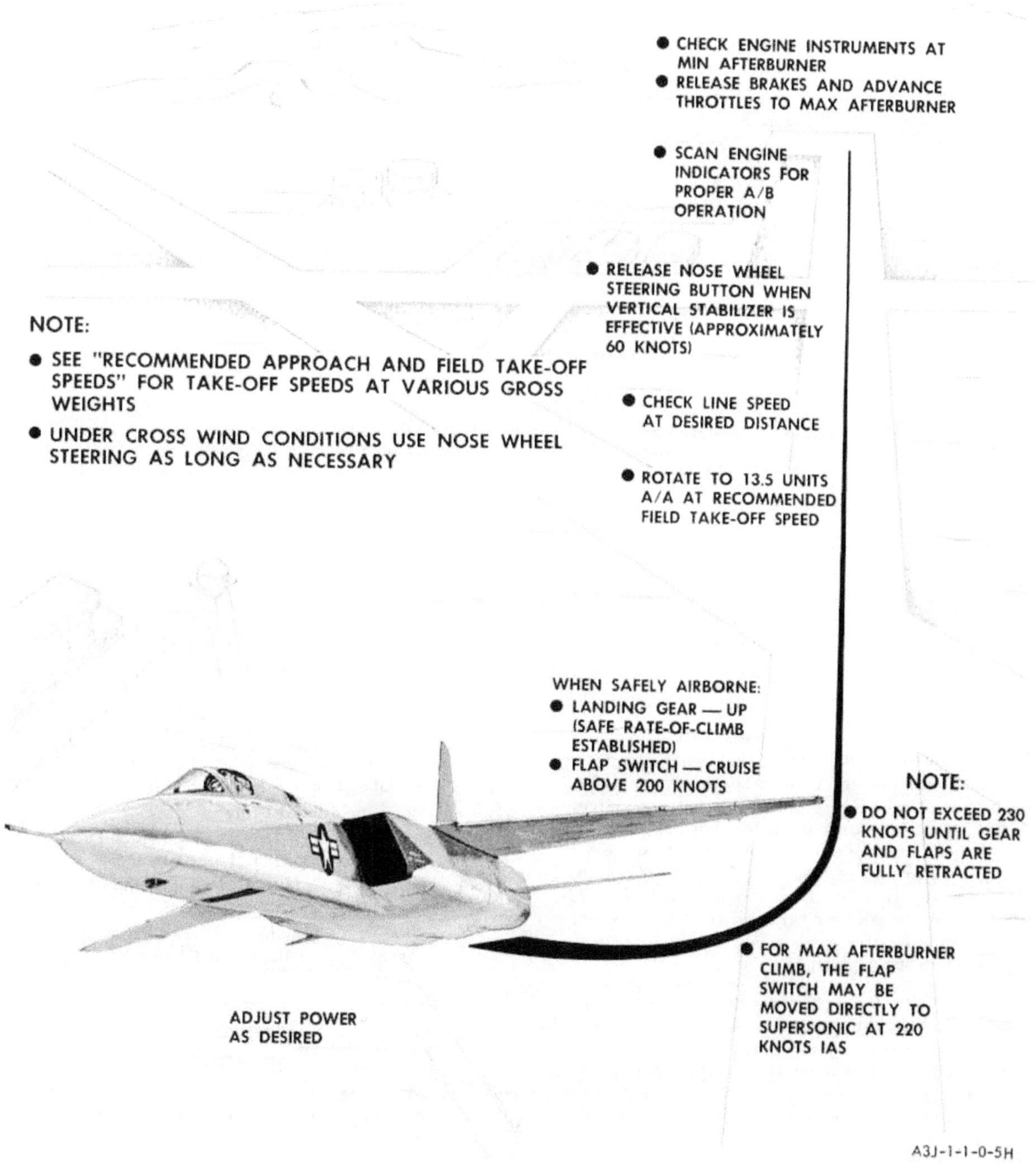

- CHECK ENGINE INSTRUMENTS AT MIN AFTERBURNER
- RELEASE BRAKES AND ADVANCE THROTTLES TO MAX AFTERBURNER

- SCAN ENGINE INDICATORS FOR PROPER A/B OPERATION

- RELEASE NOSE WHEEL STEERING BUTTON WHEN VERTICAL STABILIZER IS EFFECTIVE (APPROXIMATELY 60 KNOTS)

NOTE:
- SEE "RECOMMENDED APPROACH AND FIELD TAKE-OFF SPEEDS" FOR TAKE-OFF SPEEDS AT VARIOUS GROSS WEIGHTS
- UNDER CROSS WIND CONDITIONS USE NOSE WHEEL STEERING AS LONG AS NECESSARY

- CHECK LINE SPEED AT DESIRED DISTANCE

- ROTATE TO 13.5 UNITS A/A AT RECOMMENDED FIELD TAKE-OFF SPEED

WHEN SAFELY AIRBORNE:
- LANDING GEAR — UP (SAFE RATE-OF-CLIMB ESTABLISHED)
- FLAP SWITCH — CRUISE ABOVE 200 KNOTS

NOTE:
- DO NOT EXCEED 230 KNOTS UNTIL GEAR AND FLAPS ARE FULLY RETRACTED

- FOR MAX AFTERBURNER CLIMB, THE FLAP SWITCH MAY BE MOVED DIRECTLY TO SUPERSONIC AT 220 KNOTS IAS

ADJUST POWER AS DESIRED

A3J-1-1-0-5H

Figure 3-4

a delay in obtaining IFR clearance is expected, the clearance should be obtained prior to starting engines. It is necessary to use cooling air to operate the radios without engines.

Note

Depressing the cooling air switch in the external cooling air receptacle connector to operate cooled equipment without cooling air will damage the aircraft and is *prohibited*.

CHECKOFF LIST

1. The pilot will ensure that all checks have been accomplished prior to take-off.
2. The S/O will ensure that all checks have been accomplished and so inform the pilot prior to take-off.

BEFORE TAXIING INTO POSITION

1. COCKPIT PRESS switch—NORM (RAM EMERG if high humidity exists).
2. COCKPIT TEMP knob—position 2 (to prevent fogging).
3. Caution indicators—OUT, except ENG DOOR (ELEC F/C, PITCH AUG if desired).
4. Harness—LOCKED.
5. Speed brakes—IN.
6. Engine rpm—80%.
7. Flaps/droops—40/30 degrees.
8. Pitch trim—4 units ND.
9. Aft tank quantity—check for transfer.
10. Bomb bay CANS transfer switch—ON.
11. Bomb bay cans quantity—check for transfer.
12. PRESS SUIT FLOW knob—OFF.
13. MIC SEL switch—HOT.

Note

Under conditions where the aircraft has been subjected to heavy precipitation prior to flight, the windshield and canopy defrost system should be turned on at full flow, and the engines operated at 85% rpm for at least 20 seconds to purge water from the air conditioning system. If a 20-second run-up is not feasible, move the COCKPIT PRESS switch to RAM EMERG.

TAKE-OFF PROCEDURES

The take-off roll will not be initiated until the approved take-off check list, posted on the canopy molding, has been completed. Flaps will be set at 40 degrees for all normal take-offs. The entire runway length will be utilized for take-offs. Take-off distance and airspeed will be determined prior to each take-off. See figure 3-4 for a typical take-off.

1. After assuming the take-off position and ensuring that the nose wheel is straight, apply brakes and advance throttles to MIL thrust.
2. Check:
   RPM—100 (±0.5) % (at 5°C, OAT and above)
   EGT—625 (±10) °C
   Oil pressure—45—70 psi (37—67 psi*)
   Nozzles—1/4
   Fuel flow—700 to 10,000 pph

MILITARY THRUST RPM vs AMBIENT TEMPERATURE
(INLET AIR TEMPERATURE INDICATOR — STATIC CONDITIONS)

OAT (°C)	% RPM (±0.5)
5 and higher	100
0	99
−10	98
−20	96.5
−30	95

3. Select MIN AFTERBURNER and determine that both afterburners light off (3 seconds maximum from MIL).

Note

If aircraft gross weight is insufficient, tire skidding may be experienced.

4. Check nozzles—3/4.
5. Engage nose wheel steering.
6. Release brakes.
7. Advance throttles to MAX AFTERBURNER.
8. Check:
   EGT—625 (±10) °C
   Nozzles—full open and steady

TAKE-OFF TECHNIQUE

1. Acceleration at MAX AFTERBURNER is quite rapid at all gross weights.
2. Use nose wheel steering until rudder control is effective (about 60 KIAS).
3. Rotate the aircraft to take-off attitude (13.5 units angle of attack) as it accelerates to 10 knots below take-off speed. See figure 3-5.
4. Allow the aircraft to fly off.
5. Establish a positive rate of climb, then raise the landing gear.
6. Raise the flaps at 200 KIAS and 200 feet (VFR), or 1000 feet (night/IFR).
   Ensure that landing gear and flaps are retracted prior to exceeding 230 KIAS.

CAUTION

Severe crosswind conditions may require longer use of nose wheel steering and higher take-off speeds.

*Aircraft not having Engine Bulletin 104 complied with

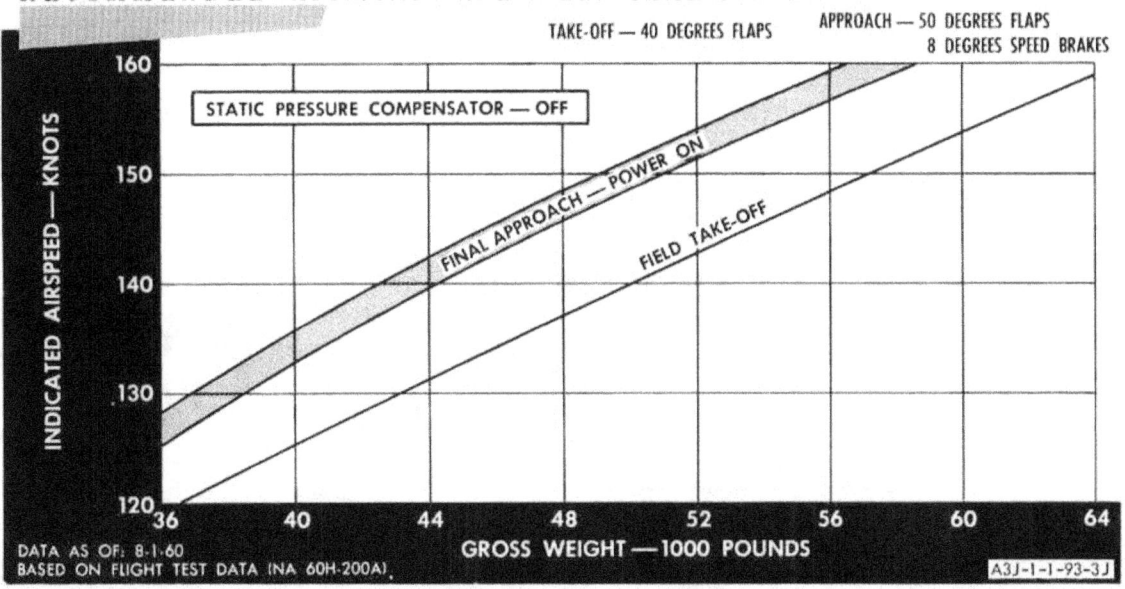

Figure 3-5

AFTER TAKE-OFF

1. SPC—ON (Depress).
2. HYD SUB-SYS ISOLATION switch—FLIGHT.
3. COCKPIT PRESS switch—NORM.
4. DROP TANK TRANSFER buttons—ON (Depress).
5. PRESS SUIT FLOW knob—ON (as desired).
6. MIC SEL switch—as desired.

PENETRATION AND LANDING

COMMENCING DESCENT

1. SPC button—OFF (Depress; Release up).
2. HYD SUB-SYS ISOLATION switch—TAKE OFF/LANDING.
3. Defrost—as required.
4. Pilot's radar altimeter—Override.
5. Altimeter—set.
6. PITOT ANTI-ICE button, ENGINE ANTI-ICE switch—as desired.
7. MIC SEL switch—HOT.

NORMAL APPROACH AND LANDING

1. Enter the landing pattern for break at 250 KIAS (SPC OFF) and at the specified break altitude for the field. See figure 3-6. At the break, establish not more than a 45-degree bank, open speed brakes, and reduce power to 78% rpm (detents). Adjust upwind turn to place the downwind leg 1½ to 2 miles abeam. Below 230 KIAS, select 50-degree flaps and extend the landing gear. On downwind, check speed brakes retracted to 8 degrees (use mirror).

2. On the downwind leg, when the aircraft is level, complete the landing check list.
   (a) AFCS—off.
   (b) Flaps/droops—50/30 degrees.
   (c) Wheels—down.
   (d) Speed brakes—8 degrees (OUT).
   (e) Hook—as required.
   (f) Harness—LOCKED.
   (g) PRESS SUIT FLOW knob—OFF.

3. Plan the base leg to allow for a 1½-mile final. Altitude at the 90-degree position should be 600 to 800 feet, with angle of attack stabilized at 13.5 units. Maintain 13.5 units throughout the remainder of the approach. Stabilize rate of descent with power and hold 13.5 units until touchdown.

4. Fly the aircraft onto the runway, holding approach speed and attitude.

5. Do not attempt to salvage a bad approach. Touchdown should be made in the first 500 feet of runway or on the designated GCA or mirror touchdown point.

In the event the landing looks long or a porpoise occurs, the correct course of action is to take a wave-off.

Section III
Part 3

NAVWEPS 01-60ABA-1

TYPICAL FIELD LANDING

ENTRY
- 250 KIAS (OR AS LOCALLY PRESCRIBED)
- FLAP SWITCH — CRUISE
- HYDRAULIC SUBSYSTEMS ISOLATION SWITCH — TAKE-OFF/LANDING

STATIC PRESSURE COMPENSATOR — OFF

BREAK
- 78% RPM (DETENTS)
- SPEED BRAKES — OUT
- ESTABLISH MAXIMUM OF 45° BANK

DOWNWIND
- 1½ TO 2 MILES ABEAM
- BELOW 230 KNOTS IAS, FLAPS — 50°
- LANDING GEAR — DOWN
- LANDING CHECKLIST — COMPLETE

RECHECK
- HARNESS — LOCKED
- LANDING GEAR INDICATORS — DN
- FLAP/DROOP INDICATORS — 50°/30°
- HYDRAULIC PRESSURES — NORMAL
- SPEED BRAKES — 8°
- YAW TRIM — 0 UNITS

NOTE:
- FOR APPROACH SPEEDS AT VARIOUS GROSS WEIGHTS, SEE "RECOMMENDED APPROACH AND FIELD TAKE-OFF SPEEDS" CHART IN THIS SECTION

BASE (90°)
- 600 FEET ABOVE GROUND
- 13.5 UNITS ANGLE-OF-ATTACK

WAVE-OFF
- THROTTLES — MIL
- SPEED BRAKES — IN
- FLAPS — 40°

IF LEAVING PATTERN
- LANDING GEAR — UP
- FLAP SWITCH — CRUISE (ABOVE 200 KNOTS IAS)

FINAL
- LEVEL 1½ MILES OUT
- 13.5 UNITS ANGLE-OF-ATTACK

AFTER TOUCHDOWN
- THROTTLES — IDLE
- USE AERODYNAMIC BRAKING
- LOWER NOSE WHEEL AT 100 TO 80 KIAS
- CENTER PEDALS AND ENGAGE NOSE WHEEL STEERING FOR TAXI

Caution:
ON LANDING ROLL OUT, ENSURE THAT THROTTLES ARE RETARDED PAST 78% RPM DETENTS

A3J-1-1-0-15E

Figure 3-6

6. On touchdown, retard throttles to IDLE and commence aerodynamic braking.

CAUTION

Ensure that throttles are retarded past the 78% detents.

7. Continue aerodynamic braking until:
   (a) The nose drops through at about 100 KIAS, or
   (b) Only 4000 feet of runway remains, whichever occurs first.
8. With all three wheels on deck, continue holding the stick aft and commence steady braking.
9. Maintain directional control with rudder and differential braking. Be prepared to use nose wheel steering if any evidence of a directional control problem exists.

CAUTION

- Center pedals before engaging nose wheel steering.
- Braking on slippery runways must be commenced lightly and with caution, increasing in amplitude as the aircraft decelerates. Otherwise, a blown tire may result. Should this occur, it is *most important* to maintain directional control with nose wheel steering.
- Check for normal braking prior to passing runway abort gear. If normal braking is not available, immediately check for emergency brakes. If both brake systems have failed, LOWER THE ARRESTING HOOK.

WARNING

During a normal landing approach, DO NOT retard the throttles aft of the BLC decay warning detents. Reducing rpm below 78% results in a rapid loss of lift and an abrupt nose-down pitch because of boundary layer control airflow decay.

LANDING TECHNIQUE

The constant rate of descent to touchdown landing technique shall normally be employed for all landings. If the aircraft is "on" angle of attack, thus having the correct speed for a given gross weight, and pitch attitude is not undergoing any transition at the moment of touchdown, the aircraft will touch down comfortably on the main wheels, rock forward on the nose wheel, and exhibit no tendency to bounce. A bounce or porpoise can be initiated by landing nose wheel first or pushing the nose down at touchdown, and should be avoided. If a porpoise develops, take an immediate wave-off.

CROSSWIND LANDINGS

Normally, no serious problems are to be expected when landing in a cross wind with a 90-degree component up to 15 knots. The wing-down (forward slip) method may be used in cross winds of up to 10 knots at 90 degrees. A combined wing-down/crab technique must be used for 90-degree components between 10 and 15 knots. If the 90-degree component exceeds 15 knots, change runways or go to an alternate airfield (if available) where acceptable wind conditions prevail. Lower the nose shortly after touchdown (nose-high aerodynamic braking is not recommended if the component exceeds 10 knots) and utilize nose wheel steering if necessary to maintain directional control. Lateral correction should be used during the rollout. At approximately 80 knots, the aircraft will tend to "heel" due to the cross wind. The amount of "heel" in a 10- to 12-knot cross wind may be uncomfortable, but directional control available is more than adequate. Full stick into the wind is effective in reducing the "heel" due to cross wind, thus increasing brake effectiveness on the upwind wheel.

1. Make a wing-down approach, combined with "crabbing" as required.
2. Immediately upon touchdown, retard throttles to IDLE.
3. Use aerodynamic braking if 90-degree crosswind component is less than 10 knots.
4. With all three wheels on the deck, commence steady braking.
5. To reduce "heel" due to cross wind, hold stick into the wind.
6. Use nose wheel steering to maintain directional control, if required.

TOUCH-AND-GO PRACTICE

Touch-and-go landing practice will be accomplished using the same technique as described in NORMAL APPROACH AND LANDING, in this section. After landing, retard the throttles to IDLE and allow the aircraft to settle down on a short runout prior to applying power for the take-off. Leave the speed brakes at 8 degrees and flaps at 50° as take-off power is applied. Be alert for yaw in case the engines do not accelerate evenly. The landing gear and flaps will not normally be retracted after a touch-and-go landing.

NIGHT LANDINGS

Night landings will employ the same techniques described for day landings; that is, power-on approach using a constant rate of descent to touchdown. The taxi light may be used on final approach during shore-based operations only if the pilot keeps the following points in mind:

1. Use of the light is recommended when doubt exists as to construction clearance, line-up, etc.

2. Switching on the light may cause radical readjustment of depth perception at a critical point.
3. Ground personnel, such as runway watches, may be temporarily blinded and unable to perform their duties.
4. Use of the light is prohibited aboard ship; its use ashore should be minimized.

STOPPING THE AIRCRAFT

The in-flight performance and handling qualities of this aircraft tend to mask its overall size and gross weight. It is extremely important, therefore, to know the proper braking techniques and limitations in order that landings may be safely accomplished.

TOUCHDOWN SPEED

To stay within its capabilities, the brake system must be given the advantage of a properly executed approach with touchdown at the optimum speed for gross weight. A touchdown above recommended speed creates greatly increased kinetic energy over that created by a landing at the correct speed. This energy must be absorbed by the brakes in the form of heat. The hotter brakes become, the less effective they are.

AERODYNAMIC BRAKING

In order to gain the most effective use of the energy-absorbing capabilities of the brakes, aerodynamic braking must be used to decrease the kinetic energy present at touchdown.

NOSE-HIGH METHOD

Optimum aerodynamic braking is obtained by raising the nose after touchdown, keeping the main wheels lightly on the runway. Aft stick travel is increased steadily as speed decreases until full aft stick is attained. The drag rise in this attitude, with flaps at 40 or 50 degrees, results in noticeable deceleration. The nose will fall through at approximately 100 knots with normal fuel remaining, but the stick should be held aft to obtain the drag of the displaced horizontal stabilizers.

Note

Flaps should be left at 40 degrees for aborted take-offs, or 50 degrees for landings, since the total deceleration of full aft stick and extended flaps decreases ground roll distance more than if flaps are retracted and wheel braking is started early.

THREE-POINT METHOD

An alternate method of aerodynamic braking is to lower the nose immediately on touchdown and steadily increase aft stick travel, leaving the nose wheel on the runway. *This method is approximately 80 percent as effective* as the nose-high method, but is effective at high gross weights and safer for use in strong cross winds.

WHEEL BRAKING

Approximately 36 million foot-pounds of energy may be absorbed before brake fading occurs. This figure is much lower if brakes are hot from previous use. Up to 6 million pounds of energy are absorbed during normal taxiing to the runway, with no external stores, at average taxi speeds. For an aborted take-off, total capacity is then far less than design. It is, therefore, important that taxiing be accomplished at speeds requiring minimum use of brakes. The following table shows recommended wheel braking initiation speed to obtain 80 and 100 percent of the energy-absorbing capacity of a set of NEW brakes:

		MAXIMUM SPEED FOR BRAKING INITIATION IN KNOTS (SPC — OFF)	
GROSS WEIGHT (Pounds)	APPROACH SPEED (Knots)	80% CAPACITY (20% remaining when stopped)	100% CAPACITY (Faded when stopped)
36,000	127	127	—
40,000	134	124	—
44,000	141	118	131
48,000	147	114	126
52,000	153	109	121
56,000	159	105	116
60,000	165	101	112

Note

During aborted take-offs or landings at high gross weights, constant wheel braking should not be commenced until speed is approximately 100 knots. Intermittent braking may be used if speed is below that shown in the 80 percent column of the table. Refer to BRAKING TECHNIQUE, in this section.

Initiation of constant braking at the speeds shown in the 100 percent column of the table results in brake fade to zero capability as speed approaches zero. The 80 percent capacity speeds assume use of the three-point method of aerodynamic braking from touchdown to stop. The speeds shown are all above 100 knots; however, it must be remembered that these figures correspond to a set of new brakes with full design capacity.

Note

A speed of 100 KIAS is considered adequate for initiation of wheel braking for all conditions and will provide a safe margin for old or slightly heated brakes.

BRAKING TECHNIQUE

After using aerodynamic braking to the recommended initiation speed (or light intermittent braking at high gross weights), and with all three wheels on the runway, brake pressure should be applied gently until the pedals feel "solid." Firm pressure should then be applied and held, increasing pressure as speed decreases until the aircraft is stopped or taxi speed is reached. Exercise care, however, since it is difficult to detect tire skidding, even on dry runway.

Intermittent Braking

It has been established that very little effective brake cooling is gained through intermittent braking. However, chances of skidding or blowout due to excess brake pressure are reduced. Calculations reveal that landing rollout distance is increased considerably by intermittent braking, inasmuch as there are short periods of zero braking effect. As much as 400 feet may pass between applications of pressure if released for 2 to 3 seconds.

Note

Since no significant cooling results from intermittent braking, it is recommended that constant brake pressure be used for normal landings. Above 100 knots, light, steady braking should be used if required. As speed decreases, pedal pressure should steadily increase.

FIELD ARRESTMENTS

Field arrested landings will be made when the aircraft has suffered physical damage which might have rendered braking ineffective (e.g., a blown tire). When available, fly-in type arresting gear will be used for emergency arresting landings. Refer to FIELD ARRESTMENT in Section V.

POSTFLIGHT

AFTER LANDING

When clear of the runway:

1. Hook — up.
2. Flap switch — SUPERSONIC.
3. Anti-ice switches — OFF.
4. Trim — neutral.
5. Canopy — as desired.
6. SUMP switch — LOW.
7. Wings, tail — Fold as required.

ENGINE SHUTDOWN

The engines should be stabilized at IDLE for 2 to 3 minutes (including taxi time) to allow temperature stabilization.

1. Air and electrical units — as required.
2. Chocks — in place.
3. Pedal adjust — full aft.
4. Gear safety locks — check installed.
5. CNI power — OFF.
6. RADAR/TV POWER — OFF.
   Check with S/O before shutdown.
7. Throttles — OFF.
8. Engine MASTERS — OFF.
9. Generator dropout (28% — 30%) — check.
10. Engine rundown (120 seconds) — check.
11. Seat and canopy jettison pins — installed.
12. Canopy uplock — ENGAGED.
13. Aircraft discrepancies — check.

DEBRIEFING

Debriefing will be conducted in accordance with Part 1 of this section.

PART 4 — CARRIER-BASED PROCEDURES (PILOT)

COMMAND RESPONSIBILITY

When carrier-based, the squadron is under the administrative and operational control of the Air Group Commander and the ship. All official reports or requests will be processed through the proper chain of command. It is reasonable to assume that operational procedures will vary between ships. For this reason, it is mandatory that the Command review standard ship operating procedures to determine, prior to the commencement of operations, that there are no variations which, in the opinion of the Command, are dangerous to the safe and orderly operation of squadron aircraft. Published NATOPS procedures will not be violated without the approval of the Commanding Officer or his duly authorized representative. The Operations Officer shall provide the ship's Air Officer and Air Operations Officer with all data required for the proper operation and employment of the A-5A prior to embarkation.

SCHEDULING

FLIGHT SCHEDULING

The Air Operations Officer of the carrier is responsible to the ship's Operations Officer for the daily flight schedule (Air Plan). The schedule is normally published the evening before any scheduled air operations and includes all pertinent information, such as fuel loads, ordnance, mission, etc, for the entire air group. Squadrons will submit flight requirements to the Air Operations Officer. The squadron Operations Officer will assign tactical crews to the flight commitments assigned by the ship's Air Plan. Day and night flights normally will be equally divided among crews. A day flight normally will be scheduled prior to a night flight after long in-port periods. The flight assignments will be indicated on the ready room scheduling board. At the end of each operating day, the completed commitments shall be transcribed to a daily corrected flight schedule. It shall be the responsibility of the squadron Operations Officer to keep Air Operations advised as to aircraft and crew lineup for each scheduled sortie. Air Operations will be notified promptly of any changes.

GROUND TRAINING SCHEDULES

1. Weekly ground training requirements will be determined and published in order to allow time for those affected to make adequate preparation.

2. Daily ground training schedules will cover the events listed on the weekly schedule and will be posted with the daily flight schedule.

3. In port, the daily ground training schedule will be posted in lieu of a flight schedule.

MANNING READY ROOM

Though this topic is generally given little formal consideration, flight efficiency begins in the ready room. Flights are often delayed because crews do not man the ready room on time for adequate briefing. Such procedure can result in failure of the mission. Therefore, it is mandatory that the ready room be manned at least 1 hour prior to scheduled launch time when operating aboard. In the event of multi-plane flights, all pilots and crews shall ensure that they are briefed thoroughly on all phases of the mission.

"Tail-end Charlie" may find himself leading the entire flight and, if he is not properly briefed, the resulting confusion may very well prove to be more than embarrassing. At the completion of the briefing, all crew members will man their aircraft when directed by Air Operations.

BRIEFING

Briefings will be in accordance with Part 1 of this section.

FLIGHT OPERATIONS

Note

Only those procedures which differ from shore-based procedures are described herein.

TOWING

Whenever the aircraft is towed without external hydraulic pressure applied, braking is dependent upon the two accumulators. Towing will not be started unless the normal brake accumulator has at least 1200 psi and emergency 2000 psi. Whenever the foot brake (normal) accumulator is exhausted, pull the emergency brake handle and do not move the aircraft further until both accumulators are recharged. The accumulators may be recharged by motoring over one of the engines with an external start air unit for about 1 minute, with external electric power supplied.

MANNING AIRCRAFT

Aircraft will be manned as directed by Air Operations; however, pilots shall man their aircraft in sufficient time to ensure an adequate preflight inspection. Normally, 25 minutes before scheduled launch should be adequate. Crew members will man their aircraft in a smart, expeditious manner. Helmets will not be worn on the flight deck until after manning the aircraft. The Plane Captain will meet the pilot and accompany him throughout the preflight inspection. Double-check aircraft gross weight written on the side of the fuselage.

PRESSURE SUITS

If the pressure suit is worn, the helmet may be worn, if desired, but under such conditions the crewman will be accompanied by another person without a helmet. The aircraft may be preflighted by the Plane Captain and a qualified crew other than the flight crew. The aircraft will be ready for manning upon arrival of the flight crew. When pressure suits are used, or on any flight using the AN/ASB-12 bomb directing set, external cooling air will be required. For other flights, cooling air is optional; however, the ship must know that, without cooling air, no radio communication with the aircraft is possible until engines are started.

NAVIGATOR (B/N)

The B/N will ascertain the status of the alinement prior to manning aircraft and complete such alinement as remains. The aircraft should not be moved during alinement. If such movement is unavoidable, the B/N shall advise the pilot of probable weapons system capability and possible compensation effects available in regard to overall mission capability. If the mission will be thus compromised, the facts will be reported to the ship's Operations Officer prior to launch.

Note

Accuracy of the autonavigator, and thus of the bombing solution, is dependent on accuracy of the initial alinement, and hence on the quality of the initial inputs, as well as on the time duration of alinement. If ship-based, it is also dependent on the maneuvers of the ship during alinement. For best results, a 30-minute alinement is required; a 15-minute alinement is marginally acceptable.

STARTING AND POSTSTART PROCEDURES

1. Engines will be started on order from Pri-Fly.
2. A 5-minute warm-up of all systems (other than the bomb directing set) is required after engine start.
3. Complete all items of the check list except (a) flap setting, (b) pitch trim setting, (c) compass synchronization, and (d) wing spread, prior to taxiing. A complete flight control system check is mandatory—do not allow yourself to be rushed. Make all checks in a thorough and expeditious manner.

CAUTION

Prior to extending wing droops and flaps, ensure adequate folded wing clearance exists in order to prevent droop damage.

4. When the Yellow Shirt director holds a thumb "up" to determine whether or not you are ready to pull tie-downs, do not answer (thumb up) unless ready to taxi in all respects. If not ready, hold your hand up, palm out, as a signal to stand by.
5. When an aircraft is determined to be "down," the pilot will immediately indicate this to the Plane Captain, the Plane Director, and to Pri-Fly Control by radio, if conditions of radio silence are not in effect. It is important that discrepancies which will down an aircraft be discovered as soon as possible and communicated to Flight Deck Control in order to avoid interfering with the launch. For this reason, it is paramount that pilots make every effort to determine the status of their aircraft prior to taxi from the spot position. If the aircraft is determined to be "down," the crew will remain in the cockpit until relieved by the Plane Captain or the aircraft has been chocked and tied down.

TAXI PROCEDURES

Taxiing on a carrier flight deck, which often may be wet, pitching, rolling, or heaving, calls for extreme care on the part of all pilots. The Plane Director's signals must be followed religiously. Know your signals and answer them without delay. Taxi speeds shall be restricted to a fast walk. Keep the director in sight at all times. If the signal is not understood or you lose sight of the director—STOP.

1. Use only as much power as is required to taxi. Use nose wheel steering, not brakes, for taxi; however, have feet up in such a manner that brakes may be quickly applied.
2. Spread wings, aline compass, set flap control switch at 40°, and set pitch trim in accordance with current Catapult Launching Bulletins (approximately 3 degrees ND) prior to taxiing onto the catapult.

Note

With flaps extended, nose wheel steering is restricted to approximately 45 degrees left and right.

CAUTION

Ship's magnetism may cause compass errors. Recheck compass after launch and synchronize if necessary.

3. Check:
   (a) COCKPIT PRESS switch—NORM.
   (b) COCKPIT TEMP knob—position 2.
   (c) Caution indicators—OUT, except ENG DOOR (ELEC F/C and PITCH AUG if desired).
   (d) Harness—LOCKED.
   (e) Speed brakes—IN.
   (f) Flaps/droops—40°/30°.
   (g) Pitch, yaw, and roll trim—Set.

(h) Bomb bay CANS transfer switch—AUTO.
(i) Sump fuel over 4000 pounds (with bomb bay can fuel) or 2200 pounds (without bomb bay can fuel).

4. Taxiing onto the catapult is a relatively simple maneuver if the director's signals are followed explicitly. As the nose wheel rolls over the shuttle, apply full brakes. At this point, ease forward in small increments while the hold-back fitting and bridle are rigged. Continue easing forward until the hold-back fitting is tensioned. When this is accomplished, the director will give the "take tension" and "release brakes" signal. Advance both throttles to MIL and adjust quadrant friction.

LAUNCH PROCEDURE

1. Never launch with a partial wing fuel load of more than 1200 pounds as a swerve during the catapult power stroke will result. For partial fuel launches such as carquals, fuel only the sump, aft tank, and bomb bay cans; leave the wings empty.

2. The Catapult Officer will pick up the aircraft with a two- (five-) finger turnup signal. Do not use afterburner unless (a) such a launch was previously agreed upon, and (b) the Catapult Officer gives the AB signal (five-finger turnup). If the flight was planned as an AB launch, and the Catapult Officer does not give the AB signal, do not salute until the situation is clarified. If the aircraft is inadvertently launched while still at MIL thrust, immediately select MAX AFTERBURNER during the launch stroke. The afterburner should light off at, or very slightly after, the completion of the power stroke. Normally, minimum afterburner will be utilized for all launches at gross weights of 55,000 pounds and above.

3. At the turnup signal, position body properly with head back against the headrest, check all engine and system indicators and, when ready, salute the Catapult Officer (day) or move the exterior lights master switch to ON (night). The launch normally will occur within 2 to 4 seconds. In the event the catapult is suspended, maintain MIL power until the Catapult Officer walks directly in front of the aircraft and signals to throttle back.

4. If, after the salute (or exterior lights master switch ON) signal, the aircraft goes down, transmit "SUSPEND—SUSPEND" on L/L frequency. This signal will be heard in Pri-Fly, and the suspend button may be pushed in time to hold the launch.

5. During the power stroke, back up the stick near the neutral position and either back up the throttles or use the catapult handgrip. Do not grasp the throttles without using the catapult handgrip as power may be inadvertently retarded.

6. If longitudinal trim has been properly set, the aircraft will, upon bridle release, fly off smoothly with no substantial control input required. Do not overrotate; however, ensure that a positive rate of climb is established.

7. During the latter phase of the power stroke and immediately after becoming airborne, the static pressure instruments will temporarily indicate erroneously, i.e., rate of climb approximately 500 fpm down, pressure altimeter at or below zero altitude. Additionally, the AAI may precess in pitch. For these reasons, utilize the angle-of-attack indicator (14 units) as the primary means of maintaining an appropriate pitch attitude and the AAI to maintain wings level.

8. Do not be in a hurry to retract the gear after launch. Drag increases momentarily while the gear retracts, so wait until positive rate of climb is established prior to gear retraction. Do not retract the flaps until 200 KIAS and 200 feet (VFR), or 1000 feet (night and/or IFR), are attained.

9. Stay below 500 feet until 3 to 5 miles ahead of the ship and clear of the recovery pattern.

10. If AB is used during the launch, do not retard power to MIL thrust until the flaps are retracted.

11. Try to avoid excessive use of lateral control immediately after the launch, as drag increases markedly with large lateral inputs. If turbulence is experienced immediately after the launch, try only to level the wings; do not try to return to course until speed builds up and the increased drag, due to lateral inputs, is less critical.

12. If pitch augmentation monitors off during the launch, be prepared for a longitudinal trim change accompanied by considerably increased longitudinal stick forces. This situation is uncomfortable but entirely manageable.

RENDEZVOUS AND DEPARTURE

Rendezvous and departure will be in accordance with Section IV and NWIP 41-3, Chapter 8.

RECOVERY PROCEDURES

MARSHAL

1. The flight operating sectors for a formation of two or more carriers are set forth in ATP-1(A).

2. Returning aircraft will normally call for marshaling instructions 20 minutes prior to the scheduled recovery time, reporting position and fuel state. A Marshal altitude and sector will be assigned by the ship. While proceeding to the assigned Marshal point, do not approach the ship any closer than the assigned Marshal distance, except under positive control of the ship.

3. On arrival at the assigned Marshal point (usually 10 minutes to the scheduled recovery time), aircraft will report arrival and fuel state and commence rendezvous with the remainder of the flight, if scheduled and if weather permits.

TYPICAL CARRIER LANDING

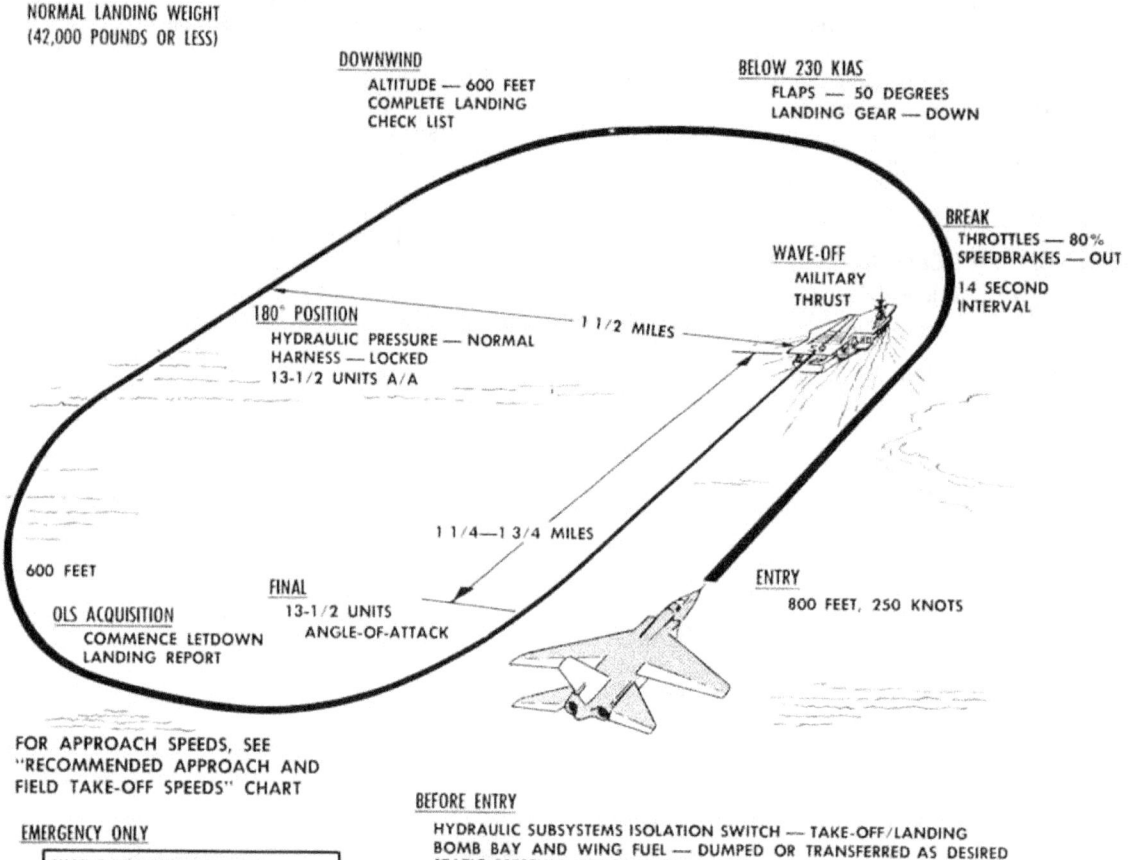

Figure 3-7

4. When rendezvoused, fuel permitting, extend arresting hooks and conduct visual inspection of the arresting hook bumper to ensure that it is in the overcenter position. Limit airspeed to 250 KIAS for extension.

APPROACH

Control and recovery of aircraft from the Marshal point will be in accordance with the individual ship's operating procedures. Generally, aircraft will penetrate as a division at 250 KIAS down to 600 feet. Flight leaders will report "see you" after passing the 10-mile Gate. At this time, the flight will switch to the recovery frequency and enter the landing pattern.

LANDING PATTERN

1. Generally, the landing pattern (figure 3-7) is entered at 600 feet, 250 KIAS, by flying in right echelon, parallel to the ship's course, close aboard the starboard side.

2. If the pattern is full, the flight should go around and reenter to avoid extending the landing pattern too far ahead of the ship. The tower should be advised of the go-around and the flight should climb to 1500 feet until passing the abeam position.

3. The leader will break, as necessary, to maintain a proper interval (40 seconds at the ramp) on the last aircraft upwind.
4. Break smartly (14-second interval), extend speed brakes, reduce power to 80%, slow to 230 KIAS, lower gear and flaps, check SPC—OFF.
5. On the downwind leg, maintain 600 feet, distance abeam 1½ miles. Complete the landing checkoff list and assume appropriate speed to maintain landing interval, decelerating to 13.5 units angle of attack by the 180-degree position.
6. Turn abeam the stern of the ship. A consistent pattern must be flown to realize a proper landing interval. Do not vary the pattern to make amends for the aircraft ahead at the expense of those behind. Generally, aircraft that are long in the groove will be waved off.
7. A report to the tower will be made when intercepting the ball. The report will include side number, fuel state, and type aircraft.
8. The maximum landing weight is 42,000 pounds. Configuration (pylons, drop tanks, bomb bay cans, etc) must be considered when computing maximum allowable fuel remaining for landing. Drop tanks will be empty and bomb bay cans will have a maximum of 2000 pounds fuel for an arrested landing. Plan fuel to be at or below maximum landing weight prior to reaching the abeam position.

CARRIER APPROACH

1. The aircraft is easy and comfortable to fly during a carrier approach. Pilot's vision is good, and aircraft response is adequate if proper speed is maintained. Excess thrust available for wave-offs is exceptional. The lateral control system, by means of spoiler/deflectors, is adequate if speed is maintained; however, if speed is allowed to drop below that required for 13.5 units angle of attack, lateral control becomes marginal.

CAUTION

At approach speeds, large spoiler deflections resulting from lateral control movements will cause a high sink rate. This condition will be amplified in a slow or decelerating approach, particularly when any ramp turbulence is encountered. This condition is extremely difficult for the pilot or LSO to detect at night, and a dangerous low-at-the-ramp situation may develop. Ramp turbulence and burble increase sharply when wind over the deck optimums are exceeded.

2. Each pilot is expected to fly his own approach. The LSO will offer advisory comments as he deems necessary; however, the wave-off is mandatory. A pilot may take a voluntary wave-off at any time he considers an unsafe condition exists; however, late wave-offs are extremely dangerous.

ARRESTMENT

Treat every carrier landing as a touch-and-go. As soon as the gear touches the deck, advance throttles to MIL thrust and hold until all forward motion stops. As the runout is completed, sharply reduce power to IDLE, engage nose wheel steering, stay off the brakes, and allow the aircraft to roll back. As the pendant clears the tail hook, the director will give a "hook up" signal, then retract the hook. As the hook retracts, the director will give a series of rapid come-ahead signals. Add power and taxi smartly out of the gear and across the foul line. Once clear of the foul line, retard power and check for normal braking. If none is available, use the emergency system and advise Primary of the loss of normal braking and that a tow will be required. While taxiing, fold the wings and remain alert for nose wheel steering malfunctions. Should a malfunction occur, release the nose wheel steering button, and use normal braking for directional control. If the aircraft is to be struck below, the radome must be folded. Do not initiate the radome folding cycle until spotted on the elevator, due to restricted forward vision.

CAUTION

The pilot must ensure that the B/N has properly secured the bomb directing set prior to folding the radome.

Should the aircraft hang up in the gear and it becomes necessary to pull it back with the arresting gear engine, ensure that nose wheel steering is engaged to prevent the nose wheel from swiveling.

BOLTERS

If the aircraft bolts the deck, allow it to fly off smoothly, then rotate nose-up slightly as the round-down is cleared, to establish a positive rate of climb. After the climb is established and comfortably airborne, take up a heading parallel to the FOXTROT CORPEN. Reenter downwind, taking a normal interval to other aircraft in the pattern.

BINGO FUEL

Bingo fuel is that fuel required to reach the break of a diversionary field (not nearest land) under VFR conditions with 1500 pounds remaining. In addition, sufficient fuel shall be computed to complete a standard jet penetration unless the weather at the diversionary field is 5000 feet and 5 miles or more and forecast to remain so for 1 hour after estimated arrival time. Know the Bingo fuel and be prepared to advise the ship of DOG time remaining or the number of passes that can be made before reaching Bingo fuel (a tight pass requires about 400 pounds of fuel). "Low state" will be declared at any point in the pattern or during the approach when usable fuel remaining reaches "Bingo." Should the pilot be confronted with a low fuel state, he will either be given priority in the pattern, directed to the emergency tanker, or diverted. Bingo data is set forth in the NATOPS Pocket Check List (NAVWEPS 01-60ABA-1B). When operating at sea, where diversionary fields are not available, all flights shall be planned to arrive at the break with a minimum of 4000 pounds of fuel. In this case, "low state" shall be declared any time usable fuel remaining reaches 1700 pounds. This fuel quantity should be adequate for three or four tight passes. A minimum of 500 pounds of fuel at the 180-degree position is needed to commence the final pass. The decision to use the barricade will be made by the Commanding Officer of the ship.

BROKEN WIRE OR HOOK

If a wire or hook breaks during an arrestment, it will be felt as an initial deceleration, followed by a sudden release. At this time, select MAX AFTERBURNER on both engines. Allow the aircraft to fly off the round-down, then deliberately but not too hurriedly rotate the nose up. In an emergency, at landing weights and with MAX AFTERBURNER, the aircraft can be flown in excess of 20 units angle of attack. Under these conditions, lateral control will be virtually nonexistent, but the aircraft will not stall and will accelerate and climb rapidly. The aircraft has been flown as slow as 95 KIAS under test conditions. Flight under such emergency conditions, although very uncomfortable and even dangerous, is still better than hitting the water. Under most conditions of broken wires or hooks, the aircraft will still have 90 or more knots airspeed, and with proper pilot techniques and MAX AFTERBURNER, should accelerate sufficiently so that the situation can be saved.

PITCH AUGMENTATION FAILURE

If pitch augmentation monitors off during the approach, wave off, if possible. After wave-off, retrim and make subsequent pass(es) without pitch augmentation. If pitch augmentation monitors off at any time during flight, the landing (carrier-based) will be without pitch augmentation.

CAUTION

A pronounced nose-down trim change occurs when pitch augmentation monitors off in power approach configuration. Large, heavy, aft stick control is required to maintain pitch attitude.

SINGLE ENGINE

Single-engine carrier landings will be made only in emergencies. Should a single-engine carrier landing be necessary, use only 40-degree flaps. Fly at 13 units angle of attack until on final, then slow to 13.5 units. Power response (both for acceleration and deceleration) is sluggish but adequate.

CAUTION

Use MAX AFTERBURNER for all bolters or wave-offs when single engine. Fuel per pass (using afterburner) will be about 200 pounds higher than a normal circuit of the same size.

CARRIER INSTRUMENT PROCEDURES

CLIMB-OUT AND RENDEZVOUS

Carrier Air Traffic Control Center (CATCC) information will be furnished for ready room briefings and will contain detailed information to meet the changing tactical situation. However, the following mandatory evolutions and criteria will be met under IFR conditions.

1. Prior to launch, each aircraft shall have positive radio communications with, and remain on, the assigned control frequency until directed to shift to another control agency.

2. The Air Officer will broadcast any necessary prelaunch information to aircraft on deck on their assigned frequency.

3. Pilots will not change radio frequencies after launch until at least a 2500-foot altitude has been reached and the aircraft is in a climbing wings level attitude. Those aircraft assigned operating altitudes below 2500 feet will not change frequencies until level attitude and cruise configuration have been attained at assigned altitude. The navigator may perform these functions below 2500 feet when directed to do so by the pilot.

4. An expected approach clearance (EAC) and alternate Marshal will be assigned each aircraft, and preflight briefings will include procedures to be followed in the event of radio or navigational aid failure.

5. The instrument climb-out should be accomplished, using the following procedures:

    (a) Retract the landing gear when safely airborne; maintain wings level and a positive rate of climb. Climb on launch heading, maintaining a sufficiently nose-high attitude to ensure that airspeed does not exceed 230 KIAS until the landing gear and flaps are fully retracted.

    (b) At 1000 feet of altitude, 200 KIAS, retract the flaps.

(c) Accelerate to climb schedule airspeed and commence a 30-degree maximum bank turn to intercept the assigned climb-out radial.

(d) Maintain climb schedule and climb-out radial to assigned altitude or "on top."

6. In the event a formation flight is planned *after* "on top" conditions have been reached, employ the following procedures:

(a) Level off at the planned cruise airspeed and altitude and maintain heading.

(b) Thirty seconds after the last aircraft reaches altitude (as reported by pilot), the leader starts a timed holding pattern to allow the last aircraft in the flight to reach the original starting point of the race track pattern simultaneously with the leader. The time consumed in the leader's holding pattern should equal the time elapsed from his arrival at altitude to that of the arrival of the last aircraft at altitude. This position (using TACAN) may be transmitted for use by all pilots in the flight.

(c) The leader may transmit on UHF to permit other pilots to use the UHF/ADF for homing.

CCA

All recoveries during instrument conditions (IFR) will be under close electronic control. IFR weather for shipboard operation is defined as ceiling of 1500 feet or less and forward flight visibility of 3 miles or less. Marshal, expected approach clearance (EAC), and jet emergency marshal (JEM) information will be given prior to the launch. Pilots will check in with Center 20 minutes prior to assigned EAC and plan their flight to arrive at Marshal 10 minutes prior to EAC. After check-in, the Center will confirm Marshal, altimeter setting, EAC, final controller frequency, expected final bearing, and time check.

PENETRATION

Holding will be accomplished at the assigned altitude in a left-hand, 6-minute, race track pattern at 250 KIAS. Plan the pattern in order to reach the holding fix inbound at the assigned EAC. The EAC is not a clearance to commence an approach until verified by Approach Control. Report commencing approach. It is very important that pilots commence the approach on the second, but if this is not possible, report the actual deviation ("departing Marshal 20 seconds late") to Approach Control.

Prior to commencing the peneration, depress the radar altimeter override button, depress and release the SPC button (OFF), and turn on the windshield and canopy defrost in order to prevent fogging at lower altitudes. Execute the entire approach with the pilot's radar altimeter in the override mode. Plan the rate of descent to arrive at Platform at 5000 feet and 18 miles. Proper altitude versus distance from the ship may be determined readily by applying a simple rule of thumb. The distance of Marshal from the ship is equal to 1 mile for every 1000 feet of altitude, plus 15 miles (Angels plus 15). The pilot can, accordingly, quickly determine proper altitude during the penetration, provided that aircraft is proceeding directly toward the ship, by applying "Angels plus 15." For example, at 30,000 feet the distance should be 45 miles, at 25,000 feet—40 miles, at 20,000 feet—35 miles, and at 10,000 feet—25 miles. Rate of descent may be regulated to arrive at these checkpoints (4000 to 6000 fpm will work nicely under normal operating conditions). It is mandatory that the pilot execute the entire penetration to the 10-mile Gate at 250 KIAS. This may be accomplished by selecting 80% rpm on both engines and regulating airspeed and rate of descent with speed brakes.

On reaching Platform, reduce rate of descent to 2000 fpm, but maintain 250 KIAS. Adjust the speed brakes to maintain the desired rate of descent. A mandatory, unacknowledged report will be made upon reaching Platform. Continue the penetration at 2000 fpm and 250 KIAS to the 10-mile Gate, to reach the gate in level flight at 1000 feet and 250 KIAS. Report reaching the 10-mile Gate. After passing the 10-mile Gate, slow the aircraft, extend the landing gear and flaps, and complete the landing check list prior to reaching the 6-mile Gate. Report reaching the 6-mile Gate. All requirements preparatory to landing shall be accomplished prior to passing the 6-mile Gate. A gradual descent to 600 feet will be commenced departing the 6-mile Gate. CCA will vector the aircraft to intercept the meatball at 600 feet, approximately 1¼ miles from ship. The requirement for calling fuel state will vary between ships; however, a fuel state report is normally mandatory on departing Marshal and reporting the 6-mile Gate.

FOULED DECK HOLDING

In the event the deck becomes fouled or an excessive number of aircraft bolter or are waved off, the Center will take action to prevent overloading the traffic pattern. Normally, a maximum of six aircraft will be allowed in the landing pattern at any one time. Should the pattern become saturated and you have not reached the Platform, Center will transmit, "All jet aircraft above 5000 feet DOG. DOG radial is............." Upon receiving this transmission, the pilot will level off at the next odd altitude and hold on the assigned radial. When holding is established, report distance and altitude. If you have passed Platform, and the landing pattern is saturated, you will be given an assigned holding altitude. Upon receiving the altitude assignment, you will be directed to proceed to a holding fix 10 miles ahead of the ship, oriented on the extension of the final bearing. Proceed to the holding fix at your assigned altitude and commence holding in a 6-minute, left-hand race track pattern. You will be fed into CCA wave-off/bolter pattern from this point.

CCA WAVE-OFF/BOLTER PATTERN

In the event of a bolter or wave-off, Bolter/Wave-off Control will come up with immediate instructions, and vector you downwind. If other aircraft are in the pattern, you will normally be vectored out ahead of the ship, prior to turning downwind. If you are alone in the pattern, you will normally be cleared to turn downwind upon reaching a safe altitude. Pilots will climb to a minimum of 500 feet prior to commencing a turn downwind during bolters or wave-offs at night, or when ceilings are less than 600 feet. After turning downwind, you will be vectored around the pattern for another approach.

NIGHT CARRIER OPERATIONS

Night operations begin in the ready room. All crews will be thoroughly briefed with regard to their assigned mission. Each crew member will be completely night-adapted prior to manning his aircraft (normally 30 minutes of adaptation will be satisfactory). Ready room lighting shall be governed accordingly. Crew members shall be issued and required to wear red lenses while proceeding from the ready room to the flight deck if red-lighted routes are not available.

LIGHTS

1. Exterior lights will be kept OFF on deck. The exterior lights panel should be set up prior to taxiing, with the wing and tail light switches at DIM and the fuselage light and the exterior lights master switches OFF.
2. The status (up/down) of the aircraft is signaled by waving a red-lensed flashlight as follows:
   Up—vertically, up and down.
   Down—horizonally, fore and aft.

SIGNALS

Standard wand signals, as prescribed in NWP 41(A), will be used on the flight deck. All pilots are required to receive a night catapult signals lecture, by the ship's Catapult Officer, prior to operating from any carrier during the hours of darkness. This is a one-time requirement and will normally be met prior to commencement of initial night operations. Pilots are, however, charged with the responsibility of remaining familiar with all flight deck signals.

LAUNCH

Taxi on the catapult as directed. Taxi speeds, during night operations, will be reduced to a normal walk. Checkoff lists should be completed prior to taxiing on the catapult. Exterior lights will be OFF. After you are "hooked up," the director will give the "take tension" signal and turn you over to the Catapult Officer. Apply MIL thrust at this time. The Catapult Officer (the only man with a red and green wand) will normally pick you up with a "one-finger" turnup signal, i.e., red wand to stern and green wand to the bow, held vertically. If a down signal is not received from the aircraft, the Catapult Officer will then put the red wand behind his back, with the green remaining vertical and slowly rotating for MIL thrust, or cycling vertically up and down for afterburner. Make your last-minute checks and turn the exterior lights master switch ON when ready to go. The fire signal is a downward sweeping motion of the green wand.

RECOVERY

All night recoveries will be under CATCC control. Under normal conditions a complete penetration, with CCA to final approach bearing and interception of the glide path (meatball), will be accomplished. Position lights (wings and tail only) will be turned on bright upon departing Marshal. Pilots may use additional external lights, including Grimes lights, if they desire, but additional lights shall be turned off prior to departing the 6-mile Gate. Pilots are reminded that they should fly the penetration, approach, and, if unfortunate, the wave-off/bolter pattern strictly on instruments until they are on final bearing and have visually acquired the meatball. After arrestment, move the exterior lights master switch to OFF.

Note
Use of the taxi light is prohibited aboard ship.

LOST COMMUNICATIONS

In the event of lost communications, prior to reaching Marshal, the pilot will proceed to emergency Marshal at the assigned Marshal altitude and enter the normal left-hand, 6-minute holding pattern. Another aircraft will be dispatched to the emergency holding fix to lead you through the penetration. Should lost communications occur after commencement of holding at Marshal, a penetration will be initiated at last *acknowledged* EAC. Should communication failure be experienced after initiation of the penetration, the pilot will continue a normal approach on TACAN or UHF homer. If lost communications occur in the wave-off bolter pattern while proceeding upwind, the pilot will climb to 600 feet, proceed to a point 2 miles ahead of the ship, and turn downwind. If the failure occurs while proceeding downwind, the pilot will proceed to a point 4 miles astern of the ship and turn crosswind. In both instances, the subsequent turn to final will be accomplished with TACAN or UHF homing.

COMMUNICATIONS EMERGENCIES

Additional lost communication procedures are as follows:

1. Lost aircraft with no navigational aids available—pilot must navigate to recovery position by dead reckoning.
2. Lost aircraft with radio receiver—Fly right-hand triangular pattern, 1-minute legs, maintain altitude, and conserve fuel. Squawk Mode II, and

await recovery instructions. Be alert for aircraft vectored to join you.

3. Lost aircraft without radio receiver—Fly left-hand triangular pattern, 1-minute legs, conserve fuel, and fly highest possible altitude consistent with the situation to facilitate radar acquisition. Squawk Mode II and be alert for aircraft vectored to join. After being intercepted, inform lead aircraft of all emergency conditions with appropriate hand signals in order to reduce the possibility of separation during penetration or letdown. Use auxiliary receiver or monitor GUARD as a stand-by receiver.

EMERGENCY SIGNALS

Refer to NWP 41(A) for emergency communications procedures.

PART 5 — NORMAL PROCEDURES (SYSTEMS OPERATOR)

CREW DUTIES

Refer to FLIGHT CREW REQUIREMENTS, in Section II.

BEFORE ENTERING AIRCRAFT

1. Assist pilot in conducting exterior inspection.
2. TV scanner—check.
3. Radome—locked (flags in).
4. TRAINING TONE switch — TRAINING (nose wheel well).
    For actual missions—COMBAT.
5. External stores—check.
6. External units—connected and operating.

ENTERING AIRCRAFT

1. RED FLOOD LIGHTS switch—as required.
2. Canopy uplock—check ENGAGED.
3. Inspect seat and canopy.
4. Canopy cam-off block—check (NAVIGATOR).
5. Canopy emergency air bottle—2800 psi (minimum).
6. Emergency oxygen—1800 psi (minimum).
7. Oxygen—OFF.
8. Scott disconnect—Fasten/check knob seated.
9. Oxygen—ON.
10. Ballistic adapters—check.
11. Harness—Fasten/Adjust.

Note

Crew members will personally fasten and become proficient at fastening and releasing the "Rocket-Jet" fittings and adjusting the integrated harness.

12. ICS—check.
13. Seat and canopy safety pins—Stow.
14. Pylon and armament safety pins—removed.
15. Canopy uplock—disengaged.

COCKPIT CHECK (A/N PREALINED)

1. Interior lights—as desired.
2. G-suit valve—Set.
3. PRESS SUIT FLOW knob—Set.
4. SIGNAL LIGHTS switch—BRT (day), DIM (night).
5. HOSE CONTROL switch—REWIND.
6. EMERG FUEL FLOW switch—NORM.
7. HOSE CUT switch—NORMAL.
8. Fuel transfer indicators—Set as desired.
9. Compass mode knob—SLAVED.
10. Ground speed dial—Set.
11. LAT dial—Set local.
12. Hemisphere switch—local.
13. Compass command button—as desired.
14. Weapons preflight check list—completed.
15. RELEASE SELECT buttons—disengaged (up).
16. MAN ARMING switch—SAFE.
17. REL TONE MODE switch—OFF.
18. PYLON SELECT switch—OFF.
19. MANEUVER switch—as desired.
20. ALTITUDE mode knob—BARO (Set to field elevation).

Note

The BOMB COMPUTER POWER switch cannot be turned ON with cooling air applied at the forward (autonavigator) access only. The ALTITUDE SET function is not required for alinement.

21. RANGE & BEARING knob—NAV.
22. SPEED switch—GROUND.
23. BOMB COMPUTER POWER switch—ON.*

Note

All steps marked (*) must be delayed until after engine start if A/N auxiliary cooling only is used.

24. RADAR/TV POWER switch—STBY.*
25. SEAT ADJUST switch—as required.
26. Audio select buttons—as desired.
27. UHF radio, TACAN, ICS, ADF—Set as desired.
28. IFF and SIF—Set desired modes and codes (STBY).
29. XMT CONT switch—ICS CALL.
30. Command lights—as desired.
31. Utility lights—as desired.
32. IND LTS TEST—Press/Test.
33. Heat control lever—as desired.
34. Present position—check.
35. AML—check blinking.
36. A/N MODE knob—OPERATE.

Section III
Part 5

AUTONAVIGATOR ALINEMENT

HANDSET ALINEMENT

PREHEAT INSTALLED (AFC 112)

1. External electrical power—connected.
2. Autonavigator PREHEAT switch—PREHEAT (ground crew).

Note

Do not apply cooling air to the left or forward (autonavigator) receptacles during preheat.

3. On completion of required warm-up, proceed with alinement.
    Refer to PREHEAT REQUIREMENTS.
4. Autonavigator PREHEAT switch—NORM (ground crew).
5. Apply cooling air to aircraft (ground crew).
6. ATTACK MODE knob—ALL WEATHER LEVEL.
7. COORD SELECT knob—NORMAL.
8. WIND knob—AUTO.
9. A/N MODE knob—STBY-NAV.
10. SYSTEM MODE knob—SET PP.
11. BOMB COMPUTER POWER switch—ON.
12. Radar/barometric altimeter—Set to deck or field elevation.

Note

The BOMB COMPUTER POWER switch cannot be turned ON with cooling air applied at the forward (autonavigator) access only. The ALTITUDE SET function is not required to complete alinement.

13. HANDSET/AUTOMATIC switch—HANDSET.
14. AN POWER switch—ON.
    Note AML out in 40 seconds or less.
15. OFFSETS—zero.
16. CARRIER HEADING indicator—Slew to aircraft true heading (ashore), or ship's true heading (afloat).
17. DIFFERENTIAL HEADING indicator—Slew to zero (ashore); Slew to angular difference, ship's true heading to aircraft true heading in degrees (afloat).
18. CARRIER VELOCITY indicator—Slew to zero (ashore); Slew to ship's speed in knots (afloat).
19. Set and store present position.
20. A/N MODE knob—DECK ALINE.
21. AN POWER switch—START, Release to ON.
    Note AML out in less than 50 seconds.
22. Present position—check, Reset as required.
23. Set and store target channels 1 through 4.

Note

Target channel 5 cannot be stored until the A/N MODE knob is moved to OPERATE.

24. SET/CORR knob—5 (alinement monitor).
    $\Delta\alpha$ in TARGET POSITION (LATITUDE).
    α in TARGET POSITION (LONGITUDE).
    Time in alinement in TARGET ALTITUDE.
25. ADVANCE MODE light—check blinking at end of programmed alinement period.

Note

For short (14-minute cutoff) alinement, note TARGET ALTITUDE display approaching 130 (14 minutes), then check AML. Upon *illumination of AML*, OPERATE may be selected.

26. A/N MODE knob—OPERATE.
27. Set and store target channel 5.
28. SET/CORR knob—desired channel.
29. NAV/BOMB knob—desired channel.

CAUTION

Ensure that the A/N MODE knob is moved to OPERATE before the aircraft is moved.

PREHEAT REQUIREMENTS

For best results, inertial platform preheat is required. When ambient temperature is below 65°F, and when tactically feasible, the inertial platform should be preheated as follows:

AMBIENT TEMPERATURE (°F)	PREHEAT TIME (MINUTES)	
	30-MINUTE ALINEMENT	SHORT ALINEMENT CUTOFF OR TVP
100	5	40
90	5	40
80	10	45
70	15	50
60	20	53
50	25	55
40	30	60
30	35	65
20	40	67
10	45	72
0	50	75

PREHEAT NOT INSTALLED

1. Equipment cooling air—connected.
2. External electrical power—connected.
3. ATTACK MODE knob—ALL WEATHER LEVEL.
4. COORD SELECT knob—NORMAL.
5. WIND knob—AUTO.
6. A/N MODE knob—STBY-NAV.

7. SYSTEM MODE knob—SET PP.
8. BOMB COMPUTER POWER switch—ON.
9. Radar/barometric altimeter—Set to field or deck elevation.

Note

The BOMB COMPUTER POWER switch cannot be turned on with cooling air applied at the forward (autonavigator) access only. The ALTITUDE SET function is not required to complete alinement.

10. HANDSET/AUTOMATIC switch—HANDSET.
11. AN POWER switch—ON.
    Note AML out in 40 seconds or less.
12. OFFSETS—zero.
13. CARRIER HEADING indicator—Slew to aircraft true heading (ashore), or ship's true heading (afloat).
14. DIFFERENTIAL HEADING indicator—Slew to zero (ashore); Slew to angular difference, ship's true heading to aircraft true heading in degrees (afloat).
15. CARRIER VELOCITY indicator—Slew to zero (ashore); Slew to ship's speed in knots (afloat).
16. Set and store present position.
17. On completion of required warm-up time, proceed with alinement.
18. A/N MODE knob—DECK ALINE.
19. AN POWER switch—START, Release to ON.
    Note AML out in less than 50 seconds.
20. A/N MODE knob—OPERATE for 10 seconds (to end preheat).
21. A/N MODE knob—DECK ALINE (to restart alinement).
22. Present position—check, Reset as required.
23. Set and store target channels 1 through 4.

Note

Target channel 5 cannot be stored until the A/N MODE knob is moved to OPERATE to end alinement.

24. SET/CORR knob—5 (alinement monitor).
25. ADVANCE MODE light—check blinking at end of programmed alinement period.

Note

For short (14-minute cutoff) alinement, note TARGET ALTITUDE display approaching 130 (14 minutes), then check AML. Upon *illumination of AML,* OPERATE may be selected.

26. A/N MODE knob—OPERATE.
27. Set and store target channel 5.
28. SET/CORR knob—desired channel.
29. NAV/BOMB knob—desired channel.

CAUTION

Ensure that the A/N MODE knob is moved to OPERATE before the aircraft is moved.

AUTOMATIC ALINEMENT (SHIP-BASED)

When operating aboard ship, it is assumed that preheat of the inertial platform on modified aircraft is accomplished prior to boarding. This requires use of deck-edge electrical power only. Alinement may be accomplished with complete external provisions (electrical and air) or with engines operating.

PREHEAT INSTALLED (AFC 112)

1. External power/cooling air or engines operating.
2. SINS umbilical cable—check connected.
3. ATTACK MODE knob—ALL WEATHER LEVEL.
4. COORD SELECT knob—NORMAL.
5. WIND knob—AUTO.
6. A/N MODE knob—STBY-NAV.
7. SYSTEM MODE knob—SET PP.
8. BOMB COMPUTER POWER switch—ON.

Note

BOMB COMPUTER POWER switch cannot be turned on with cooling air applied at the forward (autonavigator) access only. The ALTITUDE SET function is not required to complete alinement.

9. Radar/barometric altimeter—Set to deck elevation.
10. HANDSET/AUTOMATIC switch—AUTOMATIC.
11. AN POWER switch—ON.
    Note AML out in 40 seconds or less.
12. OFFSETS—Slew distance from velocity reference point (SINS).
    (a) East/West (starboard/port)—_____ feet.
    (b) North/South (forward/aft)—_____ feet.
13. DIFFERENTIAL HEADING indicator—Slew to angular difference, ship's true heading to aircraft true heading in degrees.
    Example: Ship—090 degrees.
             Aircraft—330 degrees.
             DIFFERENTIAL HEADING—240 degrees.

Note

Carrier heading and velocity are supplied by SINS.

Section III
Part 5

NAVWEPS 01-60ABA-1

14. Set and store present position.
15. A/N MODE knob—DECK ALINE.
16. AN POWER switch—START, Release to ON.
    Note AML out in less than 50 seconds.
17. Present position—check, Reset as required.
18. Set and store target channels 1 through 4.

Note

Target channel 5 cannot be stored until the A/N MODE is moved to OPERATE.

19. SET/CORR knob—5 (alinement monitor).
    Δα in TARGET POSITION (LATITUDE).
    α in TARGET POSITION (LONGITUDE).
    Time in alinement in TARGET ALTITUDE.
20. Note PRESENT POSITION updating (automatic).
21. ADVANCE MODE light—check blinking at end of programmed alinement period.
22. A/N MODE knob—OPERATE.
23. OFFSETS—zero.
24. Set and store target channel 5.
25. SET/CORR knob—desired channel.
26. NAV/BOMB knob—desired channel.

Note

Ensure that the A/N MODE knob is moved to OPERATE before the SINS umbilical cable is removed.

27. SINS umbilical cable—check removed before taxiing.

PREHEAT NOT INSTALLED

1. External power/cooling air or engines operating.
2. SINS umbilical cable—check connected.
3. ATTACK MODE knob—ALL WEATHER LEVEL.
4. COORD SELECT knob—NORMAL.
5. WIND knob—AUTO.
6. A/N MODE knob—STBY-NAV.
7. SYSTEM MODE knob—SET PP.
8. BOMB COMPUTER POWER switch—ON.

Note

BOMB COMPUTER POWER switch cannot be turned on with cooling air applied at the forward (autonavigator) access only. The ALTITUDE SET function is not required to complete alinement.

9. Radar/barometric altimeter—Set to deck elevation.

10. HANDSET/AUTOMATIC switch—AUTOMATIC.
11. AN POWER switch—ON.
    Note AML out in 40 seconds or less.
12. OFFSETS—Set as required.
13. DIFFERENTIAL HEADING indicator—Slew as required.
14. Set and store present position.
15. A/N MODE knob—DECK ALINE.
16. AN POWER switch—START, Release to ON.
    Note AML out in less than 50 seconds.
17. Set and store target channels 1 through 4.

Note

Carrier heading and velocity are supplied by SINS.

18. On completion of required warm-up time, proceed with alinement.
19. A/N MODE knob—OPERATE for 10 seconds (to end preheat).
20. A/N MODE knob—DECK ALINE (to restart alinement).
21. Present position—check, Reset as required.
22. Set and store target channels 1 through 4.
23. SET/CORR knob—5 (alinement monitor).
24. Note PRESENT POSITION updating (automatic).
25. ADVANCE MODE light—check blinking at end of programmed alinement period.
26. A/N MODE knob—OPERATE.
27. OFFSETS—zero.
28. Set and store target channel 5.
29. SET/CORR knob—desired channel.
30. NAV/BOMB knob—desired channel.
    Ensure that A/N MODE knob is moved to OPERATE before the SINS umbilical cable is removed.
31. SINS umbilical cable—check removed before taxiing.

STAND-BY NAV TURN-ON

1. External power/cooling air or engines operating.
2. A/N MODE knob—STBY-NAV.
3. AN POWER switch—ON.
    Note AML out in 40 seconds or less.
4. ATTACK MODE knob—ALL WEATHER LEVEL.
5. BOMB COMPUTER POWER switch—ON.
6. COORD SELECT knob—as required.
7. SYSTEM MODE knob—SET PP.
8. Set and store present position.
9. A/N MODE knob—DECK ALINE.

10. SYSTEM MODE knob—SET TARGET.
11. Set and store channels 1 through 5.
12. SYSTEM MODE knob—NAV.
13. COORD SELECT knob—NORMAL.
14. Wind indicator—Set to best known speed.
15. Wind indicator—Set to best known wind direction.
16. A/N MODE knob—STBY-NAV (just prior to launch).
17. Present position—check, Reset as required.

AFTER STARTING

RADAR-TV CHECK

RADAR TURN-ON

1. TRANSMIT MODE switch—SILENCE.
2. DISPLAY switch—NORM.
3. Radar-TV MODE knob—NORM.
4. RADAR/TV POWER switch—ON.
   Allow 3½ minutes after selecting STBY.
5. GAIN BRIGHTNESS knob—Adjust and check scans.
6. CURSOR & CIRCLE BRT knob—Adjust.
7. RANGE switch—check all ranges.
8. TRANSMIT MODE switch—TRANSMIT.

Note

- During shipboard operations, DO NOT select TRANSMIT until airborne.
- In close proximity to areas of combustible material, delay selection of TRANSMIT until clear.

TV CHECK

1. Radar-TV MODE knob—TV.
   Check blue filter.
2. FILTER switch—OUT.
3. APERTURE knob—AUTO.
4. BRIGHTNESS knob—Adjust.
5. VIEW ANGLE switch—as desired.
6. RETICLE knob—check as desired.
7. SYSTEM MODE knob—SEARCH.
8. VIEW switch—AFT.
   Check TSPI—12 o'clock, 30 degrees down.
9. VIEW switch—FWD.
10. Cursor control operation—check.
11. SYSTEM MODE knob—NAV.
12. FILTER switch—IN.
13. Radar-TV MODE knob—NORM.

BEFORE TAXI

1. External power and cooling air—check removed.
2. SET/CORR knob—as desired.
3. NAV/BOMB knob—as desired.
4. OFFSETS—recheck zero.

BEFORE TAKE-OFF

1. ADVANCE MODE light—out.
2. Present position—check.
3. SPEED switch—GROUND.
4. TAS— 5 knots.
5. Wind speed— 125 knots.
6. MIC SEL switch—as desired.

PRELAUNCH CHECK

1. Canopy—recheck CLOSED.
2. Utility lights—as desired.
3. Gyro horizon—Cage, Release.
4. Compass—check.
5. Caution lights—check.
6. Loose gear—Stow.
7. MIC SEL switch—HOT.
8. Harness—LOCKED.
9. Altimeter (BARO)—check "FAIL" flag (SPC OFF). Reset elevation if required.

AFTER TAKE-OFF

1. Check gear retraction with TV.
2. IFF—NORM (SIF as required).
3. TRANSMIT MODE—TRANSMIT.
4. SPC—check ON.
   Check "FAIL" flag out.

IN-FLIGHT PROCEDURES

TERRAIN AVOIDANCE CHECK (PILOT)

1. Scope mode—TA.
2. Crossover (400 feet terrain clearance)—check 2.5 miles.
3. CM operation (STEER/TERRAIN)—check.
4. Alpha (AUTO/MAN)—check.
5. LOW ALTITUDE warning light—check.

RADAR/BAROMETRIC ALTIMETER CALIBRATION

1. Approaching checkpoint, ALTITUDE mode knob— RADAR.
2. Radar/barometric altimeter—check.

3. Over checkpoint, hold ALTITUDE mode knob in BARO CAL.
   Hold until altimeter stabilizes.
4. ALTITUDE mode knob—as desired.

NAV MODE

The azimuth and range indicator (and pilot's HSI) reflects the correct steering path to the NAV/BOMB selected position. Range and bearing to SET/CORR selected checkpoint is provided to the pilot if range is less than 186 nautical miles.

1. In range, locate checkpoint (SET/CORR) on radar.
2. If not under cursors, use cursor handle to correct.
3. In TV range, select TV and identify checkpoint.
4. If not under reticle, use cursor handle to correct.
5. Over checkpoint, BARO CAL altimeter.
6. SET/CORR knob—Select next checkpoint.
7. If required, set new coordinates in address of previous SET/CORR knob position.

Note

If a checkpoint or secondary target is within 20 miles of both present position and NAV/BOMB selected destination, the following procedure is required to obtain usable steering information:

(a) NAV/BOMB knob—desired position.
(b) SYSTEM MODE knob—BOMB.
(c) ATTACK MODE knob—O/S.
(d) OFFSETS—zero.

RECON MODE

To locate targets of opportunity or to determine position coordinates of radar-TV targets, proceed as follows:

1. SYSTEM MODE knob—RECON.
2. Radar cursors or TV reticle—Place as desired.
3. Read coordinates on TARGET POSITION indicator.
4. If RECON target storage is desired:
   (a) SET/CORR knob—usable position.
   (b) COORD STORAGE button—Depress.
5. SYSTEM MODE knob—desired mode.

Note

Target altitude, as set in before flight, remains unchanged. For precise navigation to, or bombing of, this point, subsequently correct TARGET ALTITUDE indicator using SET TARGET mode.

SEARCH MODE (TV)

1. SYSTEM MODE knob—SEARCH.
2. Radar-TV MODE knob—TV.
3. To slew sight, use cursor handle.

BOMB MODE

Within 186 nautical miles of NAV/BOMB target, proceed as follows:

1. SYSTEM MODE knob—BOMB.
   (a) TARGET POSITION and DESTINATION RANGE read to NAV/BOMB target.
   (b) Steering reads to computed release point.
   (c) Azimuth and range indicator reads to NAV/BOMB target (186 to 46.5 miles), then switches to bomb release point (less than 46.5 nautical miles).
2. DISPLAY switch—FIXED or VAR, as desired.
3. Use radar for range corrections.
4. If conditions permit, make a final azimuth correction with TV prior to release.
5. Weapon—armed as applicable.
6. BARO CAL altimeter prior to release.
7. Ballistic adapter knob—as briefed.

SPECIAL WEAPONS

Refer to applicable NAVWEPS Special Weapon Check List.

CONVENTIONAL WEAPONS

AN/AWW-1

1. Function knob—STBY.
2. Pause 20 seconds.
3. OPTION SELECTOR—as briefed.
4. Function knob—READY.
5. PRESS TO TEST button—Depress.
6. HV D.C. CHECK light—check on.

Without AN/AWW-1

1. MAN ARMING switch—briefed position.
2. RELEASE SELECT button—Depress as required.

OFFSET BOMBING

DIFFERENTIAL BALLISTIC WIND (DBW)

1. Target coordinates—Store at desired channel.
2. Ballistic wind error (in hundredths of nautical miles in polar form)—Insert as OFFSET in the same direction as differential ballistic wind.

3. Slew cursors to target.

Note

After the run, present position will be in error by the amount of DBW correction until NAV is selected or the OFFSETS are removed and a cursor correction is made.

REMOTE AIMPOINT WITH DBW

1. Target coordinates—Store at desired channel.
2. Add ballistic wind error algebraically to OFFSET.
3. Slew cursors to aimpoint.

Note

After the run, present position will be in error by the amount of DBW correction until NAV is selected or the OFFSETS are removed and a cursor correction is made.

RADIATION SILENCE

To achieve maximum protection against detection, proceed as follows:

1. TRANSMIT MODE switch—SILENCE.
2. ALTITUDE mode knob—BARO.
3. IFF MASTER function selector—STBY.
4. XMT CONT switch—ICS CALL.
5. Maintain 4000 feet or more above ground level.

DELIVERY MODE CHECK LISTS

Refer to Section IX of the Supplemental NATOPS Flight Manual (NAVWEPS 01-60ABA-1A).

REFUELING TANKER PROCEDURE

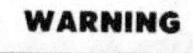

To prevent possible damage to the buddy tanker reel and hose, ensure that the HOSE CONTROL switch is at REWIND before engine start.

REEL RESPONSE CHECK

1. Stabilize speed at 280—300 KIAS.
2. Radar-TV MODE knob—TV.
3. VIEW switch—AFT.
4. HOSE CONTROL switch—TRAIL.
   (a) IN TRANSIT light—on.
   (b) FULL TRAIL light—on.
   (c) IN TRANSIT light—out.
5. Note hose is fully extended.

6. Reduce speed at least 20 KIAS.
   Hose should slowly rewind nearly full in.
7. Accelerate to original speed.
   Hose should slowly extend full out.

BUDDY FUEL TRANSFER

1. EMERG FUEL FLOW switch—NORM.
2. TO BE TRANSFERRED indicator—Set.
3. TOTAL FUEL TRANSFERRED indicator—Set zero.
4. Establish contact with receiver aircraft as required.
5. SIGNAL LIGHTS switch—BRT (day), DIM (night).
6. HOSE CONTROL switch—TRAIL.
   (a) IN TRANSIT light—on.
   (b) FULL TRAIL light—on.
   (c) IN TRANSIT light—out.
7. VIEW switch—AFT.
   TV as desired.
8. Check CANS fuel partly transferred and pitch augmentation—STBY.
   Check with pilot.
9. Ensure receiver's radar is secured or silenced and clear aircraft for hookup.
10. FUEL ON light—note on, FULL TRAIL light out.
    TOTAL FUEL TRANSFERRED indicator—note running.

Note

For speed changes of more than 10 knots and/or altitude changes of more than 1000 feet, momentarily depress REEL RESPONSE button prior to receiver contact.

11. On disconnect, note FUEL ON light out, FULL TRAIL light on.
12. Mission completed, HOSE CONTROL switch—REWIND.

Note

If hose does not rewind, momentarily depress REEL RESPONSE button.

MALFUNCTION CHECK LISTS
RADAR FAILURES

SWEEPS MISSING

Blank scope after required warm-up.

1. Cycle RADAR/TV POWER switch to STBY, then ON.
2. Increase brightness.
3. Cycle TV VIEW switch AFT, then FWD.

SCANS MISSING

1. Change ranges—20 to 60 or 60 to 20 miles.
2. Ensure ATTACK MODE knob is in ALL WEATHER LEVEL.
3. Try expanded modes under 46.5 miles to target.
4. Roll aircraft and check for movement of sweep.
5. Check PPDI mode knob—OFF.

NO TARGETS

1. Check for cursors and circles.
2. Check TRANSMIT MODE switch.
3. BEAM switch to FLAT/IF GAIN and VIDEO GAIN knobs to maximum/antenna to TILT for ground/sea return.
4. Use manual tuning.
5. Try TV, MRI, NORM, ANTIJAM modes in all ranges.
6. Lower nose of aircraft.

WEAK TARGETS

1. Check PPDI mode knob—OFF.
2. Cycle BEAM switch.
3. IF GAIN and VIDEO GAIN knobs to maximum.
4. Try manual tuning.
5. Try TV, MRI, NORM, ANTIJAM modes in all ranges.

SHORT RANGE

1. Cycle BEAM switch.
2. Check IF GAIN and VIDEO GAIN knobs/antenna to TILT.
3. Try manual tuning.
4. Check PPDI mode knob—OFF.
5. Pull up nose of aircraft.

NOISY DISPLAY

1. Adjust IF GAIN, VIDEO GAIN, BRIGHTNESS knobs separately.
2. Adjust FREQUENCY.
3. Adjust antenna to TILT.
4. Try all radar modes, ranges, and beam patterns.
5. Change heading.
6. Check TV for similar presentation.

WEDGED VIDEO

1. Try manual tuning.
2. Switch ranges.
3. Shift frequency.
4. Check TV for pulsating video.

VIDEO LOST OR UNUSUAL DISPLAY

1. If in OPERATE mode, check for normal operation.
2. If in STBY-NAV mode, check pilot's AAI/note if FRS has a wing-down error.
3. Roll aircraft/note any change in video return.
4. BEAM switch to FLAT—check video pattern.

NO RANGE CURSOR

1. Ensure BOMB COMPUTER POWER switch ON/check blower operation.
2. CURSOR & CIRCLE BRT knob—Increase.
3. Check ARI range less than radar range selected.
4. Check ARI range over and under 46.5 miles.

WAVY RANGE CURSOR

1. Check for oscillations in ARI, PDI, and TSPI.
2. Check TV presentation in NAV and BOMB modes.
3. Change ballistic adapter selection (BOMB mode).

RADAR/TV COINCIDENCE

1. Store an optically and radar significant target.
2. BARO CAL altimeter.
3. Cursor correct on radar within 46.5 miles.
4. Check placement of TV reticle.

RANGE CURSOR ERROR

1. Store an optically and radar significant target.
2. BARO CAL altimeter.
3. Select BOMB and O/S within 46.5 miles.
4. Cursor correct.
5. Steer to target.
6. Check ARI readout at visual passage over target.

ALTERNATE RANGE CURSOR CHECK

1. Store coordinates of TACAN station.
2. Cursor correct on selected target.
3. Compare TACAN with ARI range read-out when range is greater than 10 times altitude but less than 46.5 miles.

NO RANGE CIRCLES

1. Check RANGE CIRCLES switch.
2. Vary CURSOR & CIRCLE BRT knob.

RANGE CIRCLES ACCURACY CHECK

If range circles are used, do not assume they are accurate. Measure range to each circle with range cursor using RECON mode and ARI read-out.

NO AZIMUTH CURSOR

1. Ensure BOMB COMPUTER switch ON/check blower operation.
2. Vary CURSOR & CIRCLE BRT knob.
3. Check relative aimpoint on ARI to ensure that it is within ±45 degrees of aircraft heading or reciprocal.
4. Try expanded display.

MULTIPLE AZIMUTH CURSOR

1. Select RECON and slew azimuth throughout scan limits to ensure that interference is a multiple azimuth cursor.
2. Reduce CURSOR & CIRCLE BRT knob setting.

TELEVISION FAILURES

NO RASTER

1. Increase TV BRIGHTNESS knob setting.
2. Check radar sweeps.
   Note FILTER operation.

NO VIDEO

1. Check FILTER switch OUT.
2. Cycle VIEW switch FWD, then AFT.
3. Vary TV BRIGHTNESS knob.
4. Try manual APERTURE control.
5. Repeat steps 3 and 4 with SYSTEM MODE knob in SEARCH.
6. Try all view angles.
7. Note weather conditions.

PULSATING VIDEO

1. Select manual APERTURE control.
2. Check radar for wedged video.

RETICLES MISSING

1. Increase reticle brightness.
2. Select other filament.

TV SCANNER POSITION INDICATOR (TSPI)

No Pitch or Azimuth Indication

1. Try operation with SYSTEM MODE knob in SEARCH.
2. Check TV presentation for similar malfunction.
3. Check bombing computer fuses.

Pitch/Azimuth Error or Oscillation

1. Check TV presentation for similar malfunction.
2. Attempt correction by moving SYSTEM MODE knob to SEARCH.

No Aft Indication

1. Check TV presentation for similar malfunction.
2. Cycle SYSTEM MODE knob through SEARCH.

PROJECTED DISPLAY (PILOT'S PPDI) FAILURES

NO SWEEPS OR SCANS

1. Check PPDI mode knob.
2. Increase brightness.
3. Check S/O's radar/TV indicator for similar malfunction.

DISPLAY APEX INTERMITTENT OR JUMPY

Check S/O's radar/TV indicator for similar malfunction.

NO AZIMUTH OR RANGE CURSOR

1. Check PPDI mode knob.
2. Increase PPDI gain.
3. Check S/O's radar/TV indicator for similar malfunction.

NO STEERING CURSOR

1. Check PPDI mode knob in STEER, AIM, or TA.
2. Check AAI and HSI steering.

LOCKED OR ERRATIC STEERING CURSOR

1. Check AAI for similar malfunction.
2. Check ALINE/HOLD switch OFF (course line steering out).

NO ELEVATION STEERING CURSOR

1. Check PPDI mode knob in STEER or AIM.
2. Check TV depression angle on TSPI.

NO ARTIFICIAL HORIZON

Check PPDI mode knob out of OFF.

NO ROLL INDICATION

Check AAI for similar malfunction.

NO RETICLES

1. Increase RETICLE DIMMER setting.
2. Check PPDI mode knob in STEER, TA, or CM.
3. Check reticle filament switch in FIL 1 or FIL 2.

NO RADAR VIDEO

1. Check S/O's radar/TV indicator for similar malfunction.
2. Vary PPDI GAIN and MEMORY knobs.

INSUFFICIENT HORIZON CENTERING

Check AAI for similar malfunction.

NO CLEARANCE SET ACTION

Check PPDI mode knob in TA or CM.

ANTENNA NOT FOLLOWING A/A IN TA AUTO ALPHA

1. Check A/A indicator for similar malfunction.
2. Select manual alpha.

AUTONAVIGATOR FAILURES

ALINEMENT (PRESTART)

For alinement prestart, check A/N MODE knob in STBY-NAV, AN POWER switch at ON.

No AML

1. Depress IND LTS TEST button.
2. Press test AML.
3. Check A/N COOLING AIR switch—ON.

Steady AML

1. Ensure that A/N MODE knob is in STBY-NAV.
2. Check slewing and storing/if normal, proceed.
3. Cycle AN POWER switch to 1 minute, then to ON.
4. Proceed with alinement.

No PP Slewing or Storing

1. Ensure that SYSTEM MODE knob is in SET PP and COORD SELECT knob is in LAT or LONG.
2. Cycle AN POWER switch OFF 1 minute, then to ON.

Counterslewing Limited

If PDI slewing is limited to one direction only, proceed as follows:

1. Move COORD SELECT knob to opposite direction.
2. Slew in desired numerical value.
3. Move COORD SELECT knob to correct direction and STORE immediately.
4. Recheck slewing after selecting OPERATE.

ALINEMENT (AFTER START)

For alinement after start, check A/N MODE knob in DECK ALINE, AN POWER switch at START.

Steady AML

1. Ensure HANDSET/AUTOMATIC position is correct.
2. Check slewing and storing/if normal, proceed.

3. If no slewing and storing, move A/N MODE knob to STBY-NAV, wait 1 minute, check for slewing and storing. If normal, launch in STBY-NAV.

No Gimbal Caging

- Wind speed not equal to TAS ± 10 knots (BOMB COMPUTER POWER switch—ON).
- Large carrier heading error.
- Present position drifting.

1. Ensure correct carrier velocity is set in (HANDSET).
2. Switch A/N MODE knob to STBY-NAV, wait 2 minutes; then, A/N MODE knob to DECK ALINE, AN POWER switch to START.
3. If trouble persists, launch in STBY-NAV.

Alpha Read-out Excessive

If alpha read-out is greater than 10 degrees, check carrier and differential reading inputs. If in error, switch A/N MODE knob to STBY-NAV for 2 minutes, reset carrier or differential heading, and move A/N MODE knob to DECK ALINE, AN POWER switch to START.

1. If alpha error is south, decrease carrier or differential heading.
2. If alpha error is north, increase carrier or differential heading.

Note

Degraded autonavigator performance may possibly result if Δ alpha exceeds 20 minutes (Δ alpha = the difference between 14-minute and 30-minute alpha).

IN OPERATE

Erratic/Unusual Winds

1. Do not switch to STBY-NAV until the following checks are made.
   (a) Check accuracy of PP tracking, cursor tracking, and ground speed.
   (b) Check BOMB COMPUTER POWER at ON and check bomb computer fuses.
2. If PP and cursors track properly, remain in OPERATE.
   If abnormal, switch A/N MODE knob to STBY-NAV.
3. Obtain IMN, IAS, CIT, and altitude from pilot (SPC ON). Compute TAS and compare with TAS read-out. Retain figures for yellow sheet entry.

AML On

1. WIND knob to SPEED, change value and return to AUTO. If new value remains, switch A/N MODE knob to STBY-NAV.
2. Check PP tracking, cursor tracking, slewing, and storing.
   (a) If normal, remain in OPERATE.

(b) If no slewing or storing, switch A/N MODE knob to STBY-NAV, AN POWER switch to OFF for 5 minutes, then back to ON.

Excessive PP Drift

Determine drift rate as follows:

1. Using VAR expanded display under 25 miles, correct PP on a known checkpoint and note time.
2. Select next checkpoint, wait at least 5 minutes, turn SYSTEM MODE knob to RECON.
3. Slew cursors to checkpoint and note time, RECON coordinates, and course.
4. Compute the difference between RECON coordinates and actual coordinates in miles.
5. Compute drift rate.
6. If drift rate exceeds 15 knots, switch A/N MODE knob to STBY-NAV.

Stand-by Navigation

1. A/N MODE knob—STBY-NAV.
2. WIND select knob—DIR/SPEED.
   Set best known wind direction and speed.
3. SYSTEM MODE knob—SET PP.
4. Set and store best known present position.
5. SYSTEM MODE knob—NAV.
6. COORD SELECT knob—NORMAL.
7. Compass TAKE CMD button—Depress.
8. Hemisphere switch—check.
9. LAT dial setting—check.
10. Compass mode selector—DG.
11. Ground speed dial—Set to best known ground speed.
12. HDG set knob—Set ARI to aircraft true heading.
13. Perform cursor or "pickle" correction at checkpoint.

NAV/BOMB Steering Error

ARI relative bearing does not equal drift angle with AAI steering at zero. Check inputs as follows:

1. Ensure pilot's and S/O's RANGE & BEARING knobs are both in NAV.
2. Ensure SYSTEM MODE knob is in NAV or BOMB.
3. Check SET/CORR and NAV/BOMB knobs at same channel.
4. Ensure WIND SELECT knob is in AUTO.
5. Recheck accuracy of coordinate storage.

Check coincidence of AAI, ARI, and HSI as follows:

1. Turn SYSTEM MODE knob to RECON and store a visible target greater than 20 miles either upwind or downwind.
2. Fly zero AAI (HSI and ARI should point dead ahead).
3. Turn SYSTEM MODE knob to BOMB, ATTACK MODE knob to O/S—all indicators should remain the same.
4. Fly AAI steering to checkpoint and note any bearing deflections on HSI and/or ARI enroute.
5. If AAI is in error, fly HSI bearing.

Course Line Steering (ALINE/HOLD Switch)

1. Use course line steering procedures to check for proper operation.
2. If errors occur after repeated reciprocal flight paths are flown, extend straight and level inbound legs (15 miles minimum) to allow for FRS erection.
3. Resynchronize compass at start of each inbound run.

Bombing Errors

1. Perform practice release check with ballistic adapters.
2. If release range is in error:
   (a) Ensure correct altitude, ground speed, and cursor tracking.
   (b) Convert release range error into impact error.
   (c) Using offset conversion table, convert impact error into offset.
   (d) Add this offset algebraically to normal offset.
   (e) Make next bomb run on release check heading.

CURSOR CONTROL FAILURE

NO NAV OR BOMB CORRECTION

1. Check AML.
2. Ensure that COORD SELECT knob is in NORMAL.
3. Move SYSTEM MODE knob to RECON and check for cursor operation.
4. Check VERDAN storing capability—Select different target and note if cursors move to new target position.
5. Check for normal pickle correct operation.
6. Store new present position, using SET PP.

WIND CONTROL FAILURES

CANNOT SLEW SPEED OR DIRECTION

1. Ensure BOMB COMPUTER POWER switch is at ON. Check for blower operation.
2. Check bombing computer fuses.

MAXIMUM READING OR ZERO IN AUTO

1. Ensure BOMB COMPUTER switch is at ON. Check for blower operation.
2. Check bombing computer fuses.
3. Slew wind manually.

ARI ERRATIC OR INOPERATIVE

1. Ensure BOMB COMPUTER POWER switch is at ON. Check for blower operation.
2. Check bombing computer fuses.
3. Cycle RANGE & BEARING knob from TACAN to NAV.

TAS/GS INDICATOR ERRATIC OR INOPERATIVE

1. Check with SPC OFF ("FAIL" flag showing).
2. Ensure BOMB COMPUTER POWER switch is ON. Check for blower operation.
3. Check bombing computer fuses.

POSITION/DESTINATION FROZEN OR ERRATIC

1. Check VERDAN storage capability.
2. Select different target and note if counters move.
3. Try RECON operation.

ALTIMETER FAILURES

BARO ERRATIC OR FAILED

1. Check SPC both ON and OFF.
2. Check mode flag is same as selected mode.

BARO CAL INDICATION ERROR

Indication should read 0 (± 22) feet.

1. Check mode flag is same as selected mode.
2. Ensure that "FAIL" (SPC ON) flag is blank.

RADAR ALTITUDE ERROR

1. Ensure that "FAIL" (SPC ON) flag is blank.
2. Ensure that aircraft attitude is less than ± 10 degrees pitch and roll, and aircraft altitude is above 500 feet.
3. Check normal operation of RADAR CAL mode.
4. Compare RADAR altitude reading with BARO altitude reading.

BARO CAL ALTITUDE ERROR

1. Check mode flag is same as selected mode.
2. Ensure that "FAIL" (SPC ON) flag is blank.
3. Ensure that aircraft attitude is less than ± 10 degrees pitch and roll, and aircraft altitude is above 500 feet.
4. Compare BARO CAL reading with BARO reading.
5. Compare BARO CAL reading with RADAR reading.

PILOT'S HSI — FROZEN RANGE OR AZIMUTH

1. Cycle SYSTEM MODE knob between NAV and BOMB.
2. Check ARI range and bearing.
3. Cycle RANGE & BEARING knob from TACAN to NAV.

PILOT'S AAI — STEERING POINTER FROZEN

1. Ensure that BOMB COMPUTER POWER switch is at ON. Check for blower operation.
2. Check bombing computer fuses.
3. Store target coordinates in new channel and check.
4. Turn course line steering off if on (ALINE/HOLD—OFF).
5. Check ARI/HSI for proper operation.

EMERGENCY TANKER

In the event of failure of the No. 2 hydraulic system or a buddy tanker system malfunction, proceed as follows:

1. EMERG FUEL FLOW switch—EMERG. Check hose extends.
2. EMERG FUEL FLOW switch—OFF.

CAUTION

Ensure hose is fully extended before reselecting OFF.

3. After receiver hookup is made, move EMERG FUEL FLOW switch to EMERG.
4. On disconnect, move EMERG FUEL FLOW switch to OFF.
5. If hose cannot be rewound, check terrain below and move HOSE CUT switch to CUT when directed.

WARNING

If the HOSE CUT switch is used, do not return the switch to NORMAL, as fuel may collect in the bomb bay.

BEFORE LANDING

1. IFF/SIF—as required.
2. ALTITUDE mode knob—BARO/CAL, then BARO.
3. TARGET ALTITUDE indicator—Set field elevation (ashore).
   —Set to zero (afloat).
4. SPC—check OFF ("FAIL" flag).
5. Armament—check off/SAFE.
6. ARM MAST'R ON light—out.
7. Loose gear—Stow.
8. Harness—LOCKED.
9. MIC SEL switch—HOT.
10. Check gear extension with TV.

AFTER LANDING

1. IFF—OFF.
2. TRANSMIT MODE switch—SILENCE.

SYSTEMS SHUTDOWN

1. Oxygen—OFF.
2. T-375 selector—GND (with Aero 8A PBC).
3. RETICLE knob—OFF.
4. FILTER switch—IN.
5. APERTURE knob—AUTO.
6. VIEW switch—FWD.
7. TV BRIGHTNESS knob—full down.
8. Radar/TV MODE knob—NORM.
9. CURSOR & CIRCLE BRT knob—full down.
10. DISPLAY switch—NORM.
11. IF GAIN knob—full down.
12. BEAM switch—NORM.
13. TILT knob—midposition.
14. VIDEO GAIN knob—full down.
15. Radar BRIGHTNESS knob—full down.
16. FREQUENCY knob—midposition.
17. SYSTEM MODE knob—NAV.
18. COORD SELECT knob—NORMAL.
19. WIND knob—AUTO.
20. ATTACK MODE knob—ALL WEATHER LEVEL.

Do not turn RADAR/TV POWER switch to OFF with ATTACK MODE knob in VIS LEVEL.

21. RADAR/TV POWER switch—OFF.

Ensure pause of at least 30 seconds after turning off radar/TV power before engines are shut down.

22. A/N MODE knob—STBY-NAV.
23. BOMB COMPUTER POWER switch—OFF.
24. AN POWER switch—OFF.
25. Canopy—open.
26. Lights—off.
27. Safety pins—installed.
28. Canopy uplock—ENGAGED.
29. Note systems' discrepancies.

flight procedures

Section IV

TABLE OF CONTENTS

Familiarization and Transition 149	Formation Flight 157
General Flight Procedures 149	Air Refueling 160
Navigation 149	Flight Test Procedures 161
Cruise Control 150	Weapon Delivery Tactics 162A
Flight Characteristics 151	

FAMILIARIZATION AND TRANSITION

Familiarization and transition will be accomplished in the replacement training squadron. The ground training and flying training accomplished will be in accordance with current directives. Refer to Section II.

GENERAL FLIGHT PROCEDURES

The professional approach to flying is mandatory. All phases of any mission will be thoroughly planned. Each crew must know the aircraft systems, planning, and in-flight procedures thoroughly.

1. The following procedures are common to all flights:
   - Use NATOPS and applicable NAVWEPS check lists.
   - Maintain an alert watch for other aircraft.
   - Both crew members will remain on oxygen at all times. In the event either crew member fails to receive oxygen, descend to 10,000-foot cockpit altitude if sufficient fuel is available to land safely when flying at this lower altitude. If the fuel situation prohibits this action, and it is necessary to fly in excess of 10,000-foot cockpit altitude for more than 15 minutes without oxygen, the emergency oxygen system will be actuated 5 minutes prior to landing.
   - The maximum allowable 90-degree cross-wind component for take-off or landing is 20 knots.

2. Simulate and review emergency procedures regularly.

3. Check all radio equipment.

4. For procedures to be followed in the event of intercom loss, refer to INTERCOMMUNICATIONS SYSTEM FAILURE, in Section VII, and LOST AIRCRAFT PROCEDURES, in Section V.

5. Whenever crew members are wearing full pressure suits, pressure suit air shall be secured and one glove opened for take-off and landing.

NAVIGATION

METHODS OF NAVIGATION

INERTIAL AUTONAVIGATOR

The primary mode of navigation will be by the full use of the N5H inertial autonavigator (A/N). Except when specifically restricted, the AN/ASB-12 radar or television will be used to improve the accuracy of the autonavigator. The autonavigator, using the inertial gyro platform, will be used on all flights on which it is operating normally.

The stand-by navigation mode, utilizing the flight reference set gyro platform, will be used when the inertial gyro platform fails.

Present position, winds, and time will be recorded and plotted at least every 15 minutes on a navigation flight.

DEAD RECKONING NAVIGATION

Dead reckoning (DR) navigation is the most basic tool available to the navigator. The navigator shall keep a complete DR plot throughout any navigation flight. This plot shall consist of standard textbook symbols for fixes, courses, positions, etc, and will include a DR position and an air plot and wind vector for each navigation leg. The DR plot normally will not be started anew from a plot of present position, except immediately following correction of present position (A/N) on some known point.

DR navigation is only as good as the information used. To get good information, the crew must use proper navigation procedures. The systems operator may judge the adequacy of his DR plot by his ability to show: (1) present position, (2) heading to the next checkpoint, and (3) ETA at that point, at any time.

RADAR NAVIGATION

The AN/ASB-12 radar may be as a secondary mode of navigation in the event of complete autonavigator failure. Following an A/N failure, a fully stabilized radar picture normally remains. Using the fixed range circles, relative bearing scale, and aircraft compass, the navigator has all the information necessary to obtain navigation fixes, ground speed, and track information.

RADIO NAVIGATION

Radio navigation (TACAN) will be used on all airways flights, scoring, or navigation flights to check autonavigator accuracy.

LOW-LEVEL NAVIGATION

Low-level navigation flights may use either radar or visual fixes. Training flights will normally be limited to radar fixes in order to further navigator training. In the event of loss of radar, or radar silence conditions, the pilot may use visual fixes to correct the A/N. In addition to using radar to obtain fixes, the pilot may use terrain avoidance radar, or the navigator may use contour mapping radar, to control aircraft altitude above the terrain.

A plot of present position or a fix is required once each minute.

Low-level flights shall be conducted only over previously approved low-level routes.

CARRIER-BASED NAVIGATION

In general, carrier-based navigation is the same as land-based navigation; the extra variable is the mobility of the launch point and the return point. The systems operator must know the ship's intended movement (PIM) to know the ship's position at the time of his return.

A dead reckoning plot will be maintained on every flight from the carrier.

NAVIGATIONAL PLANNING

Complete navigational preplanning is required for all flights. Refer to Section III. In addition to thorough route planning, careful attention will be given to airspace reservations, Air Defense Zones, high-altitude routing, and cruising altitudes. NOTAMS shall be checked, enroute frequencies verified, and destination and alternate fields checked for current status.

SYSTEMS OPERATOR RESPONSIBILITIES

The systems operator will be thoroughly versed in the use of navigational charts, publications, and procedures associated with airways navigation, as well as operational use of available electronic aids. The systems operator shall be familiar with applicable VFR/IFR flight rules under routine and special conditions and have sufficient knowledge of instrument approach and GCA/CCA procedures to monitor the approach and render assistance to the pilot as required. The systems operator shall be capable of making all position reports and taking flight clearance reports.

CRUISE CONTROL

PREFLIGHT

As much of the checkoff list shall be completed prior to turnup as possible to minimize engine ground operation and ground fuel consumption. On IFR flights, a fairly substantial saving of fuel can be realized by using external power and delaying starting of engines until such time as the IFR clearance has actually been received from ATC. An accurate fuel check shall also be made prior to starting engines, as required by the prestart check list. If proper techniques are employed, a minimum amount of fuel will be expended during ground operation.

TAKE-OFF AND CLIMB

After the aircraft has been positioned for take-off and MIL thrust applied, the systems operator shall record total fuel aboard prior to commencement of the take-off roll.

CRUISE

Optimum performance figures for all profiles and configurations of the A-5A are included in the Supplemental NATOPS Flight Manual (NAVWEPS 01-60ABA-1A). It is the responsibility of the pilot to exploit every means to obtain the maximum performance, consistent with the assigned mission, from his aircraft.

The A-5A is capable of a wide range of altitude/speed combinations. This demands that each flight be thoroughly preplanned, utilizing the latest available fuel planning data for cruise control. This planning must consider the portions of the profile at high, low, and medium altitudes, as well as acceleration schedules and supersonic flight.

When flights are scheduled utilizing point-to-point navigation which will permit positive electronic fixes, a normal route card fuel log will suffice for cruise control purposes. This will provide an instantaneous evaluation of the progress of the flight and will enable the pilot or systems operator to extrapolate actual fuel consumption to predict the progress of the remainder of the flight.

DESCENT AND LETDOWN

The procedures to be employed in descent and letdown are categorized as follows:

1. Standard Instrument Penetration — The standard penetration is flown at 250 KIAS (SPC ON) with approximately 80% rpm (friction gates) and a 4000 to 6000 feet per minute rate of descent. Speed brakes are adjusted to attain the desired rate of descent. From commencement of penetration, a fuel state of 5200 pounds will permit completion of the penetration to a wave-off, a 150-nautical-mile flight to an alternate (optimum altitude), and an arrival over the alternate approach fix with 2000 pounds of fuel remaining.

2. Maximum Range Descent — The maximum range descent can be used in a descent from high cruising altitudes to the initial approach altitude, or during descent on a high/low profile. The aircraft configuration is throttles at IDLE, speed brakes IN, flap control switch in CRUISE (below 0.92 Mach), and 250 KIAS. For planning purposes, the maximum range descent charts in the Supplemental NATOPS Flight Manual (NAVWEPS 01-60ABA-1A) may be used.

3. Maximum Rate of Descent — This type of descent would most likely be required during carrier operations when it is necessary to meet a specified recovery time after a period of operation in the DOG circle, or in an emergency situation when immediate descent is mandatory. Maximum rate of descent is obtained by placing throttles at IDLE, extending speed brakes, and maintaining maximum allowable airspeed consistent with visibility, possible turbulence, and altitude.

FUEL MANAGEMENT

Pilots shall thoroughly plan all flights and ensure that the proper fuel load is aboard prior to manning their aircraft. The fuel system is essentially automatic and has proven to be reliable, however, the pilot must periodically monitor individual fuel tank quantities in flight to determine whether the system is functioning properly. Prior to take-off, the pilot shall ensure that the bomb bay CANS transfer switch is positioned to AUTO if cans are installed, OFF if not installed. When drop tanks are employed, it is prudent to ensure that both tanks will transfer (drop tank fuel should be used as early as possible during the flight). Shortly after take-off, the pilot shall monitor the aft (saddle) tank to ensure that the fuel has transferred. If it has not, the pilot should closely monitor fuel sequencing to ensure that it is functioning properly. Failure of the aft tank to transfer is the first indication of a fuel sequencing failure. Should this occur, check the fuel sequencing (FUEL SEQ) circuit breaker. If it has "popped" or cannot be reset, select LOW SUMP (normal gravity feed rates from the wing tanks are not available in HIGH SUMP). Should a fuel sequencing failure occur, avoid flight regimes that will require high fuel flow, and closely monitor sump fuel. When carrier-based, pilots will hold any excess fuel until assured of getting into the landing pattern; however, during night or instrument conditions, pilots will be down to authorized landing weight prior to departing the 6-mile Gate. Dump rates are approximately 1200 pounds per minute. Fuel will be dumped in LOW SUMP ONLY.

FLIGHT CHARACTERISTICS

Refer to Section IV of Supplemental NATOPS Flight Manual (NAVWEPS 01-60ABA-1A) for information concerning:
- SUBSONIC FLIGHT
- SUPERSONIC FLIGHT
- MANEUVERING FLIGHT
- PILOT-INDUCED OSCILLATIONS
- ALTITUDE LOSS IN DIVE RECOVERY
- ANGLE-OF-ATTACK RELATIONSHIP

LOW-SPEED FLIGHT

Low-speed flight characteristics are straight forward and similar to other high performance aircraft. With the droops in the SUPERSONIC (retracted) position at 41,000 to 43,000 pounds gross weight, light buffet commences at 200 to 220 KIAS, depending on altitude. With the droops in the CRUISE position (5 degrees), buffet commences at 170 to 190 KIAS. As speed is decreased, buffet intensity increases, becoming moderate at about 150 KIAS. After moderate buffet is noticed, lateral control deterioration begins, and as speed is further decreased, full lateral stick deflections are required to maintain wings level.

Note

Minimum control speeds, defined as the speeds where both lateral and directional control requirements to maintain level flight become excessive, are presented for various configurations in figure 4-1. Spoiler effectiveness deteriorates at airspeeds *higher* than those shown, but proper use of directional control will pick up a wing after lateral effectiveness is lost.

The aircraft should not be flown at speeds lower than those corresponding to 15 units angle of attack unless ample altitude is available for recovery from an unusual attitude.

STALL AND POSTSTALL GYRATIONS

UPRIGHT ATTITUDE

At approximately 15 units angle of attack, lateral control deteriorates and the pedal shaker operates as an artificial stall warning. As speed is further decreased, buffet becomes heavy in intensity, increasing difficulty is encountered in longitudinal and directional control and rate of sink starts to build up. It is possible to maintain controlled wings level flight in a high sink condition until the stabilizer reaches its full leading edge down position. When the horizontal stabilizer reaches full leading edge down, the aircraft loses directional stability rather abruptly and will generally yaw in one direction or the other. This applies to the gear and flaps down configuration as well as the clean configuration. Lateral trim position affects yaw direction tendency. With lateral trim to the right, the aircraft tends to yaw left, and vice versa. Slight asymmetry between aircraft probably will dictate to a large extent the direction in which yaw occurs.

During the stall and poststall phases of flight, the aircraft behaves as a heavy aircraft would be expected to behave. It is reluctant to enter the poststall condition, but once it has entered, it is somewhat reluctant to recover rapidly. The poststall gyration is not physically uncomfortable, but the lack of immediate response to recovery controls is disconcerting. Depending on gross weight, individual aircraft asymmetry, and other variables, the aircraft will continue to yaw in an uneven manner in the initial direction or may possibly reverse direction. Aircraft pitch attitude varies from nose-down past vertical to above the horizon and yaw rate decreases at the minimum and maximum pitch attitudes. Indicated airspeed oscillates from 0 to approximately 100 KIAS.

ACCELERATED FLIGHT

Accelerated stall characteristics are similar to the preceding 1-g stall characteristics description, and commensurate stall warning is provided. During maneuvering flight while decelerating from supersonic to subsonic Mach numbers (particularly in the speed range around 0.92 indicated Mach), a very slight tendency for the aircraft to "pitch up" may be noted. This tendency is easily controlled but caution should be exercised. With pitch augmentation off, or in the event of a pitch augmentation failure, a push force will be required to keep from increasing "g" when decelerating through this speed range.

WARNING

Avoid abrupt, large magnitude, longitudinal control motions in maneuvering flight. If the stall warnings of lateral control deterioration, moderate to heavy airframe buffet and rudder pedal shaker actuation are ignored, or if extreme control motions cause the aircraft to depart abruptly from controlled flight, the aircraft may enter a developed spin from which recovery is highly unlikely.

INVERTED ATTITUDE

The outstanding characteristic of inverted stall approach is loss of lateral control effectiveness, making it difficult to hold the aircraft inverted. Inverted stall approaches have been performed by rolling the aircraft inverted at approximately 200 KIAS at 20,000 to 25,000 feet in a 30-degree, nose-up attitude. The wings could not be held level inverted with full lateral control deflection under about 150 KIAS, and full directional control, opposing the tendency to roll out, was utilized to maintain the inverted attitude. With full forward stick maintained, the airspeed decreased to about 120 KIAS, where the nose began to drop and airspeed increased with no tendency to yaw in either direction. The inverted stall approach is characterized by very light buffet as opposed to moderate-to-heavy buffet during upright stall approaches.

MINIMUM CONTROL SPEEDS

KNOTS INDICATED AIRSPEED
STATIC PRESSURE COMPENSATOR — OFF

TAKE-OFF   FLAPS 40° GEAR DOWN

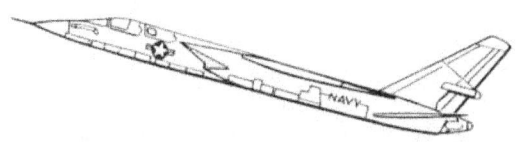

CRUISE   POWER-ON

GROSS WEIGHT-POUNDS					ANGLE OF BANK	LOAD FACTOR "G"	GROSS WEIGHT-POUNDS				
36,000	42,000	48,000	54,000	60,000			36,000	42,000	48,000	54,000	60,000
104	112	120	127	135	0°	1.0	120	130	139	148	162
112	121	129	137	144	30°	1.2	129	140	150	159	178
124	134	143	152	159	45°	1.4	143	155	166	177	187
148	160	171	181	192	60°	2.0	171	185	198	211	228

LANDING
FLAPS — 50°, GEAR DOWN, SPEED BRAKE OUT (8°)

NOTE: MINIMUM CONTROL SPEEDS ARE DEFINED AS THOSE AT WHICH CONTROL REQUIREMENTS BECOME CRITICAL; THEY ARE NOT TO BE CONSIDERED AS APPROACH SPEEDS.

POWER — ON (82% RPM AND ABOVE)				ANGLE OF BANK	LOAD FACTOR "G"	IDLE POWER			
GROSS WEIGHT-POUNDS						GROSS WEIGHT-POUNDS			
36,000	42,000	48,000	54,000			36,000	42,000	48,000	54,000
103	111	119	126	0°	1.0	107	116	124	131
111	120	128	136	30°	1.2	115	125	134	141
123	133	142	151	45°	1.4	128	139	148	151
147	158	169	179	60°	2.0	148	165	177	186

NOTE: IN APPROACH SPEED RANGE, SPC ON CAUSES AIRSPEED TO READ 7 TO 9 KNOTS HIGHER THAN ACTUAL

BASED ON: FLIGHT TEST DATA (NA 60H-200A)
DATA AS OF: 8-1-60

Figure 4-1

2. If pitch attitude is past vertical as noted on the attitude indicator, the stick should be pulled aft to achieve an inverted attitude.
3. If pitch attitude is short of vertical, the stick should be pushed forward to achieve an upright attitude.
4. If pitch attitude is so nearly vertical that there is no real choice, forward stick should be applied, as forward stick is much more effective in rotating the aircraft than is aft stick.

Note

With an airspeed of 100 KIAS in a vertical attitude, the aircraft can be rotated to an upright level attitude with forward stick.

WARNING

IT MUST BE REMEMBERED THAT ANY TIME THE AIRCRAFT IS FULLY STALLED OR FLOWN VERTICALLY TO A LOW AIRSPEED, THERE IS A DEFINITE POSSIBILITY THAT A DEVELOPED SPIN WILL BE ENTERED FROM WHICH RECOVERY IS HIGHLY UNLIKELY.

SPINS

WARNING

INTENTIONAL SPINS ARE PROHIBITED. During the spin test program, a spin mode was encountered from which no satisfactory recovery, using the production design control system, was possible.

DEVELOPED SPIN

The developed spin is characterized by higher yaw rate (rotation) and less pitching oscillation than is encountered in poststall gyration. Pitch attitude is from 40 to 60 degrees nose-down and fairly steady. There are some generally diminished roll and yaw rate oscillations. There may be some transverse (back-to-front) "g" imposed upon the crew members, which is quite uncomfortable.

WARNING

In the event the poststall gyration progresses to a fully developed spin, it is highly unlikely that recovery can be effected.

SPIN RECOVERY

Should a developed spin be encountered at high altitude, the best control positions are:

1. Control stick—FULL AFT and laterally FULL IN DIRECTION OF SPIN.
2. Directional control pedals—FULL AGAINST SPIN.
3. Controls neutralized as yaw rate (turn needle) approaches 0.

During the contractor's spin test program, insufficient altitude was available to determine the number of turns required for the above control combination to effect recovery. Tests determined that the above combination will possibly effect recovery from a low yaw rate developed spin if the initial altitude is high enough.

WARNING

EJECT IMMEDIATELY on reaching 15,000 feet above the terrain if the aircraft is not under control.

LOW-SPEED FLIGHT (LANDING CONFIGURATION)

Low-speed flight with the landing gear and flaps extended results in a relatively flat pitch attitude, affording excellent pilot visibility in approach and landing. Aircraft control in this configuration is good and lateral control remains "solid" down to minimum control speed. See figure 4-1. Undesirable flap buffet occurs above 160 KIAS, but this buffet becomes generally unnoticeable below 140 KIAS.

BOUNDARY LAYER CONTROL (BLC)

With boundary layer control, the effects of approach airspeed and engine power setting are greatly increased. BLC effectiveness varies with engine rpm. During final approach, retarding the throttle below 78% rpm results in a quick reduction in BLC flow, BLC drops off sharply, and the required angle of attack for approach and touchdown airspeeds is greatly increased. Because of BLC decay below 78% rpm, it is recommended that during approaches with the flaps at 50 degrees and speed brakes extended 8 degrees, normal approach power (82% to 88% rpm) be maintained until touchdown, at which time the throttles may be retarded to IDLE. If a decision is made to wave off during an approach, the application of Military Thrust is accompanied by an easily controlled nose-up pitch.

PITCH AUGMENTATION INOPERATIVE

Without the aid of pitch augmentation, available aircraft nose-up stabilizer displacement is reduced. If power is cut to IDLE prior to touchdown, the aircraft exhibits a sharp nose-down pitch and an abrupt increase in rate of sink due to BLC decay. Even at higher than normal approach speeds, the nose-down pitch plus reduced nose-up control may result in the aircraft dropping onto the runway before the pilot can effect sufficient flare for a safe landing. Under aft cg conditions, flap extension should be limited to 40 degrees, in case a wave-off is required, to preclude uncontrollable pitch-up.

LANDING WITH AFT CG

APPROACH CHARACTERISTICS

Under normal operating conditions, approaches and landings, as described in Section III, Parts 3 and 4, can be accomplished with aircraft center of gravity as far aft as 37 percent of the mean aerodynamic chord. However, flight tests show that the static longitudinal stability of the aircraft at an aft cg becomes weak, which provides poor flying qualities during a landing approach, particularly in turbulent air. The flying qualities are further aggravated when the pitch augmentation system is disengaged as evidenced by a decrease of precise control. However, control power is more than adequate to safely maneuver the aircraft in severe turbulence.

Note

Present requirements dictate that aircraft center of gravity be limited to 33 percent MAC.

33 PERCENT MAC

Extra caution and pilot effort are required when flying the aircraft in the landing configuration in turbulent air with a center of gravity aft of approximately 33 percent MAC, especially with the pitch augmentation OFF. With no external stores and empty bomb bay cans, 33 percent MAC is reached with approximately 1500 pounds total fuel remaining. Improper fuel management or failure of the fuel sequencing system can result in exceeding cg limits [refer to Section I, Part 4, of the Supplemental NATOPS Flight Manual (NAVWEPS 01-60ABA-1A)]. If the bomb bay cans cannot be transferred or dumped, it is strongly recommended that such bomb bay loads be jettisoned prior to attempting a carrier landing, particularly with pitch augmentation inoperative.

APPROACH TECHNIQUE

Adequate longitudinal control authority is available under all conditions to the aft cg limit for a power approach. Aft cg approaches should be conducted with a maximum of 40-degree flaps, controlling altitude with power and making required pitch attitude changes with firm, positive movements — do not let the aircraft "fly" you. Speed control will not be precise, although the aircraft will respond promptly to small thrust variations and airspeed can be maintained within desired limits. Concentrate on maintaining attitude prior to touchdown and ease the aircraft onto the runway by addition of power — not by attempting to abruptly flare with aft stick.

PITCH AUGMENTATION OFF

When a landing in turbulent air with pitch augmentation inoperative is anticipated, plan your return so that adequate fuel is available in the sump tank to maintain a center of gravity near or forward of 33 percent MAC. If the bomb bay cans will not transfer, it is recommended that the SUMP switch be moved to HIGH to maintain the sump tank at greater than 4000 pounds.

In addition, the bomb bay CANS transfer switch should be cycled from AUTO to OFF to ON, allowing 2 minutes between cycles, in an attempt to pressurize the cans to transfer the fuel. If the cans remain full, they should be dumped prior to a carrier landing, particularly under adverse conditions such as excessive turbulence.

If the bomb bay cans cannot be dumped and the fuel cannot be transferred, utilize a maximum of 40-degree flaps for landing. This will increase longitudinal control authority and provide adequate control for a field landing. With the bomb bay cans full, and with 2000 pounds of sump fuel remaining (wings empty), the cg is approximately 36 percent MAC. The cg moves aft approximately 1 percent for each 400 pounds of sump fuel used below 2000 pounds.

AFTER TOUCHDOWN

After touchdown, a throttle chop will kill lift, but if a bad bounce should occur, corrective action would be the addition of power for a complete wave-off. It is emphasized that adequate control authority is available under all conditions to safely counteract any pitch change due to thrust increase. However, remember that initial longitudinal response will be slow and no abrupt large-magnitude longitudinal stick inputs should be applied in attempting to correct for a bad bounce. Admit to yourself that a bad landing was made and wave off. Utilize the same technique following a carrier landing bolter, add power as necessary for a wave-off, and avoid abrupt, large-magnitude longitudinal stick inputs — fly the aircraft, do not let it "fly" you.

POWER APPROACH AND LANDING STALLS

Stall characteristics with gear and flaps extended are similar to clean configuration stalls, except that pitch attitude is less pronounced.

As angle of attack is increased to 15 units (115 KIAS at 40,000 pounds gross weight), the pedal shaker operates, followed by lateral control deterioration similar to that encountered in clean configuration stall approaches. Accompanying this characteristic will be a heavy "pounding" buffet impressed on the normal, mild flaps down buffet. Rate of sink will begin to increase, but the aircraft remains controllable, with difficulty, until the stick is near the aft stop. Roll attitude is controllable with directional control pedal input alone from approximately 16.5 units angle of attack, where sink rate becomes excessive, to approximately 20 units, where control is lost in roll and yaw.

156A/156B

INLET BUZZ

Inlet shock wave instability and rapid oscillation constitute a phenomenon known as "inlet buzz." This may occur above 1.4 Mach when engine airflow demand is suddenly reduced by an abrupt change in rpm, flameout, or compressor stall. At high Mach numbers, inlet buzz can occur below 95% rpm, as well as at low engine airflow (idle rpm or windmilling) conditions. Inlet duct airflow instability is caused by incorrect scheduling of the inlet ramp controls and/or hotter-than-standard ambient air temperatures.

The disturbance begins as a low-amplitude, moderate frequency airframe buffet, or "nibble," usually under high-altitude and airspeed conditions. Buffet increases to moderate and heavy as Mach number increases. Corrective action is to reduce airspeed by reducing throttles to Military Thrust and extending speed brakes. Fully developed inlet buzz is considered unlikely to occur unless the ramps or rpm sensing switches should fail during throttle chop at high supersonic speed. It is characterized by extremely heavy airframe buffet combined with aircraft lateral/directional oscillations of low amplitude and high frequency. This phenomenon is violent and abrupt, calling for immediate pilot action to slow the aircraft to a subsonic speed by extending the speed brakes and retarding the throttles to Military Thrust. If fully developed buzz is initiated by a throttle reduction with malfunction of rpm sensing switches, the intensity of the buzz can be decreased by advancing the throttles to Military Thrust, while slowing by use of the speed brakes.

Note

- When inlet ramps are fully extended, either by the rpm switch above 1.3 Mach, or by turning engine MASTER switch to OFF above 0.3 Mach, rapid engine acceleration to high rpm may cause compressor stall.

- To avoid compressor stall below 1.3 Mach with ramps extended, inlet ramp control should be reset prior to rapid throttle movements.

- Above 1.3 Mach, inlet ramp will extend full down whenever engine speed decreases below 95% rpm. Therefore, compressor stall can be avoided by slowly accelerating (5 seconds from the IDLE position) to the above engine rpm limits. When the RAMP CONT caution light illuminates, reset the inlet ramp control and continue acceleration.

- Resetting the ramp control system is unnecessary if engine power is maintained at 100% rpm, or higher, above 1.3 Mach.

Refer to AIR INDUCTION SYSTEM OPERATION, in Section I, Part 2.

FORMATION FLIGHT

Formation tactics will normally be conducted in accordance with NWIP 41-3, Chapter 8, and as discussed in the following paragraphs.

GENERAL

Most tactical missions of the heavy attack squadron will be single aircraft; however, carrier operations require a considerable amount of formation flying in the vicinity of the ship and it is essential that each pilot be adept in these procedures. A thorough and specific briefing shall be accomplished prior to conducting a formation flight.

A formation is designed to afford tactical concentration, ease of control, and mutual defense. The governing factors are:

1. It must be maneuverable.
2. It must be flexible enough to meet any situation.
3. It must be simple and arranged so that the flight leader can see all elements of the flight.

BASIC FORMATIONS

PARADE

The parade formation will be used when passing in review, orbiting the ship or station (shore-based), or when participating in aerial demonstrations.

Maneuvers performed in parade formation are relative to the leader and the wingman maintains a fixed wing position on the leader. On turns into the wingman, he will rotate about the leader's axis. On turns away from the wingman, he will rotate about his own axis while maintaining a safe stepped-down position.

Parade formations are flown in section, division, or squadron strength.

CRUISE

The cruise formation is used for cross-country formation and, at other times, to reduce pilot fatigue and to conserve fuel. The cruise formation provides maximum maneuverability.

ECHELON

This formation will normally be used prior to breakup and during rendezvous. The echelon to the right or left will be signaled by the leader. If the leader's wingman is on the same side as the echelon to be formed, the second section will cross under and join on him. If the second section is on the side to which the echelon will be formed, it will move out to make room for the wingman. Turns into an echelon will be avoided.

Section IV NAVWEPS 01-60ABA-1

FORMATION ELEMENTS

The section, consisting of two aircraft, is the basic formation unit from which other elements are formed. The division consists of four aircraft formed from two sections: a division leader with his wingman in the No. 2 position, and the second section leader in the No. 3 position, with his wingman in the No. 4 position.

PARADE AND ECHELON

In these two basic formations, the wingmen position themselves on a line slightly ahead of the leader's wing, 45 degrees relative to the longitudinal axis of the lead aircraft, and stepped down sufficiently to allow clearance between the tip of their vertical stabilizer and the bottom of the leader's fuselage. This position may be maintained by lining up the outboard leading edge of the engine inlet duct with the aft upper area of the rear canopy. Lateral separation is approximately 10 feet between wing tips.

CRUISE

In cruise formation, the wingmen position themselves on a 60-degree relative bearing, and extended laterally sufficiently to provide 20 feet of clearance between the nose of their aircraft and the tail of the preceding aircraft. This position leaves one space between each aircraft. When maneuvering, the wingmen may slide as necessary to maintain the same nose-to-tail distance between aircraft.

SQUADRON FORMATION

The squadron formation shall consist of three four-plane divisions with the second section of each division outboard from the formation leader. Sufficient space shall be left between the first and third divisions for the second division to maneuver.

BRIEFING

When formation flying is scheduled, the designated leader, or senior pilot if no leader is designated, will conduct the required briefing. The briefing will cover the following points:

1. Radio frequencies.
2. Location, altitude, airspeed, and type of rendezvous.
3. Position of each aircraft in the formation.
4. Alternate leaders.
5. Type of mission to be flown.
6. Lost communication procedures.

RENDEZVOUS AND DEPARTURE PATTERN (SHORE-BASED)

NORMAL RENDEZVOUS

1. The purpose of the rendezvous is to join a flight aircraft in the minimum amount of time and proceed on an assigned mission. The 180-degree rendezvous is the basic type.

2. Prior to leaving the line, the flight will check in with the leader on squadron frequency with side number and aircraft status. All aircraft will then switch to ground control frequency, and the leader will call for taxi for the entire flight. The aircraft will leave the line in order and taxi to the head of the runway in column, maintaining sufficient taxi interval to preclude FOD.

3. After switching to tower frequency and receiving appropriate take-off clearance, two aircraft will spot on the runway at a time.

4. The take-off interval shall be 30 seconds, or as briefed, and after take-off all aircraft shall conform to the leader's flight path.

5. After take-off, the leader will climb straight ahead at 300 KIAS (SPC ON) with 90% rpm. The leader will allow 20 seconds (30 seconds if less than four) for each aircraft in the flight before commencing the rendezvous turn.

6. At the proper time, the leader will commence a 30-degree banked turn and continue climb to briefed altitude.

7. Once the leader commences the rendezvous turn, the succeeding aircraft shall hold a straight course until the leader bears 20 degrees to left or right, at which time a 45-degree banked turn will be executed to establish the relative rendezvous bearing. Once established, the bank angle should be decreased.

8. In joining, the wingman should concentrate on working in the rendezvous cone, which is generally considered to be an imaginary cone 225 to 255 degrees relative to the leader. When there is considerable distance between aircraft, the relative bearing should be further forward; as the distance decreases, the bearing should approach to optimum 225 degrees. Maintaining this rendezvous cone will give a steady closing rate. Each aircraft should stay inside of the leader's turn until joined up, and then cross under to their assigned position. Do not tail chase in the rendezvous turn.

9. After completing 180 degrees of the turn, depending on whether all aircraft have joined, the leader will proceed on course, accelerating to climb schedule speed, or return to the departure point, leveling off at the briefed altitude at 300 KIAS.

RUNNING RENDEZVOUS

1. A running rendezvous may be accomplished at the discretion of the flight leader when time and fuel are critical.

2. After take-off, the leader will immediately turn to the briefed departure heading, maintaining 300 KIAS and 90% rpm.

3. Each succeeding aircraft shall take off with a 30-second interval and conform to the leader's flight path, utilizing MIL thrust.

4. Speed differential will be utilized to close the distance between aircraft. As the distance is reduced, the speed differential should be reduced accordingly. A speed differential in excess of 20 knots can be dangerous when in close proximity to another aircraft.

5. Wingman will join on the left side of the leader, then cross under to the assigned position.

RENDEZVOUS AND DEPARTURE (CARRIER-BASED)

NORMAL RENDEZVOUS

The rendezvous sector will be changed with respect to the number of carriers and the relative position of the specific carrier in the formation. For single carrier operations, the rendezvous area for A-5A aircraft is normally forward of the carrier and outside of the recovery pattern. On launch, the leader will execute his clearing turn and proceed straight out at 300 KIAS until all aircraft are airborne. Departure Control will give you an off count and clear you to controller or tactical frequency. The lead aircraft shall then proceed to a point 10 miles ahead of the ship and commence a 180-degree, 30-degree banked, climbing turn accelerating to 350 KIAS. When all aircraft are joined, the leader shall accelerate to climb schedule and proceed with the assigned mission. After each frequency shift, the flight shall count off, "one up, two up, etc." Lead pilots shall ensure that their flight remains clear of Marshal points and penetration courses.

RUNNING RENDEZVOUS

After launch, the leader will maintain 300 KIAS and climb out on the assigned departure radial. Following aircraft will join, using power settings as required. On completion of the join-up, the leader will accelerate to climb schedule and proceed with the mission.

FORMATION BREAKUP

1. The formation will always break from an appropriate echelon and signal from the flight leader.

2. All breaks will be executed in a 60-degree banked level turn or as briefed.

3. Breaks into a landing pattern shall normally consist of 14 seconds when shipboard (40-second landing interval), and 20 seconds when shore-based, to allow sufficient time for the aircraft ahead to clear the runway.

4. In order to avoid extension of the landing pattern, do not break more than one division at a time. Succeeding divisions shall circle 500 feet above preceding divisions entering the break in order.

FORMATION IN CLOUDS

1. Should a formation enter clouds, it can be kept intact if proper wing positions are maintained. Wingmen should maintain the same relative position during all turns, i.e., roll about the leader's axis for both turns into and away from the wingmen.

2. Should an aircraft lose sight of a preceding aircraft, an easy turn away will be in accordance with the following rules: first aircraft to the right of the leader turns 10 degrees right, second aircraft to the right of the leader turns 20 degrees right. Aircraft to the left make similar left turns. These headings will be held for 1 minute, then return to base course. The leader will maintain base course.

NIGHT FORMATION

1. The same general rules for day formations apply to night formations.

2. It is difficult to determine relative motion at night; therefore, no abrupt maneuvers should be attempted and changes in formation should be kept to a minimum. Rendezvous should be accomplished with low closing speeds.

3. While in formation, all aircraft, except the last, should set wing and tail light DIM, formation lights ON, and anticollision lights OFF. The last aircraft shall have all lights on bright and the anticollision lights ON. When not in formation, all aircraft shall keep lights on bright and the anticollision lights ON.

4. Cockpit lights shall be dimmed to improve exterior visibility.

5. Night breakup will be signaled by flashing position lights and by radio, if radio silence is not imposed. Position lights of all aircraft will be turned on bright following the break.

BASIC FORMATION RULES

1. Rendezvous as briefed.

2. Never lose sight of the aircraft ahead. If a preceding aircraft gets "sucked" in a rendezvous, all succeeding aircraft will drop back.

3. Never pass an aircraft during the rendezvous.

4. In the event an unsatisfactory join-up occurs due to an excessive closure rate, level your wings and go to the outside. Never throw a wing up to stop an excessive closure rate.

5. Do not join another aircraft or formation of aircraft without prior approval of the flight leader.

6. When maneuvering a parade and echelon formation, the leader should be smooth, avoid rapid roll rates and steep bank angles, and maintain constant power settings where possible.

7. Leaders should not use MAX AFTERBURNER, military, or IDLE power settings, thus allowing maneuvering power for the rest of the formation.

8. The flight should always be warned prior to using afterburner, speed brakes, and changing configuration, i.e., gear, flaps, etc.

AIR REFUELING

RECEIVER PROCEDURE

To successfully complete an air refueling hookup, the following procedure is recommended:

Note

- Prior to any air refueling operation, it shall be positively determined that tanker and receiver equipment are compatible.
- Normal airspeed range for refueling is between 250 and 270 KIAS.

1. Below 280 KEAS, place the fuel probe switch to EXTEND.

1A. Flap control switch—CRUISE.

2. Drop tank transfer—off.

3. PITCH AUG and ELEC SYS switches—STBY (if desired).

    Extinguish master caution indicator and trim aircraft as required.

4. Approach the tanker aircraft from the rear and below. Line up with the left edge of the drogue, stabilize aircraft position, and retrim slightly below and approximately 10 to 15 feet astern.

5. Increase power and maintain an even rate of closure.

    Maximum rate of closure recommended is 5 to 8 feet per second (3 to 5 knots). Do not hesitate; drive the probe directly into the drogue. If engagement is missed, retard the throttles and attempt a second engagement.

CAUTION

- A rapid rate of closure will move the drogue forward too fast for proper reel action, causing slack in the hose. This may result in a violent whipping action which could cause structural damage to the probe or drogue.
- If the hose loops on initial contact, or will not retract, a malfunction in the tanker exists. DO NOT ATTEMPT FURTHER ENGAGEMENTS unless an emergency exists.
- If the hose or drogue fouls on the probe, back out very slowly.

6. After hookup is accomplished, push about 10 to 15 feet of hose into the reel. Reduce speed to that of the tanker and maintain the required position during fuel transfer operations.

Note

When the drogue has extended the proper distance, an amber light is illuminated on the tanker aircraft. After contact is made, movement of the drogue inward approximately 6 feet automatically starts fuel transfer from the tanker. This is indicated by a green light on the tanker. When the green light comes on, the yellow light will go out. The sequence is reversed when the receiving aircraft moves the drogue back to full trail to break contact.

7. Note progress during fuel transfer by observing the fuel quantity indicator.

    The maximum transfer rate of the A-5A buddy tanker unit is in excess of 2040 pounds (300 gallons) per minute. A steady increase in power will be required as fuel transfer progresses.

8. When the refueling is complete, reduce power slightly to pull the hose out at 2 to 3 knots to full trail, disengaging the probe from the drogue reception coupling.

CAUTION

High rates of separation should be avoided when breaking contact. Sudden separation may damage the probe. If the drogue and/or parts of the hose break off and become entangled on the probe, do not retract the probe. Land as soon as possible.

WARNING

Broken parts or pieces may enter the port engine duct. Anticipate reduced power or erratic performance from the port engine due to foreign object damage.

9. Fuel probe switch—RETRACT.

BUDDY TANKER PROCEDURE

PREFLIGHT CHECK

Add the following to the normal preflight inspection:

1. Check paradrogue for snagged risers.
2. Check for disconnected, missing, or broken attach rings.
3. Check paradrogue for proper freedom in tunnel.

WARNING

Ensure that the HOSE CONTROL switch is at REWIND prior to engine start.

FLIGHT PROCEDURE

1. Check with pilot to ensure that several hundred pounds of bomb bay fuel have been transferred and that the CANS transfer switch is OFF.

2. Fuel TO BE TRANSFERRED indicator—Preset as desired.

Note

Fuel will not transfer with the indicator set at zero unless the emergency fuel flow switch is placed in EMERG.

3. TOTAL FUEL TRANSFERRED indicator—Set to zero.

4. After contact is established with the receiver and airspeed is stabilized, move the HOSE CONTROL switch to TRAIL.

Check that the IN TRANSIT light extinguishes and the FULL TRAIL light illuminates.

5. If installed, the television sight may be used in the aft viewing position as a monitor.

6. Check with pilot—pitch augmentation STBY.

7. At contact, note illumination of FUEL ON light and TOTAL FUEL TRANSFERRED indicator running.

Note

If airspeed changes more than 10 knots and/or altitude more than 1000 feet between receiver hookups, momentarily depress the REEL RESPONSE button prior to next hookup.

8. When fuel TO BE TRANSFERRED indicator reads zero, note TOTAL FUEL TRANSFERRED indicator stopped.

9. When receiver contact is broken, note FULL TRAIL light on and FUEL ON light out.

10. When refueling is complete, move the HOSE CONTROL switch to REWIND.

11. On rewind, check that the IN TRANSIT light goes out when the hose is fully stowed.

If the hose will not rewind, momentarily depress the REEL RESPONSE button.

Note

Remaining can fuel should not be dumped until hose rewind is completed; otherwise, wing fuel may also be inadvertently dumped.

BUDDY TANKER EMERGENCY PROCEDURE

In the event of failure of the No. 2 hydraulic system, or malfunction of the buddy tanker system, proceed as follows:

0. HOSE CONTROL—TRAIL.
Check indicator lights and fuel flow.

1. Move EMERG FUEL FLOW switch to EMERG.
The hose will trail to the fully extended position.

2. After hose is fully trailed, move EMERG FUEL FLOW switch to OFF.

CAUTION

The hose will stop, and may be damaged, if the EMERG FUEL FLOW switch is placed in the OFF position prior to full hose extension.

Note

Placing the EMERG FUEL FLOW switch to OFF removes fuel pressure from the drogue, allowing receiver hookup. Normally, the hose is "dead" (no response) during hookups in emergency.

3. After receiver hookup is achieved, return the EMERG FUEL FLOW switch to EMERG for fuel transfer.

Note

Emergency refueling without buddy tanker hydraulic power will require longer than normal, as buddy tank pressurization and gravity are transferring fuel.

4. If the buddy tanker hose cannot be rewound onto the reel after a refueling mission, momentarily depress the REEL RESPONSE button.

If rewind does not then take place, the HOSE CUT switch should be moved to CUT. This action fires a guillotine charge, which cuts the hose, closes all system valves, and secures all buddy tanker system electrical circuits.

WARNING

If the HOSE CUT switch is used, do not return the switch to NORMAL, as fuel may collect in the bomb bay.

FLIGHT TEST PROCEDURES

Pilots assigned for flight testing must be designated, in writing, by the Commanding Officer. Fuel loadings and crew requirements will be determined by the Commanding Officer or his designated representative and will take into account safety of flight and the purpose for which the test flight is conducted.

RAM-AIR TURBINE OPERATIONAL CHECK

Following major inspection:

1. Check that both hydraulic systems are operating normally and within pressure limits.
2. HYD SUB-SYS ISOLATION switch—FLIGHT.
3. Airspeed—200 to 400 KIAS.
4. PITCH AUG, YAW AUG, and ELEC SYS switches—STBY.
5. Buddy tanker power—off.
6. TRIM SEL switch—ALTR.
7. Extend RAT and check HYD EPU ON and ELEC EPU ON advisory lights.
8. Reduce speed to less than 230 KIAS.
9. HYD SUB-SYS ISOLATION switch—TAKE-OFF/LANDING.
10. Extend flaps and landing gear.
11. Check generators individually for proper reset.
12. Trim aircraft for 150 KIAS, and move both GEN switches to OFF.
    Check for proper operation of essential a-c and d-c systems. Monitor HSI and angle-of-attack indicator for proper operation. Check UHF EMER PWR indicator on, and check transmitter for operation.

Note

HYD PRESS caution indicator will illuminate after deenergizing both a-c generators.

13. NO. 1 GEN, NO. 2 GEN switches—RESET/ON.

Note

Generators do not require electrical power for reset.

14. Reset flight control augmentation systems and select normal trim.
15. Retract RAT.

FLIGHT CONTROL AND PRETAXI CHECK (COMPLETE)

1. Canopy—closed (Listen for "pop").
2. Flap control switch—SUPERSONIC.
3. Check surface travel:
    (a) Horizontal stabilizers—8 degrees nose down, 18 degrees nose up.
    (b) Spoilers—40 degrees inboard and mid, 48 degrees outboard.
    (c) Vertical stabilizer—2 degrees left and right.
4. TRIM SEL switch—ALTR.
5. ALTR ROLL/YAW TRIM switch—check trim in each direction. Trim indicator:
    (a) ROLL—3 units left wing down and right wing down.
    (b) YAW—1½ units left and right.
6. Alternate pitch trim—check full NU and ND. Trim indicator:
    (a) ND—6.5 units.
    (b) NU—9 units.
7. TRIM SEL switch—NORM.
8. Roll trim—check travel. Trim indicator:
    (a) 3 units left wing down and right wing down.
9. Yaw trim—check travel. Trim indicator:
    (a) 1½ units left and right.
    (b) Leave trimmed full out.
10. Normal pitch trim—check travel. Trim indicator:
    (a) NU—9 units.
    (b) ND—6.5 units.
    (c) Leave at 6.5 units ND.
11. YAW AUG switch—ON.
    (a) YAW AUG caution indicator—out.
12. RAMP CONT switch—RESET.
13. ELEC SYS switch—RESET.
    (a) Check ELEC F/C caution indicator out.
    (b) Check PITCH and ROLL indicators blank.
14. Hold stick full left or right.
    (a) Check spoilers partly open 40 degrees.
15. Flap control switch—CRUISE (Hold stick).
    (a) Check spoilers full open (70 degrees).
    (b) Check spoilers with full opposite stick.
16. Speed brakes—OUT.
    (a) Check spoilers open to 55 degrees.
17. PITCH AUG switch—RESET.
    (a) Hold in RESET until PITCH AUG caution indicator goes out, then release to ON.
    (b) As system engages, check that the switch moves to center and the PITCH trim indicator moves to 1.3 units NU.
18. Move stick full forward and aft.
    (a) Check horizontal stabilizers reach 15 degrees nose down, 18 degrees nose up.
19. Pitch trim—check friction and travel.
    (a) Leave at 8 degrees nose up.
20. PITCH AUG switch—STBY.
21. Move stick rapidly forward, then full left, then rapidly right.
    (a) Check ELEC F/C caution indicator on and ROLL and PITCH indicators barber-poled.
    (b) ELEC SYS switch—RESET.

22. Move stick rapidly aft, then full right, then rapidly left.
    (a) Check ELEC F/C caution indicator on and ROLL and PITCH indicators barber-poled.
    (b) ELEC SYS switch—RESET.
23. HYD SUB-SYS ISOLATION switch—FLIGHT.
24. Flap control switch—50°.
    (a) Note flaps do not extend.
    (b) Yaw trim centers.
    (c) Check speed brakes close to 8 degrees.
25. HYD SUB-SYS ISOLATION switch—TAKE-OFF/LANDING.
    (a) Check flaps extend to 50 degrees.
    (b) Check droops extended fully.
    (c) Check PITCH trim indicator—6 to 7 units ND.
26. Move stick full left and right.
    (a) Check spoilers for full 70 degrees travel.
27. Directional control pedals full left and right.
    (a) Check for 8 degrees travel.
28. Flap control switch—40°.
    (a) Check speed brakes fully retracted and indicate IN.
29. Flap control switch—50°.
30. PITCH AUG switch—RESET.
31. Disable "kill" button—Depress/Push stick full forward and Hold.
    (a) Check horizontal stabilizers 15 degrees aircraft nose down (LEU).
32. PITCH AUG and ELEC SYS switches—RESET.
33. Push stick full forward and depress disable "kill" button. IMMEDIATELY pull stick full aft and hold.
    (a) Check PITCH trim indicator reaches 6.5 units NU IMMEDIATELY and observe centering to 12 units NU.
34. Flap control switch—CRUISE.
    (a) Check flaps retract, droops stop at 5 degrees.
    (b) PITCH trim indicator—1.3 NU.
35. PITCH AUG and ELEC SYS switches—RESET, if desired.
36. CNI command lights—as desired.
37. Compass—Set and SLAVED.
38. External power and cooling air—removed.
39. Bomb bay CANS switch—ON.
40. Refueling probe—check operation.
41. Canopy defrost and windshield anti-ice—check operation.

WEAPON DELIVERY TACTICS

Refer to Section VIII.

emergency procedures

Section V

TABLE OF CONTENTS

Engine Start Malfunctions	163
Take-off Emergencies	164
After Take-off	165
Emergency Escape	166
In-flight Emergencies	167
Fuel System Failures	174
Electrical System Failures	176
Hydraulic Failures	179
Pitot-Static System Failure	180
Flight Control Systems Failures	181
Lost Aircraft Procedures	182
Downed Aircraft Surveillance	182A
Ditching	182A
Helicopter Water Rescue	182B
Landing Emergencies	182B
Carrier Arrestment	182G
Field Arrestment	182H
Brake Failure	182J
Emergency Cockpit Entrance and Escape	182J

ENGINE START MALFUNCTIONS

FALSE START

Should an engine fail to light off within 30 seconds after the throttle is moved to IDLE, proceed as follows:
1. Throttle—OFF.
2. Allow engine to crank for 40 seconds.
3. START & IGN circuit breaker—check.
4. Engine MASTER switch—check.
5. START switch—STOP.
6. Inspect engine.
7. Commence restart.
8. Depress EMER IGN button and advance throttle to IDLE, continuing to hold button down.
   If start was initiated using EMER IGN, attempt normal start.
9. If engine fails to light off, move throttle to OFF and down the aircraft for investigation.

HOT OR HUNG START

Should starting EGT exceed limits, down the aircraft for engine inspection. Should rpm build up, then hang short of normal idle, proceed as follows:
1. Throttle—OFF.
2. Allow engine to crank for 40 seconds.
3. Instruct Plane Captain to check start air and electrical connections.
4. Attempt additional start only if the cause is determined to be other than an engine malfunction.

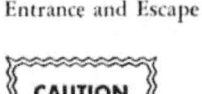

CAUTION

Do not attempt additional starts if EGT limits have been exceeded.

AUTOACCELERATION

If an engine autoaccelerates above idle rpm, proceed as follows:
1. Throttle—OFF.
2. If the engine does not shut down, ENGINE FIRE switch—TOWARD AFFECTED ENGINE.

Note

If the ENGINE FIRE switch is used, it should be left in the selected position and the corresponding engine MASTER switch should then be turned to OFF to prevent reopening of the firewall shutoff valve. Ground inspection of all engine systems is required before any further start attempts are made.

ENGINE FIRE DURING START

If a fire warning indicator comes on during a start, or if there are other indications of fire, the following procedures are recommended:

TAIL-PIPE FIRE

If a tail-pipe fire should occur during a start, the condition will probably be detected by the ground crew

Section V   NAVWEPS 01-60ABA-1

rather than by illumination of a fire warning indicator. If a tail-pipe fire exists, the pilot should proceed as follows:

1. Both throttles—OFF.
2. Appropriate START switch—START.
   Motor engine until the ground crew signals fire is out.
3. If fire is not extinguished by motoring, instruct ground crew to direct a stream of CO_2 agent into the tail pipe.
   Evacuate the aircraft as soon as possible and have the ground crew disconnect external electrical power and cooling air.

OTHER THAN TAIL-PIPE FIRES

Should a fire occur other than in the tail pipe during starting, it normally will be indicated by illumination of a fire warning indicator. Should a fire warning indicator illuminate, the pilot should proceed as follows:

1. Both throttles—OFF.
2. ENGINE FIRE switch—TOWARD FIRE.
   Instruct ground crew to direct a stream of CO_2 agent into the first door on the outboard side of the forward engine door.

Note

Opening the fire door requires a sharp rap with the fire extinguisher nozzle.

3. Instruct ground crew to disconnect external power and cooling air.
4. Leave the aircraft immediately.

TAKE-OFF EMERGENCIES

NOSE WHEEL STEERING FAILURES

Should the aircraft fail in any way to respond normally to nose wheel steering, immediately release the STEER/TERRAIN button and use differential braking or rudder.

ENGINE FIRE ON TAKE-OFF

BELOW REFUSAL SPEED

Should a fire warning indicator illuminate or a fire be otherwise confirmed during take-off below refusal speed, ABORT. Refer to ABORTED TAKE-OFFS, in this section.

ABOVE REFUSAL SPEED

Should a fire warning indicator illuminate or a fire be otherwise confirmed during take-off above refusal speed (safe stop cannot be made), CONTINUE TAKE-OFF and proceed as follows:

1. Throttles—MAX AFTERBURNER.
2. External stores—JETTISON.
3. Execute maximum climb after lift-off.

4. Affected engine throttle—OFF.
5. ENGINE FIRE switch—TOWARD FIRE.
6. If fire persists and is confirmed, EJECT WITHOUT DELAY.
7. If fire goes out, land as soon as possible.

ENGINE FAILURE ON TAKE-OFF

BELOW REFUSAL SPEED

Should an engine fail during take-off below refusal speed, ABORT. Refer to ABORTED TAKE-OFFS, in this section.

ABOVE REFUSAL SPEED

Should an engine fail during take-off above refusal speed (safe stop cannot be made), CONTINUE TAKE-OFF and proceed as follows:

1. Throttles—MAX AFTERBURNER.
2. External stores—JETTISON.
3. Execute maximum climb after lift-off.
4. Affected engine throttle—OFF.

Note

If a safe take-off or abort cannot be made, ejection is feasible at speeds above 100 KIAS.

ABORTED TAKE-OFFS

Aborted take-offs must be planned and executed prior to reaching refusal speed if they are to be accomplished successfully. The most important considerations are (1) a quick, positive decision, and (2) immediate action. An immediate decision must be made to either retain external stores or to jettison to reduce gross weight during deceleration and stop. In the event of an abort, total braking capacity is realistically only about 80 percent of normal total capacity, since approximately 20 percent is used in taxiing.

Note

During aborted take-offs at high gross weights, steady wheel braking should not be commenced until airspeed is reduced to 100 knots or 4000 feet of runway remains, whichever occurs first.

Should aerodynamic braking prove only marginally effective and runway remaining become critical, light braking may be used to the recommended maximum speed for braking initiation (MSBI). If arresting gear is available, extend arresting hook.

CAUTION

Relax wheel brake pressure before engaging arresting gear.

Where no field arrestment gear is available, nearly all aborted take-offs starting above refusal speed result in accidents of varying degrees of seriousness. The refusal speed charts in Section XI of the Supplemental NATOPS Flight Manual (NAVWEPS 01-60ABA-1A) should be consulted and a refusal speed computed prior to every take-off. For additional information, refer to STOPPING THE AIRCRAFT, in Section III, Part 3. For a discussion of landing on wet or icy runways, refer to Section VI.

WARNING

Aborted take-offs at speeds above 130 knots will require use of field arrestment gear or barrier. Applying brakes at 130 knots could result in arrival at 40 or 50 knots with completely faded brakes. If no loss of thrust is involved, no arrestment gear is available, and speed is more than 130 knots, CONTINUE TAKE-OFF.

Note

During heavy braking, brake disc temperatures may exceed 1000°F. Most of this heat is transmitted into the atmosphere, but some is transmitted into the wheel and tire. Wheel overheat conditions may cause tire failure due to melting of fusible wheel plugs, which are designed to prevent wheel explosions.

AFTER TAKE-OFF

FAILURE OF ONE ENGINE

Should one engine fail immediately after take-off (flaps retracted or retracting), the tendency of the aircraft to roll and yaw into the failed engine is accentuated by reduced rudder effectiveness due to the directional ratio changer. Proceed as follows:

1. Throttles—MAX AFTERBURNER.
2. Flap control switch—40°.
3. External stores—JETTISON, if required.
4. Landing gear—UP.
5. On reaching 200 KIAS, retract flaps in increments. DO NOT SACRIFICE ALTITUDE.
6. Throttle of inoperative engine—OFF.
7. If nature of failure permits, attempt air start.
8. If performance is marginal, dump fuel as required to reduce weight.

WARNING

- At runway temperatures above 90°F, rate of climb after lift-off is marginal at and above 55,000 pounds gross weight.
- With flaps retracted, sufficient control for safe flight may not be available below 200 KIAS.

AFTERBURNER BLOWOUT

Afterburner blowout may or may not cause an emergency situation, depending upon phase of flight at time of blowout. In flight, afterburner blowout is recognized by a distinct loss of thrust or rate of acceleration, unexpected change in nozzle position, slight yawing, and a trail of fuel vapor. Should afterburner blowout occur on take-off, a safe take-off is possible with one engine at MAX AFTERBURNER and one at Military Thrust. If refusal speed is passed and take-off cannot be safely accomplished, the decision to jettison stores or to use field arrestment gear must be weighed against ejection. Refer to ABORTED TAKE-OFFS, in this section.

Note

At speeds above 100 knots, ground ejection is feasible.

EXHAUST NOZZLE FAILURES

NOZZLE FLUCTUATION

An oversensitive nozzle control system can cause nozzle fluctuations at any throttle setting. To stabilize exhaust nozzle position, retard the throttle below MIL to obtain mechanically scheduled nozzle area control. Should each throttle movement cause fluctuations, plan to land as soon as practicable.

ONE NOZZLE FULL OPEN

If one nozzle fails open, loss of thrust in that engine can be corrected by advancing power on the fully operational engine.

1. Select Military Thrust on engine with open nozzle.
2. Reduce gross weight to practical minimum.
3. Use 40-degree flaps for landing.

Note

Night carrier approaches are not recommended with a nozzle failed open.

BOTH NOZZLES FULL OPEN

If both nozzle systems fail in the fully open position, engine thrust may be extremely marginal at throttle settings up to MAX AFTERBURNER. Afterburner light-off is very unreliable with the nozzle in the full open position, the most probable light-off being at the MAX AFTERBURNER throttle setting. In addition, an afterburner operating at MIN AFTERBURNER will probably blow out when the nozzle opens. Should both nozzles fail open, select MIL.

WARNING

Should both nozzles fail open below 150 knots during a MIN AFTERBURNER take-off, insufficient power remains below MAX AFTERBURNER for safe flight.

Under Standard Day conditions, level flight, clean configuration cruise at reduced altitude can be maintained at Military Thrust with both nozzles failed open. With 30-degree flaps, the clean aircraft can maintain approximately 5000 feet (gear DOWN) or 8000 feet (gear UP).

1. Advance throttles as required to maintain safe flight.
2. Reduce gross weight to minimum.
3. Use 30-degree flaps for landing.
4. If low power response makes the airplane unmanageable, EJECT.

Note

- Carrier approach attempts are not recommended with both nozzles failed open.
- If available power and altitude conditions permit, the use of a precautionary landing pattern and field arresting gear is recommended.

For performance capabilities with exhaust nozzle full open, refer to Section XI of the Supplemental NATOPS Flight Manual (NAVWEPS 01-60ABA-1A).

WARNING

Careful monitor of speed control and drag is required to avoid operation on the back side of the power curve. Jettison external stores and/or dump fuel if safe altitude or airspeed cannot be maintained.

NOZZLE FULL CLOSED

Serious engine overtemperature can result from a failure of the EGT regulating system, causing the nozzle area to be reduced to the minimum mechanically scheduled condition. If the EGT limitations are exceeded, retard the throttle to below MIL and regulate EGT manually with the throttle. Power settings of MIL or above must be avoided to prevent further engine overtemperatures.

LANDING GEAR EMERGENCY RETRACTION

Should the gear fail to retract after take-off, lift the red guard from the EMERG GEAR UP switch and raise the switch to UP. This action bypasses the landing gear handle and should result in normal gear retraction.

Note

If the emergency gear up switch is used, gear extension for landing requires placing the switch to NORM and using emergency extension procedure.

EMERGENCY ESCAPE
CONTROLLED EJECTION

In the event controlled ejection is required and feasible, reduce airspeed to 250 KIAS. The pilot will accomplish as much of the following procedure as time permits:

1. Order the S/O to PREPARE FOR EJECTION.
2. Both crew members will check the following:
   (a) Helmet—TIGHT.
   (b) Parachute lap and shoulder straps—TIGHT.
   (c) Oxygen mask—TIGHT.
   (d) Helmet visor—DOWN.
   (e) Assume ejection position.
3. Cockpit pressurization—RAM EMERG.
4. If the situation and time permit, obtain an altitude between 8000 and 10,000 feet.
5. IFF—EMERGENCY (MODE 3, Code 77).
6. Sending the following radio report:
   (a) MAYDAY, MAYDAY, MAYDAY.
   (b) Identification.
   (c) Position, heading, and altitude.
   (d) Situation.
   (e) Intentions.
7. Order S/O to EJECT.
8. Initiate ejection, using the face curtain or alternate knobs, keeping elbows in. See figure 5-1.

Note

Low-altitude condition or altitude control may dictate keeping one hand on the stick and using an alternate ejection knob.

9. After seat separation (below 10,000 feet):
   (a) Inflate MK 3C life preserver (over water).
   (b) Survival kit—RELEASE.
   (c) Mask/faceplate—OFF/OPEN (over land).

MANUAL SEPARATION FROM SEAT

1. Leg retainer release slides—PUSH to release.
2. Knee bar—PUSH FORWARD AND DOWN.
3. Harness release handle—PULL UP.
4. Roll clear of seat.

Note

The personal parachute will deploy approximately 0.75 second after separation, if below 10,000 feet.

NAVWEPS 01-60ABA-1

Section V

EMERGENCY EJECTION

In an emergency situation requiring immediate ejection, the pilot will:

1. WARN S/O AND EJECT.

Note

Whenever possible, the S/O should initiate his own ejection. This will ensure proper positioning. Use the face curtain, if possible, to ensure the maximum protection from wind blast. Use of the face curtain will also tend to prevent arm flailing in the absence of arm retention. See figure 5-1 for ejection seat operation.

2. During parachute descent, pull the "D" ring housing free of the riser strap to aid in separation from the parachute after landing.
3. Keep in mind that it is ALWAYS preferable to eject rather than to attempt crash landing or ditching.

Note

In any ejection using the face curtain, be sure to "slam" the curtain out and forward rather than just pull. If ejection does not take place, either "bang" the curtain against the stops or use the alternate knobs or handgrips.

EJECTION SEAT FAILURE

EMERGENCY BAIL-OUT

In the event the seat positioning devices operate but seat fails to eject or fails completely, use the following procedure as required to escape:

1. Leg retainer release slides—PUSH FORWARD.
2. Knee bar—PUSH FORWARD AND DOWN.
3. Emergency oxygen ring—PULL.
4. COCKPIT PRESS switch—RAM EMERG (high altitude).
5. Canopy jettison handle—PULL (if not jettisoned).
6. Trim aircraft nose-down, if possible.
7. Invert aircraft and maintain positive "g."
8. Harness release handle—PULL.
9. Push free of cockpit as required.
10. Free fall if required, then manually PULL "D" RING.

WARNING

When emergency bail-out is accomplished without use of the ejection seat, automatic personal parachute deployment is NOT AVAILABLE. PULL THE "D" RING AT YOUR LEFT SHOULDER.

IN-FLIGHT EMERGENCIES

COMPRESSOR STALLS

Compressor stall is a breakdown of airflow in the engine compressor due to separation of airflow from the compressor blades, similar to the separation from a wing during an aircraft stall. Such stalls usually result from an inlet control or engine fuel control unit malfunction or compressor blade damage. Compressor stalls are recognized by (1) loss of rpm or "hanging" acceleration, (2) rise in EGT and abnormal change in nozzle area, or (3) a pulsating, explosive sound, possibly accompanied by light to severe vibration. During normal operation, the main fuel control unit automatically controls compressor stator vane angle by servo fuel pressure. Vane angle is modulated to regulate airflow rate and pattern through the early stages of compression to reduce the possibility of stall. The main fuel control unit also schedules engine rpm as a function of CIT and inlet guide vane angle to maintain adequate compressor stall margin. If compressor stalls are encountered, the following procedure is recommended:

1. Throttle—OFF, then immediately above IDLE.
2. Emergency ignition button—Depress, Hold.
3. Below 1.3 Mach, reducing throttle setting may improve engine performance.

Note

To preclude stall at less than 1.3 Mach with the ramps extended, hold RAMP CONT switch in RESET prior to rapid throttle movements.

ENGINE FLAME-OUT OR FAILURE

Engine flame-out or failure is generally caused by engine material failure or failure of the engine fuel control system. Should loss of thrust be caused by engine internal failure, flame-out may be preceded by sharp rise in EGT and accompanied by explosions, compressor stalls, or severe vibration. Should a partial loss of power be encountered, yaw trim is not greatly affected due to the proximity of the engine thrust lines to the aircraft centerline. Failure of one engine immediately after take-off, however, results in a marked rolling tendency into the failed engine. Refer to FAILURE OF ONE ENGINE AT ALTITUDE, in this section. Increased power in the remaining engine is required to maintain cruising airspeeds and in the landing pattern. With one engine inoperative, the aircraft has sufficient power and control to handle satisfactorily at medium and low altitudes.

Note

Should one or both engines fail during flight with no evidence of fire, attempt to regain operation by depressing the EMER IGN buttons before an excessive amount of rpm is lost.

Section V NAVWEPS 01-60ABA-1

EJECTION SEAT OPERATION

① Prepare to Eject...

A. REDUCE SPEED TO 250 KNOTS OR ZOOM-CLIMB IF NECESSARY: INITIATE EJECTION BEFORE SINK-RATE CANCELS LOW ALTITUDE EJECTION CAPABILITY.

B. TRANSMIT MAYDAY AND TURN AIRCRAFT AWAY FROM POPULATED AREAS AS TIME PERMITS.

C. WARN CREW MEMBER TO PREPARE TO EJECT

D. ORDER CREW MEMBER TO EJECT

> 1. SEAT INITIATORS FIRE.
>   - CANOPY IS JETTISONED.
>   - SEAT BUCKET IS BOTTOMED.
>   - SHOULDER HARNESS IS RETRACTED.
>   - RETENTION DEVICES ACTUATED.
> 2. CATAPULT-ROCKET FIRES.
>   - EMERGENCY OXYGEN ACTUATED AS SEAT RISES.
>   - IFF SWITCHED TO EMERGENCY (PROVIDED PILOT'S IFF SWITCH IS IN AUTO POSITION).
>   - LIFT-PLATE IS EXTENDED.
> 3. DROGUE PARACHUTE DEPLOYED.

NOTE: IF PILOT INITIATES EJECTION, EJECTION OF PILOT'S SEAT IS AUTOMATICALLY DELAYED UNTIL 0.75 SECOND AFTER AFT SEAT EJECTS.

③ When Clear of Cockpit...

- IF ABOVE 13,000 FEET, RELEASE LEG RETRACTORS — PLACE THUMB AND FOREFINGER AROUND SLIDE RELEASE AND PUSH FORWARD.

CONTROLLED EJECTION

② Initiate Ejection

PULL FACE CURTAIN

- "SLAM" CURTAIN OUTWARD AND DOWN UNTIL REACHING FULL TRAVEL. BANG AGAINST STOPS IF REQUIRED

OR ...

TURN AND PULL EITHER KNOB

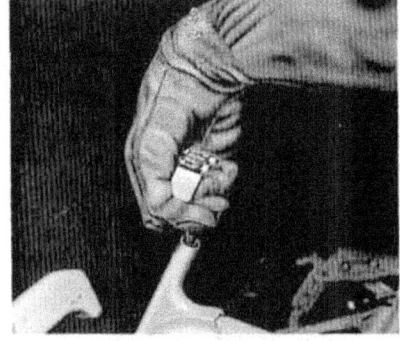

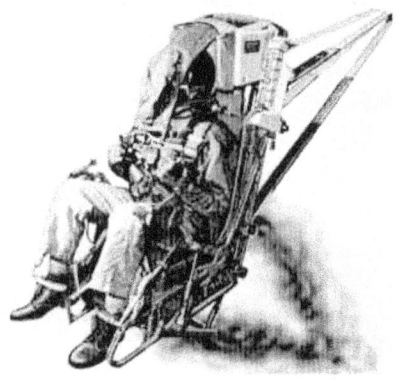

A-5C-1-73-5 A

Figure 5-1 (Sheet 1)

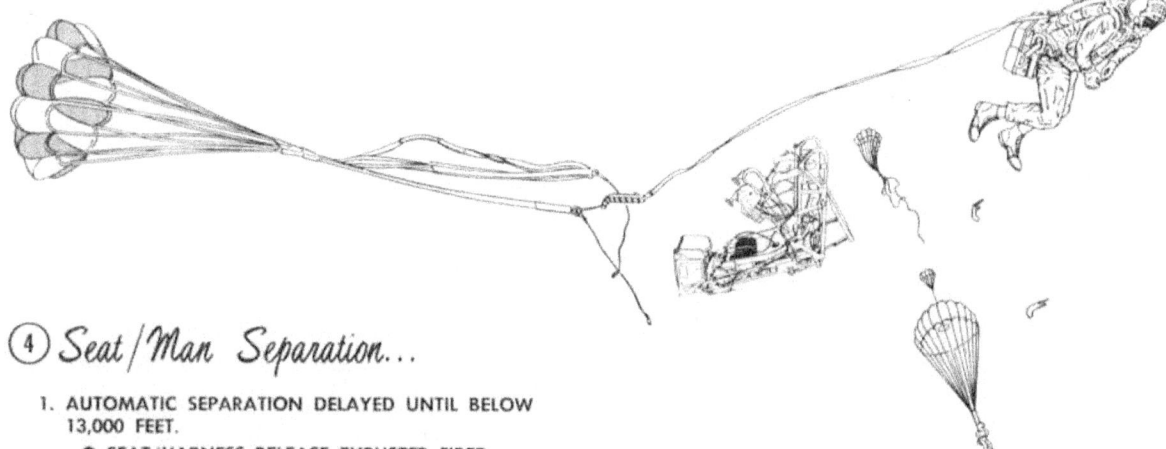

④ Seat/Man Separation...

1. AUTOMATIC SEPARATION DELAYED UNTIL BELOW 13,000 FEET.
    - SEAT/HARNESS RELEASE THRUSTER FIRED
    - FACE CURTAIN CABLES CUT
    - LEG RETRACTORS JETTISONED
    - KNEE-BAR RELEASED
2. SEAT SEPARATION BLADDERS INFLATE, SEPARATING CREW MEMBER FROM SEAT AND KNOCKING KNEE BAR CLEAR.

⑤ Descent and Survival...

1. BEFORE GROUND OR WATER CONTACT, ENSURE THAT RIPCORD GRIP IS REMOVED FROM RETAINER CLIP POCKET AND SEPARATE FROM HARNESS/RISER STRAP. FAILURE TO DO THIS WILL RESULT IN FIXED ATTACHMENT BETWEEN PARACHUTE CONTAINER AND RISER EVEN WITH ROCKET-JET FITTINGS RELEASED
2. INFLATE MK-3C LIFE PRESERVER (OVER WATER)
3. PULL SURVIVAL KIT RELEASE HANDLE TO DEPLOY LIFE RAFT.

NOTE

- THE SURVIVAL KIT SHOULD BE DEPLOYED AT SUFFICIENT ALTITUDE TO ALLOW FULL EXTENSION OF THE KIT LANYARD, WHICH ACTIVATES THE CO_2 CYLINDER, INFLATING THE LIFE RAFT.

- DO NOT RELEASE EITHER LOWER ROCKET-JET FITTING PRIOR TO SURVIVAL KIT DEPLOYMENT AND WATER ENTRY.

4. OXYGEN MASK SHOULD BE REMOVED OR FULL PRESSURE SUIT FACEPLATE RAISED TO PREVENT SUFFOCATION ON EMERGENCY OXYGEN DEPLETION.
5. ON CONTACT, RELEASE SHOULDER-HARNESS ROCKET-JET FITTINGS TO SEPARATE FROM PARACHUTE.

IF AUTOMATIC SEPARATION FAILS:

1. LEG RETRACTORS — RELEASE SLIDES.
2. KNEE BAR — PUSH FORWARD AND DOWN.
3. HARNESS RELEASE HANDLE — PULL UP.
4. ROLL CLEAR OF SEAT; PARACHUTE WILL DEPLOY 0.75 SECOND AFTER SEPARATION IF BELOW 10,000 FEET.

Figure 5-1 (Sheet 2)

ERRATIC OPERATION

If erratic operation is encountered in one engine, it is recommended that the defective engine be secured and a single-engine landing be accomplished as soon as practicable. Refer to SINGLE-ENGINE LANDINGS, in this section.

BOTH ENGINES FAILED AT ALTITUDE

If both engines fail, it is necessary to extend the emergency RAT to supply electrical power to the ignition and fuel systems, and to supply hydraulic pressure for flight control operation. Electrical power furnished by the RAT is sufficient for air starts and emergency communications. If the engines fail to respond to immediate restart, use the procedures outlined under AIR STARTS, in this section.

1. Emergency RAT—EXTEND.
2. If the nature of the failures permits, attempt immediate restart with the EMER IGN buttons.
3. If the engines do not respond, move both throttles to OFF.
4. Retrim as required and descend below 45,000 feet.
5. Attempt single air starts, using both emergency and normal ignition as required.
6. IFF/SIF—EMERGENCY (MODE 3, Code 77).
7. External stores—Jettison, if required.
8. If engines will not start, EJECT.

Power-off landings will not be attempted.

FAILURE OF ONE ENGINE AT ALTITUDE

Failure of one engine in cruising flight is accompanied by an easily controlled yaw and roll into the failed engine. Should failure occur at high Mach (above 1.4), these tendencies may be sharply increased. Cautious use of controls is required, especially if the yaw augmentation system is inoperative. Satisfactory single-engine cruise, with no external stores, may be obtained at altitudes below 25,000 feet. The drag of one inoperative engine may be simulated with the left engine at IDLE and the right engine at the required power setting.

Note

Simulated single-engine touch-and-go landings are not recommended.

Should one engine fail in flight, proceed as follows:

1. If the nature of the failure permits, attempt immediate restart using the EMER IGN buttons.
2. Throttle of inoperative engine—OFF.
3. Retrim as required.
4. Attempt air start.
5. If engine does not start, land as soon as practicable.

SINGLE-ENGINE OPERATION

In the event of in-flight failure of an engine, satisfactory single-engine handling and cruise is obtained at all altitudes below about 25,000 feet, depending on gross weight and configuration.

Single-engine landings are entirely manageable, but are not normally permitted aboard ship except in an emergency. Single-engine landing gross weight should be as low as possible. At high-gross weights (i.e., with drop tanks and a buddy tanker package installed), it is necessary to dump fuel as required or jettison external tanks to attain a low gross weight for landing (38,500 pounds or less). Refer to SINGLE-ENGINE LANDINGS, in this section.

AIR STARTS

Air starts may be attempted within a wide range of altitudes and airspeeds. See figure 5-2. Best conditions are found below 45,000 feet at less than 1.10—indicated Mach. Below 25,000 feet, optimum speed for air starts is 300 KIAS. Although in an emergency it is not expected that all engine limits will be observed, the EGT and windmill rpm limits stated in Section I, Part 4, of the Supplemental NATOPS Flight Manual (NAVWEPS 01-60ABA-1A) should be kept in mind.

CAUTION

Unless there is definite immediate evidence of engine failure (such as fire warning, EGT rise above limit, or rapid loss of oil pressure to zero well ahead of rpm decay), initiation of engine air start should not be delayed, following in-flight shutdown or flame-out, to prevent the possibility of engine seizure. If one or both engines flame out, depress the EMER IGN button(s) before too much engine rpm is lost.

If the engine(s) fails to start, use the following procedure:

1. Throttle(s)—OFF.
2. Hold 300 to 400 KIAS (12% to 30% rpm).
3. If both engines are out, pull the RAT handle and check that the ELEC EPU ON indicator illuminates.

ENGINE OPERATING ENVELOPE

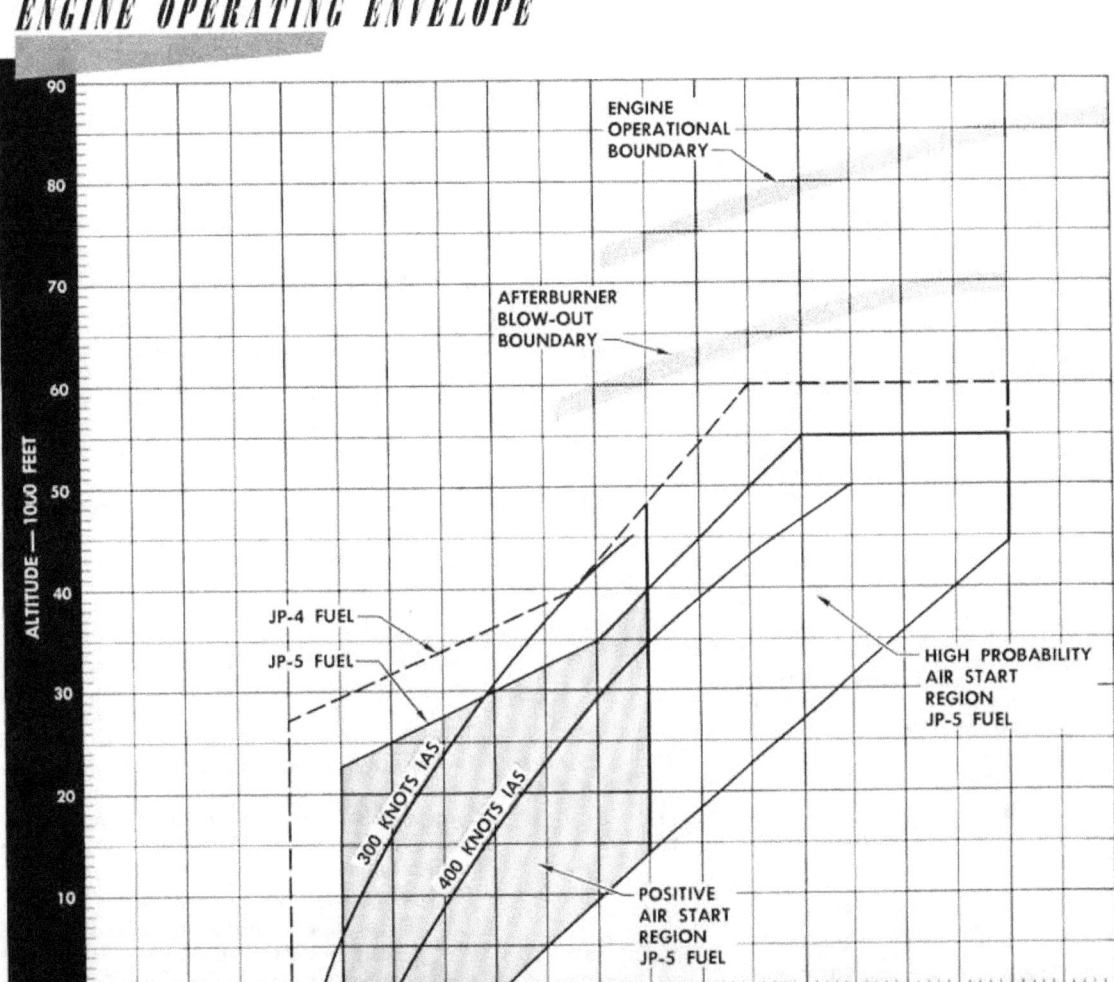

Figure 5-2

4. Depress and hold the EMER IGN button and advance the throttle above IDLE.

    If both engines are out, best procedure is to attempt start on one engine at a time.

5. If light-off does not occur within 30 seconds at IDLE while holding the EMER IGN button, continue holding the button and advance the throttle to MIL.

Note

Light-off is indicated primarily by increasing rpm and fuel flow. EGT may rise slowly until rpm increases to flight idle for that altitude.

6. After light-off, hold RAMP CONT switch in RESET and release.

    (a) At speeds above 1.3 indicated Mach, hold the RAMP CONT switch in RESET after 95% rpm is reached.

(b) At speeds below 1.3 indicated Mach, hold the RAMP CONT switch in RESET before attaining 95% rpm.

> **WARNING**
>
> When using the RAT for electrical power, do not move the flight controls more than required to maintain wings level flight while attempting air starts. The emergency hydraulic unit may take priority over the emergency electrical generator, preventing adequate electrical power for engine ignition.

NO-THRUST GLIDE

Maximum glide distance is obtained by jettisoning all external stores and maintaining 250 KIAS. The RAT must be extended to ensure No. 1 hydraulic system power for flight control operation.

NO-THRUST GLIDE PERFORMANCE
NO WIND — STORES JETTISONED — 250 KIAS
GEAR AND FLAPS UP/DROOPS — CRUISE (5 DEGREES)

ALTITUDE (X 1000 FEET)	DISTANCE (NMI)	TIME (MINUTES)
45	70	11.0
40	60	10.0
35	50	9.0
30	45	8.0
25	35	7.0
20	30	6.0
15	20	4.0
10	15	3.0
5	8	1.5

Note

Optimum glide distance and time are reduced approximately 5 percent with droops at SUPERSONIC.

ENGINE OIL OVERHEAT

Overheating of an engine oil system (OIL HOT caution indicator on) may be accompanied by associated constant-speed drive and generator failure. Refer to ELECTRICAL FAILURES, in this section. Should an OIL HOT caution indicator come on, the following procedure is recommended:

1. Set throttle of affected engine at cruise power or higher.
2. If caution indicator remains on, place associated generator switch to OFF and descend to allow increased fuel flow through main fuel/oil cooler.
3. If caution indicator remains on, monitor oil pressure and land as soon as practicable.

OIL SYSTEM FAILURE

Early indications of oil system failure are exhaust nozzle failure, low or fluctuating oil pressure, and generator failure due to CSD oil starvation. Oil pressure fluctuations of more than 5 psi from the established pressure for a given engine speed should be investigated. For oil pressure limitations, refer to Section I, Part 4, of the Supplemental NATOPS Flight Manual (NAVWEPS 01-60ABA-1A). Excessive oil pressure fluctuations and generator failure are reason enough to make preparations for landing, but premature engine shutdown should be avoided. An engine need not be secured because of low oil pressure. It is recommended that the engine power setting not be reduced to less than cruise power; however, if continued engine operation appears dangerous because of oil pressure drop to zero or vibration, and if flight safety will not be compromised by the loss of thrust, engine shutdown can be accomplished in the normal manner. If the engine is secured, attempt to maintain windmill rpm above 7%, since oil vapor accumulation in the oil sump may constitute a fire hazard if engine restart is attempted. In the event of oil system failure indications, proceed as follows:

1. Monitor oil pressure indications.
   If generator failure occurs (reset attempts fail), prepare to land as soon as practicable.
2. Periodically check the nozzle position indicator.
   If the nozzle should freeze in a closed position, EGT must be monitored during throttle movements to preclude overtemperature damage to the engine. Do not operate the engine in afterburner range.
3. Continue to utilize thrust from the affected engine until safe landing is assured, unless further operation appears hazardous.

> **CAUTION**
>
> Unless necessary for safe flight, air start of an engine after shutdown because of oil starvation is not recommended.

ENGINE FIRE DURING FLIGHT

Should a fire warning indicator illuminate and engine overheat is suspected, reduce power on the affected engine to IDLE and change speed to 300 KIAS, using the other engine as required.

Note
Engine overheat is most probable in the speed range between 165 and 180 KIAS.

If the indicator does not go out, and evidence of fire exists, move the throttle to OFF and operate the ENGINE FIRE switch. If the indicator remains on, a serious emergency exists. If fire remains confirmed, immediate ejection is recommended.

SMOKE AND FUMES

If smoke or fumes are detected in the cockpit, proceed as follows:

1. Throttles—Reduce power.
2. COCKPIT PRESS switch—RAM EMERG.

Note
Control of cockpit temperature is inoperative and, at altitudes above 8000 feet, cockpit pressure will be dumped.

3. To control temperature after clearing smoke or fumes, move the COCKPIT PRESS switch to OFF, if desired.
4. Prepare for landing as soon as practicable, continuing to check for contaminants.

ABNORMAL COCKPIT TEMPERATURE

Should cockpit supply air temperature become too hot or too cold, proceed as follows:

1. Check AUTO/MAN switch—AUTO.
2. Check temperature response to changing setting of COCKPIT TEMP knob.
3. If too hot, check temperature of defrost air; if excessive, move WINDSHIELD & CANOPY DEFROST knob to OFF.
4. If automatic control is inoperative, switch to MAN and check response to changing setting of COCKPIT TEMP knob.
   Temperature response to this procedure indicates inoperative temperature controlled or sensor.
5. If temperature is still too hot, descend and switch cockpit pressurization OFF.
   Select RAM EMERG for ventilation if required.
6. Turn WINDSHIELD ANTI-ICE switch ON to carry hot air away from cockpit if necessary.
7. Pulling the windshield defrost and anti-ice circuit breaker may isolate the source of continuing hot air.

Note
Abnormal temperature of defrost and anti-ice air supply indicates inoperative or "frozen" primary cockpit heat exchanger modulating bypass valve.

8. Flap extension (greater than 25 degrees) will also assist in diverting hot air away from the cockpit.
9. If temperature is intolerable, select RAM EMERG, jettison canopy, and land as soon as possible.

OXYGEN SYSTEM FAILURE

The first indication of oxygen supply pressure exhaustion will be illumination of the OXYGEN warning indicator. If the warning light circuit is defective and the liquid oxygen quantity indicator is not periodically checked, system supply pressure exhaustion will be indicated by a sudden onset of difficult inhalation. If this occurs, immediately pull the emergency oxygen supply ring and descend immediately to an altitude where oxygen is not required.

WARNING

- Should the OXYGEN warning indicator illuminate in flight and more than 0.8 liter of oxygen is aboard, a system malfunction has occurred. Check Scott upper block for positive connection. Descend to a safe cockpit altitude and be prepared to pull emergency oxygen supply ring upon noting a restriction to inhalation.
- Emergency oxygen flow is not available if the Scott block assembly is disconnected.
- If difficult emergency oxygen inhalation occurs, a restriction may exist between the emergency supply and the mask or suit helmet. Remove mask or raise faceplate at a safe breathing altitude.

SUIT EMERGENCY PRESSURIZATION

The oxygen system supplies suit pressurization in the event of complete failure of the aircraft air conditioning and pressurization system above 35,000 feet. The sequence of events which results in the aircraft oxygen system being used for suit pressurization is completely automatic and requires no attention from the crew members. With the pressure suit, oxygen system pressure will adequately protect the crew members for descent

Section V NAVWEPS 01-60ABA-1

and landing from any altitude. Refer to SUIT EMERGENCY OXYGEN DURATION (FULL BOTTLE), in this section.

Note

Complete suit pressurization by the emergency oxygen system blocks the exhaust port, and ventilation exists only in the form of minute suit leakage. Some discomfort may result due to insufficient ventilation.

SUIT EMERGENCY OXYGEN DURATION (FULL BOTTLE)

ALTITUDE (X 1000 FEET)	DURATION TO DEPLETION (MINUTES)	
	CABIN PRESSURE FAILED	CABIN PRESSURE NORMAL
70	20.5	25.0
65	20.5	24.0
60	20.5	23.0
55	20.5	21.0
50	20.5	20.0
45	21.0	19.0
40	23.0	17.0
35	45.0	16.0
30	33.0	14.0
25	25.0	12.0
20	20.0	11.5
15	16.0	11.5
10	13.0	11.5
5	10.5	10.5
Sea level	9.0	9.0

FUEL SYSTEM FAILURES

BOOST PUMP FAILURE

With JP-5 fuel and fuel system pressurization operating, the engines should operate normally with both sump tank boost pumps inoperative. With JP-4 fuel, under these conditions, some loss of power will be noted at altitudes above 40,000 feet. Should fuel system pressurization failure occur with both boost pumps out, Military Thrust operation may not be obtainable above approximately 24,000 feet (JP-5 fuel), or 15,000 feet (JP-4 fuel).

Note

There is no direct indication of boost or transfer pump failure except subnormal engine operation.

Should engine surging or partial power loss occur, proceed as follows:

1. Immediately reduce power and/or descend until satisfactory engine power is obtained.
2. Afterburner operation is not recommended.

3. Land as soon as practicable, avoiding excessive deceleration and steep descent angles.

CAUTION

If both sump tank boost pumps are inoperative, the forces produced by large decelerations and high angles of descent may cause the sump tank suction feed valve to become uncovered, resulting in flame-out.

FUEL FILTER BYPASS

Illumination of a low-pressure fuel filter caution indicator indicates impending fuel filter bypass. In this event, proceed as follows:

1. If fuel flow indications are normal (no fluctuations greater than ±300 pounds per hour), continue the mission, checking fuel flow periodically.
2. If the fuel flow indication fluctuates excessively, land as soon as practicable, or power loss may occur.

DROP TANK TRANSFER FAILURE

Failure of drop tanks to transfer is readily apparent, since bomb bay can transfer will start prematurely and the sump will fall to about 4200 pounds, instead of being maintained at the normal 4700-pound level. Procedure to attempt to regain drop tank transfer is limited to cycling the transfer buttons off and on, allowing at least 2 minutes in each position.

1. Cycle the DROP TANK TRANSFER buttons off (up) and on (down).
   Check for a rising fuel level in the sump tank.

2. Transfer may be prevented by a sticking tank empty float switch. To remove electrical power from the normally open float switch, notify the systems operator of intentions to secure generators and extend RAT. When ELEC EPU ON indicator is illuminated, move generator switches to OFF until fuel transfer is indicated.

3. If drop tank fuel cannot be transferred, fly final at 13 units angle of attack or jettison tanks as desired.

4. For landing with one full tank, use full opposite lateral trim.

Note

Carrier landings with fuel in drop tanks are prohibited; however, one empty drop tank may be brought aboard. If the CANS switch is at AUTO or ON, sump tank level should be maintained at 4250 pounds. If drop tank transfer is obtained, sump fuel will rise to the 4700-pound (full) level.

BOMB BAY CAN TRANSFER FAILURE

Failure of bomb bay can fuel to transfer poses a potentially more serious problem than drop tank failure, since two full cans provide about a 4000-pound contribution to aft center-of-gravity problems. Sump level drops to about 2000 pounds (after drop tank transfer), with possible illumination of the FUEL LOW caution indicator. Recommended procedure is to maintain economical altitude and power settings while allowing normal wing fuel transfer and attempt to regain can transfer. Move the CANS transfer switch to OFF, wait 2 minutes, then return to ON. If unsuccessful, rock and porpoise the aircraft to check for a sticking level control valve or a can empty float switch. Pull the FUEL SEQ circuit breaker to cut power to the can pressure valve (held closed electrically). If sump fuel level rises, transfer can be controlled by alternately pulling and resetting the breaker until can fuel is exhausted. If operational necessity requires more fuel in the sump, move the SUMP switch to HIGH to transfer wing fuel. If all attempts to transfer bomb bay can fuel fail, pull the FUEL DUMP handle to the first detent and check the fuel quantity indicator for dump reaction.

Note

Return the SUMP switch to LOW before pulling the dump handle, or wing and sump tank fuel will be dumped in lieu of can fuel.

1. CANS switch—OFF, then ON.
   Allow 2 minutes in ON position.
2. Porpoise and rock aircraft in attempt to unseat a possible sticking can level control valve or can empty float switch.
3. FUEL SEQ circuit breaker—Pull.
   Reset if fuel does not transfer or reset after transfer is complete.
4. SUMP switch—LOW.
5. Can fuel—Dump (first detent).
   If pressurization of cans is not accomplished, the aft can should gravity-dump (2000 pounds) in 10 to 15 minutes.
6. SUMP switch—HIGH (wing transfer).
7. Execute first landing approach with maximum sump fuel for optimum cg location.

CAUTION

- If a bomb bay can or the buddy tank will not dump, use 40-degree flaps for landing.
- If divert is possible, do not attempt a carrier landing with more than 2000 pounds bomb bay fuel.
- When dumping can fuel, be certain the SUMP switch is at LOW, or wing fuel and some sump tank fuel may be inadvertently dumped along with can fuel.

WARNING

If wing tank fuel has been transferred and the bomb bay fuel cans and/or buddy tank remain full, an aft center-of-gravity condition exists. Under these conditions, pitch control is sensitive and marginal. Should dumping of bomb bay or buddy tank fuel fail, and if the bomb bay cans cannot be jettisoned, use 40-degree flaps during the landing approach. Divert to shore rather than attempt a carrier landing unless optimum conditions exist.

WING FUEL TRANSFER FAILURE

After transfer of drop tank and bomb bay fuel, failure of normal wing tank transfer is indicated by a drop in sump tank fuel level to below 2300 pounds and possible illumination of the FUEL LOW caution indicator. Should wing fuel fail to transfer, the following procedure is recommended:

1. FUEL SEQ circuit breaker—check in.
2. SUMP switch—HIGH.
3. If no fuel transfer results, pull and turn FUEL DUMP handle to dump wing fuel.

Note

If wing fuel dumps at normal rate, this indicates normal operation (high duty) of the wing transfer pumps.

4. FUEL DUMP handle—OFF (in).
5. Advance one throttle to MIN AFTERBURNER and monitor sump tank fuel level.

Note

- When sump level reaches 4200 pounds (high sump), retard throttle to normal power setting as desired.
- If single-throttle procedure is successful, altitude and power setting are not restricted.

6. If high-duty wing pump operation is not available, return to LOW sump in order to take advantage of gravity flow transfer.

Note

- Maintain cruise or higher power setting (angle of attack 8 units or less).
- Sump fuel level will increase to 2300 pounds after a prolonged nose-down descent.
- Sump level will decrease to 800 pounds with 1200 pounds remaining in the wings.
- Land as soon as possible.

ELECTRICAL SYSTEM FAILURES

Failure of one generator should pose no serious problem as long as the d-c converters continue in operation. Several reset attempts may be made. However, if the generator will not reset after two attempts, it is recommended that the associated generator switch be moved to OFF and a landing be made as soon as practicable. Failure of both generators is unlikely. However, if dual failure does occur, immediate results, especially at night, may be startling. Since no battery is installed, dual generator failure results in complete failure of all electrically powered components, and at night, complete "blackout." All circuits essential to safe flight may be powered by extending the RAT (i.e., restoring communications, intercom, cockpit floodlighting, fuel sequencing, and sump aft boost pump control). Under these conditions, alternate roll and yaw trim must be used, and the standby trim switch is used to control pitch trim. Altitude should be reduced to less than 39,000 feet to ensure sufficient gravity flow of wing tank fuel. If the RAT is used alone to obtain electrical power, extended speed brakes must be dumped prior to landing, and gear and flaps must be extended by emergency means. The arresting hook will extend normally when selected. Should both d-c converters fail, the RAT may be extended to power essential d-c bus items. However, even with both generators operating, failure of both d-c converters results in loss of normal operation of the following systems: (1) landing gear extension, (2) speed brake operation, (3) pitch and yaw augmentation, (4) electric flight control system, (5) nose wheel steering, (6) normal flap extension, and (7) all isolated hydraulic subsystems.

FAILURE OF BOTH GENERATORS

Failure of both generators is a rather remote possibility. However, if a complete electrical power failure should occur, or if for any reason it becomes necessary to turn off the generator switches, follow this procedure:

1. Extend ram-air turbine and return to base.
    With the ram-air turbine extended, power is supplied to the a-c and d-c essential buses and operation of the sump tank aft boost pump will be regained.

Note
Proper output from the emergency electrical power unit is indicated by illumination of the ELEC EPU ON indicator.

2. To regain control of roll and yaw trim, move the TRIM SEL switch to ALTR.
    For trim, use the ALT ROLL/YAW TRIM switch.
3. Use the stand-by pitch trim switch for the remainder of the flight for pitch trim changes.
4. If necessary, reduce altitude and/or engine rpm to maintain engine operation, as fuel flow may be impaired because of loss of fuel boost pressure at altitudes above 39,000 feet.

5. Dump bomb bay fuel prior to landing.
    Wing fuel cannot be dumped at normal rate without generator operation since the wing transfer pumps are not powered by the essential bus.
6. For landing, the flaps can be extended by emergency air pressure from the pneumatic system and the hook will extend, when selected, by gravity and accumulator action.
    If extended, speed brakes must be dumped. The landing gear must also be extended by emergency means.

Note
If the ram-air turbine is providing both hydraulic and electrical power, electrical power may be temporarily cut off whenever hydraulic flight control power requirements take the full output of the ram-air-turbine.

FAILURE OF ONE GENERATOR

Generator failure is indicated by illumination of a generator-out caution indicator located on the pilot's instrument panel. When this occurs, all bus loads are assumed by the remaining generator, except for monitor bus powered components with either or both throttles in the afterburner range. Proceed as follows:

1. Hold generator switch momentarily in RESET, then release.
    The caution indicator may extinguish momentarily with the switch in RESET, even though the fault may still exist.
2. If the indicator remains extinguished, the temporary fault may have been due to overvoltage, undervoltage, open phase protection, or differential current protection.
3. If the indicator does not extinguish, the remaining generator will assume all electrical loads through the action of line contactors.
    If both generators fail, follow the procedures covered under FAILURE OF BOTH GENERATORS, in this section.

Note
If unable to reset a failed generator, leave the generator switch OFF.

D-C POWER FAILURE

The essential d-c bus provides the minimum requirements for d-c powered equipment. Illumination of the DC PWR caution indicator reflects failure of the primary d-c converter. The DC PWR caution indicator is powered by an a-c source so that, if both converters fail, the DC PWR indicator will be the only indicator illuminated and all d-c powered indicators will be inoperative. With both the primary and alternate d-c converters inoperative, electrical power can be supplied to the essential d-c bus by extending the ram-air turbine. *With both converters inoperative, the following systems remain inoperative with the ram-air turbine extended:* (1) normal landing gear operation, (2) speed brakes, (3) nose wheel steering, (4) pitch augmentation, (5) yaw augmentation, (6) electric flight control systems, (7) angle of attack and rudder shaker, (8) position lights, (9) cockpit pressurization, (10) all fuel system pumps except the sump tank aft boost pump, and (11) normal flap extension. If d-c power failure is caused by double generator loss, the ram-air turbine should be extended to provide power to the essential a-c and d-c buses for starting and ignition during air starts. After air start, when a-c generator output is restored, the ram-air turbine can be retracted by means of the EPU RETRACT button on the pilot's center pedestal (HYD SUB-SYS ISOLATION switch must be in TAKE-OFF/LANDING).

ELECTRICAL FIRE

1. If practicable, generator switches—OFF.
2. Secure all electrical equipment switches except engine MASTER switches.
3. Generator switches—RESET.
4. Land as soon as possible.

CIRCUIT FAILURES

Following is a resumé of losses encountered due to failure of circuits controlled through the cockpit circuit-breaker panel.

CIRCUIT BREAKER	LOST	REMARKS
EMERG JETTISON CONT	External jettison	Use normal manual release (MASTER ARM and trigger)
NAV ESS TRANS	In aft cockpit:	
	Console lights	
	White floodlights	Use red lights
	Chart lights	
	Utility lights	
	CNI command	Pilot has command
	Compass command	Pilot has command
	Warning lights	
	Caution lights	
	Store station select	Jettison as required
	Radar advisory lights	
Cφ CTR PED	Stand-by attitude indicator	Cross-check. Turn-and-slip indicator may run sluggishly
FUEL GAUGE DC	Quantity selector	Total and sump operative. Trim pitch to neutral to check cans. Watch for roll with roll trim neutral to check drop tanks
WINDSHIELD DEFROST & ANTI-ICE	Canopy defrost knob	
	Windshield anti-ice switch (associated safety factors)	If failed on, reduce power and land. Not available if failed off
EMERG FLAP	Emergency flap switch	If No. 2 hydraulic system has failed, reduce to minimum fuel and land no-flap
CABIN PRESS	Pressurization lost (dumped) ALTERNATE COOL reset inoperative	Land as soon as practicable
NAV ICS	Systems operator cannot receive or transmit, ICS or UHF COMM, in NORM, ALT ICS, or ALT RAD	Use UHF sidetone in ICS EMER mode
PILOTS ICS	Pilot cannot receive or transmit, ICS or UHF COMM, in NORM, ALT ICS, or ALT RAD	Use UHF sidetone in ICS EMER mode
ICS RELAY PWR	ICS completely dead in both cockpits in NORM, ALT ICS, ALT RAD	Use UHF sidetone in ICS EMER mode
NO. 1 FUEL SHUT-OFF NO. 2 FUEL SHUT-OFF	Applicable engine firewall valve will not close on operation of ENGINE FIRE switch	

Section V

NAVWEPS 01-60ABA-1

CIRCUIT BREAKER	LOST	REMARKS
PILOTS ESS TRANS	DC PWR caution indicator	
	ECM mode indicators	
	Indicating lights dimming	
	CNI emergency power indicator (light)	
	Armament indicator	Confirm verbally
	Hook warning light	Use TV (day)
	LABS advisory light	Use o/s mode
	HSI mode lights	
	Range/bearing selection	
	Emergency lights	
	Floodlights	
	CNI command lights	Check channel change for control
	CNI command transfer	
	ECM indicator	
	Console lights	
	AFCS indicators	
FIRE EXT SHUT-OFF	ENGINE FIRE switch OFF position will not open valves	Firewall shutoff
NO. 1 START & IGN	Applicable emergency ignition button inoperative (air start impossible)	
NO. 2 START & IGN		
FLAPS & DROOP CONT	Normal flap/droop control	Use emergency
	Engine door control relays	
	Yaw trim recentering	Trim manually after flap emergency extension
FUEL SEQ	Sump level control (HIGH/LOW)	On RAT power only with HIGH sump selected, wing dump and transfer valve remains open
	Bomb bay can pressure on (fail-safe)	
	Fuel transfer and boost pumps	Sump forward boost pump operative on RAT power. Use wing gravity feed
INFLIGHT REFUEL	Fuel system internal pressure vented	
	Fuel probe switch inoperative:	
	Probe extended	Normal transfer*
	Probe retracted	Normal transfer
IND TEST NO. 1	Fire warning system	
	Master warning indicator	
	Master caution indicator	
	Systems caution indicators	
	OXYGEN warning and test	
	WHEELS warning indicator	
IND TEST NO. 2	CNI emergency power indicator	
	Low-altitude warning light	
	Radar altimeter low-altitude override button	
	Landing gear advisory light	
	ECM indicators test	
	Armament indicator test	
	HYD EPU ON and ELEC EPU ON advisory lights test	
	Radar advisory lights test	
	Pilot's and systems operator's lights test	

*If *circuit* or *switch* fails with probe extended, bomb bay fuel may be transferred by pulling circuit breaker

HYDRAULIC FAILURES

Should the HYD PRESS caution indicator and master caution indicator illuminate with no accompanying loss of pressure in either system, a fluid leak in the No. 2 system is indicated. The most common failure would be located in one of the isolated secondary systems, such as the landing gear, nose wheel steering, or arresting hook retract cylinder. If no pressure loss or fluctuations occur following illumination of the HYD PRESS caution indicator, it may be assumed that automatic isolation of the secondary systems has stopped the loss of hydraulic fluid, and emergency methods must be used to extend landing gear and flaps.

PUMP FAILURES

Failure of one pump in the No. 1 system has no adverse effect on flight control or secondary systems operation. Failure of one pump in the No. 2 system can however, cause automatic pressure monitor shutoff of pitch and yaw augmentation, electric flight control systems, and the inlet ramp control system, should flight control demands reduce No. 2 system pressure sufficiently. The failure of a hydraulic pump will normally be indicated by a drop of pressure on the appropriate needle of the hydraulic pressure indicator. Should one pump fail on either system, the pilot may continue an *operational* mission with caution. Failure of both pumps on either system shall be considered an emergency and a landing shall be made as soon as practicable.

Failure of both No. 1 system pumps or total loss of pressure in the No. 1 system may cause monitor shutoff of augmentation, electric flight control and ramp control, which are powered by the No. 2 system. Should No. 1 system failure occur, the "kill" button should be depressed prior to landing.

NO. 1 OR NO. 2 SYSTEM FAILURES

Failure of both No. 1 or No. 2 system pumps is indicated by illumination of the HYD PRESS caution indicator and loss of pressure from the pumps and/or in the system to less than approximately 650 psi.

1. With one pump failed (one needle indicating zero), continue operational mission with caution.
2. Check HYD SUB-SYS ISOLATION switch — FLIGHT.
3. With complete loss of either hydraulic system, or reservoir (automatic) isolation of No. 2 system (HYD PRESS caution indicator on), land as soon as practicable.
4. Reduce speed to less than 1.3 IMN.
5. "Kill" button — Depress.
6. YAW AUG and RAMP CONT switches — STBY.
7. Speed brake dump handle — pull, if necessary.
8. Buddy tanker HOSE CONTROL switch — REWIND.
9. Buddy tanker FUEL FLOW switch — OFF.

CAUTION

- Do not extend air refueling probe unless absolutely required.
- Do not extend RAT if No. 1 system is operating normally, or if No. 1 system leakage is suspected.
- Do not retract the RAT once it is extended.

10. Extend flaps, using emergency procedure.

Note

- In the event of complete No. 2 system failure, droops will not extend. See figure 5-4 for emergency approach speeds with various flap/droop conditions.
- If No. 2 hydraulic failure occurs following normal flap extension, place EMERG FLAP switch to DOWN to prevent possible flap airload retraction during landing approach.

CAUTION

Wing droop leading edge extension may or may not be available when the flaps are extended by the emergency system. If all No. 2 system fluid is lost, or the hydraulic subsystem isolation valves remain closed, the droops will remain in the last selected position. In order to improve the potential of droop extension, the HYD SUB-SYS ISOLATION switch should be moved to FLIGHT and the flap control switch moved to 50° prior to using emergency procedures to extend the landing gear, flaps, and arresting hook. This procedure may return sufficient fluid to the No. 2 system reservoir to open the automatic isolation valve and allow normal droop extension.

11. Extend landing gear, using emergency procedure.

CAUTION

Ensure that flap control switch is at 50° and landing gear handle is in the DOWN position.

Section V   NAVWEPS 01-60ABA-1

12. Utilize short-field arresting gear *if immediately available.*

Note

In the event of a divert, the flaps may be retracted by airload pressure by moving the EMERG FLAP switch to UP. Under this condition, ensure that the normal flap control switch is in the same relative position as the EMERG FLAP switch (50°/DOWN) prior to landing. A second extension of the flaps may be possible if sufficient pneumatic pressure is available.

13. If short-field arresting gear is not utilized, use emergency brakes initially, saving auxiliary brake accumulator pressure for directional control. Normal braking and nose wheel steering will not be available.

Note

- With No. 1 system failure, the HYD SUB-SYS ISOLATION switch can be returned to TAKE-OFF/LANDING after the aircraft is completely stopped and prior to taxiing.
- If failure involves No. 1 system only, and if crosswind conditions warrant the use of nose wheel steering, the HYD SUB-SYS ISOLATION switch may be moved to TAKE-OFF/LANDING at the short final approach position.
- If nose wheel steering is not available, do not attempt to taxi.

COMPLETE HYDRAULIC FAILURE

Complete failure of both hydraulic systems (four pumps) is an extremely remote possibility. In the event of complete failure, all hydraulically operated systems are lost, followed closely by "freezing" of all flight controls and complete loss of control of the aircraft. Landing with RAT hydraulic power only requires increased final approach speed to ensure adequate flow rate for flight control operation. Flight control movement must be restricted to absolute minimum to prevent momentary stick stiffness and loss of control. Speed on final approach should be maintained at not less than 150 KIAS to ensure efficient RAT operation, especially in any turbulence. The gear and flaps should be extended by emergency means as soon as possible and all effort concentrated on completing the landing if landing is elected. Proceed as follows:

1. RAT—EXTEND.
2. Check HYD EPU ON advisory light illuminates.

WARNING

If control stick action is not restored, EJECT IMMEDIATELY. Control is not possible without hydraulic pressure.

3. Prepare to land as soon as possible. Carrier landing should not be attempted.
4. Extend gear and flaps by emergency method.
5. Fly final approach at 150 KIAS, under optimum conditions, flaring prior to touchdown.

WARNING

- In order to ensure maximum RAT output under all conditions, approximately 160 KIAS should be maintained. This is especially important in turbulence. Control movements must be restricted to a minimum to avoid loss of pressure at a critical point during landing.
- Should the HYD EPU ON advisory light go out and control "lock" occur while using RAT hydraulic power only, release all control pressure. Should control fail to be restored, EJECT IMMEDIATELY.

PITOT-STATIC SYSTEM FAILURE

The airspeed indicator will show characteristic reactions in the event of total pressure loss (such as might be caused by ice forming on the pitot boom) or static pressure loss (caused by water frozen in the static lines). Refer to ICE AND RAIN, in Section VI.

Note

If the airspeed indicator is suspected of inaccuracy for any reason, the landing gear can be safety extended at a 1-g stabilized angle of attack of 9 units.

CAUTION

Should the pitot anti-icing system fail under icing conditions, pitot boom ice may cause the inlet ramps to be driven toward full down, reducing engine airflow and possibly causing a flame-out.

TOTAL PRESSURE SOURCE FAILURE

1. If the aircraft is in a climb, the indicated airspeed increases as the decreasing static pressure is sensed. Altimeter and vertical speed indications are not affected.
2. If the aircraft is in a descent, increasing static pressure is sensed, resulting in decreasing airspeed indications.

180

STATIC PRESSURE SOURCE FAILURE

1. Altimeter and vertical speed indications will be incorrect, since they tend to remain at their last indications before failure.
2. Airspeed indications will be low during a climb and high during descent.

Note

Angle-of-attack equivalent data for use during pitot-static failures is available in the NATOPS Pocket Check List (NAVWEPS 01-60ABA-1B).

FLIGHT CONTROL SYSTEMS FAILURES

PITCH CONTROL MALFUNCTION

Should the aircraft display unusual or undesired pitch action, failure of pitch augmentation, autoflight, pitch electric, or pitch trim systems may have occurred. For example, internal failure of pitch augmentation gyros may cause such action without "monitoring" the system to stand-by or illuminating the PITCH AUG caution indicator. To return the aircraft to normal positive control, proceed as follows:

1. Disable ("kill") button—Depress.
2. Check that the AFC switch has been moved to OFF, and that the PITCH AUG and ELEC SYS switches have been moved to STBY.
3. Check that the PITCH AUG and ELEC F/C caution indicators are illuminated.
4. Check that the PITCH and ROLL (electric flight control) indicators are blank. On some aircraft,* check for barber poles.
5. If the malfunction continues on releasing the "kill" button, the normal pitch trim circuit may have malfunctioned. Hold the "kill" button down and move the TRIM SEL switch to ALTR.
6. Retrim as required, using alternate pitch trim.
7. Return the TRIM SEL switch to NORM. If the malfunction returns, the pitch trim circuit is defective. Return the TRIM SEL switch to ALTR and use alternate pitch, roll, and yaw trim for the remainder of the flight.
8. If normal pitch trim has not malfunctioned, attempt to reset PITCH AUG and ELEC SYS switches. If a malfunction occurs, move the switches to STBY and *do not make further reset attempts.*

Note

- Pitch augmentation cannot be "monitored" off by opposing aircraft motion with stick forces.
- The yaw augmentation system is not disabled by depressing the "kill" button.

PITCH AUGMENTATION MALFUNCTION

Malfunctions can occur in the augmented longitudinal flight control system without resulting in pitch augmentation monitoring off and without illumination of the PITCH AUG caution indicator.

WARNING

A malfunctioning pitch augmentation system cannot be monitored off by the use of opposing control stick forces. Disable the augmented longitudinal flight control system by (1) pressing the "kill" button, or (2) moving PITCH AUG switch to STBY.

In the event of longitudinal control system malfunction, proceed as follows:

1. "Kill" button—Depress.
2. If the condition is a trim runaway, select ALTR position of the TRIM switch prior to releasing the "kill" button.

PITCH AUGMENTATION FAILURE

Failure of pitch augmentation will result from loss of No. 2 hydraulic system pressure or electrical malfunction within the longitudinal series system. Failure is indicated by illumination of the master caution and PITCH AUG caution indicators and the inability to trim the aircraft through the PITCH AUG trim control. When evidence of an unreliable system is exhibited during the take-off or landing phase, while conducting loft bombing, and at speeds in excess of 450 KIAS below 5000 feet, the system will be secured. A pronounced trim change may occur within 5 seconds after the system monitors off. Failure occurring during the landing approach, particularly a carrier approach, can result in an extremely hazardous flight condition.

Note

Should pitch augmentation fail just prior to touchdown, a hard landing or porpoise may result, due to the abrupt longitudinal trim change which occurs. For these reasons, a wave-off should be executed immediately when failure occurs during a critical point of the landing approach.

EMERGENCY WAVE-OFF

Should pitch augmentation fail (PITCH AUG caution indicator on) at a critical point close-in to the ramps, proceed as follows:

1. Advance throttles to MIL and retract speed brakes.
2. Pull stick aft as required to counteract trim change.

*Aircraft not having ASC 42 complied with

3. Retrim as required, using stand-by pitch trim.
4. Check PITCH AUG switch at STBY prior to final landing.

The pitch augmentation system shall be secured prior to entering the landing pattern when an indication of impending failure of the No. 2 hydraulic system is observed.

Should attempts to reset pitch augmentation result in an abrupt nose-up or nose-down pitch, move the PITCH AUG switch to STBY and do not make further attempts to reset the system.

PITCH AUGMENTATION DISENGAGED

Flight without pitch augmentation requires that pitch trim be controlled through the five-position pitch and roll trim switch. Large changes in airspeed require more adjustment of pitch trim than is required with pitch augmentation operating. In addition, flight in or through the transonic speed range is accompanied by stick force lightening or reversal. For landing, larger and heavier stick movement and force are required to correct pitch attitude, and firm, positive attitude corrections are required for glide path correction.

Note
Stick position on final approach is appreciably aft of that with pitch augmentation engaged.

YAW AUGMENTATION FAILURE

Failure of yaw augmentation may indicate loss of No. 2 hydraulic system pressure or electrical malfunction within the directional series system. Should failure occur at high speeds (above 550 KIAS), speed and/or roll rate should be restricted. Should attempts to reset the system fail, move the YAW AUG switch to STBY. Landing in turbulence or cross wind with yaw augmentation inoperative may result in directional or lateral/directional oscillation, requiring pilot control with rudder. Due to the long moment of the fuselage, these oscillations tend to be of a low frequency (4 seconds per cycle average), allowing adequate pilot damping.

ELECTRIC FLIGHT CONTROL FAILURE

Should the electric flight control system malfunction, the following action should be taken.

1. "Kill button—Depress.

2. ELEC SYS switch—STBY.
3. Apply stick force in the desired direction to override the electric system and revert to the mechanical system.

Note
Any of the above actions should disable the electric flight control system in the axis concerned (pitch or roll). After the "kill" button is depressed, pitch augmentation must be re-engaged if operation is desired.

TRIM FAILURE

Failure of the normal roll or yaw trim systems does not present a serious problem unless asymmetrical external loads are involved. Should one or both of these systems fail, the TRIM SEL switch should be moved to ALTR, and the ALT ROLL/YAW TRIM switch should be used to remove control forces.

Note
Failure of the roll or yaw trim *actuators* cannot be corrected by selecting alternate trim.

Failure of the stand-by pitch trim circuit (pitch augmentation disengaged) results in heavy, fatiguing stick forces if not relieved. Should pitch trim fail, moving the TRIM SEL switch to ALTR switches the stand-by pitch trim actuator to an alternate source of power (essential bus). Control is maintained through the same stick-mounted switch.

Note
- Failure of the stand-by pitch trim actuator is not corrected by selecting alternate trim.
- Selecting alternate trim for any trim axis requires that all axes be trimmed by the alternate method as long as the TRIM SEL switch is in ALTR.

If the yaw trim actuator fails at "full travel," the vertical stabilizer will increase trim input from $1\frac{1}{2}$ to $7\frac{1}{2}$ degrees on extension of flaps. The only corrective action is to use control pedal deflection to counteract yaw. Should this failure occur, nose wheel steering should not be used on landing rollout.

LOST AIRCRAFT PROCEDURES

Publications used for developing lost aircraft procedures are NWP 41(A), ACP 125B and 130, and FLIP, Enroute Supplement.

IF YOU ARE LOST

1. Admit to yourself that you are lost.

2. Use and cross-check all available navigation equipment.

3. CONSERVE fuel by flying at maximum endurance airspeed.

4. Select IFF EMERGENCY (SIF MODE 3, Code 77).

VOICE PROCEDURE

1. PAN, PAN, PAN.
    Use MAYDAY if immediate assistance is required.

2. Aircraft identification three times.

3. Type aircraft.

4. Estimated position and time.

5. Magnetic heading, true airspeed, and altitude.

6. Fuel remaining (hours and minutes).

7. Situation.

8. Intentions.

9. Assistance required.

10. COMPLY with instructions when contact is established.

ADDITIONAL PROCEDURES (SHORE-BASED)

To aid radar facilities, depending upon radio communications, proceed as follows:

1. With a radio receiver, fly right triangular patterns, using 120-degree turns, 1-minute legs.

2. Without a radio receiver, fly left triangular patterns, using 120-degree turns, 1-minute legs.

3. Fly two complete patterns before proceeding on course.

4. Repeat pattern every 20 minutes.
    Refer to FLIP, Enroute Supplement, for complete procedures.

ADDITIONAL PROCEDURES (CARRIER-BASED)

1. Lost procedures under EMCOM conditions will be established during briefing.

2. When EMCOM conditions allow, make radio report using procedures listed under VOICE PROCEDURE.

3. Select proper IFF/SIF mode/code.

4. When over the carrier's estimated position, commence a square search, using left turns.

5. Use AN/ASB-12 radar, transmitting 1 minute and silent 1 minute.

6. If carrier is not located, land at a friendly field, fuel permitting.

DOWNED AIRCRAFT SURVEILLANCE

If two or more aircraft are present at the scene of an accident, the senior aviator present shall take immediate charge and carry out the following:

1. Instruct all aircraft at the scene to squawk MAYDAY.

2. Designate one aircraft to climb to altitude (if necessary), establish communications with a ground station, and act as relay. Transmit the following on GUARD frequency:
    (a) CRASH, CRASH, CRASH.
    (b) Identify yourself.
    (c) Position of crash.
    (d) Estimate of the situation.
    (e) Your intentions and endurance.
    (f) Request immediate coverage.

3. Designate one aircraft to remain on the scene and keep survivors in sight. This aircraft will:
    (a) Transmit any pertinent information to the relay plane.
    (b) Remain on station until aid arrives or as fuel permits.

DITCHING

WARNING

Rather than attempting to ditch and risking needless injury, ejection should be accomplished when feasible.

If conditions preclude ejection, the pilot must accomplish as much of the following procedure as time permits:

1. Notify systems operator.

2. Landing gear—UP.

3. RAT—Pull.

4. Flap control switch—50°.

5. Speed brakes—IN.

6. Arresting hook—DOWN.

7. Stores—JETTISON.

8. EMERG IFF switch—EMERGENCY (MODE 3, Code 77).

9. Harness—LOCKED.

10. Transmit MAYDAY, MAYDAY, MAYDAY.
    Refer to CONTROLLED EJECTION, in this section.

11. Dump all possible fuel.

12. Canopies—JETTISON.

13. Observe and use to best advantage the wind and/or sea state.

14. Emergency oxygen ring—PULL PRIOR TO TOUCHDOWN.

Section V   NAVWEPS 01-60ABA-1

15. Maintain 160 KIAS until flare for touchdown.
16. Touchdown at 100 fpm or less, in a nose-high attitude.
17. FLY THE AIRCRAFT UNTIL ALL FORWARD MOTION IS STOPPED.
18. Harness release handle—PULL.
19. Turn right and exit backwards over left side of cockpit.

DITCHING INFORMATION

If the sea is calm, land into the wind. If there is a swell running, touch down parallel to the swell crest or just after the crest has passed. In the event of high winds or a rough sea, land into the wind, touching down on the crest of a wave. Generally, the advantage gained from a slower touchdown speed will offset the disadvantage of a head-on impact with a wave crest. Rate of descent and airspeed at touchdown are the most important variables under the pilot's control. High touchdown speeds will greatly increase deceleration forces and increase the possibility of the flight crew being rendered unconscious. High rate-of-descent landings are likely to cause high impact forces and serious structural failures, resulting in a very short flotation period. A rate of descent of 100 feet per minute or less should be maintained at touchdown, if at all possible.

WARNING

If the aircraft is touched down in a flat attitude (less than 8 degrees) it may dive violently after contact. *Because of the shoulder wing mounting, the cockpits will be under water when forward motion stops.* If a properly adjusted mask is maintained, an underwater breathing supply is provided by the emergency oxygen system for approximately 5 minutes.

HELICOPTER WATER RESCUE

To ensure that survival equipment does not interfere with helicopter rescue from the water, perform the following procedures:

1. Remove oxygen mask or raise pressure suit face plate.
   Retain helmet for protection.
2. Ensure that the parachute canopy is completely released from the torso harness at both the "Rocket-Jet" fittings and the manual "D" ring pocket.
3. Pull Scott disconnect knob to release oxygen mask hose from seat pan.
4. Release "Rocket-Jet" fittings at hip attach points.
5. Disconnect life raft lanyard from torso harness.
6. Abandon life raft to avoid being blown from beneath helicopter by rotor downwash.

Note
Avoid high hand hold on shank of rescue seat.

LANDING EMERGENCIES
SINGLE-ENGINE LANDINGS

For single-engine landing procedure, see figure 5-3. To avoid possible directional control difficulty after touchdown, check and set yaw trim to 0 units after extending flaps, and ensure that the control pedals are centered when engaging nose wheel steering.

WARNING

Should final approach speed be allowed to reduce below 13.5 units A/A, sink rate may exceed safe limits.

SINGLE-ENGINE CARRIER LANDINGS

Single-engine carrier landings are normally not permitted except in an emergency. For emergency single-engine carrier landings, gross weight must be reduced to 38,500 pounds or less. Aircraft response to power changes, both for acceleration and deceleration, is sluggish. The normal carrier pattern is flown, except as follows:

1. Check/cycle afterburner to ensure proper operation.
2. Flaps—40°.

CAUTION

Single-engine performance and wave-off capability is seriously degraded with more than 40 degrees of flaps selected.

3. Hold 12 units A/A downwind, slowing to 13.5 units at the 180-degree position.

SINGLE-ENGINE WAVE-OFF

Use MAX AFTERBURNER on all single-engine bolters or wave-offs. A single-engine wave-off and landing pattern requires about 200 pounds more fuel than a normal pattern without afterburner. If leaving pattern, retract landing gear only when safe climb is established, as touchdown may be required in the event of a late wave-off. Retract flaps above 200 KIAS, when clear of all obstacles.

CAUTION

Be prepared to counteract yaw as the flaps retract. Rudder effectiveness decreases with flap retraction.

182B

SINGLE-ENGINE LANDING

NOTE:
SINGLE-ENGINE CARRIER LANDINGS ARE NORMALLY NOT PERMITTED EXCEPT IN EMERGENCY.

BEFORE ENTRY
- REDUCE GROSS WEIGHT TO 38,500 POUNDS OR LESS.
- PRE-LANDING CHECKS — COMPLETE.
- ENTER AT NORMAL SPEED AND ALTITUDE.
- SPC — OFF
- HYD SUB-SYS ISOLATION — TAKE-OFF/LANDING

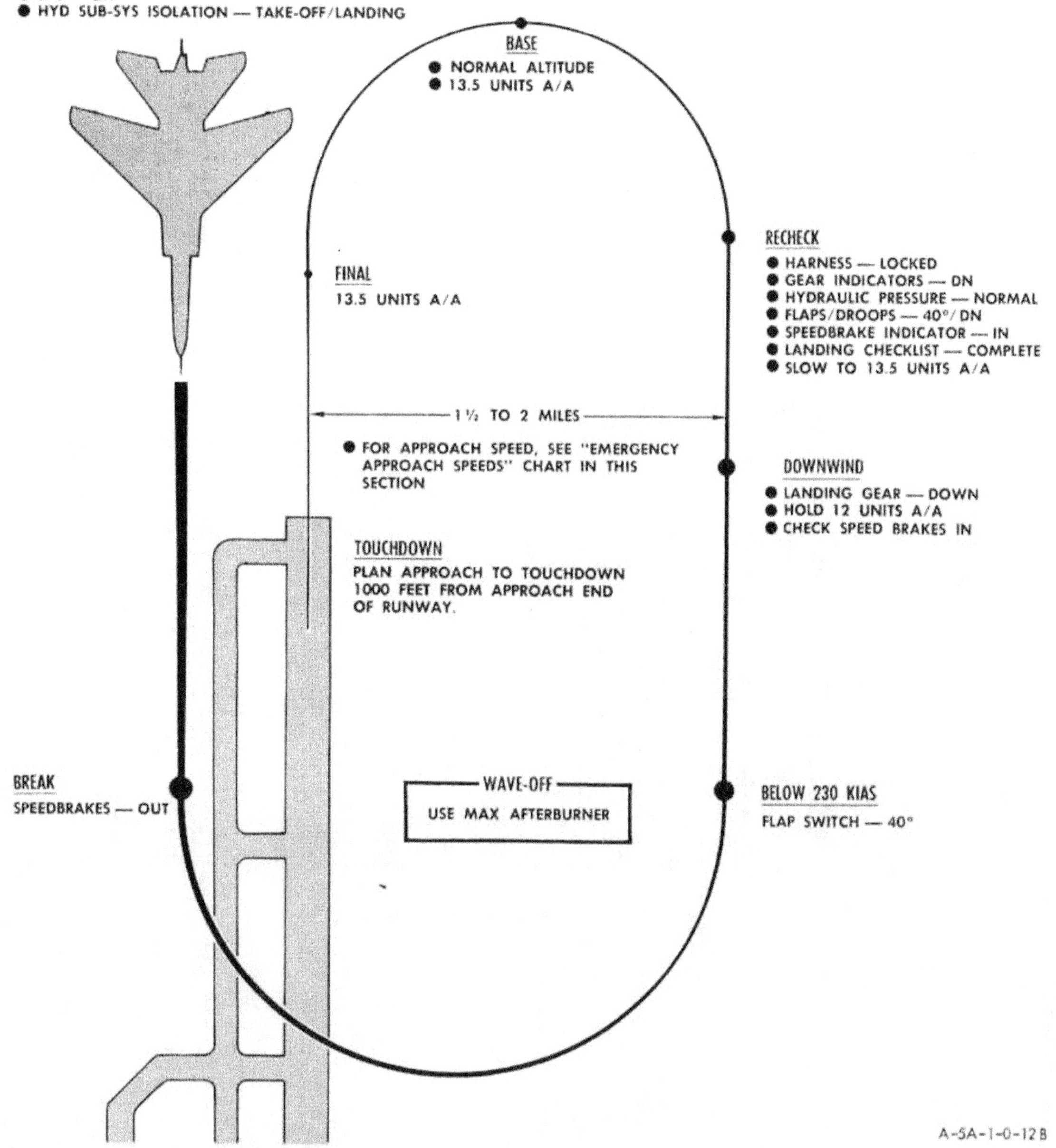

BASE
- NORMAL ALTITUDE
- 13.5 UNITS A/A

RECHECK
- HARNESS — LOCKED
- GEAR INDICATORS — DN
- HYDRAULIC PRESSURE — NORMAL
- FLAPS/DROOPS — 40°/DN
- SPEEDBRAKE INDICATOR — IN
- LANDING CHECKLIST — COMPLETE
- SLOW TO 13.5 UNITS A/A

FINAL
13.5 UNITS A/A

1½ TO 2 MILES

- FOR APPROACH SPEED, SEE "EMERGENCY APPROACH SPEEDS" CHART IN THIS SECTION

DOWNWIND
- LANDING GEAR — DOWN
- HOLD 12 UNITS A/A
- CHECK SPEED BRAKES IN

TOUCHDOWN
PLAN APPROACH TO TOUCHDOWN 1000 FEET FROM APPROACH END OF RUNWAY.

WAVE-OFF
USE MAX AFTERBURNER

BELOW 230 KIAS
FLAP SWITCH — 40°

BREAK
SPEEDBRAKES — OUT

A-5A-1-0-12B

Figure 5-3

Section V

NAVWEPS 01-60ABA-1

EMERGENCY APPROACH SPEEDS

APPROACH SPEED VARIATION FOR
VARIOUS FLAP AND DROOP SETTINGS

SPC-OFF

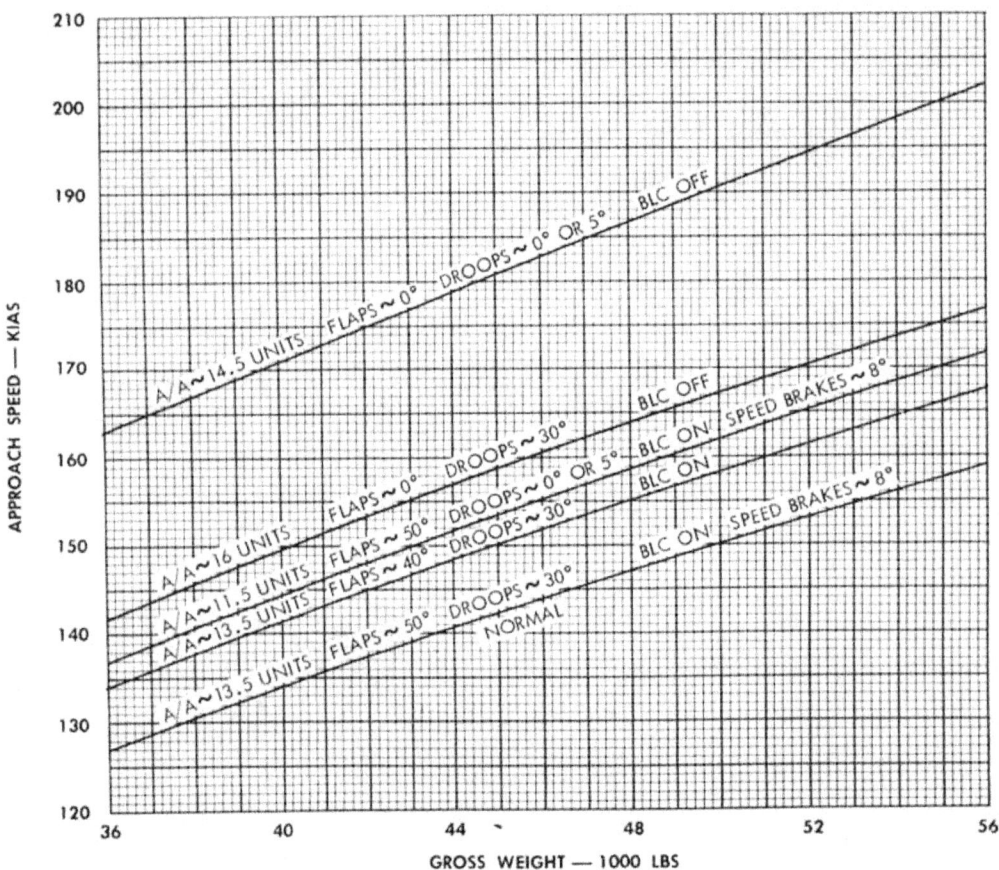

Figure 5-4

LANDING WITH ABNORMAL FLAP/DROOP SETTINGS

With flaps extended, extend speed brakes to between 8 and 15 degrees if available. This reduces undesirable pitch and yaw dynamics induced by lateral control inputs, particularly when rolling out of a turn or during large lineup corrections. No abrupt or large lateral control input should be made, especially in close.

> **CAUTION**
>
> Use of angles of attack at or above 13 units with abnormal flap/droop settings invites lateral control ineffectiveness and pitch-down with turns. Use of vertical stabilizer to aid lateral control will reduce pitch-down during rolls, particularly if speed brakes are not available.

The additional drag of partial speed brakes allows use of power settings above the BLC decay rpm (78%) and reduces the possibility of inadvertent loss of BLC effectiveness which causes undesirable pitch-down. Pitch trim change during speed brake extension and retraction is quite pronounced; therefore, speed brakes should not be retracted during wave-off.

WAVE-OFF

During MAX AFTERBURNER wave-off with PITCH AUG switch in STBY, reduced nose-down trim authority necessitates pilot anticipation with forward stick on selection of afterburner to prevent pitch-up. With PITCH AUG switch at ON, increased nose-down trim authority and improved stick-to-stabilizer ratio minimizes the pitch-up problem. Prior to landing, reduce gross weight as necessary to remain within maximum engagement speed limitations.

CARRIER APPROACH

Single-engine approach to a carrier with an abnormal flap/droop configuration is not recommended due to reduced trim authority and pronounced pitch changes with lateral control inputs. No-flap carrier arrestments are not recommended due to maximum engaging speed limitations.

TIRE FAILURE

In the event of a main gear tire failure, immediately maintain directional control with nose wheel steering. The aircraft may be held in the center of the runway until the last 10 to 20 knots of rollout. During landings, brake disc temperature may exceed 1000°F. Most of this heat is dissipated into the atmosphere, but some is transmitted into the tire. Although the fusible plugs in the main wheels should deflate the tire of an overheated wheel, a tire blowout is possible for as long as 30 minutes after a brake has been used to capacity.

> **CAUTION**
>
> Allow sufficient time between flights or after aborted take-offs for adequate cooling. If operational necessity dictates immediate take-off, gear should be left extended as long as possible (at least 3 minutes) to permit maximum cooling.

LANDING WITH TIRE FAILURE

For landing with any tire failure, use short-field arresting gear if available. Refer to SHORT-FIELD ARRESTMENT, in this section. In the event field arresting gear is not available, proceed as follows:

NOSE GEAR TIRE

1. Dump and consume fuel to 4000 pounds or less total.
2. Make normal approach with minimum sink touchdown, lowering the nose gently after touchdown.
3. Stop aircraft straight ahead.
   Do not attempt taxi.

MAIN GEAR TIRE

1. Dump and consume fuel to 4000 pounds or less total.
2. Make normal approach with minimum sink touchdown.
   LAND ON SIDE OF RUNWAY NEAR GOOD TIRE.
3. Lower nose on touchdown and engage nose wheel steering if required.
4. Use steering and differential braking as required to stop the aircraft.

LANDING GEAR UNSAFE INDICATION

An unsafe indication of the landing gear may be the result of a malfunction of the landing gear selector valve, the hydraulic system, the electrical system, or the landing gear position indicating system. If an unsafe indication is encountered, proceed as follows:

1. Maintain airspeed below 230 KIAS.
2. Cycle landing gear handle twice.
3. If unsafe indication persists with gear handle down, pull EMER LDG GR handle and hold until a safe indication is obtained.
4. If a safe indication is not obtained, retract gear.
5. HYD SUB-SYS ISOLATION switch — FLIGHT.
6. Landing gear handle — DOWN.

Section V

NAVWEPS 01-60ABA-1

7. EMER LDG GR handle—PULL and HOLD.
8. On safe indication—Return handle.
9. Remain in FLIGHT position and follow procedures under HYDRAULIC FAILURES for landing.

CAUTION

Do not return to TAKE-OFF/LANDING, as gear unsafe condition may recur.

10. After landing, have downlock pins installed as soon as possible.

Note

If a safe indication cannot be obtained, use procedures described under LANDING WITH UNSAFE GEAR, in this section.

LANDING GEAR EMERGENCY EXTENSION

For complete procedures, see figure 5-5. Landing gear emergency extension procedure may be used to extend the gear in the event of hydraulic failure, electrical failure, or both. In the event of failure, pulling the handle results in gear extension from gravity and air stream load.

Note
- During landing gear emergency extension, pull the emergency handle to *full travel* (approximately 15 inches) and HOLD until the gear is safe ("DN" indication or visually checked down). DO NOT ALLOW THE HANDLE TO FLY BACK, AS DAMAGE TO THE INSTRUMENT PANEL MAY OCCUR.
- On landing gear emergency extension, the fairing doors and gear doors DO NOT close after extension.

CAUTION

Do not attempt to retract the landing gear after emergency extension because of failure of the No. 2 hydraulic system.

LANDING GEAR EMERGENCY EXTENSION

1. REDUCE AIRSPEED TO BELOW LANDING GEAR AIRSPEED LIMITS

2.
- PLACE LANDING GEAR HANDLE DOWN
- CHECK EMERGENCY GEAR UP SWITCH AT NORM

3. PULL EMERGENCY LANDING GEAR EXTENSION HANDLE FULL OUT AND HOLD

4. CHECK LANDING GEAR POSITION INDICATOR SAFE AND RELEASE HANDLE

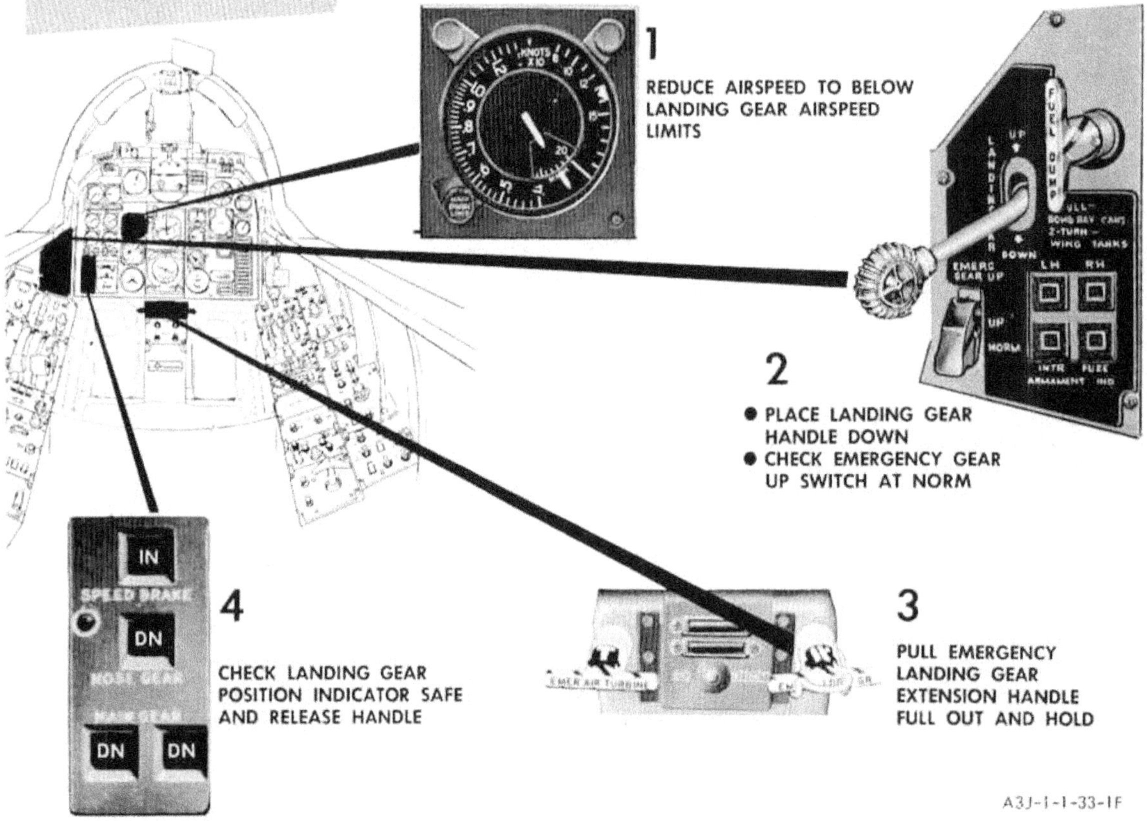

Figure 5-5

FLAP EMERGENCY EXTENSION

The wing flaps may be extended to 50 degrees by the pneumatic emergency system in the event of hydraulic or flap system electrical failure. Operation of the spoiler control lateral ratio changer is dual for fail-safe full spoiler-to-stick ratio with the flaps extended through either the normal or emergency system. Loss of power to the lateral ratio changer results in full (70-degree) spoiler authority without regard to the position of the flaps or the flap control switch. For flap emergency extension, proceed as follows:

1. Reduce airspeed to less than 190 KIAS.
2. HYD SUB-SYS ISOLATION switch—FLIGHT.
3. Flap control switch—50°.
4. EMERG FLAP switch—DOWN.
5. Droop, flap, and trim indicator—check.
6. Speed brake operation—check; Dump if required.

Note

For recommended final approach speeds in various flap/droop configurations, see figure 5-4.

LANDING WITH UNSAFE GEAR

If the landing gear indicates unsafe after extension for landing and if fuel permits, every resource should be used to determine gear position before attempting to land or ejecting. Should fly-by for inspection prove the gear to be "cocked" or unsafe, the following factors must be considered:

1. Fuel state.
2. Crosswind effect.
3. Runway length.
4. Availability of field arresting gear.
5. Runway foam equipment capability.

WARNING

- Ejection is recommended if combined landing factors are not entirely favorable.
- In case of unsafe gear indication, do not retract the landing gear once a safe indication is obtained.

If the decision is made to land with unsafe or partially extended gear, proceed as follows:

1. Dump and consume excess fuel to minimum weight.
2. Loose gear—STOW.

WARNING

If landing with unsafe nose gear, jettison canopies prior to touchdown.

3. Harness—LOCKED.
4. Make a normal approach.
    If a main gear is unsafe, land on the side of the runway nearest the good main gear. If the nose gear is unsafe, land in the center.
5. On touchdown, throttles—OFF.
6. Hold unsafe main gear off as long as possible.

Note

For unsafe nose gear, lower nose gently immediately after touchdown to minimize contact forces. As the nose touches, move the throttles to OFF.

7. Use rudder, nose wheel steering, or differential braking, as available, to control direction.
8. Abandon aircraft as soon as possible when all motion has stopped.

CAUTION

If directional control is lost and/or the aircraft is leaving the runway, JETTISON THE CANOPIES IMMEDIATELY.

CARRIER ARRESTMENT

EMERGENCY ARRESTMENT

If an emergency situation dictates that a carrier landing be attempted at gross weights approaching 47,000 pounds, damage to the aircraft must be anticipated. Recommended emergency procedures for a 47,000-pound gross weight carrier landing are as follows:

1. Maintain high sump fuel.
2. Use a normal approach.
3. Flaps—50 degrees.
4. A/A—13.5 units.
5. For approach speed, see figure 5-4.
6. For maximum arresting gear engagement speed, refer to current Aircraft Launch and Recovery Bulletins.

By maintaining high sump tank fuel until wing fuel is exhausted, aircraft cg will remain within acceptable limits down to a sump level of 3600 pounds. Landings at gross weights less than 47,000 pounds are therefore recommended if possible. At gross weights less than 47,000 pounds, linear interpolation between current ALRB information and the airspeeds in figure 5-4.

LOW SUMP LEVEL

If high sump cannot be maintained and sump level falls below 3600 pounds, the procedures for carrier emergency arrestment should be modified as follows:

1. Flaps—40 degrees maximum.
2. A/A—13 units.
3. Minimum approach speed—154 KIAS.

Note

- If sump level falls below 2500 pounds, an aft cg condition will exist. Jettisoning of external stores is recommended to provide increased stability during approach.
- For additional information about aft cg landing and emergency procedures for bomb bay fuel can transfer failure, refer to Section IV and BOMB BAY CAN TRANSFER FAILURE, in this section. Increased approach speeds consistent with maximum engaging speed and available wind over the deck will increase aircraft stability during an approach with an aft cg.

BARRICADE ENGAGEMENT

In the event it becomes necessary to use the barricade, jettison all external stores and fly a normal approach at 13.5 units A/A. When possible, wind over the deck (WOD) should be that value considered optimum for the carrier involved, but not less than 30 knots. In the event WOD values in excess of 30 knots are necessary, the pilot shall be briefed accordingly.

WARNING

FLY THE BALL. There is a tendency for pilots to "spot the deck" and go low in the groove.

Pilots should be reminded that lens roll angle will be decreased and hook-to-ramp clearance will also be decreased with a centered ball. The dangers associated with a late wave-off are obvious and should be avoided. Attempt to land on centerline in the prescribed landing attitude. The aircraft should engage the barricade on the deck in a three-point attitude. Landing signal officers should avoid giving a cut signal prior to touchdown, as large power reductions result in an abrupt aircraft pitch-down. The cut signal should be given after touchdown and both engines secured after the aircraft has stopped completely.

Note

For maximum permissible engaging speed and aircraft gross weight for barricade engagement, refer to the Supplemental NATOPS Flight Manual (NAVWEPS 01-60ABA-1A).

CAUTION

In the final portion of the approach, the pilot will lose the ball *momentarily*, due to the location of the port barricade stanchion.

FIELD ARRESTMENT

Several types of field arrestment equipment are available. These types of arresting gear include the anchor chain/cable type, the aircraft brake/cable type, and/or water squeeze gear. At most USAF bases and many USN/USMC fields, some form of jet barrier is installed. It is imperative that all pilots be aware of the type, location, and load limitations of the gear in use. In general, the arresting gear is engaged on the centerline at as slow a speed as possible.

1. Reduce fuel aboard to 4000 pounds or less.
2. Obtain assistance of LSO, if possible.
3. Fly a low-angle pass, landing at minimum sink rate. Touch down between 500 and 1000 feet short of the cross-deck pendant and taxi into the gear in a slightly nose-high attitude. If the hook skips the wire, apply power and go around for another attempt.

SHORT FIELD ARRESTMENT

Any time before landing, when it is known that a directional control problem exists or a minimum rollout is desired, the short-field equipment is used. In addition, an LSO equipped with a radio should be stationed near the touchdown point to aid the pilot in landing. The hook should be lowered while airborne and a positive hook check made. The aircraft is touched down just short of the arresting gear, with shoulder harness locked and the pilot's feet off the brakes, engaging the gear slightly nose-high. Be prepared for a wave-off if the gear is missed.

LONG-FIELD ARRESTMENT

This situation occurs when a stopping problem exists, such as failed brakes or failure of the No. 2 hydraulic system. Lower the hook in sufficient time for it to effectively extend (normally 1000 to 2000 feet in front of the arresting gear. If arrestment is to be made at night, the pilot should request illumination of the arresting gear position. For normal long-field arrestment, proceed as follows:

1. Make a normal approach and landing.
2. Hook—down.
3. Use nose-high aerodynamic braking.
4. Direct the aircraft to enter the arresting gear as close to the center as possible, and attempt to engage the gear slightly nose-high.

FIELD BARRIER

If a field barrier is to be engaged, the aircraft should be in the three-point attitude and the engines secured prior to barrier engagement. For engagement of USAF BAK-6, BAK-9, or MA-1 type barriers, ensure that the hook is extended at least 1000 feet short of the barrier to prevent the possibility of the hook skipping over the cable.

BRAKE FAILURE

In the event of any brake system malfunction, the aircraft should be maneuvered off the duty runway. Should brake failure be suspected before landing, use long- or short-field arresting gear, as applicable.

Note

For wheel brake failure accompanying failure of the No. 2 hydraulic system, use emergency braking for initial deceleration, saving normal braking for terminal rollout directional control.

EMERGENCY COCKPIT ENTRANCE AND ESCAPE

For emergency cockpit entrance and rescue information, see figure 5-6.

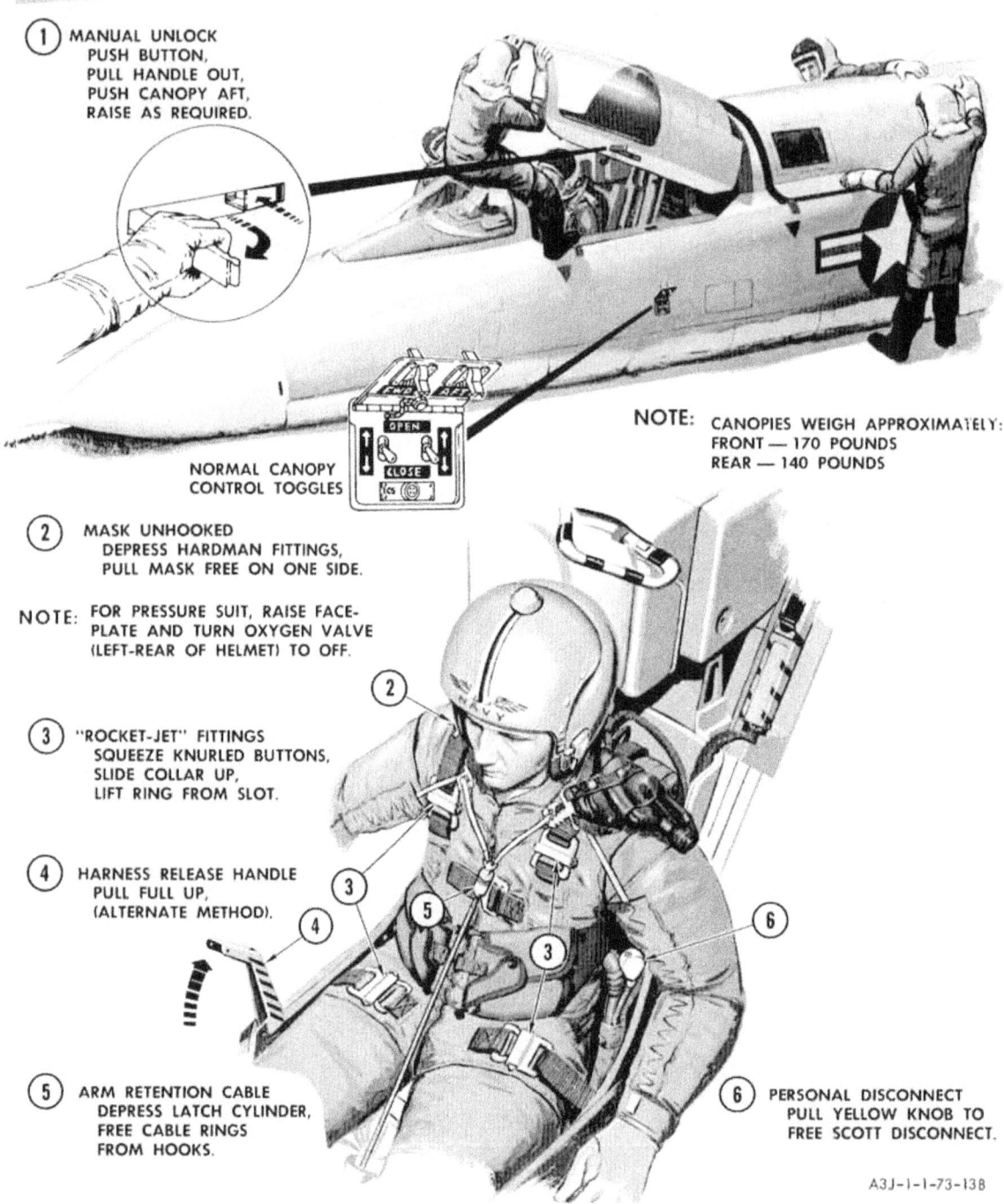

Figure 5-6

all-weather operation

Section VI

TABLE OF CONTENTS

Introduction	183
Instrument Flight	183
Penetration	184
Instrument Approaches	184
Night Flight	187
Flight in Turbulence	187
Ice and Rain	187
Cold Weather Procedures	188A
Hot Weather Procedures	189
Simulated Instrument Flight	189

INTRODUCTION

All-weather operation is discussed in this section for such conditions as instrument flight, ice and rain, turbulence, and temperature extremes. This material supplements the information contained in other sections of the manual and is not intended as a substitute for normal operating procedures. Procedures for simulated (hooded) instrument flight are also included.

INSTRUMENT FLIGHT

The capabilities of this aircraft make it highly adaptable for instrument flight. Mission accomplishment is enhanced by the effectiveness of the autoflight control, CNI systems, and the bomb directing set. However, thorough preflight planning and current instrument proficiency are always necessary for successful instrument flight operations. Effective aircraft range may be reduced by air traffic control procedures and unexpected weather developments. The hazard of icing can be reduced by use of engine, windshield, and pitot anti-ice systems. Thunderstorms should be circumnavigated through the use of radar.

Control of the UHF communications, IFF, ADF, and TACAN is available from either cockpit. Control of the SIF is possible from the rear cockpit only. Flights in positive control areas cannot be accomplished without a crew member in the rear cockpit.

FUEL PLANNING

1. The following fuel reserves and allowances shall be used as a guide for instrument flight fuel planning on nonoperational flights.

Landing reserve	2000 pounds
Holding reserve	1500 pounds
GCA allowance	800 pounds
Teardrop penetration	1000 pounds
Arcing penetration with extended low approach	1500 pounds

2. A departure fuel allowance must be provided if an adverse departure must be used.
3. All instrument flights shall be planned to arrive at the approach fix at cruising altitude. Enroute descent fuel savings shall not be planned.

TAKE-OFF

Normal operating procedures apply to preparation for instrument flight, with increased necessity for proper operation of the CNI and lighting systems. Before take-off, make the following additional checks.

CAUTION

To prevent the formation of fog and frost in the cockpit during take-off under conditions of high humidity, or to clear the cockpit anti-ice and defrost ducting system of moisture, set the cockpit temperature control knob at "3" (HOT) during ground engine operation and perform steps 1 and 2 of the following check. Any visible moisture will clear within 10 to 20 seconds.

1. Pitot anti-ice—ON.
2. Windshield and canopy defrost—ON (if required).
3. Windshield anti-ice switch—as required.
4. Pressure suit flow—OFF.
5. Check stand-by gyro horizon.
6. Lighting controls—check.
7. Anticollision lights—ON.

If take-off is made under conditions of extremely reduced visibility, rotate the aircraft to approximately 10 degrees (14 units angle of attack) nose-up pitch attitude as lift-off speed is reached. When catapulted ITO's are made, the flight instruments must be carefully cross-checked for precession produced by the catapult acceleration. A wings level, 1000 fpm climb should be maintained during post-take-off transitions.

Note

After lift-off, an increase in pitch attitude may be required to limit airspeed until landing gear and flaps are retracted.

CLIMB

Under IFR conditions, or at night, it is recommended that 1000 feet of terrain clearance and 200 KIAS be attained before retracting flaps to CRUISE. Turns to departure heading should not be commenced until reaching 1000 feet and a minimum of 250 KIAS. This procedure will avoid low-level turns at changing airspeeds and altitudes. Since Maximum Thrust may result in excessively steep climb angle, Military Thrust is recommended during the instrument portion of departure climbs. The systems operator shall handle all frequency changes below 2500 feet, so that the pilot may devote his full attention to controlling the aircraft.

CRUISE

All instrument flights, except those involving an operational clearance, shall be conducted in accordance with current regulations. All radio traffic involving reports, requests, or acknowledgements, shall be clear and concise. Requests for weather and miscellaneous information should be requested from Pilot-to-Forecaster Service (METRO) or Airways Communications Stations. Pilots shall monitor destination and alternate weather closely, especially when the weather at these two points is marginal. If the weather at the filed alternate station goes below authorized minimums, some other suitable alternate shall be requested or, lacking one, the destination shall be changed.

RADAR NAVIGATION

The AN/ASB-12 radar may be used as a secondary mode of navigation in the event of complete autonavigator failure. Following an autonavigator failure, a fully stabilized radar picture normally remains. Using the fixed range circles, relative bearing scale, and aircraft compass, the systems operator has all the information necessary to obtain navigation fixes, ground speed, and track information.

HOLDING

Holding airspeed is 200 to 250 KIAS, with the flap control switch at CRUISE (5-degree droops). Bank angles of more than 30 degrees may require added power to maintain altitude and airspeed. The following table may be used to determine recommended holding airspeed.

ALTITUDE (FEET)	FUEL REMAINING (LBS X 1000)			
	2	4	6	8
	KNOTS IAS			
10,000	200	215	230	235
20,000	215	220	235	245
30,000	230	235	245	250
40,000	240	245	250	250

DESCENT

Maximum-range enroute descent should be made at IDLE, holding 250 KIAS, speed brakes IN, flaps CRUISE. Rate of descent will average 2500 feet per minute.

PENETRATION

Prior to descent, pitot heat, engine anti-ice, windshield anti-ice, and canopy defrost should be checked ON. Airspeed and altitude control will be smoother if angle of bank is limited to 30 degrees. Normal penetrations will be the published jet penetration for the facility. Maintain 250 KIAS and 4000 feet per minute rate of descent with the speed brakes extended when compatible with the published penetration. At 1000 feet above level-off, close speed brakes while maintaining 250 KIAS. The last 500 feet prior to level-off altitude should be used to slowly transition the aircraft to level flight. GCA pickup from the penetration point will be used whenever possible.

Note

If failure of the cockpit temperature controller causes fog to form in the cockpit upon descent, fog can be dissipated most rapidly by utilizing full windshield and canopy defrost airflow and turning the cockpit pressure switch OFF.

Throughout the penetration, the systems operator should monitor both barometric and radar altitude, keeping the pilot informed of the lower indicated altitude at each 5000-foot level until reaching 5000 feet above terrain; then calling out each 1000-foot level until level-off. At start of descent, a fuel state of 4000 pounds will allow an instrument penetration followed by a wave-off, 150-mile flight to a VFR alternate base with 1000 pounds of fuel remaining at landing.

INSTRUMENT APPROACHES

With the use of TACAN for continuous bearing and distance reference and surface radar for approach and traffic control, the remaining factor in an instrument approach is control of altitude and airspeed. The effectiveness of boundary layer control depends upon maintaining the rpm above 78% until touchdown. See figure 6-1 for suggested typical procedure.

> **CAUTION**
>
> Changes in airspeed exceeding 35 knots per minute during or before turns may cause the all-attitude indicator to display a transient, erroneous wing-down bank attitude indication of up to 5 degrees.

AN/ASB-12 APPROACHES

The execution of successful instrument approaches with AN/ASB-12 equipment to land stations or to carriers is limited only by crew interest, effort, and experience in developing the necessary techniques. All practice and actual weather approaches should be executed with the AN/ASB-12 tracking the station being approached and, if possible, the runway being approached. AN/ASB-12 altitude, range, airspeed, and bearing information can provide the S/O with aids to monitor the pilot's approach which might not otherwise be available. With experience and satisfactory equipment conditions, the AN/ASB-12 may be relied upon as the sole approach aid. The following factors and restrictions must be observed:

1. The AN/ASB-12 system can be used to make an approach under actual instrument conditions or as a navigational aid in following a duly approved and published instrument approach pattern.

2. Measured and reported surface winds will be set into the system when commencing an approach using the stand-by navigation mode.
   This is necessary since automatic wind solution is not available in this mode.

3. The AAI steering signal is accurate for only a few degrees either side of zero.
   For large corrections, the AAI should be crosschecked with the HSI.

4. The HSI needle may be used, as on a normal instrument approach, to maintain proper outbound track, and may also be used on an arcing approach to the station. The HSI or AAI may be used on the initial part of the inbound approach but, for the final approach, the AAI steering display is more sensitive and accurate.

5. In the AN/ASB-12 approach, it is not necessary that the radar aimpoint coincide with the approach end of the runway, but if an offset distance is used, it must be carefully measured prior to the flight.

Any AN/ASB-12 instrument approach depends on the accuracy of either the inertial autonavigator or the flight reference set gyro platform, and air data computer and wind inputs. This accuracy must be monitored and updated throughout the approach.

RECOMMENDED PROCEDURE

The systems operator should store the coordinates of the ADF or TACAN facility and set the SET CORR and NAV/BOMB knobs to this channel. The pilot then selects the NAV position of the RANGE & BEARING knob (HSI) and the systems operator selects the NAV position of the SYSTEM MODE knob. The pilot may then execute a published instrument approach by using the HSI, as on a TACAN or ADF approach. The main limitation is that the pilot cannot select a desired radial for HSI steering. However, when established on an inbound radial, the systems operator may select course line steering (with the OP V tape program) to provide the pilot with AAI steering in order to stay on the radial. During the approach, the S/O should monitor the accuracy of the autonavigator by momentarily switching SET/CORR channels to check cursor position on some known checkpoint.

> **CAUTION**
>
> When distance to the stored ADF or TACAN facility position is less than 20 miles, AAI steering will be erroneous unless course line steering or the BOMB mode is selected.

A more precise final approach is possible if the S/O stores the coordinates of and tracks the approach end of the runway. If the runway cannot be "broken out" of the surrounding radar ground return, a radar-significant point near the end of the runway should be stored in another channel. The operator may then select this channel periodically during the approach for radar cursor corrections. When established on the inbound bearing to the runway, the systems operator should select course line steering for proper tracking.

An alternate method is to track the approach end of the runway or an offset radar target in the BOMB mode (O/S). However, with this procedure, AAI steering is toward the end of the runway, *not* to the inbound bearing. HSI bearing and range indications are toward the offset aimpoint, making lineup for landing transition more difficult. The pilot must be aware of the procedure being used, and he must know when HSI and AAI presentations are correct. In general, for any procedure, the pilot should follow HSI bearing and monitor HSI range during the penetration (AAI course line steering may be utilized when established on an inbound radial), and AAI steering should be used on final approach. (Correct HSI bearing and range will be available when the systems operator has the SET/CORR knob set to the position for the end of the runway and has course line steering selected).

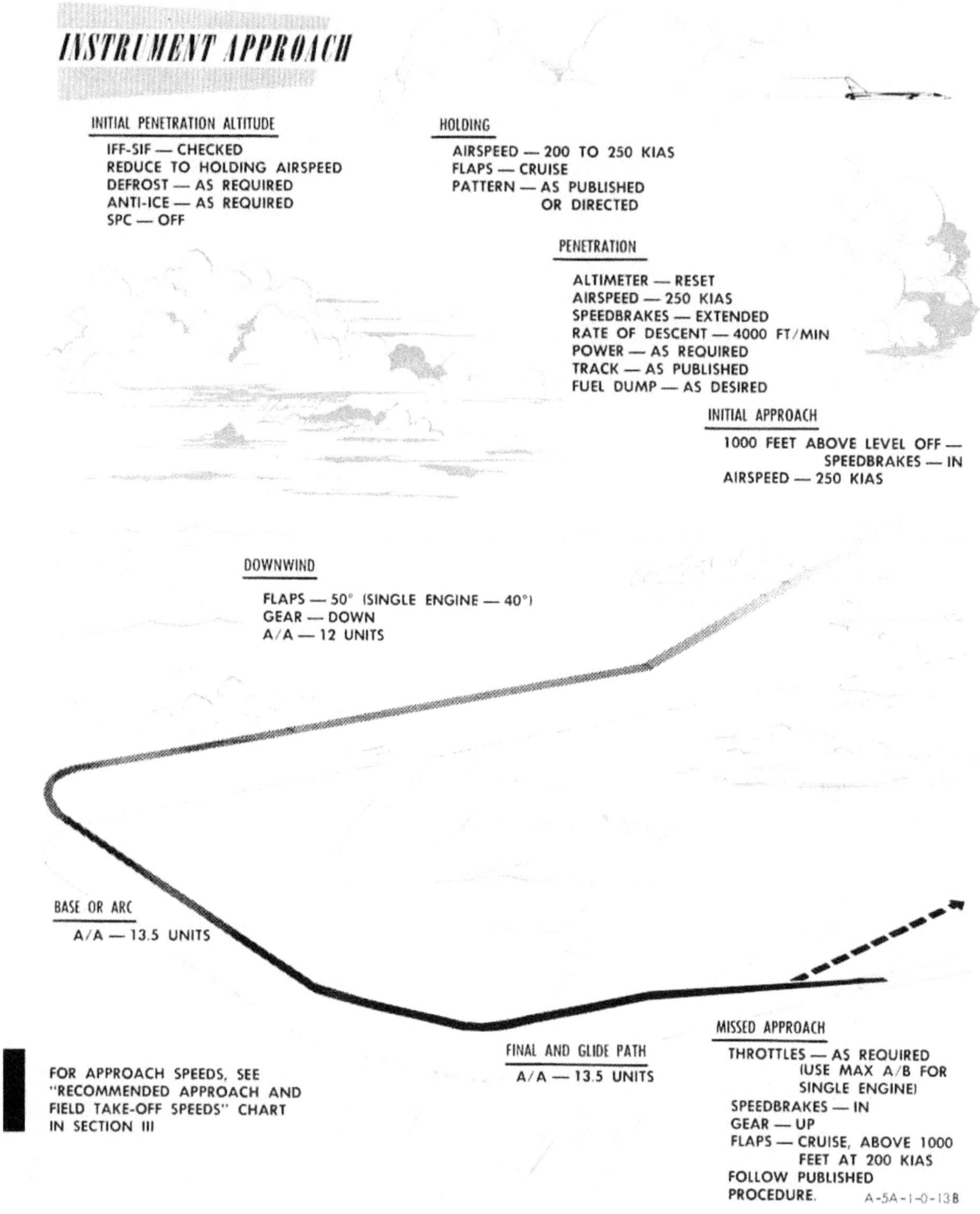

Section VI NAVWEPS 01-60ABA-1

INSTRUMENT APPROACH

INITIAL PENETRATION ALTITUDE
IFF-SIF — CHECKED
REDUCE TO HOLDING AIRSPEED
DEFROST — AS REQUIRED
ANTI-ICE — AS REQUIRED
SPC — OFF

HOLDING
AIRSPEED — 200 TO 250 KIAS
FLAPS — CRUISE
PATTERN — AS PUBLISHED
 OR DIRECTED

PENETRATION
ALTIMETER — RESET
AIRSPEED — 250 KIAS
SPEEDBRAKES — EXTENDED
RATE OF DESCENT — 4000 FT/MIN
POWER — AS REQUIRED
TRACK — AS PUBLISHED
FUEL DUMP — AS DESIRED

INITIAL APPROACH
1000 FEET ABOVE LEVEL OFF —
 SPEEDBRAKES — IN
AIRSPEED — 250 KIAS

DOWNWIND
FLAPS — 50° (SINGLE ENGINE — 40°)
GEAR — DOWN
A/A — 12 UNITS

BASE OR ARC
A/A — 13.5 UNITS

FINAL AND GLIDE PATH
A/A — 13.5 UNITS

MISSED APPROACH
THROTTLES — AS REQUIRED
 (USE MAX A/B FOR
 SINGLE ENGINE)
SPEEDBRAKES — IN
GEAR — UP
FLAPS — CRUISE, ABOVE 1000
 FEET AT 200 KIAS
FOLLOW PUBLISHED
PROCEDURE.

FOR APPROACH SPEEDS, SEE
"RECOMMENDED APPROACH AND
FIELD TAKE-OFF SPEEDS" CHART
IN SECTION III

A-5A-1-0-13B

Figure 6-1

Carrier Approaches

An AN/ASB-12 instrument approach to a carrier may be accomplished by periodically acquiring the ship in RECON mode and using the same penetration procedures as those used to a shore base. The final approach, however, should be made in the normal (ground-mapping) radar mode, with steering, lineup, relative bearing, and range information being called out to the pilot. If operating in STBY-NAV mode, false winds may be set in so that the system "tracks" the ship. The same final approach technique may then be used as is used during an approach to a shore station.

Voice Procedure

A constant flow of information between the system operator and the pilot is required to accomplish an AN/ASB-12 instrument approach. The following is an example of crew communcations procedure:

1. S/O: "Your outbound heading is 290, maintain HSI bearing 110 to NRJ."
2. S/O: "Shifting channels for cursor correction, maintain heading, disregard HSI."
3. S/O: "Cursor correction complete, HSI on NRJ."
4. Pilot: "Fifteen miles out, commencing penetration."
5. Pilot: "Commencing penetration turn, 14,000 feet."
6. S/O: "NRJ bears 098 at 20 miles, should bear 094."
7. S/O: "On bearing, course line steering selected, follow AAI steering."
8. Pilot: "Sixteeen miles out, altitude 2500."
9. S/O: "Shifting channels to runway coordinates, course line steering out, fly HSI to 090 bearing."
10. S/O: "On bearing, course line steering selected, follow AAI steering."
11. Pilot: "Seven-mile Gate, gear and flaps down, check list complete."
12. S/O: "Shifting channels for cursor correction, HSI on tower, AAI steering to runway, follow AAI."
13. S/O: Cursor correction complete, HSI and AAI on end of runway, follow AAI."
14. S/O: "Range 4½ miles, intercepting glide slope."
15. S/O: "Range 3 miles, your altitude should be 1000 feet MSL."
16. S/O: "Range 2 miles, your altitude should be 700 feet."
17. S/O: "Range 1½ miles, your altitude should be 550 feet, ½ mile from approach minimums."
18. S/O: "At approach minimums."
19. Pilot: "I have the runway in sight."

The systems operator should monitor all instrument approaches to gain proficiency in providing the pilot with accurate steering, lineup, bearing, and range information. In addition, the S/O should act as a safety observer on all approaches, using the appropriate approach plate and local charts while monitoring heading, airspeed, and altitude throughout the approach.

WARNING

The systems operator's ALTITUDE mode knob should be maintained in RADAR position for IFR approaches and altitude and true airspeed should be closely monitored throughout all approaches.

LOW-VISIBILITY APPROACHES

The low-visibility approach procedure provides final approach alinement for landing, when misalinement existed at visual pickup. The procedure is essentially a close in orientation to a circling approach and shall not be used in conditions less than those authorized for a circling approach.

EXECUTION

The aircraft should be in the power approach configuration.

1. Maintain contact with the ground; if lost, execute a missed approach.
2. Turn the shorter arc to fly the aircraft *over* the desired runway, parallel to it.
3. If proceeding upwind, immediately perform an 80—260-degree turn to proceed downwind *over* the desired runway.
4. Proceed downwind and, after passing over the approach end of the desired runway, perform an 80—260-degree turn. Commence descent to landing coming out of the 260-degree turn with the runway in sight.

HAZARDS

The low-visibility approach is not an approved maneuver except as a form of circling approach. It is not a means of salvaging a missed approach to a straight in approach if at such minima. It is not an invitation to half-instrument and half-contact flight, nor should it be combined with the transition to landing configuration. Again, if contact flight with reference to the ground is not possible, a missed approach shall be executed.

TYPICAL APPROACH

See figure 6-1 for suggested typical penetration and approach procedure. IFF and bearing indicator equipment may be desirable for assistance in orientation and traffic control under adverse conditions. Check static pressure compensator button off before final approach. An angle-of-attack indication of 13.5 units should be used for final approach.

NIGHT FLIGHT

Night flight in this aircraft presents no additional problems. Both crew members should have a reliable flashlight and should be familiar with the location of all switches and controls. Aircraft lighting and flight instruments should be checked completely before take-off. The aircraft is not equipped with landing lights; however, the nose-gear-mounted taxi light is provided for night ground operation.

FLIGHT IN TURBULENCE

Flight in light to moderate turbulence presents no serious problems. Use of the AFCS will improve the damping of undesirable aircraft motions. In moderate to severe turbulence, however, use of the AFCS is not recommended, as it may monitor off abruptly due to severe gust loads. In instrument flight conditions, its loss can induce vertigo if the pilot is not holding the stick. The relatively long moment arm between the crew and the aircraft cg aggravates the effects of severe turbulence, and the crew should keep shoulder harnesses locked to avoid injury. Instruments become blurred, making accurate interpretation impossible. Increasing airspeed increases the effects of turbulence; however, too slow an airspeed may result in engine compressor and/or aircraft stall, particularly at altitudes above 35,000 feet. The following subsonic airspeeds are recommended for flight through severe turbulence and thunderstorms:

Below 35,000 feet	250—300 KIAS
35,000 to 40,000 feet	270 KIAS to 0.92 IMN

Subsonic operations in severe turbulence above 40,000 feet are not recommended; supersonic operations in severe weather have not been evaluated at this time.

THUNDERSTORM PENETRATION

Whenever possible, flight through thunderstorms and areas of heavy precipitation should be avoided by alternate routing, vectoring by ground radar facilities, or in-flight use of the AN/ASB-12 radar. Attempting to climb above severe weather, increases the possibility of compressor stall or aircraft stall at high altitudes and low airspeeds. If penetration is unavoidable, the pilot must prepare for the disorienting effects of severe turbulence, precipitation (in the forms of hail, ice, and rain), lightning strikes, and rapid fluctuation of pitot-static instruments. The following procedures are recommended prior to entry:

1. Stabilize on penetration altitude, airspeed and attitude, using the speeds recommended above for flight in severe turbulence.
   If necessary, use afterburner to maintain minimum speeds.
2. Turn on high-altitude lights.
3. Lower helmet visor.
4. Turn on engine and pitot anti-ice switches.
5. Lock shoulder harness.
6. Maintain heading and a level attitude by reference to the AAI, using the stand-by gyro horizon as a backup.
   Do not chase altitude and airspeed.
7. Do not extend landing gear or flaps as structural damage may result.

Note

The stand-by compass may not be reliable if the aircraft is struck by lightning.

Completion of a training mission does not warrant penetration of a known thunderstorm.

ICE AND RAIN

This aircraft is not equipped to fly continuously in icing conditions. Flights shall be planned to avoid altitudes of prolonged icing. No provision is made for in-flight structural anti-icing. At moderate- to high-speed flight, impact pressure is sufficient to prevent ice build-up. Should heavy clear ice be encountered, an immediate climb should be made in order to clear the icing area. For penetrations through icing or rain, the WINDSHIELD ANTI-ICE switch should be placed in the ON position and maintained until landing is accomplished. The canopy defrosting system should be turned on well in advance of a descent to avoid fogging.

Note

If relative humidity conditions result in fogging during take-off or letdown, the cockpit temperature control can be increased to the maximum until the fog clears, at which time the heat can be lowered to a more comfortable setting.

PITOT-STATIC ICE

The PITOT ANTI-ICE button should be depressed prior to and during flight through visible moisture to prevent unreliable readings of the pitot-static system instruments.

Note

Pitot line freezing may occur when the aircraft is operated in cirrus-type clouds for extended periods of time. Melted ice crystals can reach the rear of the pitot-static tube and freeze at the connections. The pitot heater should be turned ON prior to penetration. If freezing occurs, it may be indicated by an erroneous indicated airspeed increase when altitude is increased. If this condition is noted, the angle-of-attack indicator should be used to maintain a safe attitude until aircraft altitude is decreased to a level where melting of the ice will occur.

CAUTION

Failure of the pitot anti-icing system is not positively indicated to the pilot. Should such failure allow icing to occur, the inlet duct variable ramps may be driven toward the down position, causing engine airflow reduction and possible flame-out.

ADC MOISTURE

The presence of excessive moisture in the air data computer may cause erratic, unreliable readings in airspeed, Mach number, and altitude. This is indicated by radical transients in the flight instruments and/or a barber-pole indication on the systems operator's radar/barometric altimeter. Should this occur, depress to release the static pressure compensator button and utilize the uncorrected indications of airspeed, Mach number, and altitude.

COCKPIT FOG

Under warm, humid conditions, or when the aircraft has been subjected to soaking precipitation, heavy cockpit fog and instrument frosting may form during operation at high engine power settings unless cockpit temperature has been raised sufficiently to warm the cockpit area. In addition, windshield and canopy defrost should be utilized to prevent frosting. If accomplished prior to take-off, this procedure reduces the possibility of heavy fogging and reduces frosting as high altitudes are reached. Under humid conditions, it is recommended that the cockpit temperature knob be placed at approximately the mid-position (2) and that the windshield and canopy defrost knob be turned on to a low setting as soon as the engines are started.

ENGINE ICING

The effect of moisture or icing conditions on engine operation, although predictable, is difficult to quickly and accurately detect from engine instruments. Generally, the magnitude of changes in instrument indication is small. For example, changes noted after 5 to 10 minutes of exposure to icing conditions are similar to changes resulting from an increase in altitude of 3000 feet or a decrease in Mach number of 0.15. Therefore, the absence of marked changes in indication with respect to time, and the relatively small magnitude of change, would require almost continuous monitoring of engine instruments to detect engine inlet icing. In addition to the presence of freezing moisture, other factors (such as altitude, throttle setting, rate of water and/or ice ingestion, and the amount of ice buildup) affect the direction and amount of change in engine parameters. For example, high water or ice ingestion rates can affect engine speed holding capability. At extreme ingestion rates (i.e., thunderstorms or heavy rain), engine speed will decay as a function of the water/airflow ratio. Ice buildup on the compressor inlet during high-altitude flight decreases compressor efficiency and, under extreme conditions, can result in compressor stall and engine flame-out. The number of possible interactive effects of all factors on engine instrument indication are so numerous that detection is difficult, if not impossible.

There are two basic forms of engine or inlet duct icing: water ingestion in the form of water or ice, and ice buildup on the compressor inlet surfaces. Both forms have distinct characteristics; however, actual icing progression usually begins with ingestion and culminates in combined ingestion and ice buildup. This progression requires approximately 6 to 10 minutes. Since a relatively long time is required for this progression, there will be no sudden change in engine instrument indications.

INGESTION OF ICE AND WATER

When ice and water are ingested, evaporation in the engine compressor occurs, reducing pressures and temperatures. The direction of engine parameter change will depend, however, upon engine power setting.

Low Power Settings

At low power settings (exhaust nozzles mechanically scheduled), EGT and fuel flow decrease, while nozzle position and rpm hold constant. Since the nozzle is on the fixed mechanical schedule, lowered engine temperatures caused by water evaporation will result in a decrease in EGT and fuel flow. Engine rpm holding capability will be relatively unaffected except at extreme ingestion rates.

High Power Settings

At cruise, Military Thrust, and Maximum Thrust settings (exhaust nozzles modulate to maintain EGT at rated maximum), nozzle area decreases, fuel flow increases, and rpm and EGT hold constant. At throttle settings above approximately 92% rpm, the exhaust nozzle controllers will decrease nozzle area to maintain EGT as the water evaporates. Decreased nozzle area increases tailpipe pressure, requiring an increase in fuel flow to maintain engine speed. If ingestion rate increases, the nozzles close to the minimum area scheduled by the throttle and engine operation is the same as covered under LOW POWER SETTINGS.

ICE BUILDUP

The effects of ice buildup on the compressor inlet surfaces are usually obscured by the presence of ingestion characteristics occurring simultaneously. Ice buildup results in a condition similar to engine operation at low ram pressure recovery.

Low Power Settings

At low power settings (exhaust nozzle on mechanical schedule), EGT and fuel flow increase, while nozzle position and rpm hold constant. Engine pressures are low at 80% rpm and below, and further reduction of engine pressures from ice buildup results in an increase in EGT and fuel flow.

High Power Settings

At cruise, Military Thrust, and Maximum Thrust settings (exhaust nozzle modulates to maintain EGT at rated maximum), nozzle position and fuel flow decrease, while EGT and rpm hold constant. Reduction of engine pressures from ice buildup at high engine speed tends to reduce fuel flow. Reduction in fuel flow tends to lower EGT. The nozzle control system senses the change and reduces nozzle area to maintain a constant EGT.

RECOMMENDATIONS

Serious ice buildup can occur before a significant change is noted in the engine instruments. Therefore, engine instruments should NOT be relied upon for diagnosing possible engine icing conditions. Move the ENGINE ANTI-ICE switch to ON and depress the PITOT ANTI-ICE button whenever free air temperature is 5°C or less, or prior to entering any known or suspected area of icing conditions.

COLD WEATHER PROCEDURES

PREFLIGHT

When ambient temperature is below 32°F, it may be necessary to preheat the electronic equipment compartments. Sudden surges of electrical power through extremely cold components may result in serious damage due to sudden heat expansion. In extremely cold weather, avoid touching metal surfaces with bare hands. Hot air should also be directed into the intake ducts, the landing gear wells, and the cockpits. This procedure will evaporate moisture which may have collected and frozen under controls, microswitches, etc. Ensure that all ice, snow, and frost accumulation is removed from all aircraft surfaces and activating linkages prior to flight. At starting ambient temperatures below -40°F, MIL-L-7808 engine oil should be used in place of the normally prescribed MIL-L-23699 (Wep) oil.

WARNING

Failure to remove all ice, snow, and frost from all aircraft surfaces could result in dangerous disruption of airflow characteristics and loss of lift.

GROUND OPERATION

Exercise caution when running up the engines since wheels and chocks frequently slide on ice or snow. For engine check above idle rpm, aircraft should be tied down. Taxi and take-off procedures on ice-covered taxiways and runways are hazardous. The full-power brakes may act to hinder rather than to aid in taxiing. *USE NOSE WHEEL STEERING AT ALL TIMES WHEN TAXIING ON SLIPPERY SURFACES.* If necessary, have the aircraft towed to a point close to the runway before starting engines. On icy taxiways, once a skid is started, the aircraft may slide a considerable distance before control can be regained, even when using nose wheel steering. Always taxi *SLOWLY* using a minimum of power and brakes. The retarding effect of soft snow or slush on the runway will lengthen the take-off ground run.

WET OR ICY RUNWAYS

The increase in rollout distance on wet or icy runways depends on the braking conditions encountered. Normal landings with an increase of 1000 to 1500 feet of ground roll may be accomplished on wet runways where precipitation has stopped and drainage occurred. A landing in rain or on standing water may result in up to 75 percent increase in normal rollout distance. Cross-wind conditions may affect wet or icy runway landings to an equal degree in that safe aerodynamic braking is limited. In

general, a wet runway landing should be accomplished by using the recommended final approach speed, touching down in the first 500 feet of the runway. If crosswind conditions permit, use nose-high aerodynamic braking. The nose should be held off down to 100 knots, then allowed to drop with the stick full aft. Continue to hold the stick as far aft as possible and commence cautious, steady braking. If a yaw develops, cease braking and use nose wheel steering. Continue to hold the stick aft, and as speed decreases, increase brake pressure until taxi speed is reached. For icy runways, the same factors are involved except that stopping distance may be increased by more than 100 percent. For "patchy" ice conditions, extreme care must be taken to brake on clear runway and to reduce braking on ice to prevent skidding when passing from ice to clear runway. Except for possible yawing, wheel lock is difficult to detect, and a tire may fail without warning. For landings on wet or icy runways, prepare for field arrestment if gear is available.

POSTFLIGHT

Attempt to park the aircraft on a clear spot if possible. Make sure the wheels are properly chocked and tiedowns installed before making any postflight engine run-ups. All aircraft covers and plugs should be installed immediately after postflight inspection.

HOT WEATHER PROCEDURES
PREFLIGHT

In hot weather, the aircraft surfaces may become extremely hot. Crew members and ground maintenance personnel should wear gloves to prevent injury. In extreme heat, the pilot should make as many of his operational checks as possible before starting engines. Before entering the aircraft, complete normal preflight items and devote particular attention to the following:

1. Check intake ducts for accumulated sand, etc.
2. Check tires, seals, and antenna covers for cracks and blisters.
3. Cockpit covers should be left on as long as possible to prevent excessive heating of metal surfaces and controls in the cockpit.
4. Check canopies for excessive scratches, particularly before night flight.

GROUND OPERATION

After engines are started, taxi rpm in hot temperature areas should be the lowest practical rpm for aircraft movement desired. Overheating of brakes is critical in hot weather. In most cases, small quantities of sand do no harm in passing through a turbojet engine; however, during hot weather and desert operation, pilots are reminded to:

1. Make ground run-up as short as possible.
2. With an operational bomb directing set and ambient temperature above 50°F, depress the AUX B/N COOLING button.
3. Avoid running up engines toward equipment or personnel, even from longer than usual distances. Sand blast can result in serious damage to other aircraft and injury to ground personnel.

Double-check the flight control system for proper operation and freedom of control surface movement. Hydraulic pressures which exceed or fall short of limitations should not be accepted as normal. Should system pressures exceed upper limits, return to the line and have accumulator pressures checked. Adjust cockpit air conditioning to desired temperature. If ALT COOL caution indicator is ON, reset when engine rpm is above 85%.

TAKE-OFF AND CLIMB

Power required for take-off in hot weather will depend upon aircraft configuration, weight, ambient temperature, and field elevation. During extremely hot weather and at high field elevations, maximum afterburner is recommended to avoid a prolonged take-off. This power setting should also be used to accelerate to best climb speed.

LANDING

Use of higher than normal power settings can be expected during landing approaches in hot weather. Expect gusts and turbulence at low altitudes and anticipate longer landing rollout.

POSTFLIGHT

If possible, park the aircraft cross-wind to prevent sand or dust from collecting in the intake ducts or tail pipes. Canopies should be closed and wing tips and tail should be spread and locked. All covers and plugs should be installed immediately after the postflight inspection.

SIMULATED INSTRUMENT FLIGHT

Hooded instrument take-offs will not be practiced. Simulated instrument flying under the hood will require a chase aircraft which will conduct radio checks once every 5 minutes above 10,000 feet or once a minute below 10,000 feet. The lookout chase will advise the instrument aircraft by clock code of any approaching aircraft. The instrument pilot will pop the hood and advise whether or not the aircraft is sighted. The chase pilot will continuously advise the instrument pilot of the intruding aircraft's position until it is clear or seen by the instrument pilot.

The chase pilot will fly as close formation as possible, consistent with the maneuver being performed:

1. On GCA the chase will fly 500 feet above and 500 feet astern at either the 5- or 7-o'clock position so as to be on the outside of all turns.
2. Enough separation to avoid undue concentration on formation flight vice lookout duties will be maintained.

Should the instrument pilot not receive the prescribed radio checks, or lose radio communication with the chase, he will immediately pop the hood. Should the chase pilot lose radio contact with the instrument pilot, he will fly ahead of the instrument pilot so as to cause the instrument pilot to fly through his slip stream. If the instrument pilot feels unusual turbulence, he will pop his hood.

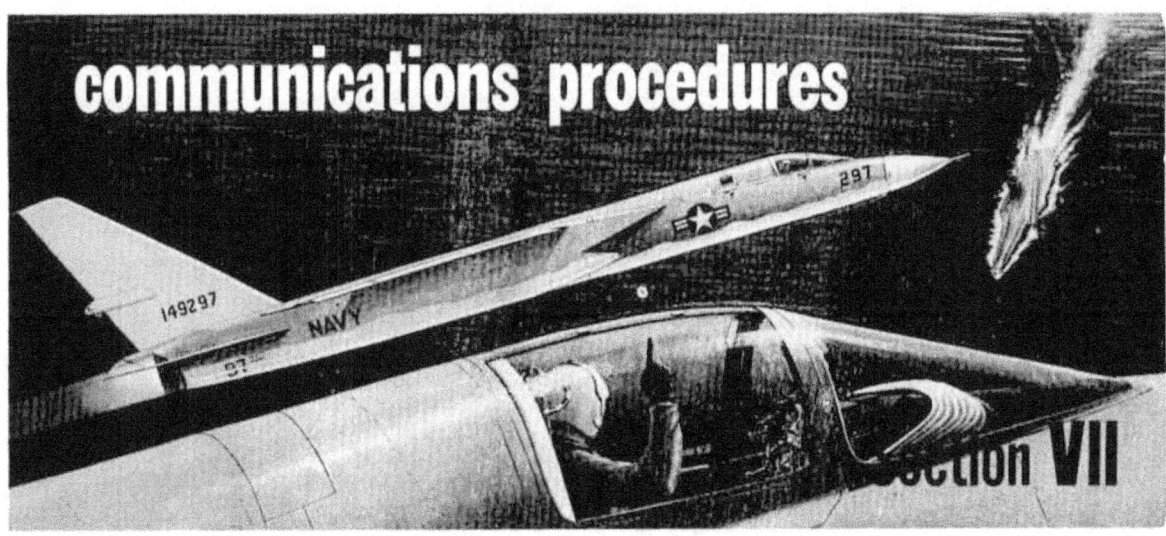

communications procedures

TABLE OF CONTENTS

Responsibility 191
Radio Communications and
   Electronic Navigation Equipment 191
Visual Communications 191
Intercommunications System Failure 192

RESPONSIBILITY

It is the responsibility of the pilot to ensure that all voice and visual communications and electronic transmissions from his aircraft are in compliance with applicable directives.

RADIO COMMUNICATIONS AND ELECTRONIC NAVIGATION EQUIPMENT

Adhere to the following instructions:

1. Do not interrupt another transmission.
2. Make only necessary transmissions.
3. Keep all transmissions brief and concise.
4. Use the phonetic alphabet.
5. Use approved phraseology.
6. Have message prepared before beginning transmission.
7. Use correct calls.
8. Be familiar with the Communications Section of USAF/USN FLIP Planning Document.

Note

Monitor GUARD frequency (243.0 mc) at all times. Do not transmit on GUARD except in an actual emergency.

RADIO COMMUNICATION EQUIPMENT

Multichannel/frequency UHF is the sole means of two-way voice communications. The systems operator will carry a copy of the current frequency plan for UHF on all flights. The auxiliary receiver may be used as a backup communications receiver.

ELECTRONIC NAVIGATION EQUIPMENT

The aircraft contains three electronic aids to navigation:
1. TACAN.
2. UHF airborne direction finder.
3. Bomb directing set, AN/ASB-12.

IFF/SIF PROCEDURES

Aircraft operating within the CONUS will operate the IFF/SIF equipment to conform with OPNAV/FAA regulations. During carrier operations, IFF will be operated as prescribed by current directives.

AUTHENTICATION

Authentication will be in accordance with the appropriate KAC-series, or as assigned by the Operational Commander.

EMERGENCY COMMUNICATIONS

Comply with OPNAV Instructions and the steps on the inside rear cover of FLIP, Enroute Supplement. Refer to Section V for aircraft distress reporting.

VISUAL COMMUNICATIONS
BETWEEN AIRCRAFT

Communications between aircraft within a formation will be conducted visually whenever practicable, provided no sacrifice in operational efficiency is involved.

Flight leaders will ensure that all aircraft in the formation receive and acknowledge signals when given. Visual signals as set forth in NWP 41(A) will be used. For emergency signaling, the FAA standard HEFOE system should be used:

1 finger	H	Hydraulic
2 fingers	E	Electrical
3 fingers	F	Fuel
4 fingers	O	Oxygen
5 fingers	E	Engine

INTERCOMMUNICATIONS SYSTEM FAILURE

If an ICS failure is experienced, the following procedures should be attempted in order to establish some degree of communications between the pilot and the systems operator.

IF PILOT LOSES ICS

To attract the systems operator's attention, proceed as follows:

1. Turn the MASTER ARM switch on and off three times.
   This will flash the systems operator's ARM MAST'R ON light.

2. Dial 333.3 on the UHF radio frequency indicator.

3. The systems operator will acknowledge by taking command of the UHF radio and redialing 333.3.

IF SYSTEMS OPERATOR LOSES ICS

To attract the pilot's attention, proceed as follows:

1. Stamp feet on cockpit floor.

2. The pilot will acknowledge by taking command of the UHF radio and dialing 333.3.

3. Refer to LOST ICS—UHF CODE in the NATOPS Pocket Check List (NAVWEPS 01-60ABA-1B).

BOTH CREW MEMBERS

Upon receiving the loss of ICS signal, both crew members will refer to LOST ICS—UHF CODE procedure in their NATOPS Pocket Check List. The following codes will be used for further communication:

333.3 Select LOST ICS—UHF CODE.
333.0 Prepare to Eject.
333.1 Squawk MAYDAY.
333.2 Squawk PAN.
333.4 Heading to nearest airfield?
333.5 Commence Emergency Descent.
333.6 Oxygen Inoperative.
333.7 Prepare to land.
333.8 Returning to home field (carrier).
333.9 TACAN Out.

320.0 Are you OK?
320.1 I read you OK.
320.2 TACAN OK.
320.3 Can we continue run?
320.4 Select proper wing station.
320.5 Follow AAI.
320.6 Depress B/N SYS button.
320.7 Select MASTER ARM—ON.
320.8 Affirmative (Yes).
320.9 Negative (No).

310.0 My UHF OK.
310.1 AAI to Home.
310.2 AAI to Nearest Airfield.
310.3 Wheels and flaps down for landing.
310.4
310.5
310.6
310.7
310.8
310.9

Note

- Use codes 310.4 through 310.9 as locally directed or as prebriefed between individual crew members.
- Before selecting a UHF frequency for transmitting, dial GUARD (243.0 mc) momentarily to let the other crew member know that the next frequency selected will be a transmitting frequency.
- The LOST ICS—UHF CODE procedure in the NATOPS Pocket Check List (NAVWEPS 01-60ABA-1B) should be used for in-flight reference.

weapon systems
Section VIII

TABLE OF CONTENTS

Armament Systems 193
Weapons Delivery 193

ARMAMENT SYSTEMS

Description and operation of aircraft armament systems are covered in Section I, Part 2, of the Supplemental NATOPS Flight Manual (NAVWEPS 01-60ABA-1A). For weapon delivery tactics, special check lists, and planning and delivery forms, refer to NWIP 41-3(A).

WEAPONS DELIVERY

METHODS

The heavy attack mission requires the delivery of special or conventional weapons in all weather conditions, including tactical support for this capability. Delivery methods used are:

1. Horizontal bombing, all-weather level:
    High level (above 55,000 feet).
    Medium level.
    Low level or laydown.

2. Maneuvering, all-weather:
    Loft, medium angle.
    Over-the-shoulder, high angle.
    Pop-up from low-altitude approach.

3. Visual bombing:
    Dive.
    Dive toss.
    Low level.

4. Alternate LABS, visual:
    Loft, medium angle.
    Over-the-shoulder, high angle.
    Laydown.

LOADING AND SAFETY PRECAUTIONS

Refer to Supplemental Handbook, Special Stores for Navy Model A-5A Aircraft (NAVWEPS 01-60ABA-13). Special weapons check lists for the A-5A are as follows:

SPECIAL WEAPON	CHECK LIST
MK 27 (Internal)	NAVWEPS 01-60ABA-15
MK 28 (Internal)	NAVWEPS 01-60ABA-16
MK 28 (External)	NAVWEPS 01-60ABA-17
MK 43 (External)	NAVWEPS 01-60ABA-18
MK 57 (External)	NAVWEPS 01-60ABA-19

ATTACK CHECK LISTS

Refer to Section IX of the Supplemental NATOPS Flight Manual (NAVWEPS 01-60ABA-1A) and to the NATOPS Pocket Check List (NAVWEPS 01-60ABA-1B).

standardization and evaluation

TABLE OF CONTENTS

PART 1—STANDARDIZATION EVALUATION
 PROGRAM 197
Concept 197
Ground Evaluation (Phases I and II) 198
Flight Evaluation (Phase III) 199
Grading Instructions 200
Forms and Records 210
Critique 210

PART 2—A-5A PILOT/SYSTEMS OPERATOR
 STANDARDIZATION EVALUATION FORM.. 211

PART 3—PILOT STANDARDIZATION EVALU-
 ATION WORKSHEETS 215

PART 4—SYSTEMS OPERATOR STANDARDI-
 ZATION EVALUATION WORKSHEETS 233

PART 1 — STANDARDIZATION EVALUATION PROGRAM

CONCEPT

The standard operating procedures described in Section I through IX represent the standardized methods of operating the aircraft. The ground and flight evaluations are intended to evaluate both individual and unit compliance with these procedures. The evaluations performed by the Standardization Instructor and the Standardization Evaluator are designed to aid the Unit Commanding Officer in improving individual and unit effectiveness through objective observation and constructive comments.

APPLICABILITY

The standardization evaluation check will be administered annually to all pilots and systems operators maintaining a current status.

IMPLEMENTATION

The standardization evaluation check will be conducted in accordance with the instructions of the Type Commander; however, instruction in and observation of individual and unit adherence to standard operating procedures must be on a day-to-day basis within each unit to realize maximum benefit.

DEFINITIONS

The following definitions will apply to terms used in this section.

GRADING CRITERIA

The parts of this section that prescribe the standards to be used in determining grades as a result of the performance observed or recorded during the standardization evaluation check.

STANDARDIZATION EVALUATION RECHECK

A standardization evaluation check administered to a pilot/systems operator who has been placed in an unqualified status. Only those areas in which an unsatisfactory level of knowledge or adherence to prescribed procedures is indicated will be observed during this check.

EMERGENCY

An aircraft component or system failure, or a condition that requires instantaneous recognition, analysis, and proper action.

MALFUNCTION

An aircraft component or system failure, or a condition that requires recognition and analysis, but which permits more deliberate action than that required for an emergency.

AREA

A routine of flight preparation, flight, and postflight procedures which is observed and graded during a standardization evaluation flight.

SUB-AREA

That portion of an area that covers a specific single procedure or a particular aspect of maneuver performance, and which is covered by a separate portion of the flight grading criteria, such as airspeed control on an instrument approach.

CRITICAL AREA

Any major area or sub-area which covers items of significant importance to the overall mission requirement or the marginal performance of which would jeopardize safe conduct of the flight. An unqualified rating in any critical area will result in an overall grade of Unqualified. Critical areas, sub-areas, or questions are preceded by an asterisk on the worksheet and in the grading criteria.

MINOR DISCREPANCIES AND/OR OMISSIONS

Minor discrepancies and/or omissions which will not adversely affect the successful completion of the mission or jeopardize the safety of the crew and/or equipment.

MOMENTARY DEVIATIONS

Deviations from the tolerances set forth in the grading criteria which are momentary in nature, and which will not be considered in marking, provided the individual being checked is alert in applying corrective action and the deviation does not jeopardize the safety of the aircraft or crew. Momentary deviations beyond the limitations prescribed for Conditionally Qualified will not be cause for downgrading unless the limit in question is marked with a double asterisk. Cumulative momentary deviations may result in downgrading in the applicable area or sub-area.

QUALIFIED (Q)

A reliable pilot or S/O who has good knowledge of standard operating procedures and thorough understanding of aircraft capabilities and limitations.

CONDITIONALLY QUALIFIED (CQ)

A pilot or S/O who meets the minimum acceptable standards and is considered safe, and who is qualified to fly the aircraft solo/unchased. He needs more practice in specific areas to become qualified, and such flying may be of the self-practice type.

UNQUALIFIED (U)

A pilot or S/O who fails to meet minimum acceptable standards as established by these criteria. He should have supervised instruction until he has gained a Qualified or Conditionally Qualified rating.

GROUND EVALUATION (PHASES I AND II)

The ground evaluation consists of two parts. Phase I is comprised of an open book and a closed book written examination and an oral walkaround exam on preflight and servicing. Phase II consists of a WST crew mission with emphasis placed on emergency procedures for the pilot and systems malfunctions for the S/O.

ORAL EXAMINATION

The oral examination will cover selected items of the aircraft preflight inspection. In addition, the pilot will demonstrate knowledge of the A-5A servicing procedure sufficient to show that he could satisfactorily supervise the servicing of his aircraft by jet maintenance personnel (not trained for the A-5A) at a strange field.

WRITTEN EXAMINATION

A bank of questions and answers will be maintained by the replacement squadron for the purpose of compiling the written examination. Examinations will be made up from these question banks by Instructors and Evaluators as they are required. Examinations will be kept in the custody of the Instructor or Evaluator concerned. The Evaluators will be responsible for the distribution, coordination, and updating of questions and answers.

OPEN BOOK

The open book examination will comprise 50 percent of the written examination for both the pilot and the S/O.

CLOSED BOOK

The closed book examination will comprise 50 percent of the written examination for both the pilot and the S/O.

COMPOSITION

Written examination questions will be taken from the sources in the percentages shown:

SOURCE	OPEN (percent)	CLOSED (percent)
PILOT		
1. NATOPS Flight Manual	30	35
2. NWIP's, NWP's	5	—
3. Supplemental NATOPS Flight Manual	10	10
4. Station Manual	5	5
SYSTEMS OPERATOR		
1. Supplemental NATOPS Flight Manual	15	35
2. A-5A Supplement, NWIP 41-3(A)	10	—
3. Flight Planning Document	10	10
4. Enroute Supplement	10	5
5. NATOPS Flight Manual	5	—

WEAPONS SYSTEM TRAINER (WST) PROCEDURES CHECK

The WST check will be a crew mission check emphasizing emergency procedures and normal procedures not observable in the flight check. The pilot grading form utilized on this check is shown in Part 3 of this section. (The S/O grading form will be published when available.)

Emphasis will be placed on the pilot's knowledge of emergency procedures and the navigator's knowledge of AN/ASB-12 system malfunctions and corrections. Normal procedures will be graded as they occur, but a grade of Unqualified in a critical area concerning normal procedures will not cause the check to be graded as Unqualified, unless Phase III is waived.

Where it is not possible to conduct WST checks for the crew, an oral examination will be administered, covering emergency procedures as outlined in Part 3. A WST check must be administered, however, in every case where Phase III is waived.

NAMT SYSTEMS CHECK

The NAMT systems check is not applicable to this manual.

FLIGHT EVALUATION (Phase III)

The flight evaluation is designed to measure the degree of standardization demonstrated by pilots and navigators in as objective a way as possible. Although the check is not meant to grade proficiency or ability, objectivity requires the use of certain limits in order to measure all flight crew members against a recognized and realistic standard. These limits have been established with the idea in mind that the vast majority of flight crew members who consistently follow standard procedures should have no difficulty staying within them.

FLIGHT EVALUATION GRADING MATERIAL

The observations of the In-flight Evaluator will be recorded on a knee-pad grading form (Part 3 of this section). This form is designed to direct the Evaluator's attention to particular items at the time they should be observed, and, in so doing, to facilitate the collection of facts rather than opinion.

The data observed by the Evaluator and recorded on the knee-pad form will be compared with the grading criteria in order that the actions performed in flight may be graded according to an absolutely objective scale. Each area of the flight check is set forth in subsections.

In order to record the grades achieved in each area and sub-area of the flight check, an evaluation report form (Part 2 of this section) will be made out for each flight crew member on every flight evaluation.

FLIGHT EVALUATION SCORE

The flight evaluation is designed to evaluate the flight crew member's standardization in every area of flight normally encountered in a mission. In those instances where all areas cannot be evaluated, the cognizant Standardization Evaluator will determine whether or not the flight will be counted as a completed check or must be reflown. In each case where all areas are not graded, the In-flight Evaluator/Instructor must include the reasons therefore, with his remarks on the evaluation report form if a waiver is being requested. The Standardization Evaluator will review each such situation individually and will grant or reject each request for a waiver, based on the individual merits of the case. Waivers will be granted or rejected in writing, with appropriate remarks, in the evaluation report form.

FLIGHT EVALUATION (PILOT)

The major areas and sub-areas listed below are those areas where adherence to standard operating procedures will be graded.

Note

An asterisk indicates a critical area, sub-area, or question, unless otherwise indicated, in Part 1.

MISSION PLANNING
1. Route Planning
2. Fuel Planning
3. Flight Plan
4. Take-off Computations

*PREFLIGHT
*1. Acceptance of the Aircraft
2. Preflight Inspection

*TAXI, TAKE-OFF, AND CLIMB-OUT
*1. Taxi
*2. Take-off
*3. Climb-out

CRUISE
1. Aircraft Control
2. Communications

*INSTRUMENTS
*1. Flight Planning
*2. Instrument Departure
*3. Cruise
*4. Holding/Penetration/Approach
*5. GCA

*EMERGENCIES
*1. Engine Malfunctions
*2. Fuel System Failures
*3. Electrical Systems Failures
*4. Hydraulic System Malfunctions
*5. Flight Control System Malfunctions
*6. Flight Reference Set Malfunctions
*7. Bomb Directing Set Malfunctions

*TACTICS
*1. High-altitude Horizontal Bombing
*2. Low-level Laydown
*3. Loft
*4. Nuclear Weapons
*5. In-flight Refueling

*VFR LANDING PATTERN
  1. Entry and Break.
  *2. Simulated Single Engine.
  *3. FMLP.
  *4. Touch-and-Go and Final Landing.

POSTLANDING, SHUTDOWN, AND DEBRIEFING
  1. After Landing.
  2. Shutdown and Postflight.
  3. Debriefing.

FLIGHT EVALUATION (SYSTEMS OPERATOR)

The major areas and sub-areas listed are those areas where adherence to standard operating procedures will be graded. An asterisk indicates a critical area or sub-area.

*MISSION PLANNING
  *1. Charts.
  *2. Navigation Log.
  *3. Forms and Check Lists.
  *4. (Deleted.)
  *5. Target Study.
  *6. Ballistic Data.
  *7. Navigation Bag Contents.
  *8. Personal Flying Equipment.

*PREFLIGHT INSPECTION
  *1. Weapon Check List.
  *2. System Turn-on Check List.

*TAXI AND PRE-TAKE-OFF
  *1. NATOPS Pocket Check List.

*OPERATING PROCEDURES
  *1. Radar.
     (a) High Altitude.
     (b) Low Altitude.
  2. VERDAN.
  3. Inertial Platform.
  *4. Bombing.
  *5. Weapons.

*IN-FLIGHT MALFUNCTIONS
  *1. Weapons.
  *2. Radar.
  3. VERDAN.
  4. Inertial Platform.
  5. Bombing Computer.

*AIRMANSHIP
  *1. Crew Coordination.
  2. Radio Procedures.
  3. Navigational Charts and Publications.

PRELANDING, TAXI, AND SHUTDOWN
  1. NATOPS Pocket Check List.

DEBRIEFING
  1. Equipment.
  2. Mission.

GRADING INSTRUCTIONS

ORAL EXAMINATION GRADING CRITERIA

The oral examination will be graded in two parts.

PART ONE

Part One will consist of selected items on the aircraft preflight inspection. A grade of Qualified will be assigned if the pilot being graded can satisfactorily explain 95 percent or more of the items selected (Conditionally Qualified, 90 to 95 percent), and none of the items not satisfactorily explained would jeopardize safety of flight or ability to accomplish the mission.

A grade of Unqualified will be assigned if the pilot being graded cannot satisfactorily explain 90 percent of the items selected, or cannot satisfactorily explain an item which would jeopardize safety of flight or ability to accomplish the mission.

PART TWO

Part Two will consist of a demonstration by the pilot of his knowledge of servicing procedures. A grade of Qualified will be assigned if the pilot being graded demonstrates sufficient knowledge of the servicing procedures to be able to supervise servicing with the help of jet maintenance personnel (not A-5A qualified) at a strange field for each of the following systems:

  1. Fuel.
  2. Hydraulic.
  3. Engine Oil.
  4. Pneumatic.
  5. Liquid Oxygen.

A grade of Unqualified will be assigned if the pilot being graded does not demonstrate sufficient knowledge of servicing procedures to supervise servicing as required for Qualified.

ORAL EXAMINATION MATERIALS

An oral examination form is shown in Part 3 of this section. Although the two parts are graded separately, only one grade is given for the entire oral examination. If a grade of Unqualified is obtained on either portion, then the entire oral examination is graded Unqualified; however, only the portion graded Unqualified will be covered on the re-examination.

WRITTEN EXAMINATION GRADING CRITERIA

OPEN BOOK EXAMINATION GRADING CRITERIA

To obtain a grade of Qualified on the open book examination, a minimum score of no lower than 3.5 must be achieved.

CLOSED BOOK EXAMINATION GRADING CRITERIA

To obtain a grade of Qualified on the closed book examination, a minimum score of no lower than 3.3 must be achieved.

WST PROCEDURES CHECK GRADING CRITERIA

Using the check form shown in Part 2 of this section, both normal and emergency procedures for the pilot will be graded as follows.

EMERGENCIES/MALFUNCTIONS

If proper corrective action is initiated within the time limits specified on the forms shown in Parts 2 and 3 of this section, the response will be graded Qualified or Conditionally Qualified, according to the reaction time. The response will be graded Unqualified if the reaction time for Conditionally Qualified is exceeded. For those emergencies or malfunctions where no reaction time is specified, the criteria will be graded as follows: If proper action is initiated with minimum delay, the response will be graded as Qualified. If action is initiated with some delay and nonstandard procedures are utilized but the emergency is successfully coped with, the response will be graded Conditionally Qualified. If action is not initiated in time to prevent jeopardizing safety of flight or if nonstandard procedures are utilized which fail to correct the emergency, the response will be graded Unqualified.

Emergencies in each section will be graded as follows: If any emergency or malfunction is graded Unqualified, the area grade will be Unqualified; if less than half the emergencies or malfunctions are graded Qualified, the area grade will be Conditionally Qualified; if more than half of the emergencies or malfunctions are graded Qualified, the area grade will be Qualified.

NORMAL PROCEDURES

Normal Procedures will be graded using the criteria in this section.

NORMAL PROCEDURES AND EMERGENCY PROCEDURES

Normal procedures and emergency procedures will be graded separately: The overall grade will be determined as follows:

Qualified	Both procedures graded Qualified, or the emergency procedures graded Qualified and the normal procedures graded Conditionally Qualified.
Conditionally Qualified	Both procedures graded Conditionally Qualified, or the emergency procedures graded Conditionally Qualified and the normal procedures graded Qualified.
Unqualified*	Either or both examinations graded Unqualified.

*If Phase III is waived. If Phase III is completed, a grade of Unqualified in normal procedures will not bring the overall grade below Conditionally Qualified.

NAMT SYSTEMS CHECK GRADING CRITERIA

The NAMT systems check is not applicable to this manual.

FLIGHT EVALUATION GRADING CRITERIA

PILOT'S GRADING CRITERIA

In answering each question: if yes, mark Qualified; if no, but these are extenuating circumstances or if only a qualified yes, mark Conditionally Qualified; if the answer is an unqualified no or if the extenuating circumstances are not an adequate explanation, mark Unqualified.

Mission Planning

1. Route Planning.
   (a) Were all necessary charts and publications drawn?
   (b) Was planning commenced in sufficient time to permit meeting the scheduled launch time without undue hurrying and/or omitting necessary items?
   (c) Was an accurate in-flight card prepared, showing distance, time, and Navaids for each leg?
   (d) Were alternate landing fields appropriate to the flight preplanned?
   (e) Were all NOTAMS and other necessary information sources checked?
   (f) Were predicted winds used in flight planning?
   (g) Was an alternate plan computed in the event fuel ran below that predicted?

2. Fuel Planning.
   (a) Were fuel checks computed at the end of each leg or each half hour and each minute of AB operation?
   (b) Was fuel, time, and speed information taken from the Supplemental NATOPS Flight Manual or appropriate REST computer?
   (c) If supersonic, was an alternate Hot Day profile computed?
   (d) Were cruising speeds computed as either Mach number or KIAS?

3. Flight Plan.
   (a) Was weather briefing completed, including wind data?
   (b) Was DD-175 or other applicable flight plan properly filled out without error or omission in accordance with existing directives?

4. Take-off Computations.
   (a) Were take-off computations accurately computed in accordance with existing directives?

*Preflight

*1. Acceptance of the Aircraft.
   (a) Were a minimum of 10 yellow sheet parts "B" checked if available?

(b) Was the Plane Captain's preflight completed and the yellow sheet part "A" properly filled in and signed prior to acceptance of the aircraft?

*(c) Did the pilot accept an aircraft with unexplained discrepancies which could affect safety of flight and/or accomplishment of the mission? (Grade either Q or U.)

2. Preflight Inspection.

(a) Did the pilot complete the external inspection, noting each item on the inspection check list?

(b) Was pilot wearing appropriate flight gear considering type of flight and time of year?

(c) Was pilot's personal equipment operable and within a current inspection period?

*Taxi, Take-off, and Climb-out

*1. Taxi.

(a) Was departure clearance properly acknowledged and read back?

*(b) Was taxiing accomplished at prudent speed and with flaps up?

*2. Take-off.

(a) Was aircraft ready for take-off before taking position?

(b) Was engine power advanced before lowering flaps?

(c) Was aircraft properly lined up?

(d) Was AB ignited before commencing roll?

*(e) Was take-off smooth and well controlled?

*3. Climb-out.

*(a) Was climb-out made in accordance with clearance?

*(b) Was aircraft controlled during instrument departure in accordance with existing directives?

(c) Was aircraft controlled within the following limits during departure:
Departure radial (± 5 degrees or 1 mile, Q; ± 10 degrees or 2 miles, CQ)?
Airspeed (± 15 KIAS or ± 0.02 IMN, Q; ± 30 KIAS or ± 0.04 IMN, CQ)?
Altitude (± 200 feet, Q; ± 300 feet, CQ)?

Cruise

1. Aircraft Control.

(a) Was aircraft controlled during the level flight portions of the flight within the following limits:
Airspeed (± 20 KIAS or 0.03 IMN, Q; ± 30 KIAS or 0.05 IMN, CQ)?
Altitude (± 300 feet, Q; ± 500 feet, CQ)?

2. Communications.

(a) Were position reports made promptly and properly?

(b) Was proper communications plan used if applicable?

*Instruments

*1. Flight Planning (do not grade here if all sub-areas of MISSION PLANNING area are also graded).

(a) Were all necessary charts and publications drawn?

(b) Were all NOTAMS and other necessary information sources checked?

*(c) Was an adequate fuel plan made?

(d) Was an accurate in-flight card prepared, showing distance, time, and Navaids for each leg?

(e) Was weather briefing completed including wind data?

(f) Was DD-175 properly filled out in accordance with existing directives?

*(g) Was forecast weather at destination and alternate within minimums prescribed by governing directives?

(h) Were take-off computations accurately completed in accordance with existing directives?

*2. Departure (IFR).

(a) Was clearance read back accurately?

(b) Were ITO and initial turns after take-off made in accordance with existing directives?

*(c) Was departure clearance followed?

(d) Was aircraft controlled within following limits:
Departure radial or course (± 5 degrees or 1 mile, Q; ± 10 degrees or 2 miles, CQ)?
Airspeed (± 15 KIAS or 0.02 IMN, Q; ± 30 KIAS or 0.04 IMN, CQ)?
Altitude (± 200 feet, Q; ± 300 feet, CQ)?

(e) Were proper voice communications procedures used throughout?

*3. Cruise (Grade under CRUISE Area).

*4. Holding/Penetration/Approach.

(a) Were destination weather and alternate (if appropriate) weather obtained before leaving cruise altitude?

(b) Was clearance to alternate obtained before commencing penetration if destination weather was marginal?

(c) Was holding pattern entered in accordance with governing directives?

(d) Was holding clearance followed?

(e) Was approach time met within following limits: (±1 minute, Q; ±2 minutes, CQ)?

*(f) Was penetration clearance followed?

(g) Was aircraft controlled within limits:

Descent and inbound radials (±10°, Q; ±20°, CQ)?

Airspeed (±10 KIAS, Q; ±20 KIAS, CQ) Rate of descent (±1000 FPM, Q; ±2000 FPM, CQ)?

(h) Was aircraft transitioned to P/A configuration in accordance with governing directives?

(i) Was minimum approach altitude maintained: (±200 ft, Q; ± 200 ft, −100 ft, CQ)?

(j) Was proper voice radio procedure used?

(k) Was aircraft at minimum approach altitude when missed approach time/point was reached: (±200 ft, Q; ±200 ft, −100 ft, CQ)?

(l) Was aircraft at proper approach speed when missed approach time/point was reached: (12-14 ± units A/A, Q; 11-15 units, CQ)?

(m) Was missed approach procedure commenced when missed approach time/point was reached: (±30 secs, ±1 mile, Q; ±1 min, ±2 miles, CQ)?

*(n) Was missed approach clearance followed?

*5. GCA.

*(a) Were the GCA controller's instructions followed?

(b) Was proper voice radio procedure used?

(c) Was pattern flown smoothly?

(d) Was transition to glide path accomplished with a minimum of oscillations in attitude and power?

(e) Were aircraft attitude and airspeed safe at touchdown point?

Note

Grade only the first complete pass. If the pilot could not accomplish a safe landing on the first pass and must make a second, the maximum grade for this area will be Conditionally Qualified.

*Emergencies

The criteria for grading emergencies will be written for use in the WST since that is normally the environment in which this section will be graded. However, if an actual emergency occurs during the flight evaluation, it should be evaluated as feasible, according to the following criteria.

Qualified — Recognized the emergency situation with a minimum of delay or within time limits specified. Took timely and appropriate action in accordance with governing directives.

Conditionally Qualified — Recognized emergency situation with delay not endangering safety of flight or exceeding time limits specified. Successfully coped with the situation but deviated from governing directives.

Unqualified — Failed to recognize situation or exceeded time limits for Conditionally Qualified. Use of improper procedures or unnecessary delay in commencing corrective action allowed controllable situation to proceed out of control. Endangered safety of flight.

Note

( ) — Denotes time limit for Qualified.

— Denotes time limit for Conditionally Qualified.

*1. Engine Malfunctions.
  (a) Wet start   (5 secs)   #8 secs
  (b) False start   (5 secs)   #8 secs
  (c) Hot start   (5 secs)   #8 secs
  *(d) Engine failure
  *(e) Engine fire   (5 secs)   #8 secs
  (f) Low oil pressure

*2. Fuel System Failures.
  (a) Failure of aft tank transfer
  (b) Failure of bomb bay can transfer

*3. Electrical System Failures.
  (a) Loss of either   (5 secs)   #8 secs
      a-c generator
  *(b) Loss of all   (3 secs)   #5 secs
       a-c power
  (c) Loss of d-c   (5 secs)   #8 secs
      inverter
  *(d) Loss of all a-c   (3 secs)   #8 secs
       and d-c power

*4. Hydraulic System Malfunctions.
  (a) Loss of either   (8 secs)   #12 secs
      pump #1 system
  (b) Loss of both   (5 secs)   #8 secs
      pumps #1 system
  (c) Loss of either   (8 secs)   #12 secs
      pump #2 system

Section X
Part 1

   (d) Loss of both   (5 secs)   #8 secs
       pumps No. 2
       system
   (e) Loss of hy-   (5 secs)   #8 secs
       draulic fluid in
       either system
*(f) Wing flap
     emergency
     operation
*(g) Landing gear
     emergency
     operation
   (h) Failure of
       gear to
       retract

*5. Flight Control System Malfunctions.
   (a) Loss of   (3 secs)   #5 secs
       pitch aug
*(b) Runaway   (3 secs)   #5 secs
     trim (roll,
     pitch, or yaw)
   (c) Failure of nor-
       mal trim system
*(d) Hard-over   (3 secs)   #5 secs
     lateral or lon-
     gitudinal signal
     with electric
     flight on

*6. Flight Reference Set Malfunctions.
    Information will be provided at a later date.
*7. Bomb Directing Set Malfunctions.
    Information will be provided at a later date.

*Tactics

*1. High-altitude Horizontal Bombing (RBS or Pin-point).
   (a) Was IP reached on time (± 1 minute, Q; ± 3 minutes, CQ)?
   *(b) Was speed on run-in to target accurately controlled (± 15 KIAS or 0.02 IMN, Q; ± 30 KIAS or 0.04 IMN, CQ)?
   (c) Was system armed for release tone at proper time?
   (d) Was AB light-off and acceleration to supersonic dash commenced at preplanned point or corrected for ambient temperature?

*2. Laydown.
   (a) Was IP reached at preplanned time (± 1 minute, Q; ± 3 minutes, CQ)?
   *(b) Was run-in speed accurately controlled (± 15 KIAS or 0.02 IMN, Q; ± 30 KIAS or 0.04 IMN, CQ)?
   *(c) Was run-in altitude within limits (± 300 feet, Q; ± 600 feet, CQ)?
   (d) Did weapon release?

*3. Loft.
   (a) Was IP reached at a preplanned time (± 1 minute, Q; ± 3 minutes, CQ)?
   *(b) Was run-in speed accurately controlled (± 15 KIAS or 0.02 IMN, Q; ± 30 KIAS or 0.04 IMN, CQ)?
   *(c) Was run-in altitude within limits (± 300 feet, Q; ± 600 feet, CQ)?
   (d) Did weapon release?
   (e) Was maneuver performed correctly?

*4. Nuclear Weapons.
   (a) Was applicable NAVWEPS check list used?
   (b) Did crew correctly analyze in-flight weapon malfunctions?

*5. In-flight Refueling.
   (a) Was tanker/receiver rendezvous accomplished in accordance with governing directives?
   (b) After getting into initial position, was a plug-in made successfully within time limits (5 minutes, Q; 10 minutes, CQ)?
   (c) Was receiver able to take on fuel?
   (d) Was breakaway accomplished in accordance with governing directives?

*VFR Landing Pattern

1. Entry and Break.
   (a) Was local traffic checked and duty runway and altimeter setting obtained prior to reaching field?
   (b) Was break entry made in accordance with governing directives?

*2. Simulated Single Engine.
   *(a) Did landing pattern conform to local traffic rules and published procedures?
   (b) Was aircraft configuration correct for S/E situation?
   (c) Was single-engine wave-off accomplished in accordance with published procedures?
   (d) Was touchdown made in safe attitude and on speed?

*3. FMLP.
   *(a) Did FMLP patern conform to local traffic rules and published procedures?
   (b) Of the first four FMLP's made, how many were graded fair or better by the LSO (2, Q; 1, CQ)?

*4. Touch-and-Go and Final Landing.
   *(a) Did landing pattern conform to local traffic rules and published procedures?
   (b) Was touchdown made in safe attitude and on speed?
   (c) Was aerodynamic braking used effectively on final landing?

Postlanding, Shutdown, and Debriefing

1. After Landing.
    (a) Were flaps retracted and canopy opened after turning off duty runway?
    (b) Was taxi-in accomplished at prudent speed, flaps up?
    (c) Were proper radio reports made?
2. Shutdown and Postflight.
    (a) Was aircraft parked and shut down in accordance with governing directives?
    (b) Did pilot perform postlanding aircraft inspection?
3. Debriefing.
    (a) Were yellow sheet entries made accurately and correctly?
    (b) Were discrepancies reported in writing, using accepted terminology and in a clear, concise manner?
    (c) Were debriefing and other required postflight forms filled out?
    (d) Was crew debriefed by applicable debriefing officer in accordance with governing directives?

SYSTEMS OPERATOR'S GRADING CRITERIA

*Mission Planning

	QUALIFIED (Q)	CONDITIONALLY QUALIFIED (CQ)	UNQUALIFIED (U)
*1. Charts	Suitable scaled charts were available for the type mission flown. An accurate intended course was plotted, with DR positions or tick marks as appropriate. Suitable enroute diversionary fields were plotted. Other information pertinent to the mission was plotted, such as bomb-safe line, radar on point, etc.	Charts were prepared with minor errors or omissions that did not jeopardize the success of the misison.	Charts were prepared with errors or omissions that materially jeopardized the mission. Positions were grossly misplotted or courses and distances were in error.
*2. Navigation Log	The navigation log was prepared with no errors or omissions. It included all items on the standard navigation log.	The navigation log was prepared with minor errors or omissions that did not jeopardize the success of the mission.	The navigation log was prepared with serious errors or omissions that adversely affected the success of the mission.
*3. Forms and Check Lists	Forms and check lists applicable to the mission were available and information required properly recorded: (a) DD-175 or appropriate flight plan (b) NATOPS Pocket Check List (c) NAVWEPS Special Weapons Check List (d) Pilot's route card (e) RBS communication card (f) NAV/Coord Data card (g) Other forms, as required	Forms and check lists were prepared with minor errors or omissions that did not jeopardize the mission.	Forms and check lists were either not available or were prepared with errors or omissions that adversely affected the success of the mission.

*4. (Deleted.)

	QUALIFIED (Q)	CONDITIONALLY QUALIFIED (CQ)	UNQUALIFIED (U)
*5. Target Study	An intensive target area study was made. Predictions were prepared using best available target information. Offset distances, target, and aimpoint altitude were established based on best available information. A suitable aimpoint, within the limits of the bombing equipment, was selected.	Target study was completed with minor errors or omissions that did not affect the successful completion of the mission.	Target study was not completed. The successful completion of the mission was adversely affected.
*6. Ballistic Data	The proper ballistic module for the type weapon and mode of delivery was used in the bombing computer, with the correct altitude and airspeed band selected.		The wrong ballistic module was used.
*7. Navigation Bag Contents	Navigation bag contained all items as listed in NAVIGATION BAG CHECK LIST (FLIGHT CREW), Section III, Part 2.		Not up to the standards of Qualified.
*8. Personal Flying Equipment	Systems operator was equipped as required in Section II.		Not up to the standards of Qualified.

*Preflight Inspection

	QUALIFIED (Q)	CONDITIONALLY QUALIFIED (CQ)	UNQUALIFIED (U)
*1. Weapons Check List	External preflight was conducted in accordance with NAVWEPS Special Weapons Check List or conventional weapons check list.	The check list was completed with minor errors that did not affect the successful completion of the mission. Safety was not affected.	The check list was not completed. Errors or omissions were made which prevented the successful delivery of the ordnance load. Safety was adversely affected.
*2. System Turn-on Check List	AN/ASB-12 system was checked in accordance with the NATOPS Pocket Check List. A review of recent system history was made.	Check list was used but minor errors or omissions were made that did not adversely affect the successful completion of the mission.	Check list was not completed or items were missed that adversely affected the successful completion of the mission.

*Taxi and Pre-take-off

	QUALIFIED (Q)	CONDITIONALLY QUALIFIED (CQ)	UNQUALIFIED (U)
*1. NATOPS Pocket Check List	Taxi and pre-take-off were conducted in accordance with the NATOPS Pocket Check List.	The NATOPS Pocket Check List was used but minor errors or omissions were made that did not adversely affect the successful completion of the mission.	Check list was not completed or items were missed that adversely affected the successful completion of the mission.

*Operating Procedures

	QUALIFIED (Q)	CONDITIONALLY QUALIFIED (CQ)	UNQUALIFIED (U)
*1. Radar (a) High altitude	Operated the radar in an acceptable manner so as to radar navigate the aircraft on its intended route and made cursor corrections when necessary to update present position.	Did not utilize all the radar modes of operation available to radar navigate the aircraft and correct present position.	Was not able to utilize the radar to navigate the aircraft or update present position.
(b) Low altitude	Showed good crew coordination in utilizing either the terrain avoidance or contour map mode of the radar to navigate the aircraft along the intended flight route, and at the same time terrain avoid.	Could either terrain avoid or navigate using the radar, but could not do both at the same time.	Unable to use the radar to either terrain avoid or navigate at low altitude.
2. VERDAN	Utilized the VERDAN to its utmost throughout the mission in navigating the aircraft and in bombing the assigned target.	Used the VERDAN sufficiently to finish the mission, but did not take advantage of all of its capabilities.	Not proficient enough with the use of the VERDAN to accomplish the assigned mission.
3. Inertial platform	The inertial platform was properly aligned, and operated throughout the flight to obtain the best system accuracy.	The inertial platform was operated in such a manner as to induce errors into the system but the mission was completed.	The inertial platform was either not properly aligned or was not properly operated in flight.
*4. Bombing	Employed all the proper bombing procedures to deliver the weapon accurately on the assigned target.	Delivered the weapon but made an error or omission that would have resulted in an appreciable error on the bomb impact point.	Bombing procedures were such that he could not deliver the weapon on the target.
*5. Weapons	Completed all items on applicable NAVWEPS check lists without error or omission. Was familiar with fuzing criteria as set forth in governing directives, if applicable.	Completed all items on applicable NAVWEPS check lists with minor errors or omissions not affecting safety of flight or ability to release the store in proper condition.	Did not complete all items on applicable NAVWEPS check lists and/or made major errors or omissions affecting safety of flight or ability to release the store in proper condition and/or made incorrect decision concerning malfunction of the store(s).

In-flight Malfunctions

	QUALIFIED (Q)	CONDITIONALLY QUALIFIED (CQ)	UNQUALIFIED (U)
*1. Weapons	Followed "go"/"no go" considerations as outlined in the appropriate NAVWEPS Special Weapons Check list.		Did not meet the requirements as outlined under Qualified; either aborted with a good weapon or continued with a bad one.

Section X
Part 1

	QUALIFIED (Q)	CONDITIONALLY QUALIFIED (CQ)	UNQUALIFIED (U)
*2. Radar	Recognized the radar malfunction immediately and took appropriate corrective action.	Was unduly slow in recognizing the malfunction and in taking corrective action.	Did not take appropriate corrective action to overcome the radar malfunction.
3. VERDAN	Quickly recognized the VERDAN malfunction and took appropriate and timely corrective action.	Was slow in recognizing the VERDAN malfunction and lost valuable time in trying to correct it.	Either did not see the malfunction or did not know how to correct it.
4. Inertial Platform	Quickly noticed the platform failure and followed the correct procedures for switching the system to the stand-by navigation mode of operation.	Noticed the platform failure but did not follow the correct procedures for going to the stand-by navigation mode of operation.	Did not notice the platform failure or did not know how to put the system in the stand-by navigation mode of operation.
5. Bombing Computer	Quickly recognized the failure of the bombing computer and switched to an appropriate mode for an alternate delivery.	Recognized the failure but switched to a mode of delivery not available without the bombing computer.	Did not recognize the bombing computer failure.

*Airmanship

	QUALIFIED (Q)	CONDITIONALLY QUALIFIED (CQ)	UNQUALIFIED (U)
*1. Crew Coordination (noncritical if crew is nontactical)	Coordinated smoothly and effectively in all crew endeavors. Anticipated demands upon his crew position. The overall performance of the crew was enhanced by his continual alertness in performing his duties.		Coordination was at a level sufficiently low so as to hinder crew performance. Was unfamiliar with crew members' duties and/or was continually interrupting them to a degree that teamwork was definitely retarded. Mission requirements were lost due to his failure to coordinate properly.
2. Radio Procedures	Demonstrated the ability to copy, understand, and read back ATC clearances in minimum time. Monitored frequencies and/or facilities at the appropriate time. Was familiar with communications equipment and facilities. Understood and correctly transmitted position reports.	Met the criteria for Qualified except for discrepancies or delays that indicated lack of thorough familiarity with procedures, equipment, or facilities.	Failed to transmit or receive mandatory reports through omission or lack of familiarity with equipment or procedures.

	QUALIFIED (Q)	CONDITIONALLY QUALIFIED (CQ)	UNQUALIFIED (U)
3. Navigational Charts and Publications	Demonstrated complete familiarity with the following charts and publications: (a) Flight Planning Document. (b) Enroute Supplement. (c) Enroute FLIP Charts. When required in flight, was able to assist the pilot in changes to the flight plan through proper use of navigational charts and publications.	Generally understood the procedures for proper use of publications and charts. Was slow in rendering assistance required by the pilot when questions concerning the route of flight came up or when changes to the flight plan occurred.	Completely unfamiliar with publications and charts. Gave the pilot no assistance in handling subject documents in flight.

Prelanding, Taxi, and Shutdown Procedures

	QUALIFIED (Q)	CONDITIONALLY QUALIFIED (CQ)	UNQUALIFIED (U)
1. NATOPS Pocket Check List	The NATOPS Pocket Check List was completed in a timely, orderly manner. The system was properly set up for landing/taxi, and proper shutdown procedures were employed.	The NATOPS Pocket Check List was completed with minor errors or omissions that would not normally affect future operation of the equipment.	The NATOPS Pocket Check List was not followed. Items on the check list were omitted that might have been damaging to the equipment.

Debriefing

	QUALIFIED (Q)	CONDITIONALLY QUALIFIED (CQ)	UNQUALIFIED (U)
1. Equipment	The AN/ASB-12 debriefing sheet was completed without errors or omissions, and included a clear, concise description of discrepancies.	The AN/ASB-12 debriefing sheet was completed with minor deviations or omissions not affecting future operation and maintenance of the system. Discrepancies were written in an understandable manner.	Major discrepancies in completing the AN/ASB-12 debriefing sheet were noted. Equipment malfunctions were either omitted from the write-up or were written in an ambiguous manner and not understandable.
2. Mission	All required debriefing forms, charts, cards, and logs were completed. In-flight data were accurately recorded. It was possible to reconstruct the mission from available information. The debrief was conducted in a concise, clear, and intelligent manner.	Minor errors or omissions were made in log keeping; however, it was possible to reconstruct the mission from available information.	Required forms, charts, cards, and logs were not complete, left out, or neglected entirely. It was impossible to reconstruct the mission from available information.

FINAL GRADE DETERMINATION

Each phase of the annual standardization check will be given a final grade of its own as follows.

PHASE I

The overall grades for the oral examination and the written examination will be determined as described under GRADING INSTRUCTIONS. A final grade of Qualified will be given for Phase I if both examinations are graded Qualified. A final grade of Conditionally Qualified will be given if either examination is graded Conditionally Qualified. A final grade of Unqualified will be given if either examination is graded Unqualified.

PHASE II

The overall grade for the WST check will be determined as described under WST PROCEDURES CHECK GRADING CRITERIA and will serve as the final grade for this phase.

PHASE III

The overall grade for the flight evaluation will be determined as described and will serve as the final grade for this phase.

In grading each sub-area question, the following numerical equivalents shall be used:

Qualified—2.0

Conditionally Qualified—1.0

Unqualified—0

The sub-area grade will be determined by the numerical average of the questions graded within the sub-area; however, a grade of Unqualified on a critical question will cause the entire sub-area to be graded Unqualified, regardless of the numerical average.

The area grade will be determined by the numerical average of the sub-areas graded; however, a critical sub-area grade of Unqualified will cause the entire area to be graded Unqualified.

The overall flight evaluation grade will be determined by the numerical average of the areas graded; however, a critical area grade of Unqualified will cause the entire flight check to be graded Unqualified, regardless of the numerical average.

Average grades must fall in the following ranges for corresponding adjective grades shown:

Qualified—1.5 to 2.0

Conditionally Qualified—1.0 to 1.49

Unqualified—0 to 1.0

FORMS AND RECORDS

FORMS

The forms described will be used in recording data and reporting grades:

1. Annual Standardization Evaluation Check Form
2. Oral Examination Stan/Check Form (pilot)
3. WST Stan/Check Form (pilot)
4. In-flight kneepad grading sheet (pilot)
5. In-flight kneepad grading sheet (systems operator)

A copy of each of these forms is contained in Parts 2, 3, and 4 of this section. Each unit will reproduce enough forms for its own use. No deviations from the format shown in Parts 2, 3, and 4 of this section are authorized.

RECORDS

The Stan/Check forms and kneepad grading sheet used on each standardization evaluation will be retained by the Unit Standardization Instructor concerned until the annual standardization evaluation for the following year is successfully completed. The Annual Standardization Evaluation Check form used on each standardization evaluation will be retained by Unit Standardization Instructor for as long as the crew member concerned is serving in that unit.

Unit Standardization Instructors will maintain a record of flight crew members assigned and the standardization evaluation phases they have completed.

CRITIQUE

Each phase will be critiqued separately as follows:

1. PHASE I. Both the oral and written examinations will be critiqued by the Standardization Instructor/Evaluator concerned within 24 hours after completion of each examination.

2. PHASE II. Each crew member will be critiqued individually by the Standardization Instructor/Evaluator concerned no sooner than 12 hours and no later than 48 hours after completing the WST check.

3. PHASE III. Each crew member will be critiqued individually by the Standardization Instructor/Evaluator concerned no sooner than 12 hours and no later than 48 hours after completing the flight check.

Critiques will be formally conducted, scheduled events. The Annual Standardization Evaluation Check form will be completed at the Phase III critique and will be forwarded immediately afterward, with pertinent comments and recommendations made at the critique, to the Unit Commanding Officer.

If the standardization evaluation is being conducted by the Standardization Evaluators, an additional critique will be held with the Unit Commanding Officer and Unit Standardization Instructors present, at which time the unit standardization program will be reviewed and pertinent comments and recommendations made.

NAVWEPS 01-60ABA-1

Section X
Part 2

PART 2 — A-5A PILOT/SYSTEMS OPERATOR STANDARDIZATION EVALUATION FORM

STANDARDIZATION EVALUATION CHECK	STAN/EVAL		
	RECHECK		DATE

INSTRUCTIONS

1. This form will be completed in accordance with instructions contained in Section X, NATOPS Flight Manual (NAVWEPS 01-60ABA-1).
2. Entries on this form will be made by the Standardization Evaluator/Instructor.
3. Comments will be made stating reason for failure to complete Sub-area/Item.

NAME	RANK/RATE	FILE/DESIG/SERIAL
SQUADRON/DETACHMENT	DATE OF BIRTH	AC TYPE/MODEL

PREREQUISITES

FLIGHT	PREVIOUS 6 MO	12 MO	TOTAL HOURS	GROUND	PREVIOUS 6 MO	12 MO	TOTAL HOURS
PILOT TIME				WST			
FIRST PILOT TIME				LINK			
A-5A SPECIAL CREW TIME							
SIM. INST. TIME							
ACT. INST. TIME							
INST. APPROACHES							
CCA/GCA							
A-5A CV LNGS D/N	/	/					
A-5A LOFTS	/	/					
BOMB DROPS							
RBS RUNS							

211

PILOT
GROUND (PHASES I AND II)

ITEM	DATE	GRADE
CLOSED BOOK		
OPEN BOOK		
WST		
ORAL EXAMINATION		

FLIGHT (PHASE III)

AREA PILOT	SUB-AREA/ITEM								AREA GRADE		
	(1)	(2)	(3)	(4)	(5)	(6)	(7)	(8)	Q	CQ	UQ
MISSION PLANNING											
PREFLIGHT INSPECTION											
TAXI, TAKE-OFF, CLIMB-OUT											
CRUISE											
INSTRUMENTS											
EMERGENCIES											
TACTICS											
VFR LANDING PATTERN											
POSTLANDING, SHUTDOWN, DEBRIEF											

NAVWEPS 01-60ABA-1 — Section X, Part 2

NAVIGATOR
GROUND (PHASES I AND II)

ITEM	DATE	GRADE
CLOSED BOOK		
OPEN BOOK		
WST		

FLIGHT (PHASE III)

AREA / CREWMAN	SUB-AREA								AREA GRADE		
	(1)	(2)	(3)	(4)	(5)	(6)	(7)	(8)	Q	CQ	UQ
MISSION PLANNING											
PREFLIGHT INSPECTION											
TAXI AND PRE-TAKE-OFF											
OPERATING PROCEDURES											
IN-FLIGHT MALFUNCTIONS											
AIRMANSHIP											
PRELANDING AND SHUTDOWN											
DEBRIEF											

Section X
Part 2

NAVWEPS 01-60ABA-1

DATE OF FLIGHT CHECK	OVER-ALL GRADE ASSIGNED	EVALUATOR/INSTRUCTOR

EVALUATOR/INSTRUCTOR: REMARKS/RECOMMENDED CORRECTIVE ACTION

Evaluator/Instructor	Date	Signature

SQUADRON COMMANDING OFFICER: REMARKS

Squadron Commanding Officer	Date	Signature

CORRECTIVE ACTION COMPLETED:

Squadron Commanding Officer	Date	Signature

PART 3 — PILOT STANDARDIZATION EVALUATION WORKSHEETS

Oral Examination Worksheet

PHASE I

Pilot_____

Squadron_____ Date_____

Evaluator/Instructor_____

Part I EXTERIOR INSPECTION

Attach Inspection Check List used.

    Number Items Checked_____

    Number Items Checked Satisfactorily_____

Q—95% or better; CQ—90% to 95%; U—less than 90%
Failure to properly check any one essential item—U.

Part I Grade_____

Part II AIRCRAFT SERVICING

Mark the questions Q or U as indicated by the level of knowledge observed. The grade for each system should indicate whether or not the pilot observed can satisfactorily supervise the servicing of the aircraft in that system.

SYSTEM	MATERIAL REQ'D	EQUP'T REQ'D	SERV. TECHNIQUE	GRADE
FUEL				
HYDRAULIC				
ENGINE OIL				
PNEUMATIC				
LIQUID OXYGEN				

A grade of Q is required in each system or the grade for part II will be U.

Part II Grade_____

Part I   Part II   FINAL GRADE

Section X
Part 3

NAVWEPS 01-60ABA-1

page 1

STANDARDIZATION/EVALUATION WORKSHEET
FOR THE WST CHECK—PILOT

SQUADRON_____ DATE_____

CREW POSITION	NAME	RANK	FILE/SERVICE

EVALUATOR/INSTRUCTOR

_____

DESCRIPTION OF SIMULATED FLIGHT

Both NORMAL and EMERGENCY procedures for the pilot will be graded as follows:

EMERGENCIES/MALFUNCTIONS: If proper corrective action is initiated within the time limits specified, the response will be graded Q or CQ, according to the reaction time. The response will be graded U if the reaction time for CQ is exceeded. For those emergencies or malfunctions where no reaction time is specified, the criteria will be graded as follows: If proper action is initiated with minimum delay, the response will be graded as Q. If action is initiated with some delay and nonstandard procedures are utilized but the emergency is successfully coped with, the response will be graded CQ. If action is not initiated in time to prevent jeopardizing safety of flight or if nonstandard procedures are utilized which fail to correct the emergency, the response will be graded U.

Standard procedures will be graded using the criteria in the NATOPS Flight Manual (NAVWEPS 01-60ABA-1).

Emergencies in each section will be graded as follows: If any emergency or malfunction is graded U, the area grade will be U; if less than half the emergencies or malfunctions are graded Q, the area grade will be CQ; if more than half of the emergencies or malfunctions are graded Q, the area grade will be Q.

I   PRESTART

    Time started check list_____

    Items missed on check list:

ITEM NO	ITEM	RESPONSE

NAVWEPS 01-60ABA-1   Section X
                      Part 3

                                                                  page 2
        Check list completed _____
        Discrepancies missed by pilot:

                                              U   CQ   Q   TIME

  II   START/GROUND CHECKS
              EMERGENCIES/MALFUNCTIONS

          1. _____

          2. _____

          3. _____

          4. _____

COMMENTS:

        Items missed on Ground Checks
        ITEM NO   ITEM

                                    TAXI TIME _____

  III   PRE-TAKE-OFF/TAKE-OFF
        Items missed on Pre-take-off Check
        ITEM NO   ITEM   RESPONSE

Full Power Check

Take-off Time _____

217

	U	CQ	Q	TIME
Emergencies/Malfunctions				
1. _____	___	___	___	___
2. _____	___	___	___	___
3. _____	___	___	___	___
4. _____	___	___	___	___

COMMENTS:

IV   DEPARTURE

	U	CQ	Q	TIME
Followed Departure Clearance	___	___	___	
Voice Reports	___	___	___	
Gear Up: _____ KIAS _____ Rate of Climb				
Flaps Up: _____ KIAS _____ Altitude				
Climb Schedule	___	___	___	
Post-take-off Items Missed	___	___	___	
1. _____	___	___	___	
2. _____	___	___	___	
3. _____	___	___	___	
4. _____	___	___	___	
Emergencies/Malfunctions				
1. _____	___	___	___	___
2. _____	___	___	___	___
3. _____	___	___	___	___
4. _____	___	___	___	___
5. _____	___	___	___	___

COMMENTS:

NAVWEPS 01-60ABA-1   Section X
Part 3

page 4

		U	CQ	Q	TIME
V	LEVEL-OFF/CRUISE				
	Voice Reports				
	Followed Clearance				
	Aircraft Control				
	Pilot's Bomb Switches For RBS				
	Knowledge of FAA Procedures				
	Emergencies/Malfunctions				
	1.				
	2.				
	3.				
	4.				
	5.				
	6.				
	7.				
	8.				
	9.				
	10.				

COMMENTS:

VI	LOW-LEVEL CRUISE/LOW-LEVEL ATTACK				
	Followed B/N Steering				
	Airspeed Control				
	Altitude Control				
	Bomb Switches Positioned				
	Run-in Airspeed				
	Run-in Altitude				
	Attack Technique				

219

	Emergencies/Malfunctions	U	CQ	Q	page 5 TIME
	1.				
	2.				
	3.				
	4.				

COMMENTS:

VII HOLDING/PENETRATION/APPROACH

Holding Pattern Entry			
Holding Pattern			
Holding Airspeed			
Holding Altitude			
Number of Circuits Made			
Penetration Procedures			
Penetration Airspeed			
Penetration Rate of Descent			
Transition to Level-off			
Transition to P/A			
Final Approach Airspeed			
Final Approach MIN ALT			
Recognized Missed Approach + _____			
Voice Procedures			
Emergencies/Malfunctions			
1.			
2.			
3.			
4.			
5.			
6.			

COMMENTS:

page 6

GRADING

NORMAL PROCEDURES   U   CQ   Q

    TOTAL GRADED

    NORMAL PROCEDURES GRADE _____

EMERGENCIES/MALFUNCTIONS

    TOTAL GRADED

    EMERGENCY PROCEDURES GRADE _____

    PHASE II GRADE _____

TRAINER INSTRUCTOR _____   NATOPS EVALUATOR/INSTRUCTOR _____

A-5 Pilot page 1
Kneepad Grade Sheet

Squadron _____ Date _____ Buno _____
Name _____ Rank _____ Serial _____

Evaluator/Instructor _____

Description of Mission Flown

NOTE: Information on the following pages will be filled in as accurately as possible. When additional comments are required to clearly describe performance, they should be placed on the backs of adjoining pages.

Kneepad Grade Sheet page 2

MISSION PLANNING

| | | YES | NO | COMMENTS |

(1) Route Planning
   1. Were necessary charts and pubs drawn?
   2. Adequate time allowed for planning?
   3. Suitable in-flight card prepared?
   4. Alternate fields?
   5. NOTAMS etc, checked?
   6. Predicted winds used?
   7. Alternate plans?

   Comments:

(2) Fuel Planning
   1. Fuel checks planned?
   2. Source for fuel planning was:
   3. Hot fuel plan made if required?
   4. Cruising speeds computed as IMN or KIAS?

   Comments:

(3) Flight Plan
   1. Complete Wx briefing obtained?
   2. DD-175 completed without error?

   Comments:

(4) Takeoff Computations

T. O. Alt_____ Gr. WT._____. Runway Temp._____. Wind_____.
                        Pilot Comp   Evaluator Comp
T. O. Roll
T. O. Airspeed

Kneepad Grade Sheet page 3

*PREFLIGHT

	YES	NO	COMMENTS

*(1) Aircraft Acceptance

    1. How many prior yellow sheets checked?

    2. Plane captain's preflight completed and yellow sheet signed off?

  *3. Plane accepted with unexplained critical gripes?

    Comments:

(2) Preflight Inspection

    1. External Inspection complete all items?

    2. Pilot's flight gear adequate?

    3. Pilot's personal equipment current?

    Comments:

*TAXI, TAKE-OFF, CLIMB-OUT

*(1) Taxi

    1. Radio calls correctly made?

  *2. Clearance read backs correct?

*(2) Take-off

    1. Aircraft ready for T. O. before taking position?

    2. Power advanced before flaps lowered?

    3. Proper lineup?

    4. AB ignited before brake release?

  *5. T. O. smooth and coordinated?

    Comments:

Kneepad Grade Sheet   page 4

                                                                    YES   NO   COMMENTS

*(3) Climb-out

   *1. Dept clearance followed?

   *2. Aircraft transitions accomplished IAW standard procedures?

   3. Aircraft control:

      Radial (or hdg) ±5° or 1 mile ____, ±10° or 2 miles ____, exceeded limits ____. Airspeed ±15 KIAS or 0.02 IMN ____, ±30 KIAS or 0.04 IMN ____, exceeded limits. Altitude ±200 ft ____, ±300 ft ____, exceeded limits ____.

   Comments:

CRUISE

(1) Aircraft Control

   Limits in level flight:

   Airspeed ±20 KIAS or 0.03 IMN ____, ±30 KIAS or 0.05 IMN ____, exceeded limits ____. Altitude ±300 ft ____, ±500 ft ____, exceeded limits ____.

(2) Communications

   1. Were position reports prompt and accurate?

   2. Was proper commplan used?

   Comments:

*INSTRUMENTS

*(1) Flight Planning (Do not grade here if all sub-areas of Mission Planning area are also graded.)

   1. Necessary charts and pubs drawn?

   2. NOTAMS etc checked?

   *3. Adequate fuel plan prepared?

   4. Adequately prepared in-flight knee card?

   5. Wx briefing adequate?

   6. DD-175 properly made out?

Kneepad Grade Sheet   page 5

                                                              YES   NO   COMMENTS

   *7. Forecast terminal and alternate Wx above minimums? _____ _____ _____

    8. Take-off computations (page ____)

    Comments:

*(2) Departure (IFR)

    1. Clearance followed?

    2. ITO and departure turns IAW standard procedure?

  *3. Departure clearance followed?

    4. Aircraft control:

        Radial (or hdg) ±5° or 1 mile _____, ±10° or 2 miles _____, exceeded limits _____.

        Airspeed ±15 KIAS or 0.02 IMN _____, ±30 KIAS or 0.04 IMN, exceeded limits _____.

        Altitude ±200 ft _____, ±300 ft _____, exceeded limits _____.

    5. Proper voice procedures used?

    Comments:

*(3) Cruise (Grade under CRUISE Area)

*(4) Holding/Penetration/Approach

    1. Dest Wx obtained before leaving cruise alt?

    2. Alt Wx obtained if appropriate?

    3. Alt flt plan filed if appropriate?

    4. Holding pattern entry:
        Entry airspeed _____
        Entry altitude _____

    5. Holding pattern:
        Airspeed _____ Altitude _____
        Maintained pattern YES/NO

    6. Missed assigned approach time by _____

        Number of holding circuits completed _____

Kneepad Grade Sheet Page 6

                                                                                                 YES   NO   COMMENTS

*7. Penetration clearance followed?

  8. Airspeed control:

      Radial ±10° _____, ±20° _____, exceeded limits _____.

      Airspeed ±10 KIAS _____, ±20 KIAS _____, exceeded limits _____.

      Rate of descent ±1000 fpm _____, ±2000 fpm _____, exceeded limits _____.

  9. Aircraft transition out of penetration:

        S/B in at _____ ft.

        Maintained _____ KIAS

        L. O. alt _____

*10. Min approach altitude deviation:

      +200, −0 ft _____, +200, −100 ft _____, exceeded limits _____.

  11. Proper voice procedure used?

  12. Deviation from min approach altitude at missed approach point:

      +200, −0 ft _____, +200, −100 ft _____, exceeded limits _____.

  13. Deviation from approach speed at missed approach point:

      12-14 units A/A _____, 11-15 unit A/A _____, exceeded limits _____.

  14. Recognized missed approach within:

      ±30 secs or 1 mile _____, ±1 min or 2 miles _____, exceeded limits _____.

*15. Followed missed approach procedure

Comments:

*(5) GCA

  *1. Followed GCA instructions

    2. Used proper voice procedures

    3. Flew pattern smoothly

    4. Transition to glide slope

      Smooth _____   Slight Oscillations _____   Rough _____

    5. Touchdown

      Attitude: OK _____   3 point _____   Nosefirst _____

      Airspeed: OK _____   Fast _____   Slow _____

      Touchdown Point: OK _____   ±500 ft _____   ±1000 ft _____

      1st satisfactory pass was # _____

Kneepad Grade Sheet

*EMERGENCIES

Actual emergencies occurring in flight should be written up as well as possible under the circumstances.

Type Emergency:

Pilot Reaction:

*TACTICS

*(1) High-altitude Bombing

Type observed: RBS_____ Pinpoint_____

1. IP time deviation:
  ±1 min_____, ±3 min_____, exceeded limits_____.

*2. Run-in airspeed deviation
  ±15 KIAS or 0.02 IMN_____, ±30 KIAS or 0.04 IMN_____, exceeded limits_____.

3. Release tone arming OK_____, early_____, late_____.

4. AB light-off for supersonic dash accomplished with_____ mins/mile of preplanned time/point.

Comments:

Kneepad Grade Sheet page 8

*(2) Low-level Laydown

    1. IP time deviation:

       ±1 min_____, ±3 min_____, exceeded limits_____.

   *2. Run-in speed deviation:

       ±15 KIAS or 0.02 IMN_____, ±30 KIAS or 0.04 IMN_____, exceeded limits_____.

   *3. Run-in altitude deviation:

       ±300 ft_____, ±600 ft_____, exceeded limits_____.

    4. Weapon release?   YES_____   NO_____

*(3) Low-level Loft

    1. IP time deviation

       ±1 min_____, ±3 min_____, exceeded limits_____.

   *2. Run-in speed deviation:

       ±15 KIAS or 0.02 IMN_____, ±30 KIAS or 0.04 IMN_____, exceeded limits_____.

   *3. Run-in altitude deviation:

       ±300 ft_____, ±600 ft_____, exceeded limits_____.

    4. Weapon release?   YES_____   NO_____

    5. Maneuver technique   OK_____   FAIR_____   UNSAT_____

    Comments:

*(4) Nuclear Weapons   YES   NO   COMMENTS

    1. Applicable NAVWEPS check list used?

    2. Correctly analyzed malfunctions?

    Comments:

*(5) In flight Refueling

    1. Rendezvous IAW SOP?

    2. Plug-in time after initial positioning 5 min_____, 10_____, exceeded limits_____.

    3. Amount of fuel transferred_____

    4. Break away IAW SOP?

Kneepad Grade Sheet page 9

*VFR LANDING PATTERN

(1) Entry and Break   YES   NO   COMMENTS

    1. Approaching the field:

        Local traffic checked?

        Duty runway obtained?

        Altimeter setting?

    2. Break entry IAW with SOP?

*(2) Single Engine

    *1. Pattern in conformance with local traffic rules and SOP?

    2. P/A configuration correct?

    3. S/E W. O. IAW SOP?

    4. Touchdown attitude   OK_____   3 Point_____   Nosedown_____

    5. Touchdown Point   OK_____   Long_____   Short_____

*(3) FMLP

    *1. FMLP Pattern standard_____   Nonstandard_____

    2. Of the first four passes   Fair or better_____

    Comments:

*(4) Touch and Go and Final

    *1. Pattern in conformance with local traffic rules and SOP?

    2. Touchdown: Attitude   OK_____   3 point_____   Nosedown_____

        Speed   OK_____   Fast_____   Slow_____

        Touchdown Point   OK_____   Short_____   Long_____

    3. Aerodynamic braking technique IAW SOP?

    Comments:

Kneepad Grade Sheet   page 10

POSTLANDING

	YES	NO	COMMENTS

(1) After landing
     1. Flaps up and canopy open after turning off the runway?
     2. Taxi speed prudent?
     3. Taxi flaps up?
     4. Proper radio reports?

     Comments:

(2) Shutdown and Postflight
     1. Aircraft parked and shut down IAW SOP?
     2. Did pilot perform postlanding aircraft inspection?

     Comments:

(3) Debrief
     1. Yellow sheet entries proper?
     2. Discrepancies written up clearly and concisely?
     3. Debrief forms filled out as applicable?
     4. Crew debriefed as required?

     Comments:

NAVWEPS 01-60ABA-1

Section X
Part 4

PART 4 — SYSTEMS OPERATOR STANDARDIZATION EVALUATION WORKSHEETS

page 1

Squadron _____ Date _____ BuNo _____

Name _____ Rank _____ Serial No. _____

Evaluator/Instructor _____

Description of Mission Flown

NOTE: A complete description of performance prior to and during the flight is desired. This worksheet contains all the areas and sub-areas listed in the NATOPS Flight Manual for mission flights. The information gathered on this worksheet will be graded using the grading criteria in the NATOPS Flight Manual.

General Comments:

Section X
Part 4

NAVWEPS 01-60ABA-1

Page 2

*MISSION PLANNING

*(1) Charts

    1. Suitable scale:

    2. Accurate route depicted:

    3. Diversionary fields annotated:

    4. Information pertinent to the mission:

*(2) Navigation Log

Errors or omissions in the following items:

1. CUS   _____
2. DIST _____
3. MH   _____
4. TH   _____
5. TAS   _____
6. GS   _____
7. ETE   _____
8. ETA   _____
9. ATA   _____
10. Winds _____
11. Leg   _____
12. Coordinates _____
13. Altitudes _____

Comments:

Section X
Part 4

NAVWEPS 01-60ABA-1

page 4

*(3) Forms and Check Lists

   1. DD-175 or appropriate flight plan
      (discrepancies noted)

   2. NATOPS Pocket Check List

   3. NAVWEPS Special Weapons Check List

   4. Pilot's Route Card

   5. RBS Comm Card

   6. NAV/Coord Data Card

   7. Other forms, as required

Comments:

page 5

*(4) (Deleted)

page 6

*(5) Target Study

    1. Predictions:

    2. Offset data:

    3. OAP selection:

    4. Target and aimpoint altitude:

page 7

*(6) Ballistic Information

    1. Appropriate ballistic adapter was available for the:

        Type of weapon _____

        Mode of delivery _____

        Envelope of the adapter was compatible with the planned bomb run _____

    2. Comments:

*(7) NAV BAG Contents: Discrepancies noted from the NAVIGATION BAG CHECK LIST (FLIGHT CREW), Section III, NATOPS Flight Manual.

*(8) Personal Flying Equipment: Discrepancies noted from the check list of flying gear in Section II, NATOPS Flight Manual.

Section X
Part 4

NAVWEPS 01-60ABA-1

page 8

List below any additional items under MISSION PLANNING that are not covered in any of the sub-areas (comments and recommendations to be used at the postflight critique).

*PREFLIGHT INSPECTION

*(1) Weapon Check List

   Omissions or errors in the use of the appropriate weapon check list.

*(2) System Turn-on Check List

   NATOPS Pocket Check List omissions or errors.

NAVWEPS 01-60ABA-1

Section X
Part 4

page 9

*TAXI AND PRE-TAKE-OFF

*(1) NATOPS Pocket Check List

Errors or omissions in the use of the NATOPS Pocket Check List:

*OPERATING PROCEDURES

*(1) Radar

(High Altitude)   YES/NO

1. Used radar to maintain the aircraft on the intended track.   _____

2. Proper checkpoint identification.   _____

3. Used the radar properly to update present position.   _____

4. Used the various operating modes of the radar to the best advantage during the flight.   _____

Comments:

(Low Altitude)   YES/NO

1. Crew displayed good coordination in the use of the TA/CM mode.   _____

2. Proper checkpoint identification.   _____

3. Updated present position with the radar.   _____

4. Kept the aircraft on track with the radar.   _____

Comments:

Section X
Part 4

NAVWEPS 01-60ABA-1

page 10

(2) VERDAN YES/NO

    1. Understood the function and use of the VERDAN. _____

    2. Used the VERDAN to maximum advantage. _____

    3. Comments:

(3) Inertial Platform YES/NO

    1. Platform was properly aligned. _____

    2. Platform was properly operated throughout the flight. _____

    3. Comments:

(4) Bombing Procedures: YES/NO

    1. Proper procedures were used for the type of delivery planned. _____

    2. Aimpoint properly identified. _____

    3. Armament check list completed. _____

    4. Comments:

page 11

*(5) Weapons   YES/NO

     1. Completed all items on the NAVWEPS or appropriate check list.

     2. Was familiar with the weapon check list and its use.

     3. Properly monitored the weapon throughout the flight.

     4. Comments:

IN-FLIGHT MALFUNCTIONS

*(1) Weapons   YES/NO

     1. Quickly recognized the malfunction.

     2. Made a correct "go"/"no go" decision.

     3. Understood the weapon completely.

     4. Comments:

(2) Radar   YES/NO

     1. Quickly recognized the malfunction.

     2. Took appropriate corrective action.

     3. Comments:

Section X
Part 4

NAVWEPS 01-60ABA-1

page 12

(3) VERDAN   YES/NO

    1. Quickly recognized the malfunction.

    2. Took appropriate corrective action.

    3. Comments:

(4) Inertial Platform   YES/NO

    1. Quickly recognized the failure.

    2. Took appropriate corrective action.

    3. Comments:

(5) Bombing Computer   YES/NO

    1. Quickly recognized the malfunction.

    2. Switched to a mode of delivery that did not utilize the bomb computer.

    3. Comments:

page 13

AIRMANSHIP

(1) Crew Coordination

    1. Coordination:

    2. Demands upon crew position anticipated:

    3. Over-all crew performance:

Section X
Part 4

NAVWEPS 01-60ABA-1

page 14

(2) Radio Procedures

    1. ATC clearance copied, understood, and correctly read back:

    2. Monitored appropriate frequencies:

    3. Position reports understood and correctly transmitted:

    4. Familiar with communications equipment and facilities:

NAVWEPS 01-60ABA-1

Section X
Part 4

page 15

(3) Navigational Charts and Publications
    1. Familiar with charts and publications:

    2. Rendered assistance as required:

Section X
Part 4

NAVWEPS 01-60ABA-1

page 16

PRELANDING, TAXI, AND SHUTDOWN

(1) NATOPS Pocket Check List

Omissions or errors in the use of the NATOPS Pocket Check List:

DEBRIEFING

(1) Equipment

1. Adequate write-up of known discrepancies:

2. Errors or omissions in completing equipment debriefing sheet:

(2) Mission Debrief

    1. Forms and data required but omitted or improperly filled out:

    2. Ability to reconstruct the flight with available information:

    3. General conduct of the debrief:

ALPHABETICAL INDEX

A

	Page
A-5A Pilot/Systems Operator Standardization Evaluation Form	211
Abnormal Cockpit Temperature	173
Aborted Take-offs	
see: Take-off	
Acceleration	17
A-C Power	37
generators	37
constant-speed drives	37
power distribution	37, 38, 39
ADC Moisture	188
Advisory Lights	
see: Warning, Caution, and Advisory Indicators	
Aerodynamic Braking	138
also see: Stopping the Aircraft	
nose-high method	138
three-point method	138
AFCS	
see: Automatic Flight Control System (AFCS)	
Aft CG	
see: Landing	
Aft Cockpit Check (Solo Flight)	127
Afterburners	14, 17
blowout	165
variable area exhaust nozzles	14, 17
After Landing	148N
After Starting	148E
radar-TV check	148E
radar turn-on	148E
TV check	148E
After Take-off	148E
Air Conditioning and Pressurization System	82, 81, 82, 84
conditioning	
cockpit	82
equipment	85, 113
pressure suit	86, 82
controls	84
defrost and anti-ice systems	87
operation	
anti-G suit	87
cockpit conditioning	83
cockpit pressurization	85, 82
defrost and anti-ice	88
equipment conditioning	86
pressure suit	86, 112, 113
pressurization	
cockpit	85, 82
cockpit pressurization schedule	82
Aircraft Service Changes	1
categories	1
immediate action	5
record purpose	5
routine action	5
urgent action	5
Flight Manual coverage	5
effectivity	5
superseded information	5
listing	7
Aircraft, The	1, 2, 3
general description	1, 2, 3
servicing	111, 112, 113
systems	11
Air Data Computer	101
Air Induction System	18, 13
engine pressure relief doors	18
engine door caution indicator	18, 16
operation	18
bypass gaps	23
inlet control	23
variable ramps	23
secondary airflow	18
Air Refueling	29, 160
also see: Buddy Tanker Refueling System	

	Page
receiver procedure	36, 160
Airspeed/Mach Indicator	103, 20, 21
Air Starts	25, 170, 171, **169**
Alinement, Autonavigator	148B
automatic (ship-based)	148C
handset	148B
All-attitude Indicator	102, 106, **103**
airspeed/Mach indicator	103, 20, 21
G-programmer	103
stand-by attitude indicator	103, 20, 21
All-weather Operation	183
cold weather procedures	188A
flight in turbulence	187
hot weather procedures	189
ice and rain	187
instrument approaches	184, 186
instrument flight	183
simulated	189
introduction	183
night flight	187
penetration	184
Alternate Cooling	85
Alternate Roll/Yaw Trim	58
Alternate Starts	24
Altimeter	
also see: Radar Altimeter	
calibration (additional checkpoint)	109
cockpit pressure	85, 73
failures	
baro cal altitude error	148M
baro cal indication error	148M
baro erratic or failed	148M
radar altitude error	148M
Altitude Mode (AFCS)	60
operation	62
AN/ASB-12 Approaches	185
Angle-of-attack System	103, 104
approach indexer	104, **104**
approach lights	104, **104**
indicator	103, 6, 7
Annunciator	105, **105**
Anti-G Suit	
operation	87
valves	87
Anti-ice System	
see: Defrost and Anti-ice Systems	
Applicability, Standardization Evaluation Program	197
Approaches	
also see: Landing	
AN/ASB-12	185
carrier	142, 143
characteristics, landing with aft cg	156A
instrument	184, 186
low-visibility	185
power approach and landing stalls	156A
recommended field take-off and approach speeds	135
technique, landing with aft cg	156A
typical	187
Approach Indexer	104, **104**
Approach Lights	98A, 104, **104**
ARI Erratic or Inoperative	148M
Arresting Gear	69
handle, arresting hook	70, 72
light, hook warning	70
servicing snubber and bumper	118
Arrestment	
carrier-based	143, 182G
broken wire or hook	144
emergency	182G
low sump level	182H
field	138, 182H
field barrier	182J
long-field	182H

PAGE NUMBERS IN BOLD DENOTE ILLUSTRATIONS

Index
Attack Mode Procedures—Button

	Page
short-field	182H
Attack Mode Procedures	195
Augmentation Systems	
see: Pitch Augmentation System	
Yaw Augmentation System	
Automatic Alinement (Ship-based)	148C
preheat installed (AFC 112)	148C
preheat not installed	148D
Automatic Flap Trim	58
Automatic Flight Control System (AFCS)	59, 60
controls and indicators	61, 60
mode	
altitude	60
auto-LABS	61
MACH — aircraft having ASC 42 complied with	60
NAV	61
normal	59
operation	61
altitude mode	62
auto-LABS	62
MACH mode	62
NAV mode	62
normal mode	61
Autonavigator Failures	148K
alinement (after start)	148K
alpha read-out excessive	148K
no gimbal caging	148K
steady AML	148K
alinement (prestart)	148K
counterslewing limited	148K
no AML	148K
no PP slewing or storing	148K
steady AML	148K
in operate	148K
AML on	148K
bombing errors	148L
course line steering (ALINE/HOLD switch)	148L
erratic/unusual winds	148K
excessive PP drift	148L
NAV/BOMB steering error	148L
stand-by navigation	148L
Autonavigator, Inertial	149
Auxiliary B/N Cooling and Heating — Aircraft Having ASC 29 Complied With	86
Auxiliary UHF Receiver	94
also see: UHF Communications Unit	
knob	
channel	94, 93
volume	94, 93
operation	94
auxiliary UHF/ADF procedure	94

B

	Page
Bail-out	171
Barometric Calibration	
see: High-altitude System	
Barricade Engagement	180
Basic Formations	
see: Formation Flight	
Before Entering Aircraft	127, 148A, 128, 129
aft cockpit check (solo flight)	127
Before Landing	148M
Before Take-off	148E
prelaunch check	148E
Before Taxi	148E
Before Taxiing into Position	134
also see: Taxi, Take-off, and Landing	
Bingo Fuel	143
Blowout, Afterburner	167
B/N Auxiliary Power Unit	111
Bolters	143
wave-off/bolter pattern, CCA	146
Bomb Bay Fuel Cans	25
fuel transfer failure	175
Bombing Systems	
also see: Weapons Systems	
mission performance considerations	194

	Page
preflight considerations	193
Bomb Mode	148F
conventional weapons	148F
special weapons	148F
Boost Pump Failure	174
see: Pump	
Boundary Layer Control (BLC)	67, 156
Braking	
also see: Speed Brakes	
Stopping the Aircraft	
Wheel Brakes	
failure	182J
with hydraulic failure	71
Breakup	
see: Formation Flight	
Briefing and Debriefing	121
debriefing	122
formation flight	158
general briefing	121
mission performance considerations, weapons delivery	194
operational briefings	122
final	122
mission planning	122
formation (flight leader's briefing)	122
general operations	122
navigation	121
operational mission planning	122
weapons	122
target	122
intelligence planning/briefing	122
weather	122
Broken Wire or Hook	
see: Arrestment	
Buddy Tanker Refueling System	32, 160, 33, 34
button, REEL RESPONSE	33, 34
control panel	34
indicator	
fuel TO BE TRANSFERRED	35, 34
TOTAL FUEL TRANSFERRED	35, 34
light	
FUEL ON	34, 34
FULL TRAIL	34, 34
IN TRANSIT	34, 34
operation, fuel system with buddy tanker	35
emergency	36, 161
procedure	35, 160
flight procedure	161
preflight check	160
switch	
emergency fuel flow	33, 34
HOSE CONTROL	32, 34
HOSE CUT	34, 34
SIGNAL LIGHTS	34, 34
Button	
alternate cooling reset	86, 84
audio select	90, 93
auxiliary B/N cooling — aircraft having ASC 29 complied with	86, 84
check lists and stand-by compass	99, 100
CNI power	92, 8, 9
command	105, 105
communications command	92, 93
control systems disable ("kill")	57, 61, 56, 60
drop tank transfer	30, 4
emergency ignition	15, 16
fuel probe light	99, 100
indicating lights test	101, 100
MODE 2 and MODE 3	97, 93
override	108, 108
pitot anti-ice	88, 84
REEL RESPONSE	33, 34
SPC	102, 4
STEER/TERRAIN	70, 56
synchronizing	105, 105
taxi light	99, 100
turbine retract	44, 6, 7
emergency hydraulic indicator	49, 6, 7

PAGE NUMBERS IN **BOLD** DENOTE ILLUSTRATIONS

Index
Bypass Gaps—Conditioning

	Page
warning lights test	99, 101, **100**
Bypass Gaps	23
duct airflow instability	24

C

	Page
Calibration	
see: High-altitude System Mode and Calibration Controls (Navigator)	
Canopies	74
handles	
canopy jettison	74, **10**, **72**
canopy manual release	74
disconnect override	75
external release	74
internal release	74
manual uplock	75
inspection	130
lights, canopy caution	75
valves	
canopy toggle	74, **4**
external toggle	74
Cans	
see: Bomb Bay Fuel Cans	
Carrier Arrestment	**182G**
barricade engagement	**182H**
emergency	**182G**
low sump level	**182H**
Carrier-based Procedures (Pilot)	139, 142
approach	142, 143
briefing	139
command responsibility	139
flight operations	139
instrument procedures	144
CCA	145
climb-out and rendezvous	144
penetration	145
launch procedure	141
lost communications	146
lost aircraft procedures	164
navigation	150
night carrier operations	146
recovery procedures	141
rendezvous and departure	141
scheduling	139
single-engine landings	144, **182B**
typical landing	142
Catapult Rockets	76
Caution Indicators	
see: Warning, Caution, and Advisory Indicators	
CCA	145
wave-off/bolter pattern	146
Check List	
also see: Mission Planning	
aft cockpit check (solo flight)	127
flight control and pretaxi	132
mission	125
navigation bag (flight crew)	125
prestart	127
taxi procedures	134
weapons system trainer (WST) procedures check	198
Circuit	
circuit breakers and limiters	**40**
electrical circuit protection devices	40, **40**
failures	177
Climb	
climb-out and rendezvous	144
cruise control	150
hot weather procedures	189
instrument flight	184
Closed Book Examination	198
grading criteria	200
Clouds, Formation in	
see: Formation Flight	
CNI	
also see: Communications-Navigation-Identification System (CNI)	
power button	92, **8**, **9**
Cockpit	
abnormal temperature	173
aft cockpit check (solo flight)	127
check (A/N prealined)	148A
conditioning	82
operation	83
temperature knob	83, 84
emergency entrance and escape	174, **175**
entering	131
fog	188
navigator's	**110B**, **110C**
pilot's	**1**
pressurization	85, 82
operation	85, 82
pressure altimeter	85, 73
pressure switch	85, 82, 84
pressurization schedule	82
Cold Weather Procedures	188A
ground operation	188A
postflight	189
preflight	188A
wet or icy runways	188A
Command Responsibility	
see: Carrier-based Procedures	
Communications	
also see: Lost Communications	
emergencies	146
procedures	191
intercommunications system failure	192
radio communications and electronic navigation equipment	191
responsibility	191
visual communications	191
Communications-Navigation-Identification System (CNI)	92, 93
auxiliary UHF receiver	94
operation	94
button, CNI power	92, **8**, **9**
controls	93
identification units (IFF and SIF)	97
indicator	
emergency power	92, 93
horizontal situation (HSI)	96, **96**
knobs, range and bearing	95, **72**
TACAN unit	95
operation	95
UHF communications unit	92
operation	94
Compass	
also see: Gyrocompass System Stand-by Magnetic Compass	
control panel	**105**
Complete Hydraulic Failure	180
Composite Disconnect, Personal	88A
Composition	
see: Written Examination	
Compressor Stalls	24, 167
Computer	
see: Air Data Computer	
Concept, Standardization Evaluation Program	197
applicability	197
definitions	197
implementation	197
Conditioning	
also see: Air Conditioning and Pressurization System	
cockpit	82
knob, cockpit temperature	83, 84
lever, navigator's heat	83, 84
switch, AUTO/MAN	83, 84
ventilation outlets	83
cockpit operation	83
controls	84
equipment	85, 113
alternate cooling	85
auxiliary B/N cooling and heating — aircraft having ASC 29 complied with	86
button	
alternate cooling reset	86, 84
auxiliary B/N cooling — aircraft having ASC 29 complied with	86, 84
indicator, alternate cooling caution	86, **6**, **7**

PAGE NUMBERS IN **BOLD** DENOTE ILLUSTRATIONS

Index
Console—Directional Flight Control

	Page
equipment operation	86
pressure suit	86, 82
knob	
suit flow	86, 84
suit temperature	86, 84
Console	
left	4
left forward	68
right	22, 23
right forward	72
Constant Control Feel	55
Constant-speed Drives	
see: A-C Power	
Controlled Ejection	
see: Ejection	
Controls and Indicators	
also see: Indicator	
automatic flight control system (AFCS)	61, 60
button, control systems disable ("kill")	61, 60
control, HEADING TRIM	61, 60
indicators, autoflight — aircraft having ASC No. 58 complied with	61, 60
knob, PITCH	61, 60
switch	
AFC	61, 60
AUTO LABS	61
ROLL	61, 60
CNI	93
IFF/SIF	97, 93
buttons, MODE 2 and MODE 3	97, 93
code dials, SIF MODE 1 and MODE 3	97, 93
switch	
EMERG IFF	98, 93
identify position (I/P)	97, 93
conditioning and pressurization	84
electrical power supply system	41
indicator	
d-c power caution	41, 6, 7
emergency electrical	41, 6, 7
generator-out caution	41, 6, 7
lights, generator-on	41
switches, generator	41, 8, 9
engine	16
flap and droop	66
flight control systems	55, 56
button, control systems disable ("kill")	57, 56
indicator	
electric flight control caution	57, 56
pitch augmentation caution	57, 56
roll and pitch	57, 56
yaw augmentation caution	57, 56
switch	
electric system	55, 56
pitch augmentation	57, 56
yaw augmentation	57, 56
fold systems controls	73
interior lights	
systems operator's	99, 100
pilot's	99, 100
lighting	100
main fuel	11
mode and calibration (systems operator)	107
radar altimeter	108
trim systems	58
control, pitch trim	58, 56
indicator, droop, flap, and trim	59, 56
switch	
alternate roll/yaw trim	59, 56
normal roll/stand-by pitch trim	59, 56
trim select	58, 56
yaw trim	59, 56
volume, UHF communications unit	92, 93
Control Stick	49, 56
Cooling	
air, external	111, 112, 113, 114
alternate	85
auxiliary B/N cooling and heating — aircraft 148932 and subsequent	86

	Page
Crew Duties	148A
Crew Requirements	120
navigator	120
pilot	120
planning requirements	123
minimum navigation requirements	124
systems operator	120
Critique, Standardization Evaluation Program	210
Cross-wind Landings	137
Cruise	
also see: Formation Flight	
flight procedures	150
cruise	150
descent and letdown	151
fuel management	151
preflight	150
take-off and climb	150
instrument flight	184
radar navigation	184

D

	Page
Damper	
see: Yaw Augmentation System	
Danger Areas	118, 115
movable surfaces	118A
noise areas	118, 115
D-C Power	37
failure	117
power distribution	37
Dead Reckoning Navigation	
see: Navigation	
Debriefing	
see: Briefing and Debriefing	
Definitions, Standardization Evaluation Program	197
area	197
conditionally qualified (CQ)	198
critical area	198
emergency	197
grading criteria	197
malfunction	197
minor discrepancies and/or omissions	198
momentary deviations	198
qualified (Q)	198
standardization evaluation recheck	198
sub-area	197
unqualified (U)	198
Defrost and Anti-ice Systems	87
button, pitot anti-ice—aircraft having ASC 10 complied with	88, 84
indicator, engine anti-ice	88
knob, windshield and canopy defrost	87, 84
operation	88
switch	
engine anti-ice	88, 84
windshield anti-ice	87, 84
Delivery Mode, Check Lists	148G
Delivery, Weapons	
see: Weapons Systems	
Departure	
see: Rendezvous and Departure	
Descent and Letdown	135, 151, 184
Description, General	1, 2, 3
Aircraft Service Changes	1
cockpits	1, 4—7
dimensions, aircraft	1
Developed Spin	
see: Spins	
Dial	
ground speed	105, 105
latitude	105, 105
Dimensions, Aircraft	1
Directional Flight Control System	53
also see: Yaw Augmentation System	
control pedals	49
operation	63
ratio changer	63
trim	58
operation	63

PAGE NUMBERS IN BOLD DENOTE ILLUSTRATIONS

	Page
centering	63
Ditching	182A
emergency cockpit entrance and escape	174, 175
information	182B
Downed Aircraft Surveillance	182A
Drogue Parachutes	76
Droop Leading Edge	
see: Wing Flaps and Droop Leading Edge	
Drop Tanks	25
fuel transfer failure	174
transfer buttons	30, 4
Dual Hydraulic System Failures	48
Duct Airflow Instability	24
also see: Bypass Gaps	
Dumping, Fuel	29

E

	Page
Echelon	
see: Formation Flight	
EGT Indicators	15, **16**
Ejection	
also see: Ejection Seat / Escape System	
alternate ejection pull-knobs	78
separation aneroid indicator	78
controlled	171
emergency	167, 168, 169
interconnect	78
minimum safe ejection altitudes	79
seat failure	171
emergency bail-out	171
Ejection Seat	75, **77**
also see: Escape System	
catapult rockets	76
drogue parachutes	76
failure	167
emergency bail-out	167
handle, harness lock	**78**, 77
inertia reel	76
inspection	130
knee bar and foot retractors	76
operation	172, 173
separation system	76
aneroid indicator	76
survival kit	76
switch, seat adjust	**78**, 8, 9, **10B**
training	120
Electrical Power Supply System	37, **38, 39**
a-c power	37
circuit protection devices	40, **40**
controls and indicators	**41**
d-c power	37
electronics power supply	40
emergency power unit	40
external power	37
electrical requirements	111, 112, 113, 114
failures	176
both generators	176
circuit	42
d-c power	176
one generator	176
fire	177
ram-air turbine operation	41
Electronic	
navigation equipment	191
power supply	40
table of equipment	91
Elements, Formation	
see: Formation Flight	
Emergency Brakes	71, **68**
also see: Wheel Brakes	
Emergency Cockpit Entrance and Escape	182J, 182K
Emergency Ejection	167
Emergency Electrical Power Unit	40
Emergency Extension	
flap	68, 178
landing gear	178, 179
Emergency Flap Switch	67, **66**

	Page
Emergency Hydraulic Power	44
button, turbine retract	44
indicator, emergency hydraulic	49
handle, air turbine	44
Emergency Oxygen System	88A
pressure gages	88A
rings	88A
Emergency Power Indicator	92, **93**
Emergency Procedures	163
aborted take-offs	164
air starts	170, 171
barricade engagement	180
brake failure	163
ditching	171
downed aircraft	164
ejection seat failure	171
electrical failures	176
emergency escape	166
engine failure	165
engine fire	170
engine start malfunctions	164
fuel system failure	174
hydraulic failures	177
landing emergencies	178
lost aircraft procedures	164
nose wheel steering failure	163
tire failure	163
Emergency Retraction, Landing Gear	166
Emergency Signals	
see: Lost Communications	
Emergency Tanker	148M
Emergency Wave-off	181
Engine	11, **16**
also see: Air Induction System	
acceleration	17
afterburners	14, 17
characteristics	17
controls and indicators	**16**
emergency procedures	163
air starts	170, 171
failure	165, 167
afterburner blowout	167
both engines at altitude	170
engine oil overheat	168
exhaust nozzle	167
fuel filter bypass	168
high altitude	165
nose wheel steering	164
oil system	172
one engine	165
after take-off	165
at altitude	170
oxygen system	173
suit emergency pressurization	173
suit emergency oxygen duration (full bottle)	174
single-engine landings	165, 166
fire	
during flight	173
during start	163
other than tail-pipe fires	164
tail-pipe fire	163
electrical	170
flame-out	167
erratic operation	170
hot air leaks	170
on take-off	164
above refusal speed	164
below refusal speed	164
smoke and fumes	173
fuel systems	11, 12
governor override	17
icing	188
ice and water, ingestion of	188
high power settings	188
low power settings	188
ice buildup	188A
high power settings	188A
low power settings	188A

PAGE NUMBERS IN BOLD DENOTE ILLUSTRATIONS

Index
Entering Aircraft—Familiarization

NAVWEPS 01-60ABA-1

	Page
recommendations	188A
indicator	
EGT	15, 16
fuel flow	15, 16
nozzle position	15, 16
oil pressure	15, 16
oil overheat	172
oil supply systems	11, 16
operating envelope	**169**
operating procedures	24
postflight shutdown, shore-based	138
poststart procedures, carrier-based	140
pressure relief doors	18
engine door caution indicator	18, 16
servicing, engine oil	118
single-engine operation	170
starting	
air	111, 112, 113, 114
alternate starts	24
carrier-based	140
malfunctions	163
autoacceleration	163
false start	163
hot or hung start	163
operating procedures	24
shore-based	
alternate start (GTC-85 or MA-1A unit)	132
without RCPP-105 connection	132
with RCPP-105 connection	131
starting system	14, 112, 113
switch	
ENGINE FIRE	
engine MASTER	14, 16
engine START	14, 16
ramp control	15, 16
tachometers	15, 16
throttles	15, 16
variable stators and inlet guide vanes	14
Entering Aircraft	127, 148A, 130, 131, 175
Equipment	
also see: Personal Equipment Requirements	
electronic navigation	191
radio communication	191
table of electronic equipment	**91**
Equipment Conditioning	85, 113
alternate cooling	85
auxiliary B/N cooling and heating — aircraft having ASC 29 complied with	86
button	
alternate cooling reset	86, **84**
auxiliary B/N cooling — aircraft having ASC 29 complied with	86, **84**
indicator, alternate cooling caution	86, **6, 7**
operation	86
Escape System	75, 79
also see: Ditching	
Ejection	
Ejection Seat	
ejection interconnect	78
ejection seats	75, 77
emergency	166
controlled ejection	166
emergency ejection	167, 168, 169
emergency cockpit entrance and escape	174, 175
face curtain	78
harness release handle	78, 77
minimum safe ejection altitudes	79
operation	80, 79, **80**
pull-knobs, alternate ejection	78
trajectory	**80**
Evaluation	
see: Standardization Evaluation	
Examination	
see: Oral Examination	
Written Examination	
Exhaust Nozzles	14, 17
failures	165
both nozzles full open	165

	Page
nozzle fluctuation	165
nozzle full closed	166
one nozzle full open	165
nozzle position indicator	15, 16
Exterior Inspection	128, 129
Exterior Lights	98
button	
fuel probe light	99, 100
taxi light	99, 100
light	
air refueling reference	98A
anticollision	98
approach	98A
formation	98
fuel probe	98A
position	98
taxi	98
switch	
anticollision lights	98A, 100
approach lights	99, 100
exterior lights master	98A, 100
formation lights	99, 100
wing and taillight	98A, 100
External Power	37
power and air requirements	111, 112, 113
B/N auxiliary power unit	111
cooling air	111, 112, 113
electrical	111, 112, 113
engine starting air	111, 112, 113
power units (RCPP-105-1 and RCPT-105-3)	111
units	114

F

	Page
Face Curtain	78
Failure	
altimeter	148M
autonavigator	148K
bomb bay can transfer	175
boost pump	174
both engines	25
both generators	176
brake	163, 182J
braking with hydraulic failure	71
circuit	42
cursor control	148L
d-c power	176
drop tank transfer	174
ejection seat	167
electrical system	176
electric flight control	182
engine	164
on take-off	164
erratic operation, engine	25
exhaust nozzle	165
flight control systems	181
fuel system	174
hydraulic	179
complete	180
No. 1 or No. 2 system	179
pump	179
intercommunications system	192
nose wheel steering	163
oil system	168
one engine	165
one generator	177
pitch augmentation	144
pitot-static system	180
static pressure source	181
total pressure source	180
projected display (pilot's PPDI)	148J
television	148J
tire	163, 178
trim	182
wind control	148L
wing fuel transfer	175
yaw augmentation	182
False Start	164
Familiarization and Transition	149

PAGE NUMBERS IN BOLD DENOTE ILLUSTRATIONS

Index

	Page
Field Arrestment	
see: Arrestment	
Field Landing	
see: Landing	
Filter	
fuel	11, 16
fuel bypass	168
Final Briefing	
see: Briefing and Debriefing	
Final Grade Determination, Standardization Evaluation Program	209
phase I	209
phase II	209
phase III	210
Fire	
electrical	170
engine	170
during flight	173
during start	163
other than tail-pipe fires	170
tail-pipe fire	170
on take-off	164
above refusal speed	164
below refusal speed	164
hot air leaks	170
smoke and fumes	170
Flags, Wing and Tail Fold Warning	73
Flame-out or Failure, Engine	167
erratic operation	170
Flap	
also see: Wing Flaps and Droop Leading Edge	
automatic flap trim	58
emergency extension	68, 178
interconnect	67
Flight Characteristics	151
inlet buzz	157
landing with aft cg	152
low-speed flight	151, 153
low-speed flight (landing configuration)	156, 153
minimum control speeds	153
power approach and landing	152
recovery from poststall gyrations	155
spins	156
stall and poststall gyrations	152
Flight Control and Pretaxi Check	132
abbreviated	132
complete	162
Flight Control Systems	49, 50—53, 56
also see: Automatic Flight Control System (AFCS)	
controls and indicators	55, 56
control stick	49, 56
directional	53
directional control pedals	49
failures	181
electric flight control	182
pitch augmentation	181
disengaged	182
emergency wave-off	181
malfunction	181
pitch control malfunction	181
trim	182
yaw augmentation	182
horizontal stabilizers	49
lateral	52
longitudinal	51
operation	62
directional control	63
lateral control	63
longitudinal control	62
pitch augmentation	63, 50, 51
trim	63
pitch augmentation system	
modified by ASC 42	54
unmodified	55
spoiler-deflectors	54
trim systems	57
vertical stabilizer	49
yaw damper	55
Flight Evaluation (Phase III)	199
grading criteria	201
grading material	199
pilot	199, 201
cruise	199, 202
emergencies	199, 203
instruments	199, 202
mission planning	199, 201
postlanding, shutdown, and debriefing	200, 205
preflight	199, 201
tactics	199, 204
taxi, take-off, and climb-out	199, 202
VFR landing pattern	200, 204
score	199
systems operator	200, 205
airmanship	200, 208
debriefing	200, 209
in-flight malfunctions	200, 207
mission planning	200, 205
operating procedures	200, 207
preflight inspection	200, 206
prelanding, taxi, and shutdown	200, 209
taxi and pre-take-off	200, 206
Flight Operations, Carrier-based Procedures	139
manning aircraft	139
starting and poststart procedures	140
taxi procedures	140
towing	139
Flight Procedures	149
air refueling	160
cruise control	150
familiarization and transition	149
flight characteristics	151
flight test procedures	161
formation flight	157
general	149
minimum control speeds	153
navigation	149
weapon delivery tactics	162A
Flight Reference Set, AN/ASN-26	
see: Gyrocompass System	
Flight Scheduling	
see: Scheduling	
Fog	
see: Cockpit	
Fold Systems	72
controls	73
radome	73
wing and tail	72
Formation Flight	157
basic formations	157
cruise	157
echelon	157
parade	157
rules	159
briefing	158
formation breakup	159
formation elements	158
cruise	158
parade and echelon	158
formation in clouds	159
general	157
night formation	159
rendezvous and departure (carrier-based)	159
normal rendezvous	159
running rendezvous	159
rendezvous and departure pattern (shore-based)	158
normal rendezvous	158
running rendezvous	158
squadron formation	158
Forms and Records	210
A-5A pilot systems operator standardization evaluation	211
forms	210
records	210
Forward Console	
see: Console	

PAGE NUMBERS IN BOLD DENOTE ILLUSTRATIONS

Index
Fouled Deck—Horizontal Situation Indicator

	Page
Fouled Deck Holding	145
Free-play Mechanism	
see: Lateral Flight Control System	
Fuel Filter Bypass	174
Fuel Planning	
Bingo fuel	143
cruise control	151
instrument flight	183
mission planning	124
Fuel Supply System, Aircraft	25, 26, 27
also see: Air Refueling	
Buddy Tanker Refueling System	
Fuel Systems, Engine	
Refueling	
buttons, drop tank transfer	30, 4
cans, bomb bay fuel	25
dumping	29
failure	174
bomb bay can transfer	176
boost pump	174
drop tank transfer	176
wing fuel transfer	176
handle, fuel dump	30, 68
indicator	
fuel low caution	31, 6, 7
fuel quantity	31, 4, 6, 7
operation	31
inverted flight	32
normal sequence	31
touch-and-go	32
quantity data	28
refueling	29
switch	
CANS transfer	30, 4
INFLIGHT FUEL PROBE	30, 4
SUMP	30, 4
tanks	
drop	25
internal fuel	25
transfer	28
venting	29
Fuel Systems, Engine	11, 12
engine-driven pumps	11
fuel filter bypass	168
fuel filters	11, 16
fuel flow indicator	15, 16
main fuel controls	11
oil coolers	11
Fumes	
see: Smoke and Fumes	

G

	Page
GCA Approach	187, 186
Gear	
see: Arresting Gear	
Landing	
General Arrangement	2, 3
General Briefing	
see: Briefing and Debriefing	
General Flight Procedures	
see: Flight Procedures	
Generators	37
constant-speed drives	37
failure	
both	176
one	177
Governor Override	17
flight idle reset	17
rpm/EGT cutback	17
G-programmer	103
Grading Instructions, Standardization	
Evaluation Program	200
final grade determination	209
flight evaluation grading criteria	201
NAMT systems check grading criteria	201
oral examination grading criteria	200
written examination grading criteria	200
WST procedures check grading criteria	201

	Page
Grading Material, Flight Evaluation	199
Ground Evaluation (Phases I and II)	198
oral examination	198
weapons system trainer (WST) evaluation check	198
written examination	198
Ground Handling	118A
towing	118A
turning radius	118A, 116
Ground Operation	
cold weather procedures	188A
hot weather procedures	189
Ground Pressure Refueling	
see: Refueling	
Ground Training Schedules	
see: Scheduling	
Gyrocompass System	105, 105
annunciator	106, 105
buttons	
command	105, 105
synchronizing	105, 105
compass control panel	105
dial	
ground speed	105, 105
latitude	105, 105
indicator	
all-attitude	106, 103
horizontal situation	106, 96
knob, heading set	106, 105
operation	106
COMP (emergency)	106A
DG (alternate)	106
SLAVED (normal)	106
selector, mode	105, 105
stand-by magnetic compass	106
switch, hemisphere	105, 105

H

	Page
Handgrip, Catapult	15, 16
Handle	
air turbine	44, 6, 7
arresting hook	70, 72
canopy jettison	74, 10, 72
canopy manual release	74
disconnect override	75
external release	74
internal release	74
fold control	73, 22, 73
fuel dump	31, 68
harness lock	78, 77
harness release	78, 77
landing gear	68, 68
landing gear emergency extension	69, 6, 7
manual uplock	75
speed brake dump	65, 4
Handset Alinement	148B
preheat installed (AFC 112)	148B
preheat not installed	148B
preheat requirements	148B
Hazards	
see: Low-visibility Approaches	
Helicopter Water Rescue	182B
High-altitude/High-speed Flights	
see: Personal Equipment Requirements	
High-altitude System (Systems Operator)	107
also see: Mode and Calibration	
Controls (Systems Operator)	
operation (systems operator)	109
altimeter calibration (additional checkpoint)	109
barometric calibration	109
barometric calibration without bomb directing set	109
High-pressure Air Valves, Servicing	118
High-speed Operation, Pitch Augmentation	64
Holding	145, 184
Hook	
see: Arresting Gear	
Horizontal Situation Indicator (HSI)	96, 106, 96
ADF mode	96, 96
NAV and BOMB modes	96
TACAN mode	96, 96

PAGE NUMBERS IN BOLD DENOTE ILLUSTRATIONS

Index
Horizontal Stabilizers—Instrument Approaches

	Page
Horizontal Stabilizers	
see: Stabilizers	
Hot Air Leaks	170
Hot or Hung Start	164
Hot Weather Procedures	189
ground operation	189
landing	189
post flight	189
preflight	189
take-off and climb	189
Hydraulic Power Supply Systems	41, 42, 43
emergency	44
air turbine handle	44, 6, 7
turbine retract button	44, 6, 7
indicator	49, 6, 7
failure	179
complete hydraulic failure	180
No. 1 or No. 2 system	179
pump failures	179
No. 1 system	41
No. 2 system	41
pressure caution indicator	44, 6, 7
pressure indicators	44, 6, 7
subsystems isolation switch	44, 4
servicing	118

I

	Page
Ice and Rain	187
also see: Defrost and Anti-ice Systems	
ADC moisture	188
cockpit fog	188
engine icing	188
ice buildup	188A
high power settings	188A
low power settings	188A
ingestion of ice and water	188
high power settings	188
low power settings	188
recommendations	188A
pitot-static ice	187
wet or icy runways	188A
ICS	
see: Intercommunications System (ICS)	
Identification Units (IFF and SIF)	97
IFF procedures, pilot's	98
IFF/SIF controls	97, 93
buttons, MODE 2 and MODE 3	97, 93
selector, MASTER function	97, 93
SIF MODE 1 and MODE 3 code dials	97
switch, EMERG IFF	98, 93
switch, identify position (I/P)	97, 93
IFF/SIF operation (systems operator)	98
IFF/SIF procedures	191
authentication	191
emergency communications	191
Implementation, Standardization Evaluation Program	197
Indicator	
also see: Controls and Indicators	
Light	
airspeed/Mach	103, 6, 7
all-attitude	102, 106, 103
alternate cooling caution	86, 6, 7
angle-of-attack	103, 6, 7
autoflight—aircraft having ASC 58 complied with	61, 60
caution	101, 6, 7
channel/frequency	94, 93
d-c power caution	41, 6, 7
droop, flap, and trim	59, 56
EGT	15, 16
electric flight control caution	57, 56
emergency electrical	41, 6, 7
emergency hydraulic	49, 6, 7
emergency power	92, 93
engine anti-ice	88
engine door caution	18, 16
fire warning	1, 101, 6, 7
flap/droop position	67
droops caution	67, 6, 7
fuel flow	15, 16

	Page
fuel low caution	31, 6, 7
fuel quantity	31, 4, 6, 7
fuel TO BE TRANSFERRED	35, 34
GEAR STIFF caution	69, 6, 7
generator-out caution	41, 6, 7
horizontal situation (HSI)	96, 106, 96
HYD PRESS caution on	45
hydraulic pressure	44, 6, 7
hydraulic pressure caution	44, 6, 7
inlet air temperature	103, 72
landing gear position	69, 6, 7
low-altitude (pilot)	108, 108
master warning and master caution	101
nozzle position	15, 16
oil pressure	15, 16
oxygen quantity	88A, 6, 7
oxygen warning	1, 88A, 100
pitch augmentation caution	57, 56
ramp control caution	17, 16
roll and pitch	57, 56
separation aneroid	76
speed brake	65, 6, 7
stand-by attitude	103, 6, 7
TOTAL FUEL TRANSFERRED	35, 34
warning	1, 101, 6, 7
WHEELS warning	69, 6, 7
yaw augmentation caution	57, 56
Indoctrination	119
crew requirements	120
introduction	119
personal equipment requirements	120
training	119
Inertial Autonavigator	149
Inertia Reel	76
In-flight Fuel Probe Switch	30, 4
In-flight Emergencies	167
abnormal cockpit temperature	173
air starts	170
both engines failed at altitude	170
compressor stalls	167
engine fire during flight	173
engine flame-out or failure	167
erratic operation	170
engine oil overheat	172
failure of one engine at altitude	170
no-thrust glide	172
oil system failure	172
oxygen system failure	173
suit emergency oxygen duration (full bottle)	174
suit emergency pressurization	173
single-engine operation	170
smoke and fumes	173
In-flight Procedures	148E
mode	
bomb	148F
delivery, check lists	148G
nav	148F
recon	148F
search (TV)	148F
offset bombing	148F
radar/barometric altimeter calibration	148E
radiation silence	148G
refueling tanker	148G
terrain avoidance check (pilot)	148G
Inlet Air Temperature Indicator	103, 72
Inlet Buzz	157
Inlet Control	23
Inlet Guide Vanes and Variable Stators	14
Inspection	
canopy and seat	130
exterior	128, 129
oxygen, preflight	89
Instrument Approaches	184, 186
AN/ASB-12 approaches	185
recommended procedures	185
carrier approaches	186A
voice procedure	186A
low-visibility approaches	185

PAGE NUMBERS IN BOLD DENOTE ILLUSTRATIONS

Index
Instrument Flight—Light

	Page
execution	185
hazards	185
typical approach	187
Instrument Flight	183
climb	184
cruise	184
radar navigation	184
descent	184
fuel planning	183
holding	184
simulated	189
take-off	183
Instrument Panel	20, 21
Instrument Procedures, Carrier	144
CCA	145
climb-out and rendezvous	144
penetration	145
Instruments	101
air data computer	101
airspeed Mach indicator	103, 6, 7
all-attitude indicator	102, 103
G-programmer	103
inlet air temperature indicator	103, 72
stand-by attitude indicator	103, 6, 7
static pressure compensator (SPC)	102
SPC button	102, 4
Intercommunications System (ICS)	90, 91
buttons, audio select	90, 93
failure	192
both crew members	192
if pilot loses ICS	192
if systems operator loses ICS	192
knob, volume	90, 93
operation	92
selector, function	90, 93
switch	
microphone	90
microphone select	90, 93
Interconnect	
ejection	78
flap	67
Interior Lights	
pilot's	99
controls	99, 100
button	
check lists and stand-by compass	99, 100
warning lights test	99, 100
knob	
console lights	99, 100
instrument lights	99, 100
light, emergency	99, 8, 9
switch	
floodlights	99, 100
high-altitude lights	99, 100
systems operator's	99
controls	99, 100
button, indicating lights test	101, 100
knob, compartment lights	99, 101, 100
switch, red floodlights	101, 100
Internal Fuel Tanks	25
Inverted Flight	
see: Fuel Supply System, Aircraft	
Stalls and Poststall Gyrations	

K

	Page
Knee Bar and Foot Retractors	76
Knob	
alternate ejection pull-knobs	78
altitude mode	107, 108
channel, auxiliary UHF receiver	94, 93
channel, TACAN	95, 93
cockpit temperature	83, 84
compartment lights	99, 100
console lights	99, 100
heading set	106, 105
instrument lights	99, 100
PITCH (AFCS)	61, 60
range and bearing	95, 72

	Page
suit flow	86, 84
suit temperature	86, 84
volume, auxiliary UHF receiver	94, 93
volume, ICS	90, 93
volume, TACAN	95, 93
windshield and canopy defrost	87, 84

L

Landing	
also see: Approaches	
Low-speed Flight	
Penetration	
Postflight	
Taxi, Take-off, and Landing	
aft cg, landing with	156A
33 percent MAC	156A
after touchdown	156A
approach characteristics	156A
approach technique	156A
pitch augmentation off	156A
power approach and landing stalls	156A
carrier-based landing pattern	142, 142
single-engine landing	144
typical carrier landing	142
emergencies	182B
abnormal flap/droop settings	182E
field arrestment	180
flap extension	182G
single-engine landings	182B, 182C
carrier	182B
wave-off	182B
tire failure	182E
unsafe gear	182E, 182G
gear	68
emergency extension	182F, 182F
emergency retraction	166
handle	
emergency extension	69, 6, 7
landing gear	68, 68
indicator	
GEAR STIFF caution	69, 6, 7
landing gear position	69, 6, 7
WHEELS warning	69, 6, 7
light, landing gear warning	69, 68
operation	69
servicing landing gear struts	118
switch, emergency gear up	68, 68
hot weather procedures	189
shore-based penetration and landing	135, 136
after landing	138
braking techniques	138
commencing descent	135
cross-wind landings	137
field arrestments	138
landing technique	137
night landings	137
normal approach and landing	135, 136
touch-and-go practice	137
typical field landing	136
Lateral Flight Control System	54, 52
also see: Spoiler-Deflectors	
free-play mechanism	54
operation	63
effectiveness	63
ratio changer	54, 52
trim	58
operation	63
Launch Procedure	141
night carrier operations	146
Left Console	4
Left Forward Console	68
Letdown, Descent and	151
Lever, Navigator's Heat	83, 84
Light	
also see: Exterior Lights	
Indicator	
Interior Lights	
Miscellaneous Lighting	
Warning, Caution, and	
Advisory Indicators	

PAGE NUMBERS IN **BOLD** DENOTE ILLUSTRATIONS

	Page
advisory	101
air refueling reference	98A
anticollision	98
approach	98A, 104, **104A**
canopy caution	75
emergency	101, **8, 9**
formation	98
FUEL ON	34, **34**
fuel probe	98A
FULL TRAIL	34, **34**
generator-on	41
hook warning	70
IN TRANSIT	34, **34**
landing gear warning	69, **68**
low-altitude warning	109
night carrier operations	146
position	98
taxi	98
Lighting Systems	98, **100**
also see: Warning, Caution, and Advisory Indicators	
controls	**100**
exterior lights	98
interior lights, pilot's	99
controls	99, **100**
interior lights systems operator's	99
controls	99, **100**
miscellaneous	101, **112, 113**
Line Operations, Shore-based Procedures	127
before entering aircraft	127, **128, 129**
aft cockpit check (solo flight)	127
entering aircraft	127, **130, 131**
flight control and pretaxi check	132
manning aircraft	127
prestart check	127
starting engines (without RCPP-105 connection)	132
starting engines (with RCPP-105 connection)	131
Loading and Safety Precautions, Weapons	193
Long-field Arrestment	
see: Arrestment	
Longitudinal Flight Control System	54, **50, 51**
also see: Spoiler-Deflectors	
operation	62
pitch augmentation off	62
pitch augmentation on	62
Lost Communications	146
communications emergencies	146
emergency signals	147
Lost Aircraft Procedures	182
additional procedures	
carrier-based	182A
shore-based	182A
if you are lost	182
voice procedure	182A
Low-altitude System (Pilot)	107
indicator (pilot)	108, **108**
button, override	108, **108**
light, low-altitude warning	109
operation	109
Low-level Navigation	
see: Navigation	
Low-pressure Chamber, Training	119
Low-speed Flight	151, **153**
landing configuration	156, **153**
boundary layer control (BLC)	156
pitch augmentation inoperative	156
Low-speed Operation, Pitch Augmentation	63
Low-visibility Approaches	186A
execution	186A
hazards	186A

M

	Page
MACH Mode (AFCS)	60
operation	62
Main Fuel Controls	11
Main UHF/ADF Procedure	
see: UHF Communications Unit	
Malfunction Check Lists	
altimeter failures	148M
ARI erratic or inoperative	148M
autonavigator failures	148K
cursor control failure	148L
pilot's AAI — steering pointer frozen	148M
pilot's HSI — frozen range or azimuth	148M
position/destination frozen or erratic	148M
projected display (pilot's PPDI) failures	148J
radar failures	148G
TAS/GS indicator erratic or inoperative	148M
television failures	148J
wind control failures	148L
Manning Aircraft	
carrier-based procedures	139
systems operator	140
pressure suits	140
shore-based procedures	127
Manning Ready Room	
see: Scheduling	
Manual Brakes	71
Manual Separation from Seat	166
Marshal, Recovery Procedures	141
Master Warning and Master Caution Indicators	101
Methods of Navigation	
see: Navigation	
Methods, Weapons Delivery	
see: Weapons Systems	
Military Specifications Servicing	114
Minimum Control Speeds	153
Minimum Safe Ejection Altitudes	79
Miscellaneous Lighting	101, **112, 113**
Mission Performance Considerations, Weapons Delivery	194
bomb release	194
briefing	194
in flight	194
postflight	195
pre-take-off	194
tactical	195
Mission Planning	123
also see: Briefing and Debriefing	
crew planning requirements	123
minimum navigation requirements	124
fuel planning	124
fuel requirements	124
Bingo fuel	125
speed	124
fuel control log	124
single-engine flight	124
subsonic missions	124
supersonic missions	124
mission check list	125
aircraft armament	126
bomb system	126
detection	125
fuel management	125
navigation	125
reports	126
tactical	126
weapons	125
navigation bag check list (flight crew)	125
navigation planning	123
factors	123
operational mission planning	123
planning forms	123
specific responsibilities	123
pilot	123
pilot and systems operator	123
systems operator	123
subsonic/supersonic missions	123
Mode and Calibration Controls (Systems Operator)	107, **108**
knob, altitude mode	107, **108**
switch, altitude set	108, **108**
Modes	
AFCS	
altitude	60, **62**
auto-LABS	61, **62**
MACH—aircraft having ASC 42 complied with	60, **62**
NAV	61, **62**
normal	59, **61**

PAGE NUMBERS IN **BOLD** DENOTE ILLUSTRATIONS

Index
Movable Surfaces—Operation

	Page
compass system	
COMP (emergency)	106A
DG (alternate)	106
SLAVED (normal)	106
horizontal situation indicator (HSI)	
ADF	96, 96
NAV and BOMB	96
TACAN	96, 96
ICS operation	
alternate mode, loss of	92
normal mode, loss of	92
Movable Surfaces	118A

N

	Page
NAMT Systems Check	199
grading criteria	201
Navigation	149
also see: Mission Planning	
carrier-based	150
electronic equipment	191
methods of navigation	149
dead reckoning	150
inertial autonavigator	149
low-level	150
radar	150
radio	150
minimum navigation requirements	124
mission check list	125
planning	123, 150
factors	123
radar	184
systems operator responsibilities	150
Navigation Bag Check List (Flight Crew)	125
Navigator's Cockpit	1, 6, 7
NAV Mode	
(AFCS)	61
operation	62
normal procedures	148F
Night Flight	187
carrier operations	146
launch	146
lights	146
recovery	146
signals	146
formation flight	159
landings	137
No. 1 System, Hydraulic Power Supply	41
failure	179
No. 2 System, Hydraulic Power Supply	41
failure	179
indicators	
hydraulic pressure	44, 6, 7
hydraulic pressure caution	44, 6, 7
switch, hydraulic subsystems isolation	44, 4
Noise Areas	118, 115
Normal Brake System	71
also see: Wheel Brakes	
Normal Fuel Sequence	31
Normal ICS Operation	92
Normal Mode (AFCS)	59
operation	61
Normal Oxygen System	88, 89
indicators	
oxygen quantity	88A, 6, 7
oxygen warning	88A, 100
operation	89
preflight	89
oxygen duration	89
valves, oxygen supply	88A, 4
Normal Procedures (Systems Operator)	148A
after landing	148N
after starting	148E
after take-off	148E
autonavigator alinement	148B
before entering aircraft	148A
before landing	148M
before take-off	148E
before taxi	148E
cockpit check (A/N prealined)	148A
crew duties	148A
emergency tanker	148M
entering aircraft	148A
in-flight procedures	148E
malfunction check lists	148G
stand-by nav turn-on	148D
systems shutdown	148N
Normal Rendezvous	
see: Formation Flight	
Nose Wheel Steering	70
button, STEER/TERRAIN	70, 56
failure	163
No-thrust Glide	172
Nozzle	
see: Exhaust Nozzles	
Nozzle Position Indicator	15, 16

O

	Page
Offset Bombing	148F
differential ballistic wind (DBW)	148F
remote aimpoint with DBW	148F
Oil Coolers	11
Oil Pressure Indicator	15, 16
Oil Supply Systems	11, 16
failure	168
engine oil overheat	168
servicing, engine oil	118
Open Book Examination	198
grading criteria	200
Operation	
also see: All-weather Operation	
Flight Operations, Carrier-based Procedures	
Line Operations, Shore-based Procedures	
Night Flight	
AFCS	61
mode	
altitude	62
auto-LABS	62
MACH — aircraft having ASC No. 42	
complied with	62
NAV	62
normal	61
air induction system	18
bypass gaps	23
duct airflow instability	24
inlet control	23
variable ramps	23
ramp monitor	23
anti-G suit	87
auxiliary receiver	94
auxiliary UHF/ADF procedure	94
buddy tanker emergency	36
cockpit conditioning	83
cockpit pressurization	85, 82
compass system	106
COMP (emergency)	106
DG (alternate)	106
SLAVED (normal)	106
defrost and anti-ice	88
ejection seat	172, 173
engine	24
operating envelope	169
starting	24
equipment conditioning	86
escape system	80, 80
flight control systems	62
directional control	63
ratio changer	63
lateral control	63
effectiveness	63
longitudinal control	62
pitch augmentation off	62
pitch augmentation on	62
pitch augmentation operation	63, 50, 51
high-speed	64
low-speed	63
pitch damping	64
trim operation	63

PAGE NUMBERS IN **BOLD** DENOTE ILLUSTRATIONS

	Page
directional	63
lateral	63
fuel system	31
inverted flight	32
normal sequence	31
touch-and-go	32
fuel system with buddy tanker	35
high-altitude system	109
altimeter calibration (additional checkpoint)	109
barometric calibration	109
barometric calibration without bomb directing set	109
ICS	92
alternate mode, loss of	92
external stations	92
normal	92
normal mode, loss of	92
IFF/SIF	
pilot	98
systems operator	98
landing gear	69
low-altitude system	109
oxygen systems	88A
emergency	89
normal	88A
preflight	89
pitch augmentation	63, 50, 51
high-speed	64
low-speed	63
pitch damping	64
pressure suit	86, 112, 113
ram-air turbine	41
flight check	44
single-engine	25
speed brakes	65
characteristics	65
TACAN	95
touch-and-go	32
trim	63
directional	63
centering	63
lateral	63
UHF communications	94
main UHF/ADF procedure	94
wheel brake systems	71
emergency	71
normal brake system	71
Operational Briefings	
see: Briefing and Debriefing	
Operational Mission Planning	
see: Mission Planning	
Oral Examination	198
grading criteria	200
materials	200
part one	200
part two	200
Over-water Flights	
see: Personal Equipment Requirements	
Oxygen Systems	88
emergency	88A
normal	88, 89
operation	88A
oxygen duration	89
personal composite disconnect	88A
servicing	118
suit emergency pressurization	90

P

	Page
Panel	
buddy tanker control	34
compass control	105
instrument	6, 7
Parade	
see: Formation Flight	
Pedals	
see: Directional Flight Control System	
Penetration	
all-weather operation	184
carrier-based penetration	145

	Page
CCA wave-off/bolter pattern	146
fouled deck holding	145
shore-based penetration and landing	135, 136
braking techniques	138
commencing descent	135
cross-wind landings	137
field arrestments	138
landing technique	137
night landings	137
normal approach and landing	135, 136
touch-and-go practice	137
typical field landing	136
thunderstorm	187
Performance	
see: Mission Performance Considerations, Weapons Delivery	
Personal Composite Disconnect	88A
Personal Equipment Requirements	120
high-altitude/high-speed flights	120A
over-water flights	120A
temperate climate (low and medium altitude)	120
Pilot's AAI—Steering Pointer Frozen	148M
Pilot's Cockpit	1, 4, 5
Pilot's HSI—Frozen Range or Azimuth	148M
Pilot Standardization Evaluation	
also see: Flight Evaluation (Phase III)	
form	211
worksheets	215
Pitch Augmentation System	
also see: Longitudinal Flight Control System	
disengaged	182
failure	181
malfunction	181
modified by ASC 42	54
constant control	55
pitch damping	55
off, landing with aft cg	156A
operation	63, 50, 51
high-speed	64
low-speed	63
pitch damping	64
unmodified	55
Pitch Control Malfunction	181
Pitch Damping	55, 64
Pitch Trim	57
stand-by pitch trim	58
Pitot-Static Ice	187
servicing pitot-static drains	118
Pitot-Static System Failure	180
static pressure source	181
total pressure source	181
Planning	
see: Briefing and Debriefing, Fuel Planning, Mission Planning, Navigation	
Pneumatic Power Supply System	49
servicing	118
Position/Destination Frozen or Erratic	148M
Postflight	138
after landing	138
cold weather procedures	189
debriefing	138A
engine shutdown	138A
hot weather procedures	189
mission performance considerations, weapons delivery	195
Poststall	
see: Stalls and Poststall Gyrations	
Poststart Procedures, Carrier-based	140
Power	
also see: A-C Power, D-C Power, Emergency Hydraulic Power, External Power	
approach and landing stalls	156A
distribution	
a-c	37, 38, 39
d-c	37

PAGE NUMBERS IN **BOLD** DENOTE ILLUSTRATIONS

263

	Page
unit, emergency electrical power	40
units (RCPP-105-1 and RCPT-105-3)	111

Power Supply System
  see: Electrical Power Supply System
       Electronic
       Hydraulic Power Supply Systems
       Pneumatic Power Supply System
Precautions
  see: Danger Areas
       Loading and Safety Precautions, Weapons
Preflight

cold weather procedures	188A
considerations, weapons delivery	193
aircraft	194
bombing systems	193
weapons system	193
cruise control	150
hot weather procedures	189
oxygen systems normal operation	89
Prelaunch Check	148E

Pressure Gages
  see: Emergency Oxygen System
Pressure Relief Doors
  see: Engine
Pressure Suit

carrier-based procedures	140
conditioning	86, 82
knob	
suit flow	86, 84
suit temperature	86, 84
emergency pressurization	90
operation	86, 112, 113

Pressurization
  also see: Air Conditioning and Pressurization System

cockpit	85, 82
altimeter, cockpit pressure	85, 73
pressurization schedule	82
switch, cockpit pressure	85, 82, 84
cockpit operation	85, 82
controls	84
suit emergency	90
Prestart Check	127
Pretaxi Check	162

Program, Standardization Evaluation
  see: Standardization Evaluation

Projected Display (Pilot's PPDI) Failures	148J
antenna not following A/A in TA auto alpha	148K
display apex intermittent or jumpy	148J
insufficient horizon centering	148K
locked or erratic steering cursor	148K
no artificial horizon	148J
no azimuth or range cursor	148J
no clearance set action	148K
no elevation steering cursor	148J
no radar video	148J
no reticles	148J
no roll indication	148J
no steering cursor	148J
no sweeps or scans	148J

Protection Devices, Electrical Circuit
  see: Circuit
Pull-knobs
  see: Knob
Pump

boost pump failure	174
engine-driven fuel	11
failures, hydraulic system	179

R

Radar Altimeter	106A, **108**
controls and indicators	**108**
high-altitude system (systems operator)	106A
operation	109
low-altitude indicator (pilot)	108, **108**
low-altitude system (pilot)	107
operation	109
mode and calibration controls (systems operator)	107, **108**
Radar/Barometric Altimeter Calibration	148E

	Page
Radar Failures	148G
alternate range cursor check	148H
multiple azimuth cursor	148J
no azimuth cursor	148J
noisy display	148H
no range circles	148H
no range cursor	148H
no targets	148H
radar/TV coincidence	148H
range circles accuracy check	148H
range cursor error	148H
scans missing	148H
short range	148H
sweeps missing	148G
video lost or unusual display	148H
wavy range cursor	148H
weak targets	148H
wedged video	148H
Radar Navigation	184
methods	150
Radar-TV Check	148E
radar turn-on	148E
TV check	148E
Radiation Silence	148G

Radio Communications and Electronic
Navigation Equipment

	191
electronic navigation equipment	191
IFF/SIF procedures	191
authentication	191
emergency communications	191
radio communication equipment	191
Radio Navigation	150
Radome Fold	73
switch	73, **73**
external control	73

Rain
  see: Ice and Rain

Ram-air Turbine Operation	41
flight check	162

Ramps
  see: Variable Ramps

Range and Bearing Knobs	95, **72**

Ratio Changer

directional flight control system	63
lateral flight control system	54, **52**
Receiver Procedure, Air Refueling	36, 160
Recon Mode	148F
Records and Forms, Grading	210

Recovery

carrier-based procedures	141
approach	142
arrestment	143
Bingo fuel	143
bolters	143
broken wire or hook	144
carrier approach	143
landing pattern	142, **142**
marshal	141
night carrier operations	146
pitch augmentation failure	144
single engine	144
typical carrier landing	**142**
from poststall gyrations	155
inverted and vertical attitude recovery	155
spins	156
unusual attitude	155
Refueling	29, 114

also see: Air Refueling
         Buddy Tanker Refueling System

ground pressure	29, 116
normal procedure	116
partial fuel load procedure	117

Refusal Speeds
  see: Engine
Rendezvous and Departure

carrier-based procedures	141
climb-out and rendezvous	144
formation flight	

PAGE NUMBERS IN **BOLD** DENOTE ILLUSTRATIONS

	Page
carrier-based	159
normal rendezvous	159
running rendezvous	159
shore-based	158
normal rendezvous	158
running rendezvous	158
Responsibility	
command responsibility	139
communications procedures	191
mission planning	123
navigator	150
Right Console	8, 9
Right Forward Console	72
Rings	
see: Emergency Oxygen System	
Roll Trim	
see: Alternate Roll/Yaw Trim	
Lateral Flight Control System	
Running Rendezvous	
see: Formation Flight	

S

	Page
Safety Precautions	
see: Loading and Safety Precautions, Weapons	
Scheduling	
carrier-based	139
flight	139
ground training schedules	139
manning ready room	139
shore-based	127
daily flight schedule	127
long-range planning schedules	127
Score, Flight Evaluation	199
Search Mode (TV)	148F
Seat	
see: Ejection Seat	
Secondary Airflow	
see: Air Induction System	
Selector	
communications mode	94, 93
compass mode	105, 105
function, ICS	90, 93
function, TACAN	95, 93
MASTER function, IFF/SIF	97, 93
Separation System	76
separation aneroid indicator	76
Service Changes	
see: Aircraft Service Changes	
Servicing, Aircraft	111, 112, 113
danger areas	118A, 115
external power and air requirements	111, 112, 113
ground handling	118A
military specifications	114
refueling	114
systems servicing	118
Shore-based Procedures (Pilot)	127
line operations	127
lost aircraft procedures	182
scheduling	127
stopping the aircraft	138
taxi, take-off, and landing	132
Short-field Arrestment	
see: Arrestment	
SIF	
see: Identification Units (IFF and SIF)	
Signals	
emergency, lost communications	147
night carrier operations	146
Simulated Instrument Flight	189
Single-engine Operation	25
failure of one engine	165
after take-off	165
in-flight	165
landings, single-engine	182B, 182C
carrier	182B
wave-off	182B
Smoke and Fumes	170
Specifications	
see: Military Specifications, Servicing	

	Page
Speed	
also see: Mission Planning	
approach speeds, recommended field take-off and	135
minimum control speeds	153
touchdown	72
Speed Brakes	65
handle, speed brake dump	65, 4
indicator	65, 6, 7
operation	65
characteristics	65
switch	65, 4
Spins	156
developed	156
recovery	156
Spoiler-Deflectors	54
longitudinal and lateral electric systems	54, 50—52
free-play mechanism, lateral	54
ratio changer, lateral	54, 52
Squadron Formation	
see: Formation Flight	
Stabilizers	
horizontal	49
vertical	49
Stall and Poststall Gyrations	152
accelerated flight	152
compressor stalls	24
inverted attitude	152
recovery from poststall gyrations	155
upright attitude	152
vertical attitude	155
Standardization Evaluation	197
form, A-5A pilot systems operator	211
program	197
concept	197
critique	210
flight evaluation (phase III)	199
forms and records	210
grading instructions	200
ground evaluation (phases I and II)	198
oral examination	198
weapons system trainer (WST) procedures check	198
written examination	198
NAMT systems check	199
worksheets	
systems operator	233
pilot	215
Stand-by Attitude Indicator	103, 6, 7
Stand-by Magnetic Compass	106A
Stand-by Nav Turn-on	148D
Stand-by Pitch Trim	
see: Pitch Trim	
Starting	
after, radar-TV check	148E
radar turn-on	148E
TV check	148E
Starting Engines	
see: Air Starts	
Engine	
Fire	
Starting System	14, 112, 113
switches	
engine MASTER	14, 16
engine START	14, 16
Start Malfunctions	
see: Engine	
Static Pressure Compensator	102
SPC button	102, 4
Static Pressure Source Failure	181
Steering	
see: Nose Wheel Steering	
Stick	
see: Control Stick	
Stopping the Aircraft	138
aerodynamic braking	138
nose-high	138
three-point	138
postflight	138A
after landing	138A

PAGE NUMBERS IN BOLD DENOTE ILLUSTRATIONS

	Page
debriefing	138A
engine shutdown	138A
touchdown speed	138
wheel braking	138
braking technique	138
intermittent braking	138A
field arrestments	138A

Subsonic/Supersonic Missions
 see: Mission Planning
Suit
 see: Anti-G Suit
  Pressure Suit

	Page
Sump Switch	30
Survival	
kit	76
training	120
mobile	120
Switch	
AFC	61, **60**
alternate roll/yaw trim	59, **56**
altitude set	108, **108**
anticollision lights	**98A**, **100**
approach lights	99, **100**
AUTO LABS	61
AUTO/MAN	83, **84**
CANS transfer	30, **4**
channel/frequency slew	94, **93**
cockpit pressure	85, 82, **84**
electric system	55, **56**
emergency flap	67, **66**
emergency fuel flow	33, **34**
emergency gear up	68, **68**
emergency IFF	98, **93**
engine anti-ice	88, **84**
ENGINE FIRE	15, **16**
engine MASTER	14, **16**
engine START	14, **16**
exterior lights master	**98A**, **100**
flap control	67, **66**
floodlights	99, **100**
formation lights	99, **100**
function control	94, **93**
generator	41, **8**, **9**
hemisphere	105, **105**
high-altitude lights	99, **100**
HOSE CONTROL	32, **34**
HOSE CUT	34, **34**
hydraulic subsystems isolation	44, **4**
INFLIGHT FUEL PROBE	30, **4**
I/P (identify position)	97, **93**
microphone	90
microphone select	90, **93**
normal roll/stand-by pitch trim	59, **56**
pitch augmentation	57, **56**
radome fold	74, **73**
external control	73
ramp control	15, **16**
caution indicator	17, **16**
red floodlights	101, **100**
ROLL	61, **60**
seat adjust	78, **73**
SIGNAL LIGHTS	34, **34**
speed brake	65, **4**
SUMP	30, **4**
tail control	73, **73**
trim select	58, **56**
windshield anti-ice	87, **84**
wing and taillight	**98A**, **100**
yaw augmentation	57, **56**
yaw trim	59, **56**
Systems	11
air conditioning and pressurization system	82, 81, **82**, **84**
angle-of-attack system	103, **104**
arresting gear	69
canopies	74
communications-navigation-identification system (CNI)	92, **93**
electrical power supply system	37, **38**, **39**

	Page
engines	11, **16**
air induction system	18, **13**
characteristics	17
emergency procedures	24
operating procedures	24
escape system	75, 79
operation	80, **80**
flight control systems	49, 50—53, **56**
automatic flight control system (AFCS)	59, **60**
operation	62
fold systems	72
radome	73
wing and tail	72
fuel supply system, aircraft	28, **26**, **27**
air refueling procedures (receiver)	36
buddy tanker refueling system	32, **33**, **34**
operation	31
gyrocompass system	105, **105**
hydraulic power systems	44, **42**, **43**
failure	45
instruments	101
intercommunications system (ICS)	90, **91**
failure	192
landing gear	68
lighting systems	**98**, **100**
nose wheel steering	70
oxygen systems	88
pneumatic power supply system	49
radar altimeter	107, **108**
ram-air turbine operation	44
speed brakes	65
stopping the aircraft	72
warning, caution, and advisory indicators	101
wheel brakes	70
wing flaps and droop leading edge	65, **66**

Systems Operator Standardization Evaluation
 also see: Flight Evaluation (Phase III)

	Page
form	211
worksheets	233
Systems, Servicing	118
arresting gear snubber and bumper	118
engine oil	118
high-pressure air valves	118
hydraulic	118
landing gear struts	118
oxygen systems	118
pitot-static drains	118
pneumatic systems	118
tires	118
Systems Shutdown (Normal Procedures)	148N

T

	Page
TACAN	95
knob	
channel	95, **93**
volume	95, **93**
operation	95
selector, function	95, **93**
Tachometers	15, **16**

Tail Fold
 see: Wing and Tail Fold
Take-off
 also see: Taxi, Take-off, and Landing

	Page
aborted	164
cruise control	150
emergencies	164
engine fire on take-off	171
above refusal speed	171
below refusal speed	171
failure of one engine after take-off	165
hot weather procedures	189
instrument flight	183
pre-take-off mission performance considerations, weapons delivery	194
procedures	134, **133**, **135**
after take-off	135
technique	134, **135**
recommended approach and field take-off speeds	135

PAGE NUMBERS IN **BOLD** DENOTE ILLUSTRATIONS

	Page
typical take-off	133
Tanks	
drop	25, **176**
internal fuel	25
Target Briefing	
see: Briefing and Debriefing	
TAS/GS Indicator Erratic or Inoperative	148M
Taxi, Take-off, and Landing	132
before taxiing into position	134
penetration and landing	135, **136**
postflight	138
pretaxi check	132
take-off procedures	134, **133**, **135**
taxi procedures	
carrier-based	140
shore-based	132A
air conditioning/defrost procedure	132A
checkoff list	134
fuel conservation	132A
Television Failures	148J
no raster	148J
no video	148J
pulsating video	148J
reticles missing	148J
TV scanner position indicator (TSPI)	148J
no aft indication	148J
no pitch or azimuth indication	148J
pitch/azimuth error or oscillation	148J
Temperate Climate (Low and Medium Altitude)	
see: Personal Equipment Requirements	
Terrain Avoidance Check (Pilot)	148E
Throttles	15, **16**
catapult handgrip	15, **16**
emergency ignition buttons	15, **16**
Thunderstorm Penetration	187
Tires	
failure	163
landing with tire failure	178
main gear tire	179
nose gear tire	179
servicing	118
Total Pressure Source Failure	180
Touch-and-Go	
see: Fuel Supply System, Aircraft Landing	
Touchdown	
landing with aft cg	156A
speed	138
Towing	118A, **139**
Training	119
ejection seat	120
low-pressure chamber	119
survival training	120
mobile	120
weapons system trainer (WST)	119
procedures check	198
grading criteria	201
Trajectory, Escape System	80
Transfer, Fuel	28
normal sequence	31
Transition, Familiarization and	149
Trim Systems	57
alternate roll/yaw	58
automatic flap	58
controls and indicators	58
directional	58
failure	65
lateral	58
operation	63
directional	63
centering	63
lateral	63
pitch	57
stand-by pitch	58
Turbulence, Flight in	187
thunderstorm penetration	187
Turning Radius	118A, **116**

U	Page
UHF Communications Unit	92
also see: Auxiliary UHF Receiver	
button, communications command	92, **93**
control, volume	92, **93**
indicators, channel/frequency	94, **93**
operation	94
main UHF/ADF procedure	94
selector, mode	92, **93**
switch	
channel/frequency slew	94, **93**
function control	94, **93**
Upright Attitude	
see: Stalls and Poststall Gyrations	

V	
Valve	
anti-G suit	87
canopy toggle	74, **4**
external toggle	74
high-pressure air, servicing	118
oxygen supply	88A, **4**
Variable Area Exhaust Nozzles	
see: Exhaust Nozzles	
Variable Ramps	23
ramp monitor	23
Variable Stators and Inlet Guide Vanes	14
Ventilation Outlets	83
Venting, Fuel	29
Vertical Attitude	
see: Stalls and Poststall Gyrations	
Vertical Stabilizer	
see: Stabilizers	
Visual Communications	191
between aircraft	191
intercommunications system failure	192

W	
Warning, Caution, and Advisory Indicators	101
buttons, warning lights test	101
indicators	
caution	101, **6, 7**
master warning and master caution	101
warning	101, **6, 7**
lights, advisory	101
Wave-off	
CCA wave-off/bolter pattern	146
single-engine	165
Weapons Systems	193
trainer (WST)	119
procedures check	198
grading criteria	201
emergencies/malfunctions	201
normal procedures	201
normal procedures and emergency procedures	201
weapons delivery	193
Wind Control Failures	148L
cannot slew speed or direction	148L
maximum reading or zero in auto	148L
attack mode procedures	195
delivery tactics	162A
loading and safety precautions	193
methods	193
mission performance considerations	194
preflight considerations	193
Wet or Icy Runways	188A
Wheel Brakes	70, **138**
also see: Stopping the Aircraft	
braking technique	138
intermittent braking	138A
emergency brakes	71, **68**
emergency operation	71
braking with hydraulic failure	71
emergency brakes	71
manual brakes	71
operation	71
normal brake system	71
Wing and Tail Fold	72
handle, fold control	73, **73**

PAGE NUMBERS IN **BOLD** DENOTE ILLUSTRATIONS

	Page
flags, warning	73
switch, tail control	73, 73
Wing Flaps and Droop Leading Edge	65, 66
boundary layer control	67
controls	66
droop leading edge	67
emergency extension, flap	68
indicator	
flap/droop position	67
droops caution	67, 6, 7
switch	
emergency flap	67, 66
flap control	67, 66
wing flaps	65
flap interconnect	67
Wing Fuel Transfer Failure	175
Worksheets, Standardization Evaluation	
systems operator	233

	Page
pilot	215
Written Examination	198
closed book	198
composition	198
grading criteria	200
closed book	200
open book	200
open book	198

Y

Yaw Augmentation System
  also see: Directional Flight Control System
  failure 182
  yaw damper 55
Yaw Trim
  see: Alternate Roll/Yaw Trim
      Directional Flight Control System

PAGE NUMBERS IN **BOLD** DENOTE ILLUSTRATIONS

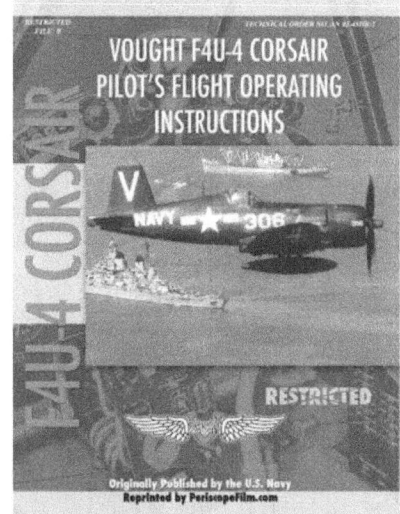
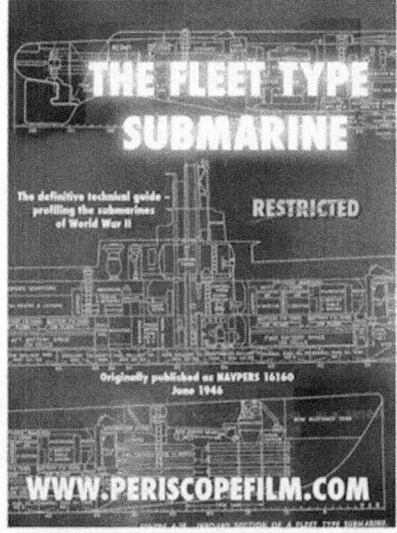

ALSO NOW AVAILABLE
FROM PERISCOPEFILM.COM

©2012 Periscope Film LLC
All Rights Reserved
ISBN #978-1-937684-72-3

www.ingramcontent.com/pod-product-compliance
Lightning Source LLC
Chambersburg PA
CBHW080725230426
43665CB00020B/2621